**CHRISTOPHER J. LUCAS**

*University of Missouri—Columbia*

# FOUNDATIONS OF EDUCATION

## *Schooling and the social order*

**PRENTICE-HALL, INC.,** Englewood Cliffs, New Jersey 07632

*Library of Congress Cataloging in Publication Data*

Lucas, Chriistopher J.
  Foundations of education.

  Includes bibliographies and index.
    1.  Educational sociology—United States.    2.  Education
—United States—Aims and objectives.    I.  Title.
LC191.4.L8 1983     370.19'0973       83–10969
ISBN 0-13-329581-8

Editorial/production supervision and
  interior design: Kate Kelly
Cover design: Diane Saxe
Manufacturing buyer: Ron Chapman
Cover photos: Reproduced from the collections of the
  Library of Congress and Laimute & Druskis

© 1984 by Prentice-Hall, Inc., Englewood Cliffs, New Jersey 07632

Printed in the United States of America

10   9   8   7   6   5   4   3   2   1

ISBN 0-13-329581-8

Prentice-Hall International, Inc., *London*
Prentice-Hall of Australia Pty. Limited, *Sydney*
Editora Prentice-Hall do Brasil, Ltda., *Rio de Janeiro*
Prentice-Hall Canada Inc., *Toronto*
Prentice-Hall of India Private Limited, *New Delhi*
Prentice-Hall of Japan, Inc., *Tokyo*
Prentice-Hall of Southeast Asia Pte. Ltd., *Singapore*
Whitehall Books Limited, *Wellington, New Zealand*

# CONTENTS

## CHAPTER THREE
# EDUCATIONAL CONSERVATISM
## *The Liberal-Arts Tradition*                               80

## CHAPTER FOUR
# VOCATIONALISM
## *Education for the World of Work*                       147

# CHAPTER FIVE
# VOCATIONALISM
## *Career Education and Development*    216

# CHAPTER SIX
# HUMANISM
## *Education for Self-Realization*    284

## CHAPTER SEVEN
# SOCIAL RECONSTRUCTION AND FUTURISM
## *Education for Human Survival*    372

# PREFACE

The writing of this work was prompted by what I felt was a need for a more integrative, or cohesive approach to the study of education as a sociocultural phenomenon than the potpourri of topics, issues, and themes commonly treated in so many "foundations of education" courses. My hope was to offer a text that would avoid the near-encyclopedic survey of trends and specific topical issues typical of the genre, yet still be suitable for use in a variety of undergraduate and graduate-level foundational courses. My decision was to focus on what experience suggests prospective educators find far more helpful and relevant; namely, *the logic of very basic ideas about school purposes and processes.*

The challenge, first, was to construct a framework highlighting fundamental differences of opinion over educational aims, values, and larger social objectives. Second, the intent was to illustrate the shape of "real-world" debate as it actually occurs, drawing upon a representative sample of writings from the vast literature of school criticism. Third, in outlining the various positions people defend, it seemed necessary to set them briefly in some sort of historical context. Finally, my aim was to reconstitute the main theme of each as a formal argument for purposes of further analysis and assessment. In short, what I had in mind was a "topographical survey" of, or mapping out of issues and ideas in, contemporary American education. The resulting overview is perhaps broader in scope though less "topic-oriented" than most surveys of educational theory and practice.

Throughout an unexpectedly lengthy gestation, I have benefited greatly from the helpful criticisms of students and colleagues alike. I am particularly indebted to Norm Gysbers, Bill Wickersham, Gary Fox, Michael Dyrenfurth, and Richard Erickson for assistance with source materials.

Thanks are owed the several authors and publishers cited elsewhere who extended permission to paraphrase or quote directly from selected works. The support and encouragement of Susan B. Katz and her associates are also deeply appreciated, Kate Kelly in particular. Without the help of Lori Vincent, Deborah DeClue, and Janet Thornton, the preparation of the manuscript in its several drafts would have been virtually impossible. This was particularly the case during the long, painful process of paring down the original version to more manageable proportions.

A special debt is owed Jeannie Schuffman for her patience in providing a ''sounding board'' for many of the ideas expressed here. To her, to my students, and to my son Greg this labor is gratefully dedicated.

C. J. L.

Everything has been thought of before but the difficulty is to think of it again.

—Goethe

# CHAPTER ONE
# INTRODUCTION

John Dewey once claimed that controversy over schools was basically healthy, because it was a sign of public concern and support. True or not, next to religion, sex, and politics, the topic most likely to arouse impassioned debate today is education. In disagreement with Jacques Barzun, who thought it was ''the dullest of subjects,'' most people believe there are large issues at stake and weighty matters to be resolved. Parents especially are apt to be concerned over what happens—or fails to happen—in schools, believing perhaps that their children's future well-being hinges on the direction and quality of instruction they receive. Whatever the reasons, educational questions figure at the center of much public controversy. Discussion typically is framed by the question, ''What's wrong with our schools today?''

A writer drafts a hard-hitting exposé, *How Education Is Failing Us And What We Can Do About It.* If the book makes it to the bestseller list (and one occasionally does), the author is virtually assured national prominence. Sometimes it is a major research study that captures the public's attention. Either way, alarms are sounded. In due course the work is reviewed in scores of journals. School critics and defenders alike solemnly dissect the principal allegations. Conflicting pronouncements ensue as pundits fall to quarreling among themselves over why it is schoolchildren nowadays apparently cannot read or write or compute. Amidst growing public confusion, charges and countercharges fly freely.

As in most discussion of public policy, debate about education rarely displays a high level of sophistication. This is especially the case when the issues involved have no simple straightforward answers or when even the experts disagree among themselves. More widespread and influential by far are simplistic judgments appearing in the popular press, as, for example, when mass-circulation magazines offer their readers such articles as "How Good Is Your Child's School?" or "Rating The Schools In Your Community: A Checklist." Arguably, newspaper editorialists and other journalistic popularizers exert more control over public opinion than do professionals. Rightly or wrongly, when it comes to pondering educational questions, everyone is a self-styled expert. The schools, it is said, are much too important to be left to educators alone.

Symptomatic of this popularization of debate is the favorite national pastime of finding culprits to blame for all the ills (real and imagined) in public education. Attempting to account for the schools' shortcomings, some critics point to professional "educationalists" and the inadequate preparation they offer those who work with children in the nation's classrooms. Others as often assert the problem rests with teachers themselves, many of whom are charged with being lazy, indifferent, or simply incompetent. Or it may be the children they try to teach who are at fault. Today's youngsters, runs the complaint, are apathetic, lacking in motivation, and woefully undisciplined. Negligent parents who do not seem to care enough also receive a share of the blame.

Again, absenteeism, school disruption, and classroom disorder are sometimes traced back to a more general permissiveness at work in society at large. Television violence is likewise indicted. Some analysts cite the decay of the family, cultural deprivation, or economic hardship as contributing factors. Still others find in problems of the schools signs of a more profound spiritual malaise in contemporary society, possibly even a portent of disintegration in the social fabric itself. The diagnoses are endless.

Buck-passing becomes commonplace. University professors assail the system for graduating academic incompetents. The diversion of scarce resources for remediation, it is said, would be unnecessary if the secondary schools would insist on higher standards of performance. Beleaguered high-school teachers in turn complain they can do only so much with the students they inherit from the lower grades. Elementary-school teachers for their part deplore lack of support from the home. Parents blame their children's peers and other ill-defined influences they only dimly comprehend and can scarcely control. And so the search for scapegoats continues.

Part of the problem, of course, as many observers have noted, is that Americans collectively have never quite made up their minds about what schools are supposed to accomplish. And because so little consensus exists on the basic aims of schooling, differences of opinion are pronounced when it comes to deciding what can or should be done to correct deficiencies. Everything depends on the standards used in making judgments. Thus society gets the schools it deserves, it has been said, and the result is a system reproducing in microcosm much broader conflicts within the social order over the relative importance of different, competing values.

Where there is consensus, it is apt to be more formal than substantive in nature. Overall, people seem to want schools to

teach children basic learning skills and transmit useful or important knowledge;

sort pupils out for future roles by testing and grading them, thereby providing an ostensibly fair way of rationing socioeconomic opportunity;

encourage the development of desirable personality attributes or characteristics such as creativity, critical thinking, self-reliance, or interpersonal sensitivity;

provide daytime custodial care for children;

socialize children to society's core values and provide an orderly transition between the home and adult society.[1]

The public wants and expects much else besides from schools, but these five functions are probably most important and would win greatest agreement. Trouble surfaces when the discussion gets down to specifics. For example, few would disagree that schools have a responsibility to teach the ''basics.'' But which skills are most basic, and why? Just the so-called ''three R's''? Is ''learning to get along with others'' a basic? Is ''effective oral communication'' fundamental? Are the ''basics'' the *same* for everyone, in any time and place? Can or should they all be taught in schools?

Again, it is said that schools should stress useful and important knowledge. Often overlooked is the point that terms such as ''useful'' or ''important,'' like ''basic,'' are not necessarily self-defining. Does ''useful'' knowledge mean the various subject-matter disciplines such as history, mathematics, the sciences, language, and literature? If so, *what kind* of history should be taught? How *much* science? Should everyone be exposed to literature? *Which* disciplines should be stressed?

A different way of looking at ''useful'' knowledge might be to define it in terms of vocational training: useful knowledge is whatever one needs to know in order to fulfill one's economic role in the social order. The utility of knowledge, in other words, is a function of whether or not it enables the learner to secure gainful employment. As an alternative, useful knowledge could be construed as whatever an individual student finds most meaningful or relevant in his or her own life—in which case the category of ''usefulness'' becomes entirely a matter of subjective opinion. Or, one might argue, the most useful knowledge anyone can acquire in school has to do with ''survival skills'' needed for everyday living—preparing for a job interview, deciding upon a career, deciphering legal documents, understanding one's legal rights and responsibilities, comparison shopping, balancing a checkbook, computing interest, or figuring price discounts, and so on.

Another question has to do with whether ''useful'' knowledge, however defined, is necessarily the same thing as ''important'' knowledge, and vice versa. Are there some types of information eminently worth knowing that cannot be used directly in some immediate practical sense? For example, if a person never intends to become a professional artist or musician, is it still worthwhile learning to appreciate good art or music? Is it important to become well informed about current events around the world? Does everyone need to know that the planet Neptune is the eighth planet out from the sun, that plants use photosynthesis as an energy-conversion process, or that William the Conqueror invaded Britain in the year 1066?

The fact that hard questions like these are so often left unresolved testifies to the lack of popular agreement on answers. The resulting confusion also serves as a measure of the lack of clarity and precision common to most discussions of the issues involved. Hence, most people are uncomfortable when confronted with the question, "What are schools *for?*" The typical response is, "Why, to educate people, of course!" But to educate them *in what,* and for what purposes? At this point many people shrug their shoulders—which affords scant help in planning school programs—or respond vaguely that schools should try to do everything—another retort that is also not especially helpful.

Frequently, arguments over school policy concern priorities among functions or goals. Thus, for example, critics may assail public education for trying to do so much that schools allegedly neglect basic learning skills and the teaching of the academic disciplines. The fundamental purpose of schooling, it is held, should be cognitive competence and the fostering of intellectual ability. But others with equal vehemence deplore excessive preoccupation with cognitive objectives as too one-sided. They recommend instead that more time and effort be given over to promoting "balanced" affective growth and development. Teaching should be directed to shaping attitudes, emotions, and feelings.

Still other school critics hold out for different aims: promoting good citizenship, ethical character and moral values, adaptability to social change, good mental health and a positive self-concept, proficiency in decision making, and so on *ad infinitum.* It seems safe to say that at one point or another practically every human attribute or characteristic and almost any set of skills imaginable has been held up as a proper end of educational endeavor. Nor is it uncommon for writers to fix on a single aspect of human functioning—say, decision making—and to insist that it constitutes the most important *desideratum* to which schools should give their attention.

Complicating matters still further is the varied array of "ancillary" social services schools are called upon to perform, not to mention the incredibly diverse range of societal problems or concerns to which they are asked to respond. Historically, the power of education has been considered almost infinite, in the dual sense as cure for social, moral, economic, and political maladies and as the means for enforcing overarching values and responsibilities. Sooner or later, almost everyone with a cause to advance or a concern to defend concludes, "Basically, it comes down to properly educating people." Hence, at various times schools have been expected to inculcate religious orthodoxy, to instill moral values, to foster patriotism and love of country, and to teach order, discipline, and democracy. They have been depended upon to help acculturate successive waves of immigrants; to reinforce the virtues of thrift, cleanliness, and the work ethic; to preach the evils of alcohol, tobacco, atheism, communism, drugs, war, peace, and sex; and to ensure a universally high standard of literacy. In one way or another, all this and more has been taken as the province of education.

Commenting on the interpenetration of the school as a social institution and its surrounding cultural or societal milieu, James J. Gallagher of the University of North Carolina once observed, "Education is, in fact, a mirror of our society. Whatever problems bedevil school and educators, they merely reflect problems facing our larger society." He added, "To discover the current and future problems schools must deal with, one need only look at the problems of the larger society. Also, we can surmise on past experience that the schools may likely be held responsible for both the problem and its solution, whatever its origin."[2] Needless to say, how well schools in the past have contributed to the solution of various societal issues remains a lively topic of debate. So too does the question of what responsibility schools *should* bear for dealing with social problems, now or in the future.

Meanwhile, socializing children to society's present-day norms and values similarly furnishes ample scope for disagreement. Identifying "core" values in a pluralistic, heterogeneous culture is always problematic; selecting out specific mores and values for emphasis in schools is more difficult still. The whole question gets clouded when people disagree over both "instrumental" values (ways of achieving goals) and the end goals themselves. For instance, certain critics are prone to fault the schools for excessive authoritarianism and needless regimentation, which, it is alleged, tend to thwart the very educational aims schools exist to promote. Others insist even stricter discipline and order are needed if educators are to achieve important instructional or social objectives. A further complication arises with the disparity between the values people profess to endorse in schools—critical thinking, creativity, independence of judgment, autonomy—and those they actually approve and reward—compliance, obedience, and conformity. Oftentimes, too, socialization is less a matter of deliberate or explicit instruction, and more a matter of "tacit" learning through the ways the official curriculum is organized and imparted.

Overall, the perennial dilemma in both educational theory and practice is how to reconcile the function of the school as an agency for social control with the democratic aspiration to "liberate" persons and educate them as free citizens. Profound differences of opinion prevail. Some factions want schools to safeguard traditional verities. Others urge schools to promote social reform. One segment of popular opinion sees the transmission of a cultural inheritance as the school's major task. Another recommends educators look to the future and help young people anticipate and learn to adapt to change.

As if deciding on what schools are for and what priorities should hold were not enough, constant disagreement surrounds questions of *how* educational institutions discharge their functions. The sorting-and-selection mission of schooling, to cite a case in point, is highly controversial. Sometimes critics object to the standards or criteria by which pupils are screened, sorted, and assessed. Other times it is the instrumentation of testing and how it is deployed that provides the focus of debate. Just as often the mechanism of selection in some broader sense is attacked on the grounds that the system works to the disadvantage of certain classes or groups of students. Finally, the concept of a hierarchical social order itself is condemned by those who reject the legitimacy of using schools as tools for apportioning or distributing opportunity. In recent years, questions having to do with the mainstreaming of exceptional children into regular classrooms, programs of early intervention and compensatory education for minorities and the culturally disadvantaged, multi-cultural education, and selective-admissions policies have all touched in various ways upon the issue of how schooling is functionally related to the equalization of socioeconomic opportunity in society.

Nonetheless, the most fundamental debates over education usually concern matters of purpose or goals. Over the past hundred years or so, in fact, a good part of the history of schooling in the United States could be written around the story of how one faction or another sought to redirect the course of school instruction so that it emphasized one set of objectives rather than another. While this was always the case to some extent, the tendency to disagree and to advance contending—sometimes incommensurate—aims for education has grown more and more pronounced with the passage of time.

Oversimplifying somewhat, the gradual escalation of debate over educational aims that has reached a crescendo in the present era began in the waning years of the nineteenth century. Up until then, school criticism appears to have been relatively muted, thanks in part to a widely shared system of beliefs and a consensual scheme of values held in common throughout most of society. In the era of the one-room schoolhouse, people's expectations of education were both modest and finite. Answers to questions of purpose, process, and content therefore were fairly simple and straightforward.[3] The school's task was to impart the rudiments of literacy. It was to inculcate prevailing norms and to ready students for participation in social life. The limited curriculum purveyed was organized as an accounting of information believed to be useful or thought helpful in improving mental-reasoning faculties. Just as the body is strengthened by exercise, nineteenth-century pedagogy held that the mind was like a muscle enhanced through an equivalent kind of exercising. The more difficult the traditional subjects, such as geometry and Latin, the more the student had to exercise the mind, and hence the greater value of the subject.[4] Not surprisingly, drill, rote memorization, and recitation were the order of the day.

The new social order emergent around the turn of the century spelled a dramatic expansion and elaboration of the nation's school system. Industrialization, urbanization, and a rapidly growing population swollen by immigration, among other factors, brought new forms of educational governance, including more centralized bureaucratic control. And with changing societal needs came growing appreciation for the fact that basic education in the three R's—readin', 'ritin', and 'rithmetic—and in civic morality was not nearly enough. For one thing, the enactment of compulsory-attendance legislation meant more and more young people were enrolled in schools for longer periods of time. Educators and the lay public alike began questioning the classical curriculum, the age-old emphasis on mental discipline, and reliance on incessant drill.

A strong reaction against traditional pedagogy came from at least two different directions. On the one hand were leaders in business and industry, whose increasing inclination was to look upon educational institutions as important suppliers for a specialized labor force. An education founded on the classics, they argued, was hopelessly obsolete in a modern industrial age. The need now was for vocational training for the great mass of students who would never lead lives dedicated to scholarly pursuits. The task of the school was to sort out the young and train them more directly for the specific roles they would later assume in life.

On the other were progressive educators who saw the need for school activities and subjects designed to meet the everyday-life needs of all children. They condemned passive learning as meaningless, opposed old-fashioned discipline as artificial, and urged an infusion of new subjects into curricula. Traditionalists recoiled in horror. So deeply entrenched was the idea of mental discipline and the stress on intellectual self-cultivation that any proposal to emphasize practical studies over classical disciplines appeared positively heretical.

Especially offensive to educational conservatives were the injunctions of John Dewey and his followers to educate "the whole child," and the notion that the principal goal of schooling was preparation for "complete living." The proposed substitution of a curriculum organized around basic human needs—health, vocation, faculty, citizenship, and leisure—as recommended in a 1918 statement of "Cardinal Principles" for the established regimen of traditional academic and literacy disciplines was vigorously opposed. Gradually, however, the impetus to broaden courses of study and to devise a new methodology based on problem solving and active learner-involvement gained support. By the 1920s or thereabouts, progressive educational ideals appeared to enjoy widespread acceptance, in theory at least if not always in actual classroom practice.

A three-way tug-of-war among vocationalists, traditionalists, and progressivists for control over school curricula marked debate throughout the 1920s and 1930s. Proponents of job training worked hard for the idea that schools should serve as recruitment agencies for business, agriculture, and industry. Progressivists (many of them, at any rate) opposed vocationalism as a primary emphasis and continued to push for school programs organized around the needs and interests of children themselves. Conservatives, who by now had more or less dropped their preoccupation with classical studies, held out for programs based on generic learning skills and systematic exposure to academic subject-matter disciplines. Schools, as always, were caught in the middle, trying to please everyone. Predictably, they ended up satisfying no one.

By the mid-thirties even the progressivists themselves were splintered. One wing continued to preach the doctrine of the child-centered classroom. Their focus of concern remained that of humanistic instruction, creating a supportive environment in which learning could be both enjoyable and meaningful in the lives of young children. Another faction, however, was troubled over the dislocations American society was experiencing in the middle of a Depression. With unemployment reaching an all-time high, with many youth out of school, and amidst growing fears that capitalism was failing, progressivist educators of a more radical persuasion wondered what role public education had to play in helping to bring about needed political, economic, and social reforms. If schools tried to stay out of the fray, they argued, they ran the danger of becoming obstructive. Classroom informality was all fine and good, but unless schooling became more directive or goal-oriented, more attuned to shifting social currents, it could end up being irrelevant. The pressing need, some claimed, was for schools to serve as catalysts in a socialist reconstruction of the social order.

Hardly anyone paid attention. More acceptable by far were the goals enunciated in a 1938 report entitled, *The Purposes of Education in American Democracy,* issued by the Educational Policies Commission of the National Education Association (NEA).[5] Among the list of aims cited were "self-realization" (associated with an inquiring mind, literacy skills, good health habits, recreation, intellectual and esthetic interests, and so on); productive "human relationships" (friendship, cooperation, respect for others); "economic efficiency" (consumer judgment, occupational information, job training); and "civic responsibility" (respect for law, devotion to democracy, social understanding, economic literacy, tolerance for others, justice, critical judgment, and the like). All told, the NEA document offered something for everyone—which was precisely the problem, according to educational traditionalists.

On the eve of World War II a small group of educators styling themselves "Essentialists" banded together to register their protest against the alleged domination of educational theory by progressivism. Though they made no direct reference to the 1938 Educational Policies Commission document, they might have seized on it as a symbol for everything they most opposed about American schooling.

The trouble with formal education, they complained, is that it tries to be all things to all people. Educators attempt to do too much, thereby dissipating their efforts and rendering themselves ineffectual. They misunderstand their democratic responsibilities, mistakenly assuming that "democracy" means that children should be allowed to determine of their own accord what they will learn. Or they assume "democracy" means schools have an obligation to respond to each and every external demand placed upon schools. A sense of priorities is missing. A wiser course of action would be for educators to recognize what specific tasks schools are best adapted to fulfilling. They should then abandon efforts to attempt anything more.

According to traditionalists, the school's central mission was to teach children the skills needed for further learning. Teachers also should insist upon mastery of these subject-matter disciplines that past experience had shown to be "essential" for individual self-fulfillment and social well-being. Schools cannot accept responsibility, it was said, for "social adjustment," or for the teaching of specific coping skills used in everyday life. These should be entrusted to the home, the church, and other institutions in society. Formal education should concern itself with more fundamental forms of learning. Under the aegis of progressivist doctrine, however, conservative critics maintained, discipline had grown lax. Academic standards of performance had plummeted. The time had come to restore rigor in schools and to return to the teaching of basic skills and "core" subjects.

Again, for a time nobody seemed to be paying much attention. The next official attempt to outline school purposes came in a postwar report of the NEA's Educational Policies Commission entitled, *Education for All American Youth.*[6] On a superficial reading, its statement of "imperative needs of youth" closely resembled earlier formulations of educational goals in the progressivist mold: good health and physical fitness; community and citizenship duties; consumer skills; scientific skills; literary, artistic, and musical skills; leisure activities; ethical values; thinking ability; family life; and economic and vocational competence. Closer inspection, however, would have revealed how the Commission had ended up endorsing most of the cherished aims of vocationalist educators. Outlined in the report was a detailed scheme to relate school curricula more closely to occupational training, with the bulk of time, energy, and effort going to prepare youth for employment. Had the Commission's recommendations been adopted in schools, the character of the nation's educational system might have changed drastically. In point of fact, no such dramatic transformation occurred.

Meanwhile, the cardinal tenet of progressivism, that schools should be concerned with the total growth and development of the child, not just with certain selected mental functions, was running into trouble. In the postwar years more and more critics renewed the Essentialists' attack on schools for usurping responsibilities properly belonging to the family and other segments of society. Once again, allegations were heard that schools were neglecting cognitive processes. Calls were issued for educators to emphasize the three R's, to get back to basics. As the pendulum of public opinion swung back to a more conservative position, progressive education began to lose its appeal. By the late 1940s and early 1950s, it was moribund.

Whatever lingering vestiges of progressivism remained were held up for ridicule and scorn throughout the rest of the Cold War era. Symbolizing popular fears that the schools had been overly permissive was a widely reprinted newspaper cartoon of the day, portraying a harried classroom teacher, the children clearly out of control, with one small pupil tugging at her skirt asking plaintively, "Please, teacher, do we *have* to do what we want today?" A new generation of critics proclaimed schools were socially irresponsible, that indulgent teachers had been negligent in the performance of their duties, and that the country was being sold out by a cabal of soft-headed teacher-educators responsible for a generation of ignoramuses. Some critics even hinted at a deliberate conspiracy perpetrated by leftist subversives lurking within the ranks of the nation's educators. In any case, life adjustment was out; rigor and discipline were in.

Then came *Sputnik I.* In the fall of 1957, the Soviets lofted the world's first mechanical satellite into orbit. Americans gazed up at the heavens with mingled awe and envy, wondering why it was Americans had not been the first to achieve this technological miracle. The reaction that followed assumed near-hysterical proportions. Seeking scapegoats, politicians, academics, and military leaders turned upon the schools. Their indictment ran somewhat as follows: America was paying the price for having allowed control over the schools to fall into the hands of the likes of John Dewey. Progressive education amounted to a tragic blunder. Lulled by the rhetoric of personal adjustment, individual needs, and discovery learning, the public had been misled. It was painfully apparent now that important skills had been neglected, that children could neither read nor write nor even think clearly. Ivan could read; Johnny could not. Public education had become a vast "wasteland," as one prominent critic phrased it, dominated by quackery, another alleged. The United States as a result had lost its traditional scientific preeminence in the world. Many feared perilous times lay ahead.

Testifying before a U.S. Senate Committee in 1958, the German-educated missile expert Werner von Braun urged the adoption of the European educational system, with its stress on academic achievement and scholastic rigor. Reminiscing about his own training, he observed:

> I do not remember that I ever attended any classes in Europe on "family life" or "human relations," or subjects like "boy-girl relations at college." We just learned reading, writing, and arithmetic in the lower schools. Later on they taught us technical and scientific subjects, but nothing else.[7]

Von Braun was joined by scores of others deriding the schools for incompetence, academic flabbiness, and alleged preoccupation with "frills," to the virtual exclusion of such "hard" subjects as mathematics, science, and foreign languages. Admiral Hyman Rickover, father of the nuclear-submarine program, for example, was ferocious in his denunciations of public education. More moderate in tone but no less insistent was John Gardner, president of the Carnegie Corporation, who spoke repeatedly about the "desperate need" not only for technicians and scientists but for gifted leaders in all walks of life. The pursuit of "excellence," he claimed, had become an overriding consideration for America's educational system.

Indicative of the shifting national mood was the 1959 report of the Educational Policies Commission. Whereas previously the Commission had lent its support to a whole-child, student-centered approach to schooling, now the emphasis was upon disciplinary training for the gifted. "The academically talented student, as a rule, is not being sufficiently challenged, does not work hard enough, and his program of academic subjects is not of sufficient range," claimed Commission Chairman James B. Conant.[8] The same theme was sounded in a White House Conference on Education and reiterated five years later, in 1960, by the President's Commission on National Goals. Henceforth, it was announced, top priority would be given to science, foreign languages, and mathematics as subjects of instruction. The Commission further called for a stringent program of testing for all students, beginning in the early grades and continuing through high school. Ability grouping, enrichment programs for academically exceptional students, and stricter discipline were essential, the Commission affirmed, if the nation was to meet its goals in years to come.[9]

Leading critics in the post-*Sputnik* era made it plain what they believed schools should be doing: turning out skilled scientists and engineers as quickly as possible. The nation was locked in confrontation with the Soviet Union; and education was a weapon to be wielded in the Cold War. Anything smacking of softness, of permissiveness, was a luxury the United States could no longer afford.

In retrospect, it is not at all clear that criticism of schools in the fifties was well founded. If schools were not the citadels of quality their more adulatory defenders claimed, neither were they hotbeds of know-nothing life-adjustment education. To paraphrase Will Rogers, "The schools ain't what they used to be and probably never were." Dewey's influence was vastly exaggerated; and in their workaday features, contrary to critics' allegations, schools reflected at best a very limited version of the reforms once urged by progressivists. For good or for ill, the reality of public education was the product of many different concerns and influences. What counted, however, was not the actual condition of classrooms but public perceptions of how they functioned. And what people wanted was something very different from what they thought they were getting.

The next phase of reform came in the early 1960s, and was marked by efforts on the part of such leading academics as Jerrold Zacharias of the Massachusetts Institute of Technology and Harvard's Jerome Bruner to devise new curricular strategies in tandem with more effective methods of instruction. The aim, as was explained at a now-famous conference held at Woods Hole, Massachusetts, was to develop efficient schools capable of producing competent mathematicians, technicians, and language specialists. The product of an eventual collaboration between subject-matter specialists and curriculum planners was the New Math and New Science, followed by a New English and then a New Social Studies.

Ironically enough, almost unnoticed in all the excitement over the supposed innovations being introduced was the extent to which curriculum theorists had returned to John Dewey.[10] Bruner, for example, in a best-selling report on the Woods Hole conference called *The Process of Education,* ended up arguing that the mission of the school was to teach children how to think—specifically, how to deal with questions and forms of inquiry posed by the "structure" of various disciplines. For Bruner, every subject offered a unique way of organizing material. The trick was to lay bare the conceptual building blocks that made up the discipline's organizational pattern. This "structure," in essence, was what students ought to learn. Knowledge of the motive concepts underlying each disciplinary structure could not be handed down intact or implanted, as it were, in the minds of children, he emphasized. Rather, young learners had to be led inductively to "discover" it for themselves, through a problem-solving process.[11] Dewey himself would have heartily agreed.

Hard on the heels of curriculum reform came another movement to increase the schools' efficiency. Borrowing industrial analogies or metaphors, proponents began arguing that children could be likened to "raw materials" to be processed and fitted to predetermined ends. Systematic planning required goals to be specified operationally, preferably in terms of what learners would be able to *do* once they had received instruction. "Inputs" into the system (money, materials, instructional processes, staff, and training programs) would be monitored closely and analyzed. Outcomes, or "outputs," would consist of measures of the degree to which stated goals had been met, usually expressed as changes in learner characteristics.[12] Politicians, industrialists, and some educators welcomed this prospect of applying business-management techniques to education problems. If "systems analysis," as it was called, proved successful, it would be a technocratic dream come true. Skeptical critics, on the other hand, considered the whole scheme an Orwellian nightmare.

The decade of the sixties, however, also ushered in a period of reawakened social conscience as concern grew over problems of poverty, urban decay, racial discrimination, and the special needs of minorities. Educational priorities shifted away from programs for the gifted and more toward those aimed at helping disadvantaged youth. Popular support began to appear for equal-opportunity legislation and affirmative-action policies, both of which profoundly influenced education. If questions of fundamental purpose had receded into the background, at least the nation appeared to have embarked upon a quest to achieve greater social justice for all. Many believed fervently that schools were indispensable in the building of what prevailing political rhetoric called a "Great Society." For a time, this seemed more than enough to worry about.

A challenge to the dominant view that schools should service the corporate social order came unexpectedly around the midpoint of the decade. It was to assume the form of a radical protest, expressed mainly through the writings of classroom teachers themselves who recounted in concrete specific detail how the conventions of schooling—grading, grouping, labeling, teacher-centered instruction, record keeping, bureaucratization—alienated students from learning. Before long such practicing educators as James Herndon, Herbert Kohl, and Jonathan Kozol were joined by journalists, among them Nat Hentoff, George Dennison, and George Leonard, and by psychologists and sociologists (William Glasser, Carl Rogers, Edgar Friedenberg, Jules Henry) in exposing all the ways schools suppressed children's natural curiosity and love of learning. Their message was the same. Far from helping the young to grow as autonomous individuals, they alleged, the rigidity of school worked in just the opposite direction. Instead of nurturing children's interests and allowing each pupil the freedom to develop in his or her own unique way, schools functioned in ways guaranteed to frustrate learning. They were, so-called "romantic" critics complained, profoundly inhumane institutions.

By the late 1960s the outpouring of protest had become a deluge. Remarked one critic:

> It is strange, indeed, that young people who are responsible enough to walk a mile to school are not viewed as responsible enough to walk through a school corridor or use the restroom properly. Students report that they are denied the right to question their punishment, feel that they are degraded or treated with disrespect, and report that the school does not tell students of their rights as citizens in a democratic social order. . . . Thousands upon thousands of students both young and old feel degraded, that their opinions do not count and that their teachers perceive them as unable to be responsible for their own behavior. . . .[13]

Reminiscent of the progressivists half a century earlier, radical humanistic reformers pressed their attack. Once again, critics claimed, schools had fallen into the trap of teacher-based instruction, classroom passivity, and the substitution of punishments for rewards in motivating students to learn. Degrading and demeaning practices such as comparative grading and standardized achievement testing that destroy a child's feeling of worth or self-esteem should be abolished, they argued. The purpose of schooling is not to stamp out obedient conformists who will fit into society's tidy little boxes. It is not to win the Cold War, or to beat the Russians to the moon, or to fulfill any other external policy objective. Rather, the aim of decent public education is to place people in charge of their own lives. It is to nurture the development of thinking, feeling human beings who are free and autonomous in their own right. And if children are to grow up to understand the meaning of freedom, they must experience it for themselves. Schools must become places where children can explore on their own without fear and without being penalized for making errors. They must be allowed to exercise initiative and to discover for themselves the personal significance of whatever they learn.

The American educational scene had not witnessed such ferment since the heyday of the progressive-education movement. Caught unawares, professional educators hastened to catch up with what was fast becoming a new orthodoxy. School journals soon overflowed with articles about open-space classrooms, schools without walls, nongraded schools, individually guided education, confluent education, "discovery" learning, affective curricula, and a host of other novelties. Public-school districts began experimenting (albeit cautiously and mostly on a piecemeal basis) with ways of "humanizing" and "individualizing" and "personalizing" instruction.

Meanwhile, fearful that the innovations would not go far enough, groups of concerned teachers and parents were setting out to organize their own independent "free" schools, separate and apart from controls exercised by the public-school establishment. Some of them, reflecting the youth counter-culture of the day, were begun in hopes of creating a learning environment freed of all traditional middle-class constraints. A few were designed to appeal specifically to racial and ethnic minorities. Still others scarcely resembled schools at all, in their efforts to bring incidental and formal learning closer together.

"We are in the beginning stages of a sweeping redefinition of the purposes and functions of education in our society," announced John Fischer of Teachers College, Columbia University. "Before the task is finished, we shall have to reconsider not only the nature and operation of existing institutions but also the entire question of how multiple means of education, old and new, can best be used to liberate the possibilities of individuals and to enhance the scope and meaning of human life." [14]

More radical by far were proposals in the early seventies to abolish schools altogether. Reforms *within* schools miss the point, a few critics insisted. By its very nature, institutionalized education is an enterprise designed to reproduce the established order by perpetuating its dominant values, ideology, and organizational structures. Breaking up the public-school monopoly by creating private alternatives therefore does not go far enough. True reform would require, at a minimum, an end to compulsory school attendance and the elimination of all academic certificates and credentials. Most of the important functions served by the traditional school could and should be reallocated to other agencies in society. "We are witnessing the end of the age of schooling," asserted Ivan Illich. [15] "The belief that a highly industrialized society requires twelve to twenty years' of prior processing of the young is an illusion or a hoax," agreed writer Paul Goodman. Education in the sense of socialization, Goodman asserted, is a natural and inevitable process to which formal schooling is a reasonable auxiliary whenever an activity is best learned by singling it out for special attention under someone else's tutelage. But it by no means follows "that the complicated artifact of a school system has much to do with education, and certainly not with good education." [16] Until relatively recent times, he pointed out, most education had taken place through first-hand observation and experience: in families and peer groups, in community labor and in apprenticeship arrangements, through games, play, and ritual. [17] It could do so again, and thereby regain the meaningfulness such learning had once possessed.

Repeatedly, proponents of "de-schooling" society stressed the point that only within the past century had society required a lengthy period of formal education. John Holt, among others, felt that attendance should be voluntary and that schools should "compete with other educational resources for the time and attention of children." [18] Psychologist Carl Bereiter likewise believed there was little evidence that schools were capable of achieving much beyond simple training and providing custodial care. "Education," he alleged, "amounts to an empty claim, but in trying to make good on the claim, schools waste money and energy, subject people to endless tedium, and end up doing an inferior job . . ." [19]

Everett Reimer, author of a 1971 volume entitled *School Is Dead, Alternatives In Education,* was one of several critics who concluded that the formal institution of schooling had outlived its usefulness altogether. The time had come to end its "scholastic monopoly." What was needed was the replacement of schools by an informal, noncompulsory network of other types of educational resources. [20]

Reactions to the deschooling proposal ranged from incredulity and disbelief to derisive scorn. Typical was philosopher Sidney Hook's dismissal of Illich's *Deschooling Society*[21] as a "smart, silly book . . . whose absurd criticism warrants little attention from anyone endowed with a normal portion of common sense."[22] Because schools at present are not the voluntary, noncoercive centers of innocence and pleasure deschoolers want them to be, objected Mortimer Smith, is no reason for scrapping them. Nor, he claimed, was it realistic to think children in the modern world could acquire needed skills and knowledge informally.[23] Philip W. Jackson, of the University of Chicago, agreed it was naive to imagine school-age children in a postschool era learning solely through contact with real-life situations.

"Guided by nothing more than natural curiosity and an instinctual love for learning," Jackson mused,

> our children will presumably wander over the streets and fields of our land, gathering rosebuds of wisdom along the way. Adults, gladdened by the sight of these wandering scholars, will hail them as they pass and will invite them into the shops and factories and offices and hospitals, where they will become apprentices and learn at the feet of their elders those skills and trades that will equip them to take a productive place within our society.[24]

So idyllic a scenario, he remarked, was as improbable as it was unrealistic.

Having begun with an exaggerated notion of how bad schools were, critics argued, proponents of deschooling ended up with an overly romanticized vision of a social order without formal education. But were schools as oppressive as deschoolers claimed? Jackson, once again, thought not. "Much as it might dampen the critic's flame," he remarked, "a calm look at what goes on in our classrooms reveals them to be neither Dickensian nor Orwellian horrors. They are neither prisons, presided over by modern-day Fagins who take delight in twisting ears and otherwise torturing children, nor are they gigantic Skinner boxes, designed to produce well-conditioned automatons who will uncritically serve the state."[25]

Many others agreed. And as quickly as it had begun, the impetus for humanistic educational reform collapsed. Radical critics—those urging fundamental changes in schools and those who wanted to abolish them altogether—suddenly found themselves without a constituency. Once again the climate of opinion had shifted abruptly; and by the mid-seventies, in an uncanny replay of events of the fifties, reaction set in. Now the trend was back to basics, back to core subjects, back to more rigorous accountability in education. Some school critics, chastened by failure and newly appreciative of the difficulty of bringing about lasting reforms, turned their attention elsewhere. Others simply faded away, never to be heard from again.

Yet most of the societal problems that earlier had given rise to so much turmoil and indirectly led to radical school criticism remained. Crime and violence continued to plague the streets and schools. Resentment over racial and sex discrimination persisted. The question in the 1970s was whether schooling could do anything at all to alleviate society's ills. In its 1973 report, entitled, *The Reform of Secondary Education,* for example, the Kettering Commission noted that large urban high schools appeared "on the verge of complete collapse." It voiced concern that schools across the country seemed lackluster and teachers uninspired. Truancy had increased, as had drug and alcohol abuse. Educators, as though exhausted by all the crusading fervor of the decade preceding, appeared uninterested in any bold new initiatives.[26]

Contrasting with earlier reports, the Commission's recommendations for reform avoided much consideration of purpose or goals in favor of more prosaic proposals addressing processes and curricular content: school-security codes, the elimination of racial and sexual biases in instruction, better counseling programs for students, and a somewhat controversial proposal to lower the compulsory school-leaving age to fourteen. Similarly, a report by the National Association of Secondary School Principals (NASSP) entitled *American Youth in the Mid-Seventies* limited itself to such matters as fairness in grading, school discipline, problems of finance, and the need for integration and racial balance.[27]

If there was any one single focus of concern typical of the seventies, it had to do with the relationship between schooling and work. With a steady worsening of the nation's economy, high school and college graduates increasingly found themselves joining the ranks of the unemployed. Frustration and fear permeated the social order as energy costs soared and inflation crept steadily upward, adding to the general misery. Renewed interest was shown in relating school instruction more closely to the needs of the marketplace.

Indicative of burgeoning support for a vocationalist emphasis in schooling was the positive reception accorded "career education," as promoted by Education Commissioner Sidney Marland of the U.S. Office of Education. The 1973 Kettering Commission also lent its official support to the idea that schools should devise programs designed to help students learn more about various career opportunities. A 1974 Report of the Panel on Youth of the President's Science Advisory Committee, *Youth: Transition to Adulthood,* likewise urged a realignment of curricula to allow high-school youths access to job-skill training programs.[28] A similar recommendation was forthcoming in the NASSP's 1973 report when it called for "action-learning" experiences out of schools in paid or unpaid work settings. A 1979 report by the Carnegie Council on Policy Studies in Higher Education also endorsed work-study programs for low-income youth and apprenticeships for sixteen- and seventeen-year-olds.[29]

Looking toward education in the 1980s and beyond, the National Education Association in 1977 offered its attempt at an updating of the 1918 Cardinal Principles of Secondary Education. Commenting on curriculum goals for the future, panel members cautioned educators not to overextend themselves by promising too much. Schools, they noted, do not educate in isolation but only in conjunction with the home, the influence of the media, and other institutions in society. Education should be viewed as a process that takes place in many different environments, not just in classrooms. Schools have an important yet limited role to play, the NEA panel argued, in teaching youth the technological and coping skills needed for dealing with social change.[30]

Looking back on the history of school debate, historian David Tyack and his associates in 1980 were struck by what they termed "the cheerful amnesia and lack of balance" typified by reformers:

> Those with longer memories have often commented on the cyclical pattern of attempted changes in education. However, periodically, people discover with alarm problems that have been with us for decades if not centuries: poverty, wayward youth, inadequate preparation for work, and rigid schools. Specific solutions are proposed with all the hype that advertisers invest in the "new" Old Dutch Cleanser, yet often these are recycled solutions from earlier areas: accountability and business efficiency, the career motive, or teaching the "whole child."[31]

What was different in the eighties, many writers pointed out, was that popular faith in the American system of public schooling had been severely shaken. Disorder inherent in conflicting governmental policy, the inconsistent positions and demands of a variety of special interests, years of social turbulence, eroding resources, and the imminent prospect of a drop in student enrollments had all taken their toll. Increasingly, many who could afford to enroll their children in private schools were electing to do so. A flight from public education had begun, weakening the ability of those left behind to continue the work of strengthening public schools.

Part of the problem, as some analysts saw it, was that, burdened with roles and responsibilities that other agencies and institutions had given up, public education was expected to do more than was feasible. One writer commented:

> The necessary conditions for learning . . . include teachers willing and able to teach, a curriculum that everyone can learn, order and stability in the learning environment, minimal distraction from the learning process, and children willing and able to learn what they are taught. . . . The delicacies of fashion notwithstanding, all of these conditions must obtain at once to establish an effective learning context. . . . Because modern schools provide these conditions less often than before, we have indeed strayed from the fundamentals—not from the curricula or content so much as from the context that learning requires.[32]

Many observers in the eighties wondered why past school reforms had proven so ineffectual. "When I visit new schools today," lamented University of Maryland sociologist Jean Dresden Grambs, "I see the same ugly lockers in the same barren halls, the same seats in rows, the teacher at the front of the classroom talking, talking, talking, cowed boys slouching outside the vice-principal's office, the furtive (or brazen) pre-delinquents smoking behind the building, and the terrible cafeteria food."[33] Why, she asked, had so little changed, and what could be learned from this lack of change? Did past educational inertia mean that schools were impervious to reform? Why did educational institutions seem so intractable?

Searching for answers, a few educational theorists turned to "genetic" or "structural" explanations of the relationship between schooling and the social order, with the more radical among them arguing that only sweeping changes in the political and economic structure of society could bring about significant educational change. In essence, the burden of the argument they developed was that social institutions like schools simply mirror patterns of thought and economic activity of the culture they transmit. Socioeconomic structure, in other words, determines schooling, not vice versa. Hence, it was futile to believe schools could be changed without correlative changes taking place in the undergirding social, economic, and political order. By the mid-eighties, some such position had become decidedly fashionable in certain circles.[34]

Reacting against the traditional liberal belief that schooling affords equality of opportunity for all, economist Samuel Bowles, for example, earlier had argued that schools evolved "not as part of a pursuit of equality, but rather to meet the needs of capitalist employers for a disciplined and skilled labour force, and to provide a mechanism for social control in the interest [of] political stability."[35] Contrary to the central idea of political liberalism—that education is, or can be, the great solvent of social ills in a capitalist economy and that it serves as an equalizer of social and economic disparities—Bowles claimed that schools exist to reproduce the socioeconomic *inequalities* required to perpetuate capitalism as an economic system.

Depending on how rigidly some such thesis was interpreted, those who found it credible could have drawn the conclusion that disagreements over educational goals or purposes are purely "epiphenomenal"; that is, they represent so much flotsam and jetsam awash on a sea of rhetoric. Because the character and effects of schooling are determined by society's economic relations of production, and formal education allegedly services the needs of a corporate-capitalist order, disputes over specific aims or objectives are relatively meaningless. Arguments about whether schools should be authoritarian or permissive, for example, directive or nondirective, vocationally or academically oriented, miss the point. Ultimately the outcome is the same: perpetuation and reproduction of the existing social structure, with all of its intrinsic inequalities.

One interesting variation on this theme offered by some writers in the eighties was that schools are primary carriers of "technological consciousness"; i.e., the system of assumptions, values, and beliefs behind technocracy and modernity found in all advanced industrial nations, whatever their political orientation. In the most fundamental sense possible, they argued, schooling today serves to buttress a technocratic social order. So pervasive have the assumptions and latent forms of consciousness associated with technocracy become, people are neither aware of their controlling influence nor cognizant of the possibility of alternatives. The inevitability and desirability of technocratic life, in the nature of things, is never raised as an issue. The facts of rational planning, quantification, systematization of control, and management by technical expertise are taken as fixed and unalterable—as "givens."

Consequently, or so it was said, schools are not at all the conservative institutions they are sometimes made out to be. Although the school as a social institution is particularly responsive to conservative forces in a community, the primary conceptual categories of technocracy communicated through education (symbolized by efforts to translate metaphors borrowed from industrial engineering into classroom practice and by attempts to manage school administration through metaphors adapted from systems theory) are accepted and unwittingly supported even by reactionaries. They endorse them without awareness that such assumptions undermine the very beliefs such groups are attempting to protect by exerting pressures on schools.[36]

In the final analysis, if technocratic ideology controls schooling, disputes over specific educational goals, the content of curricula, instructional strategies or organizational matters are bound to be affected, amounting once again to little more than minor variations on the larger theme. Whether people are consciously aware of it or not, arguments over school policies are framed within the context of servicing technocratic values and ends. It follows then that disagreements about school aims are either relatively trivial or perhaps even meaningless.

In fact, few so-called critical theorists in the 1970s and 1980s went this far. A more sophisticated version of the neo-Marxist critique advanced held that schools do more than simply mirror society's economic system and its needs. School life does not "correspond" in any precise way with economically shaped social relations, and schools do not passively or mechanically "reproduce" the structural order of society in some simple, straightforward fashion. In other words, the situation is actually somewhat more complex than a simplistic theory of cultural reproduction might imply. As the argument had it, schools exhibit a relatively high degree of autonomy, and are only indirectly influenced by more powerful economic and political institutions. The role of the school is to act as a *mediating* force between the social culture and its underlying structural configuration. Hence, if it is true that modes of economic production influence the character of social life in only a very general and indeterminate way, formal education also must count as a cultural force in its own right, helping to shape how people live, what forms of consciousness they experience, and the alternatives for living open to them within society.

Thus divested of some of its rigid determinism, the revised analysis left room for the reality of disagreements over how schooling should be conducted and what larger ends it should pursue. In short, even within a "systemic" or "generic" critique, it became apparent it was possible to claim that questions about educational policy and goals in contemporary society were worth taking seriously.

The problem in the eighties was that so-called "structural" explanations of the limits of school reform tended to undercut the case for the gradual improvement of existing schools. Growing disenchantment with public education and skepticism over prospects for changing it in any material way simply made matters worse. Internecine conflict over how increasingly scarce resources should be utilized and the rising influence of fractionated interest groups, each promoting its own cause, further served to destroy whatever sense of common purpose had survived. All things considered, American public education at the decade's midpoint appeared to have reached a point of crisis as great as any it had ever before experienced.

Looking back upon a century or more of educational controversy, the broad sweep of debate suggests constant reiteration as old themes are periodically recycled in new guise. These conflicting views on educational aims or processes, it needs to be emphasized, stem from very real substantial disagreements, often of a philosophic character. They arise from divergent beliefs about the nature of people, learning, knowledge, and how schooling can best contribute to human fulfillment within the social order. Enduring differences are embedded in a social context, but they further trace back in part at least to the divergent assumptions or presuppositions people take for granted, the values they endorse, and the larger principles to which they give allegiance in approaching questions about education. Clarification of the underlying issues at stake therefore demands that the ideas or beliefs participants subscribe to be examined and analyzed with care.

The basic challenge is to devise a strategy for uncovering those issues and throwing them into bold relief. The closer one gets down to scrutinizing the microscopic phenomena of debate, the harder it is to discern patterns, or "trends" and "movements," at work. All one finds are many different people, expressing many different ideas, advancing many different proposals. What is needed, accordingly, are broadly gauged categorizations or "templates" that, applied to the data, allow patterns to emerge. If the typology employed "fits" without serious distortion, it can prove extraordinarily helpful in revealing interconnections and thematic continuities among ideas that might otherwise be obscured or appear inchoate. The need, in short, is for a system of idealized "types," sometimes themselves larger than life, in and through which thinking about basic educational issues can proceed.

The narrative to follow treats four broadly defined prospectives or outlooks on education. For the sake of convenience, they may be designated, respectively, as educational traditionalism or *conservatism, humanism, vocationalism,* and reformism or *reconstructionism.* Neither the terms nor the positions they identify should be taken too literally. It is safer to understand them, rather, as useful "fictions," which, abstracted and reformulated as formal arguments, allow the positions people advance in the "real world" of debate over schooling to be categorized for purposes of analysis.

First in this fourfold classification is a position that views education as a process whereby learners acquire skills needed for induction into a culture and the forms of knowing that culture affords. To say of someone that he or she is "educated" is to claim that the person has achieved a degree of mastery over, or is conversant with, a defined body of knowledge, skills, and values. The purpose of schooling from this particular perspective is initiation into the world of intellect. Information acquired may be put to practical use in a variety of ways. It can serve many different proximate ends (for example, critical thinking, character development, ethical behavior, esthetic sensibility, and so on). Implicit throughout, nevertheless, is the notion of the importance of learning for its own sake and the idea that coming to know something is a self-sufficient end, good in and of itself. From an individual's point of view, the purpose of learning is to obtain the means for extending the range and quality of experiences one is capable of having. The more one knows, the richer and fuller life becomes. In a larger social sense, the function of education is the conservation and transmission of a knowledge culture.

Closely related in aim but more broadly conceived is a second outlook. In this view, schooling is a process of facilitating personal autonomy and self-actualization, but *without* necessary reference to some determinate body of knowledge or subject matter. The end goal of self-fulfillment might be secured in as many different ways perhaps as there are differences among people, through a variety of experiences, and aided by whatever learning or knowledge proves fruitful for each individual. The subject matter of instruction cannot be defined in advance. Especially important is the enhancement of the affective dimension of human functioning. From the learner's perspective, education means discovery and exploration. It aims at progressive self-definition, the enlargement of personal freedom, and the holistic development of one's potential to the fullest extent possible. From society's vantage point, education is a matter of nurturing a "humane" social order—one in which persons interact freely and in cooperation with one another to sustain the conditions needed for the maximal self-realization of all.

Thirdly, schooling can be thought of as a mechanism to service society's need for a skilled work force. For the individual learner, the point of schooling first and foremost is to acquire the knowledge, attitudes, and skills needed for employment—for achieving economic sufficiency, or otherwise fulfilling one's economic role in the social order. From society's standpoint, the purpose of education is manpower development. The function of schooling is to meet marketplace demands by training people for jobs. Education is induction into the world of work.

Least well-defined is a fourth orientation, encompassed by all the ways schools as social institutions are employed to exert leverage on larger societal concerns or problems. Schooling is a mechanism for addressing various social, economic, and political issues. So far as the individual is concerned, the point of the school experience is to acquire the understanding needed for full-fledged participation in a political community. Broadly speaking, education is preparation for citizenship. From society's perspective, schooling is an instrumentality for social renewal or reform.

In actual public debate, none of these four positions finds expression in some pure, unadulterated state, nor are the arguments associated with each put forth quite so baldly. At any given moment, all four perspectives enjoy support, though their relative degree of influence on public opinion may fluctuate. Each, however, offers a different set of answers to certain fundamental questions:

1. What is most worth knowing? What information, skills, or values are *most* important, and to whom?

2. By what criteria or standards should the importance of certain kinds of learning be determined?

3. What are the conditions and processes necessary for effective learning? How should formal education as a collective enterprise be conducted? What is needed in order for learning to be meaningful and relevant?

4. What are the *most* important functions or missions of the school as a social institution? How should these be identified, according to what standards or principles, and by whom? Who should decide? If the school cannot do everything, how should priorities be fixed and implemented? What is learning *for?*

5. What is (or should be) the relationship between institutionalized education and the larger social order? What kind of society best conduces to maximal human growth and fulfillment, and how (if at all) can education contribute to the development of such a society?

These four viewpoints or ways of construing education are not necessarily mutually exclusive, of course, particularly in the ways they figure in real-world debate over educational objectives and still less in terms of how their influence is felt in the workaday operations of schools themselves. Differences among them, typically, are much more a matter of relative emphasis.

For example, a proponent of vocational training would probably strenuously deny he or she was concerned *only* with school-based job preparation. At the same time, however, as a matter of priorities, a vocational educator would be apt to view occupationally relevant information as the *most* important knowledge a person could acquire, and economic efficiency—how well people are prepared for employment—would serve as the ultimate criterion for measuring school success.

Advocates of "humanistic" education likewise profess strong concern for intellectual competence, for effective citizenship, for job preparation, and other worthy ends. Yet psychosocial interests revolving around individual needs and interpersonal relations in the final analysis predominate as major concerns.

Again, supporters of the view that education is to be defined as a process of acquiring academic knowledge would say, for instance, that a liberally educated person *is* best fitted for citizenship in a democracy. They might claim, for example, that someone who has received a broad, general education already possesses the vocational skills that are apt to retain their utility over the long haul. Finally, a social reformer committed to increasing the political relevance of schooling would in no way deny the need for taking other social, psychological, or economic considerations into account in designing school programs. But ultimately, he or she would argue, the kind of learning that has the highest "survival" value is linked with helping people to adapt to change, to prepare for the future, and to raise public consciousness about events and issues that threaten the very existence of civilization itself. According to some "reconstructionists," for example, education is quite literally a race with global catastrophe.

In each instance, once again, educational conservatism, vocationalism, humanism, and reformism offer, respectively, a different set of priorities, a different hierarchy of goals, and a different conception of the purpose of educational processes. Whether or not these specific labels are invoked in debate, the belief systems or ideological perspectives they represent help to inform and shape the character of public controversy involving schools.

In what follows, these four viewpoints are made to serve as facets of a prism, so to speak, each reflecting a different perspective on American education in recent decades. The focus throughout is upon ideas, beliefs, and values as these are expressed in an on-going debate over fundamental educational issues. As much as possible, through judicious paraphrasing and extensive quotation, disputants have been allowed to speak for themselves. Needless to add, the point is not to highlight any one position to the disadvantage of others, or to win endorsement for some particular point of view. Rather, the aim simply is to explore and help clarify the issues at stake as Americans ponder the present and future course of schooling in years to come.

## NOTES

1. See David B. Tyack, Michael W. Kirst, and Elizabeth Hansot, "Educational Reform: Retrospect and Prospect," *Teachers College Record* 81 (Spring 1980): 260.

2. James J. Gallagher, "Present Trends and Future Challenges in American Education," *Peabody Journal of Education* 59 (January 1982): 69–70.

3. See Robert Wiebe, "The Social Functions of Public Education," *American Quarterly* 21 (Summer 1969): 147–150; and Daniel Walker Howe, ed., *Victorian America* (Philadelphia: University of Pennsylvania Press, 1976), pp. 3–28.

4. Allan C. Ornstein, "20th Century Educational Aims: Overview and Outlook," *American Secondary Education* 2 (Spring 1981): 10.

5. Educational Policies Commission, *The Purposes of Education in American Democracy* (Washington, D.C.: National Education Association, 1938).

6. Educational Policies Commission, *Education for All American Youth* (Washington, D.C.: National Education Association, 1944).

7. *Science and Education for National Defense,* hearings before the Committee of Labor and Public Welfare, United States Senate, Eighty-Eighth Congress (Washington, D.C.: U.S. Government Printing Office, 1958), p. 65; quoted in Ornstein, "Educational Aims," p. 11.

8. James B. Conant, *The American High School Today* (New York: McGraw-Hill, 1959), p. 15.

9. See *Proceedings, White House Conference on Education* (Washington: U.S. Government Printing Office, 1955), pp. 5, 11–12; and President's Commission on National Goals, *Goals for Americans* (Englewood Cliffs, N.J.: Prentice-Hall, 1960), pp. 84–85.

10. Neil Postman and Charles Weingartner, *The School Book* (New York: Delacorte Press, 1973), p. 5.

11. Jerome Bruner, *The Process of Education* (Cambridge, Mass.: Harvard University Press, 1960).

12. See John L. Hayman, Jr., "The Systems Approach and Education," *Educational Forum* 38 (May 1974): 493–501; and Tommy M. Tomlinson, "The Troubled Years: An Interpretive Analysis of Public Schooling since 1950," *Phi Delta Kappan* 62 (January 1981): 373.

13. Morrel J. Clute, "Can Human Rights Survive the Classroom?" *Educational Leadership* 31 (May 1974): 683–684.

14. John H. Fischer, "Public Education Reconsidered," *Today's Education* 61 (May 1972): 22.

15. Ivan Illich, "After Deschooling, What?" in Alan Gartner et al., eds., *After Deschooling, What?* (New York: Perennial Library, 1973), pp. 5–6.

16. Paul Goodman, *Compulsory Mis-education and the Community of Scholars* (New York: Vintage, 1964), pp. 16–17.

17. Paul Goodman, *The New Reformation: Notes of a Neolithic Conservative* (New York: Random House, 1970), p. 69.

18. See John Holt, *Freedom and Beyond* (New York: Dutton, 1972), and ''Why We Need New Schooling,'' in Stephen C. Margaritas, ed., *In Search of a Future for Education* (Columbus, Ohio: Chas. E. Merrill, 1973), p. 60.

19. Carl Bereiter, *Must We Educate?* (Englewood Cliffs, N.J.: Prentice-Hall, 1973), p. 81.

20. Everett Reimer, *School is Dead, Alternatives in Education* (New York: Doubleday, 1971), p. 30.

21. Ivan Illich, *Deschooling Society* (New York: Harrow Books, 1972).

22. Sidney Hook, ''Illich's De-schooled Utopia,'' *Encounter* 38 (January 1972): 54ff.

23. Mortimer Smith, ''The Romantic Radicals—A Threat to Reform,'' in Daniel U. Levine and Robert J. Havighurst, eds., *Farewell to Schools???* (Worthington, Ohio: Charles A. Jones, 1971), pp. 74–75.

24. Philip W. Jackson, ''A View from Within,'' in Levine and Havighurst, *Farewell,* pp. 62–63.

25. Ibid., p. 62.

26. National Commission on the Reform of Secondary Education, *The Reform of Secondary Education* (New York: National Commission, 1973), p. 64.

27. *American Youth in the Mid-Seventies* (Washington: National Association of Secondary School Principals, 1973).

28. James S. Coleman et al., *Youth Transition to Adulthood* (Chicago: University of Chicago Press, 1974), pp. 178–201.

29. Carnegie Council on Policy Studies in Higher Education, *Giving Youth A Better Chance: Options for Education, Work and Service, Summary of Concerns and Recommendations* (Washington: Carnegie Council on Policy Studies in Higher Education, 1979).

30. Harold G. Shane, *Curriculum Change Toward the 21st Century* (Washington: National Education Association, 1977).

31. Tyack, Kirst, and Hansot, ''Educational Reform,'' p. 255.

32. Tomlinson, ''Troubled Years,'' p. 375.

33. Jean Dresden Grambs, ''Forty Years of Education: Will The Next Forty Be Any Better?'' *Educational Leadership* 38 (May 1981): 631.

34. See Michael W. Apple, *Ideology and Curriculum* (London: Routledge and Kegan Paul, 1977); Basil Bernstein, *Class, Codes and Control, Volume 3: Towards a Theory of Educational Transmissions* (London: Routledge and Kegan Paul, 1975); Pierre Bourdieu and J. C. Passeran, *Reproduction in Education, Society and Culture* (London: Sage, 1977); Jerome Karabel and A. H. Halsey, eds., *Power and Ideology in Education* (New York: Oxford University Press, 1977); and Michael F. D. Young, ed., *Knowledge and Control* (New York: Collier-Macmillan, 1971).

35. Samuel Bowles, ''Unequal Education and the Reproduction of the Social Division of Labour,'' in Martin Carnoy, ed., *Schooling in a Corporate Society* (New York: D. McKay, 1972), p. 36. See also Samuel Bowles and Herbert Gintis, *Schooling in Capitalist America* (New York: Basic Books, 1976).

36. Consult, for example, C. A. Bowers, ''Ideological Continuities in Technicism, Liberalism, and Education,'' *Teachers College Record* 81 (Spring 1980): 293–321; and C. A. Bowers, ''Curriculum as Cultural Reproduction: An Examination of Metaphor as a Carrier of Ideology,'' *Teachers College Record* 80 (Winter 1980): 268–269.

# CHAPTER TWO
# EDUCATIONAL
# CONSERVATISM
## *A Traditionalist Perspective*

## INTRODUCTION

What is—or should be—the primary purpose of the school? Is it academic training? Vocational preparation? Promoting positive mental health and healthy psychological development? All of these, and more? Which is *most* important? When hard choices have to be made, where should educators concentrate their energy, time, and limited resources? How should teachers and administrators, trying to respond to many different external demands, fix priorities?

If the main goal of the school is to impart knowledge, what kind of knowledge is *most* worth having? Are there certain concepts, skills, values, and bodies of factual information so vital they should be acquired by *everyone?* If so, should there be a common core curriculum required of all children in school? What would be its component elements? Do individual differences among students in terms of ability, motivation, interests, needs, learning styles, and life goals need to be taken into account in planning a curriculum? If people differ, can the elements of some common learning be taught to all learners, to the same degree, or in the same fashion?

Historically, one set of responses to questions such as these has been represented by a theory about the proper aims of schooling that, for want of a better rubric, may be referred to as educational *conservatism*. Although its influence on public opinion has waxed and waned over the years, as a formal argument its basic contours have not changed appreciably in over half a century. The dominant theme throughout has been *the importance of the school's "conserving" role in society*. It comes closest, one might argue, to supplying a "mainstream" tradition, not because it has always been followed, but because alternative views usually have been advanced in reaction to, as modifications of, or as rival claimants upon, public attention to the conservative position.

Unfortunately, the label is apt to be somewhat misleading. In its educational bearings, the term "conservatism" has little to do directly with any point on a political spectrum of opinion. Rather, it denotes advocacy of the part played by the school as a social institution *in preserving the established culture of the past and transmitting it to successive generations*. Hence, *educational* conservatism ought not to be identified too closely with *political* conservatism, even though admittedly at times the association between the two has been very real and intimate. Thus, for example, many—but not necessarily all—political conservatives today are likely to espouse some kind of an educationally conservative point of view. Contrariwise, however, a number of people of decidedly liberal convictions in the political realm also claim the position as their own and enthusiastically defend its major tenets.

## THE CONSERVATIVE REACTION TO PROGRESSIVISM

Conservatism in educational theory first found systematic expression in the 1930s as a reaction against the alleged dominance of progressivism in educational practice, a movement widely—though not always accurately—linked with the pragmatist philosophy of John Dewey and his disciples.[1] Briefly, progressive education as it evolved in the early part of this century had arisen as a protest against rigid classroom convention and, more broadly, as an effort to revitalize and "humanize" the schools. As one historian has observed, speaking of traditional schooling:

> The realm of the classroom was totally set off from the experience of the child who inhabited it. The teachers' lessons encrusted by habit, the seats all arranged in formal rows, and the rigid etiquette of behavior all emphasized the difference between school and life. Hence learning consisted of the tedious memorization of data without a meaning immediately clear to the pupil.[2]

What progressivist reformers hoped for therefore was to bridge the gap between life and learning, to lessen the authoritarian character of old-fashioned education, and to individualize curricula and instruction in order to take into account very real differences in students' abilities, interests, and needs.[3]

Progressivist pedagogy allowed students much more freedom than ever before. Pupils helped plan school activities. Instead of using techniques requiring passivity and rote memorization, teachers encouraged learners to explore their own individual interests, to solve problems, and to "learn by doing." Subject matter, as John Dewey insisted, properly consisted of "whatever is recognized as having a bearing upon the anticipated course of events" in the lives of learners.[4] Consequently, the curriculum could not be defined in terms of rigid bodies of knowledge, separate and isolated from one another. Nor of course was it expected that students would necessarily pursue the same subjects.

Conservative school critics of the Depression era were aghast at what they saw as the results. American education in recent decades, they argued, had been diverted from its historical mission of defining, preserving, and reproducing a stable cultural inheritance. It was all very well to try to make learning as meaningful and pleasant as possible. But not all learning is equally important, they asserted. Certain facts and values are "essential" for everyone in society and should be shared in common. To the school therefore must fall the task of prescribing a uniform course of instruction. The curriculum should consist, minimally, of an irreducible care of academic skills and basic disciplines that all students must master whatever their personal inclinations or interests. Unfortunately, or so critics claimed, under the influence of progressivist doctrine many educators had lost sight of the need for priorities, for standards, and for some measure of commonality in school curricula.

## ESSENTIALISM

The opening salvo in what later evolved into a national debate was sounded by William Chandler Bagley (1874–1946), a professor of education at Teachers College, Columbia University. In his book, *Education and Emergent Man,* published in 1934, Bagley took an uncompromising stand. "Paradoxical as it may seem," he argued, "it is the conservative functions of education that are most significant in a period of profound change." The most important purpose of schooling, he avowed, is to transmit the funded wisdom, knowledge, and values of the past, and in so doing to preserve for society a measure of stability or equilibrium otherwise lacking in the midst of change.

"The very time to avoid chaos in the schools," Bagley wrote, "is when something akin to chaos characterizes the social environment. The very time to emphasize in the schools the values that are relatively certain and stable is when the social environment is full of uncertainty and when standards are crumbling." He continued, "If education is to be a stabilizing force it means that the school must discharge what is in effect a disciplinary function."[5] Regardless of what dislocations or upheavals mark the social order at any given moment, the school's mission remains the same. Its primary objective is to impart to the young those values and systems of knowledge that historical experience has revealed to be most important over the long haul. Particularly during periods of crisis or rapid change, the school's role in serving as a sort of "anchor" for society assumes special significance. For Bagley and other conservative educators, it followed that schools as social institutions are charged with a threefold mission.

First and foremost, *formal education should aim at helping all students acquire basic learning skills.* Only when learners have achieved proficiency in the application of such fundamental tools as reading, writing, and arithmetic can they hope to profit from further instruction and thereby progress in their mastery of academic subject matter.

Secondly, *institutions of learning have responsibility to emphasize truly important learning.* The pedagogical challenge is to sort out the trivial from the profound, to abstract what is of enduring significance from that which is only of transient interest, and to stress whatever is of central rather than peripheral concern. From an almost infinite array of possibilities, instruction should be directed toward basic disciplines and the most fundamental branches of human learning. That which has withstood the test of time deserves the most attention.

Thirdly, *schools should endeavor to foster morality.* Civilized life would be impossible unless members of society acknowledged the importance of honesty and truth-telling, of loyalty, personal integrity, justice, and so on. Certain ethical imperatives never change, no matter what the time or place. The task of the schools, accordingly, is to inculcate in students a knowledge of, and appreciation for, those overarching cultural values that, as Bagley put it, "will be just as significant a thousand years from now as they have ever been in the past."

Bagley was convinced that the educational philosophy promoted by John Dewey and the progressivists had served to dilute the true purpose of schooling. Worse yet, its influence had contributed materially to an erosion of academic standards. Less and less was expected of students. As he phrased it, "Our dominant educational theory is based upon the philosophy of pragmatism. What works passing well is not necessarily good but what works well enough is good enough." American schools, he believed, distinctly encouraged a "get-by" attitude. "It is difficult to conceive of an attitude more fatal," he commented, "than that which is developed in the practical implications of such a theory when spread over from eight to sixteen of the most impressionable years of life."[6] According to Bagley, the neglect of excellence was a sure prescription for academic mediocrity.

Not long afterwards, a like-minded critic by the name of Michael Demiashkevich coined the term "Essentialism" to refer to the position of all those who subscribed to the importance of schools stressing learning "essentials."[7] Together with Bagley, he was instrumental in helping to form The Essentialist Committee for the Advancement of American Education. Its members first assembled as a group in Atlantic City, New Jersey, in February of 1938 to hammer out a formal statement of Essentialist principles.

Those in attendance, besides Bagley and Demiashkevich, included Walter H. Ryle, M. L. Shane, F. Alden Shaw, Louis Shores, and Guy M. Whipple. Bagley agreed to accept major editorial responsibility for the drafting of "An Essentialist's Platform For The Advancement of American Education." It was to appear in print shortly thereafter, in the April 1938 issue of the journal *Educational Administration And Supervision.*[8] According to a prefatory note, an unauthorized advance release of the text to the press already had given rise to widespread publicity and "fiery denunciations" by several prominent educators.

"In spite of its vast extent and its heavy cost to society," Bagley began, "public education in the United States is in many ways appallingly weak and ineffective."[9] Elementary-school students lagged far behind their European counterparts in their mastery of learning fundamentals. They learned less and acquired it more slowly. American high-school graduates likewise fared poorly in comparison with graduates of secondary schools in many other countries. Growing numbers of pupils in junior and senior high schools, he alleged, were "essentially illiterate." Weaknesses in basic computational skills and the rudiments of English grammar were widespread. A major cause of these deficiencies, according to Bagley, was the relaxation of academic standards that had accompanied the upward expansion of mass education. Formerly, under a rigorously selective system, less able students had been excluded from the system's upper echelons. But when high schools and then colleges opened their doors to more and more students, the result was pressure to lower achievement norms for all.

Bagley's feeling was that, however desirable it might have been to extend educational opportunity to everyone, educators were prone to accept any theory or philosophy that could justify or rationalize the undesirable consequence entailed—any theory, in other words, that could convert a necessity into a virtue. As he put it:

> Under the necessity which confronted American education of rationalizing the loosening of standards and the relaxation of rigor if mass-education were to be expanded upward, the theories which emphasized interest, freedom, immediate needs, personal experience, psychological organization, and pupil-initiative, and which in so doing tended to discredit and even condemn their opposites—effort, discipline, remote goals, race-experience, logical sequence, and teacher-initiative—naturally made a powerful appeal.[10]

Such theories, he judged, had increasingly influenced the conduct of public schooling since the turn of the century.

The Essentialist Platform spelled out in detail the most flagrant abuses and misconceptions ostensibly condoned by permissive educational doctrine. Among these cited:

1. The virtual abandonment of achievement standards for determining grade promotion;
2. A disparagement of "systematic and sequential" instruction in favor of "incidental" learning;
3. A tendency to assume that "richness" of experience alone would lead pupils to acquire meaningful, important knowledge;
4. A downgrading of "exact and exacting" studies such as Latin, algebra, and geometry in secondary schools;
5. The substitution for difficult subject matter of less demanding "social studies" in school curricula;
6. Lack of uniformity in school requirements and in the grade-placement of crucial topics.

By and large, Bagley argued, the main thrust of educational usage had been "to minimize basic learnings, to magnify the superficial, to belittle sequence and system, and otherwise to aggravate the weakness and ineffectiveness of schools."[11] Discipline was lacking. Students were allowed to decide for themselves what they wished to learn. Following the line of least resistance and least effort, all too many educators refused to impose learning when necessary. Classroom teachers failed to insist upon obedience or to correct unruly students. In short, public schooling was in disarray.

Apart from shortchanging individual students, the Essentialist Platform affirmed, permissive education was also having a corrosive impact upon society at large. Democracy has a "vital, collective stake in the informed intelligence of every individual citizen," the author asserted.[12] The very survival of democratic institutions depends upon a literate electorate. If freedom is to be preserved, everyone must possess a modicum of social understanding and insight. Citizens must be taught how to exercise their franchise intelligently. The height of folly, therefore, would be to leave the development of informed reasoning to the whim or caprice of either learner or teacher.

Furthermore, Bagley went on to say, "An effective democracy demands a community of culture. Educationally this means that each generation must share a common core of ideas, meanings, understanding, and ideals, representing the most precious elements of the human heritage."[13] It is not necessary for everyone to learn *all* the same skills or knowledge. But people of otherwise diverse interests, backgrounds, needs, and goals must share *some* common frame of reference; and it is the job of the school to supply its foundation by teaching the essentials.

Two years later, paraphrasing the formulation supplied previously in the Essentialist Platform, Bagley outlined the sort of program he believed should frame a democratic system of education:

> There can be little question as to the essentials. It is no accident that the arts of recording, computing, and measuring have been among the first concerns of organized education. Every civilized society has been founded upon these arts, and when they have been lost, civilization has invariably collapsed. Nor is it accidental that a knowledge of the world that lies beyond one's immediate experience has been among the recognized essentials of universal education, and that at least a speaking acquaintance with man's past and especially with the story of one's country was early provided for in the program of the universal school. Investigation, invention, and creative art have added to our heritage. Health instruction is a basic phase of the work of the lower schools. The elements of natural science have their place. Neither the fine arts nor the industrial arts should be neglected.[14]

To the objection that not all students are capable of mastering a rigorous course of studies, Bagley's response was that "all except those hopelessly subnormal" *are* competent to achieve proficiency in the educational fundamentals.[15] The school should not adopt an easy policy of "leveling down" the curriculum. Quite the contrary, its challenge is to "level up" learning for all. Success depends upon the quality of instruction offered. Bagley freely conceded that not all learners progress at the same rate. Some in fact advance at a much slower pace. Still others find it difficult even getting started. But once initial handicaps are overcome, improvement follows quickly for the overwhelming majority of students.

The ultimate objective, however, should be much the same for everyone. "Let us not stigmatize failure as we have done in the past," he advised. "On the other hand, if education abandons rigorous standards and consequently provides no effective stimulus to the effort that learning requires, many persons will pass through twelve years of schooling only to find themselves in a world in which ignorance and lack of fundamental training are increasingly heavy handicaps." [16]

For Bagley, the corollary was obvious. "Should not our public schools," he asked rhetorically, "prepare boys and girls for adult responsibility through systematic training in such subjects as reading, writing, arithmetic, history, and English, requiring mastery of such subjects and, when necessary, stressing discipline and obedience?" [17]

The label Essentialism seems not to have survived very long as a term for designating educational conservatism—except possibly in the imagination of textbook writers of later years. Nonetheless, the basic positions staked out by Bagley rather quickly won new adherents in the decade following. Among the more articulate of its advocates in this period were such educators as Franklin Babbitt, Thomas H. Briggs, Henry C. Morrison, Charles H. Judd, William W. Brickman, and Isaac L. Kandel, editor of the influential journal *School and Society*. [18] Discounting individual differences of emphasis in their writings, the basic outline of the Essentialist perspective they shared could be discerned as follows:

1.  Human culture has an identifiable "core" of information and values;
2.  Core knowledge refers to the most important learning available within a culture;
3.  Certain basic values are absolute and enduring;
4.  The test for what information, skills, and values are most fundamental is what in the experience of successive generations proves useful and relevant for a majority of people;
5.  Societal stability requires the preservation and transmission of the core culture;
6.  The school's primary mission is to pass on this cultural inheritance;
7.  Formal education has fallen under the influence of those who would divert the schools from their historical function of handing down the established culture;
8.  The expansion of mass education in order to broaden and more nearly equalize educational opportunity has contributed to a weakening of academic-achievement standards;
9.  Owing to misconceptions of what democracy and egalitarianism require, schools fail to challenge their ablest students; curricula and instruction have been "leveled down" to the lowest common denominator;
10. Students at all levels in the American school system do not perform as well academically as do their counterparts in other countries;
11. As a result of abandoning rigorous academic standards and attempting to "popularize" curricula, schools lack coherence and a sense for educational priorities;
12. Schools cannot be all things to all people; nor can they do everything worth attempting equally well;

13. Peripheral social and educational concerns have been brought to the fore, thereby obscuring and confusing the schools' most important goals;

14. Democratic society and its institutions require a literate, informed citizenry schooled in the essentials and sharing in a common culture;

15. Schools neglect the teaching of basic learning skills, fundamental knowledge, and values of enduring significance;

16. Educational institutions have forsaken achievement norms as the condition for grade promotion and graduation, thereby producing "overgraded" pupils who are increasingly handicapped by learning deficits as they progress through the school system.

17. Schools disparage system and sequence in instruction; incidental learning and "learning by doing" are poor substitutes for mastery of the various academic disciplines, as taught in some logical, sequential, and systematic fashion;

18. Formal education should emphasize more rigorous, intellectually demanding disciplines, the skills required for scholastic competence, and those traditional values that provide both the basis of American culture and the accepted norms for personal morality. Schools should stress the "essentials."

## POSTWAR CRITICISM: SCHOOLING FOR AMERICANISM

Debate over school policy between Progressivists and Essentialists was soon eclipsed by America's entry into the Second World War; and for the duration, rather obviously, public attention was engaged elsewhere. But with the restoration of peace, popular interest again returned to the question of what direction American schooling should assume in the postwar period. Reflecting back upon the disputes of the late 1940s and the first half of the decade following, two distinct if overlapping phases are easily recognizable. The first thrust of criticism alleged that public education was failing to safeguard the values of "Americanism" and to conserve the nation's political heritage. The second wave developed amidst charges that school curricula remained vapid, that standards were anemic, and basic educational objectives misconceived. Each of the two initiatives will be considered in turn.

It is important to recall that the decade or so after World War II was a convulsive, oftentimes tumultuous era in American life. For many who sought only a return to "normalcy" and the imagined simplicity of an earlier day, the postwar years were proving to be much more a time of heightened frustration and anxiety. America had lost its innocence. At home the country was beset by unforeseen problems: inflation, an unprecedented baby boom, rapid industrial expansion, and uncontrolled urban sprawl. Abroad, the picture looked equally problematic. In the euphoria accompanying the close of the war, most people had looked forward with confidence to the irresistible advance of freedom, democracy, and prosperity throughout the world. Subsequent events, however, suggested these roseate expectations would go unfulfilled. It was increasingly clear that the military victory that had put an end to the most destructive conflagration in all history would bring no respite. Once again the United States found itself involved in a succession of conflicts in distant lands. Worse yet, as the Cold War deepened and the world's two major superpowers moved toward confrontation, the possibility of a still more terrifying holocaust loomed large. To growing numbers of people, prospects for a nuclear Armageddon appeared imminent.

The old enemies, Japanese militarism and Nazism, had been vanquished. But they in turn had been supplanted by an even more formidable adversary—world Communism. In the face of the apparent threat posed by this monolithic global conspiracy, the domestic response in the late 1940s and early 1950s therefore was a proliferation of ultraconservative leagues, societies, councils, committees, and other crusading organizations, all bent on stemming the tide of Communist influence. Near-hysterical alarms were sounded. According to Senator Joseph McCarthy, whose rise to national prominence symbolized the nation's mounting paranoia, Communists and Communist sympathizers were everywhere. Traitors had burrowed their way in, infiltrating all facets of American society. Subversives were to be rooted out wherever they might be found, their seditious machinations awaiting exposure by right-thinking citizens. The critical imperative, it was said, was to eradicate whatever insidious influences were at work corrupting the hearts and minds of otherwise-loyal Americans.

Predictably, it was not long before right-wing radicals turned their attention to the schools. There ensued a great number of campaigns against godlessness, moral laxity, subversion, lack of patriotism, and ''un-Americanism'' in public education. Superpatriots worked assiduously to rebuild the schools as bastions of anti-Communism. Religionists, fearful that creeping secularism was eroding public virtue, urged renewed emphasis upon classroom prayer and direct instruction in religion. Cost-cutters for their part extolled the values of belt-tightening and sharp reductions in expenditures for education. And in more than a few cases, the ranks of school critics were added to by professional agitators and propagandists who hoped in various ways to profit by whatever discontent and suspicion they might implant in the public mind.[19]

Commenting on the escalation of controversy over school policy, one writer aptly summed up the situation. ''Since World War II,'' she observed, ''there is virtually no aspect of public education that has gone unquestioned by one source or another. . . . Not only is American education under fire; the practice of criticizing our schools is well on its way to becoming a national pastime.'' She added, ''For some it is already a favorite armchair sport. For others, it has become a full time career.''[20]

A variety of national organizations emerged in the late forties dedicated to safeguarding public education from un-American influences. Typical in its formulation was the charter of a group calling itself ''Guardians of American Education.'' Their purpose, the text announced, was ''to preserve among the principles of public school education the ideal of upholding faith in the American form of government and of maintaining belief in our traditional tenets of social and economic freedom.''[21] Still more widespread in its activities was an organization, headed by Allen Alderson Zoll, called the National Council for American Education (NCAE). The January 1951 issue of *Nation's Schools* described the NCAE as "devoted to the stimulation of sound education and the eradication of Marxism and Collectivism from our schools' national life."[22]

Council literature somewhat extravagantly claimed it was "the *only* organization in America specifically and exclusively opposing, on a national basis, subversive influences in schools and colleges."[23] To this end the NCAE issued an extensive list of pamphlets bearing such provocative titles as *How Red Are the Schools?; Harvard Red Hunting Ground; Reducators at Harvard University; Harvard Crimson Harvard; Socialism is Stupid; Awake, Awake, and Pray!; They Want Your Child; A Fifty-Year Project to Combat Socialism on the Campus;* and *Should Americans Be Against World Government?* As one critic noted, NCAE tracts were calculated to lead readers to believe that "deadly fifth columns of un-American propagandists have been vigorously at work in the schools for the last three decades."[24]

NCAE Executive Vice-President Zoll made it clear he believed that America's leading educators such as John Dewey and George S. Counts were involved in nothing less than a deliberate conspiracy. Their aim, he declared, had always been to undermine the basic precepts of American democracy, to inculcate among unsuspecting youth a philosophy of godless materialism, and to destroy all traditional moral and spiritual values. "I tell you frankly," Zoll informed one audience, "that their precepts, if carried on, will absolutely ruin the United States of America."[25] Given their degree of influence upon teacher education, he claimed, Dewey and his cohorts more than any others were responsible for the ruinous state of affairs existing in the nation's schools and colleges.

Supporters of the schools more often than not found it difficult, if not downright impossible, to counter accusations that public education in America was tainted with subversion, that many educators were actively engaged in efforts to undermine the Republic, or that schools for the most part had fallen victim to the international Communist conspiracy. Many organizations, such as the National Education Association and the Association for Supervision and Curriculum Development, organized special political-action groups to mount a counteroffensive. Nonetheless, their efforts were to enjoy only modest success in the climate of opinion prevailing throughout the McCarthy era. When compulsory loyalty oaths were commonplace, when unsubstantiated charges of treason circulated freely, and anything resembling political liberalism was suspect, even the wildest accusations could be expected to command a hearing.

## THE CONSERVATIVE ATTACK UPON LIFE-ADJUSTMENT EDUCATION

Part of the crisis, as a small but highly vocal number of right-wing alarmists saw it, was that through public indifference or naïveté, the schools had been allowed to fall into the hands of Communist sympathizers, fellow travelers, and liberals.

Having succumbed to subversive influences, it was only natural that public educa-tion should fail to promote the virtues of loyalty, patriotism, and love of coun-try—in a word, "Americanism." The challenge was clear. For ultrarightists, what was needed was a rescue operation, an assault aimed at wresting control from those who were "soft" on Communism. Above all, if, as many of the fringe element had long suspected, progressive education was but a manifestation of left-ist doctrine at its worst, it should be eradicated once and for all.

Less hysterical conservative critics shared with the extremists strong an-tipathy toward progressivism, though they did not necessarily subscribe to the no-tion of conspiracy. Yet they too believed that the time was long overdue for adopt-ing what was called a no-nonsense approach to the education of the young. Frills should be jettisoned. Curricula should be overhauled. "Flabby" pedagogy should be thrown out and replaced by a stress on "hard-core" learning. Hence, the con-trapuntal theme to charges that schools were not conserving American values was that they lacked discipline and academic rigor. This in essence was the dominant motif of the second major postwar wave of criticism against the nation's schools.

Ironically enough, just at the moment when progressivism had already entered upon a decline and educational conservatism was again in the ascen-dancy, critics were furnished with a convenient new target, a *bête noire* called "Life-Adjustment Education," which rather quickly came to symbolize for con-servatives everything fundamentally wrong with modern public education. Nur-tured originally in the Vocational Education Division of the U.S. Office of Educa-tion, life adjustment was acclaimed by such proponents as Charles A. Prosser and others as a fresh, innovative response to the "real-life" needs of students ill-served by traditional academic curricula. Conservative opponents, on the other hand, saw in this nascent initiative merely an attempt to perpetuate in new guise the worst errors of progressive education. The issue was quickly joined, and with fatal results.

Life-adjustment education as a concept appears to have been put forth in response to fears that many students of high-school age were not profiting by the established program of the secondary school. Among vocational educators especially, a push was begun for a curriculum more directly geared to the diverse abilities and career aspirations of high-school youth. What was required, it was alleged, was a course of study through which students could acquire basic survival skills needed in daily life; that is, tools for "adjustment" to society and the rudiments of vocational training, preparatory to entering the work force.

The Educational Policies Commission, for example, in its 1944 report en-titled, *Education For All American Youth,* called for a more "balanced" program in the nation's high schools designed to help each student grow in "occupational pro-ficiency; in competence as a citizen; in satisfying relationships in family, school, and other personal associations; in health and physical fitness; in discriminating expenditure of money and of time; in enjoyable and constructive use of leisure; and in understanding and appreciation of [the] cultural heritage."[26] The Com-mission went on to recommend what it called "a continuous course for all, planned to help students grow in competence as citizens of the community and the nation, in understanding of economic processes and of their roles as producers and consumers; in cooperative living in family, school, and community; in appreciation of literature and the arts; and in use of the English language."[27]

An officially sponsored Commission on Life Adjustment Education for Youth was subsequently created. Its charter, it was announced, was to promote a new kind of education and what was termed a more "practical" curricular approach centering upon everyday problems. It would be directed toward teaching citizenship, the productive use of leisure, good hygiene, knowledge of consumer affairs, home and family life, and the world of work. For various reasons, however, little progress was achieved in translating these broad themes into a practical, usable curriculum.

In retrospect, the term "life adjustment" was ill-advised, because it lent itself to so much ridicule. It is doubtful too whether the abortive movement launched under its banner ever exerted even a fraction of the influence its detractors imputed to it. In point of fact, various curricular proposals offered through the U.S. Office in the name of life-adjustment education had little if any impact upon the schools. Even among teachers themselves, acceptance was limited. Nonetheless, hostile critics never tired of castigating professional educators for having allegedly subscribed to the philosophy of life adjustment; and they spared no effort in trying to discredit it. Their criticisms were to furnish the substance of debate over school policy for years to come.

Bernard Iddings Bell, in a 1949 diatribe entitled, *Crisis in Education,* set the pattern followed by later opponents. It is not the school's business to foster social "adjustment," he claimed. Nor should an educational institution attempt directly to prepare youth for employment. Still less should it be distracted with promoting self-satisfaction, informed decision-making, the judicious use of leisure time, or the niceties of personal hygiene. No matter how worthy the ends, it does not follow that the schools have a major role to play in advancing these and other social objectives. The school's basic task is to provide academic instruction. Educational functions extending beyond the purview of the school are best left to the home, the church, civic associations, business and industry, and community youth organizations. The problem is one of priorities. Schools cannot take on too much, except at the risk of neglecting their primary function of promoting sound learning.[28]

Arthur E. Bestor, a professor of history at the University of Illinois and one of the most eloquent conservative school critics of the period, reserved special contempt for the life-adjustment concept. The school, he avowed, is not designed to provide all kinds of services indiscriminately. "The idea that the school must undertake to meet every need that some other agency is failing to meet, regardless of the suitability of the schoolroom to the task," Bestor claimed, "is a preposterous delusion that in the end can wreck the educational system without in any way contributing to the salvation of society."[29]

Bestor was willing to say that the school could respond to certain noneducational needs of youth, but only provided the effort did not interfere with its more fundamental educational mission. "The first duty of the school, if it values its own educational integrity,'' he wrote, ''is to provide a standard program of intellectual training in the fundamental disciplines, geared to the needs of serious students and to the capacities of the upper two thirds of the school population.''[30] Above and beyond this, the school should make provision for an enriched or more intensive program for the exceptionally able. Thirdly, the school should provide remedial programs for slow learners. Fourth-ranked in Bestor's order of priorities was physical education, followed next by vocational training. Extracurricular activities came last. But always foremost in his scheme was instruction in basic skills and academic disciplines.

The real crisis in American public education, Bestor argued, was one of muddled purpose; and he lay the blame squarely at the feet of professional educators. ''Professional educationists in their policy-making role,'' he alleged, ''have lowered the aims of the American public schools. In the last analysis, it is not lack of effort but lack of direction that has resulted in the mediocre showing of our public schools.'' The educational establishment, he judged, had ''undermined public confidence in the schools by setting forth purposes for education so trivial as to forfeit the respect of thoughtful men.''[31] Bereft of any sense of scale or proportion, educators had allegedly drafted curricula that freely intermingled the trivial and the important, the frivolous and the essential. ''Regressive education,'' as Bestor satirically called it, offered courses of study so ''trivial, unbalanced and so out of harmony with the thinking of trained scientists and scholars that they constitute a mere parody of education.''[32]

Under the influence of progressivist doctrine, Bestor complained, new educational purposes had supplanted traditional ones: ''Intellectual training, once the unquestioned focus of every educational effort, was pushed out to the periphery of the public-school program. Into the vacuum rushed the pedagogical experts . . . the curriculum doctors . . . the life-adjusters and the specialists in know-how rather than knowledge.'' What they offered in place of real learning as the school's primary objective were ''lesser aims, confused aims, or no aims at all.''[33]

Mortimer Smith, author of *And Madly Teach* (1949), heartily agreed. ''Educationists,'' as he called them, were chiefly responsible for the anti-intellectualism and moral myopia so rampant in public education; and he urged an end to the stranglehold they exerted on the schools. ''If anyone will take the trouble to investigate,'' he observed,

> it will be found that those who make up the staffs of the schools and colleges of education, and the administrators and teachers whom they train to run the system, have a truly amazing uniformity of opinion regarding the aims, the content, and the methods of education. They constitute a cohesive body of believers with a clearly formulated set of dogmas and doctrines, and they are perpetuating the faith by seeing to it, through state laws and rules of state departments of education, that only those teachers and administrators are certified who have been trained in correct dogma.[34]

The ''dogma'' to which Smith referred, of course, was progressivism and its later incarnation, life adjustment. And however implausible the allegation that professional educators collectively shared allegiance to a monolithic doctrine, the charge was repeated over and over again in the writings of school critics. Attacks upon progressivism-life adjustment were advanced by Paul Woodring in *Let's Talk Sense About Our Schools* (1953), by Albert Lynd in *Quackery in the Public Schools* (1953) and again by Mortimer Smith in *The Diminished Mind* (1954).[35] John Keats, writing in the *Saturday Evening Post* in 1957, summed up the most common complaint. ''Most of this nation's public schools,'' he claimed, ''now offer America's children an education that is anticultural, anti-intellectual, narrowly utilitarian at best and utterly vapid at worst.''[36]

George Leonard, writing for *Look* magazine in the same year, propounded the identical theme. ''Firm standards of actual achievement are lost in a haze of concern for the child's emotional well-being,'' he alleged. Today's children, he went on to say, ''mainly are being schooled in 'how-to'—adjustment to life has replaced the absorption of knowledge as the highest goal of a public-school education.''[37] Schools ought to stop coddling children, ran the refrain. Instead of insipid lessons in social conformity and ''living skills,'' in personal grooming and social adjustment, teachers should offer rigorous intellectual and moral training. Nothing less should be allowed to substitute—least of all ''life adjustment.''

## ANTIACADEMIC EDUCATION: A CONSERVATIVE INDICTMENT

The most serious charge proffered by critics was that public education was antiacademic and anti-intellectual. Once again Arthur Bestor's critique, as developed in his lengthy *Educational Wastelands, The Retreat from Learning in Our Public Schools* (1953) and its expanded version, published three years later as *The Restoration of Learning,* offers the most vivid illustration of how the case for educational conservatism was presented in the early 1950s. Even today his arguments sound a distinctly contemporary note.

Bestor's thesis was devastatingly simple. A decent education, he argued, should provide ''sound training in the fundamental ways of thinking represented by history, science, mathematics, literature, language, art and other disciplines evolved in the course of mankind's long quest for usable knowledge, cultural understanding, and intellectual power.''[38] That certain skills and facts are more basic and more important than others he had no doubt. The criterion to which he appealed was utility:

> Certain intellectual disciplines are fundamental in the public-school curriculum because they are fundamental in modern life. Reading, writing, and arithmetic are indispensable studies in the elementary school because no intellectual life worthy of the name is possible or conceivable without these particular skills. Science, mathematics, history, English, and foreign languages are essentials of the secondary-school curriculum because contemporary intellectual life has been built upon a foundation of these particular disciplines. Some, but by no means all, of these studies can

be described as "traditional." This fact, however, has next to nothing to do with the case. It is not tradition, but a realistic appraisal of the modern world, that points out these disciplines as fundamental.[39]

The purpose of formal education, boldly stated, is intellectual training. Schools exist to foster the ideal of disciplined intelligence, the power to think. The founders of the American public-school system, Bestor avowed, meant by "education exactly what Thomas Jefferson meant by it and exactly what thoughtful people have always meant by it." They understood that ignorance was a liability and disciplined intelligence a source of power. In a democracy, they believed, society has an obligation to make intellectual training available to every individual citizen, rich and poor alike. So greatly would the state benefit from a diffusion of knowledge and intelligence that it was legitimate for the government to support a school system by taxation and even to employ the coercive authority of law to force the populace to attend school and acquire an education.[40] What was true in the early nineteenth century remains valid today.

The school's role, then as now, is "to provide training in every field of activity where systematic thinking is an important component of success." At the elementary level, the task is to foster basic literacy, to teach pupils to read, write, and calculate. At the secondary-school level, students must acquire a sound knowledge of science, history, economics, philosophy, and other fundamental disciplines.[41]

The curriculum, Bestor argued, should present not just isolated facts, but knowledge organized in logical and sequential patterns. It should reflect not some random or haphazard arrangement of data, but the various academic disciplines that, respectively, offer generically different modes of understanding. There is nothing arbitrary about how human knowledge is ordered. Disciplines represent ways of organizing human thought and experience. Each has something irreducibly different to offer. And as each learner grows in his or her capacity to abstract, to integrate generalizations based on the facts and concepts deployed within the disciplines, so then is the student's power to reason coherently and to think painstakingly enlarged.

Good public education therefore demands a common course of studies. All should pursue essentially the same curriculum, even though not everyone will proceed at the same pace. Students should be grouped by their actual levels of educational development, not by age or ability. Strictly enforced prerequisites should govern advancement through the system, perhaps assuming the form of a succession of essay examinations administered at various points to measure each student's academic attainment. Only when some such standardized program of intellectual training in the fundamental disciplines is instituted, Bestor was convinced, would popular discontent and "general dissatisfaction" with the schools disappear.

Bestor had little patience for the argument that "academic" education is somehow elitist, or fitted mainly to the needs of the few. Popular education, he claimed, should be designed to endow the people as a whole with precisely the kinds of intellectual power that once had been monopolized by the privileged classes. The idea of a general education, rooted in a command of basic learning skills and conversance with many branches of human learning, is neither unrealistic nor class-bound. If mass education offers anything less, he argued, it is bound to be ''a cheap and shoddy substitute'' for the real thing.[42] Merely gathering students of varying backgrounds and socioeconomic circumstances together in classrooms is not enough. The school, Bestor claimed, ''becomes an agency of true democratization only if it sends them forth with knowledge, cultural appreciation, and disciplined intellectual power—with the qualities, in other words, that have always distinguished educated men from uneducated ones.''[43]

Bestor was willing, albeit reluctantly, to concede that so-called ''deprived'' learners might find it difficult to master the ''fundamental'' curriculum he considered essential. Nevertheless, in a way characteristic of many of today's proponents of ''back to basics,'' he appeared to feel that the school environment was capable of providing resources sufficient to overcome whatever deficits a child might bring to the learning situation.

He also felt that provision should be made for the varying rates at which students learn. Yet in the final analysis, as he put it, ''The public school system has a solemn responsibility to the ninety percent of our children and young people whose intelligence is nowise defective.'' That responsibility, he reiterated, ''is to provide sound and rigorous training in the basic intellectual disciplines.'' To the objection that it might be difficult to instruct all students in such a program, Bestor's response was that it was ''primarily a matter of intelligent and imaginative teaching.''[44]

## "SURVIVALISM" AND THE TRAUMA OF *SPUTNIK*

The launching of *Sputnik I* by the Soviet Union in October of 1957 sent shock waves reverberating throughout American society, including its system of public education. Within a very short time the search for a scapegoat was underway. Why, it was asked, had the Russians rather than the Americans been the first to succeed in placing the world's first satellite in orbit? What had become of America's much-vaunted technological excellence, its commanding lead in all branches of science and technology? Was U.S. technical know-how somehow inferior to that of the Soviets? Did the Russian triumph presage the eclipse of American power, and had the country lost its ability to compete successfully in the international arena? What factors were responsible for so calamitous a setback? Who was responsible?

It soon became fashionable in certain quarters to blame the schools for the nation's traumatic humiliation. ''Since Soviet Russia launched its first globe-circling satellite in the fall of 1957,'' one group of contemporary commentators observed, ''shrill criticism of public education has reached a new crescendo. The unexpected achievement of the Russians has been attributed to their educational system; conversely, our failure to be the first launcher of a successful satellite has been laid at the door of public education. . . .'' They continued:

> The gravity of the situation cannot be overestimated. If we fail to educate the present and immediately future generations appropriately and well, we may lose the current conflict with the Soviet powers and cease to be free to educate and live as we see fit. This is the grim prospect before us.[45]

Amidst cries that American education had let its people down, crash programs were begun to develop new school curricula in mathematics, science, and foreign languages. In a desperate race to regain lost time, conferences were hastily convened, reports issued, and prescriptions drafted to correct all the ills, real and imagined, plaguing the nation's schools. It was clear to many that the stimulus of Cold War competition had lent new urgency to educational reform.

Max Rafferty, one-time Superintendent of Public Instruction for the State of California, posed the issue in the starkest terms possible. ''A race of faceless, godless peasants from the steppes of Asia strives to reach across our bodies for the prize of world dominion,'' he warned. While the Soviets dropped an Iron Curtain around themselves in the mid-1940s, behind which they built and starved and plotted, ''we erected around our satisfied selves a picket fence composed of chrome bumpers, king-size filter tips, and empty bottles of imported Scotch whiskey behind which we—quite frankly—had fun,'' he explained with characteristic hyperbole. ''Nothing was taken too seriously. Nothing was allowed to disturb our composure. Above all, no hint of coming austerity or sacrifice was suffered to ripple even for a moment the brimming pool of full prosperity.''

The ascent into the heavens of a silvered sphere bearing Cyrillic letters and the emblem of the hammer and sickle had now changed everything. ''The time is obviously here,'' Rafferty asserted, ''for a girding of loins and a measured marshaling of our resources.''[46] ''It is up to us, as educators, to determine whether in the onsurging and billowing wave of the future, mankind will hear the laughter and the shouting of free men, or the murmuring of innumerable bees.''[47]

Education had a leading role to play, he claimed, in making possible national survival. To defeat the purposes of the Soviets would demand ''the massed wisdom and understanding of the great minds that have gone before us. . . . It follows that the first duty of the schools is to impart that accumulated wisdom of the race to our children.'' Surveying the condition of the schools as he found them, however, Rafferty found little reason to feel confident. He wrote, ''I submit that our national school curriculum, particularly in the elementary and junior high schools, has had little or no relation to the only really basic issue of . . . national survival.''[48]

High schools he judged to be no better. Instead of offering a four-year program of studies in mathematics, history, foreign languages, and other disciplines, he alleged, they encouraged students to divert themselves with ceramics, stagecraft, table decorating, upholstering, and second-year golf. With scant evidence but unequaled fervor, Rafferty concluded that subject matter was "undervalued, despised, kicked into the gutter and left to shift for itself." Schools were succeeding only in the teaching of trivia, thereby producing "a race of barely literate savages."[49]

Rafferty left no doubt as to what was needed: intensive instruction in basic subjects, emphasis upon repeated drill and memorization, a raising of standards, the restoration of classroom discipline, and the teaching of "the basic principles of the American free enterprise system."[50] So long as the United States was locked in conflict with the Soviet Union, he insisted, the most urgent arm of public education would remain that of "survivalism."

Others echoed Rafferty's recommendations, though perhaps in somewhat more measured tones. Admiral Hyman Rickover's several suggestions for improvements included a more rigid and fixed school program, more demanding courses, and the establishment of national academic achievement standards.[51] James D. Koerner, addressing a 1963 symposium sponsored by the American Association of Colleges for Teacher Education, also adopted a hard-line approach. "Almost all children," he declared unequivocally,

> are capable of sustained academic study and . . . it is the proper business of a public school system to give this study to them through the medium of what Matthew Arnold called "the best that has been thought and said in the world." In this system all students run on the same track but at their own best speeds; and all concentrate their education in a relatively few areas that encompass the most significant of man's knowledge.

"It is a competitive system," Koerner admitted, "authoritarian if you like . . . and built on strong assumptions about the importance of priorities in education and on a highly optimistic assessment of the intellectual possibilities of most men."[52] More than a few other writers shared Koerner's optimism as well as his "strong assumptions." Paul Woodring, for one, author of an influential critique entitled *A Fourth Of A Nation* earlier had called for much the same system, one accenting a rigorous course of study including algebra, geometry, English grammar and composition, history, the sciences, and so on.[53] Along similar lines was the proposal offered by James B. Conant in *The American High School Today* (1959), urging as the basis for high-school organization a core of "general education" courses for all students, including science, mathematics, English, and social studies.[54]

Extending ideas defended by Bestor, Koerner, Conant, Smith, and many other leading critics, in 1961 the Educational Policies Commission argued that the central purpose of American education should be to develop in students the power to think effectively. The Commission urged a retreat from performance-based subjects and increased attention to fostering intellectual skills. Helping students to expand their capabilities for logical reasoning, it concluded, offered them the best hope for an education of long-range utility; only academic preparation was likely to retain its applicability in an uncertain and unpredictable future.[55] Many of the curriculum reform movements sponsored by the National Defense Education Act in the post-*Sputnik* era, most notably as defended in the writings of Jerome Bruner, Joseph Schwab, John Goodlad, and Ralph Tyler, likewise emphasized the importance of cognitive understanding and stress upon the fundamentals of academic disciplines.[56]

A full review of the many works authored by educational conservatives throughout the late 1950s and 1960s would be impossible to encompass briefly; and in any event most of the books condemning progressive and life-adjustment education all labored to much the same conclusion: that there is a common core of ideals, values, meanings, and understandings, bound up with the accumulated knowledge of a culture, whose preservation depends upon educational endeavor. The school's role is to transmit this fundamental knowledge and thereby conserve the best of the past as a legacy to future generations. Lacking basic skills and essential knowledge of the academic disciplines, a person can neither reach his or her fullest potential as a human being nor contribute materially to the betterment of the social order.[57]

## THE COUNCIL FOR BASIC EDUCATION

As is so often the case in the history of social movements, precisely at the time when the precepts of Bestor, Conant, Rickover, and Smith seemed assured of a secure place in the newly established educational orthodoxy, a host of new critics appeared on the scene in the 1960s, proclaiming the total moral bankruptcy of public education. Unlike their predecessors, they did not call for more and better schooling of the traditional variety; they wanted nothing less than a complete inversion of the conventional order. Some observers wondered if the ghost of John Dewey had not been resurrected in different guise.[58]

The new critics rarely spoke with a single voice. They constituted a diverse group without an identifiable or definite program for school reform. But all seemed to share an intemperate anger, even contempt, directed at prevailing usage. "Because adults take the schools so much for granted," wrote Charles Silberman, author of an influential and widely discussed book, *Crisis in the Classroom* (1970), "they fail to appreciate what grim, joyless places most American schools are, how oppressive and petty are the roles by which they are governed, how intellectually sterile and esthetically barren the atmosphere, what an appalling lack of civility obtains on the part of teachers and principals, what contempt they unconsciously display for children as children."[59]

He and others deplored what they characterized as the dehumanization, apathy, and boredom prevalent in classrooms. Public schools were repeatedly assailed for their repression, for authoritarianism, and their obsessive preoccupation with irrelevant trivia. Given viable alternatives stressing activity, joyfulness, and spontaneity, such as those provided by the example of certain "open-education" institutions, most Americans, Silberman believed, would opt for a system in which learning was more informal, humane, and individualized.

For a time, it appeared that expectation would be fulfilled. The closing years of the sixties and the first half of the decade following brought a remarkable surge of interest in "humanistic" education and the "open classroom." So favorable was the popular response to the critique advanced by Silberman, John Holt, Jonathan Kozol, George Dennison, Herbert Kohl, Paul Goodman, and others too numerous to mention, that pundits such as Joseph Featherstone were moved to observe that "what was once a point made by a handful of radical cultural critics is now very close to being official wisdom." [60] All indications pointed to the eclipse of educational conservatism as an influence upon American schooling.

One of the few organized lobby groups that stoutly resisted the trend toward open education was an organization called the Council for Basic Education. Founded in July of 1956 by Arthur Bestor, a romance languages professor from Grinnell College named Harold Clapp, and botanist Harry Fuller of the University of Illinois, the Council (CBE) was organized, according to a 1958 Statement of Purpose, to support "high academic standards" in public education. The Council, it was explained, stood in support of measures to ensure:

1. That all students, excepting only those few whose intellectual equipment is clearly too limited, receive adequate instruction in the basic intellectual disciplines, especially English, mathematics, science, history, and foreign languages;
2. That the fullest possible opportunity is afforded to students of high ability to reach mature levels of achievement without waste of time;
3. That clear standards of actual accomplishment are used to measure each student's progress and to govern promotion to higher levels of the educational system;
4. That teachers are thoroughly educated in the subjects they teach and in current developments therein;
5. That vocational training is offered in due subordination to the school's fundamental purpose of intellectual discipline;
6. That school administrators are encouraged and supported in resisting pressures to divert school time to activities of minor educational significance, to curricula overemphasizing social adjustment at the expense of intellectual discipline, and to programs that call upon the school to assume responsibilities properly belonging to the home, to religious bodies, and to other agencies.[61]

In 1981, on the twenty-fifth anniversary of the Council's founding, former Executive Secretary Mortimer Smith wryly observed, "It would be nice to be able to report that after the Council for Basic Education came on the scene in 1956 and pointed out the shortcomings of public education, there was immediately launched a wave of reform that culminated 25 years later in sweeping away many educational ills and fevers." That, he lamented, had not been the case: "My impression is that the old agues and chills have not been substantially reduced."[62]

Smith reported his impression that many of the "ailments" of public education in 1956 still prevailed a quarter of a century later. Many schoolchildren could not read or write properly. Languages, history, and the sciences were still neglected. Teacher training, in his judgment, was more concerned with how to teach than with knowledge of subject matter. Controlling organizations among professional teachers and administrators persisted in their preoccupation with power and money, neglecting the cause of high-quality education, which should be their exclusive concern.

All this notwithstanding, in Smith's view, the Council *had* made piecemeal gains in forcing public attention upon the deficiencies of the schools. Among his fondest projects from the Council's early years was the publication of *The Case for Basic Education,* a layman's primer that defined the nature of the basic subjects and described what grasp students should have of them after twelve years of schooling.[63]

The initial announcement describing the project explained that the undertaking had arisen from a need for "an authoritative statement, emanating from the learned world, that would explain the importance of the basic subjects and set forth what knowledge and understanding" a student ought to be equipped with at the conclusion of his or her formal education.[64] A list of eight basic subjects cited was subsequently lengthened to include twelve areas of study: American history, European history, political science, English composition, literature, classical languages, modern languages, geography, mathematics, biology, chemistry, and physics. Sixteen contributors offered ideas on what constitutes "basic education" in these disciplines.

If Smith's assessment of the Council's accomplishments over the years was relatively modest, it was not for want of effort. From the outset, the Council assumed an active role in attempting to influence public policy by molding public opinion. It saw itself as a pressure group, not merely a forum for the exchange of ideas. It provided for organizational membership by learned societies and activist professional organizations. It maintained a speakers' bureau. Initially, at least, it offered its services in evaluating specific school systems (an offer the Council later withdrew for lack of response). The Council also published a bulletin and a series of occasional papers.

In the pages of its newsletter (later renamed *Basic Education*), the Council adopted a consistent stand on behalf of an educationally conservative viewpoint. It rejected characterizations of its position as "old-fashioned" or "no-nonsense," however, claiming such words were, in the public arena where school policy is made, "simplistic battle cries of doubtful merit."[65] Its representatives vociferously denied recurrent allegations that the Council was interested only in promoting the three R's—reading, writing, and arithmetic. Although it took a jaundiced view of including home economics, driver education, and other activities in school curricula, it supported, for example, a place for music and art in public schools as "basics" alongside mathematics, languages, history, and literature. "Our quarrel is not with these subjects," a 1960 editorial explained,

> but with the manner in which they are all too often taught. Music, for example, is often presented entirely from the standpoint of performance, resulting in that often distressing phenomenon, the school band, in which gaudily costumed youths play banal music badly. In our opinion, the primary emphasis in the schools should be on appreciation for the majority, not performance for the few.[66]

When the *National Observer* in 1976 identified the Council as an organization "that has been pushing for a return to the basics since 1956,"[67] the *CBE Bulletin* took strong exception to the characterization. "Let there be no mistake," it objected, "CBE favors all efforts that promise to raise levels of reading and writing, and to increase skills in computation. . . . At the same time, it must be understood that basic education, in the Council's conception, is by no means limited to the Three R's." The writer quoted Clifton Fadiman, one of the original contributors to its publication, *The Case For Basic Education:*

> Basic education concerns itself with those matters which, once learned, enable the student to learn all the other matters, whether trivial or complex, that cannot properly be the subjects of elementary and secondary schooling. In other words, both logic and experience suggest that certain subjects have generative power and others do not. . . . Among these subjects are those that deal with language, whether or not one's own; forms, figures and numbers; the laws of nature; the past, and the shape and behavior of our common home, the earth.[68]

Repeatedly, writers for Council publications returned to the same theme: the need to concentrate on the most generically fundamental forms of knowledge as the proper subjects of school instruction. Officially, the Council took no specific position on various teaching methods or approaches; its concerns were limited to goals, more general strategy, and academic results. It favored individualized instruction, but only when it could be shown to be superior to more structured management techniques. The Council also gave a lukewarm endorsement to calls in the 1970s for career education and for acquainting students with the world of work, but with the important caveat that this not be allowed to take precedence over responsibility for basic education.[69]

Writing at the decade's midpoint, Associate Director George Weber renewed the Council's plea for "a basic and limited curriculum." He asked: "Do you believe all children should learn to read and write? How about fundamental mathematics? Science? History? Government? Geography? If you answer yes to these questions, you probably believe in 'basic education.'"[70] If "frills" were eliminated and educators directed their exclusive attention to academic considerations, Weber asserted, American parents would at long last achieve the quality schooling most desired for their children.

## BACK TO BASICS

In the early 1970s, however, public attention was still focused on open education. The "cutting edge" of experimentation, so to speak, was represented by self-paced learning, individualized instruction, diversified curricula, mini-courses, alternative free schools, and flexible learning "modules." Not that the general public necessarily endorsed all the innovations undertaken in the name of "humanistic education"—opinion polls indicated otherwise. But the viewpoint long espoused by the Council For Basic Education did seem to represent a minority position. Among professional educators especially, it was assumed that a popular mandate existed to "humanize" the schools and make them more immediately "relevant" in the lives of young learners. Nonetheless, a considerable number of other writers continued to defend what in the aftermath of the sixties had become a distinctly unfashionable stance.

In a 1972 article entitled, "What Are Schools For?" educational psychologist Robert Ebel, for example, was to throw out a direct challenge to the reigning orthodoxy.[71] Schools, he argued, are not social-research agencies or experiment stations to which society can delegate responsibility for devising solutions to various societal ills. Schools are not custodial institutions for coping with emotionally disturbed youth or the incorrigible. They are not intended for keeping nonstudents off the streets or out of the job market. Schools are not "adjustment" centers either, responsible for helping young people develop positive self-concepts *in vacuo,* to solve personal problems, or to come to terms with life. Least of all, said Ebel, are schools recreational facilities for amusement and entertainment, though they often are considered as such. Educators, he claimed in a now-familiar refrain, had been far to willing to accept responsibility for dealing with all the problems of young people and trying to meet all of their immediate needs.

Schools, Ebel insisted, are for *learning,* and what ought to be learned mainly is *useful cognitive knowledge.* Affective dispositions, emotions, and feelings are undoubtedly important by-products of instruction. But they should not be made the principal targets of educational effort. They cannot be taught directly. What schools should concentrate on is helping pupils acquire factual information as presented in the curriculum. "Knowledge," in the final analysis, is a "do-it-yourself" endeavor, the outcome of a long process of building up a structure of perceived relationships among concepts. With the conversion of raw data into knowledge come the kinds of insight and understanding schools are uniquely adapted to help foster. It is what they can do best.

Schools cannot accept responsibility for every student's success in learning, Ebel claimed, since the results depend ultimately upon factors lying outside their control. Chief among these is the effort expended by learners themselves. What the school can be held accountable for, nevertheless, is a good learning environment; that is, capable, enthusiastic teachers on the one hand and an abundance of appropriate instructional materials on the other.

Gradually, as the decade wore on, the country's political mood turned more conservative, and with it came deepening disaffection with open-education reforms. Now the pendulum of opinion began to swing away from permissiveness and toward support for education of a more traditional character. A variety of factors was involved. One was a widely held perception that discipline in schools had seriously deteriorated. Respondents in public opinion surveys consistently cited "lack of discipline" most frequently as the single greatest problem confronting American education. If some press reports were to be believed, the blight of inner-city "blackboard jungles" had long since spread into the suburbs. In many instances, schools bore more resemblance to holding pens for the young than to centers for learning. Complaints grew of disruption, insolence, and back talk from students. Felonious assaults were up. More and more teachers came to see themselves as casualties in a losing battle for classroom order in an indulgent age; and "burn-out" among educators became an increasingly familiar phenomenon.

More than a few critics attributed the apparent rise in violence and school misbehavior to the demise of the autocratic teacher and the long-standing tendency to grant immature students more autonomy.[72] Predictably, conservatives, both political and educational, issued calls for firmer discipline as the answer to a situation seemingly grown out of control.

For Paul Copperman, director of a private school for the training and supervision of reading teachers, the locus of the problem with public education in the 1970s was "the degeneration of authority relations" in schools. In his book, *The Literacy Hoax: The Decline of Reading, Writing, and Learning in the Public School and What We Can Do About It* (1978), Copperman characterized the entire educational system as a "sick 130-billion-dollar-a-year social institution." The "hoax" was the alleged deception perpetrated by educators on students, who, he claimed, were led to believe they were doing adequate or even excellent work in school when in fact they were performing poorly. "Many of these students suffer from a delusion of adequacy, engendered by an educational system which is lying to them," he caustically observed.[73]

Copperman's indictment seemed confirmed by numerous studies throughout the seventies reporting a marked decline in the scholastic performance of high-school seniors, as indicated by scores on the Scholastic Aptitude Test (SAT), administered by the College Entrance Examination Board, and the ACT examinations, given by the American College Testing Program.[74] Again, according to a national survey conducted by the National Assessment of Educational Progress, the performance of American seventeen-year-olds in science, writing, social studies, and mathematics had been dropping continuously over a ten-year time span. It was widely alleged that growing numbers of high-school graduates could neither read nor write. They were, to all intents and purposes, functionally illiterate. Upwards of one-fifth or more of all adult citizens, some authorities claimed, shared the same predicament.

Explanations for the apparent failure of the schools to help students achieve even minimal literacy varied. Some analysts blamed the general social turbulence of society in the sixties and seventies, citing increased television-watching, the apparent breakdown of the family, marital discord, skyrocketing divorce rates, and a lack of law and order in other social institutions. Others were more specific, pointing to factors internal to schools: tolerance of excessive absenteeism, grade inflation, easier textbooks, a noticeable diminution of motivation on the part of students, a proliferation of elective courses that allegedly had led to neglect of instruction in verbal and computational skills, lowered standards, and, overall, diminished seriousness of purpose in the learning process. Prescriptions for reform ranged from the establishment of clear standards of achievement for students, "performance-based" assessment, "criteria-mastery" as the basis for grade promotion, greater teacher accountability, increased attention to academic subjects, and more rigorous evaluation of educational innovations.

Such proposals struck a responsive chord among the American public. The 1975 George Gallup Poll, for example, revealed that over half of all parents of public-school children agreed that elementary schools were not making youngsters work hard enough and did not require enough homework. About the same percentage of parents felt the same way about public high schools. Almost 60 percent of all respondents nationwide indicated support for strict discipline, school dress codes, and greater emphasis on the three R's. These results were not dissimilar from earlier findings, nor did they change much in the years following.

Indicative of the second thoughts many educators themselves were having was the appearance of a book by Neil Postman entitled, *Teaching As A Conserving Activity* (1977). Postman's analysis was notable on two counts: first, because it rang a novel variation on the theme of the school as a "conservative" force in society, and, secondly, because it amounted to a reversal of the position assumed by the same author a decade earlier in a book coauthored with Charles Weingartner called, *Teaching as a Subversive Activity.*[75]

Postman admitted *Teaching as a Conserving Activity* was "the result of a change in perspective." His thesis was twofold: (1) "The means by which people communicate comprise an environment just as real and as influential as the terrain on which they live"; and (2) "It is the business of education, at all times, to monitor and adjust the information environment whenever possible so that its inherent biases and drift do not monopolize the intellect and character of our youth."[76]

The contemporary information environment, Postman explained, is a structure of electronic media in which television occupies a central place. Like the school, television purveys a curriculum as real, influential, and as readily defined as any course of instruction offered in a formal educational institution. The "First Curriculum" of television and the biases of its lessons will inevitably prevail.

Traditional education, Postman went on to argue, is the only cultural force capable of countering the prevalance of the television curriculum, and it should be deployed with precisely this aim in mind. Acknowledging that he had once "joined in the fun," he was now prepared to forswear the "soppy philosophy" of his previous writings. "If a traditional school exerts influences that make visible and modify the biases of the new media," he wrote, "then it is obviously an institution to be aggressively preserved." Formal education should be relieved of the staggering burden of social-service functions they perform so poorly. His suggestion was that "the school may be the only remaining public situation in which [traditional] roles have any meaning at all" and that it is "the commonsense view that the school ought not to accommodate itself to disorder."[77]

Phrasing the point differently, the school should be a place of order and discipline, dedicated to a very few, carefully defined academic tasks. Above all, Postman believed, formal education should counterbalance the "antihistorical, nonanalytical, nonsequential, immediately gratifying biases of the present information environment." The school could best accomplish this objective by affording schoolchildren "education that stresses history, the disciplined use of language, a wide-ranging knowledge of the arts and religion, and the continuity of human enterprise."[78]

For all its McLuhanesque flourishes and the author's explicit disavowal of what he called the "baleful philosophy" of traditional education, the thrust of Postman's thesis appeared to put him squarely in the conservative camp. So persuasive were his arguments that *The Washington Star*'s leading editorialist was moved to ask, "How can so fundamental a perspective have been so widely and devastatingly discarded?"[79]

By the mid-seventies, the popular demand for more school discipline and a return to mastery of basic skills had assumed the proportions of a full-fledged reform movement. The rallying cry was, "Back to basics."[80] Manifestations of the movement in various parts of the country, as James R. Norton noted, ranged from "the ridiculous to the sublime, lacking similarity of philosophy, goals or method." He further observed, "Within states and even within districts there is a lack of coordination, and the results in some cases have bordered on chaos."[81]

Many educators resented the implication in the slogan "back to" that the schools had been somewhere else, that they had been doing something different than previously, possibly off adventuring in "open education," and that the paramount need was to recapitulate an antecedent state of affairs located somewhere in the 1940s or 1950s.[82] "We never really *left* the basics," came the rejoinder. But that was precisely what many proponents of the movement believed, and they intended to lose no time in restoring "basic education" to the school agenda.

The problem was how to define the "basics." "Obviously," Norton wrote, "anyone's definition of basics will include something about reading, writing, and arithmetic. Beyond that, there is almost total lack of agreement, and even within the three basic R's there is great controversy as to what skills are to be considered basic and necessary for everyone."[83] The 1976 Gallup poll, for example, showed that over half of those responding felt that schools should return to a strong emphasis on the teaching of basic skills. A 1979 survey conducted by *Better Homes and Gardens* magazine demonstrated the same concern: fully 94 percent of over 300,000 respondents agreed that schools "should place a stronger emphasis on fundamental skills—reading, writing, and basic arithmetic." Commenting, the author wrote, "Most people concur that proficiency in the three R's is a basic educational requirement, but beyond that, consensus disintegrates. For many people, the arts are basic. For others, career education, health, and personal finance are equally basic. Still others believe any subjects outside the three R's, history, and science are 'frills.'"[84]

From a popular literature not much distinguished for its conceptual clarity or precision of usage, many illustrations could be adduced to show how ambiguously the term "basics" was employed. Typical was the "explanation" supplied by an ultraconservative lobby group based in Dallas, Texas, called the National Congress For Educational Excellence. In an undated newsletter issued in early 1981, the following two lists were juxtaposed:

| **WHAT THE BASICS ARE NOT** | **WHAT THE BASICS ARE** |
|---|---|
| Including but not limited to: | Develop skills in: |
| Sensitivity training | Reading |
| Social & self-awareness | Writing or penmanship |
| Magic circle | Mathematics |
| Personal diaries | Vocational areas |
| Human development programs | Fine arts |
| Situation ethics | Intellectual development |
| Values clarification | English |
| Moral value alteration | Science |
| Behavior modification | Our heritage/History |
| Education in sexual attitudes | |
| Values changing curricula | Translation: The cognitive domain |
| Personal and family emotional | & the psycho-motor domain |
| development | |
| The occult | |
| Introspective examination of social | |
| and cultural aspects of family life | |
| Translation: The affective domain | |

"If you agree with this designation of basics as what you want for your child," an editor's note advised readers, "present it to your state and local school boards." [85]

If popular characterizations of the basics in education left something to be desired, parallel attempts by professional-educator's groups fared no better. A position paper by the National School Public Relations Association on reading, for example, characterized "basics" in reading in terms of perceptual skills, word identification skills, practice in oral reading, skills to improve study habits, "learning to use the library," and techniques for textual interpretation." [86]

The enumeration of "basic skill areas" in mathematics proposed by the National Council of Supervisors of Mathematics was similarly nonspecific, encompassing, in addition to computational skills, use of measurements, basic geometry, "computer literacy, alertness to the reasonableness of results," and a number of other locutions as well. [87] The comingling of categories—information, tasks, skills, competencies, learning outcomes—was exceeded only by another writer's adumbration of mathematical "basics" as practical *applications* of arithmetic performances, such as food pricing, figuring checking-account balances, computing savings-account interest rates, and maintaining logs of travel schedules. [88]

Even in the exact sciences, candidates for a "basic" ranged from "learning to live harmoniously within the biosphere" to "exploring values in new experiences" and "developing intellectual and vocational competence." [89] Nor were the pronouncements of the Council for Basic Education in this period particularly helpful for *defining* the basics. Apart from claiming that "*some* subjects ought to be studied and mastered by *all* students . . . [and that] some subjects are more important . . . than others," the substance of a "basic and limited curriculum" was not spelled out in meaningful detail.[90]

Statements by practicing administrators and teachers offered scant improvement over the very general formulations issued by official bodies. Robert F. Madgic, principal of Los Altos High School, in Los Altos, California, felt that learning to think independently was most fundamental and basic as fostered through reading, writing, and mathematics. Yet he failed to outline what skills or concepts *within* these areas were best adapted to promoting thinking ability.[91] The principal of a junior high school in Fort Stockton, Texas, on the other hand, argued that "discipline" and the "Puritan work ethic" were *most* basic. "There can be little doubt that a need to return to the basics is both imperative and urgent," he asserted. "The debate lies in defining what we consider to be basic. A quick review of history," he went on to say, "will reveal that it is a peculiar and unique system of values which has contributed to the greatness of this country and its people, and it has been this value system which has been basic." The writer asked, "Can any teaching purport to be basic which does not address itself to instilling the Judeo-Christian values of our forefathers in today's youth?"[92]

Also of interest were the findings of a survey undertaken among 209 randomly selected principals and superintendents in Texas, who were asked, "If your budget were drastically reduced and you were told to 'teach only the basics,' what courses would you teach?" In order of frequency, "reading" headed the list—the only course to receive a unanimous endorsement. Arithmetic was close behind, cited by 99 percent of all respondents. But writing was edged out of third place by "personal hygiene." The list of top-ranked courses and the frequency percentage for each ran as follows: (1) reading, 100; (2) arithmetic, 99; (3) personal hygiene, 95; (4) writing-cursive, 92; (5) biology, tied with spelling, 91; (6) life-time sports, 88; (7) life science, tied with national history, 86; (8) state history, 85; (9) civics, 82; (10) earth science, 81; (11) algebra, 80; (12) vocabulary, 79; (13) chemistry, 75; (14) basketball, tied with punctuation, 74.6; (15) Spanish, 74; (16) chorus, 73; (17) world history, 72; (18) band, 71.5; (19) track, 71; (20) geometry, 69; (21) wood shop, tied with football, 68; (22) geography, 67.6; (23) sentence structure, 67; (24) business education, tied with first aid, 64; and (25) arts and crafts, 62.

Athletics, shop courses, band, and art activities, significantly, were ranked far above courses in physics, trigonometry, economics, literature, public address, calculus, and foreign languages. "How," the authors of the study asked, "can we expect the public to determine what the basics are when there is so much disparity among school administrators?"[93]

Before it had run its course, the back-to-basics movement had generated an enormous literature. Most obvious was the extraordinarily broad range of constructions placed on the term "basics." It was plain that many writers had a more extensive agenda in mind than simply renewed emphasis on the three R's. Linked with appeals to return to basics were demands for any or all of the following:

TWO DISSENTING VIEWS

There is a story, often repeated in Tanzania, about the Christian missionaries who took over the schooling in a Wachagga village and taught with great dedication the basic skills of readin', 'ritin', 'rithmetic, and reverence for the Lord. The missionaries did a fine job, sanctified by their own zeal, and when they left, all the young Wachaggans in the village had mastered the basics and could 'rite, 'rithmetize, and revere. By *all the young Wachaggans,* that is, we mean the sole two youngsters who accidently survived the lions, sharks, drought, heat, European clothing, etc. This experience gave rise to the old Tanzanian proverb, "Caveat disciplus," which translates roughly "Beware of pedagogues peddling basic skills."

> —Jon Dunn et al., "A New Kind of Writing," *Media & Methods* 6 (April 1970): 39.

We are reading much more now about the need to get back to the basics. Face it, with many of our students we have not been to the basics *once.* . . . If we have criticized students' writing because words were misspelled rather than because of specious arguments and misstated facts, then we deserve to read correctly spelled nonsense for the rest of our lives. If we have insisted that students say every word they read errorlessly but are only given token criticisms when they miss the author's point, then we deserve to listen to people pronouncing and declaiming inanities as if they were words of wisdom. By alll means, let's go back to the basics. . . .

> —Peter Hasselriis, "Reading Instruction: Why Go Beyond the Reading Class?" *Report of The State Reading Council* (Jefferson City, Mo.: Department of Elementary and Secondary Education, 1976), p. 21.

1. Renewed emphasis upon reading, writing, and arithmetic in the primary grades;
2. Reassertion of the directive authority of the classroom teacher, together with a corresponding decline of pupil-directed activities;
3. Elimination of curricular "frills" and elective courses;
4. Reduction of the school's "social services," such as guidance and counseling, sex education, driver education, physical education, and sundry "enrichment" programs;
5. A moratorium on "nontraditional" curricular and programmatic innovation;
6. More and better school "accountability" for learning outcomes, such as proficiency or competency-based assessment and performance-based curricula;
7. Increased emphasis upon vocationally related instruction and curricula;
8. Inculcation of "core values" thought essential for maintaining societal stability (e.g., patriotism, religion, respect for tradition and authority);
9. Strict discipline and control, including student dress codes and corporal punishment;
10. Drill, recitation, daily homework, and frequent testing;
11. Stricter community control over schools;
12. Reduction of costs, to be achieved through less-expensive new plant construction,

consolidation of existing facilities, deprofessionalization of teachers (i.e., apprenticeship training and the proscription of collective bargaining), and elimination of special student programs.[94]

Commenting, one author summed up the confusion:

> Educational talk over the past few years has been replete with a number of slogans, including injunctions to "individualize instruction," to make schooling 'relevant,' " to "humanize" education, ad infinitum. . . . What marks out the phrase "back to basics" from so many others of recent vintage, however, is the extraordinarily *wide* range of connotative associations it has attracted, perhaps to the point where even its emotive impact as a slogan has been seriously vitiated. . . . When the injunction to get back to basics fails even to conjure up a common universe of discourse within which debate can proceed, it is difficult to imagine the point of its further deployment at all.[95]

## FUNDAMENTAL SCHOOLS

Whether, as some observers had claimed, the impetus to return to basics in education was only a minority crusade launched by a few political extremists or an authentic mass movement remained an open question as the decade of the 1970s drew to a close. What was clear was that many public-school districts throughout the country were beginning to respond to its pressure. Sometimes the response assumed the more limited form of piecemeal curricular revisions and the imposition of stricter classroom control in regular schools. Occasionally, however, larger school districts acted to create alternative "fundamental schools," to which parents might make special application for their children's enrollment.

What distinguished fundamental schools from their "mainstream" counterparts was the attention they gave to basic skills and academic subject matter. All told, perhaps no more than a hundred or so special elementary schools of this type were operating in the late 1970s, and a still smaller number of middle, junior high, and high schools. But they were distributed from Anchorage, Alaska, to Dade County, Florida; and their numbers were to increase considerably in the years immediately following. Indicative of the support they enjoyed was the fact that, with few exceptions, most reported long waiting lists of prospective students. Some were conceived as "magnet schools," drawing children from different neighborhoods to help bring about voluntary desegregation. In the Los Angeles Unified School District, for example, by 1982 there were half a dozen such elementary and three junior high fundamental schools. Others had sprung up in Louisville, Kentucky; in the Charlotte-Mecklenburg district in North Carolina, in Montclair, New Jersey; in San Diego, California; in Arlington, Virginia; in Cupertino, California; in Mesa, Arizona; and elsewhere.

No single organizational pattern predominated, and often they employed quite different approaches in matters of curriculum, instruction, administration, and daily operation. But for all their differences, fundamental schools did tend to share certain characteristics in common. Among them were: (1) *teacher-centered instruction,* with little student involvement in decision making and planning; (2) *rigorous academic curricula,* with maximum emphasis on reading, writing, and arithmetic in the primary grades, and with subjects broken down into their component elements (for example, separate attention in Language Arts given to grammar, spelling, punctuation, and penmanship; Social Studies broken down into separate courses in history, geography, and civics; and so on); elimination or reduction of electives and ''mini-courses''; required foreign languages; and stress on biology, chemistry, physics, and mathematics; (3) *traditional pedagogy* based on repeated drill and recitation; (4) *self-contained classrooms;* (5) *strict discipline,* including corporal punishment, suspension for violations of school rules, and dismissal for repeated offenses; (6) *dress codes;* (7) *frequent homework;* and (8) *competency-based assessment and evaluation,* involving regular report cards bearing letter grades, frequent testing, and with grade promotion and graduation dependent on successful mastery of predefined skills and subject matter, and so on.

Fundamental-school advocates argued that the academic performance of students under such a regimen typically surpassed that of pupils enrolled in more permissive institutions. They emphasized as virtues the advantages of having clearly defined educational goals, classroom orderliness, promotion based on merit alone, respect for order and discipline, extensive parental involvement and support, and high standards of academic achievement. While skeptics detected an uncomfortable resemblance between fundamental schools and military academies or even penal institutions, defenders pointed out that the fundamental-school concept came closest to the demanding educational program conducted in a safe and businesslike atmosphere that more and more parents found appealing.

## EDUCATION AND THE NEW RIGHT

To what extent the emergence of the fundamental school and the trend in education to return to basics were connected with the nation's political move to the right in the late seventies and early eighties is difficult to ascertain. What was evident, however, in this period was a resurgence of social, economic, political, and religious conservatism in all aspects of American life. As Patrick P. McDermott observed, a ''mini-Cultural Revolution'' of sorts was underway, and it was perhaps inevitable that it should impact more or less directly upon the schools.[96] Education professor J. Charles Park characterized the phenomenon as follows: ''During the last few years a rather sophisticated coalition has emerged on the political right. Calling itself the New Right, a series of well-heeled organizations, operating outside traditional Democratic or Republican organizations, have used issue politics for the purpose of turning America back to God and away from uncertainty.''[97] The organizations it spawned were manifold. Aside from strictly political groups such as the Committee for Survival of a Free Congress, the Conservative Caucus, and the National Conservative Political Action Committee, the

New Right was represented in the 1980s by such single-issue organizations as Life Advocates, Stop-ERA, the Leadership Foundation, a Life Amendment Political Action Committee, the National Federation for Decency, Save Our Children, the Heritage Foundation, Educational Research Analysts, Citizens for Educational Freedom, National Christian Action Coalition, the Moral Majority, Conservative Caucus Research and Education Foundation, the Catholic League for Religious and Civil Rights, the American Legislative Exchange Council, as well as many others.

Specific targets of the New Right included the Equal Rights Amendment, abortion, homosexuality and gay rights, pornography, feminism, secularism, school integration and forced busing, the teaching of evolution in schools, official proscription of prayer in the classroom, and numerous other alleged evils.

"On the surface," wrote McDermott, "the New Right symbolizes a call for the return to simplicity and to 'tried and true' conservative values."[98] Underneath, it represented a response to an inchoate but deep revulsion on the part of many groups within society against modernity and the dominant values of contemporary Western culture. On its seamier side, he felt, the New Right was radically anti-intellectual. Its appeal was owed partly to an oversimplified view of the world that glossed over many of the complexities that must be considered in formulating sound public policy. Yet he fully appreciated the strength of that appeal. "The New Right," he conceded, was proving successful in "attempting through various means not only to inject its own view of morality . . . into the public domain but also to make sure it is accepted by legislating it into the fabric of our laws and thus our lives."[99]

Whatever its genesis, protagonists of this "new" conservatism had firm convictions on how society should be remolded. And like ultraconservatives of the 1940s and 1950s, they were resolved to enlist the schools to further their cause.

Among religious fundamentalists especially, the struggle to remake the social order was cast in apocalyptic terms. Battle lines were clearly drawn. Arrayed on the side of truth and light were all those dedicated to the restoration of traditional moral, religious, and political values. Opposing them were the forces of evil and godlessness. Not surprisingly, public education, with its commitment to pluralism and religious neutrality, was cast in the role of arch villain.

The basic problem with public schools, fundamentalists alleged, was that they were permeated with the "religion" of "secular humanism." As propagated by "humanists" in government, the media, and in schools, claimed the Moral Majority's Reverend Jerry Falwell, "secular humanism has become the religion of America." It had, he declared, "taken the place of the Bible."[100] With a virulence strongly reminiscent of the anti-Communist crusades of the McCarthy era, fundamentalists began a campaign to discredit what they insisted was a profoundly subversive doctrine—godless, relativist, immoral, and calculated to lead to the destruction of American society. A pamphlet distributed by the Pro-Family Forum entitled, *Is Humanism Molesting Your Child?* (1980), for example, claimed humanism

. . . denies the deity of God; denies the existence of the soul, life after death, salvation and heaven, damnation and hell; denies the Biblical account of creation; believes in sexual freedom between consenting adults, regardless of age, including premarital sex, homosexuality, lesbianism, and incest; believes in the right of abortion, euthanasia, equal distribution of America's wealth, control of the environment, control of energy and its limitation; and in the removal of American patriotism and the free enterprise system.[101]

In the classic mode of what American historian Richard Hofstadter once termed "the paranoid style in American politics," fundamentalist antihumanists suspected conspiracy within the leading ranks of the nation's executive, legislative, and judicial systems, its labor unions, universities, and the media industry. "We must remove all humanists from public office and replace them with pro-moral political leaders," declared Tim Lattaye, a self-styled Biblical family counselor and founder of the right-wing Council for National Policy.[102] So too was the threat of humanism in the schools described in conspiratorial terms: "Skilled change agents [teachers] can manipulate discussion to create peer pressure to conformity to non-Christian values." "Let's protect our families from child molesters." "Slowly he [the child] is conditioned to view his parents with distrust and disrespect," claimed *Is Humanism Molesting Your Child?*[103] Reverend Falwell, for one, warned his readers that "the liberals and humanists are slowly 'sneaking in' perverted and anti-moral sex educational material among public school systems."[104]

In vain, mainstream religious organizations rejected as unfounded, fundamentalist allegations of a conspiracy and claims that humanism as a philosophy or religion was being propagated in the nation's classrooms. James E. Wood, executive director of the Baptist Joint Committee of Public Affairs, for example, denounced as a "myth" charges that schools were engaged in a deliberate effort to foster any particular viewpoint. "Much of the myth," Smith argued, "has been predicated by those who seek to harass the public schools, to make them more responsive to their own particular moral and religious values, rather than remain schools in which a secular or nonreligious approach to the study of history, science, and government and literature prevails."[105]

Others pointed out the semantic confusion inherent in fundamentalist rhetoric on this particular issue. "Humanism," properly understood, is not a discrete "philosophy" in the Western cultural tradition. Rather, it is an attitude that stresses the dignity of humanity and the importance of culture to its full realization. Again, "humanism" *can* be understood as a religious doctrine—or, more precisely, an antitheological stance—adopted by nontheists; but, contrary to the impression encouraged by evangelical traditionalists, it is neither indifferent to questions of morality nor opposed to ethical standards for regulating human behavior. Paul Kurtz, editor of *The Humanist,* categorically denied the charge of a religion of secular humanism in schools. "The majority of the more than two million school teachers identify with the Judeo-Christian tradition, nominally or otherwise, whereas the official membership of the humanist religious bodies are numerically only a small portion of the total,'' he declared. ''Moreover, the organizational activities of secular humanists have no role in the schools, hence they are in no way leading to the establishment of a religion.''[106]

Finally, as many critics pointed out, ''humanism'' in education connotes ''humaneness'' and sensitivity to students' differing needs and abilities. It does not speak to any particular religious beliefs (or the lack thereof); it assumes no particular stand on specific social, economic, or political issues; and it is concerned primarily with the means or processes of instruction.

Undeterred, militant fundamentalists continued efforts to restore prayers in schools, to ban textbooks failing to meet certain ideological standards, and to influence the shape of school curricula. Their strongest demand was the substitution of ''creationism'' for the teaching of evolution as an account of the origin of life in the universe, or at least equal time for the former theory. Education, they appeared to believe, should be a means of imposing or instilling absolute truths as enshrined in Biblical scripture. Whoever opposed that viewpoint was considered by definition to be anti-Christian, atheistic, and ''humanistic.'' As one ultraconservative put it succinctly, ''There are people—millions of them—in the

---

### THE NEW RIGHT: SIGNS OF THE TIMES

As long as the schools continue to teach *abnormal attitudes* and *alien thoughts,* we caution parents *not* to urge their children to pursue high grades and class discussion, because the harder students work, the greater their chances of brainwashing.

> —Excerpt from Handbook No. 1, published by Educational Research Analysts

Some stuff is so far out you have to ban it. . . . I would think that moral-minded people might object to books that are philosophically alien to what they believe. If we have the books and feel like burning them, fine.

> —Chairman, Illinois Moral Majority

The Bible instructs parents to whip their children with a rod. . . . Welts and bruises are a sign that a parent is doing a good job of discipline. . . . If you haven't left any marks, you probably haven't whipped your children.

> —Head of Moral Majority of Indiana

Don't discuss the future, Don't exchange "opinions" on political or social issues, Don't participate in any classroom discussion which begins with such phrases as "What is your opinion of . . ." or "Do you think . . .?"

> —From a list of "26 Don'ts" to help parents purge certain teaching methods from local schools, circulated by Parents Actively Concerned (North Carolina)

USA . . . who adhere to the great tenet of Judeo-Christian civilization: that truth exists, and that we can know it. A logical corollary is that we want our children to also know it.''[107]

## CURRICULAR CENSORSHIP

A further corollary for many was that schoolchildren needed to be protected against whatever they regarded as ''objectionable'' or untrue. Their campaign, as an editorial comment in *The Christian Century* pointed out, had become ''widespread and well orchestrated,'' and followed ''a pattern of intimidation of local and state school and library officials.''[108] The ostensible goal of the New Right was to reverse the alleged trend of ''permissiveness'' in public schools by insisting that society not tolerate books containing material (particularly material related to sex) contrary to what was termed ''traditional American values.''

Repeatedly, in New York, Alabama, Illinois, Washington, and other states, legal suits were brought to remove from public and school libraries texts that, as it was claimed in one instance, ''undermined parental values, taught disrespect for law, encouraged dependence on welfare, contained profanity, included discussion of abortion and divorce, were anticapitalist and pro-labor, were hostile to the Bible, supported equal rights for women, and did not stress that the United States is 'a republic and not a democracy.' ''[109] Sex-education materials in particular provoked the greatest opposition.

The Dallas-based National Congress for Educational Excellence, for example, in an undated quarterly newsletter observed, ''The [original] purpose of sex education programs was to *decrease* the incidence of sexual intercourse which leads to teenage pregnancy and venereal disease.'' Citing national studies showing sex education had *not* decreased sexual activity among teenagers, the writer remarked, ''Parent concerns about the adverse effects of Sexual Education courses have been borne out. . . .''[110] With righteous indignation, quotations were reproduced from a book allegedly used by the Dallas Independent School District Parenting Materials and Information Center:

> I have known cases of farm boys who have had a loving sexual relationship with an animal and who felt good about their behavior until they got to college . . .

> Premarital intercourse can also be a training ground, so that when people get married they already have experience in one of the most important aspects of learning to live with someone else in marriage.

> If it happens that a particular premarital intercourse experience doesn't lead to marriage, because of dissatisfaction with the sexual relationship, it is less upsetting and complicated than if it had happened after marriage . . .

> If, however, his attitude is that only a virgin is good enough for him to marry, maybe he had better examine his values . . .[111]

A 1981 survey sponsored by the Association of American Publishers, the American Library Association, and the Association for Supervision and Curriculum Development found that more than one-fifth of all the nation's school districts and upwards of a third of its school libraries were embroiled in challenges to literary works and textbooks.[112] Many of the attacks had proved successful. Included in the roster of distinguished writers censored were works by Ferlinghetti, Heller, Huxley, Orwell, Salinger, Vonnegut, Solzhenitsyn, Malamud, Hughes, and scores of lesser authors.

As ultraconservatives saw it, schools are extensions of the home, and concerned parents have a right to ban from the classroom or library any books they would not allow in the home. Opponents of censorship responded by asking, "*Whose* home is the public school?" As one writer posed the issue:

> In any other setting, the right of free expression would be held to prohibit the government or political majority from controlling the content of communication. In schools, however, the accepted practice is local government control of the indoctrination of children. The problem is how to distinguish appropriate indoctrination from instances of censorship that undercut freedom of thought, hobble community tolerance, and turn schools into ideological battlefields.[113]

Central to disputes over book banning was the search for a legal expedient capable of reconciling the principle of majority control of schooling with the First Amendment rights of parents and students who dissented from community values. On one side, the question was whether there were *any* actions that a school board might take in an effort to inculcate local mores without running afoul of First Amendment guarantees. On the other side, the issue was how to protect the rights of dissenting minorities. For persons whose values were threatened by the dominant culture, the defensive response was to use every means possible to prevent their children from being exposed to alien ideas in schools. On the other hand, when school officials acceded to demands for the removal of certain books or instructional materials, they also exposed themselves to the threat of litigation from those opposed to any prior restraint of ideas. The control of schools by a minority was unacceptable, yet majority control could also be equally tyrannical. No acceptable resolution of the dilemma immediately suggested itself, and so debate continued.

## CHRISTIAN ACADEMIES

When fundamentalist attempts to reshape public education stalled in the courts or met with stiff opposition from those not sharing their views, an alternative suggested itself: private schools. In the nineteenth century, Catholics had felt compelled to build an independent parochial-school system because of fears that the public schools were too Protestant. Ironically enough, much the same pressures lay behind the Christian-fundamentalists' drive in the 1980s to create their own separate schools, except that now secession was prompted by a conviction that public education had grown too secular.

Some parents withdrew their children from public schools in flight from declining academic standards and disciplinary problems. But others did so more out of a desire for an explicit moral framework for instruction. As a 1981 piece in *Newsweek* phrased it, "They don't like the ban on prayer in school. They are unhappy about library books that reflect the less-than-chaste realities of contemporary society. Drugs dismay them and sex education horrifies them." [114] Above all, what supporters wanted was the kind of pervasive religious environment the public schools could not offer. By some estimates, conservative religious academies numbered 10,000 or more in the early eighties and were opening at about the rate of three or four daily.

Most were elementary schools, offering a curriculum up through the first six grades. Others combined primary-level and secondary instruction. Some enjoyed their own lavish physical facilities; others operated out of more humble church Sunday-school rooms. But whatever the size of their enrollment or number of teachers, in the classroom religious and moral concerns were foremost. Fiercely independent and resistant to all state attempts at regulation or certification, organizers of fundamentalist academies were determined to offer a brand of education strictly informed by Biblical precepts.

---

Students of this school are expected to refrain from talking about or engaging in cheating, swearing, smoking, gambling, rock or country music, dancing, Hollywood movies, drinking alcoholic beverages, or using narcotics. . . . Students are expected to act in an orderly and respectful manner, maintaining Christian standards in courtesy, kindness, language, morality, and honesty. Students must agree to strive toward unquestionable character in dress, conduct and attitude.

Christian Americanism places emphasis upon the greatness of America's heritage and the sacrifices of its heroes. America is a republic which guarantees liberties to educate to preserve freedom. We unashamedly teach the Biblical doctrines of self-discipline, respect for those in authority, obedience to law, and love for flag and country.

Students must at all times conduct themselves in a manner becoming a Christian. *Griping is not tolerated!*

Use only words which glorify the Lord.

—From the *Student Handbook,* Apostolic Christian Academy (Columbia, Missouri)

---

## CONTEMPORARY VOICES

Political, social, and religious fundamentalists were not alone in their criticism of American public education. Mirroring the nation's mounting conservatism in all areas, increasing numbers of educators themselves began joining in the chorus. McDermott, for one, noted early in the 1980s that "academe has already gone conservative, from the competency-based, back-to-basics approach in elementary and secondary education to the renewed interest in science, engineering and job skills in higher education.''[115] What some critics lacked in originality, it appeared, they more than compensated for with fervor.

Typical was the salvo fired by John Carver, a former educator and teacher of broadcasting, who, like Bestor, Smith, and others a quarter of a century earlier, blamed the educational establishment itself for the quality schools were lacking. ''Amidst the flack of damning evidence,'' he wrote somewhat unkindly, ''the placid and confident denials of culpability by professional educators carry all the conviction of a Marine battalion being led into combat by a transvestite.''[116] The spectacle of nineteen million American illiterates aged sixteen or over and the fact that over half of all college students were required to take remedial English, he avowed, amounted to a national disgrace.

Carver assigned blame freely. G. Stanley Hall and his disciple, John Dewey, he alleged, were initially responsible for ''liberating'' schoolchildren from ''the tyranny of subject matter'' and emphasizing instead values clarification, self-concept development, and what came to be known as human potential psychology. The fifties witnessed the full flowering of ''a galvanic urge to assure the people that what they were doing was best.'' ''Succumbing to its heady fragrance, teachers thought to elevate the egos and sublimate the aggressions of the underprivileged by sheltering them from the need of even minimally conforming to the prevailing cultural standards.''[117] Discipline was abandoned, as was the concept of a structured curriculum.

Under the aegis of ''democratizing'' American education, Carver continued, there gradually developed an uncritical reverence for the spoken tongue, and a corresponding contempt for correct usage and semantics in its written expression. Grammar was relegated to the trash heap. Phonics as a method of teaching reading was given up. Frills, not skills, were emphasized; and such ''holistic'' goals as ''psychic integration'' and ''spiritual validation'' were made to substitute for such functional aims as competence and carefully cultivated ability.

''We are facing the prospect,'' Carver warned, ''of a world packed with people who will be, no doubt, very sensitive, very earnest, visceral communicators with nothing of interest or relevance to communicate.''[118]

Bill Freeman, a professor of education and chair of the Department of Teacher Education at Austin College, in Sherman, Texas, confessed that under the influence of ''liberal professors'' in his undergraduate days, he had been indoctrinated into a permissive philosophy of life and education. He was imbued with liberal theology and ethical relativism. He subscribed to the progressivism of John Dewey. In his subsequent career as a classroom teacher, principal, and then college professor, he practiced what he had been taught. His goal was to make all teaching and learning easy, fun, and exciting. In his personal life, he ''kept silent as society became more and more permissive while it abandoned traditional moral values.''

Gradually, however, Freeman reported, he woke up to the results of permissiveness in the public schools. "I came to see such problems as grade inflation, promotion for merely social reasons, laxity in discipline, lower academic standards, and general disrespect for people and property as reflections of our culture and its system of education." [119]

Ultimately, Freeman repudiated his earlier views. In his own teaching, he began to stress the need for teachers to provide exemplary models for their pupils. He came to appreciate the need for "order, respect, responsible behavior, and decency in the classroom." He counseled his students preparing to become educators to "establish high expectations and standards in all aspects of teaching." To counter the "spiritual void" in contemporary society created by self-centeredness, unbounded freedom, and relativism, Freeman concluded, the job of teachers was "to point out the nature of society's dilemma, its causes, and the things we can do to correct it." [120]

For Carver, the root of the problem with American education was confusion among educators over the meaning of equality and democracy in learning. For Freeman, it was the growing permissiveness of society among educators and the unwillingness of teachers to set high standards of accomplishment. For Illinois School Superintendent Donald R. Gill, among others, a major deficiency in public education was its failure to stress moral values. Mindful that moral education could easily become a vehicle for introducing religion into the schools or for teaching values repugnant to ethnic or cultural minorities (thereby proving seriously divisive), Gill proposed a statewide series of hearings in the early 1980s to discover what values might command general support. [121]

According to Reo M. Christenson, a professor of political science at Miami University, in Oxford, Ohio, schools could not help teaching certain values. "Schools have always been teaching morality," he insisted; they "always will and always must. They teach students to do their work well, to avoid cheating, to be punctual, courteous, law-abiding and respectful of school and private property, and so on."

In the Talawanda School district in Ohio, Christenson reported, officials had managed to identify a set of values and attitudes to be fostered that had not aroused opposition from community groups. They included self-discipline, trustworthiness, truth-telling, honesty, personal integrity in the face of group pressure, respect for individual and collective rights, good sportsmanship, courtesy, the golden rule, respect for property, obedience to the rule of law, respect for democratic rights and values, physical and emotional health, conscientiousness in work performance—and abstinence from "premature sexual experience."

"These values and attitudes can be taught with the acceptance and approval of all parents—religious believers or unbelievers, liberals or conservatives, white, brown or black," Christenson argued. "They represent a consensus of what democratic societies, and responsible people, have learned from experience about human behavior and about constructive attitudes toward life and society." If the first responsibility of every society is to pass on the best of its ethical heritage to the young, he observed, the schools must share in that responsibility.

Schools have an obligation to try to compensate for the failure of some parents to inculcate sound values, he further stated. The most difficult challenge was not to identify values but to discover how to instill them most effectively.[122]

According to Gordon Cawelti, executive director of the Association for Supervision and Curriculum Development (ASCD), American education had always been plagued by the persistent notion that for every societal problem that exists, an educational program should be devised to respond to that problem. Particularly in high schools, Cawelti felt, the curriculum had been "optionalized" to the point where any substantive reconsideration of what *common* learning should be provided was impossible. Seldom had anyone asked what would be *excluded* when secondary schools were required to develop instructional programs dealing with drug abuse, sex education, moral education, values, leisure time, nutrition, parenting skills, energy, global affairs, ecology, population, careers, death, or ethnic studies. Neither was much thought given to the legitimacy or prospects for success of such programs. "As a result," he claimed, "we have a badly overloaded or 'patchwork' curriculum which lacks coherence and serves poorly its purpose of providing a general education for American youth."[123]

Cawelti's argument found broad support among other educators. "Inasmuch as the curriculum is a zero-sum game, with only a certain number of hours each day, every course added to a student's schedule displaces some other course," observed education professor Diane Ravitch. In recent decades, she complained, every felt need within society had produced pressure for new courses. Eventually the proliferation of new courses and the easing of requirements had proved fatal to any universally shared course of instruction: "In many high schools the requirements and the common curriculum collapsed like eggshells."[124]

Judith S. Siegel, a program officer for the National Endowment for the Humanities, and Edwin J. Delattre, writing in the *New Republic,* likewise deplored public clamor for schools to serve a vast array of purposes, from vocational training and citizenship development to the promotion of social reform. The erroneous idea that a "quick fix" for social problems is available through the schools, they argued, "undermines the kind of intellectual preparation necessary for making conscientious and informed judgments about personal well-being and social policy." If the trend toward curricular fragmentation continued, they warned, "we will finally lose sight of the idea that there is any shared experience and understanding which defines an educated people."[125] Serving the same point was the observation of psychology professor Joseph Adelson that "in an era marked by a multiplicity of aims, or by competing aims, the schools tend to become ambivalent, or confused, or inhibited—often all three at once."[126]

Jacques Barzun, author of *Teacher in America* (1945) and numerous other works on education, was bitter in his indictment of American public education, which, he was convinced, had degenerated into "a wasteland where violence and vice share the time with ignorance and idleness, besides serving as battleground for vested interests, social, political, and economic.''[127] The new product of that debased system, he judged, the functional illiterate, now numbered in the millions. The manifest decline of a once-proud institution he found ''heartbreakingly sad,'' but he insisted that it represented what the public had chosen to make of it in its confusion over priorities:

> Instead of trying to develop native intelligence and give it good techniques in the basic arts of man, we professed to make ideal citizens, supertolerant neighbors, agents of world peace and happy family folk, at once sexually adept and flawless drivers of cars. In the upshot, a working system has been brought to a state of impotence. Good teachers are cramped or stymied in their efforts, while the public pays more and more for less and less. The failure to be sober in action and purpose, to do well what can actually be done, has turned a scene of fruitful activity into a spectacle of defeat, shame, and despair.[128]

ASCD Executive Secretary Cawelti recognized the desirability of retaining an extensive offering of elective courses in American high schools. At the same time, he stressed the urgent need for ''common learnings deemed essential for *all* students to function well in a free society.'' His recommendation was a ''base line'' or required ''core'' of interdisciplinary courses encompassing six major areas:

1. *Learning Skills*—minimal competencies established in mathematics, composition, speaking and listening, problem-solving, computer literacy, and critical thinking.
2. *Emotional-Physical Health*—integrated, interdisciplinary courses in physical education, nutrition, drug abuse, stress management, use of leisure time, lifetime sports, and so on.
3. *Career-Vocational*—cooperative work-study programs in industrial arts, career education, vocational education, distributive education, etc.
4. *Cultural Studies*—a unified ''course or courses'' in art, music, drama, aesthetics, literature, history, multicultural education, ethnic studies, foreign language.
5. *Science-Technology*—applied courses in biology, physics, chemistry, earth science, physiology, and environmental education.
6. *Citizenship-Societal Studies*—one or more team-taught ''problems of democracy'' courses, utilizing community resources and compelling student participation in data collection and analysis, in: history, economics, social sciences, citizenship; to include such topics as poverty, urban life, the economy, global studies, war, population control, and energy sources.[129]

Cawelti anticipated the objection that many teachers would tend to resent any intrusion on the ''purity'' of their respective disciplines. ''While any number of restraints can be anticipated,'' he advised, ''most can be overcome through good planning skills, effective participation on techniques, and strong instructional leadership.''[130] Overall, however, the enumeration of topics, subject matter, and activities encompassed by his six ''curriculum areas'' was astonishingly broad in scope; and it was difficult to imagine how any room would be left for electives. Many critics might very well have faulted him for the same failure to make hard choices and to decide upon priorities that he himself claimed had so bloated and fragmented school curricula in the past.

Less well-defined but more limited in scope were recommendations offered by the Council for Basic Education. In an era of retrenchment when financial exigency was forcing drastic cutbacks in expenditures for public schools, the Council warned against measures threatening the integrity of "respectable public education." Advised one editorial, "Cut back on any school activities except those that are necessary to assure young people sound, basic education." In partial agreement with Cawelti, the editorialist urged educators to distinguish between what is necessary in education and what is "nice or useful or convenient" for children and adolescents to do in school: "The necessity to cut back provides the opportunity to cut out the expense of much that has long been improperly charged against education—extraneous 'educations' like career, consumer, death, and driver education; soft elective courses that take credit for hard requirements; big-time interscholastic athletic competition and all that goes with it." [131]

The only "sane" posture, the editorialist commented in a paraphrase of the Council's by-laws, was to husband available resources carefully and to stress such essentials as: (1) adequate instruction in such intellectual disciplines as English, mathematics, science, history, foreign languages, and the arts; (2) clear standards of achievement for student promotion; (3) competent teachers thoroughly trained in subjects taught; and (4) opportunities for high-ability students to achieve their full potential as quickly and efficiently as possible. [132]

A long line of conservative school critics, extending from Bagley and Demiashkevich through Bestor, Conant, Koerner, Barzun, and others would have warmly endorsed the suggestion.

Richard Mitchell, an English professor and self-styled "underground grammarian," doubted any such appeals would ever receive a hearing, and, once again, placed blame directly on the Educational Establishment. In a trenchant and witty analysis entitled, *The Graves of Academe,* he pressed the attack with a vengence not seen since the heyday of Rafferty, Smith, or Rickover. [133] Unlike similar indictments of an earlier day, his scathing criticism, while polemical, was carefully constructed, detailed, and, for many, highly persuasive.

Mitchell's proximate target was what he called "that special and unmistakable kind of mendacious babble" commonly employed by "professionals" in education. [134] Citing numerous examples of convoluted prose with devastating effect, he ridiculed at length the propensity of educators to speak and write in jargon-ridden "educationese." It was, he asserted, a particularly odious kind of noncommunicative "vaporing"—puerile, inflated, innane, and utterly mindless. [135] With its "special, ludicrous combination of ignorance and pretentiousness," educationist talk, he said, enjoys that rarest of literary qualities, "absolute immunity to parody." [136] Given to reinventing the wheel every few years and belaboring the obvious at interminable length, educators, he further asserted, by word and deed reveal their own incapacity to think or write clearly about anything. "Educationists," he observed acidly, "love to sound technical, and they have a penchant for giving important sounding names to things that need no names at all.''[137] But in their ponderous, overblown rhetoric about "outcomes" and "interactive relationships" and "learning variables: and "transpersonal instruction" and "competencies," *ad infinitum, ad nauseum,* Mitchell believed he had found the key to why ''Johnny can't read'' and why schools turn out generations of "thoughtless, unskilled unproductive, self-indulgent, and eminently dupable Americans.''[138]

In disagreement with other critics, Mitchell professed to believe that complaints about the schools arise from a lack of understanding as to how and why education functions as it does. Public education is *not* failing, he avowed; it does its work superbly, almost perfectly, in accordance with the dictates of its own implicit, elaborate ideology, of which the general public is largely unaware.[139] Children *do* learn, always, every day. But what they learn is that errors have no consequences, that failure carries no penalty, and that hard effort will go unrewarded. They learn to disregard subject matter and to turn inward in narcissistic self-absorption. They are taught to pay attention only to themselves, their likes and dislikes, their whims and fancies, their private hopes and fears and interests.[140]

Mitchell believed it was futile to expect professional educators, those he derided as intellectual "pygmies," to institute reforms. The "problem" of American education cannot be solved; it is, rather, an ineluctable fact of life. Because the school constitutes a "monolithic and self-sustaining institution," it is absolutely impervious to reform. It is immense and mindless, a "brooding monstrosity," capable of absorbing the shock of every criticism by pretending to "reform" itself, only to disarm whatever it claims to embrace, transforming it into nothing but more of the same. Public education might be described as an industry whose task is to generate both supply *and* demand, so the public will want from it precisely what it intends to provide. That is, the system assumes children cannot learn and then it sells an endless succession of "remedies" to compensate for that inability. Failure is built in, because every unsuccessful experiment makes room for further experimentation dressed up as innovation. The fact that people do not learn and are not taught to think in school, in the final analysis, is useful because the problems thereby created provide ever-expanding employment for the people originally responsible:

> Thus it is that, after about sixty years of organized and militant anti-intellectualism in the schools, every disorder in education brings power and profit to those who have made that disorder, and every problem is given for solution into the hands of the only people who cannot possibly solve it. The pygmies have been in charge for so long now that we are all cracking our skulls on the doorways of the public buildings; when we go to them for remedy, they urge on us the value of crawling.[141]

Could an outraged public remedy matters by insisting that schools teach only what can be objectively taught and measured? Mitchell rated the chances as slim. Given the educationist hegemony over public education, the sort of noneducation purveyed in schools has kept the mass of people stupid and uninformed. It would require a much more enlightened and thoughtful public than can exist under present conditions to demand that schools return to academic fundamentals. In other words, the intellectual climate of the public schools—or, rather, the lack thereof—assures an equally abysmal climate within society. Even following H. L. Mencken's advice to burn down all the colleges and hang the professors would avail nothing. Authentic reform would necessitate nothing less than a revolution—the obliteration and reconstitution of the entire school system. But so long as a gullible public accepts the protestations of educationists that they alone have the answers to all of society's ills, in the form of extra-academic courses, faddish new curricula, and enlarged programs in schools, Mitchell concluded, everything will remain unchanged.[142]

## IN RETROSPECT

Reflecting back upon half a century or more of school criticism, one finds in the literature of educational "conservatism" discussions and analyses ranging from the near-hysterical excesses of a fringe element to the more considered reflections of quite thoughtful critics. Judicious commentary and rhetorical hyperbole freely intermingle. At one extreme appear unsubstantiated allegations flung carelessly at an easy and convenient target—the public school. At the other have been closely reasoned critiques representing efforts to deal carefully with fundamental issues. But the underlying thematic unity shared in common has to do with a belief in the importance of intellectual and moral fundamentals and the school's role as an academic institution in conserving those fundamentals within the social order.

Historically, it might not be too far off the mark to say that subsequent discussion among educational conservatives has added very little to themes first enunciated by the original Essentialists in the thirties and forties. In basic outline, the argument has since changed scarcely if at all. Its main features might be abstracted and reduced as follows:

1. *Educational Purpose.* The role of the school as a formal institution is to nurture, preserve, reproduce, and transmit the essential elements of a cultural inheritance—the panoply of ideals, values, skills, and factual knowledge demonstrably necessary for individual self-development and the preservation of the social order. Any other set of objectives, whether promulgated by educators themselves or imposed from without, cannot help deflecting the school from its proper aim. The school enjoys no legitimate mandate to change or reform society, nor should it seek to deal directly with more specific social problems or needs.

2. *Curricula.* The school is charged with teaching basic literacy skills whose aim is proficiency in reading, writing and oral communication, and computation. Such skills, in turn, permit the acquisition of further information, skills, and values whose relevance and validity have survived the test of time. Each new generation must be placed in possession of a common core of knowledge, meanings, insights, and intellectual skills. These are best fostered through the study of basic academic

disciplines; i.e., the most generically simple and fundamental forms of understanding available within the culture.

3. *Instructional Method.* The school is an agency of social control. No matter what specific teaching or management procedures are utilized, maintaining order and discipline is essential for learning. Explicit and unambiguous standards for academic achievement are also critical. Advancement through the system should depend solely upon performance in conformity with those criteria. Repetition, drill, recitation, and memorization are useful expedients for assuring academic competence. The ultimate test of instruction is the cognitive development it renders possible.

## SUMMARY

Educational conservatism as a theory and a social movement in American education originated in reaction to the alleged dominance of progressivism in the 1920s and 1930s. It first received systematic expression as an argument under the aegis of William Bagley and the Essentialists. Pleas for a stress upon basic learning skills and academic discipline were renewed in the postwar period, though they were overshadowed somewhat by attempts to enlist the schools in a crusade to resist subversive infiltration and to buttress the traditional values of "Americanism."

Conservative school critics of the 1950s repeatedly assailed public education, first, for reflecting a "life-adjustment" philosophy inimical to true academic learning, and, subsequently, for having failed to nurture a level of excellence required in order to sustain broader social and political policy objectives. A recurrent theme was the need for academic goals, better instruction in basic skills and disciplines, and more rigorous achievement standards. Despite an upsurge of interest in the sixties and seventies in individualized "open education," critics such as Robert Ebel, Paul Copperman, George Weber (speaking on behalf of the Council for Basic Education), and many others argued consistently for a less-permissive system of schooling.

In the mid-1970s, mounting public concern over the alleged lack of classroom discipline and reports of declining academic achievement scores provided the impetus for a "back-to-basics" movement. Few concurred in their definitions of basic learning, but almost all were agreed that schools should accord greater emphasis to the teaching of the three R's. Reform proposals included calls for competency-based instruction and assessment, elevated standards of performance, a restoration of discipline, and greater teacher accountability.

By the late 1970s, the nation's political mood appeared to have shifted in a conservative direction. The emergence of the so-called New Right brought increasing attempts to eradicate "secular humanism" from the schools, to censor school curricula, and in other ways to influence both the direction and character of public instruction. Coupled with ultraconservative attempts to remold public education was the rise of fundamentalist-Christian private academies.

Much school criticism up through the mid-1980s reiterated complaints and allegations levied previously. Although analyses of the presumed faults of the schools differed, with some blaming a misguided public and others assigning primary responsibility to professional educators themselves, the general feeling was that public education had attempted to achieve too many disparate ends. For educational conservatives, meaningful reform would entail a narrower range of instructional objectives, more rigorous curricula and pedagogy, and a commitment to academic achievement.

## REVIEW QUESTIONS

1. Upon what basis, and for what reasons, did the early Essentialists oppose the alleged domination of American public education by progressivism? What were their specific complaints?

2. How did William Chandler Bagley envision the role of the school in society? What did he claim is the school's contribution to the social order in periods of change? How should the school perform its primary function?

3. By what criteria did Essentialists identify the most important kinds of skills, knowledge, and values to be fostered in schools?

4. What was the Essentialist Platform? What were its major allegations and recommendations?

5. How did conservatives in the 1930s and 1940s propose to deal with individual learner differences in the teaching of a common curriculum?

6. What was the major complaint levied against the schools by political conservatives in the McCarthy era? What explanation did they offer to account for the alleged shortcomings of American public education? How did they propose to remedy the situation? In what sense can they be termed *educational* conservatives?

7. To what specific educational needs was life-adjustment education intended as a response? Why was it commonly identified as a form of progressivist pedagogy? Why was it so strenuously opposed by educational conservatives?

8. To what criterion or standard did school critics such as Arthur Bestor appeal in defining fundamental knowledge? How and why did educational conservatives in the early 1950s indict the schools for being anti-intellectual and anti-academic?

9. What was the connection in the late 1950s and early 1960s between the U.S.–Soviet "space race" and changing attitudes toward American public education? Why the stress on "excellence" and how was this defined? How did such "survivalist" critics as Max Rafferty view the role of the school as a social institution? What did they see as its primary mission?

10. What were the main objectives of the Council for Basic Education? How did the CBE originally define basic education? Why did its representatives object to characterizations of the Council as an organization concerned exclusively with stressing the three R's in school? How was the substance of "a basic and limited" curriculum characterized?

11. Advocates of "back to basics" in the 1980s appeared to share with earlier conservative critics skepticism regarding various social services offered by public schools. What was the most common objection to these social-service functions?

12. What factors lent influence and credibility to the back-to-basics movement of the seventies and eighties? What specific complaints and criticisms were put forth by writers such as Paul Copperman, Neil Postman, and others during this period?

13. How have so-called "fundamental" schools responded to popular demands for return to basic education?

14. Summarize briefly the nature of the influence exerted by the New Right upon public education in the 1980s. How did objections by religious fundamentalists to "humanism" resemble ultraconservative protest against public education in the immediate postwar period? What values did conservatives urge schools to preserve and endorse in both periods?

15. What have been the main philosophical and legal issues surrounding attempts to censor school curricula?

16. In what sense is it plausible to argue that fundamentalist-Christian academies represent an expression of educational conservatism as a theory and a social movement?

17. Assess the viability of Christenson's argument that schools inevitably teach values. What political, social, and moral values have educational conservatives characteristically espoused over the past few decades? What factors frustrate efforts by public schools to inculcate these values?

18. A recurrent theme by educational conservatives is curricular fragmentation; i.e., a loss of common learning and a proliferation of courses designed to meet extra-academic concerns. How have critics explained this phenomenon? To what factors has it been variously attributed?

## SOME QUESTIONS FOR DISCUSSION

1. Assume for argument's sake that a major role of the school is to conserve and transmit the funded wisdom of the past. In light of this assumption, assess the following claim: "The social heritage is often glorified for its own sake and without discrimination. Learning becomes largely an acquiescent process of corresponding with, by responding to and representing, the selective stimuli of those who control the schools in the interests of their own patterns of authority. And the belief that both individual self and objective world are governed by predetermined uniformities and mandates becomes a subtle, sometimes inadvertent, but still potent means to instill habits of uniformity with what has been and hence is assumed still to be both inevitable and right." (Theodore Brameld, *Philosophies of Education in Cultural Perspective* [New York: Holt, Rinehart and Winston, 1955, p. 284].)

2. The school's transmission of the past through formal curricula is inevitably selective. Not everything that has been thought, written, or achieved, obviously, deserves a place within a program of instruction. Therefore, what principles ought to guide teachers and curriculum planners in determining what is included? Not everything can or should be preserved—but by what criteria does one decide? Is ancient history less important than modern history? If schools teach French, German, and Spanish, should they neglect Russian, Chinese, or Japanese? Is English

literature on a par with the ancient Sumerian epics? Are Shakespeare's plays more or less significant than those of Sophocles or Aristophanes?

3. What is "basic" in education? Which are *most* basic, academic skills or such "life-coping" skills as first-aid procedures, installment purchasing, understanding credit, driver safety, and so on? Is grammar more basic than style or composition? Are computational skills more fundamental than facility in the use of a calculator? How does computer literacy stack up against the ability to read and write? Which is more important in science—understanding the laws of thermodynamics or the nature of scientific inquiry? In what sense is some knowledge more "generic" than other knowledge?

4. What is an academic "discipline"? Is it an arbitrary convention or an indispensable conceptual tool for organizing thought about human knowledge? What about so-called "hybrid" disciplines such as social psychology, sociobiology, or biochemistry? Where do such subjects as "ecology" fit in as disciplines? Can all knowledge be compartmentalized in terms of disciplines? How should concepts be ordered or facts arranged in a curriculum? Do some kinds of knowledge have more "generative power" than other forms or types of knowledge? What knowledge has greatest utility, and in what sense?

5. How plausible and convincing is the argument that the purpose of formal education is *academic* training? Is the emphasis upon cognition too one-sided? What about affect—feelings, sentiments, emotions? Can attitudes be fostered and shaped? Can facts and feelings be separated in the learning process?

6. Does the school's responsibility extend beyond strictly academic considerations? Or should the school and its personnel have a concern for all the myriad forces affecting learning? Assess the claim that the school is neither designed nor equipped to provide specific services or to fulfill social needs neglected elsewhere in society. For example, if children's classroom performance is affected by nutrition and a child shows up at school inadequately fed, is the school obliged to respond? How? What about children on drugs? Or a child who misses school because the parents cannot afford to buy clothes or extracost school supplies? If a teenager is working at an outside job and is suffering from lack of sleep, who should intervene? Another common problem is schoolchildren who must take care of younger siblings while both parents work, and who therefore have neither time nor energy for work at school. What then? If an emotionally disturbed youngster cannot learn properly, what are the school's limits of responsibility? If a youth is unmotivated to learn and is contemplating dropping out of school, what should be done? When a disruptive child's behavior reflects a poor home environment, what should be the school's response? What about child abuse? Can the school be concerned exclusively with academics, either in the classroom or outside?

7. If a child repeatedly fails and lacks self-confidence, how should teachers encourage the development of a more positive self-image? What should count for success in school? Apart from treating their students with care and respect, can or should teachers seek to promote good mental health? Should healthy mental development serve as a direct and explicit aim of instruction?

8. What is "relevance" in education? "Relevant" to whom or what? If schoolchildren typically are most interested in "what's happening

today," how can instruction about the past avoid seeming irrelevant and hopelessly anachronistic? Should appreciation for the cultural legacy of the past be a paramount aim of the school?

9. Is academic education elitist? Should all students be required to master certain skills and knowledge domains in common? What if, despite his or her best efforts, a teacher is confronted with a child who cannot or will not attempt to master an academic curriculum? The student appears utterly devoid of intellectual curiosity, lacking in motivation, apathetic to learning, and totally unwilling to expend the effort needed to succeed. What then? Is it prejudicial to claim that inner-city minority children can profit more from a curriculum that differs from that offered to advantaged youths? Or is it the case that all children should be afforded equal opportunity to succeed—or fail—in the mastery of a common curriculum? What would be required to assure each child genuine equality of opportunity?

10. Experienced teachers are well aware of the fact that children differ in their ability to learn. Is the *time* variable the most critical factor? In other words, if children of differing ability are allowed to progress at different rates, is it realistic to hope that all can end up mastering much the same material at some minimally acceptable level? Or must curricula be differentiated to reflect differences among learners? Is "tracking" a defensible expedient? Does it lend itself too readily to abuse? Or is it an inevitable and necessary response to the reality of heterogeneity among public-school children?

11. Should schools be employed as instruments to further national, social, economic, or political objectives? Can schools, for example, help strengthen democratic beliefs, values, and institutions? How congruent should school curricula be with larger policy aims? Again, if severe shortages of personnel in certain important professional job categories are forecast for the future, should present-day school curricula and instruction be adapted accordingly? How?

12. Who determines school policy? What forces shape what is taught in school? Are educators primarily responsible? Where do pressures for new courses or types of curricula originate? Who should exercise ultimate control? Do administrators, teachers, and textbook publishers establish goals or determine instructional methods or do agencies external to the school establishment? How has the American tradition of local community control affected curricula, instruction, and classroom management? What are the respective degrees of influence exercised by federal, state, and local governments? How do citizens' coalitions and parents' associations exert power over educational institutions? How should professional educators respond to externally imposed guidelines, policies, directives, or recommendations? What might be the most equitable distribution of power and influence?

13. Notice how, sooner or later, in any discussion over social issues or problems, someone will say, "Well, basically, I see it as an *educational* question. What we need to do is to get the *schools* to offer a course or a program in ..." To what extent is this phenomenon responsible for the alleged curricular fragmentation, diversity, and proliferation of separate courses deplored by so many school critics?

14. Oftentimes schools are faulted for failing to devise and enforce minimum standards of academic competency. Who should select and define such standards, assuming they are both desirable and necessary? Is it possi-

ble that a stipulated "minimum" would frequently become the "maximum," thereby encouraging the growth of "mediocracy" in education? Would teachers be content to "teach to the tests" and not insist that students attempt to exceed them? Is it *politically* feasible to establish minimal standards that a certain percentage of schoolchildren could be expected to fail? If not, would lower standards serve any useful purpose?

15. Can *all* learning be assessed in terms of a performance? Testing whether a child has learned the multiplication tables, for example, is relatively simple and straightforward. The proof of success in learning to operate, say, a drill press is whether in fact the learner can do so. Evaluation instruments can be readily devised to ascertain many different levels or types of factual learning. But what about insight, appreciation, or understanding? Can affective learning outcomes be measured with an acceptable degree of precision or objectivity? If minimal competency-performance standards were inaugurated on a widespread basis in schools, would they generate a tendency among educators to teach and assess only what can be measured?

16. Assume a school district has established certain criteria governing grade promotion and graduation. What happens to children who fail? How long should they be retained at a given level?

17. Imagine (to employ an admittedly farfetched example) the parents of a schoolchild are fervent members of the Flat Earth Society. They strenuously object to the presence of a globe in their child's classroom. They take strong exception to the use of certain map projections used in teaching geography and demand their removal. They bring legal suit against the school, alleging an infringement upon their constitutional rights and those of their child. What are the issues involved? How might they be resolved?

18. Periodically, demands are renewed for tuition-tax credits or the institution of a "voucher" plan, whereby parents could enjoy greater freedom of choice as to where their children attend school. Assess the relative advantages and disadvantages of a multiplicity of competing private-school systems as compared with a common public-school system attended by the overwhelming majority of school-aged children.

19. Do schools teach values? Should they? Can they avoid doing so? What values and ideals and standards of conduct are endorsed in schools, and why? What *other* norms might they seek to instill? What are the practical difficulties—social, political, or religious—inhibiting moral education in public schools? Within what legal constraints must such institutions operate with respect to inculcating values?

20. If people disagree on what it is schools should be doing, how meaningful are public-opinion polls that ask respondents to rate the quality of American public education? Or is it the case that a sufficient consensus exists for such surveys to be informative, and schools *can* be judged according to commonly accepted criteria?

## FURTHER READING

ADLER, MORTIMER. *The Paideia Proposal: An Educational Manifesto.* New York: Macmillan, 1982.

BAGLEY, WILLIAM. *A Century of the Universal School.* New York: Crowell Collier and Macmillan, 1937.

———. *Education and Emergent Man.* New York: Ronald Press, 1934.
BESTOR, ARTHUR E. *Educational Wastelands.* Urbana: University of Illinois Press, 1953.
———. *The Restoration of Learning.* New York: Knopf, 1956.
BRODINSKY, BEN. *Defining the Basics of American Education.* Bloomington: Phi Delta Kappa Education Foundation, 1977.
CONANT, JAMES BRYANT. *The American High School Today.* New York: McGraw-Hill, 1959.
CORNOG, WILLIAM H. *What Are the Priorities for the Public Schools in the 1960's?* Washington: Council For Basic Education, 1963.
COUNCIL FOR BASIC EDUCATION. *The Case For Basic Education: A Program of Aims for Public Schools.* Boston: Atlantic-Little, Brown, 1959.
DEMIASHKEVICH, MICHAEL. *An Introduction to the Philosophy of Education.* New York: American Book Company, 1935.
POSTMAN, NEIL. *Teaching As A Conserving Activity.* New York: Delacorte, 1977.
RAFFERTY, MAX. *Suffer, Little Children.* New York: Devin-Adair, 1962.
RAYWID, MARY ANNE. *The Axe-Grinders, Critics of Our Public Schools.* New York: Macmillan, 1962.
RICKOVER, HYMAN S. *Education and Freedom.* New York: Dutton, 1959.
———. *Swiss Schools and Ours.* Boston: Little, Brown, 1962.
RUSSELL, JAMES E. *Change and Challenge in American Education.* Boston: Houghton Mifflin, 1965.
SCOTT, C. WINFIELD, CLYDE M. HILL, and HOBART W. BURNS, eds. *The Great Debate, Our Schools in Crisis.* Englewood Cliffs, N. J.: Prentice-Hall, 1959.
SMITH, MORTIMER. *And Madly Teach.* Chicago: Regnery, 1949.
WOODRING, PAUL. *A Fourth Of A Nation.* New York: McGraw-Hill, 1957.
———. *Let's Talk Sense About Our Schools.* New York: McGraw-Hill, 1953.
ZOLL, ALLEN A. *Our American Heritage.* New York: National Council for American Education, 1950.
———. *They Want Your Child.* New York: National Council for American Education, 1949.

## NOTES

1. For a good summary discussion, consult Charles A. Tesconi, Jr., *Schooling In America, A Social Philosophical Perspective* (Boston: Houghton Mifflin, 1975), pp. 63–71.

2. Oscar Handlin, *John Dewey's Challenge to Education* (New York: Harper & Row, 1959), p. 42.

3. See Lawrence A. Cremin, *The Transformation of the School* (New York: Knopf, 1962), pp. 1–24ff.

4. John Dewey, "The Child and the Curriculum," in Martin S. Dworkin, ed., *Dewey on Education, Selections* (New York: Teachers College, Columbia University), 1964, pp. 95, 96. Note also John Dewey, *Experience and Education* (New York: Macmillan, 1938), pp. 56, 138.

5. William C. Bagley, *Education and Emergent Man* (New York: Ronald Press, 1934), pp. 154–156.

6. Ibid., pp. 171, 172.

7. The term apparently first appeared in Michael Demiashkevich, *An Introduction to the Philosophy of Education* (New York: American Book Company), 1935.

8. William C. Bagley, "An Essentialist's Platform For The Advancement of American Education," *Educational Administration And Supervision* 24 (April 1938): 241–256.

9. Ibid., p. 245.

10. Ibid., p. 246.

11. Ibid., p. 250.

12. Ibid., p. 252.

13. Ibid., p. 253.

14. William C. Bagley, "The Case for Essentialism in Education," *Journal of the National Education Association* 30 (October 1941): 202.

15. Ibid., p. 203.

16. Bagley, "Essentialist's Platform," p. 254.

17. William C. Bagley, *A Century of the Universal School* (New York: Crowell, Collier and Macmillan, 1937), pp. 73ff.

18. See William W. Brickman, "Essentialism Ten Years After," *School and Society* 67 (May 5, 1948): 361–365; Gurney Chambers, "Educational Essentialism Thirty Years After," *School and Society* 97 (January 1960): 14–16; and James C. Stone and Frederick W. Schneider, *Commitment to Teaching, Volume I, Foundations of Education* (New York: Thomas Y. Crowell, 1965), pp. 25–48, 217–239.

19. See Robert C. Morris, "The Right Wing Critics of Education: Yesterday and Today," *Educational Leadership* 35 (May 1978): 625; and William Van Til, *Education: A Beginning* (Boston: Houghton Mifflin, 1974), p. 161.

20. Mary Anne Raywid, *The Axe-Grinders, Critics of our Public Schools* (New York: Macmillan, 1962), pp. 1, 2.

21. Quoted in ibid., p. 51.

22. Robert A. Skaife, "They Sow Distrust," *Nation's Schools* 47 (January 1951): 29.

23. Allen A. Zoll, *They Want Your Child* (New York: Monographs and Papers of the National Council for American Education, 1949), p. 2.

24. Robert A. Skaife, "They Oppose Progress," *Nation's Schools* 47 (February 1951): 32. For further discussion, consult Robert C. Morris, "Thunder On The Right: Past and Present," *Education* 99 (Winter 1978): 168–169.

25. Allen A. Zoll, *Our American Heritage* (New York: National Council for American Education, 1950), p. 12.

26. Educational Policies Commission, *Education For All American Youth* (Washington, D.C.: National Education Association and the American Association of School Administrators, 1944); as quoted in Frederick M. Raubinger et al., *The Development of Secondary Education* (New York: Macmillan, 1969), p. 323.

27. Ibid., as reproduced in Raubinger et al., *Secondary Education,* p. 325.

28. Bernard Iddings Bell, *Crisis in Education* (New York: McGraw-Hill, 1949), pp. 2–5ff.

29. Arthur E. Bestor, *Educational Wastelands, The Retreat from Learning in Our Public Schools* (Urbana: University of Illinois Press, 1953), p. 75.

30. Arthur E. Bestor, *The Restoration of Learning* (New York: Knopf, 1956), pp. 364, 365.

31. Bestor, *Educational Wastelands,* p. 8.

32. Bestor, *Restoration of Learning,* p. 44.

33. Ibid., p. 143.

34. Mortimer Smith, *And Madly Teach* (Chicago: H. Regnery, 1949), p. 7.

35. See Albert Lynd, *Quackery in the Public Schools* (New York: Greenwood, 1977); and Mortimer Smith, *The Diminished Mind: A Study of Planned Mediocrity in Our Public Schools* (New York: Greenwood, 1977).

36. John Keats, "Are the Public Schools Doing Their Job?" *Saturday Evening Post* 230 (September 21, 1957), as reproduced in C. Winfield Scott et al., *The Great Debate, Our Schools in Crisis* (Englewood Cliffs: Prentice-Hall, 1959), p. 8.

37. George B. Leonard, Jr., "Adjustment vs. Knowledge," *Look* (June 11, 1957), as reproduced in Scott et al., *Great Debate,* p. 43.

38. Bestor, *Restoration of Learning,* p. 7.

39. Ibid., p. 40.

40. Bestor, *Educational Wastelands,* p. 3.

41. Ibid., p. 13.

42. Ibid., pp. 26–28.

43. Ibid., p. 28.

44. Bestor, *Restoration of Learning,* pp. 296, 152.

45. Scott et al., *The Great Debate,* p. iii.

46. Max Rafferty, *Suffer, Little Children* (New York: Devin-Adair, 1962), pp. ix, 134–135.

47. Ibid., p. 93.

48. Ibid., pp. 147–148.

49. Ibid., pp. 152, 26.

50. Ibid., p. 154.

51. See Hyman S. Rickover, "European vs. American Secondary Schools," *Phi Delta Kappan* 40 (November 1958): 60–64; *Swiss Schools and Ours* (Boston: Little, Brown, 1962); and *Education and Freedom* (New York: Dutton, 1959).

52. James D. Koerner, "Theory and Experience in the Education of Teachers," in American Association of Colleges for Teacher Education, *Strength Through Reappraisal, Sixteenth Yearbook, 1963 Annual Meeting* (Washington, D.C.: AACTE, 1964), pp. 15–16.

53. See Paul Woodring, *A Fourth Of A Nation* (New York: McGraw-Hill, 1957), and his *Let's Talk Sense About Our Schools* (New York: McGraw-Hill, 1953).

54. James B. Conant, *The American High School Today* (New York: McGraw-Hill, 1959).

55. Consult James E. Russell, *Change and Challenge in American Education* (Boston: Houghton Mifflin, 1965).

56. For an overview and selected references, note the discussion in Robert E. Mason, *Contemporary Educational Theory* (New York: D. McKay, 1972), pp. 151–173ff.

57. See, for examples, Sterling M. McMurrin, "What Every Intelligent Woman Should Know About Education," reprinted under the same title as *Occasional Paper #2*, Council For Basic Education (Washington, D.C.: Council For Basic Education, 1962), pp. 1–6; and William H. Cornog, *What Are the Priorities for the Public Schools in the 1960's?* (Washington, D.C.: Council For Basic Education, 1963), pp. 9–12.

58. See Peter Schrag, "Education's 'Romantic' Critics," *Saturday Review* 50 (February 18, 1967), reprinted in Stan Dropkin et al., eds., *Contemporary American Education* (New York: Macmillan, 1970), pp. 265–274.

59. Charles E. Silberman, *Crisis in the Classroom* (New York: Vintage, 1971), p. 10.

60. Quoted in Christopher J. Lucas, *Challenge and Choice in Contemporary Education* (New York: Macmillan, 1976), p. 171.

61. *Council for Better Education, Descriptive Leaflet* (Washington: Council For Basic Education, 1968), reproduced in Raywid, *Axe Grinders,* pp. 89, 90. Raywid offers a detailed if unflattering account of the Council's early years, pp. 84–99ff.

62. Mortimer Smith, "CBE: The Early Years," *Basic Education* 25 (March 1981): 13.

63. See Council for Basic Education, *The Case for Basic Education: A Program of Aims for Public Schools* (Boston: Atlantic-Little, Brown, 1959).

64. "The Council's Basic Curriculum Study and Related Plans for the Future," *CBE Bulletin* 2 (July 1958): 1.

65. *CBE Bulletin* 21 (October 1976): 12.

66. "Worth Hearing Again," *CBE Bulletin* 21 (October 1976): 12.

67. Cited ibid., p. 12.

68. "Basic Education And The Basics," *CBE Bulletin* 21 (October 1976): 11.

69. See "Career Education's Doughty Skeptics," *CBE Bulletin* 21 (January 1977): 7–8.

70. George Weber, "Back to 'the Basics' in Schools: Here's the Case for Pushing the Current Trend into a Landslide," *American School Boards Journal* 162 (August 1975): 45.

71. Robert E. Ebel, "What Are Schools For?" *Phi Delta Kappan* 54 (September 1972): 3–7.

72. See John G. Thornell, "Reconciling Humanistic and Basic Education," *Clearing House* 53 (September 1979): 23.

73. Paul Copperman, *The Literacy Hoax* (New York: Morrow, 1978), p. 6.

74. Consult, for example, *Report of the Advisory Panel on the Scholastic Aptitude Test Schore Decline* (New York: College Entrance Examination Board, n.d.). For extensive commentary, note the discussion in Diane Ravitch, "The Schools We Deserve," *New Republic* (April 18, 1981): 24–25.

75. See Neil Postman and Charles Weingartner, *Teaching as a Subversive Activity* (New York: Delacorte, 1969).

76. Neil Postman, *Teaching as a Conserving Activity* (New York: Delacorte, 1977), pp. 4–5.

77. Ibid., p. 23.

78. Ibid., p. 101.

79. See *The Washington Star* (September 2, 1979): 48.

80. See Ben Brodinsky, "Back to the Basics: The Movement and Its Meaning," *Phi Delta Kappan* 58 (March 1977): 522–527; and Robert F. Madgic, "Reconciling Basic Skills with Education for the Future," *Educational Leadership* 36 (May 1979): 559–560.

81. James R. Norton, "Back-to-Basics and Student Minimal Competency Evaluation: How to Spell 'School' With Three R's and an E," *Contemporary Education* 50 (Winter 1979): 98.

82. Ernest Helton, "Back to Basics?" *Instructor* 85 (August/September 1975): 14.

83. Norton, "Back-to-Basics," p. 98.

84. Margaret V. Daly, "Your Child's School and the 'Back to Basics' Movement," *Better Homes and Gardens* 57 (April 1979): 16.

85. See "What The Basics Are Not," *News and Comment, National Congress For Educational Excellence* (1981): 4.

86. *Reading Crisis: The Problem and Suggested Solutions, An Education USA Special Report* (Washington, D.C.: National School Public Relations Association, 1970), pp. 15–16.

87. *NCSM Position Paper On Basic Mathematical Skills* (Minneapolis: National Council of Supervisors of Mathematics, 1972).

88. Ann Wilderman, "Math Skills for Survival in the Real World," *Teacher* 94 (February 1977): 68–70.

89. See Glenn D. Berkheimer et al., "NSTA Position Statement on School Science Education for the 70's," *Science Teacher* 38 (November 1971): 46–51; and Mary Blatt Harbeck, "Is Science Basic? You Bet It Is!" *Teacher* 94 (November 1976): 224.

90. See Weber, "Back to 'the Basics,'" p. 45; "What is Essential in Education," *CBE Bulletin* 13 (September 1968): 1–2; and "Eric Johnson: Basically Dedicated," *CBE Bulletin* 21 (January 1977): 3–4.

91. Madgic, "Reconciling Basic Skills," pp. 559–560.

92. Fred Zachary, "How Basic Is Basic?" *National Association of Secondary School Principals Bulletin* 64 (November 1980): 110–111.

93. Robert L. Carruthers and L. S. Richardson, "The End of the Three R's," *National Association of Secondary School Principals Bulletin* 64 (October 1978): 41–44.

94. Christopher J. Lucas, "On the Possible Meanings of 'Back to Basics,'" *Educational Theory* 98 (Summer 1978): 236.

95. Ibid., p. 237.

96. Patrick P. McDermott, "Education and the Turn to the Right," *Improving College and University Teaching* 29 (Winter 1981): 3.

97. J. Charles Park, "The New Right: Threat To Democracy In Education," *Educational Leadership* 38 (November 1980): 146. See also Frances Fitzgerald, "The Triumphs of the New Right," *New York Review of Books* 28 (November 19, 1981): 19–26.

98. McDermott, "Education," p. 3.

99. Ibid., p. 3.

100. Quoted in "The Right's New Bogyman," *Newsweek* 98 (July 6, 1981): 48.

101. Quoted in Park, "New Right," p. 148.

102. Quoted in "Right's New Bogyman," p. 48.

103. Quoted in Park, "New Right," p. 148.

104. Quoted in Stephen Arons, "The Crusade to Ban Books," *Saturday Review* 8 (June 1981): 19.

105. James E. Wood, "Baptist Scores 'Humanism' Charge," *Church and State* (June 1977): 17.

106. Paul Kurtz, "The Attack on Secular Humanism," *The Humanist* 36 (September/October 1976): 4.

107. Cannaught Marshner, "The Pro-Family Movement: A Response to Charles Park," *Educational Leadership* 80 (November 1980): 152.

108. "An Ominous Threat To Books," *The Christian Century* 98 (May 20, 1981): 563.

109. Quoted in ibid., p. 564.

110. "Sex Education," *News and Comment, National Congress for Educational Excellence* (1981): 6.

111. Cited in ibid., p. 6.

112. Cited in Arons, "Ban Books," p. 17.

113. Ibid., p. 18. See also Samuel M. Holton, "IT Bears Repeating, Should Public Education Yield to Christian Fundamentalism?" *High School Journal* 64 (February 1981): 229–231.

114. "The Bright Flight," *Newsweek* 98 (April 21, 1981): 68.

115. McDermott, "Education," p. 3.

116. John Carver, "Education In America, Its Decline And Possible Fall," *The Humanist* 41 (March/April 1981): 47.

117. Ibid., p. 47.

118. Ibid., p. 56.

119. Bill Freeman, "How I Slid into Education's Permissive Pit and Climbed Out Again," *Christianity Today* 25 (April 10, 1981): 41.

120. Ibid., p. 42.

121. As reported in Reo M. Christenson, "Schools Should Stress Moral Education," *Chicago Sun-Times* (December 31, 1981): 18.

122. Ibid.

123. Gordon Cawelti, "Redesigning General Education in American High Schools," *National Association of Secondary School Principals Bulletin* 65 (May 1981): 11.

124. Ravitch, "Schools We Deserve," p. 26.

125. Judith S. Siegel and Edwin J. Delattre, "Blackboard Jumble," *New Republic* 184 (April 18, 1981): 17, 18.

126. Joseph Adelson, "What Happened to the Schools," *Commentary* 71 (March 1981): 39.

127. Jacques Barzun, "The Wasteland of American Education," *The New York Review of Books* 28 (November 5, 1981): 34.

128. Ibid., p. 35.

129. Cawelti, "Redesigning General Education," p. 14.

130. Ibid., p. 13.

131. "The Time for Basic Education," *Basic Education* 25 (March 1981): 4.

132. Ibid., p. 5.

133. Richard Mitchell, *The Graves of Academe* (Boston: Little, Brown, 1981).

134. Ibid., p. viii.

135. Ibid., pp. 11, 120.

136. Ibid., p. 186.

137. Ibid., p. 53.

138. Ibid., p. 186.

139. Cf. ibid., pp. 4, 10.

140. Ibid., p. 188.

141. Ibid., pp. 147–148.

142. Ibid., p. 187.

# CHAPTER THREE
## EDUCATIONAL
## CONSERVATISM
### *The Liberal-Arts Tradition*

## INTRODUCTION

Humorist Robert Benchley, reminiscing on the theme, "What College Did to Me," once compiled a list of what he had learned during his first year at Harvard:

1. Charlemagne either died or was born or did something with the Holy Roman Empire in 800 A.D.
2. By placing one paper bag inside another paper bag you can carry a milkshake in it.
3. There is a double "l" in the middle of the word "parallel."
4. Powder rubbed on the chin will take the place of a shave if the room isn't very light.
5. French nouns ending "aison" are feminine.
6. Almost everything you need to learn about a subject is in the encyclopedia.
7. A tasty sandwich can be made by spreading peanut butter on raisin bread.
8. A floating body displaces its own weight in the liquid in which it floats.
9. A sock with a hole in the toe can be worn inside out with comparative comfort.
10. The chances are against filling an inside straight.
11. You begin tuning a mandolin with "A" and tune the other strings from that.
12. There is a law in economics called the *Law of Diminishing Returns,* which means that after a certain margin is reached, returns begin to diminish. This may not be correctly stated, but there *is* a law by that name.[1]

The more serious point perhaps is that much of what an undergraduate learns in college has nothing whatsoever to do with academics. What formal learning is acquired may be soon forgotten. Or it is recalled only hazily as unrelated bits and pieces. Hence a fundamental question arises: why go to college in the first place? What *is* the purpose of a college education?

A passage from Thomas Hughes's novel, *Tom Brown's School Days* has Squire Brown musing on sending his son to Thomas Arnold's Rugby:

> 'Shall I tell him to mind his work, and say he's sent to school to make himself a good scholar? Well, but he isn't sent to school for that. . . . I don't care a straw for Greek particles, or the digamma, no more does his mother. . . . If he'll only turn out a brave, helpful, truth-telling Englishman, and a gentleman, and a Christian, that's all I want,' thought the Squire.[2]

Strip away the quaint allusions, and an article of faith remains clear: namely, belief in the transformative power of disciplined study to strengthen character and instill basic values. Through the mastery of the liberal disciplines—languages, mathematics, music, grammar, and logic—and the exposure to great human models of literature and history, the point of education in an earlier day was intellectual and moral development, not erudition.

If ever such a time really existed, nothing could be plainer than the fact that that period has long since passed. For decades, school counselors, government at every level, and other social agencies have labored to fix in everyone's mind that a baccalaureate degree is an *economic* good. As a result, a self-generating assumption is perpetuated; and because thinking patterns die hard, many will continue to value a college degree in terms of its economic utility even if (as now appears increasingly to be the case) the bottom drops out of the academic market. Rational motives have given way to faith in schooling as the most appropriate middle-class rite of passage into adulthood, and the chief means of preparing for one's economic role in the social order.

The tradition to be considered here stands in strong opposition to this commonplace assumption. Like educational "conservatism" as a perspective on lower-level schooling, it shares a belief in the importance of the institution of higher learning as a "conserving" force in society. The primary goal of the college and university is viewed as one of nurturing and transmitting a cultural inheritance. The liberal-arts tradition, in common with other forms of conservative thought in education, stresses the importance of general fundamental knowledge, of "core" learning. It shares antipathy toward, and distrust of, proposals to broaden the mission of the college or university. It opposes the substitution of "life-adjustment" curricula, of extraneous involvements of any sort, for the major objective of teaching basic knowledge and values. Without in any way denying the need for applied vocational training, proponents of this tradition argue that careerist concerns threaten to overwhelm and finally obscure the enduring value of a liberal-arts education.

No one single rubric serves to designate a "position," as such, underlying the liberal-arts tradition. "Conservatism" might suffice (for reasons already alluded to), though not all "back-to-basics" advocates and other conservative school reformers would necessarily subscribe to its major tenets. Some might oppose them vigorously. On the other hand, proponents of liberal or general education probably *would* be sympathetic to certain aspects of the educational conservative's agenda for lower schools: improved academic-achievement standards, core curricula, the stress on academics, and so on. In this limited sense, conservatism applied to higher education expresses some of the same basic values and assumptions considered previously.

## LIBERAL ARTS AS MENTAL DISCIPLINE

E. K. Rand, in making a plea for renewed emphasis on the liberal arts, summed up the prime objective of the colonial college as one of training the mind to think well and the tongue to speak eloquently. This, he suggested, was "not so bad for the seventeenth century, and it is not an unworthy goal for education today."[3] Some of the lofty pronouncements of academics defining the purpose of higher education in an earlier day sound more than a little overblown to the modern ear. But, for all their seeming pomposity, they did reflect a spirit of assurance, a sublime confidence in the formative powers of a liberal education, which somehow has since been lost. Two hundred years ago, for example, Provost Smith of the College of Philadelphia could accept as a self-evident truth that "thinking, writing and acting well" was the "grand aim" of liberal learning. Again, the founding charter of the College of Rhode Island in 1764 proclaimed, "Institutions for liberal education are highly beneficial to society, by forming the rising generation to virtue, knowledge and useful literature and thus preserving in the community a succession of men duly qualified for discharging the offices of life with usefulness and reputation...."[4]

Higher education in the colonial and early Republican era was vastly different from what it would later become. Consistent with the aristocratic and elitist traditions it had inherited from the English model, after which it was patterned, the early American college was neither vocationally oriented nor directly professionalized. Its function was one of academic, intellectual, and moral preparation for professional life; and most of its students were studying for the major occupation of law, medicine, or divinity. To all intents and purposes, however, liberal education was thought *to be* the best possible preprofessional training. As an 1829 faculty report at Amherst College expressed it:

> Our colleges are designed to give youth a general education, classical, literary, and scientific, as comprehensive as an education can well be, which is professedly preparatory alike for all the professions. They afford the means of instruction in all the branches, with which it is desirable for a youth to have a general acquaintance before directing his attention to a particular course of study....[5]

Many other statements could be cited to give expression to what Carl Becker called the "lost cause" of the old-time college in defending a traditional conception of higher collegiate learning that had come down from at least the time of the Renaissance, and perhaps even earlier.[6] In the early nineteenth century, the collegiate curriculum was still limited in scope, prescribed, and heavily weighted with classical studies. The typical course of studies was an amalgam of the medieval arts and sciences and of the Renaissance interest in literature and belles-lettres. Its fundamental discipline was Latin—the language of the law, of the church, and of medicine, the medium through which translations of Aristotle from the Greek had dominated formal curricula for over half a millennium. Taking its place beside Latin was Greek, the language of classical humanism.[7] Together with Hebrew, logic, rhetoric, mathematics, metaphysics, and moral and natural philosophy, Latin and Greek furnished the staples of a type of learning that, as Noah Porter put it, was "preeminently designed to give power to acquire and to think, rather than to impart special knowledge."[8]

Implicit in Porter's comment and underlying the dominant philosophy of education throughout the first half of the 1800s was the Aristotelian notion of the human psyche or "soul," which, it was held, revealed itself through certain "faculties" or mental powers; for example, memory or reasoning ability. The mind was likened to a muscle that could be strengthened through proper exercise; and it was assumed that its powers could be freely transferred from one field of study to another.[9] Thus, memorization was useful training for a broad range of tasks; and the classics were studied less for their actual content than for their disciplinary power in the training of the mind.

As might be expected, defenders of such a rationale held that a college student must pursue a full range of prescribed studies over the entire four-year undergraduate course. Latin and Greek were necessary precisely *because* they were difficult subjects, uniquely adapted for disciplining the mind and preparing it for whatever tasks it might later be required to undertake. No effort was needed to train directly for the actual activities in which college graduates would engage. It was assumed instead that the rigors of metaphysics, philosophy, and classical literature would develop mental powers ultimately transferable to professional work.

The classic defense for this particular view of the college curriculum was given its most influential and long-lasting expression in the Yale Report of 1828, a faculty manifesto that with almost Olympian assurance laid down the dictum that the true end of higher education was the production of a "disciplined and informed mind." In a document undoubtedly shaped by Yale President Jeremiah Day, the argument was advanced that "the two great points to be gained in intellectual culture, are the *discipline* and the *furniture* of the mind, expanding its powers, and storing it with knowledge." In response to the question as to why each student should not "be allowed to select those branches of study which are most to his taste, which are best adapted to his peculiar talents, and which are most nearly connected with his intended profession," the Report insisted, "Our prescribed course contains those subjects only which ought to be understood . . . by everyone who aims at a thorough education.''

The Report went on to claim that ''those who are destined to be merchants or manufacturers, or agriculturists'' needed the social elevation provided by a classical education. ''Is it not desirable,'' the Yale faculty asked, ''that the new men of wealth and influence'' being created by American abundance

> should be men of superior education, of large and liberal views, of those solid and elegant attainments, which will raise them to a higher distinction, than the mere possession of property; which will not allow them to hoard their treasures, or waste them in senseless extravagance; which will enable them to adorn society by their learning, to move in the more intelligent circles with dignity, and to make such an application of their wealth, as will be most honorable to themselves, and most beneficial to their country? [10]

Dartmouth's president had declared flatly that a college education was not intended for people who planned to ''engage in mercantile, mechanical or agricultural operations.'' But the Yale faculty, in acknowledging the commercial aspirations of its clientele, based its defense of liberal education on just that fact. Public life and culture would benefit from the refining influence of liberally educated leaders in business, agriculture, and industry. The study of mathematics would bolster reasoning ability; classics would elevate popular taste, or at least afford standards against which to gauge its level; and moral philosophy would buttress canons of public and private morality. Overall, the dispersion of letters, the Report affirmed, would ''tame the masses'' and conduce to the improvement of an otherwise rude and boorish society.

So firmly did the professoriate believe in the disciplinary power of a classical curriculum that it stoutly resisted pressures to expand the collegiate course of study and admit new subjects. Alpheus S. Packard, of Bowdoin College, for example, was adamant in his insistence that the introduction of modern language and English literature would serve only to dilute the requirements of a baccalaureate degree. [11] As late as the 1860s, Packard's views continued to represent a majority position in most academic circles. Repeated suggestions that the single fixed standard for graduation be modified were dismissed out of hand.

Even before the end of the colonial era, however, there had been mounting demands for education better suited to the needs of all classes of society. By the 1820s, loud and clamorous voices were being heard on every side calling for a more practical type of higher education. Reformers urged a broadening of curricula to include, in addition to the traditional linguistic, mathematical, and literary subjects, more scientific and technical courses. Even despite declining student enrollments, however, colleges were slow to accommodate to the rising pressure for curricular diversification and change. And when reforms were instituted, they were made grudgingly, reluctantly, and only on a piecemeal basis.

Francis Wayland, of Brown University, in 1850 posed the issue in the starkest of terms. The choice, he said, was between adopting a course of study that would appeal to all classes and adhering to a course that served one class only. Summing up half a century of collegiate history, he observed, "We have produced an article for which the demand is diminishing. We sell it at less than cost, and the deficiency is made up by charity. We give it away, and still the demand diminishes. Is it not time to inquire whether we cannot furnish an article for which the demand will be, at least, somewhat more remunerative?"[12]

Responses to Wayland's question differed. University of South Carolina's President James H. Thornwell, for instance, rather defiantly proclaimed, "While others are veering to the popular pressure . . . let it be our aim to make Scholars and not sappers or miners—apothecaries—doctors or farmers."[13] Lamented Henry Tappan, soon to be president at the University of Michigan, "The commercial spirit of our country and the many avenues of wealth which are opened before enterprise, create a distaste for study deeply inimical to education. The manufacturer, the merchant, the gold-digger, will not pause in their career to gain intellectual accomplishments. While gaining knowledge, they are losing the opportunities to gain money."[14] At the same time, Tappan thought a case *could* be made for the utility of a broad, liberal education. "We ought to aim," he wrote, ". . . to make apparent the difference between a mere professional and technical education and that large and generous culture which brings out the whole man, and which commits him to active life with the capacity of estimating from the highest points of view all the knowledges and agencies which enter into the well-being and progress of society." He added, "That is not really the most practical education which leads men soonest and most directly to practice, *but that which fits them best for practice.*"[15]

President Charles William Eliot of Harvard, in his inaugural address of 1869, professed to see no conflict between the defenders of the older classical conception of liberal education and protagonists of curricular reform. "The endless controversies whether language, philosophy, mathematics, or science supplies the best mental training, whether general education should be chiefly literary or chiefly scientific, have no practical lesson for us today," he asserted. "This University recognizes no real antagonism between literature and science, and consents to no such narrow alternatives as mathematics or classics, science or metaphysics. We would have them all, and at their best."[16] The vexing question, of course, was how to "have them all."

Eliot's answer, in frank acknowledgment of the expansion of human knowledge and the growing impossibility of anyone's encompassing all that could be known, was to institute an elective system permitting students for the first time to select from *among* alternative courses and programs of study. Gone was the rigidly prescribed, uniform curriculum of yesterday. In its place evolved a multiplicity of curricular sequences and specializations. And while the institution of a limited system of elective courses may have been both necessary and inevitable, the resulting fragmentation it presaged was to have far-reaching consequences unimagined in Eliot's day.

Eliot's dethronement of the prescribed classical curriculum thus marked a kind of watershed in attitudes toward liberal education of the traditional variety. Slowly but inexorably, changes were being forced upon the nineteenth-century American college and university. Reflecting back upon these institutions during the first half of the century, a contemporary writer summarized their dominant features as follows:

> The American college . . . was centered in tradition. It looked to antiquity for the tools of thought, to Christianity for the by-laws of living; it supplied furniture and discipline for the mind, but constrained intellectual adventure. Like most institutions anchored to tradition, the ante-bellum college was also paternalistic and authoritarian. In honoring the past and depreciating the present, it drew the doubtful conclusion that age best imparts its wisdom when youth surrenders its style. Students took prescribed courses and recited their lessons by rote; professors acted like schoolmasters, drillmasters, and prisonkeeps. . . . One encounters a consistent spirit and argument: the preceptive importance of religion, the disciplinary advantage of the classics, and above all, the waywardness and immaturity of youth that called for precepts and discipline.[17]

## LOSS OF CURRICULAR INTEGRATION

In the post–Civil War period, the landscape of American higher education began to change rapidly. The elective system pioneered at Harvard and then at Yale grew widespread as other leading institutions adopted similar practices. One college after another was compelled by the rapid expansion of learning to enlarge the scope and to modify the requirements of its curriculum. The inclusion of new scientific and technical subjects in the 1860s hastened a process of accretion begun a decade or two earlier, and it was to continue unabated thereafter. Modern languages first appeared as distinct fields for specialized study in the 1870s. In the decade following, modern philosophy, literature, and the fine arts were increasingly promoted as academic studies. By the 1890s a variety of social sciences had appeared and become enshrined in college curricula. The fledgling disciplines of psychology and sociology especially were to experience remarkable growth.

Old barriers came tumbling down. By the late eighties and early nineties, land-grant colleges were offering courses in animal husbandry, agronomy, veterinary medicine, horticulture, plant pathology, farm management, and home economics. Vocational and technical education were fast becoming legitimate functions of American higher education.

Well before the turn of the century, the emergence of universities had begun to blur any distinction remaining between professional and vocational education. Universities, it was now apparent, would offer instruction for all careers for which some formal body of knowledge existed—not just divinity, law, or medicine. New professional schools began to proliferate, offering specialized training in engineering, education, journalism, and other fields. With attendant bureaucratization and departmentalization in academe came fragmented curricula and the carving up of knowledge into disciplines superintended by separate, often contending administrative units. This ''Balkanization'' of academic life simply underscored the growing conviction symbolized by the elective principle that not all educated people needed to command the same knowledge.[18]

The problem, however, was to determine whether the old conception of liberal learning retained any validity whatsoever in the modern age.[19] By 1900, if not well before, the earlier humanistic tradition with its ideal of learning as a single body of thought and values, acquaintance with which marked the educated person, was fast disappearing. The price paid for the growing connection between higher learning and the nation's economic life, it might be said, was the virtual loss of a common universe of discourse and an eclipse of the notion of the liberal arts as the passport to learning.[20]

The felt sense of a loss of unity was remarked upon by many commentators around the turn of the century, among them John Dewey. In 1902 he wrote:

> The problem of the multiplication of studies, of the consequent congestion of the curriculum, and the conflict of various studies for a recognized place in the curriculum; the fact that one cannot get in without crowding something else out; the effort to arrange a compromise in various courses of study by throwing the entire burden of election upon the student so that he shall make out his own course of study—this problem is only a reflex of the lack of unity in the social activities themselves, and of the necessity of reaching more harmony, more system in our scheme of life.[21]

Yet ''unity'' within social and intellectual life could not be generated or summoned on command, any more than it could readily be achieved within postsecondary curricula. The challenge for proponents of liberal learning therefore was to define its nature and to offer a more adequate rationale on its behalf than that provided by the now-discredited doctrines of faculty psychology and mental discipline. Breadth, as produced by the balanced development of various mental and moral faculties, had been the avowed aim at American educators throughout much of the nineteenth century. What was needed now was a more substantive interpretation of that breadth of character and understanding allegedly produced by liberal studies.

## IN DEFENSE OF LIBERAL CULTURE

The term ''culture'' accordingly figured repeatedly in the arguments of those around the turn of the century who opposed vocationalism and specialized professionalism in American higher education. Wrote Charles Eliot Norton of Harvard, ''The highest end of the highest education is not anything which can be directly taught, but is the consummation of all studies. It is the final result of intellectual culture in the development of the breadth, serenity, and solidity of mind, and in the attainment of that complete self-possession which finds expression in character.''[22] Agreeing, W. A. Merill claimed that liberal education was the most practical kind of education a student could acquire, not only because it conferred a culture of humane letters, but also because liberal studies were useful "in the elevation of character, in the more lively sympathy with the true, the good, and the beautiful, and in the increase of mental power."[23]

Vassar College's president in 1894 similarly spoke of "real, intellectual culture" and the "opening vistas of intellectual interest" as major aspects of academic purpose. Frank Thilly, a professor of philosophy at the University of Missouri, in 1901 argued that the university as a trustee "for the general intellectual capital of society" should have as its chief aim "an intellectual one", namely, "intellectual emancipation." R. M. Wenley of the University of Michigan declared the university's fundamental goal was "to elevate intelligence above all else, to make men thoroughly pervious to ideas." Robert MacDougall likewise placed the emphasis upon culture, advocating a college curriculum that stressed history, literature, and moral philosophy. "Culture" he defined as "an appreciative acquaintance with the permanent expression of human thought," involving "breadth of knowledge and catholicity of sympathy." So too did Webster Cook of Michigan argue in 1889 that appreciation for the past was the surest guide for understanding the present.[24]

J. R. Wheeler, dean at Columbia University, expressed a widely shared view when he observed that humane standards of thought and action in the Western cultural tradition had first taken shape in ancient Greece. The classic tongues therefore should still be taught, Wheeler felt, as a means for acquiring familiarity with what civilized man had said and done in antiquity. Classical literature should be related "in a broad and vital way to modern life," exhibiting its enduring relevance to modern culture and the applicability of those "absolute values" contained within the Graeco-Roman cultural legacy. To fail to do so, Wheeler insisted, was to cut off the present from its intellectual and moral roots in the past, and to deprive college students of any sense of historical identity.[25]

President Norton of Harvard, writing in the *New Princeton Review* in 1888, advanced a similar argument. The challenging task of the academic world, he was convinced, was to implant the essence of a 2,500-year-old civilization in the minds of youthful students in an uncivilized and thoroughly materialistic society. Liberal education, including the classics, he argued, needed "revival and reinvigoration, not in the interest of the few, a select and eminent class, but in the interest of the many, of the whole community."[26]

Although some college presidents made vague rhetorical obeisance to the continuing demand for "social utility," more often they returned to the theme of liberal culture as the chief preoccupation of higher learning. Sometimes a note of wistful nostalgia, a longing for the sheltered academic cloister of an earlier day, surfaced in their writings. "In the rush of American life," one author commented, "[the college] has stood as the quiet and convincing teacher of higher things. It has been preparing young men for a better career in the world by withdrawing them for a while from the world to cultivate their minds and hearts by contact with things intellectual and spiritual."[27]

Woodrow Wilson during his tenure as president at Princeton gave voice to a similar sentiment. At an alumni dinner in 1904, he declared that the university was "not a place of special but of general education, not a place where a lad finds his profession, but a place *where he finds himself.*" Wilson resolutely opposed the creeping vocationalization of academe. "If the chief end of man is to make a living, why, make a living any way you can," he advised. "But if ever has been shown to him in some quiet place where he has been withdrawn from the interests of the world, that the chief end of man is to keep his soul untouched from corrupt influences, and to see to it that his fellow-men hear the truth from his lips, he will never get that out of consciousness again."[28]

Just as often a defensive sort of militance informed arguments advanced on behalf of liberal education. Alexander Meiklejohn, for one, a philosophy professor and dean at Brown who later assumed the presidency at Amherst College, wrote at length on the mission of institutions of higher education. Over the span of several decades he left no doubt in the minds of his readers that academicians had an obligation to explain to the public at large the nature and relevance of their service. Repeatedly, Meiklejohn stressed the importance of general or liberal instruction. The task of the American college, he affirmed,

> is not primarily to teach the forms of living, not primarily to give practice in the art of living, but rather to broaden and deepen the insight into life itself, to open up the riches of human experience, of literature, of nature, of art, of religion, and of philosophy, of human relations, social, economic, political, to arouse an understanding and appreciation of these, so that life may be fuller and richer in content, in a word, the primary function of the American college is the arousing of interests.[29]

A common feeling among many writers of the period was that Eliot's elective system, begun a quarter century earlier, had borne bitter fruit. Not only had the college curriculum been fragmented beyond repair, but it had become possible now—an unthinkable proposition in the early nineteenth century—for two students to attend the same institution over a four-year period and never take a single course in common. Specialization of interest and professionalism, many warned, had advanced to the point where general education of a liberal character was suffering neglect and would soon disappear entirely.

As early as 1893, Wilson was urging that due regard be paid to the value of a liberal education before embarking upon a more specialized course of professional preparation. The current drift toward early specialization, he judged, was producing a "new ignorance." He hoped that universities would boldly challenge students' inclination for narrow practical training and their seeming indifference to general education, both antecedent to, and continuous with, professional training.

Apologists for liberal culture constantly returned to the same themes. Vocationalism had superceded liberal learning. Professionalism had grown rampant. Appreciation was lacking for that generous, broad learning that "liberated" the learner from ignorance, provincialism, and philistinism, perhaps in the Biblical sense of "You shall know the truth, and the truth shall make you free." The college or the university had lost its moorings, its sense of identity, its guiding unity. Learning was fragmented. Higher education in America had surrendered to the trade-school mentality and in the process had substituted ignoble ends for those higher values that had once given it intellectual purpose and dignity.

A. Lawrence Lowell, a practicing attorney in Boston in 1887 who would later become president of Harvard, spoke for many when he argued that the highest aim of the college was to promote general learning, not the acquisition of specific information that is expected to have immediate practical utility. A "thorough" education, he believed, "ought to make a man familiar with the fundamental conceptions that underlie the various departments of human knowledge, and with the methods of thought of the persons who pursue them." In his opinion, for an educated person, "no great region [of knowledge] should be wholly a strange unexplored wilderness, traversed only by people who utter dark sentences in an unknown tongue." [30] A cultivated learner should have some conversance with almost all knowledge domains—natural science, mathematics, history, literature, language, and the fine arts.

On one point Lowell was insistent: Not all subjects are equally useful or liberal. "Any man who is to touch the world on many sides, or touch it strongly," he argued, "must have at his command as large a stock as possible of the world's store of knowledge and experience; and . . . bookkeeping does not furnish this in the same measure as literature, history, and science." [31]

## GENERAL EDUCATION AS COMMON LEARNING: THE FIRST MOVEMENT

By the early 1900s the aristocratic image of a liberal education intended chiefly for the privileged few with sufficient wealth and leisure to pursue it had fallen into disrepute. With its traditional emphasis upon antique literature and classical languages, many questioned its relevance or utility in a scientific, technologically complex society. For others in the dawning era of mass higher education, its elitist connotations were deeply offensive. Despite aversion to a single rigid liberal-arts curriculum, however, in the years that joined the nineteenth and twentieth centuries, and increasingly thereafter, there was growing appreciation of the fact that the uncontrolled application of the elective principle offered no satisfactory alternative. If the concept of a fixed course of study for all was no longer supportable, the idea that all could freely chose whatever attracted their interest or satisfied some personal need came to be viewed as an equally undesirable alternative. Criticisms of rampant specialization and the evils of the elective system therefore grew in number and vehemence in the decades preceding World War I. Not all knowledge is equally valuable, it was said, and if the cost of curricular flexibility was total disorder, the price was too high.

More and more critics were troubled by the lack of order or design in collegiate courses of study. Their most conspicuous feature, as many pointed out, was a lack of organic unity, a system of connections and common tasks among disparate disciplines. The old concept of liberal education had assumed some sort of common humanity, and a belief that despite differing abilities, interests, needs, and vocations, people should share in the products of the accumulated wisdom of the past. Within the social order, there were certain responsibilities—for example, those concerned with citizenship—which could be discharged only in the exercise of a kind of understanding all should seek to possess.[32] Perhaps the ideal of a shared "culture" or *paideia* had been too narrowly circumscribed in the classic conception of liberal learning. Still, the social needs it addressed were very real. Some common learning, many people argued, was absolutely indispensable to the presentation of a democratic society. It was apparent that this need was going unfulfilled.

Hence, terms such as "general education," "general studies," or "general culture" came into frequent use in the early part of the century to denote the idea of a common learning shared by all educated people. Strong disagreement surrounded attempts to specify its content, though there was a growing conviction that embodied in the adjective "general" was an ideal that stood for something lacking in accepted educational usage of the day. It was further understood that the term "general education" was no longer precisely equivalent to the older meaning of "liberal education." The question was how to translate this newer ideal of common learning into the curriculum.

The specific impetus for the first general-education movement in this century occurred about the time of World War I. In 1914 President Meiklejohn of Amherst introduced a survey course entitled, "Social and Economic Institutions." It offered a broad perspective on society, intended to introduce students to the "humanistic sciences" and provide an orientation to the larger world. Then in 1919 Columbia University introduced a peacetime adaptation of a "war issues" course, now retitled "Contemporary Civilization," which was similar to the survey begun at Amherst. It was required of all entering freshmen. The Columbia course was the first of several offered that emphasized historical social development. "There is a certain minimum of . . . [the Western] intellectual and spiritual tradition that a man must experience and understand if he is to be called educated," a faculty prospectus explained.[33] Dartmouth and Reed College soon followed suit with their own survey courses.

Before long, the Columbia and Reed prototypes had been adopted on scores of campuses across the country.[34] Extensive experimentation followed as colleges and universities tried to provide their students with the broad outlines of human knowledge through various synoptic surveys and introductory overviews of the disciplines. In the search for organizing principles, some survey courses stressed subject-matter *content*. Others emphasized the basic *methods of inquiry* that were distinctive in various fields. Still others organized material around such rubrics as "The Social World," or "Contemporary Issues," "Man And His Environment," or "Problems of Democracy." At the University of Utah, for example, the unifying principle of a social ethics course around 1930 was "the ethical foundation of private and public action in human relations." Between 1924 and 1930 at the University of Chicago, a "Nature of the World and Man" sequence was based on the concept of biological and social evolution.[35]

Even as general survey courses came into vogue, however, they were severely criticized. Charges of shallowness, of superficiality and lack of depth, were frequent. A common complaint was that introductory courses treated those enrolled in them as prospective majors in the discipline of disciplines represented, thereby frustrating their original intent of providing a broad intellectual overview. Others faulted surveys for their apparent lack of structure. Alexander Meiklejohn, for example, in criticizing the typical survey course, described it as "a little music, a taste of philosophy, a glimpse into history, some practice in the technique of the laboratory, a thrill or two in the appreciation of poetry."[36] Yet discovering or inventing satisfactory principles to bring knowledge into some kind of unity was a difficult task, one not easily achieved. (In a very real sense, it could be said, the issue has never been satisfactorily resolved.)

Much of the history of higher education between 1920 and the early 1940s, in fact, could be written around the theme of how colleges devised new curricula or courses in attempting to avoid the intellectual anarchy of early specialization. Gradually it became established policy to give over all or most of the first two years of the collegiate experience to general education. Nonetheless, the most striking features of the two-year programs created were their diversity of content and approach. Breadth of intellectual experience was a common denominator, but otherwise no uniform patterns emerged. Some colleges retained the early emphasis upon "survey" or "orientation" courses. Others adopted more radical measures, including wholly new administrative arrangements. Several experimental colleges were started: at Wisconsin, Minnesota, Florida, Cornell, at Stephens College, and elsewhere, to mention only a few.

By 1935 or thereabouts, a majority of colleges had adopted some form of Harvard's original system of distribution and concentration (i.e., a diversity of required subject-fields to be studied, plus a major field of specialization in one area). The amount of freedom permitted students in selecting course work varied, depending on the institution in question. Sometimes choices were closely circumscribed. The imposition of a prescribed program was defended on the grounds that immature learners needed to be compelled to explore at least the broad divisions of knowledge in order to make more judicious choices of fields for specialization. Without some direction and guidance, a student might avoid certain subjects without adequate appreciation for what had been left out. The more permissive approach allowed students greater latitude in choosing courses, but only within the broad constraints of a distribution system.

Either way, after two years of general education students were encouraged—or required—to concentrate in greater depth in a single field of study. Choosing a "major," however, did not presume further specialized study would necessarily lead to vocational competence in any particular occupation. An undergraduate might major in psychology, for example, without expecting to pursue graduate work in that area or ever becoming a professional psychologist. The point rather was to achieve greater depth of understanding in a knowledge discipline without regard for its possible job applications.

## THE GREAT BOOKS APPROACH

Surely one of the most remarkable and hotly debated experiments with general education undertaken by a major university was that inaugurated in 1930 at the University of Chicago under the leadership of Chancellor Robert Maynard Hutchins. Counter to all prevailing trends, his was a bold initiative, aimed at nothing less than a revival of the ''classical'' tradition of the liberal arts. Accompanying the organization of a semi-autonomous ''College'' to superintend all undergraduate general education, the faculty voted to create a new required curriculum built around the study of original sources, the so-called ''Great Books'' of Western civilization. Henceforth, it was announced, general education at Chicago would be understood as ''a course of study consisting of the greatest books of the Western world and the arts of reading, writing, thinking, and speaking, together with mathematics, the best exemplar of the processes of human reason. If our hope has been to frame a curriculum which reduces the elements of our common human nature,'' it was said, ''this program should realize our hope.''[37]

The course of study prescribed was both uniform and demanding. It consisted basically of a series of one-year interdisciplinary survey courses taught by lectures and supplemented by frequent small-group discussions. Course credits and tests were dispensed with completely. In their place, students were required to submit themselves whenever they felt sufficiently well prepared for comprehensive examinations in English composition, humanities, social science, physical science, and biological science. Minimal proficiency in a foreign language was also required. Only when all examinations had been passed successfully was a student permitted to extend his or her studies at an upper-divisional level or in another college of the University.[38]

In a series of essays, articles, and books, Hutchins spelled out the educational philosophy inspiring what he was attempting to accomplish at Chicago. Best known among his many works was a collection of sarcastic, bitter, and oftentimes humorous addresses delivered at the Storr Lectures at Yale and published in 1936 as *The Higher Learning in America*. There he gave expression to a point of view which one historian aptly characterizes as ''a kind of strange and wonderful throwback to Jeremiah Day and the Yale Report of 1828.''[39]

Looking at the rest of American higher education, Hutchins found only rampant disorder, capitulation to an acquisitive materialistic society, and institutions distinguished chiefly for their trade-school or finishing-school qualities.[40] ''Love of money,'' he believed, had had the practical effect of creating a ''service-station'' conception of the university scrambling to be all things to all people. The typical university, Hutchins alleged, exists to flatter the spirit of the age and will do for people anything society is willing to pay for. The expectation is that whatever problems exist within the social order, the university must take up and frame some sort of response. In its headlong rush to meet miscellaneous, immediate, low-level needs of every sort and kind, its curricula proliferate endlessly. It offers instruction for any clientele whatsoever. It must even ''help the farmers look after their cows.'' But once this process of social accommodation begins, it has no end. Increasingly the service-station university must frame its policies to appeal to those who pay the bills—students, private donors, and state legislatures. The university is not free or independent, because it is always pursuing money to support its multitude of tasks.

In its efforts to attract students, for example, the university must go to unusual lengths in housing, feeding, and amusing them. Athletics and extracurricular social activities assume exaggerated importance. Both students and alumni come to care more for higher education as an entertainment industry than as an academic enterprise. (Imagine today the anguished howls of protest that would greet a university's proposal to abandon its athletic program, while the abolition of an academic program or department would likely go unnoticed.) Priorities become hopelessly scrambled, and academic learning suffers. Worst of all, few students care about or even understand what they have missed in their collegiate experience.[41]

An even more important factor contributing to confusion in American higher education, Hutchins asserted, was a misconception of democracy that holds that everyone is entitled to the same amount of education. Typically, the belief is that a young person should be allowed to remain in school as long as he or she wants, to study whatever is appealing, and to become a candidate for any degree the individual prefers. In fact, he argued, democracy does not require that higher learning be open to anybody indiscriminately. It should be reserved only for those with the ability and interest demanded by independent intellectual endeavor. Higher education, in other words, *should* be elitist, in the special meritocratic sense of being made available exclusively to those best able to profit from it. As for the peculiar American passion for credentials, the factor chiefly responsible for student's occupying time and space in academe, Hutchins felt it might only be assuaged by conferring a baccalaureate degree upon every citizen at birth, thereby leaving colleges and universities free to educate those few people genuinely interested in learning.

Contemporary society, Hutchins felt, was confused in its assumption that education should serve a vocational purpose. The true aim of the university, he argued at length, is the disinterested pursuit of truth for its own sake. This objective, he judged, was fast being obscured and stood on the verge of extinction. ''Every group in the community that is well enough organized to have an audible voice wants the university to spare it the necessity of training its own recruits,'' he observed. ''They want to get from the university a product as nearly finished as possible, which can make as large and as inexpensive a contribution as possible from the moment of graduation.'' Hutchins considered this a ''pardonable, perhaps even a laudable'' desire. But the consequence of vocational pressures, he claimed prophetically, would be that ''soon everyone in a university will be there for the purpose of being trained for something.''[42]

Hutchins freely conceded the need for job training. Nevertheless, he felt the university was a poor place to attempt direct instruction for employment. ''Turning professional schools into vocational schools degrades the universities and does not elevate the professions,'' he insisted. The inherent ambiguity in any training program is how to get immediate technical proficiency and at the same time some longer-range understanding of the general principles, the fundamental theoretical propositions, underlying a craft or discipline. As he put it:

> My contention is that the tricks of the trade cannot be learned in a university, and that if they can be they should not be. They cannot be learned in a university because they get out of date and new tricks take their place, because the teachers get out of date and cannot keep up with current tricks, and because tricks can be learned only in the actual situation in which they can be employed.[43]

Modern conditions require constant retraining, almost inevitably on-the-job retraining. All the university can hope to provide is the broad understanding that provides the base or foundation upon which specific skills are initially acquired or later refurbished and upgraded.

Hutchins's decidedly unfashionable proposal was for a forthright return to ''a common intellectual training,'' or general education. Without it, he asserted, a university must remain a series of disparate academic units lacking a common language, understanding, or purpose. Like an encyclopedia whose unity is found only in its alphabetical arrangement, the modern university has departments running from Art to Zoology, but nothing holds it together. It lacks cohesion. What was needed, Hutchins believed, was a ''common stock of fundamental ideas'' to overcome the ''disunity, discord, and disorder that have overtaken our educational system.''[44] In apparent defiance of a hundred years of experience, he asserted, ''Education implies teaching. Teaching implies knowledge. Knowledge is truth. The truth is everywhere the same. Hence education should be everywhere the same.'' Education, rightly understood, should be understood as ''the cultivation of the intellect'' and the single-minded pursuit of intellectual virtues.[45]

Hutchins assailed the modern heresy that all education is formal education and that formal education must therefore assume total responsibility for the individual's full development. His advice was to leave experience to life itself and to concentrate instead on intellectual training. The specific curriculum he advocated would be organized around those ''permanent studies'' that reflect elements of a common human nature, the disciplines that connect people together and link the present with the past, with the best that has been thought and written in previous ages.

For Hutchins, as for Mortimer Adler, Mark Van Doren, Jacques Maritain, Irving Babbitt, Gilbert Highet, and many others, the specific means to intellectual training would be furnished by the Great Books—those works that through the centuries have attained the status of "classics" in all fields of knowledge. A truly great book is one that has survived the test of time, Hutchins explained. As the prospectus for the Great Books Program published by Encyclopedia Britannica and the University of Chicago phrased it, a great book, first, is one that does not have to be written again, because, like any great work of art, it succeeds perfectly in accomplishing what it sets out to do. (The world, one wit has observed, does not require a sequel to Plato's *Republic,* a *Republic II,* or perhaps a *Son of Hamlet.*)

Second, a great book is always contemporary. Unlike any given current best-seller, it is a perennial best-seller. It is a best-seller for all times, enjoying the same fundamental appeal and currency in every century, in any place or time, under any political, social, or economic conditions. It endures, long after a lesser work has been forgotten. As Adler cautioned, one does not read such a work for antiquarian purposes. The intent is not archeological or philological but contemporary.

Next, a great book is readable by almost anyone. Its appeal is universal because it deals with the universal themes that always occupy thinking persons.

Finally, and most important of all, according to Hutchins, a great book is capable of helping to develop standards of taste and criticism that enable the learner to think and act intelligently, to participate fully in the social and intellectual movements of his or her own time.

In order for a Great Books curriculum to succeed, Hutchins felt, general education (ideally occupying the equivalent of the last year or two of high school and the first two years of college) should include preparatory training in grammar—the rules of reading—and in rhetoric and logic, the rules of writing, speaking, and reasoning. With the addition of mathematics, "reasoning in its clearest and most precise form," students would be ready to comprehend and more fully appreciate the riches that only great books can offer.

Hutchins did not foresee any great inclination on the part of the American public to embrace his proposed revival of the medieval *trivium* and *quadrivium.* On the contrary, he felt his proposals would be quite unpopular. Nevertheless, a quarter-century later, long after he had left the University of Chicago, his mind was unchanged. Writing in the preface to the 1962 reissue of *Higher Learning,* he saw the same tendencies at work he had warned against in 1936. "One of the easiest things in the world," he remarked acidly, "is to assemble a list of hilarious courses offered in the colleges and universities of the United States. Such courses reflect the total lack of coherent, rational purpose in these institutions."[46] In his judgment, if institutions of higher education had ever given the nation intellectual leadership, any claim of their doing so had long since lost credibility. Higher learning, he believed, had disintegrated. Educational standards had collapsed entirely. The triumph of specialization, vocationalism, and triviality, as he saw it, was well-nigh complete.

There were a few institutions, however, that did not fall under Hutchins's indictment. Thanks to the prestige of the University of Chicago and the personal charisma of its chancellor, parts of the Chicago program were replicated in experimental colleges, honors departments, and schools throughout the country. The creation of Monteil College at Wayne State University, for example, was one of several attempts to adapt the so-called Chicago Plan elsewhere. Better known was the program established by Stringfellow Barr and Scott Buchanan at St. John's College in Annapolis, Maryland, and later at a sister campus in Santa Fe, New Mexico.[47] In many ways it was a direct descendant of the Chicago program.

Two years after its beginning, in 1937, Donald P. Cottrell of Teachers College, Columbia University, reported for the National Society For The Study Of Education on what was happening at St. John's:

> In the belief that the power of the great liberal tradition of Europe and America is generally being neglected, St. John's proposes to center its program upon the recovery of that tradition. The classics and the liberal arts, the embodiments and tools of the tradition, have long been associated with the ancient languages and mathematics, but these have recently become ineffective carriers of the tradition. It is proposed to recover the tradition for education through the great classic books—the books of our Western heritage that have been read by the greatest number of readers, the books that have the largest number of possible interpretations, the books that "raise the persistent unanswerable questions about the great themes in European thought," the books that are works of fine art, the books that are masterpieces of the liberal arts.[48]

From the outset, the approach followed at St. John's was highly controversial. Alexander Meiklejohn, among others, strongly approved of what Buchanan and Barr were attempting. In a 1940 *Fortune* magazine article, he wrote,

> When St. John's College turns to Hume and Plato to find the beginning for a study of the sciences and technology, it is not looking to those writers for the last words on those subjects, it is looking for first words. . . . From the time of the Greeks, until the present, the knowledge and wisdom of men has been growing. . . . And the intention of the curriculum is that the student shall follow that growth in order that he may be better able to play his part in the intellectual and moral activity of his own time and country. As he follows a sequence of ideas, the [student] will be confronted, not with one static set of dogmatic beliefs, but with all the fundamental conflicts that run through our culture. He will find Pythagoras at war with Plato, Kant at war with Hume, Rousseau at war with Locke, Veblen at war with Adam Smith, and he must try to understand both sides of these controversies.

John Dewey, on the other hand, was highly skeptical of what the St. John's curriculum had to offer:

> The attempt to re-establish linguistic skills and materials at the center of education, and to do it under the guise of "education for freedom" or even "liberal" education, is directly opposed to all that the democratic countries cherish as freedom. The idea that an adequate education of any kind can be obtained by means of a miscellaneous

assortment of 100 books, more or less, is laughable when viewed practically. The five-foot bookshelf for adults to be read, reread, and digested at leisure throughout a lifetime, is one thing. Crowded into four years and dealt out in fixed doses, it is quite another thing.[49]

Undeterred by critics, St. John's introduced few major changes over the next four decades. Basically, its reading list remained the same as one used by John Erskine in 1916 in an honors program at Columbia University and later revised at the University of Chicago under Hutchins. Readings by Shakespeare, Yeats, Baudelaire, Freud, and Einstein were gradually added; Lucian, Quintilian, Bonaventura, Veblen, and Montesquieu were dropped. Otherwise, formal lectures, seminars, and tutorials remained much the same. Commenting, two observers in 1970 remarked that the curriculum "raises questions and doubts more than it increases confidence. It tests and encourages the development of a fairly narrow range of important skills. It teaches appreciation more than it spurs the ambition to create something at least marginally new." Yet despite their reservations, they still found much to admire about the college:

> The program that exists is remarkable. Its community is founded on a radical faith in the ability of liberal education to teach men and women to think for themselves and to become conscious of their social and moral obligations. It has embodied a vision and fostered a dialectic in the culture because it has been there to be criticized. It has kept alive an ideal of the liberal arts and a concern for the wholeness of intellectual experience in a pure form. It has been a kind of conscience of the liberal arts colleges, a goad to all of higher education, and a declaration about how men should live.[50]

The ongoing St. John's experiment originally inspired in part by Hutchins was certainly atypical. Its uniqueness notwithstanding, Barr, Buchanan, and Hutchins did not stand alone in their call for a radical restructuring of American higher education, for which Chicago and St. John's offered one possible blueprint. Many others joined in inveighing against the dead hand of vocationalism and urging the wider restoration of a type of education that would draw out and develop what is distinctively "human" about people; namely, the power to think and to reason. Nor were they in the least impressed by critics' claims that their ideal was too narrow or one-sided. As Mortimer Adler put it, "One who rejects the life of reason . . . is rejecting himself as a human being. He is living like an animal. He is merely vegetating."[51]

The distinctive—if not unique—characteristic of a human being is his or her potential for rationality, for thinking, reflecting, and conceptualizing. This capacity for intellection is what sets off humankind from the lower primates, and it is the precondition for the intelligible development of sensing, feeling, and all the other capabilities that collectively define human consciousness. The basic function of education, therefore, it was argued, is to help the individual actualize his or her potentialities as a thinking being, to bring out one's essential "humanness." An education that develops reason is superior, in and of itself; it is the best preparation for a full and satisfying life; and in the long run, Hutchins and others held, it is even the most useful form of vocational preparation.

## ANDY ROONEY ON THE GREAT BOOKS

How many books have you read?

If you had to write down the names of the 100 greatest books of all time, how far would you get? "The Valley of the Dolls" and "The Complete Scarsdale Medical Diet" are not among them, I'll give you that much of a tip.

A great teacher named Stringfellow Barr had a revolutionary idea for educating his students when he was president of St. John's College in Annapolis, Md. His idea was simply to make them read the 100 best books of all time. That was it. The four-year college course consisted of nothing but those 100 books and he made up the list.

. . . I thought it would be interesting to give you his idea of the 100 best books. I went to a lot of trouble to get the list, but now that I have it, I'm not going to pass it on because the chances are you wouldn't even read the list, let alone the books on it. I never heard of half of them. Ptolemy's "Almagest"? Aristarchus's "On the Distance of the Sun and the Moon"?

I see a few familiar faces on the list: "Gulliver's Travels," Montaigne's "Essays," "David Copperfield," "The Constitution of the United States," the Bible, Marx's "Das Capital," "Hamlet," Darwin's "Origin of Species."

Is there anyone alive who doesn't wish he'd read more? I have this terrible guilt feeling about not reading as much as I ought to, but I don't see any prospects for improving my reading record now. It *takes* so long. Whenever I have time enough to sit down and read a book, I get up and go do something else.

"I'd never read a book," President Woodrow Wilson said, "if I could talk for half an hour with the man who wrote it."

I agree with that. I think most people can tell you everything they know in half an hour, and after that they're just padding it out. I sure wish I could have spent half an hour with Plato. His book "The Republic" is on the greatest books list. We have it on our shelf at home and I often try to read it. I'll take it down and start into it, but I never get very far.

Sorry about that, Plato, but your book just doesn't grab me. I know you've got some good ideas in there, but you gab too much before you get at them.

Plato, of course, wrote his books in Greek, so there isn't much left of whatever literary grace he had. Most books that have been translated sound like the instructions that come in English for a toy made in Tokyo.

A lot more books are bought than read in this country. As a writer I'm certainly not going to object to that, but there's no doubt people often fake an interest in books that they don't feel. Some books are used like wallpaper. A full bookshelf with its variety of colors and sizes presents a pleasant face and at the very least makes the owners look as though they wished they read books.

I'm suspicious of people whose shelves are lined with books they haven't read, but mine are, too. I tend to read the same three or four books over again instead of picking up a new one.

Most libraries don't have all the books on Dr. Barr's list, but I suppose it won't be long before we all have computers where our bookshelves are now and we'll be able to call up any book we wish. Someone will certainly offer a chip for the size of the head of a pin with every one of those 100 greatest books on it. I'll hate that.

I love the books I have on my shelves, even the ones I'll never read again. They're old friends looking down at me as I live my life, ignoring their wisdom. Just glancing at their titles once in a while brings a warm glow that no computer will ever duplicate. If I ever read Stringfellow Barr's 100 greatest books, I'll do it on the paper on which they were written.

—Reprinted by permission of Tribune Company Syndicate, Inc.

According to Mark Van Doren, whose *Liberal Education* offered one of the most spirited defenses of the liberal arts in the 1940s, the fundamental purpose of education is self-realization. It is the process by which one becomes the fullest, most aware human being possible.[52] Jacques Maritain in the same year expressed a similar idea with unimprovable brevity:

> The aim of education . . . is to guide man in the evolving dynamism through which he shapes himself as a human person—armed with knowledge, strength of judgment, and moral virtues—while at the same time conveying to him the spiritual heritage of the nation and the civilization in which he is involved, and preserving in this way the century-old achievements of generations. The utilitarian aspect of education . . . must surely not be disregarded. . . . But this practical aim is best provided by the general human capacities developed. And the ulterior specialized training which may be required must never imperil the essential aim of education.[53]

Ultraconservatives were insistent that liberal education is ''self-contained,'' that it should make a person competent not merely ''to do'' but, more importantly, ''to be.'' Its prime occupation, as Van Doren put it, is with the ''skills of being.''[54] And if people were educated to become capable and sensible, their subsequent roles in society would more or less take care of themselves.[55] As John Henry Cardinal Newman phrased it almost a century earlier, ''I say that a cultivated intellect, because it is a good in itself, brings with it a power and a grace to every work and occupation which it undertakes, and enables us to be more useful, and to a greater number.[56]

In protest against the whole of contemporary culture, with its science and technology, its corporate industrialism, its controlling institutions, its ethical relativism and secularism, crusaders of the likes of Adler, Hutchins, Van Doren, Maritain, and Norman Foerster thus threw down their challenge. Modern society, they insisted, had misconstrued entirely what true education is all about. In the wisdom of the past—the classic intellectual principles, enduring values, and unchanging standards of Western civilization—humankind would find the best means for developing mental power and fostering self-development. Only as one is liberally educated—that is, steeped in history, literature, languages, mathematics, philosophy, and theology—is it possible to attain the knowledge that forms the highest type of human being. Anything different, any sort of training offering less, they argued, does not deserve to be dignified by the term ''education.'' It is unworthy of a free citizenry. In the nature of things, for genuine liberal education there can be no adequate substitute.[57]

A viewpoint so obviously at odds with prevailing trends in the 1930s and 1940s could hardly be expected to gain much popular acceptance, and in fact it did not. Nevertheless many of the more modest experiments with general education undertaken in the two decades after the First World War did share something of the spirit and concern of a Hutchins or Van Doren. But most were very much a product of the times, and they were tied to the exigencies of more specific social circumstances. Thus, for example, the movement to create a common learning was touted as a panacea for almost every imaginable academic problem, from overspecialization to excessive vocationalism.

General education, proponents argued, would serve to correct the tendency of colleges and universities to cater to individual interests. At the same time, however, supporters had other larger social goals in mind. With the rise of a new broadly educated generation, it was hoped, the way would be open to address such pressing problems as machine politics, municipal corruption, assimilating newly arrived immigrants into the mainstream of American life, and helping to revive concern for social justice:

> General education was seen as an answer to the intolerance and conformity of the 1920's. It would help young people understand and find a useful place in a complex industrial society on an interconnected globe. . . . But above all, for older Americans who were still rooted in the certitudes of the pre-1914 world, general education would revive the heady idealism and sense of national unity that had so suddenly and so mysteriously faded with the signing of the Armistice in November 1918.[58]

Yet if the surge of interest in general education was galvanized by events beyond the campus, it was another extra-academic crisis, the Depression, that served to hasten the decline of the movement that interest had inspired. By the late 1930s, as economic conditions worsened and breadlines lengthened, as student enrollments declined and those who remained pressed for vocational instruction, support for general education temporarily lessened. No matter how eloquent the pleas for a common learning or how much prestige attached to programs like those at Columbia, Chicago, or St. John's, the paramount concern of college students on the eve of World War II was not liberal culture but education for economic survival.

## POSTWAR REDEFINITIONS OF GENERAL EDUCATION: THE SECOND MOVEMENT

In 1939 the National Society for the Study of Education (NSSE) devoted its thirty-eighth yearbook to the topic of general education in the American college. A retrospective look back at the experiments of the preceding two decades, according to Stanford's Alvin C. Eurich, revealed a palpable failure to reach consensus on the meaning of general education. "Each person who uses the term has some definite connotation in mind," he wrote. "Commonly it is thought of in contrast with specialization and as implying an emphasis upon living in a democratic society." But different interpretations had led to considerable confusion as to the means or methods of implementation.

Close to everyone's mind was Hutchins's attempt at Chicago to root general education in intellectual tradition expressed through the great books of the Western world, from Homer to the present day. John Dewey, on the other hand, had emphasized the need for experience with *present-day* personal and social problems as an alternative way of providing students with a general education. For Eurich, the only commonality to be found in efforts to promote general learning was dissatisfaction with collegiate specialization and agreement on the need for greater curricular "integration." General education, he felt, was "an expression of a quest for unity and a renewed emphasis upon the democratic ideal." It designated no fixed procedures or program. General education was "what one finds in American colleges that are seriously attempting to modify their programs in order to provide more unifying experience." [59]

John Dale Russell, a professor of education at the University of Chicago, in the same NSSE yearbook shared the results of his national survey of programs in liberal-arts colleges. He too found in statements of purpose wide variation in how the term "general education" was understood. Some respondents viewed "liberal" and "general" education as synonymous. Others disagreed but felt the distinction between the two terms was unclear. A majority was agreed that general education excludes technical, vocational, and professional preparation, but others were less sure. Some felt general education need not exclude vocational or professional training so long as the subject matter pursued was integrative and interdisciplinary. Some thought general or liberal education could be defined in terms of its content. As many others disagreed, claiming that general education was distinguished more by the spirit and means of its instruction than by any specific subject matter. [60]

Henry M. Wriston, president of Brown University, offered an especially provocative essay attacking the notion that traditional liberal education was ever "aristocratic." On historical grounds, he took issue with the familiar argument that general education was ill-adapted for meeting the needs of a mass population and that its chief beneficiaries had always been a select few. "The history of American higher education," he insisted, "is replete with examples of those who have come from environments that sociologist and psychologist alike would regard with horror, and yet these students have done brilliantly in intellectual work—and in the development of social graces." [61] Nor were they isolated exceptions in some larger pattern. Cant about the need to vocationalize collegiate curricula, to accommodate "newcomers" to higher education, in his opinion, was just that—cant.

Wriston's conclusion was worth noting. "The expression of dislike of liberal education because it was 'aristocratic,' is too often an expression of an innate anti-intellectualism—a suspicion that the higher learning and more refined esthetic taste cannot be attained by all men, hence cannot be democratic," he commented. "But there is nothing whatever in democratic theory that justifies such a feeling. The 'aristocracy' of intellectualism is of a character wholly in harmony with both the theory and the practice of democracy." [62] Interestingly enough, and unfortunately perhaps, Wriston's analysis seems to have been ignored totally in subsequent discussions of the topic.

The 1939 yearbook marked a convenient dividing point between the first phase of activity on behalf of general education, extending from the First World

War to the end of the Depression, and a second general-education movement, beginning in the 1940s. This second movement was to follow a pattern similar to the first of the 1920s. Once again the revival came in the aftermath of a world war, when the country's mood very much resembled what it had been twenty years before. Joseph C. Goulden, in his popular account, *The Best Years*, claimed that the nation in the 1950s went into a "holding pattern" intellectually, morally, and politically:

> Perhaps the pause was inevitable, even necessary; the nation was weary from depression, war, and reconversions, and the Eisenhower years proved singularly undemanding. The result, regardless, was a generation content to put its trust in government and in authority, to avoid deviant political ideas, to enjoy material comfort without undue worry about the invisible intrinsic costs. America misplaced, somewhere and somehow, the driving moral force it had carried out of the world war. . . . There were times, during the 1950s, when the entire nation seemed to be saying, 'Leave me alone.'[63]

Like its predecessor, this rebirth of interest in general education was also a product of the times. As in the 1920s, general education was once again called upon to counter vocationalism, overspecialization, and the elective curriculum. The familiar themes of educating citizens for public responsibility, of promoting a common cultural heritage, and promoting "self-realization" gained new currency. In an era when the United States was locked in Cold War conflict with "world communism," a particularly urgent need felt by many was for an education that would reaffirm the cardinal values of Western civilization and American society.

The national symbol for the postwar renewal of general education was a 1945 Harvard faculty committee report entitled, *General Education in a Free Society*. Bound in red, it was promptly dubbed the "Redbook," and soon won acclaim as an articulate, authoritative exploration of the meaning of general education. The committee's analysis opened with the observation that education seeks to fulfill two objectives: first, to prepare the young for their unique and particular functions in life; and, secondly, to fit them "so far as it can for those common spheres which, as citizens and heirs of a joint culture, they will share with others."[64]

The problem was not merely to foster skills and outlooks that differentiated individuals according to their talents and differing aspirations, but also to develop the traits and understandings that people should have in common despite their differences. In an age marked by a "staggering" expansion of knowledge and consequent specialization, the report noted, the latter task had become increasingly difficult. What was required, the committee argued, was an "over-all logic, some strong, not easily broken frame" within which educational institutions could simultaneously fulfill their diversifying and uniting tasks.[65]

The Harvard Redbook stopped short of specifying what might furnish an optimal framework for unifying undergraduate learning; and it cautioned against assuming any single pattern was workable for all colleges and universities. For

Harvard, the report urged the institution of a system whereby students were required to complete at least one course each in the natural sciences, humanities, and social studies, and an additional three courses of a general nature prior to, or coincident with, advanced specialized training. A combination of survey courses and distribution requirements, in other words, would safeguard the more general or common aims of undergraduate education.

The basic need, the report concluded, was for a *balance* between "general" and "special" (i.e., specialized) education. Distinguishing between the two, general education was said to denote "that part of a student's whole education which looks first of all to his life as a responsible human being and citizen; while the term, special education, indicates that part which looks to the student's competence in some occupation." The former is "an organism, whole and integrated," whereas the latter is "an organ; a member designed to fulfill a particular function within a whole." Both are essential in a free society. Both are necessary for the development of the educated person—an individual who can think effectively, communicate clearly, make relevant judgments, and discriminate with care among values.[66]

The Harvard Committee was concerned to emphasize the point that general education should not be thought of as having to do with "some airy education in knowledge in general." Nor should it be formless, consisting merely of the taking of one course after another. Neither should it be defined negatively, in the sense of whatever is left over apart from a field of concentration and specialization. Finally (in an obvious reference to Hutchins), the report claimed, it cannot be conceived of in terms of a specific set of books to be read or courses to be given.

The task of modern democracy in a social order where all are free to pursue private ends but everyone shares responsibility for the management of the community is to preserve the ancient ideal of liberal education and to extend it as far as possible to all members of society, the Redbook concluded. Whatever its shape or specific content, and however it is organized, general education is indispensable, because it speaks to the larger ends of personal development and social service. The most critical question, therefore, the committee asserted, is "how can general education be so adapted to different ages, and, above all, differing abilities and outlooks, that it can appeal deeply to each, yet remain in goal and essential teaching the same for all?"[67] To this question, unfortunately, *General Education in a Free Society* offered no definite answer.

Ironically, the Harvard faculty ultimately rejected its own committee report. Elsewhere, however, support for the Harvard plan ran strong, and variations were adopted in dozens of colleges and universities. Two years later, a White House Commission on Higher Education for Democracy released a report enthusiastically endorsing general education along the lines sketched out in the Harvard Redbook. Meanwhile, a flurry of reform activity marked collegiate curricular development. At Denison University, a core course entitled, "Problems of Peace and Post-War Reconstruction" begun in 1942 continued to attract national attention. At Wesleyan, in Connecticut, and a number of Ivy League schools, new general-education seminars were launched with much fanfare.

Gresham Riley, Dean at the University of Richmond, writing from the perspective of 1980, judged that the mixture of required courses and limited choice within groupings of closely related disciplines like the general-education model of the 1950s had been "seriously flawed." Besides being restricted parochially to Western society and its dominant ethnic and socioeconomic groups, the typical curriculum, he claimed, focused predominantly on the subject matter of various disciplines, with little or no thought given to relationships *among* bodies of knowledge. The model, Riley felt, encouraged student passivity and dependency instead of providing opportunities for learners to gain intellectual independence and to function as active learners.

Furthermore, according to Riley, the typical introductory course, which could satisfy distribution requirements, tended to stifle student interest rather than to stimulate intellectual excitement. "I find it appropriate," he observed sardonically, "that we frequently characterized those introductory courses as providing 'an exposure' to the various disciplines. As a matter of fact, they 'exposed' students to disciplines like a smallpox vaccination exposes a child to the disease: One is 'cured for life'—in the latter case of the disease and in the former case of any possible interest in the subject matter."[68]

Horace M. Kallen, author of *The Education Of Free Men*, decried the identification of general education with a fixed historical content. Although he opposed particularistic vocational training, he was equally uncomfortable with pedagogic custodians of a traditional "body of knowledge" inherited from the past who urged schools to hand it on intact. "Any thought or thing, any vocation or technique momentous to a mind may become the base of its liberation," he claimed. "Any art or craft, any theme, datum or system of ideas, is an instrument of liberal education when it serves as a road and not as a wall for him who studies it. Whatever be the avowed field and purpose of the study—farming, engineering, business, law, medicine, the ministry, teaching, garbage collecting, archaeology—when it liberates, it is liberal."[69]

Kallen admitted that the curriculum of traditional liberal education, properly mastered, *could* serve to free a student's mind from the provincialism of his or her place and time; the experience was "liberal" at least with respect to a world past and gone. "To be liberated into the life more abundant of the actual world, however," he hastened to add, "has so obvious a priority over this other, that the recurrent debate over its dignity and worth argue an inexplicable blindness of spirit in those who deny it."[70] The past exalted by traditionalists, Kallen claimed, is a living past only as people living today cherish and study and use it to enrich their existence in the present. The criterion or standard of relevance for liberal education, then, is whether it teaches people to learn about one another; to understand, respect, and appreciate differences among themselves, and to assist them in working together for common ends.

Traditionalists, with their "mortuary cult" of a moribund past, Kallen claimed, cultivate people's perennial snobbery by exalting one phase or aspect of human culture while denigrating all others. John Dewey and the progressivists, he argued, were the true defenders of a *living* tradition whose signature was respect for diversity and cultural pluralism. Liberal education, he concluded, was "one that frees each and all safely and happily to live and to move and have his personal being in fact or in idea among the others of his choice. This is what liberal education must mean in the modern world."[71] The practical implication of Kallen's view, of course, was that liberal or general education would be undefinable in terms of any specific subject matter.

Interestingly, in the 1940s and 1950s, some writers attempted to introduce a sharp distinction *between* "liberal" and "general" education, the suggestion being that the former consists of a fixed body of traditional liberal-arts disciplines and the latter of any course of study exhibiting breadth or diversity.[72] This usage was decidedly at odds with earlier practice in the 1920s and 1930s, when the two terms were used interchangeably and almost synonymously. As always, writers harbored great expectations about what general-liberal education might accomplish but were forever in disagreement over structure and substance.

## LIBERAL LEARNING AND SOCIAL TURMOIL

As in the 1930s, when the Depression prompted renewed concern for practical utility and vocational curricula, another dramatic crisis, this time symbolized by the Soviets' *Sputnik,* slowed the second revival of general education in the late fifties. With the launching of the first artificial satellite in 1957 by the Russians, Americans fell into a state of near panic. The shift from preoccupation with individual to corporate values, and from concern with personal attitudes to intellectual and social skills in the larger society, already in process earlier in the decade, was now greatly accentuated as the fifties drew to a close. More and more the trend was toward assessing schooling for its potential contribution to national requirements and policies, and less for individual needs. As concern mounted over the possibility that the United States was lagging behind the Soviet Union in the "space race," the standard for judging education was whether it could be made politically or militarily useful. To some critics, general education was a luxury the nation could no longer afford.

Following the Eisenhower interregnum and the restoration to power of the Democratic Party, education received increasing attention in Washington. As one writer notes, in the person of President John F. Kennedy, but even more in the coterie of efficiency experts with whom he staffed high federal offices, there was dramatic exemplification of a new emphasis upon technical competence and expertise.[73] The task ahead, said John W. Gardner, was to draw upon the talents and abilities of each citizen and to educate people so that the nation could retain its position of world leadership. "The difficult, puzzling, delicate and important business of toning up a whole society," he wrote, framed the nation's most pressing educational challenge.[74]

By the early 1960s, it was widely accepted that schooling should be made to work for national ends. The need for language specialists, applied mathematicians, scientific researchers, and engineers was paramount if the country was to counter Soviet expansionism and safeguard its own security. "Excellence," not "equality of opportunity," was the watchword in American education.[75] Proficiency in the underlying concepts and processes of each discipline such as physics, chemistry, biology, mathematics, and language became an increasingly common theme in curriculum-building, as urged by such theorists as Jerome Bruner, Joseph Schwab, and several others. Particular stress was laid on the "structure of knowledge in each field and its method of inquiry as the objects of instruction."[76] Far less concern was shown for wholeness, for personal integration, or common learning. In the push for specialized competence and professionalism, the earlier preoccupation with liberal or general education now seemed less urgent, less important, in a new era fraught with danger and uncertainty.

Ironically, the cause of general education was further weakened by the subsequent social turmoil of the sixties, when a reaction *against* social efficiency and the use of education as an instrument of national policy set in. As the United States became mired in an inconclusive war in Indochina, the early glamour of Kennedy's New Frontier and his successor's Great Society began to fade. With each passing year, as the conflict wore on, American society grew more divided within itself. By the middle of the decade, military adventurism abroad had become a symbol for many of all that was internally wrong with American society. A new generation of activist students derided what was contemptuously referred to as the "military-industrial complex." Across the country, widespread dissent seriously disrupted the former tranquility of college campuses. Student demonstrations dominated the popular press. Borrowing from the tactics of confrontation developed in the Ban-the-Bomb movement and the burgeoning civil rights crusade of the early sixties, disaffected youth assailed the nation's industrial-capitalist technological culture as hopelessly corrupt and degenerate.

From the radical Left came demands for the wholesale destruction of the "Establishment" and mainstream bourgeois culture. "Middle American" manners and mores were held up to ridicule. Radical rhetoric soon reached deluge proportions and began exerting pressure upon the education system. Calls were sounded for new forms of education, for "alternatives" to traditional schools. Proponents of reform quickly won national prominence for their denunciations of conventional schools as instruments of repression and alienation. In the polemical writings of Ivan Illich, Paul Goodman, John Holt, Paulo Friere, Jonathan Kozol, Jerry Farber, and countless others, the same themes were voiced time and time again. In protest against American materialism, racism, social and economic injustice, inequality, and class divisions, against dehumanization and oppression, school critics argued for more diversity, pluralism, and individual freedom.

The "hard" counter-culture of the sixties was thoroughly political in character. Its members accounted for only a small fraction of the total population, but their protest was vocal and highly visible. Their critique of traditional education, when it occurred, scattered in thousands of separate tracts, articles, and books, took aim at the alleged "irrelevance" of schools and school curricula, their divorce from actual living, and their tendency to provide (and reflect) an ideological rationale for social repression. Needless to add, traditional notions of liberal or general education were dismissed as elitist, class-bound, and anti-egalitarian.

Overlapping that "hard" politically oriented counter-culture of protest, both in terms of span of influence and membership, was what for want of a better term might be called a "soft" counter-culture of privatism. Whereas the former rallied its participants to mount the barricades and tear down the existing social order, devotees of the latter counseled withdrawal from the fray, a retreat within, leaving the external world to its own devices. The values of political radicalism were those of engagement, commitment, and active participation in the work of reform. The values of the new privatism, which gained credence in the late 1960s and throughout much of the decade following, were ones of subjectivity, self-absorption, and psychic fulfillment.

What the soft counter-culture appeared to seek was heightened intensity of experience for its own sake, and, ultimately, some new form of internal equanimity or spiritual quietude. Whether achieved through drugs, meditation, or some other means, the goals remained the same. Once again, however, in an era marked by what Christopher Lasch several years ago termed "the cult of narcissism," the traditional ideal of general learning could hardly be expected to flourish. Extreme individualism left no room for self-subordination to the strictures of a prescribed curriculum or the demands of distribution requirements in undergraduate education. The widespread feeling instead was that everyone should do his or her own "thing." More often than not, when the cry for "relevance" was sounded, it assumed the form of a plea for social leverage; that is, for education to address directly society's immediate needs and to contribute to social reform, not longer-range goals demanding contemplation, dispassionate analysis, and the disinterested pursuit of knowledge.

Alternatively, "relevance" as a slogan was intended to denote a type of learning that would promote individual inner peace and tranquility, not some broad comprehension of the human condition in the contemporary world. Either way, what reformers had in mind bore little resemblance to what had passed for liberal learning in the 1940s and 1950s.

Traumatized by the emotion-ridden young, many educators were unsure how to respond. Were these youthful revolutionaries harbingers of a new age about to dawn, or were they simply troubled students with no one else to taunt? Leaders in higher education were uncertain, especially when they sympathized with the reformist aims of students. Their reactions reflected this basic ambivalence.[77] Gresham Riley, of the University of Richmond, later ruefully concluded that the frequent elimination of course and distribution requirements was often mindless, and effected without much thoughtful consideration of the consequences.[78] Robert Blackburn and his associates, for example, in a Carnegie Council-sponsored survey of educational reforms between 1967 and 1974, cited the case of one institution where prolonged faculty tension (exacerbated by the discovery of an FBI agent agitating students to burn the ROTC building) was relieved by an unplanned, spur-of-the-moment faculty meeting at which *all* curricular requirements were eliminated. Although this was admittedly an extreme instance, Blackburn and his colleagues concluded that major curricular change was seldom accompanied by protracted faculty debate on the aims of education or on the question of what knowledge was most worth having.[79]

One of the few major attempts to reexamine the meaning of general education in this tumultuous period was undertaken by Daniel Bell, of Columbia University, in a 1966 volume entitled *The Reforming of General Education.*[80] For him, the need was to focus on "modes of conceptualization, explanation, and verification of knowledge," while at the same time finding a way "of giving a student a conspectus of relevant knowledge as an intellectual whole."[81] Achieving this dual, sometimes paradoxical, goal of "conceptualization" and "coherence" of knowledge, he felt, required first a recognition of how knowledge is acquired in each of the three traditional subject-matter categories. In mathematics and the sciences, the acquisition of knowledge is largely sequential, and proceeds in linear fashion. Knowledge in the humanities is "concentric," as a few major themes continually reappear and recycle themselves (the nature of tragedy, different kinds of love, self-discovery, and so on). In the social sciences, knowledge or understanding is acquired by linking one kind of phenomenon to another in its appropriate setting or context.[82]

Based on these epistemological presuppositions, Bell recommended a college curriculum begin with the acquisition of a "general background" of information, followed by "training in a discipline," and capped with "the application of this discipline to a number of relevant subjects."[83] The key to curricular "coherence," as Bell saw it, was a scheme that envisaged the first year of a student's undergraduate program given over to acquiring necessary historical and background knowledge, the second and third years devoted to training in a discipline, and the fourth year occupied with a combination of seminar work in the discipline *and* synoptic courses—a "third-tier" level—which could give the student a sense of how his or her major subject might be applied to specific problems and how it related to other knowledge domains. Bell denied that he had in mind a set of survey courses or "interdisciplinary" courses, or courses of the type called "great issues." In his sequence, the concluding phase would set the fund of knowledge previously acquired into some larger appropriate context, showing its possible applications and connections.

There were of course during the same period many others besides Bell who wrestled with the question of what general education and liberal learning could mean in contemporary society. At a five-day Liberal Arts Conference sponsored by the University of Chicago in observance of its seventy-fifth anniversary, in 1966, for example, a dozen or so conferees met to ponder the question originally posed in the nineteenth century by Herbert Spencer, when he asked, "What Knowledge is of Most Worth?" Out of that meeting came a collection of papers, published the following year under the title, *The Knowledge Most Worth Having.*[84]

Editor Wayne C. Booth opened the discussion by noting how "exasperating" the conference topic was, given the common assumption that value judgments among types of knowledge cannot be defended rationally. As one faculty critic at the conference complained, since nobody can say what is *most* worth knowing, there are as many opinions as there are people who care to entertain the question. Debate is pointless. A similar feeling was expressed by a student who insisted that each person chooses his or her own answer. One person's right choice is not necessarily correct for anyone else. [85]

In objecting to such extreme solipsism or relativism, Booth argued that if we think of knowledge simply as inert information, as something we can *have,* then perhaps there is little if any data that is absolutely indispensable. He admitted that we all get along perfectly well without vast loads of learning others consider essential. Further, if we talk only about what an individual needs to know for minimal survival in the world, the knowledge required may be negligible. But, again, if we consider *collective* human survival, we might derive an entirely different answer. Much needs to be known and done, for instance, if humankind is to control population growth, avoid atomic annihilation, or refrain from exhausting the planet's natural resources. Booth, however, saw the central issue differently. For him the crux of the problem was one of deciding what *anyone* as a human being must know in order to be fully human. What knowledge beyond practical survival lore is required for living a fully human life? The answer, he believed, depends upon what sort of creature one believes a human being to be and how a person should be educated.

Booth noted, "Some educators talk as if they were programming machines, some talk as if they were conditioning rats, some talk as if they were training ants to take a position in the anthill, and some—precious few—talk as if they thought of themselves as men dealing with men." [86] Mechanistic metaphors of a person as a programmable machine, as a stimulus-response system wholly susceptible to conditioning, as a drone in a hive, or as a simple collection of psychological drives Booth found abhorrent and reductionistic. Worse yet, he felt they were profoundly misleading. Each metaphor emphasizes a partial aspect of what personhood means and mistakes it for the whole. A full conception of what it means to be a human being resists its definition in terms of anything else. A person is *more* than an ant, a rat, or a machine. The question thus becomes, "Is there any part of the educational task that is demanded of us by virtue of our claim to educate this curious entity, this *person* that cannot be reduced to mechanism or animality alone?" [87]

Booth's answer was that the education a human being must have "is what has traditionally been called liberal education." The knowledge it yields is the knowledge or capacity or power of acting freely as a person. The reason liberal education is called "liberal" is precisely that "it is intended to liberate from whatever it is that makes animals act like animals and machines act like machines.'' Consequently, first and foremost, a person must have knowledge of how to learn for himself or herself. If one cannot learn for oneself, one is at the mercy of the ideas of others—teachers, persuasive contemporaries, or machines programmed by others. Nor is it enough merely to learn *how* to learn. The person who is incapable of independent thought is still enslaved to others' ideas. ''To be fully human means in part to think one's own thoughts, to reach a point at which, whether one's ideas are different from or similar to [those of others], they are truly one's own.''[88]

Beyond certain basic reasoning skills, what is it one must learn to think *about?* Briefly, Booth's answer was that, first, a person must know something about his or her own nature and humanity's place in the world. In natural science, philosophy, literature, and the various social sciences, the learner finds accounts of the universe and of our place within it.

Second, in order to be fully human, a person must be educated to the experience of beauty. One who has not learned to comprehend, understand, and fully appreciate creative esthetic endeavor, Booth claimed, is either enslaved to caprice, bound to the testimony of others, or ultimately condemned to a life of esthetic impoverishment and ugliness.

Third, a person needs to learn about human intentions and how to make them effective in the world. The individual must come to understand something about what is possible and what is impossible, what is desirable and what undesirable, what is desirable and what is merely desired. In short, one must acquire ''practical wisdom'' in the realm of human values.

Booth admitted his threefold scheme would not lead to a list of great books that everyone must read, or to any specific pattern of requirements across the many domains of knowledge. A college cannot determine or limit what a student learns. But, he insisted, it *is* the business of an educational institution to help the person use his or her mind independently in the pursuit of knowledge of truth, beauty, and goodness (or ''right choice''), regardless of the particular course of study followed.

At the same Liberal Arts Conference, philosopher Richard McKeon offered four useful distinctions in the ways education can be ''general.'' In his view, general education can be the search for a *common learning* to be shared by all people—what a fixed prescribed curriculum seeks to supply. General education can also involve the search for principles or structures underlying all *knowledge*—what theology or metaphysics once allegedly provided and what proponents of epistemic ''unity'' and curricular ''integration'' look for in terms of modern surrogates. Again, general education can mean the search for a learning appropriate to or useful for all *experience*—whether the learning is sought in great books, in ''life-adjustment'' courses, or in interdisciplinary surveys of issues, concepts, and problems, as viewed from the varying perspectives of different bodies of subject matter. Finally, according to McKeon, general education can be understood as the search for a learning derived from or applicable to *all cultures*.[89]

However conceived, liberal or general learning denotes a planned structure of educational experiences, he emphasized; it cannot arise from "the accidental joining of particular skills and individual collections of facts and information."[90]

McKeon's distinctions surfaced repeatedly through the conference's discussions. Much of what followed was repetitive or added little to what had been said previously. For one participant, the main aim of a college was said to be that of providing "a common education in principles permitting communication and rational progress to occur among citizens otherwise variously expert and occupied." For F. Champion Ward, general education "should have the same degree of coherence for its students and teachers as does a course of professional study."[91] In the final analysis, most conferees returned to the first sense of general education as common learning. Although there was considerable unanimity as to basic goals and hoped-for outcomes, not surprisingly, reaching agreement on what specific curriculum should be offered proved as elusive as ever.

## GENERAL AND LIBERAL LEARNING: A THIRD MOVEMENT

In an incisive analysis of the interplay of social forces and educational policy, Boyer and Levine have argued that successive general-education reforms have always reflected the social concerns of their respective eras.[92] Each movement has occurred in a period of social drift. Each was the product of a time when war had destroyed a sense of community, when political participation declined, when government efforts to establish a common social agenda proved ineffectual, when international isolation was on the rise, and when individual altruism decreased. Despite apparent conflicts and contradictions, the recurrent theme in each general-education movement was the move away from social fragmentation and toward some sense of community. The consistent focus was on shared values, shared responsibilities, a shared heritage, and a shared world vision:

> During each revival, general education spokesmen consistently have been worried about a society that appeared to be losing cohesion, splintering into countless individual atoms, each flying off in its own direction, each pursuing its own selfish ends. They have been convinced that our common life must be reaffirmed, our common goals redefined, our common problems confronted. The specific agenda—the preservation of democracy, the promoting of a common heritage, the development of citizen responsibility, a renewed commitment to ethical behavior, the enhancement of global perspectives, the integration of diverse groups into the larger society—has varied. But the underlying concern has remained remarkably constant.[93]

As evidence for their thesis, the authors could point to a growing willingness within the academic community in the decade of the seventies to take a fresh look at general education. Once again official enthusiasm for liberal learning resurfaced on the nation's campuses. Once again there arose a national debate, an outpouring of articles and books on the subject, a rash of curricular experiments, and a few new proposals which in the public mind came to epitomize the movement. As in the early 1920s and again in the post-World War II period, there was a growing conviction of the need for what general education had to offer.

In the aftermath of Viet Nam and the isolationism that swept the country, many pundits began calling for education designed to foster a more global perspective, in a time when it was becoming painfully obvious that the nation's destiny was inexorably linked with the fate of other peoples around the world. Others in the wake of the Watergate scandal urged more attention to moral training. Above all, some sort of general education was argued for as an antidote to the narcissistic self-absorption of the "me" generation and its myopic obsession with immediate gratification, so pervasive in the culture of the 1970s. In academe, the cause of general education was increasingly embraced as the answer to the decline in academic performance. Liberal learning was likewise viewed as a palliative for the "new vocationalism" on campus and loss of interest among undergraduates in a liberal-arts education. Once again, a reaction against the elimination of general requirements, common in the 1960s, led to new calls for common learning.

As the seventies opened, however, there were few indications of the burgeoning interest in general education to come. In a 1971 report by the American Association of American Colleges (AAAC), the outlook appeared gloomy. "Contemporary liberal education," wrote Willis D. Weatherford, chair of the AAAC's Commission on Liberal Learning, "seems irrelevant to much of the undergraduate population and, more especially, to middle America. The concept of intellect has not been democratized; the humanities are moribund, unrelated to student interest, and the liberal arts appear headed for stagnation. Narrow vocational education has captured the larger portion of political interest." Weatherford continued:

> The liberal arts colleges are captives of illiberally educated faculty members who barter with credit hours and pacts of nonaggression among their fiefs and baronies. Illiberally educated politicians, who want a bigger gross national product with scant regard for whether the mind and lives of the persons who produce it are or are not gross, make their own negative contribution, as do illiberally educated students who imagine that real meaning can be captured in romantic abandon or existential caprice.

In the final analysis, he felt uncertain what might be needed to "re-establish the creative impulse of the liberal arts" in American higher education.[94]

Half a dozen years later, the Carnegie Council on Policy Studies in Higher Education reported the results of its study, which found that between 1967 and 1974 general-education requirements, as a percentage of undergraduate curricula, had dropped from 43 to 34 percent. "Today there is little consensus on what constitutes a liberal education," the Council found, "and, as if by default, the choices have been left to the student." General education, its report claimed, "is now a disaster area. It has been on the defensive and losing ground for more than 100 years."[95]

## LIBERAL LEARNING IN THE KNOWLEDGE FACTORY

Attempts at analyzing causes responsible for the "disaster" dominated an ever-growing body of literature. From the mid-1970s through the first half of the decade following, for example, the total number of published books and articles treating relevant topics registered a tremendous increase, more than doubling the record for the preceding ten-year period, from 1965 to 1975. Throughout, however, there was remarkable unanimity on what forces threatened to gut the substance of liberal education, leaving perhaps only an empty rhetorical shell. Writers were generally agreed that the professionalization of scholarship in higher education was a major factor contributing to fragmentation and specialization. A second factor inimical to the cause of the liberal arts was the modern tendency to treat knowledge as a commodity, something to be "used" or "consumed." Finally, the structural organization of the university itself was identified as a culprit. These allegations were hardly novel, of course, although they were given new force and clarity in the writings of those seeking to account for the apparent decline of liberal educational values. All of the factors cited were understood to be interrelated.

Much earlier, Clark Kerr, former president of the University of California at Berkeley, had pointed out in his *Uses of the University* that the American university had become a "multiversity" under pressure from its many publics.[96] Faced with an explosion of knowledge and rising demands that it serve the needs of business, government, military, and other groups and causes, the character of the university was transformed. Too harassed to lead, university administrators became mediators among competing interests, trying to balance among contradictory demands, treating students as consumers, knowledge as a factory product, course offerings as supermarket wares, and neglecting ultimately the liberal studies.[97] For Kerr, the rise of the multiversity was accounted for by the democratization of American higher education, its break with older elitist traditions, and its inability to resist social, business, and governmental needs.

Critics such as Robert Paul Wolff in his *The Ideal of the University* argued that the multiversity's response to the felt needs of society spelled a neglect of society's longer-range spiritual needs. In turning away from its founding ideals, the multiversity ceased being a critic of its own practices. It lost its own sense of intellectual vision and settled for a hodgepodge curriculum that thinking students rightly disdained as "required irrelevance." Jacques Barzun, in *The American University,* likewise had decried the university's supermarket mentality, its attempt to assume multiple roles, its muddled graduate-school professionalism, and its assembly-line scholarship. Corrupted by populism and professionalism, as Christopher Jencks and David Riesman showed in *The Academic Revolution,* the

DISSENTING VIEWS

The only advantage of a classical brain is that it will enable you to despise the wealth it will prevent you from earning.

—Anonymous British mathematician

There can be no adequate technical education which is not liberal, and no liberal education which is not technical; that is, no education which does not impart both technique and intellectual vision.

—Alfred North Whitehead, *The Aims of Education* (New York: Free Press, 1967), p. 23.

In an interdependent technological society, the development of competence to produce a fair share of commodities and services is a major objective of any realistic educational system. So is the development of ability to earn income.

—Rupert N. Evans, "Rationale for Career Education," *NASSP Bulletin* 57 (March 1973): 52.

How absurd to suggest that general knowledge for its own sake is somehow superior to *useful* knowledge. "Pedants sneer at an education that is useful," Alfred North Whitehead observed. "But if education is not useful," he went on to ask, "what is it?" The answer, of course, is that it is nothing. All education is career education, or should be.

—Sidney P. Marland, Jr., "Career Education Now," in Keith Goldhammer and Robert E. Taylor (eds.), *Career Education: Perspective and Promise* (Columbus, Ohio: Chas. E. Merrill, 1972), p. 35.

tendency of the multiversity was to offer most undergraduates simply a cutrate version of graduate education aimed at preparing them as quickly as possible for specialized professional careers.[98]

In the seventies and eighties, critics repeatedly assailed the same trends. In *The Uses of a Liberal Education* Brand Blanchard insisted that "the most searching question that can be asked about a university . . . is, What sort of person does it produce?"[99] The university or college that ignores the question, argued Robert H. Chambers, runs the risk of abandoning its integrity to marketplace flux and flow. "It is not Xerox or Gulf and Western that should be the shapers of undergraduate curricula," he emphasized. "When job charts come to determine, even indirectly, what should be taught, then the heart of the university, its dedication to perspectives on truth, has been unceremoniously cut out." An institution of higher learning should not pander to the needs of corporate society, but should resist society's materialistic thrust "by offering the tempering force of the life of the mind as a means to a better, fuller way of living." [100]

Universities have become the principal manufacturers and retailers of knowledge as a commodity, argued Barry O'Connell, professor of American Studies and English at Amherst College. Universities have many buyers: students seeking credentials to insure prosperous futures, industries wanting the skills and products of faculty researchers, and the government, needing an array of services. [101] But in the quest for social prestige and authority, the university has been forced to alter the mission of undergraduate education. The goal of providing a liberating experience has given way to the aim of advancing and transmitting knowledge and fitting people for careers. [102]

Associated with the transformation and broadening of institutional mission, as some critics saw it, was a major change in approach to the liberal arts. Exposure to great models of human conduct had become formal literary study, a more "scientific" history, and the social sciences; the disciplines through the conquest of which one won master over self became the specialized domains of advanced research. In other words, the traditional sources for personal "liberation" grew more exclusively cognitive, technical, and professional. Even in the humanities, specialized training grew more pronounced as the dominant emphasis.

In the absence of a scheme of values in society that commands broad respect and holds it together at its center, today's highly professionalized academic disciplines, it was said, seek to be value-free. Once again, knowledge comes to be seen as a commodity, packaged for consumption in tidy little packages called credit units, hours, and courses. Wrote Joseph Shoben, "It is little wonder that personally meaningful conceptions of selfhood, ideas of bravery and gentleness, and notions of justice and morality hold hardly a candle among the norms of the academy to methodological proficiency and technical competence in the generation and handling of data." [103] Philosopher Frank Harrison's dire prediction was that knowledge emptied of value content would result eventually in "a very impoverished society of machine-like individuals—individuals who in fact *do* a great deal while yet *being* nothing either to themselves or anyone else." [104]

The American university, according to conservative critics, had committed itself to all that is "objective," countable, precise, and publicly verifiable. On principle, the university concentrates on statistics, facts, logic modeled on the discourse of the physical sciences, and problems of documentation. The standing assumption is that larger questions of human meaning, purpose, or significance are unanswerable, and hence not worth asking seriously. Eventually the lesson is driven home to students that ultimate questions are nonintellectual, subjective, and unamenable to reasoned dispute.

Herbert I. London, a dean at New York University, saw the cult of neutrality most clearly exemplified in the vogue for behaviorism and competency based instruction, in which an area of learning is broken down into its component parts and each part has corresponding behavioral objectives that are carefully monitored and measured. There would be few critics of this approach, he claimed, if, like a simple equation, general or liberal learning could be reduced to its component parts. But, he believed, this is not the case: "What is worthwhile is very often not measurable; what is measurable is too often not very worthwhile." The behaviorist program, as London conceived it, had promoted a shift away from liberal educational aims to goals that are measurable and attainable but finite. "In the attempt to apply minimum standards of competence to . . . general education," he wrote, ". . . they have inadvertently created a Gresham's Law of curriculum design: That which is measurable will drive what is not measurable out of the curriculum."[105] The "minimalists," he feared, if unopposed, would eventually destroy what was left of the liberal-arts tradition in higher education.

London, like many others, was not optimistic about prospects for liberal learning in the university as presently constituted. Efforts to find a consensual view of appropriate undergraduate experiences, in his opinion, reflected compromise among faculty factions, not consensus. The issue of a possible "core curriculum," for example, had become particularly touchy at a time when many departments were more concerned with survival than principle. Behind the rhetoric of a holistic approach, specialists continue to press for a wider array of specialized courses. And in the intense competition for space, time, and resources, "a ballot to determine the complexion of the curriculum is very often simply a pork barrel bid." Anxious to save faculty jobs and bolster sagging enrollments, one department votes for another's preferred course selection in exchange for support of its own required course in the general education program. "Of what value is debate about academic issues in this climate of academic backscratching?" London asked rhetorically.[106]

Dean Robert H. Chambers, of the College of Arts and Sciences at Bucknell University, summed up the problem: "The triumph of the academic department as an autonomous unit capable of demanding greater loyalty than the institution of which it is a part is certainly the primary cause of the splintering of the liberal arts curriculum that we see all around us today."[107] American University Professor Samuel Lubell served the same point in claiming that the "feudal" structure of the university, with all of its fragmenting characteristics, was mostly to blame.[108]

## COLLEGIATE VOCATIONALISM AND CLOSET VOCATIONALISTS

Critics of American higher education in the late 1970s and early 1980s saw clearly the malaise affecting colleges and universities across the country brought on by an economic crunch, the impact of declining student enrollments, and public skepticism over the practicality of a liberal-arts education. "Career preparation is one of liberal education's most fundamental problems," admitted H. Bradley Sagen, a professor of higher education at the University of Iowa and editor of *Liberal Education*. "As a conceptual issue, the relationship of the liberal arts experience to career preparation has never been resolved to the satisfaction of those committed to either aim; and as a practical matter, many current liberal-arts graduates are not able to find positions appropriate to their abilities and educational attainment.''[109]

The poor position of liberal-arts graduates in competing for employment with graduates of more specialized applied programs, observed Lewis H. Drew, undoubtedly lent force to the attack upon liberal education. ''One cannot simply ignore or wash away these very real problems for liberal arts education or the traditional link between education and jobs, right or wrong,'' he observed.[110] Gresham Riley expressed no surprise over the obvious fact that the primary concern of many students was ''first-job-placement,'' though he noted, ''This concern exists in spite of the fact that we know that most people experience four to six job changes in their careers, that the time spent on the job represents a decreasing amount of the total time available to adults, that many of the challenging jobs of the immediate future do not yet exist, and that change rather than stability will increasingly define our lives as adults.''[111]

The possible short-lived utility of narrow specialized training notwithstanding, Elie Abel was convinced college students and their parents would not soon be disabused of the persistent notion that liberal education is next to useless by way of job preparation.[112] The question, as Herbert London saw it, was how to keep the career component of undergraduate education from swamping everything else. Students arrive at the university so career-oriented, he complained, that attempts to discuss anything else are futile. But since students vote with their feet, the total curriculum reflects their prejudices. If it was destructive for faculty to bow before every student demand of the sixties, he warned, it would be equally wrong now to surrender to the competing claims of specialists within the academy, of legislators, parents, or any other pressure group.[113]

Barry O'Connell offered a more charitable interpretation of students' expectations and desires. Students come to college in the 1980s, he thought, as they did in the sixties and seventies, deeply troubled about the world, skeptical about the capacity of most institutions to redress society's apparently intransigent failures, but vaguely hopeful their education might provide them with the understanding and skills necessary to better the world they inherit. They incline toward cynicism and resignation, but these are still tempered by a healthy idealism. Once on campus, however, taking the cues of their elders, they become obsessed with their professional futures. They elect courses most directly preparatory for their chosen vocations. Mindful of the oversupply of graduates competing for fewer desirable jobs, they feel compelled to hold everything else in abeyance as they train themselves for employment.

''This process does not conduce to much self-respect among the current student generation,'' O'Connell felt. ''Having lost their faith, as it were, they must now endure the excoriations of their teachers and the media for being narrowly obsessed with careers, and, if one believes most of the curricular reports, inept at writing, incompetent in mathematics, and moral barbarians.'' Students unquestionably need a broad general education, he argued, but their disinclination to pursue liberal learning was entirely understandable.[114]

Some authors wondered aloud if it was not possible to find a better way of integrating or synthesizing vocational preparation and liberal or general education. Sagen, for example, urged more appreciation for the legitimate need for specialized vocational expertise in a baccalaureate-degree program. More emphasis, he argued, should be given to the acquisition of specialized knowledge and the expertise required to obtain an entry-level position following graduation. Competence could be credentialed in work-related settings, he believed, without giving up the other, broader aspects of a liberal-arts education. One could, in effect, have it both ways within the confines of a typical four-year program. Accordingly, Sagen recommended expansion of a college's career counseling and placement services, more intensive student advisement, the addition of internships and career-oriented courses and programs, and other expedients in recognition of the legitimacy of career preparation as a component of liberal-arts education. He concluded with a warning:

> How effectively liberal arts institutions respond to the challenge of career preparation will determine in large measure the future of liberal learning. Capitulation to narrow specialization will deprive both the individual student and society of the humanizing influence of the liberal arts. Rejecting career preparation as a major goal, however, will result in desertion of the liberal arts by our most promising students who are striving to fulfill their potential as human beings through productive and meaningful careers. The challenge to educational leadership is to unite the liberal and the practical in a more effective pursuit of each as a worthy aim of human achievement.[115]

Generally, proposals aimed at balancing market needs with liberal-education aims drew a lukewarm or hostile response from defenders of the liberal arts. Willard F. Enteman, president of Bowdoin College, felt that catering to shortsighted notions of curricular utility would turn liberal learning into something else, and the liberal-arts college with it. "No matter how imprecise the distinction between a liberal arts degree and a vocational degree," he stated emphatically, "surely a degree with an occupational or professional major must lie on the side of the vocational. To be confused on that issue is to deny the existence of any difference.[116] Even stronger was the reaction of George M. Schurr, at the University of Delaware. The typical liberal-arts college, in his view, was already a "protograduate" school offering vocational courses even as it preached against vocationalism. Most institutions purporting to offer general learning, in their attempts to retain students, had already gone too far in "preparing diligent occupants of servile positions." In his judgment, they had "sold their birthright for a mess of vocational pottage."[117]

David French, provost and dean at Lake Erie College in Ohio, confessed he was weary of the "sometimes eloquent and sometimes turgid perorations on the need to protect the 'purity' of liberal and general studies from the dreadful barbarians now at the gates who would bury us with careerism, technological specialization, and the cult of vocational preparation." But his feeling too was that most institutions had long since opened the gates and let them in. Specifically, he accused many academics of being "closet vocationalists," even in the liberal-arts disciplines, in the sense of being committed to training students for successful completion of advanced degrees in narrowly defined areas within the liberal arts. In terms of teaching and accepted scholarships, French felt that specificity, pedantry, and narrowness of concern had obscured the large and generous goals of a traditional liberal education. "When liberal arts teaching is allowed to become little more than training for graduate study in a specialty, and then when graduate study itself demands a specialization so intense that it makes the freshly minted Ph.D's obsolete teachers before they have fairly begun," he argued, "we in the liberal arts can no longer pretend that we are more sinned against than sinning." [118]

## THE SEARCH FOR NEW MODELS

In the fall of 1976 Dean Henry Rosovsky, of Harvard University, devoted his annual report to the topic of undergraduate education. Defining six requirements as basic characteristics of a "reasonable standard" for undergraduate instruction, Rosovsky returned to the hallowed theme of liberal education and its meaning for colleges and universities. He asked that college graduates:

1.  "be able to think and write clearly and effectively . . . [and] to communicate with precision, cogency, and force";
2.  that they possess "an informed acquaintance with the mathematical and experimental methods of the physical and biological sciences; with the main forms of analysis and the historical and quantitative techniques needed for investigating the workings and development of modern society; with some of the important scholarly, literary, and artistic achievements of the past; and with the major religious and philosophical conceptions of man";
3.  that they not be "ignorant of other cultures and other times," and be able to view their own life experience in wider contexts;
4.  that they "have some understanding of, and experience in thinking about, moral and ethical problems," and be able "to make discriminating moral choices";
5.  that they possess "the capacity to reject shoddiness in all its many forms, and to explain and defend . . . [their] views effectively and rationally"; and
6.  that they "have achieved depth in some field of knowledge." [119]

By the following year the Harvard faculty's Task Force on the Core Curriculum had begun its first comprehensive reappraisal of undergraduate education since the appearance of the landmark Harvard Redbook of 1945. Eventually the Task Force called for the restoration of a year's study in at least four of five major subject areas: arts and literature, history, social analysis and moral reasoning, the natural and social sciences, and foreign cultures. Instead of such staples as

"Central Themes in American History" and "Natural Science I," students would opt from among such courses as "The Function and Criticism of Literature," "The Christianization of the Roman World," "The Theory of a Just War," "The Astronomical Perspective," and "Art, Myth, and Ritual in Africa."[120]

Fulfilling the core curriculum courses was to take up the equivalent of about one academic year. Other requirements involving expository writing, mathematics, a foreign language, and quantitative reasoning would consume a second year; and concentration requirements were planned to occupy another two years' of academic work. Associate Dean Charles Whitlock explained, "We think the new core curriculum is a strong, positive restatement of our belief in the value of liberal arts training."[121]

Reactions to the Harvard initiative were mixed, often critical. "Neither original nor particularly distinguished," was one judgment. "At best, a watered-down version of the experiments in general education conducted at Columbia in the 1920's, at Hutchins' Chicago in the 1930's, and at Harvard itself in the late 1940's," was another. "Disappointingly short of expectations," came still another response. A "rather simple and unimaginative resurrection of distribution requirements," yet another critic maintained.[122] Elizabeth Coleman, writing in the June 1, 1981 *Chronicle of Higher Education,* observed that the history of higher education in this century "is strewn with the debris of attempts to create a more integrated curriculum . . . to revitalize the liberal arts." She, like many others, questioned whether a lost common heritage or shared culture could be recaptured through simple curricular reform such as had been attempted at Harvard, Yale, and elsewhere, or whether the splintered curriculum could be put back together in any meaningful and coherent way.[123]

Jerry Gaff, Director of the Center for General Education, sponsored by the American Association of Colleges, felt that the simple reimposition of conventional distribution requirements was a "quick and dirty" approach to curricular reform. While it reasserted the importance of the liberal arts, he felt it did not go nearly far enough. "Distribution requirements," he claimed, ". . . are usually fashioned for political rather than education reasons; more often than not they constitute a trade-off among departments on how to carve up the curricular pie rather than a genuine commitment that certain kinds of knowledge are more important than others."[124]

Theodore Lockwood shared Gaff's skepticism: "The current trend at colleges of reviving distribution requirements does not convince me we are improving the quality of education. Giving the curriculum more structure doesn't necessarily give it coherence."[125] Mindful of such criticism, other colleges and universities in the 1980s began experimenting with alternative models that went beyond distribution requirements: new core programs, college-wide courses, tightened skill requirements, integrative and interdisciplinary seminars, the inclusion of global or non-Western studies to help students broaden their predominantly Western world view, administrative reorganization providing greater centralized authority over general-education programs, and other nontraditional arrangements.

Foremost in the minds of many faculty planning committees in the eighties was the need to upgrade students' ability to read, write, and compute. As an editorialist in the *Washington Post* commented, "The decline of education, when sufficiently prolonged, becomes irreversible and alters the structure of society. The point of irreversibility comes when a full generation has been mal-educated. Thereafter no one remembers what literate education was, or why it was desirable, or how to provide it." [126] An anonymous professor of history put the matter more succinctly: "Civilization is only one generation deep."

The problem as many saw it was how to develop a new model of the old liberal arts. There were those who argued for going back and recovering the old tradition, but few were sure how to find it. "Today the only thing we seem to have in common is our differences," lamented Ernest L. Boyer of the Carnegie Foundation for the Advancement of Teaching. "There is no widely shared social vision, and there is no agreement about what it means to be an educated person." Boyer added, "Curiously we have remained more confident of the length of a baccalaureate education than we have about its purpose. We are certain that a college education takes about four years, but we are uncertain as to *what* takes four years." [127] Jill Kerr Conway, president of Smith College, appeared to feel the search for a common learning was futile: "We can no longer say today what courses ought to be taught and what ones ought not to be taught. We can no longer say, for instance, that students should study the Bible instead of the Koran. Those days are gone forever." [128]

Jay G. Williams, chair of the religion department at Hamilton College, on the other hand, warned against the hazards of trying to revive uniform requirements in the undergraduate curriculum. "Educational institutions," he wrote, "must be very careful not to aim for the standardized, well-rounded person who, like a doughnut, is empty in the middle. The uniqueness of each calling, rather than individuality, is to be prized." [129]

More than a few reformers took a different tack entirely. We must begin, it was said, by determining the marks of an educated *person,* not with the knowledge he or she should possess or the knowledge all people should share in common. According to Fred D. Brown, Dean at Buena Vista College, in Iowa, for example, a liberally-educated person should share a perspective, viewpoint, attitude, or "inward sense" that consists of seven elements: holism, humanism, historical perspective, readiness to analyze beliefs, creativity, sensitivity to values, and ability to utilize recreation wisely. [130] Paul L. Dressel, a professor of university research at Michigan State, similarly felt that approaches to liberal education in terms of departmental majors, core skill requirements, and electives were "inefficient and ineffective." Attempts to define a liberal education in terms of specified content, he felt, would always run afoul of disagreements over what knowledge is most worth having. A better tactic, he argued, was to ask about the characteristics of a liberally-educated person and how one might determine whether an individual is liberally educated:

1. they know how to acquire knowledge and how to use it;
2. they possess a high level of mastery of the skills of communication;
3. they are aware of personal values and value commitments and realize that other persons and other cultures hold contrasting values which must be understood and respected in interaction with them;
4. they cooperate and collaborate with others in studying, analyzing, and formulating solutions to problems and in taking actions on them;
5. they are aware of, concerned about, and accept some responsibility for contemporary events and their implications;
6. they continually seek coherence and unity in accumulating knowledge and experience and use the insights thus achieved to further their development and to fulfill their obligations as responsible citizens in a democratic society.[131]

For many reformers in the early and mid-eighties, the paramount need was to repudiate once and for all any lingering notions that the content of a general or liberal education could be confined within the bounds of Judaic-Christian, Graeco-Roman, or Western society. Observed Richard A. Fredland, a political scientist at Indiana University-Purdue, in Indianapolis, "If ever a time was when liberal education could reasonably omit a substantial international component, that time has passed. It is now inconceivable that a sound education can ignore the international dimension of the lives graduates are ordained to live."[132]

The desirability of international education, as proponents viewed it, was emphasized by the state of collective ignorance repeatedly demonstrated on the part of the American citizenry. Evidence of American provincialism was gathered in depressing quantity. "Americans' scandalous incompetence in foreign languages," charged a President's Commission on Foreign Languages and International Studies, ". . . explains our dangerously inadequate understanding of world affairs."[133] Joseph Lurie, in an unpublished report entitled, "America, Globally Blind, Deaf and Dumb," for example, pointed out numerous instances where U.S. personnel in embassies around the world could not speak the local languages; that there are more *teachers* of English in the Soviet Union than there are *students* of Russian in the United States; that in a UNESCO survey of television coverage of international events in a hundred nations, the U.S. ranked lowest; and that according to a Roper Poll in the early 1980s, almost half of those surveyed believed that foreign trade was either irrelevant or harmful to the American economy—this despite the fact that one out of every three acres of U.S. soil under cultivation goes for agricultural export and one of every six manufacturing jobs is directly dependent on foreign trade.[134]

"Liberal arts and related curricula can continue to offer the traditional liberating potpourri of courses by which students may learn to speak a few phrases of German, list the causes of the Russo-Japanese War, arrive at the formula for red dye number 2, identify hymenoptera, or determine the volume of a lake but have no coherent view of the pressing realities of the international system,'' Fredland commented sarcastically. He warned, ''Unless the perspective of the student is consciously lifted above provincialism, not to mention ethnocentrism, of the home state and country, or more importantly above the parochialism of an academic discipline or profession, there is every likelihood that a future isolationism has been spawned.'' Calling for international literacy as a major thrust in the liberal-arts curriculum, Fredland stressed the utility of an education designed to foster awareness of global interdependency:

> . . . It is clear the future promises substantial changes with regard to interdependence. Virtually any imaginable form of interaction that we are likely to see in tomorrow's world will involve no less than a greater need for international understanding to be an effective participant much less an informed observer or decision maker. Chances are very slender indeed that future forms of international interaction are going to be less complex, less intertwined, and less intrusive on individual existence in advanced industrial states than what is now the case. Consequently, informed, responsive participation in the coming international system, which increasingly engulfs all political subsystems, will demand an international perspective.[135]

Not until the mid-eighties, however, were there signs that colleges and universities would heed the call in revamping their general-education programs.

## THE UTILITY AND CONSEQUENCES
## OF LIBERAL LEARNING

Literally centuries of debate have produced libraries of elaborate, well-crafted pious statements about what the goals and effects of liberal arts education *ought* to be, from Plato to Boyer and Levine's *A Quest for Common Learning*. But the sobering fact is, little hard or reliable evidence exists, one way or another, about the actual effects of liberal-arts education, what one group of researchers called ''this most enduring and expensive Western educational ideal.''[136] While the case for liberal or general education has never lacked rhetorical eloquence, it has not received substantial empirical attention, nor have the actual effects of such an education been demonstrated.

*Do* the liberal arts produce specific qualities of mind and character, from critical thinking and analysis, skill in formulating and criticizing abstractions, independence of thought, or learning how to learn, to self-control, leadership, emotional maturity, balanced judgment, or personal integration? Do liberally educated persons make for better citizens? Do they enjoy fuller, more satisfying lives? Is general education truly broadening? Is there any identifiable and practical ''pay-off'' that would warrant the time, energy, expense, and effort required in obtaining a humane, liberal education?

In the seventies and eighties, growing attention was paid to these critical issues. Some writers, distrusting empirical methodology, continued to rely on personal testimony, intuition, and rhetorical appeals in making their case for the liberal arts. "It is far better," advised Christopher J. Hurn, a sociology professor at the University of Massachusetts, "to base our claims . . . upon the unmeasurable benefits that are today mentioned only as afterthoughts: the expansion of intellectual horizons, growing sophistication, tolerance of diversity, self-realization, and even the pursuit of knowledge as a good in itself." [137] Others, however, shared a feeling that strength of personal conviction was insufficient to persuade a skeptical, empirically-minded society of the usefulness of liberal learning.

Many contemporary philosophers, of course, had long struggled with the issue. They included Paul Hirst, whose conception of liberal education as an initiation into forms of knowledge provoked a considerable body of critical literature; Michael Polanyi and Harry Prosch, whose theory of meaning and "tacit knowing" had direct relevance; and Harry Broudy, who relied extensively on Polanyi's work in the development of his own rationale. [138]

Broudy, for example, in a succession of essays, articles, and speeches, was to argue that there are several different senses of "knowing" something, and therefore, accordingly, different uses of what is known. "Applying" what one has learned is only one use. But, he pointed out, little of what is learned formally is directly applied in the sense of solving a problem or changing a situation. Knowing chemistry is not likely to help a person remove tablecloth stains. A knowledge of physics cannot be applied *directly* to the management of space flight or building a spaceship. Neither the construction of a spacecraft nor the removal of a stain can be deduced from some general knowledge of physics or chemistry. Rather, people have to be trained how to translate basic knowledge into specialized skills and techniques. The ordinary person applies very little of what he or she has learned outside of that individual's field of specialization.

The usual criteria for success in learning, Broudy argued, involve how much *knowing that* (knowledge that something is the case, knowledge about facts) can be reinstated on cue, or the amount of *knowing how* (knowledge of technique) that can be invoked in coping with a predicament. And by either standard, most of what one learns in school seems to be a waste of time. But there are other kinds of knowing and uses of learning, he pointed out. One is the *interpretive* use of knowledge; that is "making sense" of a set of facts in terms of some context or larger setting, understanding the facts of the case because they can be related to other facts. Closely related is another, the *associative*, "in which what is learned is recalled not by precise prespecified clues but by adventitious association and circumstance." For example, one perceives relationships between an isolated datum and other data. Both are examples of *knowing with.* [139]

Hence a liberal education, Broudy insisted, should not be judged on the criteria of *knowing that* or *knowing how,* but on *knowing with,* not on whether something previously learned can be reproduced or applied, but instead by the way that content provides a sense of meaning or context. "To *know with,*" he wrote, "is to comprehend with a point of view, a value scheme, a style of life.

Former British Prime Minister Harold MacMillan once recalled the following remarks of an Oxford University professor addressing entering students:

"Gentlemen, you are now about to embark upon a course of studies which will occupy you for four years. Together they form a noble adventure. But I would like to remind you of an important point. Some of you, when you go down from the University will go into the Church, or to the Bar, or to the House of Commons, or into various professions. . . . a few—I hope very few—will become teachers or dons. Let me make this clear to you. Except for the last category, nothing that you will learn in the course of your studies will be of the slightest possible use to you—save only this—that if you work hard and intelligently, you should be able to detect when a man is talking rot, and that, in my view is the main, if not the sole purpose of education."

—Cited in Gresham Riley, "Goals of a Liberal Education: Making the Actual and the Ideal Meet," *Liberal Education* 65 (Winter 1979): 437.

What we know *with* gives meaning to *what* we know."[140] Long after the details of instruction have been forgotten, having had the experience of studying certain "disciplinary maps," a person comprehends something new differently than the person ignorant of those "maps." This context building is a form of "tacit" knowing, in which what is peripheral in consciousness gives meaning to what is at its focus. A person can more fully appreciate a work of literature or comprehend a theorem, for example, if he or she has previously acquired a context for it than can someone who has not. On the periphery is the functional residue of all that has been previously learned, formally or informally. Some of it can be made conscious and explicit; some functions at a preconscious level. But building a reservoir of resources for tacit knowing, Broudy claimed, is still the valid goal of a liberal education:

> To study and teach the sciences and the humanities so that their noetic and normative structures become available for tacit knowing, for concept building, for imagination, and for understanding is no mean intellectual feat. . . . To the skeptical student one can point out that increasingly even their specialized vocational education will require an interpretive use of their schooling to supply contexts of the professional tasks in which their specialized knowledge is used applicatively. . . . Above all, they need to be assured that although much of what they studied is forgotten, perhaps none of it is *really* gone.[141]

Empirical evidence for Broudy's thesis was forthcoming in at least one massive study of specific changes in undergraduates in a national cross sample who had undergone a liberal-arts experience. Entitled, *A New Case for the Liberal Arts,* researchers allegedly demonstrated, among other things, that liberal-arts education: (1) increases students' capacity for mature adaptation to the environment when encountering new experiences; (2) enhances critical thinking and the use of conceptual skills in integrating novel experience; (3) fosters independence of thought and self-definition; and (4) raises motivation for leadership. The authors concluded:

> A good deal of the crisis of confidence in [liberal arts education] specifically resolves down to a *crisis of evidence*. . . . We believe that our findings help to establish a base of evidence to support the ideal of liberal arts education. . . . Liberal education seems to have at least some of the important effects that it claims to have. . . . we believe that we have established the claim of the liberal arts on a plausible and scientific basis.[142]

Whether or not in fact an empirical rationale for liberal-arts education had been established remained open to question. What was important about this particular study was that it was the largest and most exhaustive among several research efforts aimed at supplying tangible evidence for the benefits of liberal learning. In the 1980s others would follow as the search for new ways to convince skeptics continued.

## IN RETROSPECT: RECONSIDERING DEFINITIONS

As previously noted, ''liberal'' education was once permitted only to ''free men'' (in Latin, *liberi*), and it had the dual connotation of being reserved for those who were free (as opposed to those who were slaves) and as the sort of learning conducive to the realization of personal, intellectual freedom, or ''liberation'' (from the Latin *liberare*, ''to free''; *liber*, ''free''; *liberalis*, ''liberal''). In antiquity and long afterwards, ''general'' education (again, from the Latin, *generalis*, ''of or pertaining to the whole, not particular or specialized'') was used synonymously or interchangeably with ''liberal'' education to denote the same kind of learning experiences. General and liberal education, simply put, were identical. They meant the same thing.

The liberal arts—*artes liberales*—in their original sense, it may be worth adding, did not designate fixed fields of study so much as they referred to activities or techniques; they were conceived of, strictly speaking, as ways of *doing* things. This in fact was precisely what the word ''arts'' meant; as, for example, the means for engaging in rhetorical, logical, or grammatical analysis. Ancient writers categorized these liberal arts in slightly different ways, but the most common enumeration included grammar, logic, and rhetoric (the *trivium*), and music, geometry, arithmetic, and astronomy, or alternatively, philosophy (the *quadrivium*). The liberal arts were the means for achieving personal liberation, and, later, those studies that open up human knowledge and thereby liberate. A liberal-general education began with the study of the liberating arts.

When Graeco-Roman learning first passed into the medieval world, the precedent of dividing the liberal arts into two parts followed by Plato, Aristotle, Augustine, and others was extended by the fifth-century writer Martianus Capella in his influential work, *The Marriage of Philology and Mercury*. He specified grammar, rhetoric, and dialectic—the literary arts—as the *trivium,* and arithmetic, geometry, astronomy (and astrology), and the study of musical harmonics—the quantitative or mathematical arts—as the *quadrivium.*[143] Taken together, this combination of subjects, as H. I. Marrou has shown, constituted a "general" or "ordinary" education: *enkyklios paideia.* (*Enkyklios* meant "recurring," hence "regular," hence "ordinary." *Paideia* connoted the *process* of education, the *means* through which it was conducted, and also, finally, its *end* or goal, the acquisition of "culture.") From a general education in the liberal arts (and hence a liberal education) issued the "cultured" individual, one who participates in and shares a literate culture.[144] The Romans later referred to much the same thing by the term *humanitas,* the condition or state of being fully human and sharing human characteristics to the fullest possible extent.

The overarching goal of *enkyklios paideia* was the attainment of *aretē,* the "virtue" or, better yet, the "distinctive excellence" that makes of a person the highest, finest, most exemplary form of human being possible—roughly, in modern parlance, the fully "actualized" or "self-realized" individual. The word "form" is used here advisedly. "Be forever at work carving your own statue," urged one classical maxim—suggesting rather clearly that one shapes or molds or fashions the raw, unhewn "stuff" or "substance" of the self and thereby creates a self-defined person. The German word *Bildung* has also found use as a term to describe the process of "building" or making a self. The product of this act of self-definition or cultivation, once again, was "culture" (*paideia*).

Cognate with "liberal" as the type of education suited to the pursuit of *aretē,* or "self-realized excellence," and the acquisition of culture was "liberality"—broad-mindedness—and "generous," implying compassion, tolerance, and humaneness. To be educated was to be "liberated" from bigotry, intolerance, and harshness. The educated person was "freed" from the bondage of ignorance, parochialism, and ethnocentrism. The original sense of "humanism" as a belief in the importance of liberation or emancipation and of culture for attaining one's true "humanity" was also closely bound up with this classical educational ideal.[145]

In the medieval period, the study of the *artes liberales* was viewed as the necessary precondition for professional specialization. Through the study of the liberal arts, students were to acquire basic skills and facility in the use of an international language (namely, Latin) and proficiency in quantitative analysis. Thus, to speak of the study of grammar, logic, and rhetoric is but an antiquated way of referring to instruction in language, thinking, and in speech. The study of arithmetic, geometry, harmonics in music, and so forth likewise was the means for achieving skills in quantitative analysis. Thinking precisely (qualitatively and quantitatively), writing correctly, and speaking clearly were the basic aims of university instruction.

Moreover, and contrary to later perceptions, university education was not always an elitist phenomenon, at least not in the sense of being restricted to members of the privileged social classes. In many ways, students were as internationally and socially heterogeneous a group as today's college students, and even less well prepared than their modern counterparts. Universities in any event appear to have afforded many less-advantaged persons a route upward in terms of socioeconomic mobility. It is no accident, one historian has argued, that the liberal arts supplied the avenue over which the sons of Europe's poor made their way into high positions in church and state. Through practice in the liberal arts they acquired skills as well as a first introduction to the knowledge and wisdom of their age.[146] Much the same held true in the Renaissance period and in succeeding centuries.

Not until the eighteenth and nineteenth centuries did it become customary to define the liberally-educated individual almost exclusively in terms of the books he had read and the extent to which he accepted the values of a socially restrictive, class-conscious, male-dominated society. As interpreted by the dons of Oxford and Cambridge and their latter-day American imitators, liberal education became rigidly defined by the canon of books and values it bequeathed to its students and the positions in society it provided for them. It was the commitment to social exclusivity and privilege for college graduates—deliberately so in Great Britain and derivatively so in North America—that differentiated a college education in the 1800s from the practices of the *artes liberales* in the Middle Ages. And while, upon occasion, the less advantaged did gain access to a collegiate education, they did so in smaller proportion than seems to have been the case formerly.

If this historical analysis holds, it would help explain why twentieth-century defenders of general education have had to labor so assiduously to disassociate the concept from the elitist associations it inherited over the last two centuries. In the eighteenth and nineteenth centuries the tendency was to identify a liberal or general education primarily with the study of theology, ethics, some rudimentary natural science, and the language and literature of Graeco-Roman antiquity. Education in the liberal arts (now expanded to encompass formal fields of study besides techniques for qualitative and quantitative reasoning) was variously defended on the grounds of mental training and moral discipline, conserving and transmitting a cultural heritage, sustaining high culture, and as a source of cultural unity or integration. In the twentieth century, in some quarters, the term ''liberal'' was retained as a prefix to describe education organized around basic disciplines, whereas ''general'' education, more broadly, was intended to connote learning experiences unrelated to vocational or professional preparation. By mid-century, general education as a term had come to refer to any nonspecialized, nonvocational learning and to practically any educational experiences students shared in common.

The potential for confusion in the ways such terms as ''liberal'' learning, ''general'' education, and ''liberal arts'' have been used should be obvious. Hence, at the risk of appearing arbitrary or purely stipulative, but drawing on their original meanings and the history of their subsequent evolution, the following distinctions might prove useful:

1. Liberal and general education could both denote the same learning experiences, subjects, or course content. But they need not do so. A liberal education is not necessarily general, and general education is not always liberal.

2. *Liberal* education stresses the goal or results of an educational process: to the extent that the experience "liberates" the learner, enlarges understanding, or otherwise produces desirable consequences, the education is liberal.

3. *General* education has a twofold connotation. The first involves the scope or breadth of coverage of the learning involved. Its opposite is narrow or *specialized* education.

4. The second meaning of "general" education refers to the character of the learning involved; that is, "basic" knowledge. It is acquired without regard for its immediate utility. The opposite of general education in this second sense is *applied* education. It is also the opposite of *vocational* training.

All things being equal, general education and liberal education could be identical. The association between the two arises from the assumption that "liberality" is a function of "generality" in learning. Thus, if an education encompasses a broad range of disciplines, and study is pursued chiefly for its own sake, with the focus upon basic knowledge rather than the immediate short-range applications of knowledge, then presumably its effects could be liberalizing. It would qualify as liberal learning.

The first sense of general education connotating scope or breadth of content is straightforward and understandable. Insofar as a course of study includes a variety of subject matters, types of knowledge, and a range of disciplinary knowledge, it is "general" and "broadening." Its antithesis is learning confined within a single discipline, circumscribed by one type of subject matter, or concerned exclusively with a very few topics—in a word, *specialized* education.

The second sense of general education as "basic" learning is not much more difficult. In principle, at least, there is an identifiable difference between generically fundamental knowledge (for example, basic theory in a discipline) and applied knowledge (the application of knowledge to some useful end or purpose). Thus, physics might refer to the former, whereas engineering would designate the latter. There are differences, once again, between the study of psychology as an academic discipline and learning counseling techniques; between studying sociology as a knowledge domain and learning group-management processes; between esthetics and interior design, nutrition and the culinary arts, art history and graphic design, and so on. In the sense that general education concentrates on basic concepts and ideas rather than techniques or methodologies, it is the opposite of *applied* education.

General education in either or both senses—nonspecialized and nonapplied—might also be thought of as the opposite of *vocational* or professional training. Vocational education or training has as its aim the fostering of skills required for employment. Ultimately, its test is whether it enables a learner to engage in a craft or occupation—to *do* something. A program in air-conditioning maintenance, for instance, that failed to prepare people to service air-conditioners would be judged a failure.

It is only in specific, particular cases that these principles begin to break down. Thus, for example, one might assume that a course in philosophy would be a likelier candidate for inclusion in a program of liberal studies than, say, a computer-programming course. But what if the philosophy course is taught pedantically? What if it consists solely of rote memorization? If the student is untouched by the subject matter, if the knowledge remains inert and lifeless, if it has no "fermentative" qualities and fails to stimulate the learner's appreciation or understanding, can the experience be said to have been liberalizing?

Contrariwise, suppose the course in computers is taught with imagination and style. Possibly the content or material is presented in some broader context—one involving the foundations of binary logic, artificial intelligence, cybernetics, and the impact of electronic information storage and retrieval systems upon society. In this situation, it is arguable that the computer course could be more "liberal" than the course in philosophy.

In other words, there are grounds for questioning whether certain subjects have more intrinsic liberalizing potential than others. All things being equal, philosophy might be more fruitful than accounting. But of course in real-life settings, things rarely *are* equal. The relevant considerations in specific situations would be how the subject is approached, how it is taught, for what purposes, and with what results. If liberal education emphasizes consequences, the outcome therefore is relevant for deciding *ex post facto* whether an educational experience has been liberal or not.

Sometimes what is part of a vocational curriculum for one person is part of someone else's general education. If a student majoring in engineering, for example, takes a mathematics course, there is enough correspondence between the two to say the course in mathematics is part of his or her professional training. But if an art-history major enrolls for the same course as a broadening experience, the course is part of his or her general curriculum.

Conceivably, a highly specialized learning experience could be liberal. A course on economic conditions in France under Louis XIV might have a liberalizing effect. But whether liberal or not, for a history major, the course would represent an element in a professional program. For a physics major, the history course taken as an elective would be part of a general education.

Without complicating matters further, much of the foregoing can be summarized as follows:

1. *Liberal* education designates learning that leads to personal growth and development, independence of thought and judgment, heightened sensitivity and awareness, informed decision-making and effective action.
2. *General* education, as a means of achieving the goals of liberal learning, connotes breadth of content and the disinterested pursuit of knowledge. It is the opposite of specialized and applied learning, and also is distinguishable from vocational training.
3. General education can be thought of as *common* learning: in terms of actual *content;* or of *principles* for organizing and integrating knowledge; or as the basis for the use of knowledge in ordering life experiences.
4. The *liberal arts* consist of skills, disciplines, and fields of knowledge in which learning (on various grounds) has been thought to be liberalizing. Their contents furnish the main substance of a general education. They include the natural and social sciences,

mathematics, communicative arts, and the humanities. The *humanities* in turn are distinguished for having as their primary focus of interest values and questions of human meaning or significance. For some purposes, the humanities are distinguishable from the *applied* arts and technologies generally, and from the *fine arts* in particular, whose aim is the creation or production of artistic works.

Is there such a thing as a liberal-arts tradition? That is, can one identify a set of assumptions, arguments, and values that collectively define an intellectual stream or pattern? To some extent, an affirmative answer seems possible. The major tenets of this perspective might be set forth as follows:

1. The concept of "culture" has at least three interrelated meanings:
   a. First, in its broadest anthropological usage, *social* culture designates the totality of learned or acquired ways of thinking, believing, valuing, communicating, and acting shared by the people of a society. Culture is what holds the social order together. It defines or creates the social reality to which members of society respond in their relationships with one another and in their interactions with the environment;
   b. Second, and in a more restrictive sense, "culture" consists of the beliefs, values, and ideals surrounding "artifacts" (for instance, literature, works of art, architecture, music, theatre, dance, philosophy, theology) expressive of the highest forms of consciousness and creativity available within the larger social culture. This is the meaning of "high" or "literate" culture;
   c. Third, "culture" refers to a process of enlightenment and refinement of taste acquired through intellectual, moral, and esthetic training. It is a product of education. To be educated is to be "cultured."
2. Anthropological or *social* culture is enriched and extended by high or *literate* culture. The survival, transmission, and progressive enlargement of literate culture depend upon educational endeavor. To the extent that people are informed and refined through education, they come to share in and appreciate literate culture. *The range and quality of experience they are capable of having are increased.*
3. People become fully human—that is, they most fully realize their human potentiality—to the degree that they are cultured. Liberal education is the means by which human beings achieve intellectual, esthetic, and ethical freedom. Liberal learning provides the wherewithal to think, judge, and reflect more critically and rationally; to become more fully aware of choices as an ethical agent and the grounds upon which to make decisions regarding moral action; and, finally, to expand consciousness of, and appreciation for, created beauty.
4. The highest goal of learning is human liberation. In a democratic society, education must be both general and liberal. Although vocational training of a specialized and applied nature is indispensable, it is insufficient by itself. Scope must be allowed for other types of education aimed at the total holistic cultivation of human beings. A person is—or should be—more than simply a producer and consumer of goods and services in society.
5. An institution of higher learning has as its most fundamental mission the nurturance and transmission of the cultural heritage through the disinterested pursuit and dissemination of knowledge. Its subsidiary goal is certification of academic proficiency and professional preparation.
6. Colleges and universities (for various reasons) have lost their sense of priorities. The *uni*versity has become a *multi*versity. In broadening the scope of its mission, the educating institution stands in danger of losing its historic identity. Not all education

can or should occur in a collegiate setting. Not all types of learning are appropriate for academic instruction. Not all educational needs require servicing by formal institutional programs.

7. Undergraduate education should exhibit breadth or scope and generality of content. As much as possible, the totality of learning should be coherent, cohesive, and integrative. Again, insofar as it is possible to identify knowledge, values, or skills that everyone should acquire, these should frame a common learning taught to all.

8. Rampant vocationalism threatens the academic integrity of the curriculum. Premature or excessive specialization is dangerously illiberal—for both the individual and the larger social order. The *least* useful learning in the long run is that which is narrow, specialized, and tied to a specific knowledge base.

9. The key to coherent or "synthetic" higher education is *balance:*

   a. Against the legitimate demands for occupational competence must be weighed the equally important imperative of intellectual emancipation;
   b. Both breadth and depth of learning are needed;
   c. The interdependence of theory and practice, thought and action, basic and applied learning, deserves greater recognition;
   d. Necessary specialization must be compensated for by generality of learning as well;
   e. Quantitative knowledge (that is, objective, scientific, technological) and qualitative knowledge (that is, subjective, "humanistic," and esthetic) are both essential for complete human development.

The overriding question in the eighties was how much support these assumptions would continue to enjoy. To hostile critics, the entire liberal-arts tradition was a vestigial atavism, a holdover from a bygone era. Even among its staunchest supporters, optimism about the future of liberal learning in an age of specialization and technocracy was guarded at best. Compared with a time when the liberal arts were assumed to be the *sine qua non* of higher learning, more than a few proponents in the contemporary period found themselves fighting a rearguard action, arguing for no more than *some* place within academe where liberal learning could survive if not flourish.

## SUMMARY

In the colonial and early Republican era, a conception of liberal learning heavily weighted toward classical languages and literature predominated in American higher education. Liberal education was commonly assumed to provide the preprofessional preparation needed by those who attended college, and was defended on the basis of the twin doctrines of mental discipline and transfer of training. Not until the mid-nineteenth century did most colleges abandon the principle of a uniform prescribed course of studies in favor of a system of free electives. In the post–Civil War period, curricula were increasingly diversified and new subjects admitted, mirroring the large-scale expansion of knowledge available for instruction. By the end of the 1800s, curricular fragmentation had grown pronounced, and there was rising concern over the loss of academic and intellectual unity it had entailed. As the old rationale for liberal learning was thrown into question, the concept of ''liberal culture'' played an increasingly important role in defenses of general, nonspecialized, nonvocational education.

The end of World War I marked the first of three successive general-education movements; the second followed World War II, and the third occurred in the late 1970s. Reform efforts aimed at providing a more unified and integrative college curriculum initially assumed the form of broad survey courses, interdisciplinary experiences, and the revitalization of core courses or distribution requirements. The most radical of several experiments undertaken in the 1930s was the Great Books program begun at the University of Chicago under Robert Maynard Hutchins, and the adaptation of the Chicago Plan at St. John's College in Maryland, both of which proved highly controversial.

The publication in 1945 of the Harvard Report, *General Education in a Free Society*, symbolized the start of a second wave of reform in the late 1940s and early 1950s, which eventuated in a new round of experimentation with core curricula and required survey courses. Theoretical disagreements over the content and aims of general and liberal education, however, were as apparent as ever. By the late 1950s the impetus had shifted in favor of policies aimed at enhancing the social and political utility of schooling; and interest in general education temporarily subsided. Attendant upon the turmoil and social protest of the sixties and early seventies, popular support for liberal education in its traditional forms was virtually eclipsed. Neither the political counter-culture of the 1960s nor the ethos of privatism that succeeded its demise proved supportive of the values and ideals associated with liberal learning.

Not until the late 1970s and early 1980s was there any substantial reawakening of interest in the restoration of general education. Among the many factors cited as corrosive influences upon humane learning were increasing vocationalism and specialization in academe, bureaucratization, the continuing influence of positivist conceptions of knowledge, a technocratic stress upon utility, and the rise of the multiversity or ''knowledge factory'' as a dominant institutional model in higher education.

For many liberal-arts advocates in an era of rampant professionalism, the vexing question of how far to go in accommodating to vocationalist pressures assumed greater urgency than ever before. Whereas some reformers urged a reconciliation between liberal and vocational education, others felt the rise of careerism threatened to destroy whatever vitality liberal-arts ideals still retained. By the late 1970s and continuing well into the eighties, the search was for new models by which to organize programs of general education. Among those proposed were suggestions for reconceptualizing the issues in terms of the characteristics or competencies liberally educated persons should possess, not the knowledge content they ought to have mastered. Just as frequently other reformers insisted that content could and should be specified, particularly when the need for a more global, international perspective was called for as the hallmark of an educated citizenry. In addition, increasing attention began to be paid to the need for empirical support in advancing the cause of liberal learning in the modern world.

## REVIEW QUESTIONS

1.  What was the "lost cause" to which Carl Becker referred in discussing the traditional conception of collegiate higher education?

2.  Why was the concept of "discipline and furniture" cited in the Yale Report of 1828 important from an historical point of view? Upon what basis did this Report defend the social utility of the learning offered at Yale in the early nineteenth century?

3.  Why did the early American colleges attempt to resist popular pressures to introduce new subjects into the curriculum?

4.  What specific forces led to Eliot's institution of an elective system, and what were the long-range consequences in terms of the structure of college curricula?

5.  In what sense, and for what reasons, did the rise of the American university in the nineteenth century serve to blur the distinction between "vocational" and "professional" education?

6.  What was the meaning and function of "liberal culture" as understood by defenders of liberal education around the turn of the century? How did their rationale differ from that of their predecessors in the early 1800s?

7.  What factors were chiefly responsible for the first general-education movement following the First World War? Why were general survey courses and interdisciplinary sequences instituted? To what criticisms were these innovations subjected?

8.  Summarize the main complaints levied by Robert Maynard Hutchins at the modern university. To what specific factors did he attribute the disorder he perceived in American higher education? Why did he advocate a Great Books curriculum? Account for his opposition to vocationalism in the university. What did he hold to be the primary mission of an institution of higher learning?

9.  Contrast the opposing claims advanced concerning the curricular reform begun in 1937 at St. John's College. Why, for example, did Alexander Meiklejohn approve of the program, while John Dewey opposed it?

10.  How is the conception of human nature adhered to by Hutchins, Adler, Van Doren, and others related to their shared views on education?

11.  How did the 1945 Harvard Report distinguish between "general" and "special" education? What specific reforms did the Redbook advocate?

12.  Summarize briefly Horace Kallen's argument for the indeterminacy of the content of a liberal education. What, in his view, was the primary goal of liberal learning, and what subject matter was likely to help achieve that goal?

13.  Identify the shift in emphasis between the fifties and late sixties in terms of educational policies and views on the function of schooling. How did prevailing social trends of the sixties and early seventies serve to weaken traditional ideals about general or liberal education?

14. What knowledge did Wayne C. Booth argue was most worth having? Upon what grounds did he advance his argument?

15. How, according to critics cited, has the transformation and broadening of the mission of the university in modern times influenced liberal-arts education?

16. What specific approaches to curricular reform in general education appear to be unique to, or distinctive of, recent decades? In other words, what new strategies have been proposed to revive general education?

17. Explain the possible differences, in Broudy's terms, among knowing *that*, knowing *how*, and knowing *with*. Why are these distinctions important to the rationale he offers for general or liberal education?

18. Define the following: *trivium, quadrivium, enkyklios paideia, arētē, humanitas,* humanism, the liberal arts.

## SOME QUESTIONS FOR DISCUSSION

1. Which poses the greater obstacle to the realization of the goals of a liberal education—specialization of topic or specialization of point of view? Consider, for example, the common potato. Could not the examination of this humble tuber be made into a liberal study? Imagine a college course devoted solely and exclusively to the potato—one that treats its chemical makeup, its biological properties, the conditions necessary for its growth, and then reviews its role in history, in the development of trade, of economies, of whole cultures. It deals with the Irish potato famine and its consequences. Attention is given over to the role of the prosaic potato in ethnic cuisine and the variety of ways in which it can be served. Is it entirely ludicrous to conceive of an entire college course on the potato or, say, the egg, that might very well contribute significantly to a general or liberal education?

2. The result of vocational training, according to the ancient Greeks, was a "slavish" person, whether legally a slave or not, one whose only basis for decisions was his or her own perceived interest as the performer of a particular role. Some contemporary critics espouse a similar position today, maintaining that if a person's education is exclusively vocational, it amounts to a form of "slavery." Assess this claim.

3. Is there any evidence, formal or informal, to suggest that the ancient doctrines of transfer of training and mental discipline may have had some validity? Is it possible to train or educate someone to think? Can "mind" be disciplined? Is it possible that an individual trained to think critically in one particular discipline might have acquired habits of thought that could serve that person in a variety of other settings?

4. Even conceding the fact that the culture of Graeco-Roman antiquity exercised a formative influence upon the subsequent development of Western civilization, does it still make sense to single out the Greeks and Romans for special attention? Should most people be exposed to classical literature? Does it still make sense to study Greek and Latin today, especially since virtually the entire canon of Graeco-Roman learning is readily available in modern translation?

5. Controversy over the gradual elimination of Greek and Latin as required

subjects earlier in this century has been exceeded only by contemporary debate over the relaxation or elimination of *all* foreign-language requirements in degree programs, both graduate and undergraduate, at many institutions. Should holders of a baccalaureate or graduate-level degree be *required* to take courses in foreign languages, especially since English is fast becoming a global means of communication? If so, and if—as many argue—the chief benefits to be derived cannot be realized until high proficiency is attained, of what use are a few courses that fail to promote genuine fluency of use? Should computer languages be allowed to substitute for human languages in fulfilling a requirement?

6.  On historical or sociological grounds, is it accurate to assume that the college or university as an institution of higher learning was ever a citadel devoted to the disinterested pursuit of knowledge for its own sake? Was there ever a period of time when students did not demand some practical benefit to the learning they acquired?

7.  A contemporary writer has argued that American higher education is moving from a "social-service station" model of the college or university, in which the institution agrees to "serve" the community with products and services recognized as appropriate to the collegiate tradition, to a model of the "culture mart," in which the boundaries between the college and the community are progressively blurred, and all educational activities, whether on campus or off, whether by formal colleges or other institutions performing educational services, get validated and legitimized by colleges acting as educational brokers. (See the discussion in Philip G. Altbach and Robert O. Berdahl (eds.), *Higher Education In American Society* [Buffalo: Prometheus Books, 1981], p. 7.) Insofar as this might be true, is it desirable? Assess the advantages and disadvantages of a college or university as a "culture mart" in the sense specified. Does it still make sense to ask questions about *the* purpose of higher education? Or are there *many* purposes? Which might be considered *most important,* and why?

8.  Are "distribution" requirements in an undergraduate collegiate curriculum really defensible? Is it fair or just to force students to pay tuition for, and successfully complete, courses in a variety of disciplines as a degree requirement? For that matter, why should there be *any* required courses? Why not allow students to select and choose for themselves? Can compulsion ever be justified? How likely is it that a student obliged to take a course will learn as much as another student who has freely chosen to be in the course? Do unmotivated "captives" learn as well? Why not allow curricula to reflect student interests and demands?

9.  It was once estimated in the early 1970s that the number of students taking classes in witchcraft and the occult arts surpassed the total enrolled in advanced physics courses. Assuming an interested clientele, are there any courses, on any subjects, that do *not* belong or should not be included as legitimate offerings in a college or university?

10.  Can or should public educational institutions retain selective admission policies? Should a student with deficient preparation be denied access to a college education if he or she is prepared to bear the cost? Does everyone deserve a chance to succeed—or fail? Should the institution be obliged to expend resources on remedial instruction for those who need it?

11.  One student asks another about his major in college. He replies, "I'm ma-

joring in journalism, with an emphasis in public broadcasting." He in turn asks the first student what her major is. She responds, "Sumerian literature and cuneiform languages." What is likely to be the next question she will be asked? What does the posing of the question reveal about popular attitudes toward learning, knowledge, and the aim of a college education?

12. The English department at a large university, in an effort to bolster sagging enrollments, once sponsored an on-campus conference to which leaders of business and industry were invited to address the question of employment prospects for liberal-arts graduates. As the conference wore on, a succession of guest speakers praised the values of a liberal-arts education. At one session, a student in the audience tried to pin down the representative of a major manufacturer of greeting cards as to whether he personally would be willing to hire English majors. The student also wanted to know what specific type of employment they might expect. Reportedly, after some hesitation the speaker answered, "Well, I guess we could hire one or two to help write inscriptions." Analyze this scenario. Was the purpose of the conference misconceived? Did the student pose an appropriate question? How adequate was the response? What issues are raised by this illustration?

13. Extraterrestrial visitors have just landed on Earth. Assuming the possibility of two-way communication, how would these hypothetical aliens identify a liberally-educated human being? Would there be any way a human could detect a liberally-educated sentient being who was nonhuman?

14. What does it mean to claim that human knowledge lacks "unity" or "integration"? Did it ever possess more cohesion than it displays today? Is the issue important? Why or why not? What would be required for the intellectual integration of all human learning? How could it possibly be achieved?

15. What does it mean to be a "cultured" person? What differences mark off the educated individual from the noneducated? Is it still possible in any sense of the term for people to share a common literate culture? Does the ancient conception of *paideia* retain any contemporary relevance or validity whatsoever? In what sense is the imposition of a "core" curriculum an attempt to foster and preserve a common culture?

16. Evaluate the claim, frequently advanced, that universal liberal education is essential for the preservation of a democratic social order. Thus, for example, it is argued that *all* members of a democracy should be able to read, write, and speak effectively. All should possess an understanding of public issues, based on substantive knowledge in the areas of natural and social science, history, ethics, and so on. Otherwise, so it is said, a citizen cannot participate intelligently in public discussions of issues. All members of society should understand both the methods and results of scientific and other forms of investigation, all should be sensitive to esthetic experience, and all should have a knowledge of human values. Education within a democracy should not be limited to training individuals in occupational skills, for no matter what his or her vocation, each citizen is called upon to take part in decisions of public policy. Education therefore must be broad enough to enable each person to render wise decisions. Is this argument plausible and convincing? Why or why not?

17. One of the oldest questions in the history of recorded culture is whether knowledge and virtue are related. Can morality be taught? Can education produce a more ethically-responsible agent in the world of moral choice and action? Is a liberally-educated person (however defined) apt to be wiser, more responsible, or more ethical in conduct than someone who has not been liberally educated?

18. What is the difference (if any) between "education" and "training"?

19. It has been said that when a work of art or a classic in literature survives for centuries, it is not because it has been protected from criticism, but because it has survived it. The greater the reputation of a work, the more intense the scrutiny it undergoes from critics in every epoch. Its survival is evidence of its inherent strength and quality, and therefore it deserves to survive. If true, then does it not make sense to encourage people to acquire a "classical" education in terms of gaining as much familiarity as possible with the best that has survived the ages? Why concentrate on the latest popular best-sellers at the risk of neglecting more durable works of literature? Since there is always more to be known than any individual can master, why not a Great Books curriculum as the primary (though not necessarily exclusive) basis of a college education?

20. Notice how in most debates over a factual issue, sooner or later a participant in the discussion will insist on "proof" as to the factual accuracy of whatever claim is at issue. But if the controversy concerns values, the tendency is to assume not only that no proof is possible, but that the debate must always end inconclusively, with everyone agreeing simply to disagree. In matters involving artistic or moral judgments, it is often assumed, there are no rules or criteria to which one can appeal for a definitive answer. Anyone's subjective opinion is held to be on a par with, or of equal validity as compared with, everyone else's. To the extent that this is so, what does it tell us about attitudes toward human knowledge? What implications follow for the liberal study of disciplines whose stock in trade is ethical or esthetic values?

21. A favorite argument of some critics is that liberal education is wasted on the young. A typical eighteen-year-old undergraduate, it is said, cannot properly appreciate or understand the theme of tragedy in literature, for example, when the most "tragic" event in that young person's life might have been the end of a romance, or the loss of a grandparent or childhood pet. Only with the maturity and breadth of life experience possessed by the older returning student, some claim, can liberal learning be pursued profitably. For perfectly understandable reasons, undergraduates are more anxious to prepare for and embark upon a career; general or liberal education should be deferred until later on, when they are psychologically prepared for it. The opposing view holds that unless an adequate foundation is laid and a desire for liberal learning awakened early in life, later on the person is unlikely to pursue a liberal course of study. Analyze and evaluate these two competing claims.

22. Should conversance with non-Western cultures be established as a goal of liberal and general education? Is it as important to acquire in-depth knowledge of Indian, Oriental, or African civilizations as it is of Western culture? Is the expectation realistic? What do people need to know in the dawning era of the "global village"?

## FURTHER READING

ADELMAN, HOWARD. *The Holiversity.* Toronto: New Press, 1973.

ADLER, MORTIMER. *How to Read a Book.* New York: Simon & Schuster, 1940.

BELL, DANIEL. *The Reforming of General Education.* New York: Columbia University Press, 1966.

BLANSHARD, BRAND. *The Uses of a Liberal Education.* LaSalle, Ill.: Open Court, 1973.

BOOTH, WAYNE C., ed. *The Knowledge Most Worth Having.* Chicago: University of Chicago Press, 1967.

BOUCHER, CHAUNCEY S. *The Chicago College Plan.* Chicago: University of Chicago Press, 1935.

BOYER, ERNEST L., and ARTHUR LEVINE. *A Quest for Common Learning.* Washington, D.C.: Carnegie Foundation for the Advancement of Teaching, 1981.

BREED, FREDERICK S. *Education and the New Realism.* New York: Macmillan, 1939.

BROUDY, HARRY S. *Building A Philosophy of Education.* Englewood Cliffs, N.J.: Prentice-Hall, 1961.

———. *Enlightened Cherishing: An Essay on Aesthetic Education.* Urbana: University of Illinois Press, 1972.

BRUBACHER, JOHN S., and WILLIS RUDY. *Higher Education in Transition: A History of American Colleges and Universities, 1636–1976.* New York: Harper and Row, 1976.

BRUNER, JEROME. *The Process of Education.* Cambridge, Mass.: Harvard University Press, 1960.

BUTLER, J. DONALD. *Idealism in Education.* New York: Harper and Row, 1966.

CARNEGIE COMMISSION. *Priorities for Action: Final Report of the Carnegie Commission on Higher Education.* New York: McGraw-Hill, 1973.

CARNEGIE COUNCIL ON POLICY STUDIES IN HIGHER EDUCATION. *Three Thousand Futures: The Next Twenty Years for Higher Education.* San Francisco: Jossey-Bass, 1980.

CARNEGIE FOUNDATION FOR THE ADVANCEMENT OF TEACHING. *Missions of the College Curriculum.* San Francisco: Jossey-Bass, 1977.

———. *More Than Survival.* San Francisco: Jossey-Bass, 1975.

CUNNINGHAM, WILLIAM F. *Pivotal Problems in Education.* New York: Macmillan, 1940.

DEWEY, JOHN. *The Educational Situation.* Chicago: University of Chicago Press, 1902.

DRESSEL, PAUL L., and LEWIS B. MAYHEW. *General Education: Explorations in Evaluation.* Washington, D.C.: American Council on Education, 1954.

FRODIN, REUBEN. *The Idea and Practice of General Education.* Chicago: University of Chicago Press, 1951.

GARDNER, JOHN W. *Excellence.* New York: Harper and Row, 1961.

GRANT, GERALD et al., *On Competence: A Critical Analysis of Competence-Based Reforms in Higher Education.* San Francisco: Jossey-Bass, 1979.

GRANT, GERALD, and DAVID RIESMAN. *The Perpetual Dream: Reform and Experiment in the American College.* Chicago: University of Chicago Press, 1978.

GREENE, THEODORE. *Liberal Education Reconsidered.* Cambridge, Mass.: Harvard University Press, 1953.

HARVARD UNIVERSITY COMMITTEE ON THE OBJECTIVE OF A GENERAL EDUCATION IN A FREE SOCIETY. *General Education in a Free Society.* Cambridge, Mass.: Harvard University Press, 1945.

HEATH, D. H. *Growing Up in College: Liberal Education and Maturity.* San Francisco: Jossey-Bass, 1968.

HENRY, NELSON B. *General Education, Part I, The Fifty-First Yearbook of the National Society For The Study of Education.* Chicago: University of Chicago Press, 1952.

HIRST, PAUL H. *Knowledge and the Curriculum.* London: Routledge and Kegan Paul, 1974.

HOFSTADTER, RICHARD, and WALTER P. METZGER. *The Development of Academic Freedom in the United States.* New York: Columbia University Press, 1957.

HOOK, SIDNEY, PAUL KURTZ, and MIRO TODOROVICH, eds. *The Idea Of A Modern University.* Buffalo: Prometheus Books, 1974.

———, eds. *The Philosophy of the Curriculum, The Need For General Education.* Buffalo: Prometheus Books, 1975.

———, eds. *The University and the State.* Buffalo: Prometheus Books, 1978.

HORNE, HERMAN H. *This New Education.* New York: Abingdon Press, 1931.

HUTCHINS, ROBERT M. *The Conflict in Education.* New York: Harper and Row, 1953.
———. *A Conversation on Education.* Santa Barbara, Cal.: Fund for the Republic, 1963.
———. *The Higher Learning in America.* New Haven: Yale University Press, 1936.
———. *The Learning Society.* New York: Praeger, 1968.
JENCKS, CHRISTOPHER, and DAVID RIESMAN. *The Academic Revolution.* Chicago: University of Chicago Press, 1977.
KALLEN, HORACE M. *The Education Of Free Men.* New York: Farrar, Straus & Giroux, 1949.
KAPLAN, MARTIN, ed. *What Is An Educated Person?* New York: Praeger, 1980.
KERR, CLARK. *The Uses of the University.* New York: Harper and Row, 1972.
KIRK, RUSSELL. *Decadence and Renewal in the Higher Learning.* South Bend, Ind.: Regnery, 1978.
LOWELL, LAWRENCE A. *At War With Academic Traditions in America.* Cambridge, Mass.: Harvard University Press, 1934.
MARITAIN, JACQUES. *Education at the Crossroads.* New Haven: Yale University Press, 1934.
MARROU, H. I. *A History of Education in Antiquity.* New York: New American Library, 1964.
MAYHEW, LEWIS B., ed. *General Education: An Account and Appraisal.* New York: Harper and Row, 1960.
METZGER, WALTER P. *Academic Freedom In The Age Of The University.* New York: Columbia University Press, 1955.
NEWMAN, JOHN HENRY. *The Idea of a University.* London: Longmans, Green, 1852.
PARSONS, TALCOTT, and GERALD M. PLATT. *The American University.* Cambridge, Mass.: Harvard University Press, 1973.
RICE, JAMES G., ed. *General Education, Current Ideas and Concerns.* Washington, D.C.: Association for Higher Education, National Education Association, 1964.
ROCKEFELLER COMMISSION ON THE HUMANITIES. *The Humanities in American Life.* Berkeley: University of California Press, 1980.
ROSZAK, THEODORE. *The Making of a Counter Culture.* New York: Doubleday, 1969.
RUDOLPH, FREDERICK. *The American College And University, A History.* New York: Knopf, 1962.
———. *Curriculum: A History of the American Undergraduate Course of Study Since 1636.* San Francisco: Jossey-Bass, 1977.
RUDY, WILLIS. *The Evolving Liberal Arts Curriculum: A Historical Review of Basic Themes.* New York: Bureau of Publications, Teachers College, Columbia University, 1960.
SANFORD, R. N., ed. *The American College.* New York: John Wiley, 1962.
SNOW, C. P. *The Two Cultures and the Scientific Revolution.* New York: Cambridge University Press, 1962.
STADTMUN, VERNE A. *Academic Adaptations: Higher Education Prepares for the 1980s and 1990s.* San Francisco: Jossey-Bass, 1980.
TAPPAN, HENRY P. *University Education.* New York: Putnam's, 1851.
THOMAS, RUSSELL. *The Search For A Common Learning: General Education, 1800–1960.* New York: McGraw-Hill, 1962.
ULICH, ROBERT. *The Human Career.* New York: Harper and Row, 1955.
VAN DOREN, MARK. *Liberal Education.* New York: Holt, Rinehart & Winston, 1943.
VEYSEY, LAWRENCE R. *The Emergence Of The American University.* Chicago: University of Chicago Press, 1965.
WHIPPLE, GUY MONTROSE, ed. *General Education In The American College, Part II, The Thirty-Eighth Yearbook of the National Society For The Study of Education.* Bloomington, Ill.: Public School Publishing Company, 1939.
WILSON, LOGAN. *American Academics: Then and Now.* New York: Oxford University Press, 1979.
WINTER, DAVID G., and DAVID C. McCLELLAND. *A New Case For The Liberal Arts.* San Francisco: Jossey-Bass, 1981.
WOLFF, ROBERT PAUL. *The Ideal of the University.* Boston: Beacon Press, 1969.

## NOTES

1. Robert Benchley, *Inside Benchley* (New York: Harper & Row, 1927), pp. 216–217. Copyright 1972 by Harper & Row, Publishers, Inc. Renewed 1955 by Gertrude D. Benchley. Reprinted by permission of Harper & Row, Publishers, Inc.

2. Thomas Hughes, *Tom Brown's School Days* (London: Blackie and Son, 1857), p. 57.

3. E. K. Rand, "Bring Back the Liberal Arts," *Atlantic Monthly* 171 (June 1943): 80. See also Willis Rudy, *The Evolving Liberal Arts Curriculum: A Historical Review of Basic Themes* (New York: Bureau of Publications, Teachers College, Columbia University, 1960), p. 1.

4. Adapted from a quotation in Frederick Rudolph, *The American College And University, A History* (New York: Knopf, 1962), p. 12.

5. Alpheus S. Packard, "The Substance of Two Reports of the Faculty of Amherst College to the Board of Trustees, with the Doings of the Board thereon," *North American Review* 28 (April 1829): 300.

6. Carl Becker, *Cornell University* (Ithaca, N.Y.: Cornell University Press, 1943), pp. 19–20.

7. Rudolph, *American College*, pp. 25–26.

8. Cited in Lawrence R. Veysey, *The Emergence of the American University* (Chicago: University of Chicago Press, 1965), p. 24.

9. Rudy, *Liberal Arts Curriculum*, p. 2.

10. Quoted in Rudolph, *American College*, pp. 133–134.

11. Packard, *"Amherst College,"* pp. 304–306.

12. Quoted in Rudolph, *American College*, p. 220.

13. Ibid., p. 240.

14. Ibid., pp. 219–220.

15. Henry P. Tappan, *University Education* (New York: Putnam's, 1851), pp. 15–16. Italics added.

16. Quoted in Russell Thomas, *The Search for a Common Learning: General Education, 1800–1960* (New York: McGraw-Hill, 1962), pp. 24–25.

17. Walter P. Metzger, *Academic Freedom In The Age Of The University* (New York: Columbia University Press, 1955), pp. 4–5.

18. George Wilson Pierson, *Yale College: An Educational History, 1871–1921* (New Haven: Yale University Press, 1952), p. 305.

19. See Thomas, *General Education*, p. 18.

20. Rudolph, *American College*, p. 455.

21. John Dewey, *The Educational Situation* (Chicago: University of Chicago Press, 1902), pp. 85–86.

22. Quoted in Veysey, *American University*, pp. 186–187.

23. W. A. Merrill, "The Practical Value of a Liberal Education," *Education* 10 (March 1890): 441.

24. See Frank Thilly, "What Is A University?" *Educational Review* 22 (December 1901): 500; R. M. Wenley, "Can We Stem The Tide?" *Educational Review* 34 (October 1907): 253; R. M. Wenley, "The Classics and the Elective System," *School Review* 18 (October 1910): 518; Webster Cook, "Evolution and Education," *Education* 9 (February 1889): 372; Robert MacDougall, "University Training and the Doctoral Degree," *Education* 24 (January 1904): 261–276.

25. J. R. Wheeler, "The Idea of a College and of a University," *Columbia University Quarterly* 10 (1907): 7.

26. Charles Eliot Norton, "The Intellectual Life of America," *New Princeton Review* 6 (1888): 323.

27. A. F. West, "The Present Peril to Liberal Education," *National Education Association Proceedings* (1903): 55.

28. Quoted in Veysey, *American University*, p. 216.

29. Alexander Meiklejohn, "College Education and the Moral Ideal," *Education* 28 (May 1908): 558.

30. See A. Lawrence Lowell, *At War With Academic Traditions in America* (Cambridge, Mass.: Harvard University Press, 1934), pp. 5–7, 40–41.

31. Ibid., pp. 108–109, 116, 239–240.

32. Note the discussion in Thomas, *General Education*, p. 62ff.

33. See Rudolph, *American College*, p. 455.

34. M. L. Burton, "The Undergraduate Course," *New Republic* 32 (October 25, 1922): 9.

35. See Lewis B. Mayhew, ed., *General Education: An Account and Appraisal* (New York: Harper & Row, 1960), pp. 11–24.

36. Alexander Meiklejohn, "The Unity of the Curriculum," *New Republic* 32 (October 25, 1922): 2–3.

37. See Richard Hofstadter and Wilson Smith, eds., *American Higher Education: A Documentary History* II (Chicago: University of Chicago Press, 1973), pp. 924–940.

38. See Chauncey S. Boucher, *The Chicago College Plan* (Chicago: University of Chicago Press, 1935); and Reuben Frodin, *The Idea and Practice of General Education* (Chicago: University of Chicago Press, 1951), pp. 87–122.

39. Rudolph, *American College,* pp. 479–480.

40. Robert Maynard Hutchins, *The Higher Learning In America* (New Haven: Yale University Press, 1936). Quotations following are from the 1962 paperbound edition.

41. Ibid., pp. 4–12.

42. Ibid., p. 36.

43. Ibid., p. 47.

44. Ibid., p. 60.

45. Ibid., pp. 66–67.

46. Ibid., pp., xiii–xiv.

47. Consult Christopher Jencks and David Riesman, *The Academic Revolution* (New York: Doubleday, 1968), p. 494 ff. See also David Boroff, "St. John's College: Four Years with the Great Books," *Saturday Review* 46 (March 23, 1963): 58–61.

48. Donald P. Cottrell, "General Education in Experimental Liberal Arts Colleges," in Guy Montrose Whipple, ed., *General Education In The American College, Part II, The Thirty-Eighth Yearbook of the National Society For The Study Of Education* (Bloomington, Ill.: Public School Publishing Company, 1939), pp. 206–207. See also F. R. Leavis, "Great Books and a Liberal Education," *Commentary* 16 (September 1953): 224–232.

49. Both quoted in Gerald Grant and David Riesman, "St. John's And The Great Books," *Change* 6 (May 1974): 30.

50. Ibid., p. 60. See also Albert Guerard, *The Education of a Humanist* (Cambridge, Mass.: Harvard University Press, 1949), pp. 128–132.

51. Mortimer Adler, *How to Read a Book* (New York: Simon & Schuster, 1940), pp. vii–viii; see also Mortimer Adler, *Art and Prudence* (New York: Longmans, Green, 1937), p. 213.

52. Mark Van Doren, *Liberal Education* (New York: Holt, Rinehart & Winston, 1943), p. 23.

53. Jacques Maritain, *Education at the Crossroads* (New Haven: Yale University Press, 1934), p. 10.

54. Van Doren, *Liberal Education,* p. 73.

55. See the discussion in John S. Brubacher, *The University—Its Identity Crisis* (New Britain, Conn.: Central Connecticut State College, 1972).

56. John Henry Cardinal Newman, *The Idea of a University* (London: Longmans, Green, 1852), p. 145 ff.

57. Note the analysis in Robert E. Mason, *Contemporary Educational Theory* (New York: D. McKay, 1972), p. 26; and in G. Max Wingo, *Philosophies of Education: An Introduction* (Lexington, Mass.: Heath, 1974), pp. 85–136.

58. Ernest L. Boyer and Arthur Levine, "A Quest for Common Learning," *Change* 13 (April 1981): 30. The argument here is largely adapted from their analysis. Cited with permission.

59. Alvin C. Eurich, "A Renewed Emphasis Upon General Education," in Whipple, *Education,* p. 6.

60. John Dale Russell, "General Education In The Liberal Arts Colleges," in Whipple, *Education,* pp. 171–192.

61. Henry M. Wriston, "A Critical Appraisal Of Experiments In General Education," in Whipple, *Education,* p. 308.

62. Ibid., p. 307.

63. Quoted in Boyer and Levine, "Common Learning," p. 31.

64. Report of the Harvard Committee, *General Education in a Free Society* (Cambridge, Mass: Harvard University Press, 1945), p. 4.

65. Ibid., p. 39.

66. Ibid., pp. 40, 51, 64, 195.

67. Ibid., p. 93.

68. Gresham Riley, "The Reform of General Education," *Liberal Education* 66 (Fall 1980): 299.

69. Horace M. Kallen, *The Education Of Free Men* (New York: Farrar, Straus & Giroux, 1949), pp. 88–89, 316–318.

70. Ibid., p. 317.

71. Ibid., pp. 319, 323, 325–326.

72. See T. R. McConnell, "General Education: An Analysis," in Nelson B. Henry, ed., *General Education, The Fifty-First Yearbook of the National Society For The Study of Education, Part I* (Chicago: University of Chicago Press, 1952), pp. 4–13; Horace T. Morse, "Liberal and General Education: A Problem of Differentiation," in James G. Rice, ed, *General Education, Current Ideas and Concerns* (Washington, D.C.: Association for Higher Education, National Education Association, 1964), pp. 7–12; and Horace T. Morse, "Liberal and General Education—Partisans or Partners?" *Junior College Journal* 24 (March 1954): 395–399.

73. Mason, *Educational Theory*, p. 138 ff.

74. John W. Gardner, *Excellence* (New York: Harper & Row, 1961), p. xiiii.

75. Francis S. Chase, "Can Both Excellence and Quality Be Honored?" *Education Digest* 30 (October 1964): 27.

76. See Jerome Bruner, *The Process of Education* (Cambridge, Mass.: Harvard University Press, 1960); Joseph Schwab, "The Concept of the Structure of a Discipline," *Educational Record* 43 (July 1962): 199–202; John I. Goodlad, "The Curriculum," in John I. Goodlad, ed., *The Changing American School, Sixty-Fifth Yearbook of the National Society For The Study of Education* (Chicago: University of Chicago Press, 1966), p. 39 ff.; and George W. Denmark, "Concept Learning; Some Implications for Teaching," *Liberal Education* 51 (March 1965): 54 ff.

77. John S. Morris, "The Place of the Humanities in the Liberal Arts," *Liberal Education* 64 (March 1978): 44.

78. Riley, "Reform," p. 304.

79. Robert Blackburn et al., *Changing Practices in Undergraduate Education, A Report for the Carnegie Council on Policy Studies in Higher Education* (Berkeley: Carnegie Foundation for the Advancement of Teaching, 1976), p. 40.

80. Daniel Bell, *The Reforming of General Education* (New York: Columbia University Press, 1966).

81. Ibid., pp. 8, 68. See also Daniel Bell, "The Reform of General Education," in Robert A. Goldwin (ed.), *Education and Modern Democracy* (Chicago: Rand McNally, 1967), p. 103.

82. Bell, *General Education*, p. 141.

83. Ibid., p. 166. See also his "Reform," p. 115 ff.; and Daniel Bell, "A Second Look at General Education," *Seminar Reports* 1 (December 7, 1973): 4.

84. Wayne C. Booth, ed., *The Knowledge Most Worth Having* (Chicago: University of Chicago Press, 1967).

85. Cited in ibid., pp. 2–3.

86. Ibid., p. 7.

87. Ibid., p. 7–8.

88. Ibid., p. 21.

89. Richard McKeon, "The Battle of the Books," in Booth, *Knowledge,* 183 ff.

90. Ibid., pp. 21–23.

91. See Booth, *Knowledge,* pp. 194–195 and pp. 170–172.

92. Boyer and Levine, "Common Learning," pp. 29–35.

93. Ibid., p. 30.

94. Willis D. Weatherford, "Commission on Liberal Learning," *Liberal Education* 57 (March 1971): 37.

95. Carnegie Foundation for the Advancement of Teaching, *Missions of the College Curriculum* (San Francisco: Jossey-Bass, 1977), p. 11.

96. Clark Kerr, *Uses of the University,* (New York: Harper & Row, 1972).

97. See Frankin Parker, "The Future of Liberal Arts," *Educational Studies* 8 (Summer 1977): vii–xii.

98. See Robert Paul Wolff, *The Ideal of the University* (Boston: Beacon Press, 1969); Jacques Barzun, *The American University* Christopher Jencks and David Riesman, (New York: Harper & Row, 1968); and *The Academic Revolution* (Chicago: University of Chicago Press, 1968).

99. Brand Blanchard, The Uses of a Liberal Education (LaSalle, Il.: Open Court Publishing Company, 1973), p. 1.

100. Robert H. Chambers, "Educating for Perspective—A Proposal," *Change* 13 (September 1981): 46.

101. Barry O'Connell, "Where Does Harvard Lead Us?" *Change* 10 (September 1978): 38.

102. Edward Joseph Shoben, Jr., "The Liberal Arts And Contemporary Society: The 1970's," *Liberal Education* 56 (March 1970): 28–38.

103. Ibid., pp. 30–31ff.

104. Frank R. Harrison, "The Pervasive Peanut," *Modern Age* 23 (Winter 1979): 78.

105. Herbert I. London, "The Politics of the Core Curriculum," *Change* 10 (September 1978): 11.

106. Ibid.

107. Chambers, "Educating for Perspective," p. 48.

108. Samuel Lubell, "The Fragmentation of Knowledge," in Sidney Hook, Paul Kurtz, and Miro Todorovich, eds., *The Idea of a Modern University* (Buffalo: Prometheus Books, 1974), pp. 93, 94.

109. H. Bradley Sagen, "Careers, Competencies, and Liberal Education," *Liberal Education* 65 (Summer 1979): 150.

110. Lewis H. Drew, "The Greek Concept of Education and Its Implications for Today," *Liberal Education* 64 (October 1978): 303.

111. Gresham Riley, "Goals of a Liberal Education: Making the Actual and the Ideal Meet," *Liberal Education* 65 (Winter 1979): 439.

112. Elie Abel, "Liberal Learning: A Tradition with a Future," *Liberal Education* 64 (May 1978): 115.

113. London, "Core Curriculum," p. 62.

114. O'Connell, "Harvard," p. 39.

115. Sagen, "Careers," pp. 165–166.

116. Willard F. Enteman, "When Does Liberal Education Become Vocational Training?" *Liberal Education* 65 (Summer 1979): 171.

117. George M. Schurr, "On Rediscovering the Liberal Arts Curriculum," *Liberal Education* 65 (Fall 1979): 334, 335.

118. David French, "Closet Vocationalists among Proponents of the Liberal Arts," *Liberal Education* 65 (Winter 1979): 470, 476.

119. Cited in Jurgen Herbst, "The Liberal Arts: Overcoming the Legacy of the Nineteenth Century," *Liberal Education* 66 (Spring 1980): 24–25.

120. See Stephen J. Makler and Robert J. Munnelly, "Harvard in the 1980's: A Question of Adaptability," *Educational Leadership* 37 (January 1980): 304–306.

121. Quoted in ibid., p. 305.

122. See Chambers, "Educating for Perspective," p. 49; Abel, "Liberal Learning," p. 117; O'Connell, "Harvard," pp. 35–36.

123. Quoted and discussed in Kenneth R. R. Gros Louis, "General Education: Rethinking the Assumptions," *Change* 13 (September 1981): 35ff.

124. Jerry Gaff, "Reconstituting General Education: Lessons from Project GEM," *Change* 13 (September 1981): 53. See also Jerry Gaff, "General Education for a Contemporary Context," *New Models for General Education, Current Issues in Higher Education No. 4* (Washington, D.C.: American Association for Higher Education, 1980), pp. 1–5.

125. Theodore D. Lockwood, "A Skeptical Look at the General Education Movement," *Forum for Liberal Education* (November 1978): 1–2.

126. Fred Reed, "Half-Educated Generation," *Washington Post* (December 20, 1979): 43.

127. Ernest L. Boyer, "The Core Curriculum: A Search for Commonness," *Liberal Education* 66 (Fall 1980): 278.

128. Quoted in Gros Louis, "General Education," p. 34.

129. Jay G. Williams, "The Ritual of Initiation: Implications for the Liberal Arts," *Educational Record* 63 (Winter 1982): 31.

130. See Fred D. Brown, "Toward a Better Definition of Liberal Education: Seven Perspectives," *Liberal Education* 65 (Fall 1979): 383–391.

131. Paul L. Dressel, "Liberal Education: Developing the Characteristics of a Liberally Educated Person," *Liberal Education* 65 (Fall 1979): 313–322.

132. Richard A. Fredland, "Beyond Bounded Education," *Change* 13 (September 1981): 37.

133. President's Commission on Foreign Languages and International Studies, *Strength Through Wisdom* (Washington, D.C.: Government Printing Office, 1979), p. 4.

134. Cited in Fredland, "Bounded Education," p. 37.

135. Ibid., p. 41.

136. David G. Winter, David C. McClelland, and Abigail J. Stewart, *A New Case for the Liberal Arts* (San Francisco: Jossey-Bass, 1981), p. 7.

137. Christopher J. Hurn, "The Reemergence of Liberal Education," *Change* 10 (October 1978): 8–9.

138. See Jane Roland Martin, "Needed: A New Paradigm for Liberal Education," in Jonas F. Soltis, ed., *Philosophy and Education, Eightieth Yearbook of the National Society for the Study of Education, Part I* (Chicago: University of Chicago Press, 1981), pp. 37–59; Michael Polanyi and Harry Prosch, *Meaning* (Chicago: University of Chicago Press, 1975); Harry Broudy, "Tacit Knowing as a Rationale for Liberal Education," *Teachers College Record* 80 (February 1979): 446–462; and Harry Broudy, "The Brightest and the Best," *Phi Delta Kappan* 60 (May 1979): 640–644.

139. Broudy, "Brightest and Best," p. 643.

140. Ibid., p. 643.

141. Ibid., p. 644.

142. Winter et al., *Case for Liberal Arts,* pp. 177–178, 182–183.

143. R. R. Bolgar, *The Classical Heritage and its Beneficiaries* (New York: Harper & Row, 1964), p. 36.

144. H. I. Marrou, *A History of Education in Antiquity,* trans. George Lamb (New York: New American Library, 1964), p. 244.

145. Note the useful discussion in Michael Simpson, "The Case for the Liberal Arts," *Liberal Education* 66 (Fall 1980): 315–319.

146. See Herbst, "Liberal Arts," pp. 34–39.

# CHAPTER FOUR
# VOCATIONALISM
## *Education for the World of Work*

## INTRODUCTION

Throughout most of recorded history and up until the modern period, training for work was largely a matter of informal learning. It consisted for the most part of direct observation, imitation, and experience, of "learning by doing." Children acquired needed skills from their parents and other elders in the community at firsthand, in the home, the fields, the workshop, or the marketplace. From the dawn of civilization to the opening years of the nineteenth century, there were few basic changes in how people were prepared to assume their economic roles within the social order. Most common was some form of indentured apprenticeship, the first known reference to which appears in the ancient Babylonian Code of Hammurabi: "If an artisan takes a son for adoption and teaches him his handicraft, one may not bring claim against him. If he does not teach him his handicraft, the adopted son may return to his father's house."

Preparation for work was an acknowledged social need long before the advent of mass schooling. Indicative of the importance placed on vocational training among the Greeks, Solon's rules exonerated children for refusing to care for their parents in their old age if the latter had not taken pains to teach their offspring a trade. Talmudic literature likewise abounds with injunctions to educate the young for gainful employment and economic self-sufficiency. "Whosoever does not teach his son a trade teaches him to be a thief," warned one traditional saying. Advised Maimonides in the thirteenth century, "Anticipate charity by preventing poverty; assist the reduced man by teaching him a trade, and putting him in the way of business so that he may earn self-respect and a livelihood. . . ." Nevertheless, throughout the millennia when only a select few required occupational training in a formal institution of learning, the majority acquired job-related skills through informal means and without benefit of schooling apparatus.

Apprenticeship continued to be the primary method of vocational instruction down through the centuries. It was to achieve its most elaborate level of development in the guild system of the late medieval period, when it was customary for the masters in a particular trade or craft, in exchange for services rendered, to instruct apprentices in the elements of their craft. Following an extended period of tutelage, during which young boys studied under a master and assisted him in his work, apprentices acquired the experience, knowledge, and skills necessary for independent practice.[1] In most of Europe and England, and later in colonial America, apprenticeship was the main—sometimes the exclusive—route of entry into almost all vocations and the various professions.[2]

In the Jamestown colony, for example, in the absence of any system of free public education, those lacking the means to send their children to private schools were obliged under the colony's Poor Laws to indenture them to learn a craft or trade—boys for a seven-year period, extending from age fourteen to twenty-one, and girls for a minimum of four years, from age fourteen to eighteen. Apprentices were required under contract to serve a master for the duration. In return the master promised to provide adequate food, shelter, and clothing until his charges had learned the trade. Some such plan, common to all the colonies, encompassed virtually all the occupations of commerce, shipping, mercantile pursuits, handicraft production, domestic services, teaching, and in some cases even the legal and medical professions.

Not until sometime after the 1830s did the apprentice system begin to fall into disuse. The reasons for its gradual demise were manifold. An abundance of land, the freedom and mobility of the people, the willingness of pioneers pushing back the western frontier to make do with improvised implements and furnishings, and the immigration of craftsmen and mechanics who had been trained in Europe all began working against tutorial trade-training. The heaviest blow of all was delivered by industrialism and the rise of the nineteenth-century factory system.

Rapid development of labor-saving machinery contributed the most to its decline, at first in the textile industry and later in industries using the steam engine and other power sources characteristic of the emergent factory system. As many writers have noted, the industrial revolution meant a shift in production from cottage to factory, from home handicrafts to machine-powered manufacturing. Whereas formerly, in the pre-industrial era, the handworker was intimately involved in all phases of production, from the procurement of the raw materials to the distribution and sale of the finished product, the machine worker who superceded the artisan seldom if ever was involved with more than a fraction of the total production process. His or her skills were at once more specialized and more limited under a system of divided labor and large-scale mechanization.

Overcrowding in some trades and depressed wages, the enactment of legislation regulating and restricting child labor, the rise of the free public elementary school, and compulsory school attendance laws further weakened the apprenticeship system. More importantly, as vocational training ceased to be a natural incident or by-product of production, it became increasingly difficult to acquire training on the job. Industrialization and mechanization required a trained work force, one whose members had already been adapted and socialized for employment and who already possessed job skills. Consequently, as vocational preparation became more an explicit responsibility of the employer, the trend developed of looking to the school as an agency for fostering skills, values, and work habits required under the factory system. Since more and more youngsters were attending school, and for longer periods, formal education appeared to offer the most logical and efficient way of preparing people for the world of work.

By the end of the nineteenth century, schools were under strong pressure from business and industry to assume a more direct role in job preparation. The resulting controversy has continued unabated in one form or another ever since. Before turning to this story in greater detail and tracing the subsequent developments that have led to the most recent phase of what has become a perennial debate, it may prove useful to preview some of the more fundamental questions about educational purpose, priorities, and the proper relationship between schooling and the socioeconomic order brought to the fore as a result of almost a century of discussion and experimentation:

1.  Schools transmit culture. Traditionally, educational institutions have emphasized the preservation and transmission of "high" or "literate" culture—the artifacts of literary, scientific, artistic, and philosophic endeavor. Are there other aspects of the material culture, other expressions of human creativity, equally deserving of emphasis within school curricula?

2.  In a scientific, technological, industrialized society, does the school have a special obligation to foster scientific-technological-industrial literacy? That is, should the school attempt to teach about the dynamics and processes of production and distribution of goods and services within society? Should it do so to the same extent that other elements of the cultural inheritance receive attention?

3.  Should the school be utilized at all as a socialization agent for the workplace? Is it the school's proper task to instill certain attitudes, habits, and values relevant for future employment? What specific values should be emphasized? As determined by whom? To serve whose interests—the worker's or the employer's? Do these interests necessarily coincide? What is society's stake in work socialization?

4.  What is or should be the economic role of formal education? Should the school be involved directly in preparation for a specific vocation? Or should formal instruction be aimed at a much broader set of skills and knowledge? In other words, should the school confine its efforts primarily to teaching *about* the world of work? Should it

stress, for example, basic knowledge necessary for understanding the role of work in society? Or should the school attempt to foster a *discrete* set of occupational skills? Should it do both?

5.  Is it the exclusive responsibility of the school to prepare people for work? Or should responsibility be shared? Among what agencies and institutions, and to what degree? Can the knowledge and skills needed for vocational competence be acquired in school, under classroom instruction? Or can job competencies be most effectively and efficiently acquired in a work setting where they will be most immediately applied? What about job retraining?

6.  What is the long-range utility of direct vocational instruction? How quickly do specific job skills become obsolete? Are there other forms of understanding that retain their occupational relevance longer and that can be fostered best through formal training?

7.  How closely should school curricula be tied to the exigencies of the marketplace? Should the availability of vocational preparatory programs hinge upon supply or demand? What considerations ought to dictate vocational training—student interest or the requirements of the marketplace?

8.  Can or should the school attempt to prepare people for jobs that do not yet exist? How can the school keep abreast of rapid, large-scale technological innovation and the constantly changing needs of the labor force? How accurately can future trends be forecast, and what implications follow for curriculum planning and development?

9.  What is the relationship (or lack thereof) between general academic education and vocational preparation? Are they compatible or opposed to each other? What is the optimal balance between general knowledge and skill training? Could general and vocational education be integrated somehow in a common course of studies? Should they be?

10.  Should vocational preparation be organized and administered separately, apart from general academic education? What might be the relative advantages and disadvantages of a dual school system? What would be the impact of a dual system upon individuals and society at large?

11.  When should the process of occupational selection and preparation begin? What about premature specialization in an individual's educational career? Can the school facilitate the process of vocational career selection and preparation? If so, how, and in what specific ways?

12.  Is preparation for an economic role in the social order a "narrowing" or a "broadening" experience in terms of the individual's overall development?

13.  Can or should there be a single uniform pattern of schooling for everyone? Is it undemocratic or socially divisive to "track" students at some point in the system, directing some people toward courses of study that lead to nonprofessional employment while encouraging others to prepare for more extended schooling and eventual careers in the professions?

14.  Does the vocationalization of institutionalized education equate with the democratization of educational opportunity? That is, by honoring a greater range of abilities and talents than those academic competencies heretofore emphasized, can schooling become more useful and relevant to more people? Is more and better vocational education the answer to meeting the needs of alienated learners, unmotivated students, and potential drop-outs? Would increased emphasis upon career preparation reduce school attrition?

15.  Can vocational education help solve problems of unemployment and underemployment by seeking a better balance between market needs and the skills possessed by the labor force?

These sets of questions are by no means exhaustive. Nor did they all surface at one and the same time or necessarily find expression in the forms herein presented. They serve merely to illustrate just some of the multi-faceted issues raised by the relationship between schooling and work, and by the ascendancy of "vocationalism"—here understood as a generalized viewpoint or set of beliefs, assumptions, attitudes, and values whose common theme is the need for closer ties between the world of work and formal learning.

## EARLY VOCATIONAL TRAINING IN AMERICA

Early settlers in America were deeply imbued with what Max Weber in 1904 called the Protestant work ethic. As Weber, Tawney, and especially Ernst Troeltsch, in his classic *Protestantism and Progress* have argued, Protestantism—especially Calvinism—encouraged the values of diligence, frugality, and thrift.[3] It condemned indolence as sinful and endorsed work as a positive virtue. Puritan insistence on unremitting toil and the sin of wasteful consumption combined to enjoin the amassing of wealth almost as a sacred duty. This Protestant ethic became an important cornerstone in the ideology of capitalism, nicely illustrated in the English Cleric Richard Baxter's *Christian Directory,* a veritable handbook of middle-class Puritan moral theology. Baxter counseled his readers: "You may labor in that manner as tendeth most to your success and lawful gain, for you are bound to improve all your talents. . . . If God shows you a way in which you may lawfully get more than in another way, if you refuse this and choose the less gainful way, you cross one of the ends of your calling, and you refuse to be God's steward."[4]

Countless other examples must be adduced to show how theology strengthened a capitalistic ethic. In particular, the Lutheran notion of *vocatio*—"vocation" as an occupational "calling" to be pursued strenuously and exactingly, with a sense of religious purpose—reinforced among capitalists and workmen alike the values of self-application. In America, an early and enthusiastic advocate of the work ethic was Benjamin Franklin, whose homely maxims and preachments helped mold the attitudes of successive generations toward work, leisure, and vocation. Long after it had been secularized and divested of its theological underpinnings, the ideals it helped promote were to endure—among them the notion of labor as the rendering of a social service, the concept of work as a source of personal identity, vocation as self-fulfillment, a stress on competitive advancement and upward socioeconomic mobility (the "Horatio Alger" myth), and, not incidentally, a lingering distrust of leisure as a waste of time.

From the very outset, most Americans approved of the emphasis upon the practical in education. Part of the reason why demands for vocational training struck so responsive a chord stemmed from popular recognition of the fact that "fancy book larnin'" had had little to do with success in carving out a civilization in the wilderness of a new world. Survival in a sometimes harsh and demanding environment, it was realized, had not depended on how much formal education a settler had acquired. Nor, in a land of boundless opportunity, did success in achieving material wealth hinge on the possession of academic credentials. Furthermore, most immigrants traced their ancestry from the underprivileged classes of Europe, and had come to America lacking (with some important exceptions) any tradition of learning or scholarship of their own. Most, in fact, were deeply suspicious of forms of education heretofore monopolized by a privileged aristocratic elite.

Hence the widespread tendency was to react with derision and scorn to the pretensions of the learned few. That reaction was to manifest itself as a form of popular anti-intellectualism disdainful of "bookish" knowledge. For Andrew Carnegie, to cite one well-known example of the archetypal self-made man, the term "academic" was practically synonymous with "useless." In a typical comment, Carnegie was heard to denounce the study of Greek and Latin as of no more practical value than the learning of Choctaw. Considering the prevailing climate of opinion, appeals for an education having immediate and tangible benefits were bound to command a sympathetic hearing.

Concern for the formal practical education of the working classes thus arose at an early date in American history. Thomas Budd, a devout Quaker, was among the first (1685) to submit that there should be public schools established to teach useful trades and handwork skills. In 1745 the Moravians opened an industrial school near Philadelphia, which proved to be only the first of many founded throughout the eighteenth century. Benjamin Rush (1745–1813), a physician from the Philadelphia area and one of the original signers of the Declaration of Independence, applauded the growing number of vocationally oriented schools of his day, and is credited with persuading Dr. John de la Howe, of Abbeville, South Carolina, to bequeath a large tract of land for an agricultural school in 1797, the first such institution of its kind in the fledgling republic.

Well before the end of the eighteenth century, the rising merchant and trading classes were pressing for an education more appropriate to their interests. Trade, commerce, and business required skills in modern languages, navigation, surveying, and accounting. The response came through private venture schools, where business and commercial subjects such as bookkeeping, drawing, and other courses more relevant to practical pursuits than Latin and Greek were emphasized. Unfettered by tradition and free to experiment, offering instruction wherever there was a demand and the ability to pay, entrepreneurial commercial schools offered daytime classes, evening schools, even correspondence courses, for both sexes alike. It was the most popular secondary-level instruction available throughout the 1700s and early 1800s.

The nineteenth century brought a steady increase in private trade schools, mechanical and agricultural institutes, and industrial colleges. Numerous attempts were made in the early decades to open elementary trade schools where pauper children might learn a craft. In 1825, for example, the Welsh industrialist and emigré Robert Owen, whose sponsorship of schools in connection with his model textile mills had attracted widespread attention, introduced a manual-arts curriculum in his experimental schools at New Harmony, Indiana. Although Owen's experiment was short-lived, it too offered one possible blueprint for the future.

By the 1820s, societies of mechanics whose charitable purposes included provision for schools began appearing throughout the country. The Boston Asylum and Farm School, for example, founded in 1814, was devoted to the education of orphaned boys. Each student selected practical work and study in one of several trades, in addition to a basic academic course. Similar in character were the charity schools begun in 1821 under the sponsorship of the General Society of Mechanics and Tradesmen. Also important during the same period were lyceums and mechanics' institutes, of which the Gardiner Lyceum, founded in 1823, and the American Lyceum of the Science and the Arts, first proposed by Josiah Holbrook in 1826, were typical.

Mechanics' institutes directed their attention primarily to the vocational needs of their members, following a pattern first popularized in England and later imported into the United States. Most prominent among them were the Franklin Institute, which was established in Philadelphia in 1824; the Maryland Institute for the Promotion of the Mechanic Arts, founded in Baltimore two years later; the Ohio Mechanics Institute of Cincinnati, which opened in 1828; and the San Francisco Mechanics Institute, begun in 1854.

The manual-labor movement gave rise to a number of institutions in the United States, all of which attempted to meet the needs of the farmer and the mechanic. Besides academic studies, each student enrolled worked in a local shop or factory whose owner reimbursed the institution for the student's services. The theory was that this combination of studies and labor contributed to the development of better citizens while reducing the expense of obtaining an education. The Oneida Institute of New York was perhaps the best-known example of this type of work-study school. Other so-called manual-labor seminaries founded prior to 1830 included the Fellenberg Institute, in Windsor, Connecticut, the Genesee Manual Labor School, and Yates Polytechnic, both in New York. Dozens of others appeared in Illinois, Michigan, and adjoining states.

In the postwar period renewed attention was given to trade schools, of which the first was probably the private Hampton Institute, organized in 1868 by General Samuel Chapman Armstrong in an effort to combine manual training with the elements of a liberal education for blacks. Its most famous student was Booker T. Washington. The first school to offer specific trade training with supplementary studies directly related to each trade was the New York Trade School, founded by Colonel Richard Tylden Auchmuty in 1881. Training was offered in carpentry, bricklaying, plumbing, plastering, printing, tailoring, and stonecutting. Any male over seventeen years of age was eligible to enroll for both preemployment instruction and part-time evening instruction. Auchmuty urged the creation of similar schools elsewhere, arguing that the modern factory system had rendered conventional apprenticeship training obsolete.

Auchmuty also made no effort to conceal his anti-union bias. His claim was that labor unions under the control of "foreigners" were conspiring to limit on-site apprenticeship opportunities and thereby exclude "native American boys" from the trades.[5] Among the many benefactors of the school who shared Auchmuty's concern was J. Pierpont Morgan, who provided a generous endowment in 1892. Labor unions, fearful for their control over apprenticeship training, were understandably threatened by the growing network of these private trade schools, terming them "breeding schools for scabs or rats."[6]

The first agricultural high school was established by the University of Minnesota in 1888, followed by a similar institution at the University of Nebraska, and then by others in Alabama, Wisconsin, Pennsylvania, and New Jersey. According to a report appearing in the 1899 Yearbook of the U.S. Department of Agriculture, "There are a few private schools in which agricultural subjects are taught. There is some agitation in favor of the introduction of agriculture in the public schools, but no definite movement in this direction has as yet been attempted." Later, in the same Yearbook, it was observed, "Throughout the century efforts have been made from time to time to introduce instruction in agriculture into the common schools." In the writer's judgment, "these efforts have uniformly failed."[7]

More successful by far were private schools where skilled industrial workers could be trained. The relationship between the social and economic well-being of society and a skilled labor force was repeatedly enunciated throughout the latter half of the 1800s by such leaders as Calvin M. Woodward, Dean of the Polytechnic School of Washington University, and John D. Runkle, President of the Massachusetts Institute of Technology. Added impetus for institutions like Woodward's famous St. Louis Manual Training School came through the influence of Victor Della Vos, of the Russian Imperial Technical School in Moscow, whose system for training mechanics was demonstrated with much accompanying fanfare at the 1876 Centennial Exposition in Philadelphia.

In many cities, manual-training programs for both sexes in schools emulated contemporary Finnish and Swedish efforts to combine work and learning. The so-called Sloyd system was first popularized among public-school teachers in Boston by Gustaf Larsson; within a relatively short period the Sloyd system had been adopted in experimental manual-arts training courses in the upper grades of elementary schools throughout the Northeast.

Business and industry often took the lead in establishing technical and mechanical schools for full-time day students and part-time evening students, the first of which was founded in 1872 by R. H. Hoe and Company, a leading manufacturer of printing presses. Corporations such as General Electric, Westinghouse, Baldwin Locomotive Works, Pratt and Whitney, Western Electric, International Harvester, and Goodyear were in the forefront of a movement to organize plant schools for machinists and other skilled workers. Wealthy financiers often joined in the establishment of endowed trade schools along the lines of Auchmuty's New York Trade School, helping to found Philadelphia's Williamson Free School of Mechanical Trades (1888), the Baron de Hirsch Trade School of Mechanical Arts (1895), the Hebrew Technical Institution in New York City (1883), the California School of Mechanical Arts (1895), and the Manhattan Trade School for Girls (1901).

Increasingly, as high schools assumed greater importance as extensions of the lower common elementary schools rather than simply as preparatory institutions for postsecondary education, efforts were made to open public trade schools offering vocational curricula for those not intending to extend their education in a college or university. W. T. Barnard, in the Eighth Annual Report of the U.S. Commissioner of Labor warned in 1892, "Skilled labor must be had from some source, and we cannot afford to import it in bulk, if for no other reason than its expensiveness. Our own people have the first claim upon our industrial occupations, but if we are to compete for foreign trade they must be so trained as to make and keep them, in knowledge and skill, at least the equals of foreign workmen."[8]

By the 1880s and 1890s, popular sentiment was growing for publicly supported vocational training. Coincident with the expansion of student enrollments in secondary schools, pressures mounted for the inclusion of more practical subjects in the curriculum: domestic arts and homemaking, drawing, accounting and bookkeeping, manual arts, and other industry-related training. Separate public schools for trade instruction of the period included New York City's Boys' Vocational School, the Brooklyn School for Boys, and several others.

Typical of sentiment at the turn of the century was A. D. Dean's comment: "It is surely the day of specialization, the day of special training for everyone engaged in professional life; and why not training for what are called the humbler callings of life?" The writer went on to report,

> There is a growing demand on the part of people that the public schools should fit pupils more effectively for life than they are now doing. Although this demand by the people is not recognized in many educational theories, it remains true that there is an ever increasing feeling among many of our successful business and professional men that an educational system that sends its graduates into the world without the means of earning a living is lacking in a most vital way.[9]

In American higher education, interest in agricultural and industrial education was an early development. By 1850s public support for college-based vocational preparation had led numerous organizations, particularly farmers' associations, to pressure state legislatures for action. Jonathan Baldwin Turner, of Illinois College, spoke for many in urging the establishment of institutions that would relate the study of physical sciences with practical experimentation on farms. "All civilized society," Turner avowed, "is, necessarily, divided into two distinct cooperative, not antagonistic classes: a small class, whose business is . . . the true principles of religion, law, medicine, science, art, and literature; and a much larger class who are engaged in some form of labor in agriculture, commerce, and the arts."[10]

The larger class, Turner estimated, accounted for 95 percent of the nation's total population. It was manifestly unfair and unwise to neglect the educational needs of the "industrial classes," he argued, while making full provision for the academic training of the few. His proposal was for the establishment of an "industrial university" in each state, financed in part by federal aid derived from the sale of public lands.

Turner's plan attracted widespread attention, and agricultural groups in Illinois supported the idea enthusiastically. Intensive lobbying in Washington between 1853 and 1857 eventually led to the introduction of enabling legislation signed into law by President Lincoln in July of 1862. The first Morrill Act "donating public lands to the several states and territories which may provide colleges for the benefit of agriculture and the mechanic arts" called for land grants to the states, proceeds from the sale of which would provide endowments for the support of colleges emphasizing agricultural and mechanical training. A second Morrill Act in 1890 authorized further funding for land-grant colleges.

Sometimes the resulting institutions were autonomous units; more frequently they were assimilated to existing state universities. The latter was the case in Maine (1865), Illinois and West Virginia (1867), California (1868), Nebraska (1869), Ohio (1870), and Arkansas (1871). Passage of the Morrill Acts marked a significant milestone in the university movement. Not only did these acts serve to increase greatly the number of state-controlled schools; they forever changed the character of collegiate institutions. The dominance of postsecondary schooling by traditionalists to all intents and purposes was over. Henceforth, state colleges and universities would include a wide range of practical, vocationally relevant courses of instruction in their curricula. The animating spirit of the land-grant institution was most clearly articulated by Andrew Sloan Draper, president of the University of Illinois between 1894 and 1904. "Obviously, the American university, as no other university in the world," he wrote, "must regard the life and especially the employment of the people. . . . It must guard all the professions; and it must strive to aid all the industries. . . . It must stand for work, for work of hand as well as of head, where all toil is alike honorable and all worth is based upon respect for it." [11]

## THE OPENING OF A DEBATE

Much discussion around the turn of the century centered on the question of whether private enterprise or the public schools should assume the major share of the responsibility for expanding job preparation. Businessmen themselves were divided on the issue, although all were agreed on the need for more formal and extensive vocational training. Many favored public-school-based training, if only because they saw in such programs a possible opportunity for breaking a long-standing union monopoly on apprenticeships. [12] To the extent that labor restricted entry into the trades in order to keep wages up, certain industrialists were anxious to see public education offer an alternative system of job training and thereby help depress labor costs. As the president of the National Association of Manufacturers was to admit frankly in 1910, "Trade schools . . . [are] more and more demanded as a means of recruiting the ranks of skilled mechanics . . . as well as to checkmate militant organized labor on its policy of obstructing the free employment of apprentices." [13]

The response from organized labor to calls for school-based vocational training was ambivalent. On the one hand, unions supported better work preparation in that it promised to better the lot of their members. On the other, labor leaders distrusted business motives and opposed vocational instruction outside the factories when it threatened their own apprenticeship-training programs. Professional educators were also in disagreement over whether formal job preparation should be housed in separate specialized institutions or incorporated within the nation's system of public common schools.

The basic challenge confronting American business and industry as the twentieth century opened was one of expanding markets. The growing fear expressed was that the nation's capacity for consumption could not increase as rapidly as the pyramiding of production. Hence the trend was to look abroad for overseas export markets. Either industry would be suffocated by overproduction or it had to compete for business in the international arena—it could no longer hide behind the protection of a tariff system. As one historian summarized the problem: "The logic was clear. Lack of markets led to overproduction. Overproduction led to depression. Depression led to social chaos and the prospect of endemic class conflict. The solutions, then, to business prosperity and social and class harmony were new and expanded markets, no matter how secured." [14]

A direct link between the problem of export markets and schools existed in the minds of many industrialists; and their decision to promote vocational training was a key component in a concerted drive to win a role for American industry in the growing competition for world markets. Previously, the secondary school had been a luxury for most people. Workers had no need for a degree, except for schoolteaching, bookkeeping, and certain clerical occupations. As late as the 1890s it had still made little economic sense to attend a high school, since a diploma conferred no special advantage in seeking employment. This was the situation business leaders were resolved to change.

The paramount need, it was felt, was for a trained work force, reasonably disciplined, and available at an acceptable cost—which was precisely what schools could supply. By the early 1900s, manufacturers were convinced they had found in German education a blueprint or model to be followed for securing a more effective labor force. Corporate leaders of finance and industry therefore were resolved to enter the arena of school reform, interjecting themselves into what a contemporary observer of the period referred to as "the deluge of discussion [that] has overspread the entire world of secondary education." [15]

One of the earliest and most powerful voices demanding that schools teach skills needed by industry was the National Association of Manufacturers (NAM). In 1898 its president warned that the Germans were now emerging as America's chief competitors in the export markets. His claim was that Germany's industrial prowess was based directly on a system of technical and vocational schools. If industrial training could be transferred from the factory to public high schools, the resulting gain in industrial efficiency, he predicted, would enable manufacturers to compete more successfully.

American workers, NAM President Search emphasized, needed more and better formal technical training. If American workmanship was to be upgraded, classical and literary studies in high schools and colleges would have to give way to more extensive technical and scientific instruction. Traditional subjects had their place, Search conceded, "but it is unfair to the great material interests of the land to leave out of account the obvious demands of industry and commerce." Where public education was concerned, the time had come to realize that "considerable sums should be diverted from the main educational channels and put into commercial and technical schools." [16]

Seven years later the First Report of the National Association of Manufacturers' Commission on Industrial Education (1905) sounded the same theme. "The German technical and trade schools are at once the admiration and fear of all countries," the Report bluntly asserted. "In the world's race for commercial supremacy we must copy and improve upon the German method of education. Germany relies chiefly upon her . . . trained workers for her commercial success and prosperity. She puts no limit on the money to be expended in trade and technical education." [17]

The United States, it was said, could afford to do no less. "To authorize and found and organize trade schools in which the youth of our land may be taught the practical and technical knowledge of a trade is the most important issue before the American people today," the Commission's Report asserted. If the miracle of German industry was the product of matching the nation's system of secondary schooling to manufacturers' requirements, no time should be lost in following suit. "The imperative need of the industrial workers and employers of the country is that thorough going systems of industrial education be everywhere established, so that our factories may be constantly better utilized; that standards of skill and output may continuously be improved; and that foreign and domestic markets may be better held and extended." [18]

The crusade to enlarge and extend the scope of training for wage-earning occupations of every kind begun by the National Association of Manufacturers soon began attracting support from other business and labor groups, including the National Farmers' Congress, the United Textile Workers of America, and the national Chamber of Commerce. Political pressure upon state governments to take action grew rapidly. In 1905, for example, the Massachusetts state legislature authorized Governor William L. Douglas to appoint a commission to investigate the need for skill training in that state's industries: "They shall investigate how far the needs are met by existing institutions and shall consider what new forms of educational effort may be advisable." [19]

The Douglas Commission released its final report in June of the year following. Terming existing public schools "too exclusively literary in their spirit, scope, and methods," the Commission argued they "needed to be changed to meet modern industrial and social conditions." It cited widespread interest in vocational training, a lack of skilled workers throughout the state, and the seeming irrelevance of public education to practical, agricultural, and industrial requirements. Cities and towns were urged to "so modify the work in the elementary schools as to include for boys and girls instruction and practice in the elements of productive industry, including agriculture and the mechanic and domestic arts." Elective courses in "principles of agriculture and the domestic and mechanical arts" should be made available in high schools, and the secondary curricula in mathematics, science and drawing, the Report recommended, should be related to applications in local industries.[20]

Also to be established were evening courses for trade workers and part-time day classes for youths between the ages of fourteen and eighteen. The Douglas Commission concluded with a strong endorsement for "a state system of local public industrial schools," partially funded by the state, and administered under separate control from regular schools.[21]

Virtually all of the Commission's recommendations were incorporated in a bill that, once signed into law, created the nation's first dual system of industrial-vocational and regular academic schools.[22] There soon arose a feeling that what was good for the state of Massachusetts might be beneficial for the rest of the nation as well. Several other states promptly followed the lead of Massachusetts, in creating their own programs in industrial and trade training, in education for homemaking, agriculture, and the mechanical arts. Sometimes state programs of vocational training were incorporated within the existing public school system; elsewhere parallel industrial secondary schools were created. (In Massachusetts, however, by 1909 control over vocational schools had been returned under a "unit" system to a board within the state's department of public education.)

Shortly after the release of the Douglas Commission's Report in 1906, James P. Haney, director of art and manual training in New York City's public schools, joined with Charles R. Richards, a professor of manual training at Teachers College, Columbia, and several others, for a meeting at Cooper Union, New York. Some 250 people attended. The purpose of the gathering, it was announced, was to found a National Society for the Promotion of Industrial Education (NSPIE) "to unite the many forces making toward industrial education the country over." Recognizing the political potential of the new society, the National Association of Manufacturers was quick to lend its support and almost immediately became its most active participant and funding source. Henceforth, Haney and Richards explained, the NSPIE would assume a leadership role in bringing "to public attention the importance of industrial education" and promoting "the establishment of institutions for industrial training."[23]

From the very beginning it was apparent that the NSPIE's leaders had correctly estimated the mood of the country. Commenting on the rash of interest in industrial education, New Hampshire's state superintendent of schools declared,

"We are besieged with public documents, monographs, magazine articles, reports of investigations too numerous to mention. . . ."[24] Less than a year after the Society's founding, an expression of support for its objectives was forthcoming from no less than President Theodore Roosevelt himself. In a letter dated May 1907, Roosevelt wrote to NSPIE President Dr. Henry Pritchett: "Our school system has hitherto been well-nigh wholly lacking on the side of industrial training, of the training which fits a man for the shop and the farm." Terming this "a most serious lack," the President emphasized the need to "develop a system under which each individual citizen shall be trained so as to be effective individually as an economic unit. . . ."[25]

The single greatest problem confronting the fledgling NSPIE and its affiliates was how to garner popular support in its call for public schools to assume major responsibility for job preparation. In the aftermath of publicity surrounding the Society's founding and the release of the Douglas Commission Report, the question of vocational training was widely discussed, but it was not yet evident that there existed any mandate for the wholesale overhaul of public education. Practically everyone, however, was agreed that existing public high schools were deficient. Muckrakers, for example, delighted in calling attention to what they considered the failure of secondary schools to move out of the dark ages and adapt to change. Their exclusive emphasis on "culture," vocationalists agreed, might have been appropriate to an earlier era, but literary-academic education was most definitely inappropriate in the modern industrial age. Accordingly, increased emphasis on job training was touted as a remedy. Therein lay a dilemma.

The problem was clear enough. It was plain that sons and daughters of the middle class attending high schools aspired to white-collar employment. Most would never consent to training that led only into the factories. Working-class youngsters, on the other hand, typically dropped out of the system long before they reached high school.[26] The destiny of immigrants' children lay in the necessary but low-paying, semiskilled jobs of the factory sweatshops.[27] The challenge, then, was how to attract and retain those repelled by a traditional secondary-school curriculum without in the process unduly raising their life expectations following graduation. The answer as many saw it lay in industrial education. It would be designed for American working-class youths who would be led away from unskilled and semiskilled occupations into "more wholesome" trades yet who would not harbor ambitions to pursue a college education.

In a sense, vocationalist reformers were attempting the impossible—to lure young workers back into the industrial workplace without making any substantial changes in the work environment and the social conditions that had driven them away in the first place.[28] Labor unions, for example, accepted the thesis that industrial schooling would provide students with training and entry into the better factory jobs, and they recognized that school reform would offer incentives for children to remain in school until they were prepared for skilled factory supervisory positions.[29] Yet the unions were reluctant to support curricular change without qualification or reservation if the inauguration of new programs went unaccompanied by other changes as well. As W. B. Prescott, of the International Typographical Union, warned those assembled at the 1907 NSPIE convention:

> I do not think the establishment of trade or any other sort of schools will induce American boys, of what our manufacturers deem the desirable class, to go into factories and mills. Those who will do so will go unwillingly and as a last resort, as long as the present regime attains. It is not alone inability to work with their hands that keeps the desirable ones out. It is the failure of society at large and especially a class of employers—to recognize the dignity of labor. . . . The mechanic is being lowered in social esteem as a result of iniquitous shop rules, and boys with spirit and red blood in their veins will not submit to such tyrannies. So, Messieurs Employers, if you want the flower of American youth to follow industrial pursuits you will have to treat them less like prisoners of necessity and more like men. . . . Until you do, it is my belief you will look in vain for American boys to enter your factories as willing workers.[30]

Labor leaders had other misgivings too. Besides fearing that vocational education would undercut their own diminishing role in worker training and certification, they looked with suspicion on business enthusiasm for a separate vocational school system. If the German model was followed, they asked, would programs be "administered by the same authority and agency which administers our public school systems," or would there be a return to class-divided schooling along the lines of the European pattern? Following lengthy discussion, the American Federation of Labor appointed its own committee on industrial education to investigate these and other issues. At the 1908 AFL convention, a resolution was introduced and adopted, which observed in part as follows:

> There are two groups with opposite methods, and seeking antagonistic ends, now advocating industrial education in the United States. . . . One of these groups is largely composed of the non-union employers of the country who advance industrial education as a special privilege under conditions that educate the student or apprentice to non-union sympathies and prepare him as a skilled worker for scab labor, thus using the children of the workers against the interests of their organized fathers and brothers in the various crafts. . . . This group also favors the training of the student or apprentice for skill in only one industrial process, thus making the graduate a skilled worker in only a very limited sense and rendering him nearly helpless if lack of employment comes in his single subdivision of a craft. . . .
> The other group is composed of great educators, enlightened representatives of organized labor and persons engaged in genuine social service, who advocate industrial education as a common right to be open to all children on equal terms to be provided by general taxation and kept under the control of the whole people with a method or system of education that will make the apprentice or graduate a skilled craftsman, in all the branches of the trade.[31]

Eventually, the AFL and the other labor groups elected to join ranks with those urging the establishment of school-based industrial-training programs, but only if they were administered through the public-school system. John Mitchell, who chaired the AFL's Commission in a 1910 report, for example, took the position that if technical and industrial training for workers had become a public necessity, it should properly be offered through public institutions. Trade schools, separate from the general school system, might all too easily deny some students access and thereby frustrate their hopes for upward socioeconomic mobility—the great American dream.[32] By the same token, organized labor put business and industry on notice that its continued endorsement of industrial programs would depend on what sort of instruction was offered.

The AFL Committee on Education, in its 1915 report, underscored its "apprehension that this proposed industrial education may ultimately give way to an attempt on the part of large commercial interests [to restrict] opportunities of the workers' children for a more general education," and in so doing making those children "more submissive and less independent" workers. "It is not only essential that we should fit our boys and girls for the industries, but it is equally essential to fit the industries for the future employment of our young men and women." The Committee emphasized that it did not want children turned out "as machine-made products fitted only to work and to become part and parcel of a machine instead of human beings with a life of their own." Labor was willing to endorse industry's demands for schools to serve practical purposes, but it appreciated the hazards of going too far and simply turning public education into a docile servant for meeting business and industrial needs. The report ended up affirming the importance of general education over vocational training for safeguarding against any such eventuality.[33]

The torrent of debate over industrial education caught many professional educators unawares. "No single topic," a speaker at a 1907 meeting of the National Education Association (NEA) commented, "has engaged the attention of educational conventions more frequently, during the past two years, than has this topic of industrial education. Certainly there is no question which has been so insistently urged as being of immediate and vital concern to the country at large."[34]

So much did the topic monopolize discussion that the following year the NEA joined the AFL and NAM in appointing its own "Committee on the Place of Industries in Public Education." The Committee's 1910 report acknowledged "the remarkable interest in industrial education," which it characterized as "the dominant factor in the educational thought of the country." Educators, alleged Jesse D. Burke, who chaired the committee, should take "immediate, cooperative action" with other interested groups in the reform of public schools. Frank T. Carlton, a professor of economics and history at Michigan's Albion College, however, in the same report sounded a warning:

> Today one class of men who are insistently urging that the public school emphasize industrial and trade education, do so because they wish an increased supply of workers who are mere workers or human automatons. Many influential employers in the United States are demanding in no uncertain tones that the public schools be utilized to turn out narrowly trained industrial workers who may become passive links in the great industrial mechanism of the present age. Systematization and specialization are the favorite watchwords of this class. The application of factory methods to the school is demanded in the name of efficiency and economy. Standardization, not individual treatment, is the ideal of the businessman.[35]

Captains of business and industry, Carlton alleged, wanted to convert public education into a training ground for apprentices. Others believed that "the public school system should train efficient workers who are also thinking men and women capable of enjoying art, literature, and leisure, and who will be able to intelligently consider the political and social problems which will inevitably arise in the twentieth century." As he characterized the latter faction, they demanded that "a well-rounded development be given each child, and that each student be prepared for useful and efficient work in the community." [36] The two viewpoints, he claimed, were almost diametrically opposed to each other. The first group was united in its objectives. The second, however, seemed divided as to the proper scope or character of instructional programs in schools. Following the line adopted at the AFL's 1908 convention, Carlton advised educators to endorse the perspective of the latter; and he urged caution in how industrial education was introduced into schools:

> Vocational training must be indissolubly linked with other forms of training which will broaden the outlook of the student, which will make him a citizen as well as an efficient worker with hand or brain. The aim of modern education should be, if the aim be anything more than the production of a nicely articulated industrial system, to produce men, not machines. [37]

## THE BEGINNINGS OF THE VOCATIONAL-GUIDANCE MOVEMENT

Other educators rejected Carlton's plea for caution as misconceived. Charles A. Prosser, for example, executive secretary of the NSPIE, saw the schools' task in simple, forthright terms. It was, he insisted repeatedly, "to direct and train all the children of all the people for useful service," Andrew S. Draper, Commissioner of Education for the State of New York, likewise pleaded before the NEA in 1908 for trade schools containing "nothing which naturally leads away from the shop." Their sole function, Draper avowed, was "to train workmen to do better work that they may earn more bread and butter." [38] As judged by efficiency criteria, Prosser judged existing public education to be an abysmal failure. Addressing the NEA in 1912, he contended:

> Misfits in all vocations confront us everywhere. Many workers are inefficient because they are not adapted to the work they are doing and some because they have not been properly prepared for it. This lack of efficiency constitutes a permanent handicap not only to the worker but to the calling which he follows. It means lessened wage, uncertain employment, failure of promotion, economic struggle, waste in the use of material, poor workmanship, reduced output, and the lowering of the standards of skill and workmanship of American industries. [39]

It was not enough, Prosser and other like-minded critics argued, simply to overhaul school curricula. While applauding the expansion of the courses of study to include such vocational subjects as bookkeeping, commercial arithmetic, stenography, typing, commercial law, business correspondence, mechanical drawing, woodwork, ironwork, pattern-making, and home-making or domestic arts, critics argued that far more extensive reforms were needed.[40]

For former Harvard President Charles W. Eliot, the remedy was obvious and clear-cut. In a 1908 speech delivered before the NSPIE, he expressed his belief that industrial education "ought to mean trade schools, and nothing but trade schools; that is, schools directed primarily and expressly to the preparation of young men and women for trades"—either full- or part-time institutions operated entirely outside of the public school system. At the same time he argued for a major new function for public elementary education:

> But how shall the decision be made that certain children will go into the mechanic arts high schools? Where is that decision to be made? . . . Here we come upon a new function for the teachers in our elementary schools, and in my judgment they have no function more important. The teachers of the elementary schools ought to sort the pupils and sort them by their evident or probable destinies.[41]

Eliot subsequently qualified his support for a dual school system, dropping his proposal for identifying probable career prospects in the lower primary grades and the channeling of prospective workers into separate trade schools. But he never abandoned his belief that a variety of elective shop and commercial courses should be offered in the upper elementary grades. He also continued to feel that career choice and training should begin as early as possible. In no event should it be postponed beyond the age of sixteen. He further contended that students in vocational schools were more highly motivated than those in general courses of instruction; and he urged teacher appreciation for the "life-career motive" in students as a way of providing a focus for interest.[42]

Many educators were pleased at Eliot's reversal of support for separate trade schools. The NSPIE, however, continued to favor his original plan for early career selection and sorting in the elementary grades by "probable destiny." Prosser, for one, was insistent on the point that children's aptitudes and interests should be identified as early as possible in life. Once pupils were grouped along likely career lines, they could be given practical training for maximally efficient employment, according to industry's specific requirements. He, in common with many other "hard-core" vocationalists, remained skeptical of any approach that purported to integrate practical job-training with some broader, more general type of educational experience.[43]

The appearance in 1911 of Frederick Taylor's famous *Principles of Management* triggered a new wave of criticism directed against the economic inefficiency and lack of scientific management allegedly typical in American public education.[44] In their crusade to apply business and industrial values to education—to put the operation of schools on a "sound, businesslike basis," as some phrased it—efficiency experts aspired to nothing less than a total revamping of schools so as to permit them to mirror more effectively the job requirements of American business and manufacturing.

Once again, the German model of an efficient, hierarchical school structure supporting an unprecedented level of economic productivity was held up for admiration. Frank E. Spaulding, for example, in a speech before a 1913 convention of school superintendents in Philadelphia, avowed, "Academic discussion of educational issues is as futile as it is fascinating. Which is more valuable, a course in Latin or a course in machine shop?" His response was to let monetary considerations decide. If more pupil recitations in English than in Greek could be purchased for the same amount of money, he advised his listeners "to purchase no more Greek instruction."[45]

Anticipating his critics, Spaulding declared, "Let us waste no time over the obvious but fruitless objection that the ultimate and real products of a school system—those products that are registered in the minds and hearts of the children that go out from the schools—are immeasurable, and hence incomparable."[46] Confident that "scientific management" techniques as developed for business by Taylor would prove effective in education, Spaulding joined with such self-professed "educational engineers" as William H. Allen, Franklin Bobbitt, James P. Munroe, and Ellwood P. Cubberley in urging the employment of efficiency criteria in school management and administration.

Cubberly, to cite another example, was unalterably convinced that completely "objective" standards should govern the work of public education. "Our schools," he claimed in a now-famous metaphor, "are, in a sense, factories in which the raw products (children) are to be shaped and fashioned into products to meet the various demands of life. The specifications for manufacturing come from the demands of twentieth-century civilization, and it is the business of the school to build its pupils according to the specifications laid down."[47] James Munroe, a leading Boston industrialist and later NSPIE president, arguing in much the same vein, asserted at a Society meeting in November of 1911 that the introduction of industrial education in the nation's elementary schools could undoubtedly reduce what he termed "the inconceivable waste of our human resources."

Munroe reviewed for his audience the situation as he saw it—the need for more skills in industry, the inadequacy of existing training programs, a high-school drop-out rate exceeding ninety percent, the floundering of youth who did leave schools lacking entry-level skills for the trades, the tendency of drop-outs to drift into trouble with the law or to fall into despair, the dead-end jobs to which otherwise potentially productive workers were consigned, the waste to business resulting from rapid job turnover, the surplus of undereducated workers who lacked opportunities for retraining in an era of rapid technological change, and the consequent threat to continued national prosperity. His conclusion was that the time had arrived for seeking better ways of meshing workers' interests and skills with the needs of the marketplace. What was needed, according to Munroe, was a comprehensive system of vocational guidance counseling in schools along with skill-training programs.[48]

Prosser, speaking before the NEA in 1912, offered the thesis that scientific vocational guidance was the natural handmaiden of vocational education in "fitting the great mass of our people for useful employment." Over the next decade he was to assume a leading role in supporting the new vocational-guidance movement, which, as he saw it, had as its sole and exclusive aim the preparation of students for employment. He had little patience with such critics as Owen R. Lovejoy, Secretary of the National Child Labor Committee, whose views differed sharply from his own. Lovejoy, for example, had strongly criticized "captains of industry" who said, "'Here are the jobs: what kind of children have you to offer?'" Educators, he stressed, should reverse the inquiry and ask of business, "'Here are your children, what kind of industry have you to offer?'"

Even among those who supported both vocational training and guidance in schools, there were critics who felt Munroe, Prosser, and others had adopted too extreme a position in the name of social efficiency. In objecting to the notion of vocational guidance as simply a matter of adapting people to slots within the industrial system, Meyer Bloomfield, director of the Boston Vocation Bureau, asked: "While the authorities are given increasing resources to train their charges for the demands of modern vocational life, should they not be likewise empowered to deal with abuse and misapplication of society's expensively trained product?" A "searching evaluation of occupations must also be undertaken," he believed. "The job, too, should be made to give an account of itself. The desirable occupations must be studied and better prepared for; the dull and deadly being classified in a rogue's gallery of their own. Then only can reciprocal purpose mark the relation between employer and employee."[49]

Even Frank Parsons, the acknowledged father of the guidance movement, had misgivings about the advisability of concentrating solely on narrow job training to the exclusion of all else. "Book work should be balanced with industrial education," he advised, "and working children should spend part time in cultural classes and industrial science. Society should make it possible for every boy and girl to secure at least a high-school education and an industrial training at the same time."[50] Eugene Davenport, speaking at the NEA's 1909 national convention, echoed Parsons's proposal with a call for secondary-school students to spend at least one-quarter of their time in general education courses besides their vocational studies. "In this way," he explained, "we should have a single system of education under a single management, but giving to all young men and women really two educations; one that is vocational, fitting them to be self-supporting and useful, the other nonvocational and looking to their development."[51]

## PROGRESSIVIST AND EFFICIENCY REFORMERS: ISSUES OF INTENT AND CONTROL

Well before the close of the new century's first decade, it was already apparent that the motives of those behind the vocationalist movement in education differed greatly. Advocates of social efficiency, such as Prosser, wanted simply to retool schools to service the nation's economic system. Groups such as the National Association of Manufacturers, and the National Society for the Promotion of Industrial Education were primarily interested in practical job training, and they were willing to be pragmatic about how it was achieved—through curricular reforms in existing public schools, by means of new trade institutions administered through the public educational system, or, if it could be shown to be cost-effective and more efficient, through industrial trade schools operated separate and apart from public education entirely.

Of the three alternatives, the second—a dual educational system at public expense—claimed the loyalty of a growing majority of vocationalist reformers. Together with an efficient career-sorting arrangement based upon scientific vocational-guidance programs, they believed, America could equal if not exceed the industrial productivity of the much-feared German economic miracle.

David Snedden, Massachusetts's Commissioner of Education, in 1914 placed himself on record in favor of a separate system for vocational education. "The vocational school," he declared, "should divest itself as completely as possible of the academic atmosphere, and should reproduce as fully as possible the atmosphere of economic endeavor in the field for which it trains." [52] By this time the National Association of Manufacturers had also dropped its earlier allegiance to privately supported trade schools and had endorsed the idea of trade training at public expense. It too favored a dual system of public administrative control.

For most educators, however, the notion of separate vocational schools was anathema. It seemed outrageously at odds with the common school ideal, with its promise of classless education for all, producing socially mobile, self-reliant, and informed citizens instead of compliant hired hands. Not only was it undemocratic, but, if a dual arrangement were adopted, critics predicted, it would ultimately split the social fabric altogether. [53] Less often cited in opposition were educators' apprehensions about the prospect of a schooling system functioning beyond the sphere of their own control.

George Herbert Mead expressed a common view when he reiterated allegiance to the ideal of common schooling. "A democratic education," he insisted,

> must hold together the boys and girls of the whole community; it must give them the common education that all should receive, so diversifying its work that the needs of each group may be met within the institution whose care and generous ideals shall permeate the specialized courses, while the more academic schooling may be vivified by the vocational motive that gives needed impulse to study which may be otherwise, or even deadening. [54]

Frank Leavitt, of the University of Chicago, in common with Mead, felt the unitary character of common public schooling was worth preserving, and he saw no antagonism with the nation's need for a trained work force. [55]

Nevertheless, there were deep and abiding differences separating proponents of social efficiency from humanitarian progressivist reformers. Much of the rhetoric of the period served to conceal the fundamental incommensurability of their interests. But something of the underlying antagonism surfaced in an address delivered by Jane Addams at the 1908 NSPIE convention. Addams, a leader of the settlement-house movement and founder of Chicago's renowned Hull House, supported the inclusion of industrial education within public schools. She also challenged the assumption that industrial education is one thing and cultural education is of necessity another.[56] Convinced that general education could benefit greatly if informed by the study of the social, intellectual and technological changes marking production processes in an industrial era, she declared:

> Modern industry embodies tremendous human activities, inventions, constructive imaginations and records. . . . Every factory filled with complicated machines has in it the possibilities of enormous cultural value if educators have the ability to bring out the long history, the human as well as the mechanical development, which it represents. It is this cultural aspect of industrial training which is applicable to these boys of fourteen who are not yet fit to earn their living.[57]

Unlike "classicists," who resisted any move toward practical or vocational additions to public school curricula, Addams felt general academic instruction could be vitalized by industrial education—with one major caveat. Schools, she advised, should take advantage of students' natural interest in the world of work in order to enrich their understanding of commerce and industrial production. She was further willing to have youths gain real-life work experience. "To live intelligently in an industrial community and to interpret it in terms of culture," she explained, "we must have educated people who know it from the standpoint of technique." But she was utterly opposed to having schools concentrate exclusively on training for those specific job competencies immediately useful for employment.[58]

Frank Tracy Carlton voiced similar opposition to "factory-stage" education, in which children were processed by educational machinery to fit predetermined slots in a mass-production system.[59] He rejected as false and misleading the metaphor of education as a business enterprise whose goal was to cut costs and raise production:

> Children are not pots and pans to be shaped by patterns sent down from a central office. Teachers are not drudges to be ordered about by a master mechanic. Education is an artistic form of industry; its normal product leads to imperfect output. The teacher is a skilled workman, or more accurately, an artist. Methods must vary with teachers; crowded classrooms, systematic and numerous reports bound up in red tape, clock-like precision and central office management convert the school into a factory. Commercialization of the school hampers and drives out the efficient teacher and spoils the child.[60]

Stung by critics, David Snedden redoubled efforts to defend his doctrine of social efficiency and the recommendations for school practice that flowed from it. He was unalterably convinced that the growth of corporate-urban industrialism had been an unalloyed good, a forward step in the march of human progress. Against those such as Addams and Carlton who feared the mechanization and depersonalization of social life brought on by industrialization, Snedden pointed out that the higher standard of living enjoyed by most people had been achieved and was rendered possible only by modern production methods. He admitted that the factory system had condemned many to fragmented, routinized jobs. Yet this was outweighed, in his judgment, by the fact that people lived longer, more comfortably, and enjoyed far greater leisure. In his opinion, the application of mass-production methods to school life had already proven itself:

> Quantity production methods applied in education speedily gave us school grades, uniform textbooks, promotional examinations, systems of hand writing, college admission standards, nine-month school years, certification of teachers, strictly scheduled programs, mechanical discipline and hundreds of other mechanisms most of which are unavoidably necessary if our ideals of universal education are to be realized.[61]

Snedden felt it was a happy coincidence that human beings could be sorted by ability levels paralleling the hierarchical work requirements of modern society. Employing new diagnostic and assessment instruments, children could be channeled into the sort of training programs for which they were best fitted and by means of which they would ultimately fulfill themselves as individuals and so benefit the larger social order. He concluded that beyond the first few elementary grades, differentiated education should commence, based on pupils' differing capacities and "probable destinies":

> Three different kinds of differences are recognizable among children with reference to the extent and kind of education . . . they should receive. These are based on (a) native capacity, including strong interests and tastes; (b) economic conditions of the family and its capacity to support the child during the period of its higher education; and (c) probable educational destination.[62]

A realistic assessment of individual differences, in Snedden's opinion, would cause recognition that academic aptitude was only partly a function of genetic endowment. Socioeconomic influences were equally important determinants. On practical grounds, most schoolchildren were destined for commercial-business employment or factory jobs. The most efficient arrangement therefore was to offer them the specific kind of preparatory training they would need, preferably in separate business-trade schools.

Whether or not industrial education programs should be administered under a dual or unit system remained a divisive issue; and the debate for and against separately administered industrial schooling was waged continuously at educators' meetings. At the NEA's 1914 annual convention, for example, in a widely publicized debate, Snedden confronted William Chandler Bagley, then a young professor at the University of Illinois, on the question as to whether humanitarian democratic values could be reconciled with the needs of the industrial system within the same social order. As might be expected, the two construed the issue quite differently.

The thrust of Snedden's argument was that opponents of efficiency had missed the basic point. The real and pressing need, he alleged, was *not* to integrate or synthesize liberal learning and industrial knowledge within the general curriculum. The issue was *not* whether schoolchildren should acquire deeper understanding of the role of industry, business, and technology in modern life—that much could be taken for granted. The most fundamental question, one certain enthusiasts of industrial training appeared to gloss over in their concern to incorporate it as another element of liberalized education, was that its chief end was employment and the economic self-sufficiency a job provides. In short, the issue was not whether youth should learn *about* industry, but whether schools should train them *for* industrial pursuits. It was Snedden's heartfelt belief that this concern could be safeguarded adequately only by a separate system of vocational schools.

Bagley claimed in response that a dual schooling system with separate trade institutions was a sure prescription for social stratification. Weighing the choice between industrial efficiency and democratic education, Bagley aligned himself on the side of common public schooling. He also felt sure public opinion was behind him. "A stratified society and a permanent proletariat are undoubtedly the prime conditions of a certain type of national efficiency," he alleged. "But wherever our people have been intelligently informed regarding what this type of efficiency costs, they have been fairly unanimous in declaring that the price is too high." [63]

## DEWEY ON VOCATIONALISM

As John Dewey saw it, the burgeoning vocationalist movement had the potential to reform public education, making schooling more democratic and more relevant to the realities of the twentieth century. Yet he was deeply disturbed over what he saw as the narrow utilitarianism of such vocational educators as Prosser and Snedden, and was later outraged when his writings were quoted in support of their views, which he sharply distinguished from his own. He consistently refused to be "for" or "against" vocational education until its context and aims were carefully defined. As early as 1913 he was warning against the potential danger he foresaw in pressures to vocationalize the schools:

> The question of industrial education is fraught with consequences for the future of democracy. Its right development will do more to make public education truly democratic than any other one agency now under consideration. Its wrong treatment will as surely accentuate all undemocratic tendencies in our present situation, by fostering and strengthening class divisions in school and out. [64]

The most obvious "wrong treatment" encouraging "undemocratic tendencies," he claimed, was the proposal to separate industrial schooling from public education. This he termed "the greatest evil now threatening the interests of democracy in education." Once removed from public control, Dewey predicted, vocational schools would be taken over lock, stock, and barrel by business industrialists and converted into job-training centers operated with public tax funds. A bifurcated public school system would not only be an insult to the American people but "a direct danger to the future of American democracy."[65]

Dewey characterized the issue as a question of whether the school system should be split so that "a sharp line of cleavage shall be drawn as respects administrative control, studies, methods and personal associations of pupils, between schools of the traditional literary type and schools of a trade-preparatory type."[66] He anticipated numerous evil consequences if that cleavage were permitted, the most important of which would be to accentuate the separation, division, and polarization of pupils along class lines. He feared too the influence manufacturers would exert over children isolated in trade schools, ostensibly protected from "subversive ideas" allegedly fostered in the public schools. As Dewey depicted them, more than a few captains of business and industry were already notorious for their reactionary views, and many of them allegedly looked upon the public schools as hotbeds of socialism and bolshevism.[67]

Far from seeking to dovetail vocational education with industry, Dewey indicated that "the kind of vocational education in which I am interested is not one which will 'adapt' workers to the existing industrial regime; I am not sufficiently in love with the regime for that." He continued, "It seems to me that the business of all who would not be educational time-servers is to resist every move in this direction, and to strive for a kind of vocational education which will first alter the existing industrial system, and ultimately transform it."[68]

On numerous occasions Dewey reiterated his opposition to the separation of trade education and general education. To divide the two, he claimed, would create an "inevitable tendency" to make "both kinds of training narrower, less significant and less effective than the schooling in which the traditional education is reorganized to utilize the industrial subject matter—active, scientific, and social of the present-day environment."[69] Summing up, Dewey wrote:

> Instead of trying to split schools into two kinds, one of a trade type for children whom it is assumed are to be employees and one of a liberal type for the children of well-to-do, [industrial education] will aim at such a reorganization of existing schools as will give all pupils a genuine respect for useful work, an ability to render service, and a contempt for social parasites. . . . Instead of assuming that the problem is to add vocational training to an existing cultural elementary education, it will . . . remember that the future employee is a consumer as well as a producer, that the whole tendency of society, so far as it is intelligent and wholesome, is to an increase of the hours of leisure, and that an education which does nothing to enable individuals to consume wisely and to utilize leisure wisely is a fraud on democracy. . . . Such a conception of industrial education will prize freedom more than docility; initiative more than automatic skill; insight and understanding more than capacity . . . to execute tasks under the direction of others.[70]

David Snedden was deeply disappointed over the barrage of criticism to which his views had been subjected in print by Dewey. In a two-page letter to the

*New Republic,* he professed ''profound respect'' for Dewey's insights but expressed bewilderment at the attack directed against himself. ''Those of us who have been seeking to promote the development of sound vocational educational education in schools have become accustomed to the opposition of our academic brethren, who, perhaps unconsciously, still reflect the very ancient and very enduring lack of sympathy, and even the antipathy, of educated men towards common callings, 'menial pursuits' and 'dirty trades,''' he remarked. ''We have even reconciled ourselves to the endless misrepresentations of numerous reactionaries and of the beneficiaries of vested educational interests and traditions.'' He concluded:

> But to find Dr. Dewey apparently giving aid and comfort to the opponents of a broader, richer, and more effective program of education, and apparently misapprehending the motives of many of those who advocate the extension of vocational education in schools designed for that purpose, is discouraging.[71]

Snedden tried in the same letter to clarify and restate his position. He supported a dual school system because it was more efficient and would, in his opinion, best protect vocational education as ''irreducibly, and without unnecessary mystification, education for the pursuit of an occupation.'' He opposed the blending of vocational and liberal education because it would distract from the kind of training needed by those about to embark upon a career. Youths of fourteen or thereabouts, he insisted, should already have completed their general education and were now entitled to receive at public expense the same sort of specific education given to those intending to enter professional life.

Snedden brought his missive to a close with a frank admission that business leaders were suspicious of academics. That distrust, he felt, was both well-founded and helped account for industry's support of parallel school systems, one general and one vocational. Businessmen ''feel assured neither of the friendliness nor of the competency of our schoolmasters in developing sound industrial education. For that reason they often favor some form of partially separate control, at least at the outset of any new experiments,'' he explained. Snedden felt that ''school men, however well intentioned, are apt to be impractical and to fail to appreciate actual conditions.''[72]

## THE PASSAGE OF SMITH-HUGHES

While Snedden and Dewey were trading barbs in the pages of the *New Republic* and elsewhere, the National Association of Manufacturers and the National Society for the Promotion of Industrial Education were shifting the focus of their lobbying efforts from local and professional circles to the federal level. Frustrated in their efforts to induce local and state boards of education to finance vocational schools and to grant them autonomy, they now turned to the federal government for help. Traditionally opposed to the use of public tax monies by groups outside the industrial-business sphere, the NAM had no compunction about appealing for federal funding of vocational education.[73] Thus, in the years following the NAM's 1905 report from its Committee on Industrial Education, as opposition stiffened within the AFL and NEA, a campaign begun and led by Charles Prosser of the NSPIE sought to obtain federal support for trade schools.

Preceded by years of political maneuvering and careful preparation, its culmination came in 1917, with the passage of the famous Smith-Hughes Act. Forging a coalition of business, industrial, and agricultural interests was not difficult. Farmers' groups, for example, had long charged public education with being sterile and irrelevant, too "literary" and lacking in practicality. *Wallace's Farmer,* a popular farm journal of the early 1900s, in its January 19, 1913 issue urged an end to "the cut and dried formula of a period when a man was 'educated' when he knew Greek and Latin," and demanded less textbook instruction and more attention to teaching the rudiments of agriculture.[74] In Wisconsin, farm organizations were especially critical of the state's public university, deriding it as "a cold storage institution of dead languages and useless learning which costs several billions of bushels of wheat each year."[75] Hence when business approached the farmers for assistance in effecting reforms, support was readily forthcoming.

After Prosser assumed the position of NSPIE executive secretary in 1912, he lost no time in bringing together such diverse factions as the American Federation of Labor, the Chamber of Commerce, most of the major farm organizations, settlement-house leaders, and even, finally, the National Education Association, to support a "bill to cooperate with the states in encouraging instruction in agriculture, the trades and industries, and home economics in secondary schools, in maintaining instruction in these subjects in state normal schools; in maintaining extension departments in state colleges of agriculture and mechanic arts; and to appropriate money and regulate its expenditure."[76] It later became the legislative source for both the Smith-Lever Act (an agricultural extension initiative, which was passed in 1914 as a concession to farm interests in return for a promise from farmers to support vocational education) and the Smith-Hughes Act.

Chief sponsor of the 1911 bill was Senator Caroll S. Page, of Vermont. In the same year it was first introduced, President Roosevelt wrote to Page expressing his support:

> The passage of this bill would merely be putting into effect that cardinal American doctrine of furnishing a reasonable equality of opportunity and chance of development to all our children, wherever they live and whatever may be their station in life. . . . Industrial training . . . is the most important of all training aside from that which develops character, and it is a grave reproach to us as a nation that we have permitted our training to lead children away from the farm and shop instead of toward them. The school system should be aimed primarily to fit the scholar for actual life rather than for the university.[77]

White House support notwithstanding, Page's bill failed at first to win approval in Congress, and for a time it appeared Prosser's crusade had ground to a halt. Behind the scenes, however, the NSPIE remained active, its lobbying resulting in the reintroduction of the bill in the Senate in December of 1915. Its chief sponsor was Senator Hoke Smith, of Georgia. In the same month, in his annual address to Congress, President Wilson, apprehensive over the likelihood of America's entry into World War I, spoke on behalf of Smith's bill. "What is important is that the industries and resources of the country should be made available and ready for mobilization," he stressed. "It is the most imperatively necessary, therefore, that we should promptly devise means for doing what we have not yet done; that we should give intelligent federal aid and stimulation to industrial and vocational educational legislation. . . ."[78]

Two months later Dudley M. Hughes, of Georgia, introduced a near-identical bill in the House, where it was referred to the House Committee on Education. On February 12, 1916, the Hughes bill was reported back to the House with an accompanying report supporting its passage. Meanwhile President Wilson was again urging the enactment of legislation. "We ought to have in this great country a system of industrial and vocational education," he declared, "under federal guidance and with federal aid, in which a very large percentage of the youth of the country will be given training in the skillful use and application of the principles of success in maneuver and business."[79] A third appeal came in December of 1916, when he termed a bill for the promotion of vocational training "of vital importance . . . a matter too long neglected."[80]

On February 23, 1917, almost three years after the Commission had submitted its report, Wilson signed the Vocational Education Act (Smith-Hughes) into law. "Pandemonium broke loose," according to one observer's account, when news of the signing was wired to the NSPIE's tenth annual convention meeting in Indianapolis.[81] The Society had finally achieved its long-cherished goal: federal funding for a national system of vocational education administered through a separate Federal Board. For a time (until the Board's functions were transferred in 1933 to the Department of the Interior and subsequently to the U.S. Office of Education) it appeared that Prosser had achieved everything for which he had worked so long and so hard. Under Smith-Hughes, the Board had full authority to review all state plans for vocational education and guidance programs. Monies would be available for vocational teacher training, for curriculum development, for staff-development programs, for field studies and research, and for a host of other activities. It was the first and single most important piece of federal legislation in the field of vocational education, and its major provisions would remain untouched for almost half a century to come.[82]

## A COMPROMISE:
## THE COMPREHENSIVE HIGH SCHOOL

The year following the enactment into law of the Smith-Hughes Act witnessed the appearance of a report by the NEA's Committee on Reorganizing Secondary Education. Entitled "Cardinal Principles of Secondary Education," it identified seven major objectives or aims of the high school: (1) health, (2) command of fundamental learning processes, (3) worthy home membership, (4) good citizenship, (5) productive leisure, (6) ethical character, and (7) vocation.[83] Similar in tone to Herbert Spencer's *Education: Intellectual, Moral and Physical,* published almost six decades earlier, the NEA Committee's report urged a more utilitarian type of public education adapted to a range of socially desirable goals. But in endorsing "vocation" as a "cardinal principle," the NEA explicitly rejected the NSPIE's avowed aim of separating trade schools from educational institutions of a more general character.

> It is only as the pupil sees his vocation in relation to his citizenship and his citizenship in the light of his vocation that he will be prepared for effective membership in an industrial democracy. Consequently this commission enters its protest against any and all plans, however well intended, which are in danger of divorcing vocation and social-civic education. It stands squarely for the infusion of vocation with the spirit of service and for the vitalization of culture by genuine contact with the world of work.[84]

Predictably, David Snedden was dismayed at the NEA's refusal to endorse separate vocational schools or the wholesale vocationalization of public schools. "In spite of its insistence to the contrary," he remarked with some bitterness, "it is hard to believe that the Committee is genuinely interested in any vocational education that can meet the economic tests of our times."[85]

Meanwhile, events were bypassing the expectations of the NSPIE in plumbing for terminal "intermediate industrial schools" ending at the equivalent of the ninth grade. It was becoming increasingly apparent by the 1920s that an education concluded at this stage or level would be inadequate for the great majority of fourteen- to sixteen-year-olds. Thus, even while the junior high school was being established, more and more teenagers were planning to continue their education through senior high school. Snedden earlier had argued that after nine or ten years of formal schooling, most youths should have acquired all the general and vocational training they required and now be prepared to seek employment—a notion critics attacked as "social predestination" and a plan to perpetuate class differences and promote passive acquiescence to the status quo.[86] The eventual outcome of a long debate was a compromise between the ideas of vocationalists and traditionalists—the comprehensive junior-senior high school.

The emergence of the comprehensive school as a model for American secondary education, offering both academic and vocational subjects within a single institution, saved the ideal of common schooling while thwarting vocationalists' ambitions to create separate vocational trade schools. Unfortunately, in attempting to be all things to all people, it could not adequately fulfill most of its objectives. It provided the substance of curricular differentiation by "tracking" students into different programs—vocational or academic—but without the appearance of doing so, repairing the damage to democratic pretensions by bringing students back together again into what one contemporary historian has aptly characterized as "a microcosmic, quintessentially American democratic community to eat lunch, take recess, learn their 'civics,' attend assembly, and cheer their athletic teams to victory.''[87] But comprehensive high schools could not be democratic as long as they continued to segregate students by social class into vocational or academic tracks. And their efficiency was impaired, as had been predicted, by housing the vocational offerings within what were administered and celebrated as academic high schools. Because the vocational programs within the comprehensive high schools were obviously second-class in terms of funding, teaching, and, perhaps most importantly, the social class of the students enrolled, they could never attract in sufficient number, nor could they school effectively, those students for whom they had been designed in the first place.[88]

Overall, American high schools could never hope to attain the efficiency and single-mindedness of purpose exhibited by the German model so much admired in vocationalist circles. A modern historian comments:

> American schools had other purposes to serve. They had to maintain the illusion of democracy in a society where the increasing agglomeration of wealth in the hands of the few was rendering negligible the political power of the many; they had to maintain the appearance of the classless society in a new industrial order established on the separation of labor from capital; they had to maintain the pretence of unlimited upward mobility in a society where such movement was becoming much more the exception than the rule. In short, they had to preserve and present the myths of America to each new generation of Americans.[89]

## FEDERAL LEGISLATION AND THE EXPANSION OF VOCATIONAL EDUCATION

One of the most immediate and obvious consequences of the Smith-Hughes Act was a rapid expansion of enrollments in vocational-education programs. In 1918 an estimated 164,186 students of all ages were enrolled in all-day, evening, and part-time classes and schools. Within a decade, that total had increased sixfold, reaching a total of almost 1 million students by 1928. The enrollment figures practically doubled again by 1938, encompassing an estimated 1.8 million persons. By 1948 the total was close to 3 million; and by 1958 it had surpassed 3.6 million. Over 7.5 million students were enrolled for vocational instruction of one type or another by 1968; by 1978 the figure exceeded 14 million. Comparable growth was forecast for the period 1978–1988, according to the U.S. Office of Education.[90] Even taking total population growth into account, in both absolute and relative terms, the increase was nothing less than spectacular.

A major factor accounting for this impressive rise in enrollments was the federal government's part in expanding vocational education. Beginning with the first federal vocational-education act signed into law in 1917, Congress was to assume an active role in funding programs. Twelve years after the enactment of the Smith-Hughes Act, in 1929, President Coolidge approved a supplementary law, the George-Reed Act, which authorized and increased annual appropriations for education in agriculture and home economics. In 1934 a second supplementary law, the George-Ellzey Act, replaced George-Reed in appropriating funds for training in agriculture, home economics, and trades and industries. Two years later, in 1936, President Roosevelt signed the George-Deen Act into law, which for the first time authorized annual appropriations without term limitations for vocational education in agriculture, home economics, trades and industry, and distributive occupations.[91] Although the Depression after 1929 served to slow the rate of increase in federal expenditures for vocational programs, total funding in dollar amounts more than doubled, from $7 million in 1917 to $14 million by 1936.

## CRITICS AND THE ISSUE OF CONTROL

The growth of vocational education did not go unchallenged or unopposed. Traditionalists and other educational conservatives on various grounds sharply attacked vocationalism, particularly as it became an important shaping influence on public-school curricula. A typical outburst was registered by Nicholas Murray Butler, writing in the *Educational Review* in December of 1921. ''The whole scheme of vocational training,'' he fumed,

> is not only a sham, and a costly sham, but an immense injury both to the individual and to the community, if it is permitted to find its way into the six elementary school years or, in any but the most restricted fashion, into the six secondary school years. The child who while still an infant is seized upon and prepared for some specific calling, is thereafter a prisoner without possibility of becoming a free man.[92]

Butler's allegation was held out by Arthur B. Mays, a professor of industrial education at the University of Illinois, as a prime example of ''the general lack of careful study of the real meaning of the vocational education movement'' by its critics. In response Mays retorted,

> It would be difficult to find so much as a single sentence in the whole range of writing and speaking of all the responsible advocates of vocational education that even remotely suggests the desire to 'seize upon an infant' and prepare him for a specific calling, or to permit specific vocational education to find its way into the first six years of the schools.[93]

As for Butler's charge regarding the undesirability of introducing specific trade training into the secondary school, Mays spoke for almost all vocationalists in commenting upon its need:

> Vocational-education leaders have not advocated substituting vocational training for general training, or the curtailing of general education, but only the provision of vocational training in *addition* to general education. They have maintained that the meager general education acquired by the great mass of the people before the work life begins does not prepare them for that life any more than a general, academic col-

lege training prepares a physician for his work. They merely urge that the book-keeper, the machinist, the homemaker be afforded an equal chance to prepare for their work life with that afforded the preacher, the doctor, and the lawyer. It seems strange that a philosophy of education derived from the slave-owning classes of ancient Greece should still be advanced as adequate for modern America, and that the needs of the overwhelming majority of the boys and girls, who do not enter the learned professions, should be entirely neglected by the schools in the name of the protection of culture, while the most elaborate provision is made for the very few who do enter those occupations. That such discrimination still exists can be attributed only to prejudice, or to a failure carefully to examine both phases of the necessary education of the good citizen of a democracy.[94]

Responding to what apologists for vocational training saw as irresponsible criticism was a perennial problem; greater still was the threat of loss of administrative authority over the programs they were defending. Their worst fears were confirmed finally in 1933, when Congress acted to reassign most of the major powers granted to the Federal Board for Vocational Education under Smith-Hughes to the U.S. Commissioner of Education. The practical effect of this move was to divest vocational educators of the autonomy they had enjoyed heretofore and to return control over all federally supported vocational-education programs to public-education officials. Originally intended as a cost-saving measure, the decision was fought bitterly by most vocationalists as a betrayal of almost everything they had fought for twenty years earlier, in the crusade to pass the Vocational Education Act of 1917. Most felt the "tampering" was a major crisis: the AFL termed it a "serious mistake" and a step backward. Convinced it was imperative that programs intended under federal legislation remain "under the direction of persons who understood the nature and values of practical work," vocational-education groups lobbied long and hard for a reversal before conceding defeat. The issue of control, as one prominent vocationalist historian has observed, "was, and still is, a touchy subject."[95]

Years later diehard supporters of separate vocational-education programs were still treating it as a live issue. Citing the "distinct advantages" of a dual-control plan, Hawkins, Prosser, and Wright, in a 1959 volume, insisted that "in order that maximum service may be rendered the individual and the state, it is necessary that the national, state, and local administrative authority in charge of vocational education remain distinct and separate from the corresponding authority dealing with general education." Regular school authorities, they argued, lack the experience or knowledge needed for organizing and administering vocational education. Already overburdened with other responsibilities, they neglect to give vocational education the attention, resources, and other forms of support it requires in order to be effective. Most important of all, they claimed, vocational training must be protected against the "extreme emphasis" regular school officials place on education for "culture." Hence, vocational training "must be administered by authorities who are in sympathy with its aims and who attach proper importance to its social and economic value."[96]

Not until the early 1970s were vocationalists seemingly reconciled to the assimilation of job-training programs within public education. "There is growing realization," as one writer put it, "that it is no longer possible to compartmentalize education into general, academic and vocational components and that to continue any form of separatism in education is self-defeating." It would be "futile and wasteful," it was said, to attempt to preserve the distinction between general and vocational education, and hence to sustain separate systems of administrative management and control.[97]

## THE WAR YEARS

As war clouds gathered on the horizon in the late 1930s, the U.S. Office of Education began contingency planning for training programs that might be required in the event of a national mobilization. By 1938 John C. Wright, Assistant Commissioner for Vocational Education in the U.S. Office, and Layton S. Hawkins, Chief of the Trade and Industrial Education Service, were meeting regularly with staff representatives of the War Department to ascertain what would be needed. Not long after war broke out in Europe, the U.S. Commissioner of Education released a report entitled, *Training For National Defense,* which outlined the possible use of existing trade schools for emergency vocational-training programs. In May of 1940 President Roosevelt urged, in a special message to Congress, that immediate provision be made for the expansion of trade training, especially in the field of aviation mechanics.

Within a month Congress began appropriating funds to the states to train war-production workers. Following Japan's attack upon Pearl Harbor, the American Vocational Association (successor to the NSPIE), meeting in Boston on December 10–13, 1941, pledged "the united and untiring efforts of our membership and the complete utilization of our vocational schools and training facilities throughout the nation in an all-out Training for Victory program."[98] The National Defense Training Program ultimately would train over 7.5 million people for defense production at 2,600 designated training centers, supplying workers for the shipbuilding and aircraft industries at a cost of over $100 million annually, until the program's termination at the war's end, in 1945.

Considering the scope and scale of training programs organized under wartime conditions, vocationalists were outraged over an address delivered in 1944 by Robert Maynard Hutchins, who airily announced that "the thing to do with vocational education is to forget it." Whereas vocational educators were given to pointing with pride to the rapid deployment of occupational-training opportunities, Hutchins drew an altogether different conclusion. "As the war-training programs in industry have shown," he argued, "industry can train its hands if it has to, and it can do it at lightning speed." He then added, "The task of the educational system is not to train hands for industry, but to prepare enlightened citizens for our democracy and to enrich the life of the individual by giving him a sense of purpose which will illuminate not merely the 40 hours he works, but the 72 he does not. . . ."[99]

Arthur B. Mays acidly commented, "Fortunately for American youth, such narrow and uninformed conceptions of vocational education are confined to a minority of educators. . . ." Taking issue with Hutchins's contention that the best preparation for a vocation is a liberal education, Mays felt it typified "the attitude of those educators throughout the history of education who are unable or unwilling to face frankly and realistically the demands of modern social and economic life, and who turn to the educational philosophy of the past for their solutions of modern educational problems." [100]

Heartened by the success of their wartime training programs in fostering job skills for hundreds of thousands of defense-industry workers, proponents of vocational education dropped the defensive tone that had so often typified earlier rhetoric and adopted a distinctly militant attitude in their public pronouncements. In 1943, for example, the National Society For The Study Of Education devoted a fifth yearbook to the subject of vocational education. (Others on the same topic had appeared in 1905, 1907, 1912, and 1924.) Many prominent vocational educators used the occasion to stipulate and define vocational training as an integral component of *all* general education. Edwin A. Lee, a dean at the University of California at Los Angeles, avowed,

> Education is a coin, one face of which is vocational, the other nonvocational; for some the latter may be avocational, for others intellectual self-improvement, for still others purely leisure-time activity. Without both faces there is no coin, no legal tender, no true education. Even more accurately, it is true that what for one man may be liberal education is for another indubitably vocational education. Indeed, it may be one or the other for the same man or woman, depending on time, place, and circumstances. [101]

Stephen F. Voorhees, chair of the Advisory Board on Industrial Education for New York City, in the same volume observed, "The great weakness of academic education has been its detachment from life. The growing strength of general education is its search for life. The soundness of vocational education is its foundation upon life. Everybody must work; so everybody must learn to work." [102] Franklin J. Keller, principal of New York City's Metropolitan Vocational High School, who served as editor of the 1943 NSSE Yearbook, took Voorhees's argument a step further. "Everyone who can work should receive vocational education," he declared. They should have training available whenever they need it. "People should learn to work wherever they can do so most economically in terms of time, energy and money and where the environmental influences will be such as to make them desirable social beings as well as skillful workers. Such places of work-learning should be accessible and available to everyone. They should be called 'schools.'" [103]

Alexander J. Stoddard, Philadelphia Superintendent of Schools, in his address to the American Vocational Association meeting in 1944, made much the same point. "The real question is not whether there should or should not be vocational education. It is rather the extent to which the facts, knowledge, and skills in-

One of the pressing problems in the United States is the forging of a link between schools and jobs. . . . The fundamental flaw [in U.S. education] . . . is its failure to develop the occupational bent of the child. . . . We turn millions of high school students loose without any real effort to find their occupational bent or to provide directional sign posts. They must plunge around, trying to locate themselves in the economic world. They meet a million discouragements. . . .

—Inez Robb, *1980 Americanism as Foreseen by Herbert Hoover* (New York: American Newspapers, 1940), p. 48.

"What are you going to be when you grow up?" must be quite high on the list of dumb questions asked of a child. The child cannot answer, for the three bases of a stable national pattern of work—technology, the work force and social conditions—are all in flux.

In a world of rapidly developing new technology, the job of vocational education is to widen choices, to provide information about the world of work, to offer multi-faceted training for choice and for change, and to educate students in new loyalties to quality, performance and self. The key to the future is to gear students to plan for, look forward to, accept and relish a movement to new kinds of work at different times. The great opportunity for vocational education is to prepare men and women for all seasons of their lives.

—Joseph F. Coates, "The Changing Nature of Work," *Vocational Education* 57 (January/February 1982): 27, 29.

volved in certain processes of service should be taught in school or college or left to apprenticeship or direct experience on the job," he asserted. "The question is further complicated by the fact that attitudes, appreciations, and ideals are also involved with the service processes, resulting properly in a mixing of the civic, cultural, and social with the practical aspects of the service. . . ."

Stoddard then amplified his theme that vocational and general education were two complementary and sometimes indistinguishable aspects of a unitary whole.

> Vocational education and what might be called general or academic education do not differ, or should not be regarded as differing in the respect in which they are usually regarded as being different. The former is not "training of the hand" and the latter "training of the brain." The former is not for those only of low ability, capable only of learning how to work with their hands.

It followed for Stoddard that "everyone ought to be educated vocationally, according to his ability and his occupational desires and everyone ought to be educated for citizenship, for effective living as an individual, and for successful participation in the society of which he is a part." In other words, every American should be prepared adequately for productive service, that is, for employment at useful occupations, and . . . to live richly and effectively in accordance with our cultural heritage." He concluded, "Every American should know how to make a living at a useful occupation and also be able to pursue happiness with some assurance of a reasonable expectation of success." [104]

Superintendent Stoddard's address was warmly received, especially his point that vocational education should be for *everyone,* not just for those indisposed to pursue a traditional academic curriculum. More controversial was his proposal to postpone job training until after high school:

> The vocational education program of our schools should be pushed upward to the post-high school period as far as possible in accordance with the economies of employment then prevailing. The curriculum should be expanded to cover the whole range of teachable vocational areas, from the highly complicated to the very simple. Long and short courses, both unit and sequential, would be involved. Vocational education should be regarded as the common right of all the people. We should not think of general education for some types of our people and vocational education for other types. Rather we should think of *all* our people having equal opportunities, according to their abilities to acquire both the common integrating facts, knowledge, and skills essential for effective living and the facts, knowledge, and skills directly related to productive employment. [105]

Keller applauded Stoddard's general stance but took strong exception to his proposal to defer occupational training until the end of the secondary-school years. This, Keller alleged, was "one of the most curious and inexplicable" errors imaginable. "It does not make sense pedagogically, economically, socially, or historically," he insisted. "It runs counter to the psychology of learning and the philosophy of education." Finally, "it ignores all the experience derived from the operation of vocational guidance programs." [106]

The theme of the interpretation of general and vocational education soon became a favorite among vocationalist writers. After having quoted approvingly from Stoddard's address, Arthur B. Mays, once again, in 1948, summed up what was fast becoming a familiar position:

> When one specifically attempts to distinguish between vocational and cultural education, one immediately faces a difficulty common to all the generally accepted dualisms in educational thought, namely, that of locating an actual wall or partition between the two things considered. Are theory and practice two distinct things or merely different aspects of a single thing? The same question arises with reference to many other familiar pairs, such as heredity and environment, mind and matter, character and conduct, doing and knowing. At what point does cultural education end and vocational education begin? Can one be educated at one time exclusively for leisure and at another exclusively for productive work? Is there no culture to be had from the daily experience of making a livelihood, and no vocational proficiency from the pursuit of the intellectual disciplines? It is not necessary to think very far into such questions to conclude that the words denoting the dualisms in reality name only two sides of the same thing. Hence it is impossible successfully to maintain that training

in the skills, attitudes, and technical knowledge of a vocation does not increase culture, or that a study of history, language, philosophy, and science does not improve one's practice of a vocation. In a very real sense, it is true that one cannot sharply divide one's life into distinct compartments because each phase of consciousness reciprocally affects every other. . . . In the interest of administrative efficiency it seems necessary arbitrarily to differentiate among the various aspects of the educational program . . . [but] if . . . the real unity of the process is appreciated and maintained, no real injury is done. . . .[107]

As for the sequential relationship of vocational and cultural education, Mays felt it would differ from person to person and depend upon the sort of training involved, but job training ordinarily should begin sometime after the age of sixteen or "immediately before engaging in a chosen vocation."[108]

## VOCATIONALISM IN LIFE-ADJUSTMENT EDUCATION

Not surprisingly, most vocationalists welcomed the advent of "life-adjustment" education, as propounded by the U.S. Office of Education in the early 1940s. Many in fact were actively involved in launching what they hoped would become a mass reform movement in American education. Among them was the indefatigable Charles Prosser. At a 1944 conference on the theme, "Vocational Education in the Years Ahead," sponsored by the Vocational Division of the U.S. Office of Education, for example, it was Prosser who introduced a resolution calling upon the Commissioner of Education to hold a series of conferences to ponder the shape of postwar schooling. "It is the belief of this conference," the resolution announced,

> that . . . the vocational school of a community will be . . . able to prepare 20 percent of the youth of secondary-school age for entrance upon desirable skilled occupations; and that the high school will continue to prepare another 20 percent for entrance to college. We do not believe that the remaining 60 percent of our youth of secondary-school age will receive the life adjustment training they need and to which they are entitled as American citizens—unless and until the administrators of public education, with the assistance of the vocational education leaders, formulate a . . . program for this group."[109]

The strong vocationalist orientation attached to life-adjustment education was most clearly highlighted in a manifesto-like document issued by the NEA's Educational Policies Commission in 1944 in conjunction with the American Association of School Administrators. Entitled, *Education For All American Youth,* it summarized the nature of the "adjustment" schools should foster, not just in the 60 percent of the secondary-school population identified by Prosser's original resolution, but among *all* high-school youths:

1. The youth prepared to be a successful worker in any occupation should have mastered the basic skills of his occupation and as much of the related scientific and

technical knowledge as is possible within the limits of his abilities and the time available.

2. He should have had experience in productive work under conditions of regular employment (or conditions approximating those as nearly as possible), where he can learn the requirements of work for production and be helped to develop those personal qualifications of dependability, cooperation, and resourcefulness which bulk so large as factors in success.

3. He should know the requirements for entering the occupation in which he is interested—such as education, apprenticeship training, health and physical fitness, previous experience, and union membership (if required). He should know also how to go about getting a job through the public employment service, the personnel offices of employers, and (in some cases) the labor unions.

4. He should understand the functions both of management and of employees' organizations in his occupation and the relations between them. He should be acquainted with the purposes and operations of labor unions, if there are such; the obligations and privileges of union membership; and the duties and authority of union officials. He should likewise be familiar with the duties and authority of management—particularly foremen and supervisors. He should know about the machinery for handling relations between management and employees—about collective bargaining, seniority regulations, and the means of dealing with grievances and disputes. He should also be informed about the availability of credit unions, group hospitalization insurance, consumers' cooperatives, and other cooperative services.

5. He should understand the relations of government to his occupation—the applications of federal and state laws relating to such matters as unemployment compensation, old age and survivors' insurance, employers' liability, collective bargaining, and safety provisions.

6. He should know how the industry, business, profession, or service field which he expects to enter operates as a whole and about its place in the life of the city. He should be familiar with the most reliable predictions as to the future of his occupation and with the work of local planning bodies which relate to his work. And he should have some understanding of the national and possibly the international setting of his occupation and of the general economic conditions which shape its course.

7. Finally he should know how to use the public services available to him after he leaves full time school—particularly the services of placement, guidance, advanced vocational training, recreation, health, and civic education.[110]

Prosser and his associates in the Vocational Division of the U.S. Office of Education were nothing if not consistent in their ambition to tie school instruction as closely as possible to the world of work. Despite the usual ritualistic obeisances to "general culture" and other broadening elements, the curricular sequence detailed in *Education For All American Youth* made it plain that vocationalist concerns would dominate the structure of the high school. For grades 10 through 12, for example, besides science, a course in "common learnings," intended in part to help students in their "understanding of economic processes and . . . their roles as producers and consumers," and health and physical education, fully half of each school day was to be devoted to vocational preparation, including "education for industrial, commercial, homemaking service, and other occupations leading to employment. . . ." It was also to include "a period of productive work under employment conditions, supervised by the school staff."[111]

Shortly after the appearance of the Commission's report, the National Association of Secondary School Principals offered a summary of the document under the title, *Planning for American Youth* (1944). Heading a list of ten "imperative educational needs of youth" was the statement: "All youth need to develop salable skills and those understandings and attitudes that make the worker an intelligent and productive participant in economic life. To this end, most youth need supervised work experience as well as education in the skills and knowledge of their occupations."[112] Clearly, had the life-adjustment education movement garnered the popular support its advocates had hoped for, the effect would have been to enshrine vocationalism at the center of all public schooling. Under its agenda, the task of the American high school would have been threefold: (1) to familiarize learners with occupations, with entry-level requirements in various fields, the organization of work prevailing in different jobs, workers' rights and responsibilities, and a wealth of other work-related information; (2) to provide opportunities for actual employment experience; and (3) to acquire the actual skills needed for embarking upon a chosen line of work.

As it turned out, however, the push for life-adjustment education proved short-lived; and the movement begun with such high hopes in 1944, for all practical purposes had grown moribund ten years later. Many factors helped account for its demise. A chief cause was the vehement criticism to which it was subjected by writers such as Arthur Bestor, Hyman Rickover, and Albert Lynd in the late 1940s and early 1950s. Assailing what they claimed was the academic and intellectual flabbiness of progressive education, they soon broadened their attack to include life-adjustment education as a particularly objectionable manifestation of progressivist ideology at work. In any event, by the mid-fifties, the movement had died a quiet death. Over a quarter century would elapse before the life-adjustment concept would be resurrected once again in a new guise. With only minor modifications, and with all its essential features remaining intact, it would then be given a new name—career education.

## POSTWAR EXPANSION AND DEVELOPMENT

American industry had depended heavily upon trade and industrial education programs during World War II, and prospects that the alliance would be strengthened in the postwar years appeared bright.[113] Passage of the George-Barden Act of 1946, authorizing greatly increased expenditures for a wide variety of vocational education programs, symbolized the beginnings of an era of buoyant optimism and rapid expansion. Despite apprehensions as to whether retraining programs could be developed quickly enough to meet the needs of thousands of veterans returning to schools, the general mood in vocationalist circles was one of growing confidence.[114]

Enrollments in new area-vocational high schools and technical institutes blossomed. Vocational teacher-training programs were upgraded and vastly improved. Between 1956 and 1967 a rash of federal legislation relating to manpower development assured vocational educators an ever-expanding financial base, including the Health Amendments Act of 1956 (providing for practical-nurse training), a 1956 amendment to the George-Barden Act (authorizing funds for vocational training in the fishing industries), Title VIII of the National Defense Education Act of 1958 (authorizing funds for technical training), Section 16 of the Area Redevelopment Act (for vocational training of unemployed workers), the Manpower Development And Training Act of 1962 (appropriating funds to state vocational-education boards for program development), the Trade Extension Act of 1962 (containing provisions authorizing the training of displaced workers), and the Public Welfare Amendments Act of 1962 (providing contractual authority for the development of state vocational-education programs).

With adequate federal funding assured, many vocational educators once again reviewed the notion that future expansion should be undertaken independently of public education. William T. Bawden spoke for many when he asserted,

> We learned our lesson once, and we are not going to permit the traditionally minded superintendents and principals to do to vocational education what they did to the manual training movement. We intended to stay away from [public schools], keep our vocational education separate and independent, and thus avoid any grounds for suspicion that vocational education will ever be dominated by general education.[115]

Bawden felt strongly that the original impulse to separate vocational training from public schooling had been sound and that renewed efforts in this direction were called for in the postwar period.

Several factors accounted for vocationalists' fears for the fate of training programs in public schools. One was the upsurge of criticism to which American public education was being subjected by traditionalist critics and the tendency of conservative educators to respond to charges by downplaying the vocational elements of their programs in favor of more rigorous academic instruction. The actual role to be played by vocational education in the comprehensive high school of the sort urged, for example, by James B. Conant in his *The American High School Today* (1959) still appeared unclear. Vocationalists applauded Conant's comment, "When I hear adverse criticism of vocational education, I cannot help concluding that the critic just has not taken the trouble to find out what he is talking about!"[116] But at the same time they were mindful of the controversy generated by the furor over *Sputnik* and the growing popularity of proposals to reshape secondary education after European models, with the academically elite provided for either in separate schools or in noticeably separate parts of the general high school.

With so much interest focused on the needs of the college-bound, vocationalists feared their own programs would be relegated to an inferior and subordinate position within the comprehensive high school. Over and over again, they objected to what they saw as a widespread tendency to regard vocational education as a "dumping ground" for the academically untalented, fit only for the "sweaty shirt set" and for "blue-collar" types. Periodically, the AFL's committee on education called attention to what it defined as a "caste system" in the nation's educational structure.

In support of their contention, committee members cited situations where pupils with low IQ scores were advised to enroll for vocational work, while more academically talented students were told not to do so; where vocational schools were shortchanged in the allocation of school-district resources as compared with their academic counterparts; and where vocational-education teachers lacking minimum work experience but with good academic credentials were hired before skilled craftsmen without college degrees. "Vocational education, let us frankly admit," the AFL's *Labor and Education in 1953* observed, "is widely regarded as suitable for the 'educationally and socially inferior' pupil only." [117] Again in 1955, the AFL committee urged that efforts be made "to avoid vocational classes as a dumping ground for pupils who may be judged as intellectually inferior." [118]

Support for the cause of vocational education as a completely defensible enterprise was forthcoming not long afterwards from W. Willard Wirtz, Secretary, U.S. Department of Labor, who in 1963 commented, "There is no future in this country for the unskilled worker." Noting the industrial transformation brought about by automation and technological advances, Wirtz argued that new jobs demanding a higher level of skill were being created as fast as old jobs were being destroyed:

> There was a place in the old work force for the boy or girl who left high school, either dropping out or with diploma in hand, and entered the work force with no skill training. He or she could, and did, take an unskilled job and worked up from there. Now such jobs are vanishing. And so today there are over 700,000 16-to-21-year-olds out of school and out of work. Every American youngster *has* to be given today, as a part of his education, some know-how about making a living—which means, for a great many of them, vocational education. [119]

John W. Gardner, author of the much-discussed *Excellence, Can We Be Equal And Excellent Too?,* urged appreciation for "excellence" in every line of human endeavor. Although concessions to individual differences in aptitude are necessary, Gardner argued, "we may properly expect that every form of education be such as to stretch the individual to the utmost of his potentialities." We must learn to honor and demand the best in every socially accepted human activity, however humble, and to scorn shoddiness, however exalted the activity. In a widely quoted passage that could not help win approval from vocationalists, Gardner asserted, "An excellent plumber is infinitely more admirable than an incompetent philosopher. The society which scorns excellence in plumbing because plumbing is a humble activity and tolerates shoddiness in philosophy because it is an exalted activity will have neither good plumbing nor good philosophy. Neither its pipes nor its theories will hold water." [120]

In the same year that Willard Wirtz voiced his support for vocational education, the U.S. Congress was moving toward a more tangible expression, in its consideration of the Morse-Perkins bill, which proposed greatly increased federal support for occupational training programs. Early in 1963 the White House-appointed Panel of Consultants on Vocational Education released its final report, entitled, *Education For A Changing World of Work.* [121] The Panel called for nothing less than a comprehensive local-state-federal alliance to promote a national system of vocational and technical education on an unprecedented scale. In its deliberations on the Morse-Perkins bill, Congressional leaders repeatedly invoked the Panel's report to support pending legislation.

Impatient with the deliberate pace of his colleagues, Senator Joseph S. Clark of Pennsylvania complained, "We have come out with fine words; we receive wonderful messages; we make splendid speeches; and we hear excellent testimony. But . . . then, like Ferdinand the bull, we sit down under a tree, smell the beautiful flowers, and let the rest of the world go by." One senator after another rose to support the vocational-education bill. As appreciation grew for the magnitude of the problem under consideration, Senator Birch Bayh, of Indiana, said the amount recommended for allocation was like delegating "one beaver to dam the roaring Colorado." A floor committee subsequently increased the proposed funding level, and when a vote was taken, the bill passed with overwhelming support. On December 18, 1963, President Johnson signed Public Law #88–210, the Vocational Education Act of 1963. As later amended in 1968, it provided monies for research and training, for curriculum development, for work-study programs, and a variety of cooperative vocational-education programs. Supporters hailed it as the single most important piece of federal legislation in the field since the Smith-Hughes Act of 1917. All told, it was to provide the foundation for virtually all vocational-education legislative initiatives at the national level over the next two decades.

By the late 1960s and early 1970s, vocationalists could feel confident that the federal government had become a dependable ally in helping to extend opportunities for vocational training to an ever-widening segment of the American public. Programs were flourishing, on a scale unimaginable even in the heady aftermath of the enactment of Smith-Hughes; and enrollments in technical and vocational preparatory courses evidenced healthy growth. But what had still proven elusive so far was general acceptance of the intellectual or academic legitimacy of such programs. At any rate, this was the state of affairs as many proponents of vocationalism saw it at the time. Accordingly, throughout the seventies and beyond, renewed efforts were begun to locate and expose the origins of antivocational prejudice. The result was a growing body of literature attempting also to offer a more effective justification for the vocationalist agenda in American public education.

## FORMATIVE INFLUENCES UPON ATTITUDES TOWARD WORK AND KNOWLEDGE

Analyses of why vocational training should so often be viewed with suspicion and distrust differed considerably. Some located the root causes in history, sometimes extending back to attitudes toward work and knowledge inherited from Graeco-

Roman antiquity. Philosopher-historian Robert Beck, for example, writing in the 1981 Yearbook of the American Vocational Association, labored to show how sometimes-unconscious contemporary feelings traced all the way back to the classic Greek or, at least, the Platonic view of labor. We are too easily misled, Beck believed, into thinking of vocational instruction as somehow inferior to academic instruction, as something appropriate only for the less competent classes of society. "Even educators have accepted that duality, as witness the popularity of the differentiation between education and training," he observed.

> In no time at all, really in the next philosophic breath, educational theorists spell out their meaning of training by saying that it is a matter of acquiring techniques. These last are often talked down as "nuts and bolts." Precisely the same line of thought divides the pure from the applied, theory from practice. An invidious distinction is made and it is one with historical antecedents.[122]

In the highly stratified society of ancient Athens, built, as it was, on a slave economy, the tendency among the privileged classes of the social order was to look down upon what today would be classified as unskilled and blue-collar labor. Skilled artisans and craftsmen were accorded slightly higher regard—Plato respected the *technai,* skilled laborers—but ordinary workers and the great masses of menial laborers were considered members of a lesser breed. Unlike his mentor, Socrates, who apparently believed even the lowliest slave was capable of being instructed in knowledge of a very high and abstract order, for Plato, as for Aristotle, education was conceived of as the province of a select few. Learning was a matter of grasping and using abstractions in the analysis or "dialectic" that led to the discovery of principles of reality and the formulation of values by which human beings were to live. Those who could not apprehend or manipulate conceptual abstractions, he believed, were uneducable.

In Plato's view, education had nothing whatsoever to do with concrete particulars as would be included in the world of work; it was not concerned with the applied, the here and now of the marketplace. Hence the teaching of particular manual skills could have no place of legitimacy in formal education. Informal training through direct observation and rote imitation or by apprenticeship was assumed to be sufficient. The true end of life, said Aristotle, endorsing Plato, was "thought" and rational contemplation, not the grubby business of production or of making a living.

"Whatever has been said about work being good for developing and maintaining character," Beck commented, "the conventional attitude toward work is that it is really a matter of brawn, not brain, of hand, not mind, for those whose collars are blue, not white, for those who may have nimble fingers and strong hands—and backs—but are not nimble of tongue nor quick of speech, for those not at home with words and such other abstractions as numbers." Further,

> It is but a step from this to the conviction that those who can work with abstractions can understand such abstractions as statements of physical laws, laws of nature, rules governing grammar, logic and society. A small step farther allows one to greet as rulers those who can understand the rules and then, presumably, rule. These make

up the aristocracy, the *aristoi,* who govern the (*hoi*) *poloi* grouped as the *demos* who, lacking an intellectual elite and political aristocracy, would govern as a democracy.[123]

Since Plato was adamant in his opposition to rule by the people, to democracy, it followed that education would be restricted to an elite few—those best able to profit from instruction. In the Platonic vision, wise and enlightened philosopher-kings, knowledgeable of the form of perfect social justice (writ, as it were, into the heavens or the structure of reality) would preside over a pyramidal hierarchical society in which those best fitted by ability governed at the top. All others would be assigned appropriate slots within the hierarchy, based on their aptitudes and natural interests. From Plato, Beck believed, Western culture had inherited the underlying conception of education as intellectual training and as academic; that is bookish learning. (Significantly, the Greek word for "leisure" was *scholia;* in Latin, a root derivation of "liberal" is *liber,* "book.")

As evidence for his thesis as to the persistence of the Greek-Platonic view of education, Beck pointed to the fact that generations of historians went unopposed in describing the interregnum between the fall of Rome in the fifth century and the rise of the cathedral schools in the eleventh as the Dark Ages:

> It is now an old story to note that those years were said to be "dark" for only one reason: Latin was not generally known! Cultural darkness was held equivalent to not knowing Latin. The reason for that assumption was that manuscripts were in Latin and the inability to read Latin was held tantamount to living in Stygian gloom. The fact that ordinary people were developing all sorts of artifacts counted for nothing. Those inventions, those innovations may have been important for production but they did not require what Plato and Aristotle would have thought to be an education.[124]

Beck's feeling was that the same prejudices inherited from Graeco-Roman antiquity and transported across the centuries were still alive and well in the contemporary period, both in the Western democracies and (partially concealed by proletarian rhetoric exalting the dignity of manual labor) in the so-called "peoples' democracies" as well.

Rupert N. Evans, professor of vocational education at the University of Illinois, advanced an argument similar to Beck's, although he traced contemporary prejudices toward labor (and by implication toward vocational education) back to Aristotle more than to Plato. Discussing contemporary attitudes and feelings, however, Evans gave greater weight to the socioeconomic background of modern-day academics who allegedly exert a disproportionate influence upon what is taught in school curricula. "The major group determining the school curriculum," Evans argued in a 1971 volume, *Foundations Of Vocational Education,* "is made up of academics, many of whom have had little or no experience outside the school. Their social contacts are limited too often to people in the professions who share a similar school background. These academics write textbooks, sit on curriculum committees, and, as teachers, decide what will be emphasized in classrooms." As administrators and faculty members, he alleged, they also control the reward structure in the schools. As a result, "the school tends to value school for its own sake, to design each level of schooling to prepare for the next, and to regard anyone who drops out of school prior to completion of a doctorate as a failure."[125]

According to Evans, most such academics (educational philosophers in particular) are middle-class professionals whose unconscious preference is for a common school curriculum based on the requirements of the professions. Instead of asking the question, "What knowledge is needed by *each* individual?" they ask, "What knowledge is of most value for *all* people?" Their answer is a uniform curriculum for everyone, variously defended on the grounds that since everyone lives in a democracy, all citizens need to acquire an identical educational content; that because all students live in a common culture, all should receive instruction based on the demands of that common culture; that schools should teach only what cannot be learned more efficiently elsewhere; or that education should focus on that sort of learning that has the greatest "generative" power. As Harry Broudy, B. O. Smith, and Joe Burnett once phrased it:

> Some ideas are more general and consequently have a greater explanatory potential than others, and some cognitive operations are more pervasive and more strategic for understanding than others. . . . there are key ideas and criteria and . . . there are indispensable symbolic and logical operations without which interpretation cannot be adequate. A curriculum which includes these ideas can make a plausible claim to be "needed" by all human beings and therefore to be studied by all of them.[126]

For Evans, however, the concept of a fixed uniform curriculum imposed on all students was fundamentally misconceived. It ignores, he argued, the value of specialized education as a motivating force for learning; it is undemocratic; it fails to take individual differences into account; and it overemphasizes schooling for its own sake. "If these philosophers were from a lower socio-economic group," he remarked, "they might well . . . base the contents of the common curriculum on the requirements of the skilled trades." Claiming that a common curriculum based on the needs of professionals was a notion supported only by other academic professionals, Evans wrote, "Compelled by society to provide education for all, they keep control by insuring that the education offered meets their own needs. They deny the education needed by non-professionals, then (supreme irony) heap indignities on those who drop out of the educational system because of its lack of personal relevance."[127]

While endorsing general education as a basis for personal and civic development, Evans argued strongly for more "specialized occupational education" whose focus would be "the practice and the theory of practice . . . required by one or more occupations." He summarized his position as follows:

> The major untaught curriculum of the school has to do with values, especially the values of work as they affect life. . . . Youth who have been taught that work is unimportant . . . are in for a rude shock when they leave the sheltered world of the school and enter the real world of work. . . . In the final analysis . . . education

which leads to effective work is necessary simply because work is essential to the survival of society.[128]

The thesis reiterated by Evans, that professional educators in the aggregate are elitist and tend to harbor undemocratic attitudes toward work and learning, was always favored among vocationalist writers. "Throughout its history," the redoubtable Melvin Barlow wrote,

> vocational education has been plagued by a number of myths that have tended to put it on the defensive. To begin with, vocational education is concerned with preparing people to go to work—an idea that has been a bitter pill for education to swallow. Including occupational preparation as an equal partner in the subject matter of the educational institution rubs against the grain of the traditional school.

Barlow emphatically denied that vocational educators had ever sought to dispense with general education entirely or with traditional values. "What vocational education has been trying to say is that in addition to these traditional values education should adjust its philosophical position to include teaching people how to work. It is almost as simple as that."[129]

The nation's present educational system, Barlow argued, "should 'fit' people, but it doesn't." Values within the system are different from those outside the system, and it does not honor values other than its own:

> A tragic emphasis has been placed on mental (cognitive) development. The only true value the system honors is mental development; equality of other kinds of development is almost out of the question. The great myths about education imply great advantages derived from liberal education, but experience does not verify the need for more concentration in this area. Without question, the system says that the students must fit the system, but contemporary need says that the system should be forced to accommodate the students. Comparatively few gain the objectives of the present educational system and they leave the system neither scholars nor craftsmen, neither excited about learning nor with the basic attitudes and skills demanded of them as citizens. This is the tragedy of the system.[130]

---

### PALEOLITHIC EDUCATION

Men worked hard at making fish nets, setting antelope snares, and digging bear pits. The tribe was busy and prosperous.

There were a few thoughtful men who asked questions as they worked. Some of them even criticized the schools.

"These new activities of net-making and operating, snare-setting, and pit-digging are indispensable to modern existence," they said. "Why can't they be taught in school?"

The safe and sober majority had a quick reply to this naive question. "School!" they snorted derisively. "You aren't in school now. You are out here in the dirt working to preserve the life and happiness of the tribe. What have these practical activities got to do with schools? You're not saying lessons now. You'd better forget your lessons and your academic ideals of fish-grabbing, horse-clubbing, and tiger-scaring if you want to eat, keep warm, and have some measure of security from sudden death."

The radicals persisted a little in their questioning. "Fish net-making and using, antelope-snare construction and operation, and bear-catching and killing," they pointed out, "require intelligence and skills—things we claim to develop in schools. They are also activities we need to know. Why can't the schools teach them?"

But most of the tribe, and particularly the wise old men who controlled the school, smiled indulgently at this suggestion. "That wouldn't be *education*," they said gently.

"But why wouldn't it be?" asked the radicals.

"Because it would be mere training," explained the old men patiently. "With all the intricate details of fish-grabbing, horse-clubbing, and tiger-scaring—the standard cultural subjects—the school curriculum is too crowded now. We can't add these fads and frills of net-making, antelope-snaring, and—of all things—bear-killing. Why, at the very thought, the body of the great New-Fist, founder of our paleolithic educational system, would turn over in its burial cairn. What we need to do is to give our young people a more thorough grounding in the fundamentals. Even the graduates of the secondary schools don't know the art of fish-grabbing in any complete sense nowadays, they swing their horse clubs awkwardly too, and as for the old science of tiger-scaring—well, even the teachers seem to lack the real flair for the subject which we oldsters got in our teens and never forgot."

"But, damn it," exploded one of the radicals, "how can any person with good sense be interested in such useless activities? What is the point of trying to catch fish with the bare hands when it just can't be done any more? How can a boy learn to club horses when there are no horses left to club? And why in hell should children try to scare tigers with fire when the tigers are dead and gone?"

"Don't be foolish," said the wise old men, smiling most kindly smiles. "We don't teach fish-grabbing to grab fish; we teach it to develop a generalized agility which can never be developed by mere training. We don't teach horse-clubbing to club horses; we teach it to develop a generalized strength in the learner which he can never get from so prosaic and specialized a thing as antelope-snare-setting. We don't teach tiger-scaring to scare tigers; we teach it for the purpose of giving that noble courage which carries over into all the affairs of life and which can never come from so base an activity as bear-killing."

All the radicals were silenced by this statement, all except the one who was most radical of all. He felt abashed, it is true, but he was so radical that he made one last protest.

"But—but anyway," he suggested, "you will have to admit that times have changed. Couldn't you please *try* these other more up-to-date activities? Maybe they have *some* educational value after all?"

Even the man's fellow radicals felt that this was going a little too far.

The wise old men were indignant. Their kindly smiles faded. "If you had any education yourself," they said severely, "you would know that the essence of true education is timelessness. It is something that endures through changing conditions like a solid rock standing squarely and firmly in the middle of a raging torrent. You must know that there are some eternal verities, and the saber-tooth curriculum is one of them!"

—J. Abner Peddiwell, *The Saber-Tooth Curriculum* (New York: McGraw-Hill, 1939), pp. 42–44. Reproduced with permission.

Robert Miller, a professor of industrial education at Northern Arizona University, served the same argument slightly differently. Most citizens, he noted, are actively employed using skills that do not require more than a few years to master. Therefore, "it would seem logical to suppose that the educational system should adjust itself to fit more nearly the reality of life faced by most students and provide them with a means of competing in the market place." This point, Miller insisted, could not be overemphasized. "When a significant number of students are released unemployable and undirected, lost and disillusioned, the educational system seems inhumane and unresponsive to the most fundamental of human needs." [131]

Miller assailed the modern tendency in schools to stress cognitive learning, to concentrate upon the needs of the professionally bound, and to look down upon skill training as unworthy. "Those interested in nonprofessional careers have as much right to study topics of interest to them as those who wish to go into medicine, law or engineering. The truly equitable comprehensive public school should offer a selection of short skill and technological development courses at least as comprehensive as those in liberal and academic studies," he insisted. [132]

Miller offered an interesting explanation for the differential weight assigned by society to different categories of knowledge. The case for skill training as important knowledge, he claimed, was rarely made "because those who are working in nonprofessional occupations rarely write or speak to the public at large, and their life styles are generally more directed to psychomotor activity than philosophical discussions." Academics who decide upon curricular matters, on the other hand, he alleged,

> forget that their academic freedom and tenure have in effect set them economically free from the market place. Most scholars become alarmed when they are threatened, yet many seem to be completely unable to transfer their concern about economic stability into an understanding for other people who wish to secure the same measure of economic freedom with another life style but cannot because of a lack of funds, interest or capability. [133]

For Helen Loftis, of South Carolina's Winthrop College, and for Elizabeth M. Ray, a professor of home economics at Penn State, the basic issue at stake was not just economic security but personal fulfillment and satisfaction. [134] They took note of the results of one major national study showing that "for a significant fraction of the typical student body neither the reading of a page nor the writing of one is the avenue to a feeling of positive self-worth, security, and self-assurance." [135] Students lacking facility in traditional academic skill areas, they argued, are ill-served by a school system that devalues work, ignores vocation as a source of personal identity, and elevates to a place of exclusive importance a single procrustean standard of achievement. Like Miller, who pointed out that ordinary people are dependent on acquired skills for their economic freedom and lack the wherewithal to live their lives independent of the marketplace, Loftis and Ray argued that for many students, vocational education afforded the most effective means of achieving the goal of self-development through work.

## LOOKING BACKWARD:
## TWO DIVERGENT HISTORICAL INTERPRETATIONS

From a contemporary vantage point, the growth of vocational education has been a remarkable phenomenon in the twentieth century, beginning with the debate of the early 1900s over whether trade training had any legitimate place in public education and extending in a line of development that has culminated in a broad array of activities and programs as integral components of the nation's schooling infrastructure. Less clear, perhaps, has been the *meaning* or significance of that history. As American historian Charles A. Beard once observed, history is an act of choice, conviction, and interpretation. "The selection and arrangement of facts," he claimed, ". . . is controlled inexorably by the frame of reference in the mind of the selector and arranger."[136] Nowhere else is the force of Beard's famous dictum so vividly illustrated than in the divergence of interpretations accorded the history of vocational education. Two examples will suffice.

At one extreme is the so-called "revisionist" account of American educational history (of which the development of vocational education is an important part), which came to the fore in the 1970s. Striking hard at the self-congratulatory pieties of an earlier day, revisionist historians paint a picture of schools exploited for purposes utterly inimical to the nurture of individualism, personal dignity, independence of thought, or autonomy of action. Samuel Bowles, for example, has argued that the structure of institutionalized schooling evolved basically in response to political and economic struggles associated with the process of capital accumulation and the extension of the wage-labor production system.

According to his analysis, the school's major function historically has been to reproduce the social relations of production and the expansion of the forces of production in society. He concludes that "the corporate capitalist economy—with its bias in favor of hierarchy, waste, and alienation in production and its mandate for a school system attuned to the reproduction and legitimatization of the associated hierarchical division of labor"—defines the central theme around which most, if not all, of the history of education in the United States must be written.[137]

The story recounted by many radical historians is one of the triumph of self-interest by "haves" over the legitimate aspirations of "have-nots," of schools captured by corporate industrialists and utilized as instruments for sorting out, socializing, and training the labor supply for the workplace. As these critics viewed it, the protection of corporate interests, not individual liberty, has been the main thrust of American public education throughout much of its history. Although they explicitly disavow any theory of deliberate conspiracy, the impression most such writers reinforce is one of capitalist elites conniving to enlist the school's help in creating an inexpensive and docile work force at public cost, all the while concealing their diabolical machinations behind a cloak of pious rhetoric and protestations of noble purpose.[138]

At the opposite extreme lies the more roseate history fashioned by vocational educators themselves and intended chiefly for internal consumption. The account they offer is decidedly upbeat and inspirational. "In the progress of the human race," runs a typical panegyric, "the vocational education of man has been a consistent and identifiable element. Vocational education has been part of the foundation of man's creative and progressive development."[139] Similar in tone is the judgment offered by Gordon Swanson, writing for the 1981 Yearbook of the American Vocational Association: "Only through the study of the history of vocational education can one develop a depth of understanding and pride in belonging to this area of education."[140]

A dominant motif in the vocationalists' history is the reactionary character of most "mainstream" educational theory. "One would expect to find a ready acceptance of vocational education as essential to any program of democratic education," Arthur Mays observed. "Education thinking, however, has not always followed logical lines, and educational practice has seldom exhibited a logical progression." He continued, "In the early years of American educational history the mind of the educator was held in thrall by an unscientific psychology and by the tenets of an educational philosophy inherited from the Middle Ages. There was constant conflict between the rapidly changing environment and an unchanging theory of the function of the school. . . ."[141]

Prosser and Quigley offered much the same explanation: "Our school system still blindly tried to clutch a philosophy of education for an idyllic aristocratic leisure that had never existed even in the aristocracies."[142] Complained Melvin L. Barlow, American Vocational Association historian, "The 'educational mind' of America does not really understand the real values of industrial education."[143] Fortunately, as this account has had it, a few clear-eyed visionaries such as Charles Prosser and David Snedden have arisen periodically to do battle against the ineluctable force of elitist prejudice. "In every generation of educators," as one commentator put it, "there have been a few prophetic minds who have protested against the lag of the schools behind the needs of an ever-changing society and a few far-seeing ones who desired the schools to lead the way to a better life rather than always resisting changes. . . . The struggle for progress in education is a never-ending one."[144]

Half a century or more of vocationalist literature invariably ties occupational training to the values of social efficiency, progress, and democracy. "The greater the degree to which social wealth can be produced in the most efficient way," argued Prosser and Quigley, "the greater our potential resources for achieving our ends as a nation." On the whole, they claimed, organized vocational training is an "efficiency device" utilized by the state for securing social wealth. To the extent that "the vocations of the people" become the "universal channel" through which education operates, they promised, "social progress will be furthered, more social wealth will be produced at less cost, and society will be better equipped to carry on its struggle against nature."[145]

Consistently, proponents of vocational education have seen democracy, social progress, and industrialism as interdependent elements. "Modern life requires that all workers be trained for their work," Mays argued. "To train some and not to train others creates inequalities that violate the spirit of democracy. To give all the same training only aggravates original inequalities.'' [146] Here are Prosser and Quigley once again on the same theme:

> The more democratic the society, the more the citizens are interested in thinking, talking, reading, writing, and dreaming about work and the goods and services that it produces for our enjoyment. The more democratic a society, the more the production, the transportation, and the exchange of goods and services become the central theme of its individual and social life. This is . . . why *the more democratic a society, the more industrial its civilization.* [147]

According to Lowell A. Burkett, one-time executive director of the American Vocational Association, ''Vocational education is in reality a social movement. It is an educational process that, by its very nature, promotes democracy. It builds on each student's abilities and aspirations. And it is an avenue of opportunity for all who seek to become productive workers—without regard to race, creed, class, or national origin.'' [148] John A. McCarthy, Assistant Commissioner of Education for the State of New Jersey in 1951, saw the entire history of the vocational-education movement as one of ''steady progress,'' interrupted or impeded only when ''educators in other fields failed to recognize the importance of training persons to do the manual work of the world . . . and who persisted in the belief that vocational education was for those who were mentally incapacitated and lazy, and could not participate with profit in any other educational program.'' [149]

In retrospect, it is all too easy to satirize or caricature either history. From a contemporary vantage point, neither appears properly appreciative of, or sensitive to, the mixed motives of the protagonists involved and the complex interplay of social, economic, and political forces to which they reacted in various periods and which they helped shape. Neither account does full justice to the ambiguities, the occasional paradoxes, and the internal contradictions latent in the historical record. With its deeply rooted animosity toward capitalism, its predilection for conspiracy, and its tendency to exaggerate class conflict, the radical-revisionist history leaves itself vulnerable to charges that events have been distorted to fit a preconceived pattern and that historical materials have been exploited for didactic editorial purposes.

Much the same charge, of course, could be levied against the somewhat self-serving historical analysis offered by vocationalists. With its boosterism, its celebration of corporate-industrial interests, and its uncritical adulation of trade training, the vocationalist account is likewise all too often simplistic, unbalanced, and one-sided. A more adequate history of vocationalism in American education, it might be argued, has yet to be written. Meanwhile, at the very least, what is most likely to strike an impartial observer are the very different conclusions drawn by the two analyses.

For revisionists of a radical stripe, the growth of vocational education exemplifies and symbolizes the historic domination of educational policy by corporate-business and industrial elites. The extent to which they succeeded in advancing their own interests, so it is argued, is attested to today by the panoply of vocational guidance services and training programs evident throughout the educational system at all levels, from the primary grades up through university graduate schools. The clear implication throughout is that the expansion of vocational education *has* been successful and that its dominance of the contemporary educational scene should be the occasion for profound regret.

In contrast, the vocationalist interpretation *denies* that vocational education even today enjoys the full measure of popular acceptance it deserves, or that it has as yet achieved the level of development and support needed in a complex industrial democracy. Because reactionaries have not yet abandoned their antiquated values and outmoded educational theories, the argument runs, vocational education has been prevented from realizing its full potential or contributing to the economic progress and further democratization of educational opportunity it could help make possible within the contemporary American social order.

## IN RETROSPECT

Rather obviously, how one assesses the meaning or implications of the history of vocational education in the United States depends upon what prior assumptions and beliefs are brought to the analysis. These in turn are at least partly a function of whatever values, attitudes, presuppositions and beliefs a person may harbor concerning vocational education generally and, more broadly, the outlook or perspective identified as "vocationalism." If one is favorably disposed toward the use of schooling to prepare people for employment, the inclination is to look with favor upon the growth of occupationally relevant preparatory programs and to urge their further expansion. Contrariwise, if, for whatever reasons, one is less enthusiastic about tying education to economic objectives, the tendency will be to accept a less generous interpretation of how and why vocational training has come to occupy so important a role in modern education.

Either way, as in the case of educational "conservatism," when vocationalism is reformulated in the abstract as a formal argument, its main outlines are relatively easy to discern. Its practical applications and policy implications, both historically and today, have been exceedingly complex. In minor particulars, arguments offered on behalf of vocationalism have differed, depending on the time, place, and circumstances prevailing. But, in terms of its essential elements, vocationalism as a definable point of view regarding education has remained basically unchanged. Its proponents, it can be argued, would subscribe in varying degree to all or at least most of the following fundamental propositions:

1. Human knowledge is an instrumentality or tool for controlling and reshaping the natural environment. The ultimate test by which to judge the value of knowledge is its utility. The proper end of knowing is action. To the extent that information can be applied in the furtherance of some useful purpose, that knowledge is of most worth.

2. Organized social life depends upon the production, distribution, and consumption of goods and services. Human history is a record of the progressive improvement of humanity's ability to devise technologies for the improvement, expansion, and diversification of production. As production processes have grown more effective and efficient, living standards have improved. The resultant gains in economic security have meant greater freedom from want and deprivation for ever-increasing numbers of people, at least in modern industrialized societies. On balance, industrialization and the development of scientific technology have rendered possible greater opportunities for self-development and fulfillment, for more people, than at any previous time in history.

3. In contemporary society, almost everyone capable of doing so must fulfill an economic role within the social order. Practically everyone in the adult years (the incapacitated and the ultra-rich excepted) must be gainfully employed in one capacity or another. The need to work, to engage in labor activity of some sort, is virtually universal.

4. In addition to its obvious socioeconomic utility, work also has major psychological significance. It is an important source of self-identity and personal fulfillment. It offers a potential means for self-definition and expression. In this respect, at least, all labor has intrinsic dignity and worth.

5. The complexity of modern industrial society, combined with large-scale and rapid technological change, together have outstripped the capacity of informal means to prepare people for the world of work. Formal, systematic job training and periodic retraining conducted under institutionalized auspices are essential. The institution of schooling must assume a major share of the responsibility for equipping people with the knowledge, values, and skills necessary for employment.

6. In American society, the private sector of the economy cannot be expected to organize, finance or administer job-training programs. Public educational institutions have the primary—though not necessarily exclusive—responsibility for fostering occupational competencies, including good work habits, vocationally relevant knowledge, and, to some degree, specific entry-level skills for various trades and professions.

7. Heretofore, the persistence of outmoded attitudes and prejudices has prevented vocational education from coming into its own. Only when there is popular appreciation of, and support for, the need to prepare people for the world of work will vocational training assume its rightful role in American schooling.

8. Present-day school curricula tend to be too impractical and unrelated to the very real economic needs of contemporary society. All too many people leave the school system lacking knowledge and skills needed for subsequent employment.

9. Social efficiency demands a closer relationship between society's manpower development requirements and its system of schooling. Waste and inefficiency could be reduced significantly if there existed a better articulation of school programming with the needs of a market economy. School instruction should be more closely adapted to what the economic marketplace can utilize in the way of knowledge and skills.

10. Insofar as schools fail to provide opportunities to prepare for gainful employment, they fail in society's avowed goal of extending equality of opportunity for all. Democracy as a social ideal requires programs and courses of study adapted to the varying needs, abilities, and interests of a diverse, heterogeneous student population. Learners who lack an aptitude for traditional academic instruction should have access to alternative forms of education better suited to their needs and aspirations.

11. Student apathy, indifference, and lack of motivation may be accounted for in large measure by the lack of occupational relevance of most traditional school curricula. If

vocational concerns were more heavily emphasized, school discipline problems would be reduced, learner involvement would improve, and fewer students would drop out of school.

12. Vocational education should enjoy equal status with academic education. The practical effect of "tracking" students has been to accord those who enter a vocational-education "track" lower social status. Vocational-education programs frequently are exploited as dumping grounds for the academically unfit. Such programs are underfunded, looked down upon, and often neglected by elitist school officials.

13. A new curricular reform is needed that will better integrate academic and vocational instruction for all students, including both those who will seek employment directly upon graduation from high school and those who will continue their formal education beyond the secondary level. A major aim of the American high school should be to equip the majority of students not intending to attend college with entry-level skills for trades and occupations that do not require more than a high-school diploma for employment.

## SUMMARY

Training for work throughout most of history has been managed informally and without benefit of formal schooling. Children acquired the skills needed in adulthood through direct observation and imitation of their elders as they worked. They learned through firsthand experience. The only systematic provision offered for occupational instruction was through the apprenticeship system. This was to remain the chief means of preparing people for the world of work until the advent of modern industrialization.

Early American culture was profoundly influenced by the Protestant work ethic and informed by a deeply rooted aversion to elitist forms of schooling. For these and other reasons, Americans in the eighteenth and nineteenth centuries strongly approved of a practical emphasis in education. A variety of private, sectarian, entrepreneurial, and philanthropic institutions flourished whose aim was to provide vocational training for the working classes. Well before the end of the 1700s, the rising merchant and trade classes were supporting schools adapted to their interests. Private venture schools offered a range of business and commercial subjects, on both a full-time and part-time basis. In the nineteenth century, private trade schools, agricultural institutes, mechanics schools, and industrial colleges grew in number. Oftentimes vocational education was sponsored by private industries and businesses. The passage of the two Morrill Acts, in 1862 and 1890, served to encourage the creation of land-grant colleges offering programs in agriculture and mechanics, and, later, a host of other occupationally relevant courses of study.

Both American educational theory and practice took note of European experiments with vocational training for the underprivileged. In varying ways such theorists as Rousseau, Pestalozzi, Froebel, Cygnaeus, Ziller, and Basedow all lent support to the idea of manual-arts instruction and practical trade training.

By the end of the nineteenth century, public education was under pressure to offer more vocational preparatory programs. Leaders of business and industry called upon the schools to train a work force capable of helping the nation to compete more effectively in international trade and to expand markets. Organized labor echoed much the same demands, despite fears that expanded vocational training in public schools might weaken union control over factory-based apprenticeships. Professional educators generally looked favorably on calls for more and better job training. The question was whether such instruction should be offered in regular public schools or in separate specialized facilities.

Especially active in the drive to introduce vocational training in schools was the National Association of Manufacturers. Its representatives repeatedly called upon educators to learn from the German model, where schools were organized to reflect economic market needs as closely as possible. The Association's Commission on Industrial Education in 1905, for example, strongly urged adoption of the German system of education. When the National Society For The Promotion of Industrial Education was formed in 1906–7, the National Association of Manufacturers quickly became its chief supporter and funding agency. During the same period, a report of Massachusetts's Douglas Commission attracted nationwide interest with its proposal for the creation of a comprehensive state system of industrial trade schools. Particularly noteworthy was the fact that vocational training programs were to be administered under separate control from regular educational institutions.

Supporters of a burgeoning vocational-education movement in the early twentieth century were clearly divided on certain fundamental issues. Such leaders as David Snedden and Charles Prosser were primarily interested in practical job training, preferably in industrial trade schools operated apart from the existing public-school system but at public expense. Others opposed the creation of a separate system of vocational schools as an affront to the ideal of common schooling for all. Efficiency proponents wanted school-based vocational guidance to facilitate the sorting of students at an early age and to channel the majority into job-training programs. Opponents such as Jane Addams, Frank Carlton, and John Dewey strongly supported industrial education but resisted efforts to narrow it down to specific trade training. They likewise opposed the mechanical application of efficiency criteria to the conduct of schooling and the use of vocational guidance to fit people to occupational slots within the existing corporate-industrial order.

John Dewey wrote extensively on the theme of vocationalism in education. He foresaw a threat to democratic ideals in proposals to create a separate vocational-school system and to gear instructional programs too closely to market needs. His plea was for vocational studies in a broader and more liberal setting or context. Although convinced that the study of "occupations" or "vocations" could liberate "industrial intelligence," he refused to endorse narrow job training as a primary educational objective in American public schools.

Passage of the Smith-Hughes Act, in 1917, marked a significant milestone in the history of American vocational education. With the enactment into law of the Vocational Education Act, federal funding first became available for a national system of institutions designed to prepare people for employment. Until 1933, a Federal Board was empowered to approve all state plans for vocational training, to fund programs, conduct surveys, and otherwise encourage the expansion of opportunities for formal job preparation. The Smith-Hughes Act was the first in a succession of federal legislative initiatives undertaken in support of vocational education.

The outbreak of World War II in 1939 necessitated an unprecedented expansion of defense-related training programs. Critics such as Robert Maynard Hutchins concluded that their success demonstrated the fallacy of school-based vocational education. Others argued that such wartime efforts offered a useful blueprint for the type of education needed in the period of postwar reconstruction to follow. Meanwhile such vocationalists as Charles Prosser were in the forefront of a drive sponsored by the U.S. Office of Education to promote life-adjustment education as a comprehensive model for all American schooling.

Recurrent themes in vocationalist literature from the 1940s onward included the need for professional educators to divest themselves of reactionary theory and irrational prejudice against school-based job training; the social and economic progress vocational education could make possible; and the need to democratize education by offering more vocational courses. Many writers denied that vocational and general education were opposed to each other; rather, they should be thought of as interdependent and sometimes indistinguishable aspects of a total balanced educational system. Proponents repeatedly attacked any rigid separation of vocational training from academic instruction, arguing that *all* people needed *both* general education and training directly related to productive employment. Arthur B. Mays in particular insisted that a ''wall of partition'' between vocational and ''cultural'' education was wholly unwarranted.

In seeking to explain the apparent failure of vocational education to attain the same status as more traditional academic learning, some writers pointed to the persistence of attitudes toward work and knowledge extending all the way back to the inception of Western civilization itself. Others felt that educational policymakers were victims of their own middle-class background, and hence biased against the kind of education needed by students of different socioeconomic origins. The result, it was alleged, was a system feeding upon itself and founded on a blind faith in the value of common academic learning for everyone, regardless of differing needs, abilities and life goals.

Vocationalism as a formal argument underlying vocational-education programs is a recognizable point of view or perspective whose features have changed very little over the past three-quarters of a century. It emphasizes utility as a standard or criterion for determining what knowledge is of most worth; the personal and social necessity of work; the need for school-based vocational preparation; and the desirable consequences that would allegedly follow from relating more closely the worlds of work and learning. Traditionally, proponents of vocationalism have tended to appeal to pragmatic rather than philosophic considerations in defending their outlook upon the proper aims and goals of American public education.

## REVIEW QUESTIONS

1. What is the difference between "vocationalism" and vocational *education?* How is vocationalism characterized or defined? What is its major theme and how has it found practical expression in educational institutions?

2. Why were schools not needed throughout most of history for preparing people for work? In other words, how was job preparation managed in a preindustrial era? What specific factors led to the demand for school-based vocational education?

3. What might have been the chief advantages and disadvantages of apprenticeship training as an institutionalized means of preparing people for their economic roles in society?

4. How did the Protestant work ethic help shape early American attitudes toward vocational education? What other factors encouraged an emphasis upon practical education in schools?

5. Who supported the first private trade schools in America, and why?

6. Explain how the Morrill Acts led to the establishment of professional preparatory programs in American higher education. What led to the passage of the Morrill Acts, and what were their long-term consequences? How were colleges and universities affected?

7. What specific circumstances at the turn of the century prompted calls from business and industry for the establishment of formal vocational-training programs? Why was the German model for reform so widely admired?

8. Specifically, what did corporate industrial leaders want in the way of vocational training, and why? What was the response from organized labor? Why were so many labor leaders ambivalent about expanded job training? How did professional educators respond?

9. What was the Douglas Commission, and what was the historic importance of its 1906 Report?

10. What were the original purposes of the National Society for the Promotion of Industrial Education? Who supported the NSPIE, and why? What was the reform program urged by the Society in its formative years?

11. What was the main concern expressed in the 1915 report of the AFL Committee on Education? How did the NEA's 1910 report from its Committee on the Place of Industries in Public Education resemble the AFL's committee report? That is, what concern did the two documents have in common?

12. At least two distinguishable viewpoints emerged in the early 1900s on the nature and purpose of vocational training. What were they? How was the same difference reflected in divergent views on the scope and intent of vocational guidance?

13. What "new function" did Charles W. Eliot urge upon the elementary schools in his 1908 speech to the NSPIE, and in what ways did he subsequently modify his position?

14. How did Frederick Taylor's *Principles of Management* (1911) affect American educational theory? Summarize the basic arguments advanced by proponents of the efficiency movement in education. How were those assumptions or arguments attacked by critics?

15. Outline as specifically as possible the difference dividing Charles Prosser, David Snedden, Ellwood P. Cubberley, and James P. Munroe, on the one hand, from George Herbert Mead, Jane Addams, Frank Carlton, and John Dewey, on the other. What were the basic issues involved?

16. Did John Dewey welcome or oppose the vocational-education movement of the early 1900s? What did he specify as the main points of controversy? Why did Dewey oppose separate trade schools? What did he identify as the chief danger of vocationalism?

17. What were the major provisions of the Smith-Hughes Act? What was their historical importance? What specific rationale for the legislation was put forth by the Commission appointed by President Wilson? That is, upon what basis—for what reasons—did the Commission recommend passage of the Vocational Education Act of 1917?

18. In what sense may it be said that the rise of the comprehensive high school was a "compromise" between the demands of vocationalists and their critics?

19. Review the major federal acts that encouraged the expansion of vocational education between 1917 and 1936. What was the federal role in stimulating the growth of vocational-education programs?

20. Why did such vocationalist writers as Arthur B. Mays hold that American education was dominated by a "philosophy of education derived from the slave-owning classes of ancient Greece"? Explain as succinctly as possible the alternative viewpoint expressed by Charles Prosser and David Snedden.

21. Why did vocationalists so vigorously oppose the 1933 decision by Congress to transfer the powers of the Federal Board for Vocational Education to the U.S. Commissioner of Education? What were the issues involved? Were they resolved? What were the alleged advantages of a dual school system, as compared with a system of unit control?

22. What lesson did Robert Maynard Hutchins draw in 1944 from the success of wartime vocational training programs?

23. How did vocationalists in the 1940s and thereafter make the case for the interdependence of vocational and general education? What specific arguments were advanced? (Note the comments on this point by Alexander J. Stoddard, Stephen Vorhees, Edwin Lee, Arthur Mays, and Franklin Keller.)

24. How did the life-adjustment education movement of the 1940s reflect a vocationalist perspective? What rationale was offered? What were the distinguishing features of life-adjustment education? Why was the movement so short-lived?

25. Review the role of the federal government in the postwar period in promoting vocational education. How did the legislation that was enacted in this period contribute to the expansion of training programs?

26. According to Robert Beck, how have contemporary attitudes toward work and knowledge been influenced by ideas inherited from Graeco-Roman antiquity? Why did Plato look down upon vocational training? How was his general philosophy tied to his political views, and in turn how did these affect his attitudes toward various kinds of knowledge?

27. Why did Rupert Evans oppose the concept of a common curriculum? What are the major arguments for and against a uniform body of knowledge to be taught to everyone in school? What did he allege was the "major untaught curriculum" of the school?
28. What have been the main arguments opposing educational vocationalism as propounded by so-called revisionist historians? How have vocationalists tied their arguments to the cause of social efficiency, progress, and democracy?
29. According to the vocationalist position, what is knowledge? What knowledge is of greatest value? What is most worth knowing? Why is work important? Why should schools assume responsibility for preparing people for employment? What are the alleged consequences of the schools' neglect of vocational training?

## SOME QUESTIONS FOR DISCUSSION

1. Historically speaking, until comparatively recent times most people acquired necessary skills through on-the-job training. Are modern conditions so different that formal, school-based job training is always necessary? Can't most unskilled and semiskilled jobs be learned by doing them? What kind of prior training is needed by a prospective sanitation worker, mail carrier, drill-press operator, or service-station attendant? How about a short-order cook, a retail salesperson, or a crane operator? Do these jobs require extensive job preparation?
2. Could the age-old apprenticeship system be revived and adapted in many instances? Why couldn't many people learn job skills from a tutor or mentor engaged in a particular trade or craft occupation?
3. Why should schools assume major responsibility for occupational training? Why not require employers to pay for and organize vocational-education programs of their own? Do not many large corporations already have their own preparatory programs? So why should schools be required to train people for employment? Discuss the relative advantages and disadvantages of business- and industry-based vocational education compared with school-based instruction.
4. Why is it so often claimed that the work ethic is dead or dying? What's wrong with a work ethic? Why shouldn't people value work? Is craftsmanship declining? Do people generally still take pride in a job well done? Why or why not? Should not people be encouraged to respect work as a personal and social necessity and as a positive good? What does it mean to say of a person that he or she is lazy?
5. In colonial America, most vocational schools were private entrepreneurial ventures. If formal, school-based training programs are needed today, why must that need be met by the public sector? Why not let the private sector organize programs? Would it be a good idea to allow most people to attend private business schools and technical institutes as they ready themselves for employment?
6. Most people profess to accept the idea of the dignity of all labor. Why, then, do we look down upon certain trades and occupations as demeaning and unworthy even if they are socially useful? Why do we preserve the distinction between "white-collar" and "blue-collar" employment? What's wrong with being a garbage collector, a sanitation worker, or a

housekeeper? Somebody has to assume responsibility for unpleasant work. Why burden those who do it by branding them as somehow inferior?

7. How plausible is the suggestion that leaders of corporate business and industry originally supported school-based vocational training because they wanted a docile, submissive labor supply trained at public expense? (In other words, they allegedly wanted to avoid the expense of training industrial workers themselves.) What might count as evidence for such a thesis? Is there any evidence to suggest otherwise?

8. Why were American institutions of higher education the first to introduce occupationally relevant programs, even before high schools? Why were professional preparatory programs established at the postsecondary level prior to the creation of high-school vocational-education programs for those not intending to pursue a baccalaureate degree?

9. In many European and Asian nations today, schoolchildren are "tracked" into specialized courses of instruction at any earlier age than is common in the American school system. Why not allow—or require—children to specialize earlier? Did Charles Eliot have a good idea when he urged the use of elementary schools for sorting children according to their "probable destiny"? Isn't it true that an experienced sixth-grade teacher or a junior-high-school counselor can predict with a fair degree of accuracy whether a given child is likely eventually to enter a profession or seek blue-collar employment? So why not plan accordingly?

10. Vocationalists have often argued for a more or less independent parallel system of public vocational schools administered separately from regular academic schools. Would this be a good idea? What is so important about the ideal of common schooling? Wouldn't it make more sense to have specialized schools run by experts knowledgeable about what good vocational-education programs require?

11. Many of the early proponents of vocational guidance in schools urged the adoption of efficiency criteria for assessing the performance of public education. Why? Can schooling today be compared with running a business? Why or why not? Why not utilize standards of economy, cost effectiveness, efficiency, and financial accountability in educating children? Can schooling be conceived of as an engineering project?

12. Most high-school graduates are economically illiterate, critics charge. Few people have even a rudimentary understanding of how the American economy functions. Even most college graduates leave school lacking knowledge of basic economic principles. They allegedly have little or no awareness of supply-and-demand equations, of wage-price mechanisms, of the dynamics of domestic and international trade, of monetary policies, and so on. Should schools do more to inform people about the economic facts of life? What activities or subjects in school could be de-emphasized to leave room for more and better economic education?

13. Reflect back on your own high-school experience. Were students in vocational-technical courses looked down upon? What about those involved in work-study programs? Did your school district have a separate vocational school? Who took "shop" courses? Were students enrolled in courses in distributive and cooperative education different from those preparing themselves for college? Were you encouraged or discouraged from taking vocational courses? Explicitly or implicitly, were students in your school sorted into separate curricular tracks? Did those in a college-preparatory course of study enjoy more prestige and social status than those who were not? Why or why not?

14. When did you first decide to attend college? Was it a conscious and deliberate decision? Who helped you make it? What factors entered into that decision? How did you feel as a youngster when people asked you what you wanted to be when you grew up? Could you answer the question?

15. Should job training be postponed until after high school? Or does it make sense to begin earlier? Either way, what are the relative advantages and disadvantages?

16. How important is common learning? In other words, is there some knowledge *everyone* should possess, even if it means neglecting other kinds of more specialized training? Should everyone in high school have exposure to a common body of knowledge, skills, and values?

17. Ivar Berg, in his book, *Education And Jobs: The Great Training Robbery* (1971), argued that educational requirements for employment continue to rise. Employers are convinced that by raising their demands, they will be more likely to recruit an ambitious, disciplined work force that will be more productive than workers who have terminated their schooling earlier. A job that once required a high-school diploma now requires a college degree for employment, even though the requirements of the job itself have remained the same. Berg's argument, in part, was that enthusiasts of education continue to press for higher qualifications without reference to the tasks to be performed. He claimed that credentials, not competency, had become all-important. Furthermore, according to his analysis, there is only a rough correspondence between credentials and actual job proficiency in many occupations. He further alleged that changing the characteristics of workers by adding to their schooling affords no solution to the shortfall in demand for labor. In other words, vocational training cannot help solve problems of unemployment. Assuming some validity to Berg's thesis, what implications follow for organizing vocational-education programs?

18. What types of employment are open to high-school graduates? Is the need today for more people with entry-level skills to these occupations? Or is the need for highly trained, skilled workers in fields that require more than a secondary-school education?

19. Is it true that democracy as a social ideal mandates more vocational education? Does vocationalization equate with the democratization of educational opportunity? Is it elitist and unfair to emphasize "academic" education over vocational training?

20. Would more vocational education in schools enhance motivation, reduce discipline problems, and lower the drop-out rate? Is "occupational relevance" the key to contemporary school reform?

21. Is general academic education more "liberal" than vocational training? Is there a real difference between "education" and "training" or is the distinction between the two artificial and arbitrary? Properly managed, could a course of study leading directly to employment be more "broadening" for some students than a traditional regimen organized around the basic subject-matter disciplines?

22. Schools as formal institutions tend to value and reward academic aptitude. Should educators be more responsive to those students whose strengths lie in the areas of manual dexterity and mechanical aptitude rather than in cognition? Is it the case, as many vocationalist proponents frequently allege, that the typical high-school curriculum is unbalanced and weighted toward intellectual values?

## FURTHER READING

AMERICAN VOCATIONAL ASSOCIATION. *The Advisory Committee and Vocational Education.* Washington, D.C.: American Vocational Association, 1969.

APPLETON, L. F. *History of Manual and Industrial School Education.* New York: Appleton-Century-Crofts, 1926.

BARCELLA, RICHARD and THOMAS WRIGHT, eds. *An Interpretive History of Industrial Arts.* Bloomington, Ill.: McKnight Publishing Co., 1981.

BARLOW, MELVIN L. *History of Industrial Education in the United States.* Peoria: Chas. A. Bennett Press, 1967.

————, ed. *The Philosophy For Quality Vocational Education Programs.* Washington, D.C.: American Vocational Association, 1974.

————, ed. *Vocational Education, Sixty-fourth Yearbook of the National Society For The Study Of Education. Part I.* Chicago: University of Chicago Press, 1965.

BARRY, RUTH and BEVERLY WOLF. *An Epitaph for Vocational Guidance.* New York: Columbia University Press, 1962.

BAWDEN, WILLIAM T. *Twenty Years of Progress in the Manual Arts.* Peoria: Manual Arts Press, 1930.

————. *Leaders in Industrial Education.* Milwaukee: Bruce Publishing Company, 1950.

BELITSKY, A. HARVEY. *Private-Vocational Schools and Their Students.* Cambridge, Mass.: Schenkman, 1969.

BENNETT, CHARLES A. *History of Manual and Industrial Education, 1870–1917.* Peoria: Chas. A. Bennett Press, 1937.

————. *History of Manual and Industrial Education up to 1870.* Peoria: Manual Arts Press, 1926.

BERG, IVAR. *Education and Jobs: The Great Training Robbery.* Boston: Beacon Press, 1971.

BOROW, HENRY, ed. *Man in a World at Work.* Boston: Houghton Mifflin, 1964.

BOWLES, SAMUEL and HERBERT GINTIS. *Schooling in Capitalist America.* New York: Basic Books, 1976.

BURT, SAMUEL M. *Industry and Vocational-Technical Education.* New York: McGraw-Hill, 1967.

———— and LEON M. LESSINGER. *Volunteer Industry Involvement in Public Education.* Lexington, Mass.: Heath, 1970.

CALLAHAN, RAYMOND E. *Education and the Cult of Efficiency.* Chicago: University of Chicago Press, 1962.

CLARK, HAROLD F. and HAROLD S. SLOAN. *Classrooms in the Factories.* New York: New York University Press, 1958.

COHN, ELCHANAN. *The Economics of Education.* Cambridge, Mass.: Ballinger, 1975.

CONANT, JAMES B. *The American High School Today.* New York: McGraw-Hill, 1959.

DAVIS, RUSSELL G. *Planning Human Resource Development: Educational Models and Schemata.* Chicago: Rand McNally, 1966.

DEWEY, JOHN. *The Way Out of Educational Confusion.* Cambridge, Mass.: Harvard University Press, 1931.

DOOLEY, WILLIAM H. *Principles and Methods of Industrial Education.* Boston: Houghton Mifflin, 1919.

EDUCATIONAL POLICIES COMMISSION OF THE NATIONAL EDUCATION ASSOCIATION OF THE UNITED STATES AND OF THE AMERICAN ASSOCIATION OF SCHOOL ADMINISTRATORS. *Education For All American Youth.* Washington, D.C.: The Commission, 1944.

EVANS, RUPERT N. *Education For Employment.* Ann Arbor: Institute of Labor and Industrial Relations, University of Michigan, 1969.

————. *Foundations of Vocational Education.* Columbus, Oh.: Chas. E. Merrill, 1971.

FEDERAL SECURITY AGENCY, U.S. OFFICE OF EDUCATION. *Vocational Education in the Years Ahead.* Washington, D.C.: U.S. Office of Education, 1945.

FISHER, BERENICE M. *Industrial Education: American Ideals and Institutions.* Madison, Wis.: University of Wisconsin Press, 1967.

GARDNER, JOHN W. *Excellence, Can We Be Equal And Excellent Too?* New York: Harper & Row, 1961.

HAWKINS, LAYTON S., CHARLES A. PROSSER, and JOHN C. WRIGHT. *Development of Vocational Education.* Chicago: American Technical Society, 1951.

HENNINGER, G. ROSS. *The Technical Institute in America.* New York: McGraw-Hill, 1959.

KRUG, EDWARD A. *The Shaping of the American High School: 1880-1920.* Madison, Wis.: University of Wisconsin Press, 1969.

LAW, GORDON F., ed. *Contemporary Concepts In Vocational Education.* Washington: American Vocational Association, 1971.

LAZERSON, MARVIN. *Origins of the Urban School.* Cambridge, Mass.: Harvard University Press, 1971.

—— and W. NORTON GRUBB, eds. *American Education and Vocationalism: A Documentary History, 1870-1970.* New York: Teachers College Press, Columbia University, 1974.

LEE, EDWIN A. *Objectives and Problems of Vocational Education.* New York: McGraw-Hill, 1938.

LERGHBODY, GERALD B. *Vocational Education in America's Schools, Major Issues of the 1970's.* Chicago: American Technical Society, 1972.

LERWICK, LOWELL P. *Alternative Concepts Of Vocational Education.* Minneapolis: Minnesota Research and Development Center for Vocational Education, University of Minnesota, 1979.

MAYS, ARTHUR B. *The Concept of Vocational Education in the Thinking of the General Educator, 1845-1945.* Urbana, Ill.: Bureau of Educational Research Bulletin No. 62, University of Illinois, 1946.

——. *Principles and Practices of Vocational Education.* New York: McGraw-Hill, 1948.

MCCARTHY, JOHN A. *Vocational Education: America's Greatest Resource.* Chicago: American Technical Society, 1951.

MEYER, WARREN G. *Vocational Education and the Nation's Economy.* Washington, D.C.: American Vocational Association, 1977.

NASAW, DAVID. *Schooled To Order, A Social History of Public Schooling in the United States.* New York: Oxford University Press, 1979.

NATIONAL EDUCATION ASSOCIATION. *A Report of the Committee on the Place of Industries in Public Education.* Washington, D.C.: National Education Association, 1910.

PARSON, FRANK. *Choosing a Vocation.* Boston: Houghton Mifflin, 1909.

PROSSER, CHARLES A. and THOMAS H. QUIGLEY. *Vocational Education In Democracy.* Chicago: American Technical Society, 1950.

*Report of the Commission on National Aid to Vocational Education.* Washington, D.C.: U.S. Government Printing Office, 1914.

REPORT OF THE PANEL OF CONSULTANTS ON VOCATIONAL EDUCATION. *Education For A Changing World of Work.* Washington, D.C.: U.S. office of Education, 1963.

ROBERTS, ROY W. *Vocational and Practical Arts Education.* New York: Harper & Row, 1965.

ROE, ANNE. *The Psychology of Occupations.* New York: John Wiley, 1956.

SCHULTZ, THEODORE W. *The Economic Value of Education.* New York: Columbia University Press, 1963.

SMITH, H. ROSS. *Development of Manual Training in the United States.* Lancaster, Pa.: Intelligencer Print, 1914.

SPRING, JOEL H. *Education and the Rise of the Corporate State.* Boston: Beacon Press, 1972.

——. *The Sorting Machine, National Educational Policy Since 1945.* New York: D. McKay, 1976.

SUPER, DONALD E. *The Psychology of Careers.* New York: Harper & Row, 1957.

SWANSON, GORDON I., ed. *The Future of Vocational Education.* Arlington, Va.: American Vocational Association, 1981.

TERKEL, STUDS. *Working.* New York: Random House, 1972.

VENN, GRANT. *Man, Education and Work.* Washington, American Council on Education, 1964.

WIRTH, ARTHUR G. *Education In The Technological Society: The Vocational-Liberal Studies Controversy in the Early Twentieth Century.* Landham, Md.: University Press of America, 1980.

## NOTES

1. See Paul Boissonade, *Life and Work in Medieval Europe,* trans. Eileen Power (New York: Harper & Row, 1964); L. F. Salzman, *English Industries of the Middle Ages* (Oxford: Clarendon Press, 1923), pp. 340-343; and Donna R. Barnes (ed.), *For Court, Manor and Church* (Minneapolis: Burgess, 1971).

2. Robert F. Seybolt, *Apprenticeship and Apprenticeship Education in Colonial New England and New*

*York* (New York: Teachers College Press, Columbia University, 1917); and Paul H. Douglas, *American Apprenticeship and Industrial Education* (New York: Longmans, Green, 1921), pp. 55, 56.

3. See Max Weber, *The Protestant Ethic and the Spirit of Capitalism* (New York: Scribner, 1958); Richard H. Tawney, *Religion and the Rise of Capitalism* (New York: Harcourt, Brace, 1926); and Ernst Troeltsch, *Protestantism and Progress* (New York: G. P. Putnams, 1912).

4. Richard Baxter, *A Christian Directory* (London: G. Bell, 1925), p. 143.

5. Richard T. Auchmuty, "An American Apprentice System," *The Century* 15 (November 1888–April 1889): 401–405.

6. Cited in Arthur G. Wirth, *Education In The Technological Society: The Vocational–Liberal Studies Controversy in the Early Twentieth Century* (Landham: University Press of America, 1980), p. 17.

7. Quoted in Arthur B. Mays, *Principles and Practices of Vocational Education* (New York: McGraw-Hill, 1948), pp. 28, 29.

8. Quoted in ibid., p. 35.

9. A. D. Dean, "An Experiment in Teaching Trades at Public Expense," *Manual Training Magazine* (1901): 146, 147. See also Richard Barcella and Thomas Wright, eds., *An Interpretive History of Industrial Arts, Thirtieth Yearbook (1981) of the American Council on Industrial Arts Teacher Education* (Bloomington, Ill.: McKnight, 1981), pp. 144–164.

10. Cited in Arthur B. Mays, *The Concept of Vocational Education in the Thinking of the General Educator, 1845–1945* (Urbana, Ill.: Bureau of Educational Research, Bulletin No. 62, University of Illinois, 1946), p. 13.

11. Andrew Sloan Draper, *American Education* (Boston: Houghton Mifflin, 1901), p. 198.

12. Lawrence Cremin, *The Transformation of the School* (New York: Vintage, 1961), p. 33.

13. Quoted in Joel H. Spring, *Education and the Rise of the Corporate State* (Boston: Beacon Press, 1972), p. 42.

14. David Nasaw, *Schooled To Order, A Social History of Public Schooling in the United States* (New York: Oxford University Press, 1979), p. 122. See also William Appleman Williams, *The Tragedy of American Diplomacy,* second rev. ed. (New York: Delta, 1972), pp. 28–49.

15. See James Weinstein, *The Corporate Ideal in the Liberal State: 1900–1918* (Boston: Beacon Press, 1968), pp. 3–10; and Edward A. Drug, *The Shaping of the American High School: 1880–1920, Vol. 1* (Madison, Wis.: University of Wisconsin Press, 1969), p. 66.

16. Quoted in Wirth, *Education,* p. 25.

17. See Marvin Lazerson and W. Norton Grubb, eds., *American Education and Vocationalism: A Documentary History, 1870–1970* (New York: Teachers College Press, 1974), pp. 191–192.

18. Cited in Layton S. Hawkins, Charles A. Prosser, and John C. Wright, *Development of Vocational Education* (Chicago: American Technical Society, 1951), pp. 52–53.

19. *Twenty-fifth Annual Report of the U.S. Commission of Labor (1910), Revised Laws of Massachusetts* (Washington, D.C.: U.S. Government Printing Office, 1911), p. 3.

20. Ibid., p. 4.

21. See Commonwealth of Massachusetts, *Report of the Commission on Industrial and Technical Education* (Boston: The Commission, 1906).

22. For discussion, consult Charles A. Bennett, *History of Manual and Industrial Education,* Vol. II (Peoria: Chas. A. Bennett Press, 1937), p. 517.

23. *NSPIE Bulletin No. 1* (January 1907): 10. See Cremin, *Transformation,* p. 10. In 1918 the Society's name was changed to the National Society for Vocational Education, and in 1926, to the American Vocational Association.

24. Henry C. Morrison, "Vocational Training and Industrial Education," *Educational Review* (October 1907): 1,242.

25. See "A Symposium on Industrial Education," *NSPIE Bulletin No. 3* (September 1907): 6–9.

26. Marvin Lazerson, *Origins of the Urban School* (Cambridge, Mass.: Harvard University Press, 1971), p. 181.

27. Ibid., pp. 172–173; and Lazerson and Grubb, *American Education,* p. 78.

28. Nasaw, *Schooled to Order,* p. 147.

29. Berenice M. Fisher, *Industrial Education: American Ideals and Institutions* (Madison, Wis.: University of Wisconsin Press, 1967), pp. 124–126.

30. Cited in Nasaw, *Schooled to Order,* p. 148. See *NSPIE Bulletin No. 5* (April 1908): 49–50.

31. American Federation of Labor, "Labor and Education: A Brief Outline of the Resolutions and Pronouncements Adopted by the American Federation of Labor," *AFL Proceedings* (1908): 234.

32. See Irving J. Wyllie, *The Self-Made Man in America: The Myth of Rags to Riches* (New York: Free Press, 1954).

33. See *AFL Proceedings* (1915): 322–323; and Wirth, *Education,* p. 61.

34. Quoted in Nasaw, *Schooled to Order,* pp. 128–129.

35. National Education Association, *A Report of the Committee on the Place of Industries in Public Education* (Washington, D.C.: National Education Association, 1910), pp. 1–3, 8.

36. Ibid., p. 12.

37. Ibid., p. 13.

38. Andrew S. Draper, "The Adaptation of the Schools to Industry and Efficiency," *NEA Addresses and Proceedings* (1908): 74–75.

39. Charles A. Prosser, "Practical Arts and Vocational Guidance," *NEA Proceedings* (1910): 646–647.

40. For a description of the evolving high-school curriculum in the late 1890s and early 1900s, consult Patricia Albjerg Graham, *Community and Class in American Education, 1865–1918* (New York: John Wiley, 1974) pp. 79–81; and Robert S. Lynd and Helen Merrell Lynd, *Middletown: A Study in American Culture* (New York: Harcourt Brace Jovanovich, Harvest Books, 1956), p. 192.

41. Charles W. Eliot, "Industrial Education as an Essential Factor in Our National Prosperity," *NSPIE Bulletin No. 4* (1908): 9–14.

42. Charles W. Eliot, "The Value During Education of the Life Career Motive," *NEA Proceedings* (July 2–8, 1910): 133–144.

43. For example, see Ben W. Johnson, "Children Differ in Vocational Aims: Industrial Education in the Elementary School," *NEA Proceedings* (1910): 253–260.

44. Frederick Taylor, *The Principles of Scientific Management* (New York: Harper, 1911).

45. Frank E. Spaulding, "The Application of the Principles of Scientific Management," *NEA Addresses and Proceedings* (1913): 265.

46. Quoted in Raymond E. Callahan, *Education and the Cult of Efficiency* (Chicago: University of Chicago Press, 1962), p. 68.

47. Quoted in Wirth, *Education,* p. 98.

48. James P. Munroe, "President's Address," *NSPIE Proceedings* (1911): 49–56. See also James P. Munroe, *New Demands on Education* (New York: Doubleday, 1912), pp. 20–21.

49. Meyer Bloomfield, *The Vocational Guidance of Youth* (Boston: Houghton Mifflin, 1911), pp. 23–24.

50. Frank Parsons, *Choosing a Vocation* (Boston: Houghton Mifflin, 1909), pp. 161–162.

51. Eugene Davenport, "Industrial Education, a Phase of the Problem of Universal Education," *NEA Addresses and Proceedings* (1909): 277–288.

52. Quoted in Nasaw, *Schooled to Order,* p. 152. See Wirth, *Education,* pp. 122–123.

53. Wirth, *Education,* p. 123.

54. George Herbert Mead, "The Larger Educational Bearings of Vocational Guidance," *U.S. Bureau of Education Bulletin No. 14* (Washington, D.C.: U.S. Government Printing Office, 1914), p. 17.

55. Frank M. Leavitt, "How Shall We Study the Industries for the Purposes of Vocation Guidance," *U.S. Bureau of Education Bulletin No. 14* (Washington, D.C.: U.S. Government Printing Office, 1914), pp. 79–81.

56. See "Convention Addresses," *NSPIE Bulletin No. 5* (1908): 92–93.

57. Ibid., and quoted in Wirth, *Education,* pp. 94–95.

58. Ibid., p. 95.

59. Frank Tracy Carlton, *Education and Industrial Evolution* (New York: Macmillan, 1908), p. 76.

60. Ibid., pp. 309–310.

61. David Snedden, *Toward Better Educations* (New York: Bureau of Publications, Teachers College, Columbia University, 1931), pp. 330–331. See also David Snedden, "History Study as an Instrument in the Social Education of Children," *Journal of Pedagogy* 19 (June 1907): 259–268.

62. David Snedden, "Differences Among Varying Groups of Children Should Be Recognized," *NEA Addresses and Proceedings* (June 29–July 3, 1908): 753.

63. See "Educational News and Editorial Comment: Types of Leadership," *School Review* 12 (April 1914): 262.

64. John Dewey, "Some Dangers in the Present Movement for Industrial Education," *Child Labor Bulletin* 1 (February 1913): 70.

65. See Nasaw, *Schooled to Order,* p. 155. Quoted from Dewey, "An Undemocratic Proposal," in Robert Bremner, ed., *Children and Youth in America: A Documentary History, Vol. 2* (Cambridge, Mass.: Harvard University Press, 1970), p. 1,418.

66. See John Dewey, "Industrial Education—A Wrong Kind," *New Republic* 2 (February 20, 1915): 71–73; and "Splitting Up the School System," *New Republic* 2 (April 17, 1915): 284.

67. See John Dewey, "The Manufacturers' Association and the Public Schools," *NEA Journal* 17 (February 1928): 61–62.

68. John Dewey, "A Policy of Industrial Education," *New Republic* 1 (December 19, 1914): 11–12.

69. Quoted in Wirth, *Education,* p. 214.

70. Ibid., p. 217. See John Dewey, *The Way Out of Educational Confusion* (Cambridge, Mass.: Harvard University Press, 1931), pp. 26–27.

71. David Snedden, *New Republic* 3 (May 15, 1915): 40.

72. Ibid., p. 42.

73. See Fisher, *Industrial Educations,* pp. 133–136.

74. Quoted in Cremin, *Transformation,* p. 45.

75. Quoted in Theodore Saloutos and John D. Hicks, *Agricultural Discontent in the Middle West, 1900–1939* (Madison, Wis.: University of Wisconsin Press, 1951), p. 128.

76. Cited in Melvin L. Barlow, *History of Industrial Education in the United States* (Peoria, Ill.: Chas. A. Bennett, 1967), p. 76.

77. Cited in Hawkins et al., *Vocational Education,* pp. 391–392.

78. Ibid., p. 393.

79. Cited in Barlow, *History,* p. 59.

80. Ibid., p. 60.

81. Ibid., pp. 61–65.

82. Grant Venn, *Man, Education and Work* (Washington, D.C.: American Council on Education, 1964), p. 112.

83. "Cardinal Principles of Secondary Education: A Report of the Commission on the Reorganization of Secondary Education, National Education Association," *U.S. Bureau of Education Bulletin No. 35* (1918).

84. Ibid., p. 9.

85. Quoted in Edward A. Krug, *The Shaping of the American High School* (New York: Harper & Row, 1964), p. 395.

86. See, for example, Boyd Bode, "Why Educational Objectives?" *School and Society* (May 10, 1924): 531–539.

87. Nasaw, *Schooled to Order,* p. 157.

88. Ibid., pp. 157, 158. See Willis Ruhy, *Schools in an Age of Mass Culture: An Exploration of Selected Themes in the History of Twentieth-Century American Education* (Englewood Cliffs, N.J.: Prentice-Hall, 1965), pp. 164–188.

89. Ibid., p. 155.

90. See Melvin L. Barlow, "200 Years of Vocational Education, 1776–1976," *American Vocational Journal* 51 (May 1976): 87.

91. Mayor D. Mobley and Melvin L. Barlow, "Impact of Federal Legislation and Policies upon Vocational Education," in Melvin L. Barlow, ed., *Vocational Education, Sixty-fourth Yearbook of the National Society For the Study of Education* (Chicago: University of Chicago Press, 1965), pp. 186–187.

92. Nicholas Murray Butler, "The Closing Door," *Educational Review* (December 1921): 422.

93. Mays, *Principles and Practices*, p. 92.

94. Ibid., pp. 93, 94.

95. See Barlow, *History*, pp. 127–131.

96. Hawkins et al., *Vocational Education*, pp. 114, 115. See also Prosser and Quigley, pp. 235–240.

97. Gerald B. Leighbody, *Vocational Education in America's Schools, Major Issues of the 1970's* (Chicago: American Technical Society, 1972), p. 32.

98. Cited in Barlow, *History of Industrial Education*, pp. 317–318.

99. Quoted from an article in *School and Society* 60 (November 24, 1944): 339–340.

100. Mays, pp. 51, 46.

101. Quoted in Barlow, "200 Years," p. 65.

102. Ibid., p. 69.

103. Ibid., p. 69.

104. Alexander J. Stoddard, "The Vocational Emphasis in Education," *1945 Convention Book, Illinois Vocational Association* (Urbana: Illinois Vocational Association, 1945), pp. 6, 8.

105. Ibid., p. 9.

106. Cited in Barlow, "200 Years," p. 69.

107. Mays, p. 94.

108. Ibid., pp. 99–101.

109. The text of the resolution is reproduced in Frederick M. Raubinger, Harold G. Rowe, Donald L. Piper, and Charles K. West, *The Development of Secondary Education* (New York: Macmillan, 1969), p. 353.

110. Educational Policies Commission of the National Education Association of the United States and of the American Association of School Administrators, *Education For All American Youth* (Washington, D.C.: The Commission, 1944), pp. 289–290.

111. See Raubinger et al., *Secondary Education*, p. 325.

112. Cited in ibid., pp. 304–305.

113. See Federal Security Agency, U.S. Office of Education, *Vocational Education in the Years Ahead* (Washington, D.C.: U.S. Office of Education, 1945); and John C. Wright, "Reports from All the States Yield Blueprints of Progress," *American Vocational Journal* 20 (September 1945): 7–8.

114. See Gilbert G. Weaver, "Standards for Vocational-Industrial Education," *American Vocational Journal* 22 (April 1947): 4–8; and Miles H. Anderson, "Is Trade and Industrial Education Adequate?" *American Vocational Journal* 23 (December 1948): 19.

115. William T. Bawden, "The Crisis in Vocational Education," *Industrial Arts and Vocational Education* 43 (November 1954): 296.

116. James B. Conant, "Vocational Education and the National Need," *American Vocational Journal* 35 (January 1960): 15.

117. Cited in Barlow, *History of Industrial Education*, p. 398.

118. Ibid., p. 399.

119. W. Willard Wirtz, *Labor and Vocational Education* (March 26, 1963), unpublished mimeographed document cited in Barlow, *History of Industrial Education*, p. 404.

120. John W. Gardner, *Excellence, Can We Be Equal And Excellent Too?* (New York: Harper & Row, 1961), p. 86.

121. Report of the Panel of Consultants on Vocational Education, *Education For A Changing*

*World of Work* (Washington, D.C.: U.S. Office of Education, Department of Health, Education, and Welfare, 1963).

122. Robert Beck, "Toward a Managerial View of History," in Gordon I. Swanson, ed. *The Future Of Vocational Education, 1981 Yearbook of the American Vocational Association* (Arlington, Va.: American Vocational Association, 1981), pp. 12–13.

123. Ibid., p. 14.

124. Ibid., p. 15.

125. Rupert N. Evans, *Foundations of Vocational Education* (Columbus, Oh.: Chas. E. Merrill, 1971), pp. 87–88.

126. Harry S. Broudy, B. O. Smith, and Joe R. Burnett, *Democracy and Excellence in American Secondary Education* (Chicago: Rand McNally, 1964), pp. 12, 245–246.

127. Evans, *Foundations,* p. 80.

128. Ibid., p. 93.

129. Melvin L. Barlow, "Epilogue," in Melvin L. Barlow, ed., *The Philosophy for Quality Vocational Education Programs* (Washington, D.C.: American Vocational Association, 1974), pp. 262–263.

130. Ibid., p. 265.

131. Robert Miller, "Organization in the Educational System," in Barlow, *Quality Vocational Education,* p. 41.

132. Ibid., p. 41.

133. Ibid., pp. 51, 47.

134. Helen A. Loftis and Elizabeth M. Ray, "Let There Be Learners," in Barlow, *Quality Vocational Education,* p. 188ff.

135. See H. Spears, "Kappans Ponder the Goals of Education," *Phi Delta Kappan* 40 (September 1973): 31.

136. Charles A. Beard, "Written History as an Act of Faith," *American History Review* 39 (January 1934): 220.

137. Samuel Bowles, "The Integration of Higher Education into the Wage-Labor System," in Michael B. Katz, ed., *Education in American History, Readings on the Social Issues* (New York: Praeger, 1973), p. 159. See also Samuel Bowles and Herbert Gintis, *Schooling in Capitalist America: Educational Reform and the Contradictions of Economic Life* (New York: Basic Books, 1976); Samuel Bowles, "Unequal Education and the Reproduction of the Social Division of Labor," in Jerome Karabel and A. H. Halsey, eds., *Power and Ideology In Education* (New York: Oxford University Press, 1977), pp. 137–153; Samuel Bowles, "Schooling and Inequality from Generation to Generation," *Journal of Political Economy* 80 (May–June, 1972): 219–551; Samuel Bowles and Herbert Gintis, "Capitalism and Education in the United States," *Socialist Revolution* 5 (1975): 101–138; and Samuel Bowles and Herbert Gintis, "The Problem with Human Capital—A Marxian Critique," *American Economic Review* 65 (May 1975): 74–82.

138. See Colin Greer, *The Great School Legend: A Revisionist Interpretation of American Public Education* (New York: Basic Books, 1972); David K. Cohen and Marvin Lazerson, "Education and the Corporate Order," *Socialist Revolution* 2 (March–April, 1972): 47–72; Michael B. Katz, *School Reform: Past and Present* (Boston: Little, Brown, 1971); Michael Katz, *Class, Bureaucracy and Schools, The Illusion of Educational Change in America* (New York: Praeger, 1971); Joel Spring, *Education and the Rise of the Corporate State* (Boston: Beacon, 1972); Joel Spring, *American Education, An Introduction to Social and Political Aspects* (New York: Longman, 1978); Joel Spring, *The Sorting Machine, National Educational Policy Since 1945* (New York: D. McKay, 1976); and Nasaw, *Schooled To Order.* Note also the essay by Michael Katz, 'Reflections on the Purpose of Educational Reform," *Educational Theory* 30 (Spring 1980): 77–87.

139. Melvin L. Barlow, "The Challenge to Vocational Education," in Barlow, *Sixty-fourth Yearbook,* p. 1.

140. Gordon I. Swanson, "Our Important Past," in Swanson, *Future of Vocational Education,* p. 27.

141. Mays, *Principles,* p. 63.

142. Charles A. Prosser and Thomas H. Quigley, *Vocational Education in a Democracy* (Chicago: American Technical Society, 1950), p. 35.

143. Barlow, *History of Industrial Education,* p. 503.

144. Mays, *Principles,* p. 53.

145. Prosser and Quigley, *Education in a Democracy,* pp. 12, 37. See also Hawkins et al., *Vocational Education,* pp. 5–6.

146. Mays, pp. 69–76, 85.

147. Prosser and Quigley, *Education in a Democracy,* p. 16. Italics appear in the original.

148. Lowell A. Burkett, "Access To A Future," in Gordon F. Law, ed., *Contemporary Concepts In Vocational Education* (Washington, D.C.: American Vocational Association, 1971), p. 35.

149. John A. McCarthy, *Vocational Education: America's Greatest Resource* (Chicago: American Technical Society, 1951), p. 1.

# CHAPTER FIVE
# VOCATIONALISM
## *Career Education and Development*

## INTRODUCTION

The term ''career education'' apparently was first coined in a 1956 publication of the Education Policies Commission of the NEA and the American Association of School Administrators entitled, *Manpower and Education*. A passage in the Commission's report read as follows:

> Vocation has significance for all education and the individual's entire education inevitably influences his career . . . The manpower characteristics of the society into which pupils are moving and pupils' potential careers in that society are inescapable and valid concerns of general education in elementary and secondary school. In the same spirit, liberal education at the college level attains vitality and validity as it relates to each student's future, including his career future. Liberal education need not be antivocational. . . . *Career education* is not only concerned with what lies inside the individual, but also with the individual's role in society. It is concerned both with talents and with the ways and means by which talents are put to use in a society that needs all the talents of all its citizens.[1]

A decade and a half was to elapse, however, before anything resembling a career-education ''movement'' made its appearance. It began at the time Sidney P. Marland, Jr. first assumed the post of Commissioner of Education in the U.S.

216

Office of Education. By placing the full weight and influence of his office behind the idea, it was Marland, more than any other single individual, who was responsible for launching an administrative initiative on behalf of the career-education concept.

Even in the late 1960s, pressures were building to remove once and for all the stigma attached to vocational education (revealed, for example, in attitudes accepting the propriety of occupational training, but only when intended for someone else's children or for those considered academically unfit for anything better). Typical in its expression of the desire to close the gap between academic and vocational education was the 1968 annual report of the National Advisory Council on Vocational Education:

> It is time that we ended the artificial cleavage between vocational education and so-called academic education. All of our citizens require education to function effectively as citizens and to realize their potentials as human beings. Moreover we know that literacy and the basic skills which should be developed in any educational process are also necessary for people to learn work skills properly and to advance in their jobs.
>
> We also regard it as nonsense to have an imaginary line separate the individual's academic education and his participation in his life's career. Academic education would be enhanced, not compromised, if vocational preparation were introduced into our general school system. Moreover, an increase in vocational education might help to end the false hierarchy of values which educators have consciously or unconsciously introduced through their treatment of vocational education, the notion that preparation for a life career is a second-class activity for second-class citizens.[2]

The following year brought new expressions of support for a sweeping recasting of education along vocational lines. The summary recommendations of a landmark conference report sponsored by the U.S. Office of Education in Atlanta, Georgia, urged a wholesale merging of academic and vocational curricula—a grand synthesis making career or job awareness the central organizing principle of all schooling. Specific proposals included the following:

1. Vocational education should be structured as a developmental and sequential process from elementary through postsecondary and adult programs;
2. Vocational education should be viewed as the responsibility of the total school;
3. Vocational experiences should be incorporated in the teaching of basic academic skills;
4. Each student at the point of separation from school should be provided with a saleable skill as well as a basic educational preparation;
5. Career development efforts should begin at the elementary school level;
6. Career exploration programs should not be seen as a mining operation strictly concerned with the selection of certain talents for the purpose of meeting particular manpower needs, but rather as a farming approach in which all individuals are provided with opportunities to grow and develop;
7. Career development experiences should be subsequently organized from the elementary grades through high school;

8. Schools should assume responsibility for all pupils until they successfully make the transition from school to work; and

9. Schools should more fully cooperate with business and industry in the development of basic habits of industry on the part of students.[3]

The position advanced at the 1969 Atlanta Conference was being echoed elsewhere meanwhile, and not only by professional vocational educators. James B. Conant, for example, in his influential work *Slums and Suburbs,* had written, ''I must record an educational heresy, or rather support a proposition that many will find self-evident, but that some professors of the liberal arts will denounce as dangerously heretical. I submit that in a heavily urbanized and industrialized free society the education experiences of a youth should fit his subsequent employment.'' Conant then asserted, ''There should be a smooth transition from full-time schooling to a full-time job, whether that transition be after grade ten, or after graduation from high school, college, or university.''[4]

Countless others took up the refrain. In allocating educational resources, vocationalist critics complained, insufficient attention had been given to the hard social reality that sooner or later practically everyone must seek gainful employment. Preparation for the world of work—equipping people with saleable skills needed in the market economy—therefore ought to be of paramount importance for *all* educators. Repeatedly, the same argument was advanced. The institution of schooling is in serious trouble. Disaffection among the young is well-nigh universal. Boredom, resentment, and sometimes outright rebellion typify the attitudes of many, perhaps most, youngsters confined in classrooms. Criticism of the school has never before been so harsh or so ubiquitous. A breakdown in discipline has become a national scandal and a disgrace. Schools once again are in danger of becoming ''blackboard jungles.'' Teachers ''burn out'' at an unprecedented rate as they try desperately to cope, to ''keep the lid on,'' and, one hopes, time and energy permitting, to teach. All too often, however, they fail, through no fault of their own. School violence has reached an all-time high, frustrating the efforts of even the most dedicated to offer any kind of meaningful instruction.

Reform proposals, vocationalists alleged, ranging from a new regimen of traditional subjects (''getting back to basics'') to massive transfusions of expensive technology (e.g., micro-computers) fail because they depend upon conventional assumptions about the school's basic purposes.[5] For much the same reason, neither do such innovations as team teaching, modular scheduling, differentiated staffing, open classrooms, sensitivity and communications training, mini-courses, or independent study promise significant relief. They do not alter the basic philosophic framework of traditional education. At best they are only short-range expedients designed to shore up a decaying system now on the verge of collapse.[6]

According to critics, the danger signs in society pointing to a fundamental weakness in the nation's educational system were obvious: growing unemployment, a dramatic increase in the number of people on welfare, and a swelling segment of the population lacking useful skills. The rate of unemployment among younger persons, it was noted, was staggering. The reason was that they could not sell anything the labor market wanted to buy. At the root of the school's failure was its long-standing neglect of vocational training.

Such arguments were hardly new, of course; much the same charges had been levied throughout the century and even earlier. But what was new, as the decade of the 1970s opened, was the extent to which vocationalists went beyond traditional arguments in favor of more vocational training and, as though sensing that the time was ripe, now claimed vigorously that work and preparation for work should become the *primary* emphasis of *all* school curricula, for *everyone,* at *all* levels of the school structure.

"Occupational awareness, orientation, exploration, and preparation for careers," as two writers put it, "have to become *central rather than peripheral in the curriculum.* Regardless of school-leaving age, individuals should possess saleable skills and have the opportunity to return without stigma or penalty to the educational enterprise for instruction which will advance them on career ladders."[7] Typical was the call issued by Assistant Education Secretary James E. Allen, at the 1970 annual meeting of the National Association of Secondary School Principals, when he urged a "recasting of the entire education system" to favor vocational education and career development in relation to manpower needs. "It is the renewed awareness of the universality of the basic human and social need for competence," Allen asserted, "that is generating not only increased emphasis today on career education but a whole new concept of its character and . . . place in the total education enterprise."[8]

## A CONCEPT IN SEARCH OF A DEFINITION

In the summer of 1970, Sidney Marland, a former high-school English teacher and long-time suburban school superintendent, was invited to become the new Commissioner of Education under the Nixon administration. In a long talk with Health, Education and Welfare Secretary Elliot Richardson, Marland shared his feelings about the importance of occupational development as a responsibility of schools and colleges. Two years before, while serving on the Commission on Tests of the College Entrance Examination Board, Marland had prepared a paper dealing with the Board's future role in American education. In it, he put himself on record as favoring giving occupational study "the same level of respect and prestige that the liberal arts studies now have" and recognition for "excellence in areas that are not primarily intellectual. . . ."[9]

Richardson listened with interest to Marland's proposal for "a design for introducing awareness of work and the motivation intrinsic to the work idea, from early childhood education through the self-evident, work-focused functions of the graduate professional schools.''[10] As their conversation concluded, the HEW Secretary gave qualified support to the idea and encouraged Marland to develop it further.

A few weeks later, as Marland recalled it, Domestic Council Chair John Ehrlichman called and asked the U.S. Office of Education to give immediate attention to increasing the federal role in ''vocational education.'' He wanted a concrete plan and a systematic design for a major administrative initiative, *but with no increase in budget.* In essence, what Ehrlichman was demanding was a ''low-budget spectacular'' as the centerpiece of the new administration's national educational policy. Beginning in the fall of 1970, the U.S. Office of Education's planning staff began meeting with representatives of the Bureau of Adult, Vocational and Technical Education, in an effort to formulate a response to the White House's request.

''I tried out the idea of a total reform that would embrace vocational education as a significant element,'' Marland reported, ''but would relate the occupational aspects of human development to all levels of learning and all relevant parts of academic instruction.'' As yet the basic idea was still in an embryonic state, but it needed a label.

> We labored over a name. The idea had to be distinguished from the term *vocational-technical;* it had to imply a sequential system affecting all formal education. It had to be brief, hopefully shunning the mouthfuls of titles that would include Occupational-Academic-Manpower, Elementary, Secondary, Post-Secondary. We tried Liberal and Technical Education; we tried Education for the World of Work; we tried others with equal dissatisfaction.[11]

Knowingly or not, Marland and his staff ultimately settled on the term first cited in the 1956 NEA document and used previously in 1970 by James Allen in his NASSP address; namely, ''career education.'' As it happened, the U.S. Commissioner was scheduled to address the same National Association of Secondary School Principals at its convention in Houston some few months hence—it seemed a good opportunity to try out the concept on a national audience of professional educators. His address was entitled, ''Career Education Now.''[12]

Marland opened his remarks with the charge that most educators were unclear as to what they were educating children *for.* Urging them to divest themselves of lingering academic snobbery and to stop treating vocational training as ''education's poor cousin,'' he called for an end to the ''social quarantine'' in which it had been placed since time immemorial. Marland thought it was ''foolish'' and a ''pity'' that a country as dependent upon machines and technology as the United States should teach occupational skills grudgingly—''dull courses in dull buildings for the benefit of . . . young people somehow pre-judged not fit for college, as though college were something better for everyone.'' America could no longer afford such snobbery. The task of education, he argued, is to ''sustain and accelerate the pace of progress'' by meeting people's career needs in a complex technological society.

"Continued indecision and preservation of the status quo," Marland claimed, could only result in "additional millions of young men and women leaving our high schools, with or without benefit of diploma, unfitted for employment, unable or unwilling to go on to college, and carrying away little more than an enduring distaste for education in any form, unskilled and unschooled." Fully half or more of all young people in school, he asserted, were not properly equipped for work. The choice, then, as to persevere in traditional practices, at terrible human cost, or to undertake a "reformation of our entire system of . . . education in order to position it properly for maximum contribution to our individual and national life." For Marland, the appropriate course of action was clear: an end to the "abomination" known as general education.

In his Houston address, the Commissioner estimated that at least eight out of every ten high school students should be receiving occupational training of some sort—those unlikely to continue on to academic, college-level work. What about half were actually receiving, as he termed it, was "irrelevant, general educational pap," consisting of watered-down courses and knowledge "neither useful nor joyful." College-bound students, he conceded, should have access to the liberal arts and sciences of the traditional college-preparatory curriculum. But those whose aspirations lay elsewhere deserved more than a watered-down version of the same preparatory course of studies.

Marland therefore pleaded for "a new educational unity," which would break down the barriers dividing the system into parochial enclaves. What was needed, he said, was a blending of curricula, a balance of academic and vocational learning with a strong comprehensive program of "career development" for every one. Elsewhere Marland amplified his theme.[13] "We need," he declared, "to . . . improve our ability to teach vocational skills at the high school levels for those not going on to college. And, we need to guide the understanding of those who are going on to higher education so that they will take a degree with some definite purpose in mind, not simply—as is so often the case—for something to do." For all students, he insisted, "we need to provide a solid understanding of our free enterprise system and of the opportunities and obligations that the system holds out to each of us." Marland was convinced American education had failed to impart either broad understanding or specific skills to tens of thousands of young people. "Many are as a consequence unemployed or underemployed and obviously can know very little personal fulfillment." He added, "They are a reproach—and a continuing challenge—to our capacity to educate."[14]

Again Marland renewed his attack upon what he derided as "the ill-conceived, unproductive general curriculum" of the typical high school. Far too many people, he believed, were encouraged to go to college. "Given the inflexible law of supply and demand, the flood of bachelor's degrees has inevitably reduced their value as an entrée to a good professional job primarily because there simply aren't that many jobs in the American economy that require a college education." At the same time, not enough people received skill-producing training needed in the labor market. What most high schoolers were given instead, he claimed, was a "fallacious compromise between the true academic liberal arts and the true vocational offerings" made up of generalized courses "possessing neither the practicality and reality of vocational courses nor the quality of college-preparatory offerings."

"Career education," Marland wrote, "would provide the training these students require for successful employment, and it would give them the education they need to bring personal fulfillment into their lives. It would teach reading, writing, and arithmetic as the fundamental skills." It would at the same time stress the ability to think, decide, and judge—the "survival skills." While career education would "necessarily and properly embrace many of the vocational-technical education's skill-producing activities, it will also reach a large percentage of students presently unexposed to the usual vocational offerings." In sum, as Marland explained it,

> Career education . . . would reflect a far broader understanding of the purpose of education in today's highly sophisticated, technical, change-oriented society—the need not only to fit a person to function efficiently but to make him aware of why he is doing what he is doing, and to bring relevance to our classrooms for many, who, with reason, now find them irrelevant.[15]

Marland took pains to emphasize his point that "career education," as he envisioned it, would be much broader and all-encompassing than traditional vocational training, although job-skill acquisition would function as a vital component element within the larger total program he was urging schools to adopt. He further stressed the point that the model he had in mind was still in an exploratory stage. "Our present concept," he explained, "is that the learning program would contain three basic elements. The first would be a common or core program centered around the academic fundamentals and aimed at achieving the level of knowledge demanded for satisfactory employment. . . ." The second element would be "an elective program offering a range of studies to complement the core program." As examples, he cited computer programming, creative writing, business management, laboratory techniques, and manufacturing skills—"instruction that . . . provides skills and knowledge needed for living a rewarding life in the real world of work." The third element or component would be "a series of diversified work experiences specifically designed to give the student a taste of a number of possible careers, the live options that are open. . . ." Whether organized, administered, and based in schools, homes, or within business and industry, the types of career education programs Marland recommended would have as their ultimate aim fitness for employment.[16]

Marland's promise of substantial federal support for career education virtually assured it an enthusiastic reception at first. Yet his reluctance to define the central concept with any great clarity was an early source of puzzlement and confusion. "We have conscientiously avoided trying to lay down a precise definition for career education," he explained some two years after his original 1971 NASSP address. What he had simply attempted to express, he remarked, was his concern over "the continuing failure of the schools to serve fully a third of the young people attending them"—those he characterized as "the swelling numbers of young . . . boys and girls, listlessly, apparently helplessly, entering their names on the rolls of the unemployed, not because they lack talent, but because the schools have not given them a decent or fair preparation for the hard, competitive business of life—including, of course, adequate job skills. . . ."[17] The basic objective of career education, he reiterated, was to inculcate in youth an understanding of what to do with themselves when the transition to adulthood is completed.

At first some of Marland's listeners drew the conclusion that "career education" was just another label for old-fashioned vocational training. Kenneth B. Hoyt, an early exponent of career education, who in 1974 became the Director of the Office of Career Education, created within the U.S. Office of Education, nevertheless defended Marland's lack of precision in defining the concept on the somewhat peculiar ground that, like many other vague or undefined ideas in education, the meaning of career education was to grow out of controversy and debate about it. Hoyt left unclear how conceptual ambiguity might contribute positively to debate over educational goals and objectives, but during the decade of the 1970s, he was to offer at least four interpretations of his own.

The first, appearing in a 1972 publication, *Career Education: What It Is And How To Do It,* suggested that career education be looked upon as "the total effort of public education and the community to help all individuals become familiar with the values of a work-oriented society, to integrate these values into their personal value structure, and to implement those values in their lives in ways that make work possible, meaningful, and satisfying to each individual."[18]

Three years later Hoyt offered another definition, in a USOE publication entitled, *An Introduction To Career Education: A Policy Paper Of The U.S. Office of Education.* There he defined it as "the totality of experiences through which one learns about and prepares to engage in work as part of her or his way of living."[19] Again, in 1977, in yet another USOE monograph, *A Primer For Career Education,* career education was defined as "an effort aimed at refocusing American education and the actions of the broader community in ways that will help individuals acquire and utilize the knowledge, skills, and attitudes necessary for each to make work a meaningful, productive, and satisfying part of his or her way of living."[20]

Finally, in 1978, with the appearance of still another monograph entitled *Refining the Concept of Collaboration in Career Education,* Hoyt abandoned his earlier efforts to supply a simple, one-sentence definition. He offered instead a three-page description, identifying ten specific career-education skills; fourteen examples of specific kinds of career-education activities; four types of community resources needed in a career-education effort; fourteen suggested examples of community organizations that might be involved; and a dozen examples of agencies and institutions (including schools) that were potential participants in the delivery of career-education programs. Running through all four "definitions" were common themes: (1) that career education, however understood, is rooted in "work" and in education-work relationships; (2) that career education is an effort intended to be applicable to *all* persons at *all* age levels—in all kinds of educational settings; (3) that the idea of "work" is broader than paid labor; and (4) that career education would demand the joint participation of all segments of society. It would not succeed or accomplish its goals if total responsibility for its implementation was laid upon the school system alone.

Similar in tone were the many other official pronouncements, position statements, and explanations advanced in the early 1970s by various professional associations and governmental agencies active in popularizing the career-education idea. What they shared was an expressed desire to link work, career awareness, job preparation, and classroom learning. Most proposed definitions and interpretations reflected agreement with major objectives delineated early in 1971 in a conference discussion paper issued by the U.S. Office of Education's Division of Vocational and Technical Education. Listed as essential priorities were:

1. providing every high school graduate with a saleable skill and assured entry to further education or training;
2. providing an equivalent experience for students who left school prior to graduation;
3. offering career education orientation, with subsequent guidance, counseling, and placement services, to all students at all education levels;
4. emphasis on and enlargement of post-secondary and adult vocational and technical education programs; and
5. the gradual replacement of traditional general education by career education.[21]

Career education, it was implied, would begin as a general concept and gradually become more specific, so that somewhere halfway through high school, "entry-level skills" to a vocation or occupation would be gained, and in the last years of high school, more specific work skills. According to another publication, issued through the American Vocational Association (AVA), career education was to be defined as "the development of a lifelong learning process that provides for a broad approach to preparation for citizenship; provides job information and skill development; and, also helps individuals develop attitudes about the personal, psychological, social and economic significance of work in our society."[22] Implicit in the AVA characterization and rendered more explicit elsewhere was the point that career education was related to, but not identical with, vocational education. Rather, once again, job training as such was only *one* aspect or dimension (albeit an important one) of a larger concept. Career education as a proposal for educational reform would encompass several elements, including literacy training, occupational information and instruction relating to the world of work, and attention to decision-making skills involved in occupational selection and preparation.

## BUILDING A RATIONALE

Rupert N. Evans, of the University of Illinois and a long-time supporter of vocational training, warmly embraced Marland's concept of career education. "In an interdependent technological society," he observed, "the development of competence to produce a fair share of commodities and services is a major objective of any realistic educational system."[23] So, he said, is the development of ability to earn income, to use leisure productively, and to fulfill the general obligations of responsible citizenship. All are equally important and closely interrelated objectives.

Career education, Evans asserted, was an emergent part of the process by which an educational system could pursue all of those objectives simultaneously. All of the components of career education already existed in some form in today's schools, Evans believed. What was needed was to bring them together "into a coherent whole, extending from early childhood education through post-education of many types, to education for retirement." The first order of business, then, was to enshrine career decision-making as a primary goal of school instruction and curricula.

Schools, he alleged, actually discourage the development of decision-making skills among students. What the educational environment demands, and marshals its forces to enforce, is compliance. Each year of school is designed to lead to the next. The curriculum is basically predetermined. The only real choice a student has is whether or not to conform to the school's expectations. Even when students begin pondering what to do with themselves after graduation, the school in effect says, "Don't worry about it; you're too young to decide yet; a career decision can be postponed until later." When a child does project into the future and imagines what he or she will become, whether a fire fighter, a mechanic, a physician, or an airline pilot, one can be reasonably sure of three things. First, the student's tentative choice or decision has been made on the basis of inadequate knowledge of his or her abilities and skills; the school has done little or nothing to provide the wherewithal for an intelligent or informed choice; finally, the school may have actually discouraged a person from thinking seriously about his or her own future adult role.

What American education does, Evans alleged, is to encourage postponement of a career decision as long as possible, until it can be delayed no longer. Even those about to complete college oftentimes have no clear idea whether there is "life after graduation." They have no idea what they want to be when they "grow up"; and the discovery that they are already adults is apt to come as a nasty shock. On the whole, there has been little or nothing in their previous school experience to prepare them for a decision about occupation. This continual deferral of decision making is not true of all other cultures, Evans observed, and it need not be true in American society: "Avoidance of decisions can be taught, as can ability to make decisions."[24]

The ability to make decisions, he went on to argue, is learned behavior. People are not born with an automatic capability to choose wisely among alternatives. They learn—or fail to learn—through a series of experiences that affect sequences of decisions (most of them revocable) occurring throughout life. In the case of selecting a career, for example, a choice can occur by chance, based on instinct and a visceral "gut-level" feeling, so to speak, or it can be planned. Probabilities favor a more satisfying and rewarding career, Evans claimed, if it is the product of intelligent and reflective thought, of planning and careful prior consideration. Job satisfaction over the long haul is built on more than immediate earnings. The need for those contemplating a choice of career is to make a decision based upon awareness of their own needs, preferences, and talents; upon knowledge of what the work entails in some broader social context; and, finally, upon before-the-fact experience with making lesser decisions.

Some educators seem to have an almost pathological fear of teaching decision making in relationship to work, Evans observed. Their fear is that such instruction will minimize future options and lead to early, irrevocable occupational choices. That apprehension would be unfounded if the school would refuse to leave career-decisions to chance or circumstance. It should help students learn to make choices on a rational basis, he asserted. Since a career choice represents one of the most important decisions a person will make, the school should do everything possible beforehand to facilitate the process, through a long-term sequence of instruction.

Evans, like most other vocationalists, was committed to the belief that poor student motivation in school is owed more than anything else to a lack of ''fit'' or correspondence between what is taught and the learner's personal and occupational goals. If a student can be shown how instructional material relates to eventual career choice, motivation to learn is enhanced, he claimed.

Turning to the issue of work in society, Evans argued that people's basic attitudes are formed early in life. These include attitudes toward work. Even first-graders have some dim appreciation for dominant cultural assumptions—for example, the prejudice that certain occupations are desirable for males and others only for females. Again, despite society's pious rhetoric about the innate dignity of all labor, young children sense that white-collar professionals enjoy greater prestige and status than blue-collar menials. Some jobs are ''better'' than others. Elementary-school programs up until now, he observed, had done little or nothing to help break down sex-role stereotyping or to reinforce the ideal of the utility of all productive work. Schoolchildren are taught nothing about the economic facts of life—about why and how people work, about where money comes from, or about the variety of ways in which people make a living. Whereas in an earlier day young people could observe at firsthand how the farmer or blacksmith or grocer plied his trade, modern conditions make most occupations ''opaque'' and inaccessible to outsiders. A child can have little understanding and even less appreciation for the work of an attorney, an insurance salesperson, or an office worker, for the conditions under which they pursue their vocations are closed off to those not directly involved.

Work, Evans pointed out, is absolutely essential in any conceivable social order. Without it society could not exist. Even in an age of automated production, occupational activities claim the time and energy of most people for a good share of their waking hours. ''Work,'' he wrote, ''by some, if not by all, will continue to be one of life's necessities, and for many people it will remain one of life's rewards, because it provides self-fulfillment and another good reason for existence.''[25] In recent years, however, the nature of work has changed. Unskilled jobs have decreased sharply in number, while skilled and professional jobs have grown more complex. The effect has been sharply increased youth unemployment, especially among those who have had no vocational training. If the consequent drain on the economy is ever to be alleviated, he noted, people would need to understand more fully the contribution work makes to society and to individual well-being. And more important still, people would need more and better preparation for gainful employment.

Evans found it paradoxical that the American educational structure provides extensive preparation for work in certain occupations and little or none for work in others. University graduate schools turn out people for vocations in the academic and professional disciplines in great numbers, with the supply of graduates all too often exceeding market demands. Four-year undergraduate collegiate programs, many of them publicly supported, likewise offer instruction preparing people for work as journalists, teachers, health workers, agricultural managers, engineers, and other positions *ad infinitum,* once again graduating more prospective job applicants than the marketplace can assimilate. For all of these students there is substantial tax support. The propriety of offering this type of professional job training is rarely questioned. Yet far fewer opportunities are made available for work preparation in occupations requiring less than a four-year baccalaureate degree. Ironically enough, here the economic need is greatest and the educational response least adequate.

According to Evans's estimate, while no more than 20 percent of all jobs require a college degree, over half of all high-school students are bent on attending college. Only one-fourth receive vocational training for the remaining 80 percent of the jobs available. Some of that training, he felt, is of high quality, but some is obsolete or inefficient. Practically none of it is available to school drop-outs. The remainder of the labor force is trained in quite different ways, each of which is potentially disadvantageous to the trainee. First, business or industry is involved in job training and passes the costs on to the consumer. Its content is controlled by the company concerned, and to serve its own ends, not to enhance the options of the people receiving the training. Secondly, many people acquire job skills in the military. The problem, of course, is that the civilian economy needs few trained infantrymen, fire-control officers, fighter pilots, tank drivers, or skilled sharpshooters. Even if the skills acquired have applicability outside the armed services, when the reenlistment rate drops because too many trained personnel are serving employment in commercial fields, training courses often are revised to *decrease* trainee options outside the military. Private entrepreneurial or proprietary schools train another sizable percentage of the work force. But here quality varies greatly from one institution to another. Sometimes, too, the cost is prohibitive.

On balance, Evans argued, there is a strong case for specific preparation for work in a public-school setting. This is especially true if the instruction represents the most efficient way of offering job training and the best method of maximizing students' subsequent career options as compared with other training methods in alternative settings. Additionally, "the need for preparation for a broad range of occupations does not stop with entry into employment. People change jobs, and jobs change in ways which require additional knowledge," he observed. "Each change requires additional awareness, exploration, and preparation, and hence career education." [26]

## AN EXPANDING LITERATURE

In 1973 the American Vocational Association devoted its third annual yearbook to the theme of career education. The selection of this topic, explained AVA Executive Director Lowell A. Burkett, was especially fitting, "because vocational education is an essential component of career education" and because "career education promises to become the educational milieu within which vocational education will flourish." The movement already had begun "to bridge the false gap between vocational and academic education," Burkett wrote, "thereby promising to make all education relevant and useful for the majority of the nation's youth and adults." [27] Included in the volume were contributions from over thirty different writers, exploring the foundations of the career-education concept, describing conceptual models, and illustrating pilot programs planned or already in operation.

Kenneth Hoyt, among them, assembled literally scores of definitions of career education as devised by state and federal officials. They ranged from Arizona's description of career education as "combining the academic world with the world of work . . . a blending of the vocational, the general, and college preparatory education . . ." [28] to that offered by California's Director of Vocational Education:

> . . . a comprehensive, systematic and cohesive plan of learning organized in such a manner that youth at all grade levels in the public schools will have continuous and abundant opportunity to acquire useful information about the occupational structure of the economy, the alternatives of career choice, the obligations of individual and productive involvement in the total work force, the intelligent determination of personal capabilities and aspirations, the requisites of all occupations, and opportunities to prepare for gainful employment. [29]

He quoted Marland as of January 1971: "*All* education is career education, or should be. *All* our efforts as educators must be bent on preparing students either to become properly, usefully employed upon graduation from high school, or to go on to further formal education. Anything else is dangerous nonsense." [30]

From his review of definitions, Hoyt detected at least four areas of consensus: (1) that career education is a conscientious *effort*, not merely an attitude or point of view, one requiring both time and money; (2) that programs should start in the first grade and extend into adulthood; (3) that programs should serve all in-

LIBERAL EDUCATION AND VOCATIONAL TRAINING:
FALSE DICHOTOMY?

It is an everlasting pity that so sharp a dichotomy has established itself in our minds between liberal education and vocational training, with the false implication that the former is somehow higher, though useless, and the latter, useful but somehow crass and demeaning. If these two equally essential preparations for life are thus divorced, a *merely* liberal education will indeed tend to be useless, and a *merely* vocational training, crass. What is obviously needed is a truly liberal academic community in which the study of art and typewriting, of philosophy and accounting, of theology and medicine, of pure and applied science are, though admittedly very different, judged to be equally honorable and valuable in their several ways. In such a community the so-called liberal disciplines would indeed be liberal because they would be studied and taught with an eye to the total enrichment of the life of responsible members of a free society; and in such a community the acquisition of the vocational skills, from the simplest to the most complex, would be equally liberal because they would be taught, not in a spirit of predatory egoism, but in a spirit of deep social concern for the needs of others and for the common good.

—Theodore M. Greene, in Nelson B. Henry, ed., *Modern Philosophies and Education, The fifty-fourth Yearbook of the National Society for the Study of Education, Part I* (Chicago: University of Chicago Press, 1955), p. 119.

dividuals rather than some special segment of the population; and (4) that career education as an ideal emphasizes education primarily as preparation for work.

He further noted that most supporters of career education were in substantial agreement that career education as an ideal could not be translated successfully into practice in school if it was thought of merely as an "add-on," as a discrete course or even a sequence of courses grafted onto a pre-existing curriculum, leaving its other component elements intact and untouched. On the contrary, for it to succeed, career education would need to become the all-encompassing focus of, and basis for, the total school program. It would entail a fusion of academic and vocational instruction. It would mean an end to the channeling of students into curricular "tracks." It would demand sequential instruction in occupational knowledge and awareness; employer involvement in students' educational experiences through work-study and cooperative education programs; greatly expanded occupational guidance, career orientation, and placement activities; and career counseling extending from the early years through to job placement or further education.[31]

Gordon I. Swanson, of the University of Minnesota, offered an elaborate philosophical justification for career education, based on the work ethic. "Career education," he asserted, "has introduced much discussion about the validity of a work ethic and also . . . the possibility that career education is a kind of conspiracy to insure obedient and compliant workers for an industrial establishment." Swanson rejected the allegation out of hand. "To those who would argue that career education is a devious system for insuring an obedient work force," he said, "it should be pointed out that the opposite value may also be realized." Career education is an effort to upgrade job skills in a work setting, to create opportunities for recurrent education, and to help people find work roles that are satisfying and fulfilling. As for the validity of the work ethic itself, he thought it was "hardly available for refutation. Work continues to ration the goods, services and satisfactions of society. It is an accepted medium of exchange for which money is merely a proxy. Although work may have many forms and be amenable to many interpretations, it remains the most important global currency for exchanging values, statuses, and rewards." [32] Social justice and the principle of equality of opportunity, he argued, more than amply warranted the adoption of career education as a universal school agenda.

Marvin Rasmussen, director of career education for the Portland (Oregon) public schools, dealt with the practical aspects of occupational preparation called for in one influential career-education model. "Vocational education must be viewed as the core of career education," he declared by way of introduction. "In turn, occupational preparatory programs can be considered the heart of vocational education." The plan he advocated "provides for comprehensive program development at the elementary, mid-school, secondary and post-high school levels," he explained. "The articulated, continuous curriculum design is based upon a strong emphasis on guidance and counseling at every level." [33] Included were four levels or stages in an educational progression extending from kindergarten through postsecondary schooling: (1) "career awareness" (K-6); (2) "career exploration" (7-10); (3) "occupational preparation" (11-12); and (4) "occupational specialization" (posthigh-school and adult education). [34]

At the career "awareness" level, encompassing kindergarten through the sixth grade, programs would be aimed at helping young pupils develop an awareness of occupational careers and of self in relation to career roles, developing foundations "for wholesome attitudes toward work and society," fostering "attitudes of respect and appreciation" toward workers in all fields, and making tentative choices of a "career cluster" to explore in greater depth during the mid-school years. [35]

The second stage of the model cited by Rasmussen was that of career "exploration," extending from the seventh to the tenth grade of high school. Programs at this level would enable students to "explore key occupational areas" and to assess their own interests and abilities relative to those areas, to become familiar with occupational classifications and clusters, to develop enhanced awareness of the relevant factors to be considered in decision making, to gain actual experience in meaningful decision making, and to develop "tentative occupational plans and arrive at a tentative career choice." [36]

Students in the last two years of high school, following the model, would then enter upon a third stage, that of "occupational preparation." Career-cluster programs at this level would assist students in acquiring occupational skills and knowledge for entry-level employment and/or advanced occupational training. A majority of high-school experiences would be tied into generalized career goals. Students would be encouraged to develop "acceptable" job attitudes, to be involved in cooperative work experience, and to "become members of a vocational-youth organization." [37]

The stage of "occupational specialization" after high school could be carried out in community colleges, private vocational-technical schools, and in four-year colleges and universities. The goals of programs at this level would be, first, to help students develop specific occupational knowledge and preparation in a specialized job area; secondly, to give students an opportunity "to form meaningful employer-employee type relationships"; and, thirdly, to provide students with necessary retraining for upgrading skills.

The heart of this career-education model, as Rasmussen outlined it, was its provision for the study of "occupational clusters" at the secondary-school level. "Preparation for employment in a properly identified career cluster," he claimed, "helps the high school student avoid the hazards of premature commitment to a narrow work specialization. It also provides sufficient breadth to enable him to cope more effectively with occupational and employment changes." [38]

John E. Taylor, of the Center for Vocational and Technical Education at Ohio State University, discussing another comprehensive career-education model utilizing a clustering system, argued that a high-school curriculum based on the study of an array of similar occupations would "permit career preparation to be flexible, generalizable, and relatively comprehensive, allowing students to acquire broad skills and capabilities for entry into a range of related jobs. "Properly managed, it would not handicap a student by narrowing his or her training around too specific skills." [39]

The career-education movement spawned an enormous amount of writing within an astonishingly brief period of time. From the U.S. Office of Education came a flurry of monographs, brochures, planning guides, position papers, and conference reports. Organizations such as the American Vocational Association contributed to the outpouring of materials. Within two years of Marland's 1971 Houston address, where the concept was first introduced, scores of articles and books had appeared. Among them was a collection of essays assembled by the Northwest Regional Educational Laboratory in cooperation with the National Institute of Education. Each contributor had served on a panel of outside observers or critics brought to Washington by the U.S. Office of Education to review everything that had been written to date on the subject. Each was asked to render a verdict on the meaning and future significance of career education. With few exceptions, responses were uniformly positive.

Keith Goldhammer, Dean of the School of Education at Michigan State University, for example, judged that "Career Education constitutes a new, vitalizing thrust in education.'' He denied it was ''just another passing fancy'' that would soon disappear. Public reaction, he believed, expressed a hope that ''a new paradigm for educational operations has finally been found which will not only provide a basic social return consistent with the anticipated human and financial inputs, but a relevance for youth which will help them find their social identifications and secure a sense of mission and destiny as participating members of society. . . .''[40]

Speaking from an anthropological perspective, James P. Spradley worried that the concept of career education was so general that it was broad enough to include something for everyone. ''Like the Rorschach ink blot test,'' he observed, ''it becomes a projective device that enables different people to read their own meanings into the concept,'' depending on their respective cultural values. Vocational enthusiasts would endorse the idea unreservedly, in the belief it could revive the work ethic, reinforce the dignity of all work, and reduce the discontinuity between childhood and adulthood by equipping young people with occupational skills. Academic critics, on the other hand, Spradley predicted, would be highly suspicious of the concept, insofar as it encouraged the identification of education with job training. These differing perspectives, deeply enmeshed in opposing value systems, would not change easily, he believed.[41]

T. Anne Cleary, Executive Director of Examinations of the College Entrance Examination Board, also saw the fight for career education as an uphill struggle. There would be many obstacles to overcome. ''Career Education is intended to be much broader in scope than vocational education has been,'' she noted. ''It is intended to affect every student and to embrace the entire range of the school system.'' It was a ''major curriculum reform'' and a direct challenge to the ''humanistic'' conception of education:

> Career Education would place orientation to economic life at the center of the school program beginning in the earliest years. There would be study of information about occupations in the elementary school, together with activities designed to develop positive attitudes toward work and achievement. The entire community would be involved more fully than is now common in schools. Work-study opportunities would be vigorously developed. Every student would be pressed to select a vocational field and begin specific preparation for it during the secondary years. The division of the secondary school curriculum into vocational college preparatory and general curricula, which is now rather common, particularly in urban systems, would be abandoned.[42]

Could so ambitious and far-reaching a transformation of American education succeed? Cleary felt it was not impossible. But it would be difficult. Ideally, career education could provide for greater individualization in how students were treated in school. It could afford greater continuity of instruction. It might provide a greater integration of learning experiences. Possibly it would enhance motivation for learning. Finally, it would supply a successful ''closure'' to the educational sequence, by leading graduates to employment. Once implemented, career education would lead to improvement in conventional vocational education by giving such programs increased attention and greater financial support. It might "force attention to systematic and sustained planning as a central activity of the student in the curriculum and, thus, will rejuvenate and greatly enlarge what is now called the 'guidance' function of the schools."[43]

But on the negative side, she observed,

> To some extent the [career education] movement is political and counter-revolutionary—an attempt to reassert the 'work ethic' and other moral values of 19th-century capitalism. It is clearly a reaction against such popular post-World War II educational movements as general education and the Sputnik-inspired curriculum reform efforts in secondary education which were academically oriented and associated with the theme of "excellence."[44]

For Cleary, current interest in career education was the strongest return to the vocational theme the nation had experienced since the 1930s, when the Great Depression made jobs a central educational preoccupation. As an attempt to reorganize the entire school program around a dominant idea affecting all levels and all major disciplines in schools, she felt, it was likely to encounter stiff opposition from those interested in preserving diversity and pluralism in education.

Former U.S. Commissioner of Education Sterling M. McMurrin disagreed. He felt that the old distinction between vocational and liberal education was no longer warranted. All people are entitled to both, he argued, and for all practical purposes they should be combined: "Education worthy of the name is education for a career and education that liberates the mind and soul." But career education, in his opinion, was broad enough to encompass both objectives within a single unifying system. With a greater concern for the relation of education to careers, he alleged, "education as a continuing, unending process should come into its own."[45]

Many other writers expressed the same confidence. "Career development embraces the total development of youth," said Thelma T. Daley, past president of the American School Counselor Association. "It enhances academic preparation. True career development accentuates the development of attitudes, understandings, and self-awareness, as well as the development of job skills."[46]

What career education is all about, agreed Lola June May, a mathematics supervisor for the Winnetka (Illinois) Public Schools, is "helping each young person discover his interest as early as possible, then assuring that he will leave high school with both a traditional education and saleable skill."[47]

Many innovative proposals of great promise in the past did not live up to their projected expectations because they were oversold as something new and different, remarked John W. Letson, Superintendent of the Atlanta Public Schools. Career education, however, was not really new or different. "It is merely an effort to use a different kind of orientation for pupils in the belief that a new orientation can be the basis for stimulating a kind of response that the traditional academic approach has not achieved. . . . Career education is a concept that recognizes the urgent necessity of making sure that every pupil is prepared through education to find his proper place in the society and the economy."[48]

Philosopher Thomas F. Green argued much spadework needed to be done before career education could hope to serve as an overarching principle for American education. But he saw considerable promise in that possibility:

> No scheme for education in any society can be regarded as successful if it fails to prepare the young to take authentic and responsible roles within adult society. It might be argued, then, that preparation for work must receive central attention in any satisfactory arrangements for education in any society. Thus, in a society in which work is a predominant aspect of most adult roles, it follows that the process of education must pay serious attention to preparation for work. Indeed, it would seem a shaky conclusion to suggest that essential educational tasks should not be carried out in some central way by the system of schools itself.[49]

Van Cleve Morris, Dean of the College of Education at the University of Illinois at Chicago Circle, was intrigued by the "unfamiliar linkage" of "career" with "education." Writing in the newly founded *Journal of Career Education,* he was moved to analyze at some length the "new context for discussing educational goals and procedures" suggested by the conjunction.[50] The word "career" has a faint, upper-middle-class ring to it, he commented. Ordinarily, one does not speak of pursuing a *career* in construction, selling motorcycles, or working on a production line. These, by convention, are jobs, trades, or occupations. Somewhere toward the other end of a spectrum are the various "professions," such as law, teaching, and medicine. In a few cases, one may speak of a person's "vocation" (from the Latin *vocare,* to call) or "calling," a "high-toned rubric for gainful activities allegedly sponsored by some celestial voice," as when one is "called" to service as an evangelist, a missionary, a social worker, a nun, or a true-believing revolutionary. To speak of a "vocation" or a "calling," as Morris put it, "conveys the innuendo of some level of personal commitment and identification not usually associated with the other, more modest terms."

The very fact so many words exist for the gainful (i.e., income-producing) side of our lives—job, trade, occupation, vocation, career, profession, calling—suggested to him that "work" really cannot be understood in a generic sense, but must be analyzed more cautiously in its variety of idiosyncratic forms. The word "career," for example, is neither a "calling" nor an "occupation." Or it is both and more. "A career," Morris wrote, "at whatever level of the economic ladder, is at bottom, a decision—a personal decision on that work one feels fitted for, what one will settle for in terms of economic rewards, and finally—all things considered—what one wants to do with one's life." The word itself, he continued, "conveys a continuity of purpose and performance without sounding ecclesiastical; it is the secular equivalent of 'calling,' suggesting a significant initiative by the individual without the complications of a quasi-metaphysical, inner voice." It embraces the generic term "life work," a mode of existence or "life-style" extending beyond the context of "services rendered and payment received."[51]

Work, Morris believed, is the "primary dimension" of our being, of our existing in the world and striving to make our mark upon it. We need it. When it is withdrawn for any length of time, we miss it. Our reaction to prolonged idleness, for example, is to fill the released time with more work. "In some lines of activity," he remarked, "jobs develop a Parkinsonian crescendo of expectations, expanding by unnoticeable amounts the 'work' thought necessary for their proper execution."[52] Especially at the upper levels of the socioeconomic spectrum, in managerial and professional occupations, the "workaholic" syndrome is commonplace. Work becomes central to the ego and what it wishes to implant upon the environment.

Looked at in this way, choice of career becomes a choice of the "impress" one wants to make on the world. As Morris put it,

> A career decision is not merely a match-up between our abilities and outlooks on the one hand and some line of activity appropriate to them on the other; it becomes rather a selection of where best to exploit the possibilities for changing things along lines of our own personal desire. It is the choice of weapons and the determination of the arena in which our own personal influence on the world can best be capitalized.[53]

Of all our choices, he continued, it is obvious that the choice of life work is the most decisive in defining ourselves—in the largest possible sense, selecting a career is to define who one is or hopes to become as a human being. The "human project" of self-definition places "career" in a position of centrality: a career is the energy source and defining element in a person's effort to make a personal statement about his or her own existence. Hence it becomes all the more important for educators to help young people understand career choice as an act of self-definition.

Children, Morris insisted, must be helped to find spheres of activity compatable not only with their own skills and abilities but also with the subtler features of personality and make-up—each individual's view of himself or herself and what he or she wants from life. Asking the child, "What do you want to be when you grow up?" is not merely the "make-talk idle chatter of adults addressing young people." The very frequency of the question, in social intercourse, as Morris noted, suggests that the question lies close to the center of the growing-up process itself. "Indeed, career choice *is* growing up! It is the methodology by which an individual slowly brings some definition to his life."[54]

Schooling, said Morris, plays an important role in the enterprise of helping children become their fullest selves. "The design of the curriculum, the selection of materials, the style of teaching, indeed, the entire ambiance of the educational environment contributes in some subtle but definite way to the manner in which a youngster addresses this concern." Formerly, the tendency was to ignore the question of life work, or to defer the decision to a later determination in the postschool years. In fact, attending school has often been regarded as the best way of *postponing* the problem! Nowadays, Morris emphasized, there are growing doubts that delay represents the best policy. "Life is too complicated, the options too many. There is an urgency we have not felt before in bringing schooling and life into closer touch with one another—not in the class-trip-to-the-fire station sense, but in a generic locking together of what we teach and learn and what kind of growth and maturation we wish to generate in our students and in ourselves.''[55] For Morris, career education promised ''an exciting new way'' of probing that connection.

## BUILDING THE MOVEMENT

While academicians and professional educators were pondering the meaning of the career-education concept and assessing its future prospects, the U.S. Office of Education was pouring in money to fuel a movement on its behalf. Commissioner Marland in 1971 had $18 million available in discretionary funds from his budget for vocational-education development. Under law, one-half was already appropriated to the states for their use. The remainder could be allocated as the U.S. Office saw fit. Meeting in the summer of 1971 with the states' ranking school officers, Marland reached an agreement. In exchange for their promise to utilize their share of the monies—$9 million—for career-education model-building and program development, he agreed to reserve the same amount from his half for the same purpose.

Two units within the USOE immediately assumed leadership roles in promoting the development of career-education programs: the Bureau of Adult, Vocational, and Technical Education and the National Center for Educational Research and Development. The Bureau's task was to help various states establish their own centers for demonstrating, testing, and developing programs. The National Center was charged with designing and implementing strategies or models that demonstration sites could draw upon for inspiration and guidance.[56]

Much experimentation was to follow, with the bulk of activity centering on the school-based model for career education. More and more USOE agencies were caught up in promoting the movement. In 1972, the Developing Institutions and Cooperative Education unit began to explore how career education could be applied in postsecondary institutions. Another unit began producing films to support career-education curricula. The Bureau of Education for the Handicapped started considering how handicapped children could be better prepared for the world of work. A Career Education Personnel Branch was established under the National Center for the Improvement of Educational Systems. Seventy-five different universities received funding to provide faculty in-service programs on career education. By August of 1973 a center for Career Education had been founded, later becoming a division within the newly-created Office of Career Education. In the short span of two years, career education had become a significant presence in the federal structure.[57] In the same period, experimental programs and pilot projects were getting underway in almost every state. By 1975, over 5,000 local education agencies across the country had initiated some type of career-education involvement at the school-district level.

Program funding increased rapidly, by 1972 amounting to a figure in excess of $114 million. Besides the U.S. Office, the National Institute of Education began investing in various career-education efforts. Federally funded projects throughout the remainder of the decade included demonstrations, curriculum-development programs, numerous conferences and studies, technical assistance to state and local education agencies for program implementation, workshops, the publication of resource bibliographies and instructional aids, regional mini-conferences and colloquia, the founding of regional laboratories and research and development centers, the creation of a Clearing House for Career Education Materials, and the creation of a national career-education communication network or system.

By 1974 Commissioner Marland felt confident that the future of the burgeoning movement he had helped begin was assured. Unlike so many previous reform efforts, career education had become institutionalized. The administrative infrastructure was in place. The push for career education now had enough momentum to save it from the oblivion into which earlier movements had fallen. More importantly, Marland believed the American public was solidly behind his efforts. A National Institute of Education study, for example, showed most citizens according very high priority to job-skill acquisition as an educational priority. The 1973 Gallup poll of attitudes toward public education likewise revealed that fully 90 percent of all respondents surveyed agreed that schools should "give more emphasis to a study of trades, professions, and businesses to help students decide on their careers." Marland termed this " a remarkable consensus." [58]

Commenting on his findings, George Gallup wrote:

> Few proposals receive such overwhelming approval today as the suggestion that schools give more emphasis to a study of trades, professions, and businesses to help students decide on their careers. Nine in 10 persons in all major groups sampled in this survey say they would like to have the schools give more emphasis to this part of the educational program.
>
> And most of those who vote for this greater emphasis say that this program should start with junior and senior high school, although many professional educators think it should start even earlier—in the elementary grades.[59]

Kenneth Hoyt, in a position paper released in 1974, reviewed the factors that he felt justified career education and guaranteed it a useful role in years to come.[60] Too many persons leaving schools are deficient in the basic academic skills required for adaptability in contemporary society, he began. Most students fail to see any meaningful connection between what they are required to learn in school and what they will do once they leave the educational system. This is true, he claimed, of both those who remain to graduate and those who drop out of the system before the end of high school. American education, as currently structured, is adequate only for meeting the educational needs of a minority of persons, who will someday graduate from college. It fails to place equal emphasis on meeting the educational needs of the majority, who in all likelihood will never attend college at all.

Schools have also failed to keep pace with the rapidity of change characteristic of today's post-industrial society. Consequently, there exists little congruence between market needs and workers' qualifications. Some are grossly overeducated. Many more are undereducated or possess the wrong kind of skills. Worker alienation arises from the boredom of the overeducated worker and the frustration of those who lack relevant job training. Too many persons graduate at both the secondary and collegiate levels unequipped with the vocational competencies, the self-understanding and ability to make choices, or the work-related attitudes essential for negotiating a successful transition from school to work.

Women and minorities, Hoyt emphasized, traditionally had not enjoyed adequate career options. Nor had the nation's school system made sufficient provision for continuing and recurrent adult education. The general public, including the business-industry-labor community, lacked opportunity to help shape educational policy. The needs of the economically disadvantaged within society were still unmet. For all these reasons and more, American public education stood in need of overhaul from top to bottom.[61] Career education, Hoyt promised, had the potential to re-invent schooling for meeting real human, social, and economic needs heretofore neglected.

## ATTACKS FROM CRITICS

Early press reactions to career education were mixed. The *Wall Street Journal,* in a September 13, 1971 editorial, predicted Marland's effort would improve skill levels, raise productivity and job satisfaction, and help remove much of the stigma of work. Letters to the *Christian Science Monitor* run on April 22, 1972, all strongly supported the career-education concept. According to the *Salt Lake Tribune* for September 30, 1972, participants at the annual Utah Education Association warmly endorsed the idea. Again in March of 1974, the *Christian Science Monitor* devoted an entire issue to careers, discussing ways schools could prepare students for the world of work. An article in the *New York Times* in August of 1971 featured a five-column spread on Marland's plans for American educational reform. The *Anchorage Daily Times,* on August 18, 1972, reported favorably on efforts underway to develop a state career-education program.

Less enthusiastic was an editorial entitled, ''Not By Bread Alone,'' in the *New York Times* of May 22, 1972, which criticized the allegedly narrow and materialistic approach taken by career educators. The (Raleigh, North Carolina) *News & Observer,* on April 3, 1974, attacked confusion surrounding the career-education concept and claimed vague definitions offered no sound guide to policy planning. The *Times-Picayune*, (New Orleans) in March of 1972, advised caution before rushing headlong into career education; while the *Chicago Tribune* (February 17, 1972) reported Vice-President Agnew strongly supported career-education programs in the primary grades. The *Los Angeles Times,* on December 1, 1972, criticized Marland's initiative as just another name for vocational education and opposed its extension into higher education. A piece in the *Indianapolis Star* on October 13, 1974 viewed career education as an "expansion" of the vocational-education concept, and described how the former was being implemented in the city's school system.[62]

It was precisely the all-encompassing generality of career education that most troubled Harold Howe, Vice-President of the Division of Education and Research at the Ford Foundation. Speaking at a conference sponsored by the Educational Testing Service in May of 1972, Howe shared his misgivings about the career-education concept and its implementation. His feeling was that the relative lack of controversy or criticism when the idea was first introduced made its initial formulation suspect. The very fact that so many educators of diverse social, economic, and political viewpoints appeared unanimous in their support suggested to him several undesirable possibilities. People had not taken the notion seriously. Possibly they did not understand what it meant. Or, perhaps, they failed to grasp its revolutionary implications.[63]

Above all, Howe deplored what he characterized as the "intellectual imperialism" of career-education proponents. The trouble, he decided, lay with exaggerated claims, with an overemphasis upon vocationalism, and with the tacit assumption that career education would be broad enough to incorporate within itself a very wide range of educational concerns having little or nothing to do with jobs or vocational awareness. As a case in point, he cited a USOE pamphlet that alleged, "The fundamental concept of career education is that *all* educational experiences—curriculum, instruction, and counseling—should be geared to preparation for economic independence and appreciation for the dignity of work."[64] Howe disagreed, claiming that a considerable proportion of the total educational effort should be geared not just to "one-dimensional" economic man—linking work and education—but to the roles of people as citizens and as private individuals.

Career education is insufficient as a total response to needed reforms in American education, Howe went on to explain, because it is concerned primarily if not exclusively with the problems of human beings as economic producers and consumers. It deserves support, but to claim that there are no *other* aspects of human growth and development that could be served by education was narrow and too restrictive. Moreover, Howe rejected proponents' reassurances that career education was an adequate conceptual vehicle for the channeling and expression of those many other concerns. Any such claim, he believed, was unrealistic or disingenuous. He was skeptical that with career education one could have it all ways, that one could have the proverbial cake and eat it too, that a career-education program—no matter how generously conceived—would not demand "trade-offs" and the exclusion (or deemphasis) of certain other legitimate educational imperatives.

Frederick C. Neff, a professor of education at Wayne State University, articulated some of the same concerns expressed by Howe.[65] During recent decades, he observed, public education in the United States had been regularly subjected to a series of shock treatments. "These," he wrote, "have manifested themselves in a variety of ways and in terms of a bewildering array of causes, each of which has been touted as a panacea for all our educational ills." Not to climb aboard the newest bandwagon was to be branded an obstructionist, a heretic, or a reactionary by evangelists of innovation.

Neff reviewed some of the successive educational movements that had taken place since the end of World War II. Shortly after the successful launching of the Soviet Union's *Sputnik,* for instance, there appeared an abrupt change of emphasis favoring science and mathematics. "Because the Establishment became suddenly fearful that the United States would fall behind in the space race, education was pressed to emphasize the need for . . . engineers and those of satellite vocations, who obviously had little or no need for a knowledge of the humanities." This short-lived "structure-of-the-disciplines" movement was superceded during the years of the Viet Nam conflict by calls for "relevance" in education. Before long, the term "relevance" had become a symbol of student dissatisfaction with courses and studies that seemed too far removed from existing political and social concerns—"the problems of minorities, of the culturally disadvantaged, of the poor; the problems involved in racial, religious, ethnic, and sex discrimination in regard to housing and employment, and the like."[66]

Nevertheless, as Neff interpreted it, the term "relevance" was soon discovered to mean vastly different things to different people. Instead of serving as a coordinating principle, it became a rallying cry for whatever the individual student deemed most important. "For those who defined relevance in social and political terms, it meant an almost exclusive emphasis upon social and political reform. . . ." What was overlooked was that there is no such thing as relevance in the abstract. Because it is a relational concept whose meaning inheres in the connection between one thing and something else, discussion had to begin with the question, "Relevant *to what?*"

It became obvious that almost anything could be relevant: mathematics to the engineer or physicist, grammar to the novelist or journalist, history to the historian or politician, psychology to the counselor. "Beginning as a mass movement focused on social reform," Neff recalled, "relevance gradually began to become egocentric, turning inward to the individual and his own peculiar needs. Instead of asking the vague, general question, 'Is it relevant?' students began asking such questions as 'What is relevant to me and my needs and interests?' 'Who am I as a person?' 'How can I be helped in seeking my own identity?' 'What distinguishes me as a unique individual?'"[67]

Reacting to lockstep uniformity, standardization, regimentation and conformity in schools, reformers of the sixties and early seventies sought to remedy matters by setting up open schools, free schools without walls, and even non-schools. Romantic notions of the natural goodness of humanity were revived. They were to manifest themselves in the virtual elimination of external discipline, structure, and strict curriculum requirements. The new "humanism," as it was sometimes called, "attempted to rescue education from dehumanization and mechanization by making it less rigid and more humane."[68]

Each of these movements, according to Neff, had begun with the question, "What's wrong with education?" and thereby begged the question—that is, elicited answers to a question whose premises were themselves open to question. The prior question should have been, "What is education *for*?" However, he remarked, "since evangelists are notoriously shy about philosophic concerns, they have habitually avoided addressing themselves to this question." What all fervent missionaries of reform in education miss, he argued, is the point that education cannot endorse all conflicting aims at once, "any more than one can mount a horse and ride off in all directions" at one and the same time. It is unrealistic to assume that education simultaneously can fulfill national policy needs (for example, turn out more scientists, mathematicians, and engineers on demand), foster universal academic excellence, promote social and political activism, and encourage the humane development of each person as an individual.

Neff saw career education as another episode in a long history of bandwagon reform movements aimed at the total conversion of the nation's schools to a single end. "Spearheaded by former United States Commissioner of Education Sidney Marland and surfeited with funds from Washington," he commented,

> career education presents itself, not as a modest proposal nor even as a proper adjunct to the serious business of schooling—acquainting students with the democratic ideal and a knowledge of their social heritage, equipping them with the tools of critical thought and problem solving, awakening the life of the mind—but as a total concept of education.[69]

Neff recognized the ideology of vocationalism behind career education, and he was not entirely unappreciative of its value: "That public education should have a legitimate concern, among other things, for preparing its graduates to earn a livelihood is scarcely debatable. That many vocations . . . can summon a dedication in and through which one can achieve a significant measure of self-identification and self-realization cannot be denied."[70] Neff cited the old parable of the two stonemasons being asked what they were doing, to which one replied, "I am laying stone upon stone," and the other, "I am building a cathedral!" Vocation can be viewed in a larger perspective that confers meaning and purpose upon a person's life. But, Neff argued, "Although compelling arguments might be summoned in support of the contention that job and career training ought to be included as an important and even necessary component in the curricula of our schools, to demand that such training should become the focus of all education or that all education should be branded career education is little short of brazen."[71]

If education is broadly conceived as being concerned with all aspects of human life and thought—moral, esthetic, intellectual, scientific, philosophical, literary, historical, economic, political—then "it would appear to be a . . . grave mistake to presume that it is exclusively or even primarily concerned with careers." Neff was unimpressed with what he saw as attempts by advocates of career education to soften its vocationalist impact by embellishing the concept with broader adjunctive goals such as "personal fulfillment," "self-understanding," "improved decision-making," and so forth. Behind the rhetoric of balanced self-development, he detected only "evangelism, dogmatism and subservience to the System."[72] To the question, "Does career education have a proper place in the total spectrum of educational concerns?" his response therefore was an emphatic, "Yes." But to the question, "Does career education deserve a place of dominance under which all other educational objectives are to be subsumed?" his response was a still more emphatic, "No."[73]

The historical analysis offered by James Hitchcock, of St. Louis University, closely resembled Neff's.[74] He too traced the convoluted course of educational thought and practice from *Sputnik* and the emphasis on academic "excellence" in the early 1960s through to the period when "relevance" was equated with "political awareness" and social activism. Subsequently, as political concerns began to wane and the "soft" counterculture began to replace "hard" revolutionary ideologies, the theme of relevance in education changed from the objective, outward-looking scrutiny of society to the intensely subjective scrutiny of self. The irony of educational history, as Hitchcock saw it, was that "relevance" in the seventies had turned full circle. It had come to mean precisely what critics most vigorously opposed a scant few years earlier: processing students for the System. "In short, the newest version of relevance is vocationalism."

Hitchcock inclined to a "conspiratorial" theory of events surrounding the inauguration of the career-education movement. His view was that officials of an ultraconservative Republican administration had acted on a belief that students caught up in training for careers would be less likely to be radicalized or to act disruptively. Hence career education was interpreted as a way of restoring campus tranquility in the aftermath of the student riots of the preceding decade.

"Advocates of the new vocationalism," he judged, "are no doubt sincere in asserting that it is not their intention that career programs be narrow and philistine, but that they aim for students, through practical disciplinary training, to learn useful skills and also acquire the perspective and motivation to use them for the common good." Still, Hitchcock felt the long-term prospects were doubtful. "Many professional persons are indifferent to larger social questions, not through moral failure or lack of intelligence but because the time required to learn and maintain their professional abilities prevents them from acquiring a sophisticated awareness of larger issues."[75]

The net effect of renewed vocationalism, he predicted, would be to put an end to many of the myths about the youthful protestors of the 1960s. Their seeming rejection of materialism would be shown to have been a transitory phenomenon, sustained only so long as jobs were plentiful. Indifference to the marketplace could not long survive hard times. Hitchcock correctly prophesized that students in future, chastened by a growing scarcity of employment opportunities, would once again welcome a return to vocationalism in education. Discarding their placards and rhetoric, they would willingly return to the business of preparing themselves for economic survival. In essence, he felt career-education proponents had been right on at least one point. Once involved with careers, students would have no more time or energy for protest. Career education *was* an effective way of "cooling down" dissent.

Anthony Laduca and Lawrence J. Barnett, writing in the Spring 1974 issue of the *New York University Education Quarterly,* professed amazement at the "meteoric rise" of the career-education movement. They considered the selection of the term "career education," with its suggestion of professionalism and upward socioeconomic mobility, to be a "master semantic stroke," one less likely to evoke aversive middle-class reactions than terms such as "occupational education" or job training.

Even more than Hitchcock, they interpreted the beginnings of the movement against the backdrop of such events as the Viet Nam war, the protest movement against U.S. involvement in southeast Asia, the Watergate scandal, and the character of the Nixon administration itself. Prompted by fear and reinforced by arrogance, administrative officials, they believed, had been anxious to do everything possible to restore order and stifle dissent. "The president's fears about the condition of the nation, including the educational system, were displayed in his declarations about the revival of the 'work ethic'; his vice president's unrelenting attacks on dissidents; the frightening local violence with which he responded to demonstrations against U.S. violence abroad; and his threats and actions against institutions of higher education, which he seemed to perceive as the locus of indigenous threats to national security." Laduca and Barnett inferred that "these events were instrumental in developing an executive mind set for a crash educational reform strategy. The central goal of such reform would be the socialization of children and youths in ways that would make them more likely to run with, rather than against, the conservative corporate stream. At the least, it would neutralize them." [76] Born in the midst of political turmoil, career education thus appeared suspiciously to be an expedient aimed at fostering the sort of resocialization favored by top-echelon administration officials.

Laduca and Barnett themselves were directly involved with USOE Career Education Development Task Force personnel at New York City's Center for Urban Education at the time career-education models were being devised and tested. As direct witnesses to, and participants in, the crash research and development effort begun in 1971, their impression was that a genuine bandwagon phenomenon was underway. But their confusion grew when it appeared that activities formerly called something else were now subsumed under the rubric "career education":

Industrial arts, technical or vocational education, cooperative education, field trips to the firehouse, all have often been transformed overnight into career education. Frequently this has occurred with the stroke of a pen, consensus at a meeting, or just persistent iteration. In fact, it is extremely difficult to arrive at conclusions about the authenticity of career education programs. The principal reason behind this difficulty lies in the fact that it has been so variously and openly defined. A summation of its definitions leads inescapably to the conclusion that it is everything in education, both formal and informal, which bears on one's total life. Then, all of these infinite numbers of things are somehow caused to be related to the dependent variable, career.

The very fact that career education was touted as all-encompassing made it difficult to define. If it was everything, then it was at once anything and nothing.[77]

Laduca and Barnett's case study was the comprehensive career-education model developed by the Ohio State University Center for Vocational and Technical Education. They criticized the model on several grounds, in particular its progression from "career awareness" during grades K–6, "career exploration" during grades 7–9, and up through "career preparation" during grades 10–12. Thus, for example, the Ohio State model required that pupils make career choices before the tenth grade. "Implicit is the assumption that career development is a simple, continuous process during which adolescents experience a linear reduction in the number and range of career preferences," they noted. However, they argued, that assumption was wholly unfounded: what research indicates is discontinuity and an *expansion* of expressed vocational interests among adolescents. Hence, "by requiring reduction in preferences to a single definitive career choice at precisely the ages where significant numbers of adolescents are incapable of making such decisions," school-based career education as called for in the Ohio State model, they alleged, was counterproductive and ultimately unrealistic.

Like many other critics, Laduca and Barnett faulted career educators for ascribing widespread worker dissatisfaction and alienation to an erosion of the work ethic. The real culprit, they maintained, was the depersonalized and routinized character of much employment, a fact to which career-education enthusiasts seemed oblivious. "Rather than treating the problems of worker alienation," they claimed, "they construct instead a *Snow White* world in which millions of career-educated dwarfs skip gaily off to their dignified and redemptive jobs in the mines, mills, and restaurants of the nation."

Underlying career education, Laduca and Barnett claimed, is a "persistent authoritarian social philosophy," which sees "the creation of submissive workers with marketable skills as the sine qua non of the educational enterprise, and passive adjustment to occupational roles as the ultimate social goal."[78] As evidence for their claim, they cited Frank C. Pratzner's formulation:

> The ultimate goals of career education are individuals with stable work personalities who are (a) adjusted to and satisfied with their occupational role and with their roles in society; (b) satisfactory to both their employers and to the society of which they are

a part; and (c) employed in an occupation contributing to a balance in the supply and demand for professional and nonprofessional manpower.[79]

For all of its lack of research support, its confusions in theory-building and practice, its conceptual ambiguity and imprecision, career education *had* attracted powerful supporters, Laduca and Barnett concluded. Despite its "logical inconsistencies and misrepresentations," the movement had gained enough momentum to carry it on for some time to come. "The Nixon-Marland educational juggernaut will not be easily deterred from its alarming course," they warned, "nor will the magic of its name be readily dispelled."[80]

Lee Sproull, a free-lance educational consultant and former member of the Planning Unit for the National Institute of Education, was among the first to offer a critique of career education. His attack appeared as a popular article in a 1973 issue of *Learning*.[81] "To the accompaniment of a drumbeat of decrees and publicity aimed at classroom teachers from high school to kindergarten levels," he reported, "the passing months have brought a flurry of the kind of activity that always seems to attend the federal government's ambitions in the educational area." He spoke of state task forces spewing forth publications, directives, and workshops on career education, of the machinery at state and local levels mobilizing on its behalf. "Despite its attention to worthy concerns and its development of a few promising curriculum ideas," however, Sproull judged the movement was "more boondoggle than boon, a classic example of what psychiatrist Rollo Mays calls the 'old and ironic habit of human beings to run faster when we have lost our way.'"[82]

Sproull assailed career education for its vagueness and what he termed "pedagogical vapidity." In practice, he alleged, "career awareness" was "virtually indistinguishable from the old-fashioned trips to the firehouse to see what firemen do. Program guidelines are full of visits to gawk at other people doing work," a technique that "offers children no opportunity to learn through direct experience what a job might actually feel like to do, or what their own reactions to it are."[83] He cited an especially inane example from an eighth-grade unit on barbers and beauticians in Clarksville, Maryland, that asked students to learn to the tune of "Jingle Bells" the following song:

> Styling hair, styling hair!
> To make you gals look neat,
> So that hubbys when at home
> Will see their wives look neat.
> Fixing twirls, fixing swirls,
> Maybe a French bob,
> Don't let feminine society
> Look like crummy slobs.[84]

Its naïveté aside, and its seeming unawareness of the complexity of factors entering into career choices, Sproull observed, most career-education material designed for classroom use portrayed workers as "relentlessly happy," without ever dealing with the reality of worker discontent or its causes. Nor did instructional resources deal with issues of job status. Curriculum guides, in fact, went to extremes in avoiding the subject, making only "the questionable point that all jobs are important, thus implying that . . . society honors doctors and garbagemen equally." Sproull was especially offended by the "pushiness" of career education that allegedly encouraged premature career choices and the channeling children of lower socioeconomic backgrounds into low-status occupations.

The most offensive feature of career education, according to Sproull, was its uncritical defense of the prevailing social, political, and economic order, or, as he put it, its "Babbittry." A California unit on "attitude development" for first graders, for example, gave lip service to concerns about inequality but never questioned whether "the freedom we experience in our economic system" exists equally for everyone. "Both the inability of the poor to exercise meaningful economic choices and the fact that the American economy is not free but managed are ignored," he claimed.[85]

Overall, Sproull felt there was a real danger that even in the broadest of terms, career education programs would encourage the acquisition of specific skills that would become obsolete in short order. Acknowledging that "appropriate attitudes and decision-making skills" might be helpful, no matter what the shape and size of tomorrow's job markets, he still felt that because these were conveyed within the context of learning about particular jobs, the subtle distinction between what one needs to know today and what might be required in future would elude most students. The alleged anti-intellectualism of career education likewise troubled him. "In attempting to couple all knowledge with job potentials," he argued, "Career Education writes off the fact that some apparently impractical knowledge is valuable in its own right."

Sproull further felt that sexist stereotyping had made its way into career-education curricula, with little evidence that proponents of new programs were sufficiently sensitive to the need for illustrating the interchangeability of work roles among males and females. "So long as the real goals remain fuzzy, as long as the stumbling blocks remain unacknowledged and the tough questions remain unanswered," he advised teachers, the best thing to do with career education was "to forget it."[86]

A more elaborate analysis was offered by T. H. Fitzgerald, who called it "an error whose time has come."[87] Career education, as he characterized it, "as a national goal has been announced with all the promises, idealism, and enthusiasms which are the inevitable sparkling overture to new educational productions." The difficulties facing the movement, he wrote, had to do with "the realities of labor markets, of jobs and job choices, with the relationship of education to work, mobility, and social utility." On all counts, he condemned career education as "a superficial philosophy of education."

To the claim that career education offered a partial cure for the problem of unemployment, Fitzgerald responded that it was wrong to assume that youth unemployment is owed to lack of skills among the underemployed and unemployed. The problem of unemployment is primarily structural, he claimed. That is, it is a function of business cycles; of federal fiscal, monetary, and trade policies; it is related to welfare and unemployment compensation and to minimum-wage legislation. "The skills of individuals have nothing to do with employment or unemployment in situations where thousands of already qualified people are waiting on recall lists. Training youths in job skills will simply not produce more jobs," he argued. "The most that can be said about the improvement of the skills inventory of the work force as a whole is that it makes possible a more even distribution of the misery of joblessness, and reduces the discriminatory segmentation of employment at any stage of the business cycle." Education alone cannot *create* jobs.[88]

Contrary to conventional wisdom, Fitzgerald believed that most jobs require only rudimentary skills. "This is especially true of entrance-level jobs which are made available to the young by those who produce or dispense jobs," he argued. "Frying hamburgers or chicken at a franchise food operation, selling socks in a discount store, or hustling crates in a warehouse scarcely inspire curriculum development." The same is true of many adult jobs, which are unskilled or only semiskilled, and hardly qualify as "careers." Fitzgerald also questioned whether the simplification of work and the trend toward deskilling jobs was altogether undesirable. It is not at all clear, he alleged, whether routine work is really objectionable to even a substantial minority of employees. Moreover, "we do not know what it might cost to redesign and to enrich the jobs of those who do object." At present, indications are that many individuals are already *over*-qualified for much of the necessary work available, which someone must perform.

Training to make people more employable, Fitzgerald observed, mostly involves changing attitudes, deportment, and values, not developing objective skills. Entry-level jobs require few skill competencies; and movement up the narrowing ladder of occupational advancement in a majority of cases requires experience best obtained on the job. Credentials *are* important to initial employment, but for psycho-sociological reasons having little to do with the actual competencies an applicant may possess. This is not to deny that some occupations require a high level of skill, only that most jobs are not of this sort. Where skilled employment is available, the wage-price mechanism usually insures a healthy pool of prospective job holders.

Fitzgerald took issue with a fundamental premise of the career-education concept; namely, the desirability of rationalizing and systematizing the process of occupational selection. In the real world, he argued, serendipity plays an important role in determining what most people do for a living. Chance opportunities, happenstance, and changes of interest govern choices—*and this is not necessarily bad.* Few people can plan out their futures or anticipate and take into account all the possible variables involved. Most job characteristics are unknowable except to the insider; and whether or not an individual remains in a given position is decided only through personal experience or by considerations that cannot be provided for in advance through some type of organized program of instruction. Neither teachers nor counselors can provide the requisite information for deciding.

Fitzgerald appreciated the appeal of "a continuing supply of people who are work-ready, a condition which is a mixture of basic literacy, deference, flexibility as to job assignment, moderate good health, willingness to perform specialized tasks without complaint, energy, and dependability."[89] If the economy is to operate at a high level of output, it needs a trained work force. But he denied emphatically that human beings should be looked upon as "resources" to be allocated, maintained, and upgraded in accordance with market needs, or manipulated as so many "units," depending on shifts in production. Despite all the rhetoric about individual self-fulfillment, he asserted, career education was simply an expedient (and an inefficient one at that) whose major purpose was the development and deployment of people to service the needs of a corporate economy.[90]

Many other critics echoed Fitzgerald's claim that unemployment and job training are only loosely related. Harvey A. Daniels, of Northwestern University, for one, questioned whether even traditional vocational education was able to deliver on its promise of employability for graduates. "In a recent year," he noted, "when over 600,000 students graduated from vocational programs nationally, less than half found jobs in the field for which they were trained, and the unemployment rate among this group immediately matched the national overall figure for that period." Though that disappointing performance could be explained, perhaps, as a result of poor equipment, inadequate teaching, or technological change, Daniels felt it did not offer "a very inspiring example of efficiency and productivity to future workers," and he was skeptical that career education could offer anything better.[91]

Much the same point was made by a special assistant to the president of the American Federation of Teachers:

> Running through all the reports and rhetoric on career education is the idea that high unemployment among youth is somehow related to inadequate educational preparation—that schools are not providing each student with a "salable" skill after high school. The logic of this argument then moves on to suggest that the real burden for high youth unemployment falls on the schools and that if only the schools had the *right, relevant* program all high school graduates would immediately find a place in the labor force.

This line of thinking and any career education programs built upon it place an "unfair burden" on the schools for unemployment programs they did not create, the writer asserted. She continued:

> Students who are attracted to such programs on this basis will be disastrously misled into thinking that training in a "salable" skill will assure them of a job. Skills won't sell unless there is a market for them. In fact, students who short-circuit general education in search of career training will find themselves lining up for jobs behind those with more education whether the job market is open or tight. In short, youth

employment is more a matter of economic policy than it is educational policy and while students may benefit from some exposure to job skills, they should not be lured into thinking that a job skills orientation is a good substitute for basic grounding in academic skills. Career education programs that involve the substitution of on-site or hands-on experience for basic academic subjects may seriously shortchange students in their search for qualifications that will enable them to compete in the job market.[92]

University of Georgia professor George L. Newsome concurred that any defense of career education based on its ability to reduce unemployment was ill-founded. ''There is no shortage of trained manpower in this nation,'' he avowed, ''particularly at the entry levels of employment open to school drop-outs and high school graduates. There may be a shortage of jobs, [but] . . . training in high school . . . will create no new jobs. The level of production in the nation will not be altered by high school-level job training.''[93] He also took exception to what he termed the ''Cold War scare tactics'' employed by Hoyt when the latter had written:

> The basic rationale for career education is found in the need to restore the work ethic as a viable and effective force in American society. Erosion of the work ethic . . . has now reached a stage where the United States is in danger of losing its position as the leading nation in the world. The relative loss of the work ethic in our country, coupled with the relative gain of the work ethic in such countries as Russia and the Peoples Republic of China, is seen, by many people, as a basic reason why such countries appear to be catching up with the United States as leading world powers.[94]

Newsome alleged that Hoyt's statement did not speak to real issues in world trade or international politics, and it utterly failed to offer any *educational* reason for the work ethic. More broadly, Newsome disliked the whole approach taken by career educators in purchasing a national commitment by pouring out federal funds.[95] Besides the implied assumption that educators' allegiance to federal policies in education must be won by bribery, which Newsome found reprehensible, he opposed the use of schools as instruments of national policy, and the development of programs based on anything but *educational* considerations.

Glenn Smith, of Iowa State University, was only one of several critics who noted an uncanny similarity between career education and life-adjustment education.[96] Both were begun under federal auspices. Both were presented as a response to social unrest and popular discontent with the schools. Both were defended as expressions of democracy in action. Both encapsulated a strong interest in careers and employment; and proponents ended up contending their respective programs were sufficiently broad to meet the needs of practically everyone. Both movements were promoted through the pronouncements and policy recommendations of officials rather than by individual educational theorists or independent critics speaking in a purely private capacity. The rationale adduced in both cases was based primarily on external social and economic considerations. Both were touted by some influential supporters as panaceas for a host of ills. Both endorsed a work ethic, a strong emphasis upon vocational training, and a connection between learning and the world of work. Both garnered vigorous support from vocational educators and vocationalist ideologues. Finally, both stressed adaptation to the existing social, economic, and political order. As one proponent of life-adjustment education announced, for example, it was intended to equip "... all American youth to live democratically with satisfaction to themselves and profit to society as home members, workers, and citizens."[97]

The interesting feature of Smith's analysis, however, was his exploration of a further parallel between the two movements. He began by suggesting that it was an error to "personalize" career education by claiming it as the idea and program put forth by Sidney Marland. Like all his predecessors at the U.S. Office of Education, Smith claimed, Marland was a political appointee charged with defusing controversy, gathering statistics, coordinating various parts of the federal machinery involved in educational policy making, and generating programs to meet needs wherever a consensus had formed that such needs should be addressed. Although more activist than many, Marland did not so much invent a program as articulate an initiative in response to prevailing conditions. As Smith outlined it, the considerations mandating career education were as follows:

First, schooling is a form of capital—"knowledge stock." The amount and kind of schooling one receives affects the job, status, power, and affluence one enjoys. Secondly, since amount and kind of schooling represents "knowledge stock" in the same way money represents purchasing power, the possibility of inflation always exists. The value of a dollar depends upon how many dollars there are compared to goods and services. Likewise, the value of a diploma or degree depends upon how many others possess similar credentials relative to jobs and status available. Thirdly, because the "value" of schooling fluctuates, controls must be exercised. Inflation in education works the same way as in the economy—it is a way of redistributing wealth. Career education, Smith claimed, evolved as a necessary controlling mechanism, just as did life-adjustment education in the 1940s.

From 1900 to the end of the First World War, for example, the rate of university graduation was constant. Throughout the 1920s the number of degrees granted and the percentage of people with degrees increased steadily. By the end of that decade some college graduates could no longer find jobs in the fields for which they had prepared. The rate of degree-granting leveled in the thirties, reversed during World War II, and then swung upward dramatically from 1946 to 1950. It was the most severe educational inflation the nation had yet experienced. Thus, it was no coincidence when the U.S. Office of Education announced a new program—life-adjustment education.

The message to the schools and to society implicit in life adjustment, as Smith portrayed it was: "'Ease off the internal competition a little. Not everyone can graduate from college or have an upper-middle-class job. It's not important whether you are a welder or a surgeon. It's being human and part of the society that counts.'" For a while the "cool-down" message worked. But the postwar baby boom changed everything, creating new jobs throughout the economy. And when the Soviets orbited *Sputnik* and the demand grew for more highly trained technicians, life-adjustment education was no longer appropriate. "Critics had a wonderful time blasting it out of existence. It was, they said, an illiberal, vapid, naive, obsolete, anti-intellectual, vague, expensive boondoggle." The next inflationary spiral had begun.[98]

By the late 1960s, the bubble had burst. Once again educational credentials were suffering from a kind of devaluation as "inflation" set in, product of the schools' capacity to overproduce graduates. Supply quickly exceeded demand. "It is in this context of educational belt-tightening that career education must be seen," Smith argued. "It is, as some critics charge, life adjustment resurrected under a new name. Its methods are not new—field-trips to the bakery, work-study and coop programs, and guidance committees have been around for years."

Career education, he continued, "is a message to all of us about competition for and expectations about college and status. . . . If it's any comfort, most industrialized countries are in the same boat." Hardly a day goes by when the press does not report some country's deciding to give more attention to vocational and (nonuniversity) career education. Smith's conclusion was that career education would endure until the problem of educational inflation had been temporarily resolved, at which time it would fade away and a new round of inflation would then begin anew.[99]

The Council For Basic Education (CBE) was more ambivalent in its attitude toward career education. "CBE has never voiced unalterable opposition," James M. Howard Jr. explained in the Council's house organ, "but we have been candid in expressing misgivings about the aims of career education, and we are uncomfortable about the generous application of resources to activities which are of questionable worth." After reviewing the spectacular rise of the movement, *CBE Bulletin* editor Howard observed,

> Careful always to distinguish between career and vocational education, career educationists disavow interest in training students for jobs in particular. Their intention, as we read it, is to orient all boys and girls toward jobs in general, to condition them, as it were, for lifework. They want all teachers at all levels to make explicit the career implications of subjects they teach, and to undermine sex and race stereotypes of occupations. They look to people in business, industry and the professions to provide work-study opportunities.[100]

Howard felt such aims were "modest and plausible. He even thought there was "something wholesome and happy" about them. But he objected to "emphasis on education as preparation for work" and "a global reorientation of K–12 toward economic purposes." To accept it, he argued, "would be to approve that common article of faith which holds that, ultimately, education is worth supporting or paying for only to the extent that it qualifies people to make money." It would be "tragic" he insisted, "if the philosophy of economic purpose became official American policy respecting education."[101]

One of the strongest critiques written from a Neo-Marxist perspective was

ALTERNATIVE VIEWS

The entire import of the school cannot be a career one, for how could political education, what Jefferson called "citizenship," occur in such a program? The problem is not so much with what career education can do; rather one becomes increasingly aware of what it cannot do.

—Robert Paul Craig, "A Need For Moderation: Career Education And The Liberal Arts," *Journal of Career Education* 4 (Spring 1978): 50.

The feeling that vocational guidance is achieved when one's interests and abilities are measured against, and correlated with, a number of standard occupations is highly questionable. It would be difficult, perhaps, to find a single instance of a successful individual . . . whose early career was not a notorious series of false starts, often in totally unrelated fields. Experience seems to indicate that vocational adjustment is extraordinarily complex . . . Vocational objectives will have to be chosen with the implicit understanding that they often may be temporary or shortlived. Adaptability must become a literal reality, and the prospective worker must accept job change and job mobility, as well as periods of retraining, as a part of the natural course of things. . . . We also must . . . return to such basic questions as "what is an educated person?" utterly apart from the making-a-living obsession.

—M. L. Story, "Vocational Education As Contemporary Slavery," *Intellect* 102 (March 1974): 371–372.

provided in 1980 by Kenneth Wagner, a doctoral candidate in sociology from the University of Pittsburgh.[102] "Career education," he alleged, "is a reform movement which seeks to create more efficient workers for the capitalist system of production. In reducing expectations, narrowing 'skills,' and in increasing ties to work, career education limits learning to the existing social structure."[103] In arguing that the content of education must be in closer correspondence with the needs of the economy, career educators, in effect, endorse as a "given" a socioeconomic system that is inherently alienating and oppressive. He especially objected to the assumption that career education could serve students' real needs and interests.

"The interests of students do not mystically appear or become articulated spontaneously," he observed. "The types of work activity that students will learn are activities that they are likely to define as in their interest only in terms of their chances of getting a job." Furthermore, "to assume that the needs of the economy have always and will in the future coincide with the needs, interests, and potentialities of students is to accept the ideological assumption that capitalism promotes the freedom in which students can develop in autonomous and self-defined directions." This basic assumption, he believed, was utterly false:

> The economy dictates where it is possible to earn a livelihood and our schools reflect the needs of the economy in their curriculum and budget decisions. The needs of

capitalist production shape the needs and interests of students. . . . And that is the point: people do not control the means of capital investment and, therefore, are in a position where they must equate their needs with the needs of the economy if they hope to work at all.[104]

Wagner made it plain he felt there was an irreconcilable antagonism between capitalism and individual autonomy:

> Career educators do not realize the implications from implicitly recognizing that student needs are the historical product of a specific society. They self-consciously present their reforms as meeting the instrumental needs for the "technological world they are about to enter." What they don't understand is how that "technological world" is structured so that in serving capitalist society, public education helps perpetuate class domination and retard individual development. The specific skills and work habits demanded by capitalism do not serve self-defined human needs, but the alienated social relations which arise due to the needs of capital accumulation and private control. . . .
>
> The ideological equation of student interests with the present social structure presupposes that capitalist society can organize work in order that workers can self-consciously control their productive activity as well as their society. The ideology here obscures and mystifies the inherent conflict between labor and capital in capitalist societies. . . .[105]

Like many other radical critics, Wagner felt it was futile to attempt to teach appreciation for work so long as the forms and conditions of employment remain profoundly alienating. Instead of addressing the question of what social forces rob workers of control over their own lives and thereby create dissatisfaction, he claimed, career educators merely seek to disabuse students of the notion that work can be always fulfilling. For critical inspection of the social structure, they substitute moral admonitions having to do with the virtue of working hard and responding to incentives. "Capitalism is taken as fixed and unassailable. It is assumed that problems of alienation, unemployment and poverty can all be eradicated if only we think correctly and legislate the proper reforms."[106]

Ultimately, Wagner believed, the aims of career education would prove to be unattainable:

> What is not addressed by career educators is how capitalist society creates the problems career education proposes to solve. It is precisely because career educators are unaware that their reforms only make sense given the existence of capitalist society. . . . Only when the schools become part of a society which creates social relationships in which people democratically control their lives will the social relations in the classroom produce students who find work a self-satisfying activity.[107]

Summing up, the main lines of criticism directed at career education by various writers throughout the 1970s and early 1980s were as follows:

1. Career education as a concept is so imprecise and poorly defined that it can mean anything and everything in general, and hence nothing in particular;

2. Career education in intent and purpose is indistinguishable from old-fashioned traditional vocational training. The former is only a cosmetic cover for the latter;

3. Career education originated under the auspices of a politically ultraconservative administration bent on stifling dissent and social unrest. It is an expedient designed chiefly to induce compliance with a corporate business-industrial order;

4. Career education is not new or original; it is simply life-adjustment education revived in new guise, with renewed emphasis upon vocational training;

5. Career education is too all-encompassing. It seeks to impose a single uniform organizational, curricular, and instructional format on all schooling, stipulating the same educational goals for all educational activities. It thereby neglects the values of pluralism and diversity;

6. Career education is too narrow—it would neglect the common values of general education and would convert education in its broadest sense to narrow vocational training, and career education is therefore anti-intellectual;

7. Career education subscribes to a restrictive and narrowly utilitarian theory of the value of knowledge and learning;

8. Career education represents an overly ambitious agenda for American education that cannot possibly succeed in all its aims. Inevitably, certain other legitimate educational goals and values will be deemphasized, fatally compromised, or eliminated altogether;

9. Career education is based on an overly conservative political philosophy that uncritically endorses and reinforces the existing socioeconomic and political order;

10. Career education is based solely on external social and economic considerations. It lacks an adequate *educational* rationale;

11. Career education reflects an approach to manpower development and human-resource allocation that is potentially dehumanizing and depersonalizing;

12. Career education is based upon a futile attempt to refurbish a capitalist work ethic, organized around unlimited production and consumerism, which is obsolescent and no longer relevant to the realities of an emergent post-industrial society;

13. Career education is a subterfuge intended to reduce opportunities for socioeconomic mobility and to limit the life chances of the poor, of minorities, and others from culturally deprived backgrounds;

14. Career education cannot materially reduce unemployment or create jobs; hence it must inevitably fail in meeting its primary objective;

15. Career education entertains an overly romantic and idealized conception of work and the workplace. Not all people can hope to pursue a "career." Job-status equality is a myth; people cannot in principle be "overeducated"—there is no such thing as too much education;

16. Career-education theory incorrectly assumes that worker dissatisfaction and alienation are products of inadequate or inappropriate training rather than functions of the conditions of the workplace and the circumstances of employment;

17. Occupation is not the sole source of personal identity or worth, and therefore it would be a mistake to make "occupation" or "career" the focus of all educational endeavor;

18. The process of occupational selection cannot or should not be rationalized and systematized;

19. Career education encourages premature career choice, thereby oftentimes limiting subsequent work options;

20. Career-education programs and curricula lack theoretical coherence, consistency,

and an adequate research basis; they are insufficiently well developed, and cannot be implemented successfully under "real-world" conditions in the schools.

## RELATIONS BETWEEN CAREER EDUCATION AND VOCATIONAL EDUCATION

Some criticisms of career-education theory and practice were undoubtedly well founded. Others were less well considered and more easily refuted. Sometimes the disputes were over facts, and sometimes over values; usually they concerned both. In many cases, however, attacks reflected fundamental differences with proponents on matters of social, economic, and political philosophy. Easier to deal with by far were arguments over matters of fact or conceptual arrangement. The charge that career education was just another name for vocational education, for example, could be readily discounted by reference to the pronouncements of vocational educators themselves. As early as 1974, the National Advisory Council on Vocational Education, for example, had gone on record criticizing career education as "over-promised and under-delivered," as failing to benefit the groups for which it was intended, and as failing to face serious problems and "sobering facts." In its eighth report, the Council urged that the distinction between vocational and career education be kept clear.[109]

Writing in the October 1974 issue of the *AVA Journal,* Lowell A. Burkett, Executive Director of the American Vocational Association, reminded readers that the Association at its annual meeting the year before had decided to retain the term "vocational education" and to reject efforts to substitute any alternative designation. In addition, an official definition for the term had been adopted: "Any educational program of less than baccalaureate degree designed to prepare people for entry-level employment, to retrain employed workers who want or need retraining to remain in the labor market, or to upgrade employed workers for advancement in their careers."[110]

Against those who sought to improve the "image" of vocational education by proposing some such term as "occupational education," Burkett argued that no substitute offered sufficient advantages to warrant a change in the official nomenclature. More to the point, Burkett felt the introduction of the term "career education" was confusing, because it tended to cloud the nature, mission, and identity of vocational education. He deplored the fact that many local school districts throughout the country were redesignating their efforts, and that directors of vocational education were assuming titles of directors of career education. Burkett admonished his colleagues:

> My plea to the vocational education community is to stop the semantic game. Otherwise we will soon lose track of who we are and what we are all about. . . .
> There is evidence that some programs labeled vocational education are not preparing people for job entry and job progression. Even though they may be few in number, they have a negative effect on public support of the program. Like the bad

apple in the barrel, they contaminate all the rest. Every dollar of public expenditure for vocational education must be accounted for in terms of its return on the purposes for which the funds are intended. How well are the vocational graduates doing in getting jobs and progressing in them? That is the measure being applied.

Even though we may try to find some other legitimate and worthwhile rationale, it is quite clear that public support of our program is based on our ability to prepare people for job entry and job progression. That is our primary mission. Essential to this mission are the ancillary services that vocational education relies on to accomplish its goals.[111]

Reminiscent of the position taken in the early 1900s by vocationalists such as Charles Prosser and David Snedden, who wanted schools to concentrate on specific job training, as against people such as Dewey, who favored a more generalized program of industrial "awareness," Burkett argued that the true intent and hence source of identity for vocational educators lay in their concern for discrete occupational preparation. Career education, on the other hand, had to be viewed as a much broader concept encompassing a range of concerns.

Rupert Evans took a similar stance. "The easiest way to describe the relationship between career education and vocational education," he observed, "is to point out that all of the latter is part of the former." They share the same goals of meeting society's manpower needs, of increasing individual options related to work, and conveying knowledge of the relevance of general education in work. The most obvious difference between career education and vocational education is that, whereas the former typically serves youths aged sixteen and over and concentrates on meeting the needs of those of low socioeconomic status and low verbal ability, career education, Evans argued, "is designed to serve all of the people." It is intended to begin in early childhood and extend throughout the educational system.[112]

Evans also took issue with the assumption that vocational education is synonymous with the career "preparation" phase of career education. Vocational education traditionally is concerned with preparation for nonprofessional careers which require less than a college degree for entrance. Career preparation, on the other hand, has a broader aim. It seeks to service the needs of those who will enter the professions and other jobs requiring a baccalaureate for entry, mainly by promoting work-seeking skills, personal and work-evaluation skills, and general knowledge of how work is organized and conducted.[113] In the final analysis, he argued, vocational educators could only benefit when they accepted the fact that "the older, more specialized field of vocational education is an essential part of the newer, broader, concept of career education."[114]

## COUNTERING CRITICS: THE REBUTTAL

If the allegation that career education was nothing more than vocational education dressed up in new semantic trappings was easily disposed of, other criticisms of the career-education movement deserved more serious consideration. Sidney Marland, however, was always willing to respond to critics. Thus, in 1974, in his major work, *Career Education, A Proposal For Reform,* he sought at length to counter various accusations leveled at the movement.

Reacting to the claim levied by the Council for Basic Education that career education was anti-intellectual, Marland branded it a "misperception." He did not advocate abandoning basics or neglecting academics, he retorted; he wanted to *relate* their acquisition to a learner's personal goals and aspirations. Against the criticism that career education was "too fuzzy" and ill-defined, that it was deployed as a slogan without any definite meanings attached to it, Marland denied his intention of wielding it as a catch-all phrase. The term was not an empty rhetorical flourish. While it may have been a strategic error to shun any official federal definition, Marland felt in retrospect that, having avoided the convention of an early definition, "vigorous, creative . . . and constructive" debate had ensued that might not otherwise have occurred. He felt the results had been positive, and at the same time had assiduously avoided the stigma of anything smacking of federal prescription.[115] To charges that career education was simply "old wine with new labels," or that it was the same as vocational training, the Commissioner responded that irresponsible critics simply had not investigated the differences carefully enough.

Marland strongly rejected allegations that career education threatened any racial or ethnic minority. Contrary to a claim advanced by Sally Barber Spitzer, speaking for the National Urban League, who had voiced a fear that it would "be used as a weapon of oppression against the community of non-whites . . . trapping them into . . . servitude to a privileged professional class,"[116] Marland protested the intent had been just the opposite. Although not aimed especially at minority students, career education was designed to give people greater control over their own lives by equipping them with skills to enter productive work once they left their formal education behind. Far from recommending a "tracking" system that might condemn minorities to economic servitude, career education urged an end to all tracking and an elimination of separate curricula—general, vocational, and college preparatory.

So far as he was concerned, the idea of promoting greater career "awareness" in elementary schools in no way forced career *choices* at an early age, contrary to some critics' complaints. For Marland, the issue was a "red herring" that needed no further discussion. More significant in his mind was criticism that career education was solely concerned with getting jobs and filling manpower needs. While this was never thought of as a *primary* goal, he insisted, he saw nothing wrong with being concerned over jobs and manpower needs. "The critic here fails to comprehend the wholeness of career education with the ultimate utilitarian parts, now often scorned by teachers and professors," he observed.[117]

Marland accepted the objection that career education might accentuate the trend toward reduced collegiate enrollments. On the whole, he thought a reduction in the number of students in postsecondary institutions was healthy; and it was his belief that many young people in colleges and universities had no business being there in the first place. College is not for everybody, perhaps not even for a majority of high-school graduates. Possibly, he argued, career education would be part of a solution—not the problem—by encouraging more diversity and enhanced respectability for alternatives to the traditional four-year collegiate course of studies.

Nor was Marland troubled by the prospect that career-education programs would serve to dilute or divert resources away from vocational education. In fact, he felt the issue begged the question as to whether vocational education should be separated from other parts of the secondary-school curriculum. "The goals of career education," he avowed, "are no different than the goals of vocational education, except that they reach all the young people and afford them a more complete experience." [118]

The "most sobering" criticism of career education, in Marland's view, concerned the question of future employment opportunities. He conceded the strength of the argument that "the unpredictability of the manpower needs of the country makes career education a futile exercise." Of the several declarations of doubt expressed about career education, this he found most compelling. He agreed in part with Fitzgerald, who had argued that most people cannot plan their futures, and that job training by itself does not create increased opportunities for employment. Marland then went on to comment:

> Those of us who are . . . educators do not claim to have the answers to the future economic and manpower circumstances of our society. We are mindful of their uncertainty and the precariousness of prediction. It is for this very reason . . . that we urge against specific and narrowly conceived job preparation or professional development. We make the assumption that most people will need . . . and want to work. . . . We hold that readiness in attitude, values, versatility, and comprehension of work options are necessary ingredients of an educational program designed to help young people enter the work force. We declare one of the goals of career education to be the readying of young people for coping with change. . . . Coping with uncertainties and having the developed capacities to make good decisions is part of career education's offering for the young. [119]

Unwittingly or not, here Marland touched upon a fundamental set of issues to which proponents of career education never appeared to offer a satisfactory response. The question was one of fundamental purpose—or, rather, of *specificity* of purpose. Was the real goal of career education discrete job training? Or was it good decision making and "coping with change"? If the former, and if the culminating stage of "preparation" featured in most proposed career-education models was to be taken seriously, then career education at the upper secondary level would rather quickly "merge" into vocational education. Any distinction between the two would collapse, protestations to the contrary by supporters notwithstanding. This might not be objectionable, it was said, if all the other worthy goals of education that proponents professed to support could be achieved simultaneously—citizenship training, promoting broad cultural awareness and critical thinking, and so on. But considering the time, energy, resources, and ef-

---

THE ANIMAL SCHOOL, A FABLE

Once upon a time the animals decided they needed a better way of preparing themselves for life in a dynamic, rapidly changing world. So they organized a school. It had a common curriculum, consisting of running, climbing, swimming, and flying. All the animals were required to complete the same courses.

The duck was outstanding in swimming but he barely passed flying and was very poor in running. Since he was flunking running, the teacher made him stay after school for remedial instruction. Pretty soon his web feet became very worn from so much running practice. His grades in swimming slipped badly.

The rabbit was at the top of her class in running, but she nearly had a nervous breakdown because of so much make-up work in swimming. Her teacher advised her to see the school counselor. The squirrel was excellent in climbing. But he became very frustrated when his teacher made him start from the ground up instead of from the treetop down. He began to suffer from overexertion and then failed climbing and running.

The eagle was a problem child. In climbing class he beat all the others to the top of the tree, but insisted on using his own way to get there. He was reprimanded severely, but to no avail. He was finally diagnosed as "behaviorally disordered."

At the end of the year, an abnormal eel that could swim very well, and also run and climb, had the highest average. If he had learned to fly even a little, he might have become class valedictorian.

The prairie dogs stayed out of school and fought the tax levy because school officials refused to add digging and burrowing to the curriculum. They apprenticed their child to a badger and later joined the groundhogs and gophers in starting a successful private school.

—Adapted and retold after G. H. Reavis,
"The Animal School," *Educational
Forum* 17 (January 1953): 141.

---

fort needed to lay a foundation of general education, as academically oriented critics were quick to point out, little time would be left over for specific occupational preparation.

Many vocational educators, in their criticisms, took the opposite tack. Their concern—and skepticism—revolved around the question of whether an emphasis upon career "awareness" and "exploration" of job clusters might not ultimately divert attention from, or obscure the need for, equipping students with entry-level skills for actual employment. In a sense, by claiming one could have it both ways, the career-education advocate brought down criticism from both sides. Traditionalists feared vocationalist concerns would overshadow broad academic training. Vocationalists, for their part, wondered if all the conceptual paraphernalia of career education was really needed in getting on with the basic task of preparing people for work.

In essence, critics on all sides were questioning whether career education was realistic in its aspirations. Could programs offered under its auspices fulfill *both* the objectives of general learning and specialized job training? Could this twofold task be achieved without resorting to the sort of differentiated curricula and tracking system career educators ostensibly opposed? Or would the heterogeneity of the typical school-age student population inevitably frustrate attempts at an academic-vocational synthesis? Was it truly the case, as Marland and others claimed, that one could pursue a broad range of educational objectives *in and through* a learning context defined by vocationalist interests and concerns?

Even assuming the viability of some such synthesis or integration, would the need to equip all young people with entry-level skills to various occupations by the time of high-school graduation necessarily force premature choices upon students? What *kind* of skills could schools foster? Were they of the sort needed at the level of employment open to high-school graduates? Or would specific training be too limiting and become quickly obsolete? If career education was to be concerned mainly with job attitudes, values, and awareness, it might run the risk of failing in its avowed aim of preparing people for employment. Yet if it concentrated primarily on job training as a culminating activity, the question was how to avoid the likelihood of skill obsolescence and the danger of training for nonexistent jobs.

On this last point, Marland had no ready answer. Predicting manpower development needs, he claimed, was not the educator's business. Yet he did not feel teachers or school officials could wash their hands of the issue either. "Educators and employers along with labor must forge a much more fruitful alliance than we now have to help resolve this predicament," he offered. "We have to have better signals in education for what the needs will be a decade or two ahead." He added, "Career education as now conceived will not *depend* upon this new wisdom, but it would help if we had it." [120]

The allegation of an "insidious alliance" between big business and career education irritated Marland. According to critics, career education was a device for perpetrating a corporate social order reinforcing business interests and values. They suspect, as he phrased it, "a collusion between education and the business world that would constrain young people to enter conventional employment meekly. . . ." Marland's response was he was unaware of any "sinister alliance" between career education and big business. He conceded that it had enjoyed enthusiastic support from business, "yet it does attempt to address, for purposes of acquainting students with the world of work, real situations in which industrialized America is moving toward ever-enlarging corporate institutions with the danger of corresponding reductions of individuality." This, he observed "is a fact, not something that education encourages." He continued, if attitudes and practices conducive to alienation exist, young people should be mindful of them. But "no one . . . says that young people are all obliged to enter the big corporate system." Career education was broad enough to address the full gamut of callings and occupations. [121]

Rupert Evans was also unimpressed by critics' charges that career educators aimed at creating a submissive work force:

> Career education has begun to be important enough to attract critics. One of the criticisms is that it is designed to produce docile workers for the military-industrial

complex. It would appear, however, that even modest programs of career awareness, exploration, and preparation are likely to decrease docility by affording both blue-collar and white-collar workers new ways of looking at work as well as new opportunities for mobility. If this is true, one can expect soon to hear cries from other critics, that career education is producing people who expect too much from their work. Steering a course between these two groups of critics will be difficult, but it is better than using education to perpetuate the notion that work is necessarily bad and fit only for slaves.[122]

## CAREER EDUCATION AND CAREER DEVELOPMENT

A dozen or so years after Marland's historic 1971 address in Houston, most career-education proponents were professing satisfaction with the movement's progress. Joyce Rice, associate director of continuing education at the University of Wisconsin-Madison, for example, noted that programs had "blossomed" all across the country. Thousands of teachers had begun informally to "thread" the idea of work, jobs, and career planning into the K–12 curriculum. Industry and business were providing role models in classrooms and more actively collaborating with professional educators. In addition to "threading" or "infusion" (that is, incorporating career content into existing curricula), whole new courses had evolved around the themes of occupational choice and decision making, career values, life planning, and values clarification. Rice felt much work still needed to be done at the postsecondary level, however. "The thrust of career education and the career education literature has been at the elementary and secondary levels," she observed. "Only recently have educators begun the task of systematically defining career education as it applies to adults and to post-secondary education."[123]

Overall, she looked to a bright future for career education. But with astonishing naïveté she added, "Career education to date has been a relatively noncontroversial movement. It has no powerful enemies because it has generally remained aloof from taking stands on social issues and further, has shrewdly insisted that it demands no new money."[124]

Slightly more guarded in its optimism was a 1980 monograph by Kenneth Hoyt offering "a report card" for the 1970s on career education and "some predictions for the decade of the 1980's."[125] Hoyt pointed with pride to the fact that as early as 1975 more than 9,000 of the nation's 16,000 school districts were reported to have initiated some form of career-education programming. Federal funding had grown from $47 million for the period 1970–76 to almost $150 million for 1979–83. Between 1974 and 1978 another $100 million per year had been expended from other sources within the U.S. Office of Education. The future of career education throughout the 1980s, he noted, would be influenced by whether federal funding support continued, expanded, or declined. He worried that existing career-education legislation at the federal level was due to expire in 1983, and also correctly predicted that the level of federal assistance to the movement would decrease significantly thereafter.

Nevertheless, Hoyt believed "great progress" had been made, so far at least, in providing "all students at all levels of the educational system with a set of general employability/adaptability/promotability skills" enabling them to "change with change in a rapidly changing society." Career education, he emphasized, had demonstrated itself to be "an effective delivery system" for promoting basic academic skills, skills in "practicing good work habits," developing and using "personally meaningful work values," and "understanding and appreciating the private enterprise system." Thousands of students had been helped in developing "self-understanding" and "understanding of educational/occupational opportunities." Students throughout the nation were learning how to decide on careers; how to seek, find, and retain jobs; and how to make productive use of their leisure time. They were learning about ways of "humanizing" the workplace, and acquiring skills "in overcoming bias and stereotyping as they act to defer full freedom of career choice for all persons."[126]

Looking to the future, Hoyt cautioned that continued success in years to come was not assured, nor was it axiomatic that support for the career-education movement would endure. Yet he felt there was ample reason to feel "justifiably proud" of past accomplishments, and he felt reasonably sure programs would last. "The decade of the 1980's will be a crucial one for career education," he wrote. "I am worried, but I am not afraid."[127]

Theodore E. Molitor, a Minnesota high-school chemistry teacher, noted some of the changes that had accompanied the expansion and maturation of the movement. "Our concept of career education has broadened considerably since the U.S. Office of Education raised it to prominence nearly a decade ago," he observed in 1980. Whereas in the early years the term "career" was virtually synonymous with "occupation" or "vocation," and the emphasis was on preparation for paid employment, in response to critics who claimed the focus was too narrow, the subsequent tendency had been to expand or inflate "career" until its meaning encompassed practically everything referred to by the term, "lifestyle."

Commenting on this trend, Molitor wrote,

> As it has evolved, career education is a broad-based effort to help young people see the relationship between school and future life roles. "Work" refers to both paid and unpaid activities, and may include vocational and leisure pursuits as well. "Career" is no longer merely synonymous with occupation. In the broad sense, one's career is now seen as a life-long pattern of roles, including (but not restricted to) family member, student, employee, and community volunteer.[128]

The most tangible expression of the attempted equation of "career" with "life-style" was an effort to tie career education with guidance and counseling processes, and to make "career development" the common goal of both. "Career education is coming of age," argued Donald E. Super of Teachers College, Columbia University. "When the concepts of career development are more widely understood, and when its methods and materials are more visible and are put to use in the curriculum, career education will indeed have come of age."[129]

Successful implementation of career-education programs, agreed Edwin Herr and Stanley Cramer, depended on career guidance. School counselors in particular, they alleged, had a responsibility "to help individuals identify their career options, understand the personal implications of these options, plan the ways by which they can integrate the educational experiences necessary to achieve favored goals, and make decisions when they must be made." [130] Their "basis of professional practice" should be to assist young people in systematic ways "to develop effective career behavior and a personal vision of life goals. . . ." [131]

For Super, the counseling task was to be redefined as "career guidance" in its broadest sense, and its general objectives relative to career development would be identical with those of career education as well:

1. To provide students with an understanding of the nature and sequence of life stages and of career stages, of the developmental tasks which characterize these stages, and of the changing major roles which people play (in sequence and simultaneously) in the various theaters of activity in the several life stages;

2. To help students develop realistic self-concepts, with esteem for themselves and others, as a basis for career decisions;

3. To develop in students a realistic and appreciative understanding of the evolving world of work, with a broad perspective on opportunities and a specific focus on one or more clusters of occupations, together with knowledge of the educational and occupational pathways that lead to them, of the work and ways of life that they involve, and of the types of occupational changes which may be encountered;

4. To help students know and appreciate the many changing avocational, domestic, and civic outlets for developed interests and abilities, outlets which in an automated society often supplement, complement, or even supplant paid work in making a satisfying career;

5. To provide a basis for the making of sequential, increasingly specific, and sometimes recycled career decisions in which self and occupational knowledge are synthesized for self-realization in work, in homemaking, in civic life, and in leisure, in ways which meet social as well as individual needs;

6. To make these experiences available in ways appropriate to all students at each stage of their formal and continuing education. [132]

Kenneth Hoyt, once again, felt the American Personnel and Guidance Association was the logical professional organization to study and clarify the role of the counselor in career education. In a 1979 monograph, he spelled out what he termed "some basic similarities" in the "conceptual bases" of the guidance movement and of career education. Both, he argued, were born out of a concern for problems in the relationship between education and work; both shared common concerns and values; and both attempted to offer a "system solution" to a problem rather than a tailor-made response to a specific set of problems. Both were "help-giving." The early guidance movement, for example, begun by Frank Parsons, was an effort to help schoolchildren in "choosing, preparing for, entering upon, and progressing in an occupation." Like the career-education movement, school guidance stressed decision making and lifetime planning in relation to occupations. Traditionally, school counselors had always emphasized career guidance for students.

Today more than ever, Hoyt insisted, counselors should be thought of as the most "appropriate providers" of skills enunciated in the goals and objectives of career education. "As I see it," he wrote, "career education offers the guidance movement an opportunity to now use its strength . . . to return to the promotion of the basic concepts on which the guidance movement was founded. Career education, without doubt, desperately needs professional counselors as members of the career education 'team.'"[133]

Thus, although no one appears to have spelled it out explicitly, by the 1980s two important shifts had taken place. First, career education had become more diffuse and ambitious in its ambitions, coincident with the expansion of the term "career" to embrace far more than "occupation" or "vocation." Never wholly restricted to job preparation alone, as a movement, career education increasingly had become concerned with the totality of choices and activities associated with multiple life roles. Secondly, more and more attention was given over to "counseling-based" models of career development. An enormous literature was to grow up around the theme of lifelong career guidance.


## IN RETROSPECT

The career-education movement underwent many developmental changes throughout the first dozen or so years of its existence. Some of its themes remained unaltered; other basic concepts were refined and elaborated in the crucible of debate. As a concept and a movement, career education encompassed a variety of views and emphases—so much so, in fact, that its very diversity makes it difficult to abstract or pull out a discrete set of underlying assumptions to which all career educators might assent. For the most part, proponents would likely subscribe with only minor qualifications or modifications to nearly all of the tenets of vocationalism as an educational perspective or point of view. In recasting the case for career education as a formal argument, however, several additional elements or refinements would need to be added. In rough outline form, the series of propositions called for might be laid out as follows:

1. Vocational training, for a variety of reasons, has been relegated to a position of inferiority and subordination in educational thought and practice, although its second-class status vis-à-vis more traditional academic learning is wholly unwarranted and undeserved, both in terms of its potential importance to individual human development and to the general social welfare;
2. Economic prosperity is a necessary precondition for individual self-fulfillment and development. The nation's economic health depends to a significant degree upon a work force imbued with the values and ideals of a work ethic. A major task of the school is to reinforce the work ethic;
3. Work—whether paid or unpaid labor—has both personal and social significance. Whatever a person does, the activities in which he or she engages and to which time, energy, and effort are devoted, is a major source of personal identity and an important avenue of self-expression;

4. The concept of "career" denotes not simply gainful employment (what one does for a living), however important this may be, but more broadly, *the total pattern of choices and activities defining a way of living or life-style;*

5. "Career development" refers to a complex, multifaceted process extending over the individual's total life-span. Its most fundamental aim is to maximize personal and social self-realization or -actualization:

   a. Self-concept and attitudes and values relative to the self are formed early in life;

   b. A person's distinctive mode of response to the surrounding social environment is likewise a function of values, attitudes, experiences, and knowledge acquired early in life;

   c. Successful personal and social development depends upon growth in the effectiveness with which a person makes decisions. Decision-making skills are acquired; they represent learned behavior. They can be fostered indirectly and to some extent taught directly. Young children need opportunities to exercise those skills and to obtain practice in meaningful decision making;

   d. Effective decision making requires awareness and understanding of relevant factors that must be taken into account in selecting among alternatives—decisions depend upon knowledge;

   e. Effective decision making inspires self-confidence and confers upon the decision maker greater control over self and the social environment; it facilitates adaptability to change and enhances personal initiative;

   f. Insofar as work is necessary and desirable, decisions relative to one's economic role in society assume special importance. How a person functions in his or her occupational role(s) depends upon a continuous succession of choices and experiences;

   g. Education can facilitate the process of career selection and development by promoting effective decision making; by exposing learners to information about the world of work; by encouraging children to explore occupational opportunities; by teaching students to relate their own interests and abilities to job options; and by equipping them with the attitudes, values, knowledge, and skills needed in seeking employment, retaining a position, and advancing in a trade, occupation, or profession;

6. Academic and vocational education are inseparable and interdependent. What is needed is a new educational unity or synthesis in which vocationalist concerns are incorporated within the teaching of basic academic skills and subjects, and the skills and values associated with general academic instruction are integrated within the process of vocational preparation;

7. Occupational aspects of human development under a new curricular integration would be elevated to a place of equal respect and importance with academic instruction, such that the occupational or vocational aspects of human development would be related to all relevant aspects of academic instruction, at all levels of learning;

8. The net effect of a new curricular and instructional synthesis would be to enhance the effectiveness of schooling in helping to solve problems of poor student motivation, high attrition (i.e., the drop-out rate), classroom discipline, youth unemployment, juvenile delinquency, and the increasing percentage of the general population on welfare:

   a. Lack of student motivation is a function of the perceived vocational irrelevance of traditional school curricula and instruction;

   b. Classroom discipline problems stem largely from the apathy and boredom of students who would prefer, and better respond to, more occupationally relevant learning;

   c. A major reason why students drop out of school is antipathy toward forms of learning that do not lead directly to employment;

    d.  Unemployment, especially among school-age youth, is owed primarily to a lack of marketable skills and the school's failure or inability to provide entry-level skills to various trades and occupations needed in the marketplace;

    e.  Unemployment could be substantially reduced, as could the number of people on welfare, if there were a better match or congruence between labor-force skills and market demands;

9.  Heretofore, schools have not met the career-development and vocational needs of most students:

    a.  The current system of tracking and differentiated curricula is discriminatory, divisive, undemocratic, and educationally counterproductive;

    b.  Too many high-school students are encouraged to postpone or to defer indefinitely decisions about future careers; and too many are pressured into extending their schooling by going on to college;

    c.  Existing curricula and instruction are poorly adapted to helping young people manage the transition from childhood dependence to the social and economic independence of adulthood;

10.  Formal education, in cooperation with other agencies and institutions, should facilitate career selection and development for all learners:

    a.  Schooling should mark the opening phase of a systematic, lifelong learning process extending from initial awareness of the world of work, through the acquisition of occupationally relevant knowledge, to career preparation and periodic vocational retraining;

    b.  Schools should provide a common integrated curriculum based on the teaching of learning skills, academic subject matter, "coping" or "life-survival" skills, career awareness in relation to personal and social development, decision making, career exploration, occupational information and skill development, and specific vocational preparation;

    c.  Every learner upon termination from school should possess saleable work skills and the knowledge and values required for successful, continuing employment.

On balance, a verdict on how these assumptions and assertions fared under criticism as the career-education and -development movement progressed is bound to be mixed. From the perspective of the mid-1980s, it appeared that many charges levied against the movement had been countered successfully. Some allegations were defused and other controversies laid to rest. In some cases, however, it was plain that career-education advocates had talked past their critics. Many issues remained unresolved; and a few were never even discussed. Additionally, it could be argued, in several instances no satisfactory responses were forthcoming at all. Rather obviously, any overall judgment would be necessarily subjective and subject to variant interpretation. Nevertheless, by the middle of the decade of the eighties, the situation might have been summed up as follows:

The career-education movement was still alive if not necessarily robust. Debate continued, albeit in more measured terms. Career-education programs continued to function in schools across the country. The literature on career education and development was still expanding.

On the other hand, much of the early excitement and novelty was now absent. Popular attention and support were beginning to turn elsewhere. The movement had lost much of its original momentum, chiefly, perhaps, because of federal and state cutbacks in program funding. In any event, there was little to indicate that the dream of career educators to remake American education and to transform its character would be realized. Some critics already were prepared to dismiss the career-education movement as just another episode in a long history of efforts to infuse education with vocationalism.

In terms of specific criticisms and the adequacy of rebuttals offered by proponents, the record of discussion was uneven.

The palpable lack of any clear-cut definition or authoritative characterization of career education as an idea and as a movement was always a source of misunderstanding. Responding to charges of conceptual ambiguity, early supporters argued that no single locution could do justice to the entire panoply of ideas embodied in the term "career education." It now seems evident that the concept was construed differently among various writers, with some defenders adopting a fairly narrow and specific construction, and others favoring a greatly expanded definition. Thus, for example, from the outset advocates worked to preserve a clear distinction between career education and vocational education. In the main they were successful. A persuasive case was made that the latter was to be conceived of as only one component element within a much larger whole. Whereas vocational education was circumscribed by attention to job training, career education was to encompass a broader array of activities and concerns—career awareness, systematic study of occupations, career guidance and counseling, and much more besides.

The question, however, was always—how *much* more? Compounding confusion was the tendency of many enthusiasts to switch back and forth, sometimes using the word "career" in the restrictive sense of "job," and then, when challenged by critics, employing the term in a much more global sense as "anything important in a person's total life-style." Thus, for example, when proponents used the career narrowly, it referred to employment and work-related values. In principle some things were excluded from consideration. Education as a process was to have as its *primary* (though not exclusive) focus learning about the nature and importance of work, the variety of occupational opportunities available, and actually preparing for gainful employment. Critics could either accept or reject the theme as the most appropriate thrust for schooling, but at least the tie between career education and its undergirding intellectual support system—vocationalism—was readily discernible and plain for all to see.

An early qualification that "career" as a concept should not be limited to "paid employment" introduced a minor complication. Career education, proponents now argued, was to be concerned also with preparation for nonsalaried occupational roles—as, for example, the role of homemaker. The addition of leisure-time pursuits, avocations, and recreational activities as elements of a "career" further complicated matters. Finally, as the concept was freighted with still other elements, its meaning was expanded to the point where it was virtually indistinguishable from "life-style" or total "life activities" or "pattern of living."

As critics pointed out, the issue was more than an empty semantic quarrel.

The question was how far one could extend the term "career" and still preserve any definite meaning for it at all. The practical implication was whether, lacking any definite boundaries or limiting conditions, it could designate any particular program whatsoever or point to some coherent agenda. The problem was illustrated by the tendency to talk about "adaptability" and "coping" skills as well as "employability" skills, and to subsume under one rubric such diverse activities as values-clarification exercises for young children, "parenting" classes for young adults, retirement-planning seminars for older persons, and workshops on decision making in general for everyone.

"Career" in its broadest connotations, ran the complaint, excluded nothing and designated no one thing in particular. It could mean anything or everything, and hence nothing in particular. Like an overinflated balloon, some claimed, it was in imminent danger of collapsing into unintelligibility. Career education might be difficult to criticize because it was so diffuse, but proponents allegedly had purchased immunity from criticism at the price of making it utterly vacuous—education for "life" in general.

Career-education advocates, of course, would have rejected any such claim, and in fact did so strenuously when critics raised the objection. Typically, the argument was that career education *does* denote a specific content, and its underlying theme *is* socialization for life roles, including employment. The real strength of the concept, it was said, is that it is sufficiently commodious to accommodate a full gamut of legitimate educational values and concerns besides those having a vocational focus.

Most supporters vigorously rejected allegations that they were insufficiently sensitive to, or appreciative of, the liberal and humane values of general education. Their basic claim, endlessly repeated, was that career education could generate a new curricular synthesis broader and more generous than anything offered in traditional vocational education. Their aim was an entirely new "paradigm" capable of reconciling and integrating *both* academic and occupational learning. Career educators—some, at least—drew back from an early assertion that all education was or should be career education. Paradoxically, however, while insisting on the one hand that career education was for everyone and that it could provide a context responsive to the full range of subjects, values, and concerns associated with traditional academic learning, on the other, they tended to qualify the assertion by conceding career education did *not* include every type of formal learning activity now offered in schools.

The attendant confusion, it must be said, was never cleared up entirely. What was clear was the insistence that however career education was conceived, its agenda was intended for everyone. Career educators opposed any sort of "add-on," and continued to insist that career education would have to be "threaded" or "infused" into all programs. It could not possibly succeed if it was thought of in terms of an alternative and separate set of processes for only certain students.

The claim that the hidden agenda of career education was to socialize a docile and submissive work force was stoutly resisted. Defenders insisted this was not their intention. On the contrary, more informed decision making and better career choices by prospective job holders, it was held, would open up new options, expand alternatives, and otherwise increase the potential mobility of all wage earners. Career-education programs, apologists insisted, would benefit all students, especially women and members of minority populations.

Allegations that career education was a tool or instrumentality in the service of corporate industrialism drew an ambiguous response. Many career educators gave the appearance of misunderstanding the charge or missing the point. If it is fair to generalize, most supporters accepted as a self-evident truth the essentially benign character of capitalism. The inevitability of corporate industrialism went unchallenged. The virtues of free enterprise were tacitly assumed to be so obvious as not to require any defense or further discussion. Traditional liberal-democratic assumptions concerning socioeconomic mobility and equality of opportunity also remained unquestioned. Nor was the resumed relevance of the work ethic as an animating principle in career education much questioned.

Charges that career educators harbored a romanticized or idealistic notion of work prompted divided expressions of opinion. Most proponents of career education flatly denied the claim. The typical response was to say that students should be exposed to more and better information about various occupations, and through cooperative work-study programs learn at firsthand about the advantages and disadvantages of different types of employment.

The issue as to whether career education might contribute to solving problems of youth unemployment was never clearly resolved. While admitting that education alone could not *create* job opportunities where they did not exist, most career-education proponents continued to cling to the idea that a better correspondence between job-market needs and labor-supply skills might help reduce unemployment. The presumption was that the school as an institution is capable of equipping workers with needed ''entry-level'' skills.

The topic of job dissatisfaction and worker alienation was a continuing source of controversy in the literature. Most career educators endorsed efforts to improve workplace conditions, to give workers more flexibility and control, and to ''humanize'' labor activity. Nonetheless, the dominant motif was insufficient prior information and inadequate training as major factors contributing to unsatisfying employment.

As previously noted, few if any proponents of career education went so far as to claim that work by itself is the sole and exclusive source of a person's self-fulfillment. Most, however, were insistent that preparation for what an individual does with more than half of his or her waking hours over the better part of a lifetime is a fitting and appropriate educational concern.

Career educators flatly denied over and over again critics' complaints that career education programs would have the effect of forcing students to make premature career choices. At the same time, they rejected the idea that all or even most students should defer a decision about future employment until after graduation from high school.

A persistent area of disagreement was the desirability or practicality of rationalizing and systematizing the process of career selection. In the early 1970s, many career educators appeared to assume that if the awareness-exploration-preparation-specialization sequence began early enough, most students, by the time they reached adolescence, would have experienced a progressive narrowing of options, and would, ultimately, make a rational career decision based on the perceived "fit" between their own personal needs, interests, and aptitudes and the occupational opportunities available in society. Subsequently, however, many career-development theorists began softening or qualifying those claims.

On the whole, proponents of career education proved themselves willing and able to respond to criticism. Sometimes arguments were modified and the more extravagant claims withdrawn. Just as often the defense was sustained with renewed vigor. The safest thing to conclude is that where opinion remained divided, controversy was rooted in deep and perhaps irreconcilable differences in values or social philosophy.

## SUMMARY

Career education as an expression of vocationalist ideology first arose in the early 1970s. It represented an officially inspired effort to elevate occupational study to a place of equal status with academic learning. Originating with Education Commissioner Sidney Marland, the initiative promoted through the U.S. Office of Education bore a striking resemblance to the life-adjustment education movement three decades before. Like its predecessor in the 1940s, career education purported to be a bold new educational reform. It was based on a belief that schools should assume greater responsibility for teaching about the world of work and preparing all students for gainful employment. The aim was to transform schools by integrating general and vocational education within a common curricular synthesis.

Early proponents called for an end to second-class status for vocational training. Curricular tracking was decried, as were theories promoting learning for its own sake. Professional educators were criticized for alleged snobbery and elitism. Henceforth, supporters hoped, American education would become more responsive to the job-preparation needs of all youth. Schools would no longer neglect occupationally relevant instruction. Classroom discipline would improve. Apathy and alienation would be reduced. The drop-out rate would decrease. Youth unemployment would go down. A new educational unity blending academic and job-related concerns would be forged—the whole buttressed by a comprehensive program of "career development" for all students.

The key to success as career theorists envisaged it was a developmental process beginning in kindergarten and extending into adulthood. Its major phases were delineated in terms of stages of career awareness, exploration, preparation, and subsequent specialization. Without necessarily sacrificing competency in basic learning skills or the traditional academic knowledge domains, all students would move through programs introducing them to the world of work and fostering acceptance of work-related values. Initial awareness would be followed by learning experiences facilitating career choice and preparation for eventual employment in a chosen field.

Both individuals and society would benefit. Those dropping out or graduating from high school would have acquired entry-level skills to the various trades and occupations. Students intending to continue on to college would already have decided upon a course of studies leading to professional employment. Once career education became the integrative focus of all schooling, a better match would ensue between labor-force skills and marketplace requirements. By adapting to the changing manpower needs of the economy, American education would attain a new level of socioeconomic efficiency. By responding to the career-development needs of individuals, it also would at last fulfill its promise of equal opportunity for all.

Career education enjoyed considerable initial acceptance. Fueled with funds from the National Institute of Education, the USOE, and other federal sources, the movement grew rapidly. Scores, then hundreds, of school districts inaugurated career-education programs. Research and development centers began experimenting with various alternative models: school-based, home-based, rural/residential-based, and industry-based. Commercial publishers hastened to produce kits, curriculum guides, texts, and other instructional resources to service an expanding market. Public support for the school-based study of trades and occupations reached a new all-time high.

The response from critics ranged from cautious approval to scorn and derision. Some alleged career education was just another name for vocational education. More than a few claimed the movement's underlying concept was so ill-defined that it was vacuous and could refer to practically anything. Hostile opponents viewed career education as a subterfuge intended to "cool down" social dissent and coopt students in the service of corporate business-industrialism. Other detractors feared it was a conspiracy to limit the educational opportunities and life chances of minorities. A common objection was the alleged reduction of education to job training. A few took exception to the movement's narrow utilitarianism and conservative political bias. A recurrent refrain was that Marland's "brainchild" was tied to an obsolescent work ethic. Closely related was the charge that the movement romanticized work and misconstrued the source of job dissatisfaction. The most serious allegation was that career education would inevitably fail in its avowed aim of reducing unemployment.

Defenders struck back hard at hostile opponents. Some claims were refuted; others remained a subject of continuing controversy. Meanwhile, partly in response to criticism, proponents began expanding the concept of "career" so that it no longer connoted paid employment alone. According to some writers, at least, the term should encompass a totality of life activities or the pattern by which persons structure their lives. The range of activities, subjects, and objectives subsumed under the rubric ''career education'' was greatly enlarged.

Not unlike many previous reform movements in American education, career education progressed through several developmental phases. By the mid-1980s some of the original fervor and enthusiasm had been lost. The momentum had lessened, particularly as program funding decreased. It was not yet clear how extensive or permanent its influence might be. What was apparent, however, was that the pluralism or heterogeneity of American society inevitably would thwart efforts to recast the whole of the nation's system of schooling in the form proposed by career educators.

## REVIEW QUESTIONS

1. When did the term "career education" first appear and in what context? How was it defined?
2. How did vocationalists in the late 1960s and early 1970s account for an alleged lack of popular support for schooling, for school discipline problems, and the high rate of drop-outs? What did they view as the proper role of formal education in contemporary society?
3. Review briefly the circumstances surrounding the inauguration of the career-education movement. To what specific pressures and forces was Sidney Marland and the U.S. Office of Education responding? Historically, what was the importance of the 1971 speech delivered by the Commissioner of Education in Houston at the annual meeting of the National Association of Secondary School Principals? What was the substance of Marland's argument? Why did he seek to avoid any precise definition of "career education"?
4. Upon what basis did Sidney Marland oppose curricular tracking in schools? Why specifically did he oppose the so-called "general" education track at the secondary level?
5. Why did Rupert Evans feel that specific work preparation should be offered in public schools, and why did he advise *against* its postponement until after high-school graduation?
6. What is meant by the phrase "work ethic"? Why has this concept been so important in career-education theory?
7. Recount the four major steps or stages of the career-education model cited by Marvin Rasmussen. Explain what the model called for in terms of activities and goals at each level specified. In what specific ways did this early model reflect the outlook or perspective called vocationalism?
8. Keith Goldhammer spoke of career education as a "new paradigm for educational operations." What did he mean? What is a "paradigm," and how did career education purport to offer one for American schooling?
9. Cautious critics such as James P. Spradley and T. Anne Cleary warned that career education's struggle for popular acceptance would be difficult. What did they forsee as future problems?
10. With specific reference to Van Cleve Morris, what are the differences in

meaning among the following terms: work, job, vocation, career? What is the most important point of career selection as he viewed it?

11. Harold Howe, of the Ford Foundation, spoke of the "intellectual imperialism" of career-education proponents. What did he mean? What were his specific misgivings about career education?

12. What did Frederick Neff assume to be the central purpose of schooling? In what ways was his argument similar to Harold Howe's?

13. What was the "conspiracy theory" of the origins of career education alluded to by such critics as James Hitchcock, Anthony Laduca, and Lawrence Barnett? How did their arguments differ from the critique propounded by Kenneth Wagner?

14. Why did T. H. Fitzgerald, George Newsome, and other critics of career education believe it was impossible to use the schools to reduce youth unemployment?

15. In what specific ways can one find parallels between life-adjustment education and career education? How did Glenn Smith (among others) define the true meaning and purpose of the career-education movement? What was its alleged aim, and why?

16. How does career education differ from vocational education? In what ways do each reflect the common inspiration of vocationalism?

17. Why did critics charge career education with "anti-intellectualism"? How did proponents defend career education from this charge?

18. What is career development? How is this concept related to career education? How have "traditional" beliefs about career guidance and counseling allegedly changed?

## SOME QUESTIONS FOR DISCUSSION

1. Can "adaptability" be taught? Can one learn skills needed for effective decision making? Is "coping" with change a learned skill? Can these be taught directly? Or are such abilities acquired indirectly, in and through other learning? Should schools attempt in some deliberate and systematic way to teach "life skills"?

2. Schools, some claim, cannot teach everything to everyone. Hence, every decision about the curriculum is an act of choice and partial exclusion. A teacher who concentrates on teaching children to read has less class time that could be used for music or social studies, and so on. In a "zero-sum" game, everything must be balanced out against something else. To the extent that this might be true, if you were a parent of a child in school, would you prefer he or she concentrate on traditional academic subjects or would you prefer time be spent more on exploring career choices, learning about various occupations, and preparing for employment? Explain and justify your preference.

3. Assume, purely for the purposes of discussion, that in each of the instances cited below, the two alternatives are mutually exclusive. That is, a student in, say, junior high school, could learn about one thing but *not* the other. As a parent or teacher, which would you choose to emphasize, and why? (Remember, no matter how improbable the conjunctions, you

are asked to imagine a forced choice.) Select one topic or subject from each pair:

  a.  The value of the dignity of all labor *versus* the value of respect and tolerance for individual differences
  b.  effective decision making *versus* literary or musical appreciation
  c.  home electrical repairs *versus* Japanese calligraphy and poetry
  d.  computer programming *versus* theory and practice of dance
  e.  dinosaurs *versus* what it's like to work as a store clerk in retail sales
  f.  how telephones work *verus* European history
  g.  basic economic principles *versus* comparative religion
  h.  how to secure credit and keep a good credit rating *versus* biology
  i.  how to prepare for a job interview *versus* sexism and racism in contemporary culture
  j.  the impact of automation on modern industry *versus* soccer or volleyball
  k.  consumerism, comparison shopping, elementary banking *versus* origins and history of the United Nations.

Is there any pattern to your hypothetical choices? Upon what basis, or for what reasons, did you choose between each set of alternatives?

4.  Is it realistic or practical to argue that no student should drop out or graduate from high school lacking marketable skills for employment? Why or why not?

5.  Can a person be overeducated? Is there any such thing as too much learning? Is it possible to be "overqualified" for a job?

6.  Was there anything in your own personal school experience that helped you prepare for your first job interview? What information did you need that you lacked? Could you have learned it in school? How did you obtain your first job? Did you plan for it? Should you have done so—would it have been helpful?

7.  An elementary-school child hopes to be a physician someday but shows no obvious scientific bent. Another child wants to pursue an art career but has little artistic talent. A third child has no particular career aspirations whatsoever. A fourth is pushed to excel in school by his or her parents but has only average academic ability. How could a school counselor or teacher respond in each case?

8.  Suppose a severe shortage is forecast in a given occupational field five or ten years hence. For example, perhaps a severe shortage of medical technicians is predicted. How should schools respond? Should they create or expand relevant training programs? If so, when should this tooling-up effort begin—before or after a strong demand for such programs develops? What if the forecast is wrong? Or what happens when schools hasten to train more and more technicians and graduates glut the market? In short, how should school programming be related to current and future human-development needs?

9.  A major fast-food franchise corporation currently operates a so-called "Hamburger University" to train franchise holders and store managers. Many other large corporations have their own training programs. Assess the strengths and weaknesses or potential hazards of industry-based occupational preparation.

10.  Why do young people drop out of school? What are the major causes of the drop-out problem? Is it dissatisfaction with what is taught in school?

Would more occupationally relevant curricula enhance student motivation? Would career education help reduce the number of drop-outs? Is it important for everyone to finish high school? Why or why not?

11. What is the difference (if any) between holding down a job and pursuing a career? Does everyone have a career? To what does the concept of career refer—a type of activity? To the attitudes of those engaged in the activity? To the attitudes of society in general toward the particular work in question? How broadly or narrowly should the term "career" be defined?

12. What would happen to a high-school social-studies teacher if he or she actively encouraged students to decide for themselves on the strengths and weaknesses of the American economic system? What if students decided they preferred socialism or communism?

13. If colleges and universities graduate more people than can find employment, how should high schools respond? Should students be discouraged from attending college? Should they be *prevented* from selecting courses of study offering poor employment prospects?

14. Do people generally define themselves through their work? Is paid employment the chief source of individual self-indentity for most people? How else do people express and define themselves? Can schools help facilitate the process of self-definition?

15. In his 1974 book, *Working,* Studs Terkel quotes (p. 524) a woman he interviewed on her attitude toward employment: "I have a few options. Given the market, I'm going to take the best job I can find. I really tried to play the game by the rules, and I think it's a hundred percent unadulterated bullshit. So I'm not likely to go back downtown and say, 'Here I am, I'm very good, hire me.' You recognize yourself as a marginal person. As a person who can give only minimal assent to anything that is going on in this society: 'I'm glad the electricity works.' That's about it. What you have to find is your own niche that will allow you to keep feeding and clothing and sheltering yourself...." Comment on and react to this person's remarks.

16. What makes a person happy with his or her job? What factors contribute to job dissatisfaction? Is it true that all people hate dull, repetitive work? Can all employment be satisfying and fulfilling?

17. Analysts frequently claim that the single greatest need in the work force today is for people with specialized skills in high-technology areas, not those who are unskilled or who have only low-level entry skills for various occupations. If true, what implications follow for the organization and planning of school-based career-education programs?

18. Liberal-democratic ideology holds that the school is an important agency for extending and equalizing socioeconomic opportunity. More radical critics argue, however, that the school's role in a corporate capitalist economy is to reproduce social *inequality* and to meet the needs of a corporate economy. The school sorts and selects individuals, providing them with the expectations, attitudes, and skills appropriate to their future roles within a differentiated, hierarchical socioeconomic order. Schools dispense educational (and hence social and economic) opportunities unequally. Society does not equally value or reward all human capabilities, interests, aptitudes, or abilities. Status and affluence are rationed. Hence, vocational students are consigned to low-status positions at the bottom of the working-class occupational ladder—as unskilled or surplus labor. Analyze and assess this thesis.

19. In light of a previous discussion of John Dewey's theory of occupations and the importance he accorded vocationalism in his major work, *Democracy and Education,* what evidence might be adduced to suggest that if he were alive today he would be a strong supporter of career education? Or is it more likely that he would be a critic of the career-education movement?

20. Public opinion polls regularly suggest that most people want to work. Most of those surveyed report they would continue to work even if they did not have to do so. Fewer than 10 percent would stop working entirely; most would work in a part-time basis. Most people prefer a difficult job over an unchallenging one. Ranked next by most people is salary, followed by job security, and finally work with a sense of social mission. Workers want interesting jobs; they want opportunity; they want fair treatment; and they want their work to fit a total life pattern. Personal autonomy in a work setting is frequently cited as an important value. Discuss the possible educational implications of these findings.

21. Based on your general knowledge or personal experience, do job status and economic rewards always correlate? For example, how do the salaries of teachers compare with those of garbage collectors? With those of truck drivers? Should status and salary always correlate? Or should salaries compensate for low status or demanding work conditions? How does occupational environment relate to job status or wages? What are the possible educational implications involved?

22. Should career development be more nearly a responsibility of school guidance counselors or of classroom teachers? For example, should occupational information as one necessary component be a subject of *instruction* alongside the teaching of literacy skills and such subjects as mathematics, science, history, art, geography, or music? Or should such information be purveyed more informally in consultation with school guidance counselors?

## FURTHER READING

AMERICAN FRIENDS SERVICE COMMITTEE. *Working Loose.* San Francisco: American Friends Service Committee, 1971.

AMERICAN INSTITUTES FOR RESEARCH. *Career Education and the Technology of Career Development.* Palo Alto: American Institutes for Research, 1971.

AMERICAN VOCATIONAL ASSOCIATION. *Career Education: New Perspectives for Industrial Arts.* Washington, D.C.: American Vocational Association, 1972.

ARTERBURY, ELVIS. *The Efficacy of Career Education: Career Awareness.* Washington, D.C.: U.S. Office of Education, 1976.

BAILEY, LARRY J., and RONALD W. STADT. *Career Education: New Approaches to Human Development.* Bloomington, Ill.: McKnight Publishing Company, 1973.

BHUERMAN, ROBERT D. *Career Education and Basic Academic Achievement, A Descriptive Analysis of The Research.* Washington, D.C.: U.S. Office of Education, 1977.

BOLLES, RICHARD N. *The Three Boxes of Life, And How to Get Out of Them.* Berkeley: Ten Speed Press, 1978.

———. *What Color Is Your Parachute? A Practical Manual for Job-Hunters and Career Changers.* Berkeley: Ten Speed Press, 1973.

BOROW, HENRY. *Career Guidance for a New Age.* Boston: Houghton Mifflin, 1973.

BRICKELL, H. M. *Taxonomy and Profiles of Career Education.* Washington, D.C.: U.S. Office of Education, 1974.

BUFFINGTON, THOMAS and ASSOCIATES. *Profiles of Career Education Projects, Fourth Year's Program.* Washington, D.C.: U.S. Office of Education, 1979.

CAMPBELL, ROBERT E., and LOUISE VETTER. *Career Guidance: An Overview of Alternative Approaches.* Columbus, Oh.: Ohio State University, Center for Vocational and Technical Education, 1971.

COUNCIL FOR BASIC EDUCATION. *What Is Career Education? A Conversation with Sidney P. Marland, Jr., and James D. Koerner.* Washington, D.C.: Council for Basic Education, 1973.

DARCY, ROBERT L., and PHILLIP E. POWELL. *Manpower and Economic Education.* Denver: Love Publishing Company, 1973.

DAVENPORT, LAWRENCE, and REGINALD PETTY. *Minorities and Career Education.* Columbus, Oh.: ECCA Publications, 1973.

DOUGLASS, H. R., ed. *Education For Life Adjustment.* New York: Ronald Press, 1950.

EDUCATIONAL TESTING SERVICE. *Proceedings of the Conferences on Career Education.* Princeton, N.J.: Princeton University Press 1972.

EVANS, RUPERT. *Career Education And Vocational Education: Similarities and Contrasts.* Washington, D.C.: U.S. Office of Education, 1975.

———, KENNETH B. HOYT, and G. L. MAGNUM. *Career Education in the Middle/Junior High School.* Salt Lake City: Olympus, 1973.

GARNER, D. P., ed. *The Career Educator.* Charleston, Ill.: Eastern Illinois University, 1975.

GINZBERG, ELI. *Career Guidance: Who Needs It, Who Provides It, Who Can Improve It?* New York: McGraw-Hill, 1971.

GOLDHAMMER, KEITH, and ROBERT E. TAYLOR, eds. *Career Education: Perspective and Promise.* Columbus, Oh.: Chas. E. Merrill, 1972.

GOLDSTEIN, MICHAEL B. *The Current State of Career Education at the Post-secondary Level.* Washington, D.C.: U.S. Office of Education, 1977.

GREEN, THOMAS. *Work, Leisure and the American Schools.* New York: Random House, 1968.

GYSBERS, NORMAN C., W. MILLER, and E. J. MOORE. *Developing Careers in the Elementary School.* Columbus, Oh.: Chas. E. Merrill, 1973.

GYSBERS, NORMAN C., EARL J. MOORE, and HARRY N. DRIER. *Career Guidance: Practice and Perspectives.* Worthington, Oh.: Charles A. Jones Publishing Co., 1973.

HANSEN, LORRAINE SUNDAL. *Career Guidance Practices in School and Community.* Washington, D.C.: National Vocational Guidance Association, 1970.

———. *An Examination of the Definitions and Concepts of Career Education.* Washington D.C.: U.S. Office of Education, 1977.

HERR, EDWIN L., and STANLEY H. CRAMER. *The British Experience in Educational Change, Careers Education, School Counselor Role and Counselor Training: Implications for American Education.* Washington, D.C.: U.S. Office of Education, 1977.

———. *Career Guidance through the Life Span,* Systematic Approaches. Boston: Little, Brown, 1979.

———. *The Emerging History of Career Education:* A Summary View. Washington, D.C.: U.S. Office of Education, 1976.

———. *Monograph on Career Education: Conditions Calling for Education Reform: An Analysis.* Washington, D.C.: U.S. Office of Education, 1975.

———. *Vocational Guidance and Career Development in the Schools: Toward a Systems Approach.* Boston: Houghton Mifflin, 1972.

HOYT, KENNETH B. *Application of the Concept of Career Education to Higher Education: An Idealistic Model.* Washington, D.C.: U.S. Office of Education, 1976.

———. *Career Education: Contributions to an Evolving Concept.* Salt Lake City: Olympus, 1975.

———. *Career Education and the Marshmallow Principle.* Washington, D.C.: U.S. Office of Education, 1976.

———. *Career Education Resource Guide.* Morristown, N.J.: General Learning Corporation, 1972.

———. *Career Education: Retrospect and Prospect.* Washington, D.C.: U.S. Government Printing Office, 1981.

———. *Career Education for Special Populations.* Washington, D.C.: U.S. Office of Education, 1976.

———. *Career Education and Work Experience Education: Can We Join Together?* Washington, D.C.: U.S. Office of Education, 1976.

———. *An Introduction to Career Education.* Washington, D.C.: U.S. Office of Education, 1974.

———. *A Primer for Career Education.* Washington, D.C.: U.S. Office of Education, 1978.

———. *Career Education and the Elementary School Teacher.* Salt Lake City: Olympus, 1974.

——. *Career Education: What It Is and How to Do It.* Salt Lake City: Olympus, 1974.

——. *Future Farmers of America and Career Education.* Washington, D.C.: U.S. Office of Education, 1978.

HOYT, KENNETH B., and JEAN R. HEBELER, eds. *Career Education for Gifted and Talented Students.* Salt Lake City: Olympus, 1974.

——. *K-12 Classroom Teachers and Career Education: The Beautiful People.* Washington, D.C.: U.S. Office of Education, 1976.

——. *Obstacles and Opportunities in Career Education.* Washington, D.C.: U.S. Office of Education, 1976.

——. *Perspectives on Career Education, Perspectives On The Problem of Evaluation In Career Education.* Washington, D.C.: U.S. Office of Education, n.d.

——. *Refining the Career Education Concept: Part IV.* Washington, D.C.: U.S. Office of Education, 1979.

——. *Refining the Career Education Concept: Part V.* Washington, D.C.: Office of Career Education, Department of Education, 1980.

——. *The School Counselor and Career Education.* Washington, D.C.: U.S. Office of Education, 1976.

——. *Staff Development in the K-12 Career Education.* Washington, D.C.: U.S. Office of Education, 1980.

INTER-AMERICA RESEARCH ASSOCIATES. *Increasing Collaborative Efforts in Career Education K-12.* Washington, D.C.: U.S. Office of Education, 1978.

ISAACSON, LEE E. *Career Information in Counseling and Teaching.* Boston: Allyn and Bacon, 1971.

KELLER, LOUISE J. *Career Education In-Service Training Guide.* Morristown, N.J.: General Learning Corporation, 1972.

MAGISOS, JOEL H., ed. *Career Education.* Washington, D.C.: American Vocational Association, 1973.

MARLAND, SIDNEY P. *Career Education, A Proposal for Reform.* New York: McGraw-Hill, 1970.

McCLURE, LARRY and CAROLYN BUAN, eds. *Career Education Survival Manual, A Guidebook for Career Educators and their Friends.* Salt Lake City: Olympus, 1975.

——. *Essays on Career Education.* Portland, Or.: Northwest Regional Educational Laboratory, 1973.

NATIONAL ADVISORY COUNCIL ON VOCATIONAL EDUCATION. *A National Policy on Career Education: Eighth Report.* Washington, D.C.: National Advisory Council on Vocational Education, 1974.

NATIONAL ASSESSMENT OF EDUCATIONAL PROGRESS. *Objectives for Career and Occupational Development.* Denver: National Assessment of Educational Progress, 1971.

NATIONAL CENTER FOR EDUCATIONAL RESEARCH AND DEVELOPMENT. *The Career Education Program Status Report.* Washington, D.C.: U.S. Office of Education, 1971.

NATIONAL SCHOOL PUBLIC RELATIONS ASSOCIATION. *Career Education: Current Trends in School Policies and Programs.* Arlington, Va.: National School Public Relations Association, 1974.

OFFICE OF CAREER EDUCATION. *Career Education, Programs and Progress.* Washington, D.C.: U.S. Office of Education, 1974.

PATTON, THOMAS. *Manpower Planning and the Development of Human Resources.* New York: John Wiley, 1971.

PRELI, BARBARA STOCK. *Career Education and the Teaching/Learning Process.* Washington, D.C.: U.S. Office of Education, n.d.

RESSLER, RALPH. *Career Education: The New Frontier.* Worthington, Oh.: Chas. A. Jones Publishing Co., 1973.

SMOKER, DAVID. *Career Education: A Guide for School Administrators.* Arlington, Va.: American Association of School Administrators, 1973.

STERENSON, JOHN B. *An Introduction to Career Education.* Worthington, Oh.: Chas. A. Jones Publishing Co., 1973.

SUPER, DONALD E. *Career Education And The Meanings of Work.* Washington, D.C.: U.S. Office of Education, 1976.

——. *Measuring Vocational Maturity for Counseling and Evaluation.* Washington, D.C.: National Vocational Guidance Association, 1974.

——. *The Psychology of Careers.* New York: Harper & Row, 1957.

TOLBERT, E. L. *Counseling for Career Development.* Boston: Houghton Mifflin, 1974.

U.S. OFFICE OF EDUCATION. *An Introduction To Career Education, A Policy Paper of the U.S. Office of Education.* Washington, D.C.: U.S. Office of Education, 1974.

VENN, GRANT. *Man, Education and Manpower.* Washington, D.C.: National Association of School Administrators and the National Education Association, 1970.

WERNICK, WALTER. *Teaching Career Development in the Elementary School: A Life-Centered Approach.* Worthington, Oh.: Chas. A. Jones Publishing Co., 1973.

WHITELEY, JOHN M. and ARTHUR RESNIKOFF. *Perspectives on Vocational Development.* Washington, D.C.: American Personnel and Guidance Association, 1972.

WIGGLESWORTH, DAVID C. *A Guide to Career Education.* San Francisco: Canfield Press, 1974.

WILLINGHAM, WARREN W. *Career Guidance in Secondary Education.* Princeton, N.J.: College Entrance Examination Board, 1972.

## NOTES

1. Cited in Kenneth B. Hoyt, *Career Education: Retrospect And Prospect* (Washington, D.C.: U.S. Government Printing Office, 1981), p. 1. Italics added.

2. Quoted in Grant Venn, *Man, Education and Manpower,* rev. ed. (Washington, D.C.: National Association of School Administrators and the National Education Association, 1970), pp. 80–81.

3. Cited in G. Bottoms and K. B. Matheny, *A Guide for the Development and Implementation of Exemplary Programs and Projects in Vocational Education* (Atlanta: Georgia State Department of Education and the Division of Vocational Education, 1969), pp. 23–26.

4. Quoted and discussed in Sidney P. Marland, Jr., *Career Education, A Proposal For Reform* (New York: McGraw-Hill, 1974), p. 4. Used with permission.

5. Larry J. Bailey and Ronald W. Stadt, *Career Education: New Approaches to Human Development* (Bloomington, Ill.: McKnight, 1973), pp. 1–2.

6. Jack Hruska, "Vocational Education—All the Way Or Not At All," in Dwight W. Allen and Jeffrey C. Hecht, eds., *Controversies in Education* (Philadelphia: Saunders, 1974), p. 48.

7. Ibid., pp. 3–4, 51.

8. James E. Allen, Jr., "Competence For All as the Goal for Secondary Education," paper presented at the annual meeting of the National Association of Secondary School Principals (February 10, 1970), cited in Edwin L. Herr, *The Emerging History of Career Education: A Summary View* (Washington, D.C.: U.S. Office of Education, National Advisory Council for Career Education, 1976), p. 7.

9. Marland, *Career Educations* p. 6.

10. Ibid., p. 7.

11. Ibid., pp. 8, 10.

12. Sidney P. Marland, Jr., "Career Education Now," *NASSP Bulletin* 55 (May 1971): 1–9.

13. Sidney P. Marland, Jr., "Educating for the Real World," *Business Education Forum* 26 (November 1971): 3–5.

14. Ibid., p. 3.

15. Ibid., p. 4.

16. Ibid., pp. 4–5.

17. Sidney P. Marland, Jr., "Career Education: A Report," *NASSP Bulletin* 57 (March 1973): 2–3.

18. Cited in Kenneth B. Hoyt, *Career Education Resource Guide* (Morristown, New Jersey: General Learning Corporation, 1972), p. 5.

19. Quoted in Hoyt, *Retrospect And Prospect,* p. 3.

20. Ibid., p. 3.

21. E. L. Rumpf, *Vocational Education for the 1970's* (Washington, D.C.: U.S. Office of Education, Division of Vocational and Technical Education, 1971), pp. 2–3.

22. "Career Education: Perspectives; New Perspectives for Industrial Arts: An Introduction," in American Vocational Association, *Career Education: New Perspectives for Industrial Arts* (Washington, D.C.: American Vocational Association, 1972), p. 5.

23. Rupert N. Evans, "Rationale for Career Education," *NASSP Bulletin* 57 (March 1973): 52.

24. Ibid., p. 54.

25. Ibid., p. 55.

26. Ibid., pp. 60–61.

27. Lowell A. Burkett, Preface, in Joel H. Magisos, ed., *Career Education* (Washington, D.C.: American Vocational Association, 1973), p. 5.

28. Kenneth B. Hoyt, "Toward a Definition of Career Education," in Magisos, *Career Education,* p. 16.

29. Ibid., p. 19.

30. Ibid., p. 15.

31. Ibid., pp. 15–16.

32. Gordon I. Swanson, "Philosophical Bases for Career Education," in Magisos, *Career Education,* pp. 45–46.

33. Marvin Rasmussen, "Preparatory Programs in Career Education," in Magisos, *Career Education,* pp. 114–115.

34. Ibid., p. 116.

35. Ibid., p. 116.

36. Ibid., p. 118.

37. Ibid., p. 119.

38. Ibid., pp. 119–120.

39. John E. Taylor, "Occupational Clusters for Career Education," in Magisos, *Career Education,* p. 122.

40. Quoted in Sidney P. Marland, Jr., in the preface to Larry McClure and Carolyn Buan, eds., *Essays On Career Education* (Portland, Ore.: Northwest Regional Educational Laboratory, 1973), p. xi.

41. James P. Spradley, "Career Education in Cultural Perspective," in McClure and Buan, *Essays,* pp. 3–16.

42. T. Anne Cleary, "New Directions for Career Planning," in McClure and Buan, *Essays,* p. 40.

43. Ibid., p. 46.

44. Ibid., pp. 39–40.

45. Sterling M. McMurrin, "Toward a Philosophy for Career Education," in McClure and Buan, *Essays,* pp. 26–27.

46. Thelma T. Daley, "Career Development: A Cooperative Thrust of the School and Its Community," in McClure and Buan, *Essays,* p. 92.

47. Lola June May, "Who Shall Teach Career Education? The Practitioner as Teacher," in McClure and Buan, *Essays,* p. 74.

48. John W. Letson, "The Potential of Career Education," in McClure and Buan, *Essays,* p. 95.

49. Thomas F. Green, "Career Education and the Pathologies of Work," in McClure and Buan, *Essays,* p. 217.

50. Van Cleve Morris, "The Way We Work: Some Notes on Career Education," *Journal of Career Education* I (Winter 1975): 4–9.

51. Ibid., pp. 4–5.

52. Ibid., p. 6.

53. Ibid., p. 6.

54. Ibid., p. 8.

55. Ibid., p. 9.

56. See Edwin L. Herr and Stanley H. Cramer, *Career Guidance Through the Life Span, Systematic Approaches* (Boston: Little, Brown, 1979), pp. 37–43. See also National Center for Educational

Research and Development, *The Career Education Program Status Report* (Washington, D.C.: U.S. Office of Education, 1971); and Edwin L. Herr, *The Emerging History of Career Education: A Summary View* (Washington, D.C.: National Advisory Council for Career Education, 1976), pp. 8-9.

57. See Office of Career Education, *Career Education, Programs and Progress* (Washington, D.C.: U.S. Office of Education, 1974).

58. Marland, *Career Education,* p. 13.

59. Quoted in ibid., p. 15.

60. Kenneth B. Hoyt, *An Introduction to Career Education* (Washington, D.C.: U.S. Office of Education, 1974).

61. Ibid., pp. 3-4.

62. All citations appear in an annotated bibliography in Herr, *History of Career Education,* pp. 296-301.

63. Harold Howe, "Remarks Regarding Career Education," *NASSP Bulletin* 57 (March 1973): 45.

64. Cited in Howe, "Remarks," p. 47.

65. Frederick C. Neff, "Education Has Many Mansions," *Journal of Career Education* (Winter 1973): 27-32.

66. Ibid., p. 28.

67. Ibid., p. 28.

68. Ibid., p. 29.

69. Ibid., p. 29. See J. B. Moullette, "New Philosophies, Renewed Efforts, and Improved Strategies for Career Education," *Journal of Career Education* I (Fall 1972): 11-19.

70. Neff, "Education," p. 29.

71. Ibid., p. 30.

72. Ibid., p. 30.

73. Ibid., p. 32.

74. James Hitchcock, "The New Vocationalism," *Change* 5 (April 1973): 46-50.

75. Ibid., pp. 49-50.

76. Anthony Laduca and Lawrence J. Barnett, "Career Education: Program on a White Horse," *New York University Education Quarterly* 5 (Spring 1974): 7-8.

77. Ibid., p. 8.

78. Ibid., p. 8.

79. Frank C. Pratzner, "Career Education," in Keith Goldhammer and Robert E. Taylor, eds., *Career Education: Perspective and Promise* (Columbus, Oh.: Chas. E. Merrill, 1972), p. 178.

80. Laduca and Barnett, "Program," p. 12.

81. Lee Sproull, "Career Education Boondoggles," *Learning* (October 1973): 38-41.

82. Ibid., p. 38.

83. Ibid., p. 38.

84. In Career Education Boondoggles by Lee Sproull. Reprinted by special permission of *Learning,* The Magazine for Creative Teaching, October, 1973. © 1973 by Pitman Learning, Inc.

85. Ibid., pp. 39-40.

86. Ibid., pp. 40-41.

87. T. H. Fitzgerald, "Career Education: An Error Whose Time Has Come," *School Review* (November 1973): 91-105.

88. Ibid., pp. 92-93.

89. Ibid., pp. 93-94.

90. Ibid., pp. 103-105.

91. Harvey A. Daniels, "Is Career Education The Answer? *Journal of Educational Research* 67 (January 1974): 192.

92. Eugenia Kemble, "Possibilities and Shortcomings in Career Education," *Journal of Career Education* 4 (Spring 1978): 7.

93. George L. Newsome, "Career Education: Its Meaning and Rationale," *Journal of Career Education* I (Winter 1975): 12.

94. Kenneth B. Hoyt, *Resource Guide,* p. 2.

95. See Kenneth B. Hoyt, *Career Education: What It Is and How to Do It* (Salt Lake City: Olympus, 1972), p. 7.

96. Glenn Smith, "Career Education In Perspective," *Journal of Career Education* I (Winter 1975),: 20–23.

97. H. R. Douglass, ed., *Education For Life Adjustment* (New York: Ronald Press, 1950), p. 9.

98. Smith, "Education in Perspective," p. 22.

99. Ibid., p. 22.

100. James M. Howard, "Career Education's Doughty Critics," *CBE Bulletin* 21 (January 1977): 7

101. Ibid., p. 8.

102. See Kenneth Wagner, "Ideology and Career Education," *Educational Theory* 30 (Spring 1980): 103–113. Copyright 1980 by the Board of Trustees of the University of Illinois, All Rights Reserved.

103. Ibid., p. 106.

104. Ibid., pp. 107–110.

105. Ibid., p. 110.

106. Ibid., p. 111.

107. Ibid., p. 113.

108. For a partial listing of published criticisms up through 1975, consult Herr, *History of Career Education,* pp. 304–305.

109. National Advisory Council on Vocational Education, *A National Policy on Career Education: Eight Report* (Washington, D.C.: The Council, September 1974), p. 7.

110. Cited in Melvin L. Barlow, *Burkett—Latest Word From Washington* (Washington, D.C.: American Vocational Association, 1977), pp. 134–135.

111. Ibid., pp. 135–136.

112. Rupert Evans, *Career Education And Vocational Education: Similarities and Contrasts* (Washington, D.C.: U.S. Office of Education, 1975), pp. 1, 14–15.

113. Ibid., p. 10.

114. Ibid., p. 18.

115. Marland, *Career Education,* pp. 108, 113.

116. Ibid.

117. Ibid., p. 119.

118. Ibid., p. 122.

119. Ibid., p. 124.

120. Ibid., p. 125.

121. Ibid., p. 126.

122. Evans, *Career Education And Vocational Education,* p. 18.

123. Joyce K. Rice, "Career Education Comes of Age," *Journal of Career Education* 7 (March 1981): 212.

124. Ibid., p. 218.

125. Kenneth B. Hoyt, *Refining The Career Education Concept: Part V* (Washington, D.C.: Office of Career Education, Department of Education, 1980), p. 1.

126. Ibid., p. 3.

127. Ibid., p. 11.

128. Theodore E. Molitor, "Career Education: Toward A Larger View," *Science Teacher* 47 (May 1980): 28.

129. Donald E. Super, *Career Education And The Meaning of Work* (Washington, D. C.: U.S. Office of Education, 1976), p. 42.

130. Herr and Cramer, *Career Guidance,* p. 47.

131. Ibid., p. 68.

132. Super, *Meaning of Work,* p. 43.

133. Kenneth B. Hoyt, *Refining the Career Education Concept: Part IV* (Washington, D.C.: U.S. Office of Education, 1979), pp. 18–19, 24. See also Harold L. Munson, J. Jason Berman, and George E. Towner, ''What Do We Really Believe About Career Development.'' *Journal of Career Education* 8 (September 1981): 16–17ff.

# CHAPTER SIX
# HUMANISM
## *Education for Self-Realization*

## INTRODUCTION: CLASSICAL HUMANISM

A common term in the modern educational lexicon is "humanism" or "humanistic," as in "humanistic" teaching and learning or "humanistic" schooling. Vaguely cognate with "humane," some such appellation recurrently comes into vogue and enjoys popular acceptance. Clearly, the adjective "humanistic" has a positive ring to it—so much so, in fact, that hardly anyone today professes opposition to it. No one, for example, would make a forthright appeal for "*in*humane" or "*non*humanistic" education. Whether used in a general sense or as applied specifically to education, however, humanism as a concept tends to be poorly defined. Surrounding the idea are so many diverse associations that its central meaning has become obscured. No single, concise, or comprehensive definition even seems possible. Like many other words suffering rough usage, it has acquired multiple connotations throughout its long career in the history of Western thought.

   Originally, it needs to be said, humanism was closely allied with the concept of education itself. For Cicero and other Roman writers, *humanitas* meant simply the state or condition of being fully "human." By extension, it meant acquiring human characteristics through learning and instruction. Even earlier among the Greeks, humanism was associated with *paideia*—the "culture" of mind that was believed to exemplify the highest possible state of personal development. The term *paideia,* it will be recalled, also referred to the *process* of mastering the liberal arts as instruments or disciplines proper to humankind. Ever since, proponents of the liberal-arts tradition in education have claimed "humanism" for their own.

More broadly, in Graeco-Roman thought, humanism denoted an anthropocentric ("human-centered") view of the world. Its essence was captured by the Greek sophist Protagoras when he declared that man is "the measure of all things." Thus, from classical antiquity came the central tenet of humanism: the paramount importance of human beings in the larger scheme of reality. Humanity counts for something; and as Socrates implied, questions having to do with the sphere of human experience and action are more interesting and perhaps ultimately more significant than all others. A correlative affirmed the innate dignity and value of the individual person. A human being matters for what he or she is *intrinsically,* prior to any accounting of what the person has achieved or received. Also deriving from classicism was the notion that an individual's most important life work, so to speak, was one of self-development and definition, the shaping of a self in the world. Humanism therefore may be said to have evolved out of a point of view that acknowledged and stressed human concerns, or somehow took human nature and its interests as its main theme. Characteristically, humanists have always emphasized the power and worth of human personality, the inviolability or sanctity of the individual, and the importance of self-directed personal development.

## MODERN HUMANISM AND EDUCATION

From antiquity, Western humanism borrowed its human-centeredness, its concepts of human rights and personal dignity, and the theme of the autonomy of persons. As revived among Renaissance writers in fourteenth-century Italy, humanism took on a strongly individualistic flavor, with a stress on freedom and subjectivity—with passions, emotions, and feelings. It was to surface repeatedly in new forms, among the Pietists of the seventeenth century, among the rationalist *illuminati* of the eighteenth-century Enlightenment, and in many guises in the consciousness and thought of more than a few nineteenth-century figures. In more recent times, however, "humanism" has been claimed as the unique possession of an incredibly diverse range of philosophies and movements.

Marxists, for example, are prone to claim they alone are guardians of the only "true" humanism, since only under communism will it be possible through the abolition of the institution of private property and the end of class exploitation to eradicate man's age-old alienation from himself. Basically, this was the point of view put forth by Marx himself in his *Economic and Philosophical Manuscripts* of 1844. It is a position reiterated today by many contemporary Neo-Marxist critics who style themselves "humanists."

A comparable claim was advanced by F. C. S. Schiller in a 1903 book,

*Humanism,* except that he argued it was the philosophy of pragmatism that most fully exemplified the spirit of humanism in the modern era. In a now-famous essay written in 1946, *"L'Éxistentialisme est un humanisme,"* the French philosopher Jean-Paul Sartre likewise sought to show that Existentialism, which affirms that "there is no other universe than the human universe, the universe of human subjectivity," represents "authentic" humanism in its most adequately worked-out form.

Complicating matters still further have been the claims of various *religious* humanists. The Thomistic philosopher Jacques Maritain, for one, writing in his 1936 work, *Humanisme intégral,* advanced the argument that "personalism," which affirms man's capacity for contemplating eternal truths and entering into a relationship with transcendent reality, is the only type of humanism possible. Elsewhere he argued as follows:

> If civilization is to be saved, the new age must be an age of theocentric humanism. Today human dignity is everywhere trampled down. Still more, it crumbles from within, for in the mere perspective of science and technology we are at a loss to discover the rational foundations of the dignity of the human person and to believe in it. The task of the emergent civilization consists in refinding and refounding the sense of that dignity, in rehabilitating man in God and through God. . . .[1]

At the same time secularists of various loyalties and affiliations *also* claim title to humanism. Yet they construe it quite differently in agnostic or atheistic terms, as a doctrine of self-reliance and as a protest against the futility of appeals to supernatural powers. Secular humanism, thus understood, amounts to a claim that humanity is alone in the world, free to decide upon its own destiny and to find fulfillment in the fact of its own independent existence. "Man makes himself," as Gordon Childe proclaimed.[2] "We see the future of man as one of his own making," agreed Herbert J. Muller.[3] "From the angle of evolutionary humanism," explained Julian Huxley,

> the flowering of the individual is seen as having intrinsic value, as being an end in itself. In the satisfying exercise of our faculties, in the pure enjoyment of our experience . . . in individual acts of comprehension or love, in the enjoyment of beauty, in the inner experiences of peace and assurance, in the satisfactions of creative achievement, however humble, we are helping to realize human destiny.[4]

If there are many different conceptions and brands of humanism—Judaic-Christian, Marxist, literary, pragmatic, evolutionary, secular, psychological, *ad infinitum*—the conjunction with education is apt simply to compound confusion. In the absence of any one authoritative definition or consensus, humanism in education can be interpreted in an almost infinite number of ways.

Some writers, for example, use the term "educational humanism" to refer to a broad, diffuse outlook or point of view emphasizing human freedom, dignity, personal autonomy, and individualism. Humanism for others is more specifically a reaction against any theory or set of practices that reduces the idea of the person to something else (for example, to a set of biologically driven impulses or to environmentally conditioned stimulus-response reflexes). Humanism, it is said, is the opposite of mechanistic or behavioral reductionism. On the other hand, some authors find it possible to talk about something termed "behavioral humanism" or "humanistic behaviorism."

Again, some interpret humanism as a way of stressing "inner consciousness" and subjectivity, as opposed to approaches that "objectify" human beings as subjects of scientific investigation and manipulation. It is also widely assumed in certain quarters that humanism in education has to do with feelings, desires, and emotions—with "affect" more than with rational "cognition." Finally, some literature implies educational humanism provides a warrant for specific pedagogical practices and administrative arrangements, as, for example, those said to typify "free" schools or "open-space" classrooms, and "informal" education.

For all its imprecision and ambiguity, however, educational humanism still seems to be a definable position, at least in terms of broad themes or emphases. Without necessarily implying any one particular set of goals, curricula, or strategies, it is safe to assume proponents would likely accept some version of each of the following propositions:

1. The basic aim of education should be to promote each individual learner's maximal self-development—moral, spiritual, esthetic, emotional, and intellectual;

2. The educative process should be conducted in such a way as to avoid infringing upon the rights and prerogatives of each person as an individual;

3. People of all ages, young children included, have a right to be treated with respect, dignity, and kindness, with due appreciation of, and tolerance for, differences among individuals;

4. People differ in terms of interests, needs, abilities, values, ways of learning, and personal goals or aspirations;

5. Learning should be as free, open, and meaningful as possible;

6. Teaching-learning transactions should be individualized in terms of pacing and content;

7. Not everyone needs to acquire precisely the same skills, values, competencies, or knowledge;

8. The most valuable ends of learning are those that have been freely chosen by those involved;

9. The ultimate test of success in education is the degree to which each learner achieves autonomy and self-control, and the extent to which the individual acquires the ability to direct his or her own future learning in ways that are both satisfying and productive;

10. The final justification for all educational effort is the progressive enlargement of an individual's personal freedom, consistent with the reciprocal rights of all others.

Worth emphasizing is the point that the foregoing list falls well short of a complete enumeration of all the assumptions, values, and beliefs that might be involved in a characterization of humanism in its educational bearings. But it does afford a useful point of departure for further discussion. In trying to untangle some of its roots and fixing its underpinnings, several formative traditions suggest themselves as antecedents from which modern educational humanism in its several variant forms is descended. One is "romanticism" in educational thought—a tradition that arose in reaction to centuries of quite inhumane pedagogical practice.

## THE ROMANTIC TRADITION IN EDUCATION

The sad truth is that much of the history of formal education is a tale of mindless cruelty, regimentation, and pain. Down through the ages, for every schoolmaster who worked hard to make learning palatable and schooling a pleasant affair, there were hundreds more who brutalized their charges unmercifully. The tendency all too frequently was to rely upon the whip and cane to compensate for lifeless curricula and a woefully unimaginative pedagogy. Children for the most part were looked upon as willful, headstrong creatures who had to be beaten into submission. Without rigid discipline, ran the argument, there would be no learning. In the earliest known account of a formal school, penned by some anonymous scribe of ancient Sumeria about 4,000 years ago, for example, the story is told of a young boy who fears being late to the *édubba* (literally, "tablet-house") "lest his teacher cane him." In this vivid reconstruction of one day in the life of a schoolboy, the young child is repeatedly flogged for leaving his seat without permission, for talking out of turn, for loitering outside the school yard, and for failing to complete a written assignment according to the form prescribed. Centuries later, practices had changed very little if at all.

Among the ancient Romans, schooling apparently resembled nothing so much as a form of torture. Teachers provided their own school facilities. The *tabernae* were crude sheds or booths erected against a wall; sometimes schoolrooms (*pergulae magistrales*) were no more than awnings erected by spaces under the portico or veranda of some great mansion, open and accessible to all. Children were set to handwork, laboriously tracing out numbers and letters on waxen tablets. When their attention strayed, beatings quickly followed. The Iberian poet Martial, for example, authored an amusing epigram in which he lambasts the "despised pedant" beneath his window who had set up school and roused him from sleep with his disturbance. "Your direful threats and lashes stun my ear!" he complains. Apparently his derisive reference to "melancholy rods, sceptres of pedagogues" was well understood by his audience.

Ausonius too speaks of the school resounding with blows and the cries of children in pain. The cane (*ferula*) and the whip (*scutica*) seem to have been standard classroom equipment, so much so that the popular phrase "to withdraw the hand from the rod" was a common expression for leaving school. Aiding the *ludi magister* ("teacher of letters") was the *pedagogue,* usually a family retainer, referred to by Libanius as a helper in making a pupil finish his homework: "What the boy gets from the teacher, it is the pedagogue's job to preserve for him by urging him on, shouting at him, fetching out the strap, wielding the stick, and by forcing him to do his work, striving to drive into his memory the lesson he has heard." A surviving fragment of student graffiti depicts a crudely drawn donkey endlessly circling a grinding wheel. The inscription, by some unknown schoolchild, reads, "Labor on, little ass, even as I have done."

St. Augustine in his *Confessions* is typical in his reminiscences of the "miseries and mockeries" of childhood. "Nor did they that forced me to my book do very well," he recalled, "for no man does well against his will. . . ." He chafed at the discipline of his schoolwork: "One and one make two, and two and two make four was a harsh song to me, but the wooden horse full of armed men and the burning of Troy and the ghost of Creusa was a most delightful spectacle. . . ." He disliked the study of Greek intensely, precisely because it was forced upon him by his tutors:

> I believe that Virgil is no less harsh to Grecian children when they be compelled to learn him, as it was to learn Homer: for to say truth, the difficulty of learning a strange language, did sprinkle as it were with gall all the pleasures of those fabulous narrations. For I understood not a word of it, yet they vehemently pressed me and with most cruel threatenings and punishments to make me understand it.[5]

Imposing incomprehensible subject matter was bad enough in every century, but the error was invariably compounded by physical torment. The autobiography of the twelfth-century monk Guibert, Abbot of Nogent, for instance, offers a vivid picture of an ignorant teacher inflicting himself upon a hapless youth. Guibert relates how almost every day he was pelted with blows and curses as his incompetent mentor tried to force him to learn. "He took vengeance on me," Guibert recalled, "not knowing what he knew not himself; he ought certainly to have considered that it was very wrong to demand from a weak little mind what he had not put into it. Six years passed without reward. . . ."[6]

Part of the spirit of medieval learning is distilled in rules for the supervision of novices at Canterbury School, as described in the *Constitutions Lanfranci*. Students, it was ordered, "shall . . . sit separate from each other; shall never leave the place in which they are kept, except with the monk who has charge of them. . . . No youth is to talk with another, except so that the master may hear and understand what is said by both of them."[7] Penalties for the slightest infraction were harsh.

Erasmus of Rotterdam (1466–1536) was scathing in his criticism of school tyrants, and he especially appreciated Augustine's rueful admission that were he faced with the choice of death or being forced to return to school, he would choose death. He had scant patience with schoolmasters who "expect their little pupils to act as though they were but diminutive adults," and who senselessly hammered grammatical rules into children's uncomprehending heads. They caused children "to hate learning," he fumed, "before they know why it should be loved." Erasmus understood the need for flexibility and persistence. His advice to the teacher: "Lead the beginner to face his unfamiliar matter with self-confidence. . . . Attack it slowly. We must not underrate the capacity of youth to respond to suitable demands upon the intelligence. . . ." He continued, "The child, like every other creature, excels in the precise activity which belongs to it . . . follow nature, therefore, in this, and so far as is possible take from the work of the school all that implies toilsomeness, and strive to give to learning the quality of freedom and enjoyment."[8]

Michel de Montaigne, the sixteenth-century French essayist, heartily concurred. In his writings he repeatedly returned to the theme of educational repression. "We direct all our efforts to the memory and leave the understanding and the conscience empty," he complained. "Like birds which go forth from time to time to seek for grain and bring it back to the young in their beaks without tasting it, our pedants go gathering knowledge from books and never take it further than their lips before disgorging it. And what is worse, their scholars and their little ones are no better nourished by it than they are themselves." Rote learning, Montaigne insisted, "is no knowledge and signifies no more but only to return what one has intrusted to our memory."[9]

Despite pleas from a minority of enlightened theorists for more flexibility and the abolition of physical punishment, conventional wisdom always held otherwise. Most agreed, as Philoponus put it, that a school should be "a place void of all fruitless play and loitering." Richard Mulcaster voiced prevailing opinion when he urged the frequent use of the rod to spur students on. It "may no more be spared in schools than the sword may in the prince's hand," he declared. A "sharp master who will make boys learn what will afterwards be of service even though they are unwilling at the time is to be preferred to the vain shadow of a courteous master." Most teachers accepted John Brinsley's grim counsel in his *Ludus Literarious* to foster a "meet and loving fear, furthered by wise severity to maintain discipline."[10]

Not until the 1600s did there appear any substantial body of educational theory openly defending spontaneity, interest, or freedom in learning. In the writings of Archbishop François Fenelon (1651–1715), for instance, there are glimmerings of the view explicitly developed a hundred years later by Jean-Jacques Rousseau: that instruction ought not to be unduly coercive, and that the teacher should assist and be guided by the young learner's own natural development. For Fenelon, the child's attention span was like a candle guttering in the wind. It is enough to answer questions as they arise, to help satisfy youthful curiosity with simple, easily understandable responses, and to allow the student to mix recreation with instruction. His main prescription was to replace formal lessons with "*conversations gaies*"—informal lighthearted discussions. Anything that stimulated the child's imagination was to be pressed into the teacher's service. "Let us change the [usual] order," he suggested, "let us make study agreeable; let us hide it under the appearance of liberty and of pleasure."[11]

For Johann Amos Comenius (1592–1670), the great Moravian educational reformer, it was imperative that instruction be arranged according to what he called "the order and course of nature." Teaching should proceed without recourse to violence. Curricula should be organized in an orderly, graduated sequence. There should be more system and uniformity in methodology. Students, he argued, should be led inductively where possible from sensory experience to more abstract learning—things before words and concepts. His central idea, developed in the *Magna Didactica*, was to "follow the footsteps of nature" in presenting knowledge. The learner's mind should not be forced to anything "to which its natural bent does not incline it in accordance with its age and the right method." In modern parlance, Comenius's point was that teaching should be rooted in knowledge about child development and should be carried out in accordance with progressive stages of learning readiness. In his own time this was a novel idea.

Comenius abhorred punitive discipline. "No discipline of a severe kind should be exercised in connection with studies or literary exercises," he declared. "For studies, if they are properly organized, form in themselves a sufficient attraction, and entice all . . . by their inherent pleasantness. If this be not the case, the fault lies, not with the pupil, but with the master, and if our skill is unable to make an impression on the understanding, our blows will have no effect." Like others before him, Comenius saw that physical threats could work to a disadvantage. "Indeed," he argued,

> by any application of force we are far more likely to produce a distaste for letters than a love for them. Whenever, therefore, we see that a mind . . . dislikes study, we should try to remove its indisposition by gentle remedies but should on no account employ violent ones. . . . Such a skillful and sympathetic treatment is necessary to instill a love of learning into the minds of our pupils, and any other procedure will only convert their idleness into antipathy and their lack of interest into downright stupidity.[12]

The idea that teachers should refrain from beating students might strike a modern observer as a commonplace. Yet even today physical (and psychological) punishment in school is by no means unknown. The point is that Comenius was speaking directly contrary to the established pedagogical opinion of his own day. His was also challenging centuries of hallowed precedent in his plea for kindness, for toleration, and for understanding toward children in school. It may be worth recalling that in his own time and for at least another two hundred years, neither teaching practices nor accepted methods of managing classroom discipline reflected much of a humane approach to education.[13]

More common by far were floggings, imprisonment, and other forms of abuse. Children unable or unwilling to master prescribed lessons were chained, flogged, whipped, beaten, or subjected to other forms of punishment. In Dutch New Amsterdam, to cite an especially instructive case, the slightest violation of the rules met with severe punishment. No practice was considered too extreme so long as classroom order was preserved and discipline maintained. One old woodcut shows young children sitting in a circle extending out from the teacher's lectern. In the middle reposes a dog affixed to a long chain. Upon the schoolmaster's signal, the animal was trained to attack instantly any child who disobeyed!

Unquestionably, it was Jean-Jacques Rousseau (1742–1778) who most fully synthesized and elaborated upon the views of humane educators before him. His writings most clearly influenced the development of what is sometimes termed the "romantic" tradition in educational theory. Surveying the sorry history of schooling up to his own time, Rousseau was appalled by its record of insensitivity and mindless cruelty. Before him educators had tended to look upon human nature in terms of defects that education had to remedy by whatever means proved necessary. Rousseau's originality consisted in the way he tried to break with all views condemning the child as bad or sinful and to rethink the question of how best to educate people "according to nature."

Basic to Rousseau's view of education was his conviction that human nature is innately good. It followed that the child cannot develop if his or her own natural inclinations are thwarted or suppressed. In the long run coercion is unproductive because it results in submission to the feelings and values of others—and second-hand learning served up in a conventional school setting is almost always injurious.[14] Since the child is born innocent, it is the vices and errors of a malformed social order that frustrate natural human development. "Everything is good as it comes from the hands of the Creator but degenerates once it gets into the hands of man," as Rousseau put it. Children are living, growing beings who at every stage of their development are persons in their own right. They are capable of being properly prepared for later maturity only through the active interests of their own age and condition.[15] The cardinal pedagogical sin, therefore, is to impose ready-made habits, values, and beliefs on the child before he or she is capable of understanding them or of framing independent judgments.

The specifics of Rousseau's theory of education may be less important for present purposes than the basic underlying themes inherited by his successors. Collectively, they came to define "romanticism" in education: the notion of learning readiness, faith in the basic goodness of the child's nature, trust in its untrammeled expression and development, the idea of growth and discovery in the absence of inhibiting constraints, opposition to uncritical or purely verbal learning, stress on freedom, and the importance of intuition, feeling, and individuality.

Historically, Rousseau's influence was impressive.[16] Prominent eighteenth-century pedagogical theorists and practitioners, especially Basedow, Pestalozzi and Froebel, all borrowed ideas from his *Émile*. Johann Heinrich Pestalozzi (1746–1827), Rousseau's most sensitive disciple, summed up the spirit and concern of humanistic pedagogy in a passage his mentor could as easily have written himself. Pestalozzi advised teachers as follows:

> Be thoroughly convinced of the immense value of liberty; do not let vanity make you anxious to see your efforts producing premature fruit; let your child be as free as

possible, and seek diligently for every means of ensuring his liberty, peace of mind, and good humour. Teach him absolutely nothing by words that you can teach him by the things themselves; let him see for himself, hear, find out, fall, pick himself up, make mistakes, no word, in short, where action is possible. What he can do for himself let him do; let him be always occupied; always active, and let the time you leave him to himself represent by far the greatest part of his childhood. You will then see that nature teaches him far better than men. But when you see the necessity of accustoming him to obedience, prepare yourself with the greatest care for this duty. . . . Make sure of his heart and let him feel that you are necessary to him. . . . If he often asks for something you do not think good, tell him what the consequences will be, and leave him his liberty . . . Should he leave [the right way] and fall into the mire, go to his rescue, but do not shield him from the unpleasant results of having enjoyed complete liberty and of not having listened to your warnings.[17]

It would be difficult to find another equally succinct statement so fully expressive of what contemporary educational humanists have urged upon teachers and parents in their dealings with children. An abiding faith in human nature, appreciation for spontaneity and joy in learning, aversion to formalism and imposed authority, respect for freedom—these have always remained major elements in the romantic tradition.

A nineteenth-century attempt to explore the limits of freedom in education was provided in a little-known experiment once undertaken by the Russian writer Lyóf Nikoláyevitch Tolstoy (1828–1910). "All are agreed," he wrote, "that schools are imperfect; I, personally, am convinced that they are noxious." Tolstoy was intrigued and disturbed in noting the contrast between the typical child as "a vivacious, inquisitive being, with a smile in his eye and on his mouth, forever seeking information for the sheer pleasure of it" *outside of the classroom,* and that same child *in school,* where he became "a weary shrinking creature repeating, merely with his lips, someone else's thoughts in someone else's words, with an air of fatigue, fear and restlessness: a creature whose soul has retreated like a snail into its shell." Tolstoy termed this strange unhappy condition the "school state of mind." It consists, he observed," in all the higher capacities, imagination, creative power and reflection yielding to a semi-animal capacity to produce words without imagination or reflection."

He was resolved to discover whether this phenomenon was avoidable. Around the midpoint of the century Tolstoy opened his own school in the village of Yasnáya Polyána, hoping to find out whether students would learn naturally and spontaneously if given the opportunity to do so. "The only criterion of pedagogy is freedom," he asserted, "and . . . the less the children are compelled to learn, the better is the method; the more—the worse. . . . In instruction [there can be] no necessity of compelling children to learn anything that is tiresome and repulsive to them, and . . . if necessity demands that children be compelled, it only proves the imperfection of the method." For two years, Tolstoy conducted his school on the maxim that "the method which does not demand an increase of discipline is good; the one which demands greater severity is bad."

In the final analysis, Tolstoy believed his experiment had been successful.

He conceded his classroom could become noisy, explaining, "This disorder, or free order, is terrible to us only because we are accustomed to something quite different. . . ." He came to feel, however, that teachers were prone to fall back upon force "only through haste and insufficient respect for human nature . . . we need only to wait a little and the disorder (or animation) calms down naturally by itself, growing into a much better and more permanent order than what we have created." He recounted later how children themselves, if left to their own devices, would eventually become absorbed in their lessons: "To tear [a student] from his reading would now need as much effort as formerly to tear him from his wrestling." Having begun, he claimed, without any preconceived notions about education, his own experience suggested that the only kind of education fit for human beings was a "natural" one free of compulsion, drudgery, and restraint.[18]

In the twentieth century, the clearest expression of a radical humanism at work in education was that provided in the thought and practice of A. S. Neill, founder of the famous English private school Summerhill. Neill's thinking, by his own account, was much influenced by Rousseau and the early romantics, as well as by Theodore Reich, Homer Lane, and Freud. He authored a number of books, such as *The Problem Child, The Problem Parent, Last Man Alive,* and several others, but it was not until 1960, with the publication of *Summerhill: A Radical Approach to Child Rearing,* that his views become widely known. Thereafter his school, in Leiston, Suffolk, was besieged with a steady stream of applicants and visitors. Before his death, in 1973, Neill had become one of the most controversial figures in education, and an acknowledged pioneer in the movement for informal, free schooling.

In an early work, *A Domine Dismissed,* Neill retold the story of his dismissal as an elementary schoolmaster in a small Scottish village. In a moving farewell scene, he spoke to the children:

> I don't suppose any of you understand why I am going away, but I'll try to tell you. I have been dismissed by your fathers and mothers. I haven't been a good teacher, they say; I have allowed you too much freedom. I have taken you out sketching and fishing and playing; I have let you read what you liked, let you do what you liked. I haven't taught you enough. How many of you know the capital of Bolivia? You see, not one of you knows.

One of the children asked, "Please, sir, what is it?" Neill answered, "I don't know myself, Jim."[19]

In 1924 Neill founded his own experimental boarding school. The usual fare of basic subjects, homework, testing, and grading was done away with entirely. No child was obliged to attend classes. All members of the school community had a voice in developing and enforcing rules and regulations. All decisions were reached democratically. "The function of the child," Neill wrote, "is to live his own life—not the life that his anxious parents think he should live, nor a life according to the purpose of the educator who thinks he knows what is best."[20] The rule of education, in his view, should be love: "Love is being on the side of the other person. Love is approval. I know that children learn slowly that freedom is something totally different from license. But they can learn this truth and do learn it.''[21] Love should be exercised in an environment of freedom, of freedom to grow on one's own terms and in one's own unique way. Compulsion is fruitless. Healthy, happy persons must freely choose their own learning. As Neill insisted, ''The method of freedom is almost sure with children under twelve, but children over twelve take a long time to develop from a spoon-fed education.''[22]

The end of education for Neill was happiness. Whatever limits happiness is evil. If children are left alone without adult supervision they will develop naturally toward their fullest potential, because the drive for fulfillment comes from within. Like Rousseau, Neill believed children are innately wise and good. If allowed to pass through developmental stages at their own rate, and without any externally imposed effort to accelerate or direct the process, children will achieve healthy emotional maturity on their own. They can and will attain a sense of balance in adulthood. The best thing grownups can offer the young, Neill firmly believed, was freedom for children to become themselves.

Critics were shocked at the amount of freedom permitted at Summerhill. The fact that class attendance was always left to individual choice was attacked, as was the fact that Neill allowed the children themselves to help arbitrate disputes for the community and to set policy. Max Rafferty, one-time California State Superintendent of Public Instruction, for example, considered the atmosphere of Summerhill ''depraved'' and the school itself ''a dirty joke.'' He observed, ''I would as soon enroll a child of mine in a brothel as in Summerhill.''[23] But for Neill, the important thing was ''to make the school fit the child,'' and to keep in mind always that ''the aim of education is to work joyfully and find happiness.'' To the very end of his life, Neill remained convinced that the surest hope of a person's finding joy and fulfillment in life lay in a childhood marked by almost total freedom, love, and self-direction.

## MONTESSORI

More directive and structured by far was the educational theory of Maria Montessori (1870–1952), who in the twentieth century was to win acclaim as one of the world's foremost proponents of early childhood education. Her influence upon American educational thought was considerable. It continues to spread even today. She was born in Chiaravalle on the central Adriatic coast, in the province of Ancona, in the same year modern Italy was founded. When she was twelve, her well-to-do family moved to Rome, where the daughter could receive a better education in the new nation's capital. Encouraged to become a teacher, Montessori decided instead to pursue a medical career. In 1896 she became the first woman graduate of the University of Rome Medical School and joined the staff of the university's psychiatric clinic. During her two-year internship she developed a strong interest in mental disorders and became a frequent visitor of children housed in the city's insane asylums. Convinced that mentally deficient children could profit from special training, she traveled abroad extensively to study experimental programs in Paris and London.

In 1899 Montessori accepted a lectureship at the Royal Women Teachers' College (*Regio Istituto di Magistero Femminile*), where she worked helping to train teachers, while also employed as director of the Orthophrenic School for "feeble-minded" children. For two years she devoted long hours to observing children, making notes, and gradually developing her own views on their psychomotor development. In 1904 she was appointed Professor of Anthropology at the University of Rome. At the same time she continued to maintain a private medical practice and work in clinics and hospitals.

In 1907 she assumed responsibility for directing a day-care center in a housing project in the slums of San Lorenzo. Upwards of sixty children between the ages of three and seven were entrusted to her care while their illiterate parents were working. Drawing upon her experiences with special children, Montessori embarked upon an experiment with those she described as "tearful, frightened children, so shy that it was impossible to get them to speak." Their faces, she recalled, were "expressionless, with bewildered eyes as though they had never seen anything in their lives. They were indeed poor, abandoned children who had grown up . . . with nothing to stimulate their minds." [24] Here at San Lorenzo was an opportunity to test the views and methods she had developed working with mental deficients. Now, however, she would be working with "normal" children who, although suffering no obvious physical or intellectual handicaps, were poorly socialized and culturally deprived.

From the outset, she felt free to depart from established practice. Lacking conventional training as a teacher, she harbored few preconceptions on what to expect. Her background was that of a social worker and physician, not that of a formal educator. Amidst poor surroundings—a bare room with sparse furniture—Montessori set to work creating what she called a "Children's House" (*Casa dei Bambini*). Specially designed smaller-scale tables, chairs, and cupboards were constructed. Next she brought in pieces of sensorial equipment previously used with hospital children. Largely of her own invention, these were brightly colored blocks of wood that children could handle in learning how to count, large alphabetic letter cutouts for the teaching of reading, and frames children might manipulate while mastering such simple tasks as lacing their clothes and buttoning shoes. A brief period of instructing with an assistant followed. Montessori then retreated into the background to observe.

What ensued, she later wrote, was a series of surprises that left her "amazed and often incredulous." Once provided with manipulative materials—pegboards, dishes, blocks, serving containers, tools—the children almost immediately exhibited a totally unexpected depth of concentration working with the apparatus supplied. They virtually taught themselves, with minimal adult intervention. Even more astonishing, the demeanor of the children was transformed. They became animated, excited, and happy. "It took time for me to convince myself that this was not an illusion," she recalled. ". . . For a long time I remained incredulous and, at the same time, deeply stirred." [25]

Other unforeseen phenomena occurred. Montessori found that children enjoyed repeating tasks with certain kinds of equipment but ignored others. They worked without external rewards or punishments. When accidentally given the opportunity, children of their own accord selected these particular pieces of apparatus with which they wanted to work. Conventional toys failed to arouse their interest. Visitors to the Children's House were invariably impressed by the concentrated attention, the discipline, and the spontaneity the children exhibited. Even more astounding was their eagerness to engage in activities bearing on reading and writing. Many virtually taught themselves to read and write, beginning with the tracing of sandpaper letters and later connecting letters with sounds to form words.

Within a matter of months Montessori had opened a second school in San Lorenzo, followed by a third in Milan, and a fourth in Rome in 1908. By 1909 her methods were finding application in orphan asylums and children's homes in many parts of the country. By 1912 Montessori had published her first major educational work, *Il Metodo della Pedagogia Scientifica applicato all' educazione infantile nelle Case dei Bambini,* almost immediately translated into English as *The Montessori Method: Scientific Pedagogy as Applied to Child Education in the "Children's Houses."* It was to enjoy considerable success, eventually running through several editions in scores of languages. *Scientific Pedagogy* was followed in 1913 by *The Advanced Montessori Method,* and in 1914 by *Dr. Montessori's Own Handbook.* An outpouring of titles followed: *The Absorbent Mind, The Discovery of the Child, Education for a New World, The Formation of Man, Reconstruction in Education, The Secret of Childhood, Spontaneous Activity in Education, To Educate the Human Potential,* and several others.

Montessori's fame spread rapidly. In Italy a society entitled "Friends of the Method" (*Amici del Metodo*), later called the "Montessori Foundation," or "Montessori Society," was founded to promote her theories in Italian schools. Similar organizations appeared throughout Europe and Britain and then spread across to America. Montessori herself by now was engaged in a life of world travel—helping to establish schools and teacher-training centers, lecturing, and writing. Within the short span of two decades Montessori schools were flourishing throughout the world.

Throughout her writings Montessori favored biological analogies. [26] She repeatedly spoke of the child as a developing organism following innate natural laws, and of processes of continuous transformation and change that mark the child's struggles to realize its latent potentialities. At the same time, however, her view was of an "absorbent being" that soaks up experiences from the environment. Within the child is a self-generating source of energy, manifesting itself in sudden spurts of mental or physical growth and activity. The educational task, as she viewed it, is to know the child's true nature, to assist in its natural development, and to provide specific learning experiences by which human growth is facilitated.

The classroom, Montessori emphasized, should offer a "prepared environment" in which positive learning takes place, but always within a structure that anticipates the learner's innate impulses. It should, she said, reflect in advance the series of developmental tasks that, if well timed, will enable the child to achieve necessary growth. Essential to a good learning environment, she claimed, was a range of educative materials designed to foster the child's power to deal with the external world. Materials recommended included blocks, counters, beads, rods, building kits, and pegboard shapes, as well as such everyday utensils as cutlery and dishes.

Montessori's method was totally child-centered, at least in the sense that the "teacher" was to be more a facilitator of learning experiences than a direct purveyor of information. Children would learn from one another. For this reason, she endorsed an age range of several years in each class, so that older children could assist the younger ones with the materials. All would benefit from the social interaction. More mature learners could share their experience, the younger children learning the value of cooperation and seeking assistance as well as giving it. To the greatest extent possible, learning should proceed inductively, by a process of discovery. Sensory experiences, she emphasized over and over again, were the building blocks by which the powers of the mind were developed and coherent knowledge first organized.

Montessori strongly believed in freedom, but she derided Rousseau's "impractical principles and vague aspirations for the liberty of the child." What she termed "the true concept of liberty," in her view, was "practically unknown to educators." [27] True freedom did not mean simple release from authority or restraint; the removal of all controls would only subjugate the child to his or her own primitive impulses. Rather, as she observed, "No one can be free unless he is independent: therefore, the first, active manifestations of the child's individual liberty must be so guided that through this activity he may arrive at independence. . . ." [28] Freedom for the child, in other words, could be achieved only once the learner had developed his or her own will and inner discipline. "Real freedom . . . is a consequence of development . . . of latent guides, aided by education." [29] The child must be given activities that encourage independence, self-control, and self-competence.

"We admit," Montessori explained, "every lesson infringes the liberty of the child. . . ." But "it is in the subsequent free choice, and the repetition of the exercise, as in the subsequent activity, spontaneous, associative, and reproductive, that the child will be left 'free.' " [30] The educator's task is to present the child with choices and activities through which he or she can learn and grow independently: "The child, left at liberty to exercise his activities, ought to find in his surroundings something organized in direct relation to his internal organization which is developing itself by natural laws." [31] Unlike radical reformers, Montessori felt there was a definite place for socialization to society's norms and values. Children, she argued, should not be permitted to engage in violent or destructive acts; and they should be guided deliberately in distinguishing between good and evil, between what is socially acceptable and what must be prohibited: "The liberty of the child should have as its limit the collective interest; as its form, what we universally consider good breeding. We must, therefore, check in the child whatever offends or annoys others, or whatever tends toward rough or illbred acts."[32]

Montessori's ideas were to find ready acceptance in many countries. In 1919 she visited London, was honored with a civic reception, and assumed responsibility for a teacher-preparation course, which she offered every second year in England until the outbreak of the Second World War. She was showered with honors, including an honorary doctorate from the University of Durham in 1923. In her native country, her methods were eventually adopted in almost all lower schools. Interest remained strong in most of the European nations, particularly in Austria, the Netherlands, and throughout Scandinavia. In 1929 the Vatican lent its support to her views, thereby encouraging their adoption in Catholic schools and teachers' colleges.

At the same time, a wider movement was developing, as indicated by the founding of the International Montessori Congress, which hosted conventions of various national societies around the globe. In the United States, there was tremendous initial enthusiasm, followed, however, by a lapse of interest until the 1950s, when the American Montessori Society was formed and support for her ideas was rekindled. After World War II, Montessori continued to receive wide international recognition and attention. She remained active popularizing the movement that bore her name, until her death, in 1952, coincidentally the same year marked by the death of another great educational reformer, John Dewey.

Maria Montessori's influence was profound. Among her several contributions was a new statement of the need to adapt educational effort to the psychology of the child, the importance of safeguarding the child's happiness, and educating for independence and self-fulfillment. She always scorned conventional classrooms, where "the children, like butterflies mounted on pins, are fastened each to his place, the desk, spreading the useless wings of barren and meaningless knowledge which they have acquired." If given appropriate stimulus and an environment conducive to learning, she was convinced, children would blossom at a phenomenal rate and learning would become truly meaningful. In her early work with mental defectives, for example, she found to her amazement that under proper conditions, so-called retarded children regularly performed at a level far surpassing that of normal children in the conventional schools of her day.

Also important was her teaching concerning what she called the "sensitive" phases of child development. The tragedy of traditional schooling, she believed, was that it failed utterly to articulate instruction with learning readiness. Thus, for example, on the basis of a lifetime of study, observation, and analysis, Montessori concluded that if children were to learn "naturally," and in accord with their built-in biological time clocks, they needed exposure to developmental activities at a much earlier point than had been commonly supposed—activities designed to facilitate the growth of skills needed for reading, writing, and language acquisition.

Writing toward the end of her career, in 1948, Montessori recapitulated the central theme of her life's work. "The main problem," she observed,

> is the problem of freedom; its significance and repercussions have to be clearly understood. The adult's idea that freedom consists in minimizing duties and obligations must be rejected. . . . The freedom that is given to the child is not liberation from parents and teachers; it is not freedom from the laws of Nature or of the state or of society, but the utmost freedom for self-development and self-realization compatible with service to society."[33]

Although Montessori's influence upon the infant and primary schools of middle-class Europe was considerable, in America her contribution to the growth and development of humanistic education came much later. In the first half of the twentieth century, at least, educators were less influenced by such British and European reformers as Montessori or Neill and more by the writings and experiments of such figures as William T. Harris, Francis Wayland Parker, William James, G. Stanley Hall, Edward L. Thorndike, and John Dewey. The first wave of educational reform in the early 1900s, for example, owed very little to foreign influences. It was much more nearly an indigenous development growing out of a long history of its own. In the movement that has come to be known as "Progressivism," Americans embarked upon a crusade for better and more humane education that was the predecessor of all later humanistic experimentation and reform.

## EARLY PROGRESSIVISM

Progressivism in American life had its beginnings as a broad, diffuse movement for social reform in the latter half of the nineteenth century. It originated not so much among educators as within the ranks of settlement workers, temperance leaders, clergymen, directors of charitable kindergartens and industrial workers, muckraking journalists, and political crusaders. Broadly speaking, the "progressive" program called for the elimination of corruption in civic affairs, the "Americanization" of the immigrant, the regulation or destruction of business monopolies, and the rational adjudication of conflicts between capital and labor, between farmers and businessmen, and indeed, among all segments of society.[34]

The specific stimulus to educational reform, as to other types, was the series of social earthquakes that began with Emancipation during the Civil War and climaxed four decades later in a massive influx of Eastern Europeans. In the intervening decades, industrialization had led to profound dislocations in family and community life. The migration from countryside to factory towns and cities was well advanced. Society was uprooted. In a period of rapid, large-scale change, all of the institutions traditionally relied upon to educate the young—the family, the church, the factory apprenticeship, and the school—seemed inadequate.[35] Social workers, struggling to protect minorities, indigents, and immigrants, who were most victimized by social disorganization, were the first to feel the need for reform. "Idealistic and essentially conservative," as one contemporary historian notes, "they turned naturally to educational remedies, especially those which promised to rejuvenate rather than to replace traditional institutions." [36]

Basically, what proponents termed the "new education" until around 1910 combined three elements: vocational training or "education for life," social reform, and child-centered schooling. Jane Addams, Founder of Chicago's Hull House and a leader in the settlement-house movement, entered a typical progressivist plea in her demand for an educational system lending "human significance" to the lives of the poverty-striken. Felix Adler, originator of the Ethical Culture Society and an active propagandist for school reform in the late 1800s, was another eloquent partisan of progressivism. So too was Jacob Riis, a journalist who saw the importance of public education in fighting "the battle with the slum." Most progressivists shared a desire to broaden the typical school curriculum to encompass the occupational, civic, and moral training that the family seemed no longer able to provide. As many others felt the more important task was to transform the focus and process of schooling itself.

So-called child-centered schooling was the primary goal of humanitarian activists in the kindergarten movement. Important proponents included Anna Hallowell, of the Philadelphia Sub-Primary School Society, Susan E. Blow, of St. Louis, Mrs. Quincy A. Shaw in Cambridge, Massachusetts, the Public Kindergarten Society in San Francisco, the Chicago Free Kindergarten Association, and the Chicago Froebel Association, led by Mrs. E. M. Blatchford. Kindergarten leaders insisted that creative direction of the play of preschool youngsters would draw them "naturally" into the cooperative work that should characterize their training in later years. Repeatedly they urged a wholesale reorganization of the elementary-school curriculum more in harmony with the unfolding interests of the child's development. The method they advocated stressed learning by activity rather than by memorization; a correlation of subject matter with the child's own widening experiences; the enrichment of classroom study with materials drawn from the immediate natural and social environment; and the substitution of love for fear, of interest for authority, in classroom discipline. [37]

Joseph R. Buchanan's *The New Education,* first published in 1882, illustrated the tone of early progressivist educational theory. Buchanan denounced rote memorization of traditional learning and urged instead training the whole child for the practical requirements of real life. He believed that the school's primary goals should be to improve children's physical health and knowledge of hygiene; the teaching of manual arts necessary for pupils to earn a living; promoting moral and religious growth; and the development of powers of "original thought and invention," which would "point the way to a new social condition of intelligence, prosperity, and happiness." A major educational task, Buchanan argued, was to counteract the social degeneracy stemming from "the organization of society and all its institutions upon a basis of pure and intense selfishness instead of the principles of Christianity taught by Jesus."

Taking cues from Froebel and other contemporary reformers, Buchanan urged teachers to substitute "love" for classroom tyranny. Their duty, he wrote, was to make their pupils happy and contented, to avoid monotony and needless regimentation, and to make use of a variety of methods of instruction. Harmonious relationships built up through group singing, organized physical activities, and manual work were all-important. The classroom should be a place of tender benevolence and caring, not of fear and intimidation.[38]

In the same year that Buchanan's book appeared, Francis W. Parker, identified later by John Dewey as the true founder of progressive education, delivered a series of lectures to teachers at a Martha's Vineyard Summer Institute that covered much the same ground. Parker had recently attracted national attention for introducing handwork and banishing harsh, competitive discipline as superintendent of schools in Quincy, Massachusetts. Like Buchanan, his ideal was to emancipate the child from the restrictions of discipline, authority and regimentation.

Parker declared that the "true motive" of all education was the "harmonious development of the human being, body, mind and soul." The teacher's first obligation was to "know the child, and its nature." Only by the "exact adaptation of the subject . . . to the learning mind" could he or she promote "essential happiness" in the child. Schoolchildren, he cautioned, were not to be permitted to do whatever they liked; on the contrary, without self-control true personal freedom was impossible. But the starting point in education was to help them enjoy and profit from the opportunity to learn in as unfettered a manner as possible. He was irrevocably opposed to regimentation and oppression. Children do wrong, he claimed, only because they are "compelled to wrongdoing by their surroundings." In creating a proper environment for creative learning, teachers would discover that children were naturally inclined to pursue their own "proper and free development."[39]

Psychologist William James shared much of Parker's faith in the generative powers of children and the importance of freedom in learning. He posited a "stream of consciousness" as the essential aspect of the child; the total child comes to school, he wrote, and is in constant motion as his or her consciousness directs activity. The school's task, therefore, is to harness that behavior or activity toward positive, morally worthy ends, which come together in the ultimate value of freedom. Education should produce the free personality, which he characterized as the most complete cultivation of the will as possible.[40]

Having denounced rote learning, James asserted that education should consist of "the organizing of resources in the human being, of powers of conduct which shall fit him to his social and physical world." Instruction is not the imparting of facts and preexistent subject matter, no matter how skillfully organized. It is, instead, the guidance of the reacting child's total behavior. A good educational environment is one in which children learn by doing, through activities designed to instruct through firsthand experience. Holistic education, according to James, could not be conducted in an atmosphere of threats and intimidation. It could only evolve in a supportive climate of encouragement where learners were free to experiment and to pursue their own naturally developing interests.[41]

Many other theorists expressed similar views. What proponents of the new education shared in common was antipathy toward traditional schooling and for many aspects of the society undergirding schools.[42] As a reaction against prevailing educational usage, progressivists took as their special targets rigid classroom convention and the virtual isolation of formal learning from its surrounding social context. If schools were authoritarian and undemocratic, they needed to be made more consistent with democratic ideals. If, as many believed, instruction had grown rigid and mechanical, more flexibility should be introduced. If curricula had grown stale and obsolete, they were to be revamped so as to become more responsive to learner needs. If schools had become divorced from the larger social order, all the more reason to adapt them closely to the imperative demands of a changing society.

Armed with a faith in social progress and confident that critical human intelligence would eventually prevail over both institutional inertia and ideological reaction, educational progressives set to work. Theirs was a spirited, many-sided campaign to transform the nation's system of public education. At Marietta Johnson's Organic School, at Fairhope, Alabama, at Junius Meriam's Laboratory School, at the University of Missouri, and at its better-known predecessor, at the University of Chicago, in Caroline Pratt's Play School, in New York, and at Parker's Cook County (Chicago) Normal School, intimations were forthcoming of how progressive pedagogy would develop.

Students participated actively in helping to plan activities and lessons. Physical plants were designed for movement, for mobility, not simply for lecturing and reciting. Greater attention was given over to individual growth and development. Forging a new unity between education and life, the emphasis was upon "learning by doing." As John Dewey explained, the curriculum of the new education had to be based upon students' interests and their active involvement in learning activities. Learner participation was thought to be critical "if the pupil is to understand the facts which the teacher wishes him to learn; if his knowledge is to be real, not verbal; if his education is to furnish standards of judgment and comparison."[43]

The pluralism and diversity of the burgeoning progressive-education movement soon threatened to be as much a major weakness as a source of strength in its drive for acceptance. Dewey foresaw the difficulty early when, speaking of progressive educators, he observed, "If they do not intellectually organize their own work, while they may do much in making the lives of children . . . more joyous and more vital, they contribute only incidental scraps to the science of education." The founding of the Progressive Education Association, in 1919, represented a response of sorts to Dewey's caveat, when, under the leadership of Stanwood Cobb, what had formerly been a somewhat loosely defined protest against educational formalism now gained a vigorous organizational voice.[44] In the years following, an amorphous system combining ideas of freedom, self-expression, and psychological adjustment was refined and articulated with increasing clarity by theorists such as Harold Rugg, Ann Shumaker, John Childs, and, of course, by John Dewey.

By the early 1900s the main outlines of progressivist pedagogy could be discerned. Briefly, it encompassed the following:

1. concern for the child in all his or her complexity—needs, interests, feelings, and attitudes;
2. a facilitative rather than a didactic or authoritarian role for the teacher;
3. active learner participation in problem solving instead of instruction stressing pupil passivity, rote memorization, and deductive learning;
4. emphasis upon a warm, supportive, and humane classroom environment;
5. absence of coercion and harsh punishment;
6. provision of physical mobility within the classroom;
7. curricula geared to the maturational level of each child, and individualized in terms of pupil interest, initiative, creative self-expression, and personality development;
8. an abundance of instructional materials for students to explore, manipulate, and use;
9. patterns of organization encouraging cooperative, communal experiences;
10. rejection of the doctrine that education is a preparation for living rather than a part of the actual process of living.

## DEWEY

It has often been said that John Dewey's most seminal contribution was to develop a body of pedagogical theory that could encompass, refine, and sharpen the diverse assemblage of ideas and values incorporated within progressivist educational thought.[45] Without in the least denying his originality, it is worth noting Dewey's own disclaimer that he was only a man "sensitive to the movement of things about him." Although he later won acclaim as the chief architect of progressivism in education and was to dominate the American philosophy of education for half a century or more, it is clear that much experimentation went on quite independently of his own theorizing. His unique genius was to weave together into an integral theory the many disparate strands of innovation and reform that typified schooling in the United States for many decades.

Dewey was born in Burlington, Vermont, on October 20, 1859. He received the usual middle-class education of the period, including classical literature, and for his bachelor's degree, in 1879, from the University of Vermont, he studied both Greek and Latin. After graduation he taught high school in Oil City, Pennsylvania for two years, and then in Charlotte, Vermont. Between 1882 and 1884 he studied at Johns Hopkins University, in Baltimore, earning his doctorate in political science and philosophy. He worked as an instructor and assistant professor of philosophy at the University of Michigan from 1884 to 1888, and then moved to the University of Minnesota, where he was a professor of logic and moral philosophy for one year. In July of 1894 he came to the University of Chicago, where he remained until 1904 as professor of philosophy. During his tenure at Chicago he also served as head of the Department of Pedagogy (Education) and as director of the School of Education. Dewey's final academic post was at Columbia University, where he remained until his official retirement in 1930. He remained active lecturing and writing until his death, in June of 1952.

Dewey's interest in educational theory and practice was partly a result of his work with the famous Laboratory School, attached to the University of Chicago. In 1897 Dewey met with a group of parents seeking a better education for their children. With the university's approval, an experimental school was opened where he could begin testing the theories of Parker, James, and others on his own. In the beginning, there were only two teachers and sixteen children. In his *School and Society* (1899), Dewey recounted an experience which for him symbolized all that was wrongheaded about prevailing pedagogical usage:

> Some few years ago I was looking about the school supply stores in the city, trying to find desks and chairs which seemed thoroughly suitable from all points of view—artistic, hygienic, and educational—to the needs of the children. We had a great deal of difficulty in finding what we needed, and finally one dealer, more intelligent than the rest, made this remark: "I am afraid we have not what you want. You want something at which the children may work; these are all for listening." That tells the story of the traditional education. Just as the biologist can take a bone or two and reconstruct the whole animal, so, if we put before the mind's eye the ordinary schoolroom, with its rows of ugly desks placed in geometrical order, crowded together so that there shall be as little moving room as possible, desks almost all of the same size, with just space enough to hold books, pencils, and paper, and add a table, some chairs, the bare walls, and possibly a few pictures, we can reconstruct the only educational activity that can possibly go on in such a place. It is all made "for listening"—because simply studying lessons out of a book is only another kind of listening; it marks the dependency of one mind upon another. The attitude of listening means, comparatively speaking, passivity, absorption; that there are certain ready-made materials which are there, which have been prepared . . . and of which the child is to take in as much as possible in the least possible time.[46]

The problem with the old education, as Dewey saw it, was "its passivity of attitude, its mechanical massing of children, its uniformity of curriculum and method," and its substitution of "the forms and tools of learning" for the "substance of experience" itself. The traditional schoolroom, he continued, lacked space for the child to "construct, create, and actively inquire" as part of the learning process. He condemned traditionalism in education for its "imposition from above," for its tendency to stress "learning from texts and teacher," the "acquisition of isolated skills and techniques by drill," and "static aims and materials." Against those nineteenth-century assumptions, Dewey called for "the expression and cultivation of individuality," for "learning through experience," and for "acquaintance with an ever-changing world."[47]

With Rousseau, Dewey shared a belief that education was not something to be imposed from without. It should be conceived of instead as part of a process of growth, originating in large measure with the felt needs and interests of the learner, and organized around learning activities that are meaningful and relevant to the child involved:

> The child is the starting point, the center, and the end. His development, his growth, is the ideal. It alone furnishes the standard. To the growth of the child all studies are subservient; they are instruments valued as they serve the needs of growth. Personality, character, is more than subject-matter. Not knowledge or information, but self-realization, is the goal. . . . Subject-matter never can be got into the child from without. Learning is active. It involves reaching out of the mind. It involves organic assimilation starting from within. Literally, we must take our stand with the child and our departure from him. It is he and not the subject-matter which determines both quality and quantity of learning.[48]

A child-centered curriculum, of the sort he and his associates were trying to devise in the Laboratory School, he believed confidently, would produce students with "an alert curiosity about and keen interest in all life." Stressing activities rather than passive listening, Dewey argued, would result in "the growth of self-directive power and judgment" in young children.[49]

What was wrong with static "assign-study-recite" forms of instruction, with all their accoutrements of pupils at attention, fixed desks and chairs, and stern discipline, Dewey avowed, was that they failed to elicit interest, to stimulate motivation, or to promote meaningful learning.[50] More successful methods of instruction, he believed, depended "for their efficiency upon the fact that they go back to the type of situation which causes reflection out of school in ordinary life. They give the pupil something to do, not something to learn; and the doing is of such a nature as to demand thinking, or the intentional noting of connections. . . ."[51]

Progressivist pedagogy, as Dewey thought of it, would build upon the native powers, interests, and desires of learners, under whatever conditions proved most effective in stimulating them to develop habits of critical reflection and disciplined thought. The fundamental error of old-fashioned educational theory, he argued, was that it mistook the child as a passive cipher, a receptacle to be filled up almost entirely through the teacher's own initiative and efforts. Dewey, on the contrary, saw the child as an active, dynamic, and curious organism, forever seeking to better understand, direct, and control the environment. Hence, the teacher should be a guide, a resource, and an arranger of experiences. The teacher could not "force-feed" learning, but neither should he or she simply leave the child free to do whatever momentary impulses and whims dictated. Rather, the teacher was to assume an active role in working with, advising, and stimulating students. Methodology, Dewey said, is simply another name for the varied ways in which learners are helped to develop and broaden themselves, to test their skills, and to nurture their latent abilities so they become more adequate, better-adjusted human beings.

If one begins with the assumption that education must be child-centered, it followed for Dewey that conventional ideas about curricula would have to be abandoned entirely. Subject matter in a curriculum, he believed, should not be thought of in terms of rigidly defined, isolated bodies of knowledge. Nor could the content of a curriculum be divorced from considerations of process or methodology. Form and substance go together; they are interdependent. Above all, the greatest error, as Dewey saw it, was to assume that the curriculum could be predefined, independent of the varying needs of learners. Students, he said, should study "whatever is recognized as having a bearing upon the anticipated course of events" in their lives. Subject matter, in other words, should consist of "those things actually acted upon in a situation having a purpose." Over and against the received doctrine of a school curriculum as something to be "mastered" or acquired passively, Dewey taught that learning should proceed out of the unique inquiries and needs of each individual child.

"The source of whatever is dead, mechanical, and formal in schools," as he put it in an early essay, "is found precisely in the subordination of the life and experience of the child to the curriculum. It is because of this that 'study' has become a synonym for what is irksome, and a lesson identical with a task." [52] In his major work, *Democracy and Education* (1916), he commented, "The problem of the educator is to engage pupils in . . . activities in such ways that while manual skill and technical efficiency are gained and immediate satisfaction found in the work, together with preparation for later usefulness, these things shall be subordinated to *education*—that is, to intellectual results and the forming of a socialized disposition." [53]

There are two sides to the educational process, as Dewey defined them in *My Pedagogic Creed* (1897). One aspect is *psychological*. This implies that what is learned and how it is taught must be geared to the maturational level, needs, and interests of the child. No education is adequate or effective if it fails to take into account the child's psychological nature and characteristics. The other is *social*. In anthropological or sociological terms, education is another term for socialization—the process of converting the child's basic capacities, instincts, and dispositions into their social equivalents. As Dewey explained it, the psychological and social sides are "organically related." Education, he insisted, cannot be regarded as a compromise between the two, or "a superimposition of one upon the other." [54]

On the one hand, an exclusively psychological definition of education would be "barren and formal"—it yields an idea of how mental powers are to be developed "without giving us any idea of the use to which these powers are put." On the other hand, a social definition of education, socializing people to the existing culture, can appear to make of education "a forced and external process" that subordinates the individual's freedom to an antecedent sociopolitical order. We need both viewpoints simultaneously, Dewey insisted:

> In sum, I believe that the individual who is to be educated is a social individual and that society is an organic union of individuals. If we eliminate the social factor from

the child we are left only with an abstraction; if we eliminate the individual factor from society, we are left only with an inert and lifeless mass. Education, therefore, must begin with a psychological insight into the child's capacities, interests, and habits. It must be controlled at every point by reference to these same considerations. These powers, interests, and habits must be continually interpreted—we must know what they mean. They must be translated into terms of their social equivalents—into terms of what they are capable of in the way of social service.[55]

Had Dewey's less thoughtful critics paid closer attention to his argument at this point, they would not have concluded (as many did) that he was some sort of libertarian calling for classroom anarchy and the total abandonment of adult authority. His thesis, rather, was that a school closely geared to the needs and interests of its students could dispense with discipline in the old-fashioned sense of keeping order through external force. Children whose interest was engaged in active learning tasks, he asserted, would require no policing. They could be allowed maximum freedom to assume increasing responsibility for their own actions, the performance of which would evoke order from within. They would not be left to their own devices or allowed to do whatever they wanted. But if permitted to learn by doing, by discovering, "working over," and assimilating their own experiences, there would be no need for the regimentation and rigidity that had characterized schooling since time immemorial.

Education, as Dewey defined it, is "that reconstruction or reorganization of experience which adds to the meaning of experience, and which increases ability to direct the course of subsequent experience." Almost obscured by ponderous phrasing was a major generative idea: the refusal to isolate education from other aspects of life; in fact, the identification of education with the process of experiencing itself. "Since education is not a means to living, but is identical with the operation of living a life which is fruitful and inherently significant, the only ultimate value which can be set up is just the process of living itself. And this is not an end to which studies and activities are subordinate means; it is the whole of which they are ingredients. . . ."

Dewey took pains to point out that education as a process of reconstructing experience is not devoid of purpose or aim: "It has all the time an immediate end, and so far as activity is educative, it reaches that end—the direct transformation of the quality of experience. . . ." Further, "what is really learned at every stage of experience constitutes the value of that experience." An educational aim, as he put it, "must be founded upon the intrinsic activities and needs . . . of the given individual to be educated. . . ."[56]

In a larger sense, education can have no end extrinsic to or beyond itself. The criterion of the value of school education is the extent to which "it creates a desire for continued growth and supplies means for making the desire effective in fact."[57] Repeatedly Dewey returned to the same point: education is a "continuous process of growth, having as its aim at every stage an added capacity of growth." Once again:

Since life means growth, a living creature lives as truly and positively at one stage as at another, with the same intrinsic fullness and the same absolute claims. Hence education *means* the enterprise of supplying the conditions which insure growth, or adequacy of life, irrespective of age. . . . Living has its own intrinsic quality, and . . . the business of education is with that quality.

Education, it might be said, is simply growth leading to further growth—it is an "open-ended" process.[58]

Dewey was more careful than some of his supporters in emphasizing that not all experience or growth is necessarily educative. An experience is miseducative when it arrests or distorts further growth, or restricts the possibility of having richer continuing experiences. Traditional education failed, he insisted, not because it did not provide experience but because it provided the *wrong kind* of experience. Everything hinges upon the *quality* of experience had. The critical challenge for education is presenting the kind of growth experiences that "live fruitfully and creatively" in subsequent experiences. The teacher's task is to engage learners in activities that are both immediately enjoyable and conducive to further, socially desirable experiences. Educative activities are to be judged, as Dewey made clear in his *Experience and Education* (1938), on the basis of whether or not they enable students to handle future experiences in a productive manner. Always, however, for Dewey the emphasis was upon activities and concrete experiences, not as ends in themselves, but as means of evoking exploratory behavior and stimulating questions that would then set the stage for further development.[59]

## LATER PROGRESSIVISM

There were of course many other leading figures associated with the progressive-education movement besides Dewey. Among the better known was William Heard Kilpatrick, who later won national prominence as the originator of the so-called "project method" in education. Kilpatrick had met Dewey briefly in 1898 at the University of Chicago; a decade later he was to enroll as his graduate student at Teachers College, Columbia University, where he completed his doctorate in 1912. He remained at Teachers College as a faculty member for the remainder of his career. Early publications included a scholarly study of Dutch schools in colonial New York, a critical review of Montessorian methods, and an assessment of the kindergarten theory of Froebel. Thereafter, however, Kilpatrick confined his efforts to spreading Dewey's ideas and otherwise advancing the progressivist crusade for school reform. In a 1925 volume, *Foundations of Method,* which proved immensely popular with an entire generation of teacher educators, he laid out what purported to be a system for adapting Dewey's educational theory to day-to-day classroom practice.[60]

Unfortunately, Kilpatrick's adaptation was a somewhat simplistic and mechanical elevation of problem solving as the single model of instruction. According to the project method, teachers were to refrain from presenting subject-matter content. What was to be learned, rather, was always to grow exclusively out of the questions and interests of students, formulated in the form of a "problem" to be solved. Pupils were provided only with a four-step system of identifying something to be investigated, formulating a plan action, applying the plan, and evaluating the results. The virtue of Kilpatrick's method was that it was easy to communicate to teachers and easier still to apply in a classroom setting. The drawback was that it was wholly nondirective in character and readily lent itself to the kinds of abuses seized upon by progressivism's harshest critics. Such was Kilpatrick's professional standing, however, that for decades his interpretations of Dewey's views were accepted more or less uncritically as authoritative and complete—an impression Dewey himself appears to have done little to correct.

Meanwhile, confusion was growing among the ranks of progressivist educators over whether the "new" education was to be mainly child-centered or more directly tied to other, broader social reform movements. Harold Rugg's *Culture and Education in America* (1931), for example, emphasized the need for the reconstruction of society through social engineering, with the school serving as an important tool for change. The same impulse toward radical reform coming on the heels of the most devastating economic collapse the nation had ever experienced, found vigorous expression in a 1932 pamphlet authored by George S. Counts, entitled, *Dare the School Build a New Social Order?*[61] Increasingly, the membership of the Progressive Education Association was split between partisans of individualistic child-centered pedagogy in schools and more activist visionaries who sought to use the school to transform society.

Dewey, for his part, tried to steer a middle course between the two factions. On the one side, he supported the seven-point charter of aims for improving the elementary school enunciated originally in 1919 by the Association for the Advancement of Progressive Education:

1. Freedom to develop naturally,
2. Interest the motive of all work,
3. The teacher a guide, not a task-master,
4. Scientific study of child development,
5. Greater attention to all that affects the child's physical development,
6. Co-operation between school and home to meet the needs of child-life,
7. The progressive school a leader in educational movements.[62]

But at the same time, on the other side, Dewey appreciated the need for the cultivation of a social morality and the school's role in helping to effect societal reforms. His settled conviction seems to have been that in a heterogeneous, pluralistic society, the school could never be a main determinant of political or social change. "Nevertheless," he added in a 1937 article, "while the school is not a sufficient condition, it is a necessary condition of forming the understanding and the dispositions that are required to maintain a genuinely changed social order.''[63]

Society is constantly in flux, Dewey noted, and it is a commonplace to observe that schools tend to lag behind: "We are all familiar with the pleas that are urged to bring education in the schools into closer relation with the forces that are producing social change, and with the needs that arise from these changes." He then went on to observe that there was little consensus on what the schools were supposed to accomplish or how they should do it. Some claimed that schools should simply reflect social changes that were already in process. Others, with equal vehemence, were insisting that schools should assume an active role in *directing* the course of social change.

The fact is, Dewey argued, schools already do take part in determining the future of society, because they follow and reflect changes in existing social arrangements. Furthermore, they discriminate and select from among the many social forces that play upon them, emphasizing certain values, dispositions, behavior patterns, and beliefs to the exclusion of others. Nor does the effect of that selection and organization of elements within the social milieu end at the schoolhouse door—it affects the structure and movement of life for beyond. The real question is not whether the schools shall or shall not influence the course of future social life, but in what direction they shall do so and how, "whether they . . . do it blindly and irresponsibly, or with the maximum possible of courageous intelligence and responsibility."

Educators, Dewey avowed, could elect to perpetuate confusion and possibly increase it. Or they could try to use the school as a conservative force to buttress the old order and keep it intact against forces working for change. The third choice was to ally education with social reform. Under this alternative, Dewey concluded, the greatest problem would be to develop the insight and understanding that would "enable youth who go forth from the schools to take part in the great work of construction and organization that will have to be done, and to equip them with the attitudes and habits of action that will make their understanding and insight practically effective."[64]

The only course of action *not* open to teachers, he claimed, was to hide behind a facade of ideological neutrality. "Perhaps the most effective way of reinforcing reaction under the name of neutrality," he observed,

> consists in keeping the ongoing generation ignorant of the conditions in which they live and the issues they will have to face. This effect is the more pronounced because it is subtle and indirect; because neither teachers nor those taught are aware of what they are doing and what is being done to them. Clarity can develop only in the extent to which there is frank acknowledgment of the basic issue: Where shall the social emphasis of school life and work fall, and what are the educational policies which correspond to this emphasis?[65]

Dewey was writing during a tumultuous period in American history, a period in which almost every facet of domestic life was controlled by the Depression. At the same time, on the international scene events were dominated by the rise of Italian fascism, German Nazism, and Soviet communism. Hence it was understandable that progressivist reformers were questioning the school's role in a troubled social order. Boyd Bode, a leading progressivist theoretician at Ohio State University, had long urged a more sharply defined sense of purpose and mission among educators. "Unless we know where we are going," he had written in *Fundamentals of Education* (1921) "there is not much comfort in being assured that we are on the way and traveling fast. . . . If education is to discharge its rightful function of leadership, it must clarify its guiding ideals."[66]

Six years later, in *Modern Educational Theories,* Bode returned to the same point. The fault of progressive pedagogy, he felt, was that it depended too heavily in the idea that children's inner development required "nothing from the environment except to be let alone."[67] It underestimated the need for direction, for guidance, and for social relevance. As he put it in his best-known work, *Progressive Education at the Crossroads,* there was a very real danger that what had begun as a vital effort at educational reform and renewal would end up becoming doctrinaire, rigid, and, ultimately, reactionary.[68]

Dewey too shared Bode's misgivings. For some time he had been apprehensive over the direction, or, rather, the lack of direction, of the movement so closely associated in the public mind with his own views on education. In 1938, the same year *Progressive Education at the Crossroads* appeared, he published *Experience and Education,* a slim little volume that was highly critical of certain progressivist practices.[69] Likewise, in an address before the Progressive Education Association, he sounded a warning. Dewey prefaced his criticisms by conceding the positive advances registered by progressive schools. They were, he admitted, more informal, more inclined to respect individuality, and more willing to build upon the nature and experience of children instead of imposing external standards and subjects. The best among them, as he noted, emphasized activity over passivity, and encouraged a greater measure of classroom freedom than ever known before.

He questioned, however, whether romantic oversimplifications had not infiltrated progressivist thought. He wondered whether pedagogy had suffered as a result of aimlessness and unrestrained permissiveness. It was time, Dewey announced, to introduce a greater measure of intellectual rigor and clarity into educational theory. The need was to consider more carefully the conditions under which learning takes place most effectively, and to build up a systematic science of education. Failing this, he implied, progressivism was destined to fall short of effecting permanent reforms in American education.

Even as Dewey spoke, however, there were signs that reaction had set in, prompted in no small measure by the same ambiguities and weaknesses in progressive education that he himself had warned against a full decade earlier. On the eve of the Second World War, progressivists were clearly on the defensive. Critics of the likes of Robert Maynard Hutchins, Isaac Kandel, and William Changler Bagley pressed the attack. Schools, they alleged, had been allowed to drift aimlessly. Standards were falling. Curricula, it was said, were vapid, puerile, anemic. In allowing students to learn whatever they wished, or not to learn at all, the charge ran, educators had confused ''license'' with ''freedom'' and abdicated responsibility for the tasks to which they had been entrusted.

As criticism mounted, the progressive-education movement began to falter. Popular support gradually withered as pundits poked fun at its excesses. Circulation of the Progressive Education Association's official publications fell off sharply. By the end of the thirties, it seemed increasingly unlikely that the brave prophesy issued a scant decade and a half earlier by Harvard President Charles W. Eliot would be fulfilled. Writing in 1924, Eliot had declared, ''Progressive Schools are increasing rapidly in number and influence and the educational public is becoming more and more awake to their merits. They are to be the schools of the future in both America and Europe.''[70] Events, however, were to prove him wrong.

In the postwar period, internal decay and strident criticism from without quickly took their toll. By the late forties, a once-sturdy movement had declined to the point where only the tag ends of the progressivist credo remained—the tailoring of instruction to meet vocational needs, continuing interest in individual differences, and support for basing pedagogical practice upon research in child and developmental psychology. Otherwise progressivism as an animating force had grown moribund. Its final demise was symbolized more than anything else by the quiet disbanding of the Progressive Education Association in 1955—a victim of lack of support and interest.

The ultimate eclipse of progressivism undoubtedly was owed to many factors, not the least of which were critics' charges that it sanctioned soft pedagogy and was poorly adapted to changing social needs. In a sense, with so many representatives and spokesmen, and with so many diverse strains, the imprecision and confusion that turned out to be its major liabilities were perhaps inevitable. Historians are apt to point out how sloganeering so often substituted for substantive change. Furthermore, it was true that, in the hands of uninspired teachers, progressivist reforms often degenerated into classroom practices that were indefensible by almost any standard. Whatever the truth of the matter, in the final analysis, the legacy of progressivism proved ephemeral. But if, in the shift toward conservatism that characterized the political climate of postwar America, specific progressivists usages atrophied and finally disappeared, the underlying ideology did not. It would reappear a decade or so later, once the pendulum of public opinion had completed its full swing, benefiting from its previous incarnation but this time assuming a somewhat different form—as ''open'' education.

## THE REACTION AGAINST PROGRESSIVISM

Harvard psychologist Jerome Bruner, writing in the early sixties, tried to assess John Dewey's legacy and account for the loss of progressivism as a motivating force in American education. Reviewing his early writings as he attacked the empty formalism and sterility of school instruction in the 1890s, Bruner was struck by Dewey's "wholesomeness" and essential optimism. Yet he was troubled by his implicit faith in the power of society to help shape individuals in its own best image. In the intervening two-thirds of a century, Bruner noted, there had been many profound changes. "Between Dewey's first premises and our day," he observed,

> there bristles a series of revolutionary doctrines and cataclysmic events. . . . Two world wars, the dark episode of Hitler and genocide, the Russian Revolution, the relativistic revolution in physics and psychology, the Age of Energy with its new technology—all of these have forced a reappraisal of the underlying premises in terms of which we construct a philosophy of education.[71]

Bruner found it difficult to share Dewey's ready acceptance of the individual's harmonious continuity with society: "In our time, the requirements of technology press heavily upon the freedom of the individual to create images of the world that are satisfying in the deepest sense." Our era, he wrote, "has also witnessed the rise of ideologies that subordinate the individual to the defined aims of a society, a form of subordination that is without compassion for idiosyncrasy and that respects only the instrumental contribution of the individual to the progress of the society." [72] In these few words, Bruner effectively summed up much of the character of postwar America and the primary reason why the progressivists' version of humanism in education had lost so much of its popular appeal.

Resurgent political conservatism in the postwar years was a major factor, accompanied as it was by a reaction against all forms of progressivist doctrine in education. Prewar criticism from Essentialists in the late 1930s bore new fruit in the forties and fifties as critics assailed schools for poor discipline and lack of academic rigor. The successful launching of an earth-orbiting space vehicle by the Soviets in the fall of 1957 simply served to confirm the worst fears of many that the country had been betrayed by the sheer ineptitude of its educators. So monumental a scientific and engineering *tour de force,* it was argued, could not have been achieved had it not been for the Soviets' educational system, with its stress on "no-nonsense" learning and discipline. Faced now with a definite threat to American world power and influence, critics asserted, the nation could not afford to slip further behind. If the United States was ever to regain its supremacy in international affairs, thoroughgoing changes in the country's school system were imperative.[73]

Calls were issued for a massive infusion of science and mathematics into the curriculum, and for programs designed to turn out inspired scientists and technicians as expeditiously as possible.[74] A search was begun for ways to make instruction more efficient. The common refrain from leading scientists and mathematicians was that mismanagement and anti-intellectualism on the part of "educationists" were partly to blame for the mess in American education. The educational establishment therefore could hardly be depended upon to restore the proper measure of discipline and the sense of purpose now lacking in schools.

What was needed, it seemed obvious, were improvements in the technology of education, more rigorous curricula—"teacher proof," if possible, so their implementation could not be frustrated through incompetent instruction—and more effective systems of administration and control.

## TECHNOCRACY AND THE CULT OF EFFICIENCY

Given the extent and virulence of Cold War hysteria in the late fifties, it was not surprising that anything resembling a "humanistic" approach to teaching and learning was an early casualty in the nation's drive to harness schools to larger policy objectives. For those calling for a better accounting of professional educational practice, standardization, not individualization, of curricula and instruction appeared essential. For proponents of efficiency, the watchwords in education were competence, proficiency, and achievement.

The so-called "accountability" movement in education that ensued assumed many different forms. Common themes included the need to redefine educational goals more precisely, to develop more cost-effective strategies for administrative management, and the desirability of devising new ways of measuring academic progress. In the search for effective methods of assessment and evaluation, more and more educators turned to business and industry for assistance.

A pioneer at developing business-management practices in the public sector was Robert MacNamara, who had been chiefly responsible for the successful development of Program Planning and Budgeting Systems (PPBS) at the Ford Motor Company. Later, as Secretary of Defense in the Kennedy Administration, MacNamara became well known for the application of "systems analysis" to national defense-planning and budgeting. He was soon to win a reputation for efficiency in matters of decision making and executive administration. Predictably, many school critics saw in these management procedures developed for business, industry, and the military a promise for more effective educational planning as well.[75] If it were possible to clarify the goals of a school system, the argument went, it should also be feasible to design a plan for achieving those goals, together with strategies for measuring results, diagnosing difficulties, and modifying plans accordingly.[76] First, one would have to define objectives as specifically as possible. Next, educators would need to develop tests and performance standards to measure the attainment of the objectives specified, together with other subgoals identified. The next step would be to develop procedures for reaching the objectives sought. Finally, one would implement the system and then evaluate its performance with a view toward subsequent modifications or revision, as needed.[77]

Industrial and governmental leaders especially were attracted to the prospect of placing educational management on a sound, "businesslike" basis. The task of specifying ends or goals in education, it was assumed, was in principle, at least, a simple, straightforward undertaking. Tests could be devised for determining whether objectives were being met, and the results then evaluated accordingly. As experimentation with systems planning and analysis expanded in the 1960s, there was little discussion of students' needs and interests, of human growth and development, or of personal self-realization. The tendency instead, in an unintentional parody of the style of the engineer or production specialist, was to describe educational processes in terms of "inputs," "outputs," "entropy," "subsystems," and "management by objectives" (MBO)—in short, with all of the imagery and nomenclature of organizational management and design.

Talk about instructional intentions rather quickly gave way to specifications for operational goals, "delivery systems," "cost-benefit ratios," "time-to-solution criteria" and "information dissemination procedures." [78] Less was heard about experiential learning, inductive discovery, or individualized instruction, and more about "human resources," or "manpower training and development." Much of the literature on accountability and systems design in education came to rely increasingly on the metaphor of the school as a malfunctioning machine needing repair or as an inefficient, disorganized "production system" requiring readjustment. A common approach was to compare the school to a factory where learners were sent for "processing." Sometimes metaphors were cojoined, as in talk of "hooking up" students or "plugging into" a system where they would later be "turned out" as graduates. [79] Also fashionable were "performance-based" and "competency-based" training programs, for schoolchildren and their teachers alike. [80] Overall, the controlling values for educational reform in the early sixties appeared to be mainly those of objectivity, efficiency, cost effectiveness, and accountability.

## BEHAVIORISM

Coincident with the rise to prominence of an efficiency movement in education came growing interest in behaviorism and its practical applications to teaching. As a psychological theory or school of thought, behaviorism had exercised little influence upon education until the 1950s, when it was first popularized and given a wider hearing in the writings of Harvard psychologist B. F. Skinner. [81] Thereafter, and for some time to come, interest among professional educators in the application of behaviorist doctrine to problems of school instruction and management was to run strong. To all intents and purposes, support for "humanistic" education in the romantic or progressivist traditions was nonexistent.

Most historians credit John B. Watson (1878–1958) with being the father of modern behaviorism, although the movement owed much to the pioneering work of the Russian psychologist Ivan Pavlov (1849–1936) and many others as well. To the age-old question of whether psychology should deal with the data of consciousness or of behavior, or both, Watson had answered it was unprofitable to attempt the study of internal mental processes or states of mind. These, he argued in *Behavior, An Introduction to Comparative Psychology* (1914), must forever remain inferential, since they cannot be observed directly. If the fledgling discipline of psychology was ever to achieve the status of a true scientific discipline, he insisted, it would have to ignore "inaccessible states of consciousness" as objects of investigation. It should concentrate instead on formulating laws governing their "physico-chemical or functional correlates"—that is, behavior.[82]

Behaviorism was expanded and refined by a long line of theoreticians, including Edwin B. Holt, Max Meyer, Edward L. Thorndyke, Karl S. Lashley, Albert F. Weiss, and, later on, by Edward C. Tolman, Clark Hull, and Walter S. Hunter. Discounting differences in their respective formulations of specific issues, they shared a conviction that psychology could become an objective, experimental branch of natural science whose sole inquiry was observable phenomena (that is, behavior) and whose major theoretical goal would be the prediction and control of behavior. B. F. Skinner, as the best-known contemporary exponent of behaviorism, stood very much in this same tradition.

Skinner was exceptional for his strong interest in the more practical applications of behaviorism to social theory and to education. The technology involved he referred to as "behavioral engineering." The particulars of his views are less important in the present context than the reaction they prompted, even though his influence on education was to prove extensive. Suffice it to say that the apogee of his popularity in educational circles came at a time when the retreat from humanistic learning was already well advanced. Interest in behavioral objectives, programmed instruction, auto-tutorial "teaching machines," behavior modification, and a number of other innovations were all traceable to ideas he had argued for forcefully and eloquently throughout a long, distinguished career.

Like Watson before him, Skinner eschewed any analysis of mental consciousness and inner psychological states as a proper concern of science. "If psychology is a science of mental life—of the mind, of conscious experience," he argued in 1964, "then it must develop and defend a special methodology, which it has not yet done successfully. If it is, on the other hand, a science of the behavior of organisms, human or otherwise, then it is part of biology, a natural science for which tested and highly successful methods are available."[83] The use of inner states (thoughts, feelings, intentions, and so on) as explanations of observable behavior, he went on to say, adds nothing to an account of how the organism under observation is actually behaving. If to be hungry, for example, means nothing more than to exhibit a tendency to eat, the invocation of a hypothetical state of "hunger" to explain an observable tendency to eat is redundant. "If this state is purely inferential—if no dimensions are assigned to it which would make direct observation possible—it cannot serve as an explanation," Skinner insisted. "But if it has physiological or psychic properties, what role can it play in a science of behavior?"[84]

Psychology, then, for Skinner should be understood as a form of scientific inquiry whose aim is to analyze behavior by describing the conditions under which it occurs. Additionally, insofar as possible, it should seek to summarize whatever lawful relationships might be detected as a result of systematic, controlled observation. Meanwhile, however, he felt sufficient evidence had accumulated to make possible certain practical applications of what was already known. Education, for instance, in his view could be seen as nothing more or less than a process of "establishing . . . behavior which will be of advantage to the individual and to others at some future time."[85] This task of modifying behavior is accomplished through appropriate conditioning; that is, by the application of schedules of selective reinforcement. Teaching is simply a matter of arranging contingencies within the environment so that undesirable behavior is extinguished (that is, the probability of its occurrence is diminished through nonreinforcement) and desired "operants" are reinforced.[86] The "technology" of instruction, according to Skinner, amounts to shaping a person's responses by using positive conditioning to form small subunits of new behavior. These ultimately are built up to form a more complex repertoire of conditioned responses.

This, in essence, constituted the behaviorist program. Out of it grew professional interest in the formulation of measurable instructional objectives in operant or behavioral terms, criterion-referenced evaluation, the use of token economies in the classroom, programmed instruction, performance-based teaching, and, generally, behavior modification as a management system. To critics who objected that behaviorists were attempting to reduce "teaching" to mere "training," Skinner had a ready response: "The traditional distinction comes down to this: when we know what we are doing, we are training; when we do not know what we are doing, we are teaching. Once we have taken the important step and specified what we want the student to do as the result of having been taught," he emphasized, "we can begin to teach in ways with respect to which this outworn distinction is meaningless. In doing so we need not abandon any of our goals. We must simply define them. Any behavior which can be specified can be programmed."[87]

Skinner's approach to education was invariably controversial.[88] A typical response from a hostile critic ran as follows:

> Always the strategy aims to control, manipulate, or shape behavior from outside the individual. No provision is made for feelings, attitudes, mind, or inner phenomenological choice. . . . The Skinner doctrine makes man into an "empty organism" whose only right is to respond to the rewards administered by the controller or shaper. . . . For school learning, Skinner's theory is far too narrow. It emphasizes the one principle of external reinforcement to the ridiculous. . . . it makes teachers into trainers, mechanics, and technicians, rather than professional guides of learning. . . . Individual choice is lost . . . We must not train students in our schools as animals are trained in the circus.[89]

The behaviorist rejoinder was to say that more control, not less, was required if teachers were to prove effective in their work. As Skinner phrased it,

> What we may call the struggle for freedom in the Western world can be analyzed as a struggle to escape from or avoid punitive or coercive treatment. It is characteristic of the human species to act in such a way as to reduce or terminate irritating, painful, or dangerous stimuli, and the struggle for freedom has been directed toward those who would control others with stimuli of that sort.

Schooling, for instance, has a long history of using aversive controls to induce learning. Skinner felt that any effort to eliminate punishment in education was commendable, but he felt the "classical mistake" in the literature of freedom had been to suppose that children will automatically learn useful things once punishment ceases. "Students are not literally free when they have been freed from their teachers," he emphasized. "They then simply come under the control of other conditions. . . ." The student must be provided with positive reinforcements that generate a useful behavioral repertoire. This means more—not less—attention to the conditions under which learning takes place.

Learners *can* be given nonpunitive reasons for acquiring useful behavior, Skinner insisted, and it is up to educators—not immature students—to determine educational policy in advance. Goals must be established and learning outcomes specified. "The natural, logical outcome of the struggle for personal freedom in education," he wrote, "is that the teacher should improve his control of the student rather than abandon it." Only the teacher who "understands his assignment and is familiar with the behavior processes needed to fulfill it" can have students who "not only feel free and happy while they are being taught but who will continue to feel free and happy when their formal education comes to an end." [90]

Skinner himself strenuously denied charges of antihumanism. He was emphatic on the point that behavioral engineering in education was simply a better technology for doing more effectively what educators have always professed to desire: a means of facilitating learning so as to achieve defined objectives or goals believed to be worthwhile. Complaints about operant conditioning being an infringement upon the "freedom" and "dignity" of the individual, he argued, rest upon the "myth" of the inner, autonomous person and upon a profound misconception of the nature of human freedom itself. [91]

## HUMANISTIC PSYCHOLOGY

Humanistic critics (protestations to the contrary notwithstanding) held that the behaviorist agenda rested upon a confusion of human beings with lesser organisms, or that it represented at best a mechanistic attempt to reduce persons to objects for manipulation and control. Utterly different in terms of underlying assumptions were the writings of such "humanistic" psychologists as Gordon W. Allport, Rollo May, Abraham Maslow, Carl Rogers, and many others. In their general outlook or orientation, it may be said, they were worlds apart from Skinner and his disciples. More importantly, it was to people such as Maslow and Rogers that proponents of "open" education turned for legitimacy once the next movement for humanistic teaching and learning gained currency in the late sixties and early seventies.

In opposition to Skinner, Maslow, for instance, was to argue that an experimental science of behavior could only be concerned with the common features of classes or groups of behaving organisms. Its search was for general lawfulness, for uniformity and commonality. Missing in any such analysis, he claimed, was proper attention to the uniqueness or idiosyncratic features of each individual person in his or her own right.[92] Moreover, he declared, a human being cannot be understood solely in terms of environmental variables impinging upon the person or the overt responses to them that the individual may exhibit. While external circumstances undoubtedly exercise a powerful influence upon behavior, environmental influences do not even begin to exhaust the causes of human functioning. The totality of human development must be examined "from the inside out," as it were. It can be comprehended only with reference to internal forces striving to express and achieve latent potentialities.

Maslow saw the human organism neither as passively shaped by the environment nor as wholly conditioned by social forces. A person is an active, dynamic initiator of action, he believed, selecting and responding to certain features within the surrounding phenomenological "field."[93] Human experience, in other words, cannot be reduced to a set of behaviors alone, for how a person acts is affected by all the ways in which the individual perceives his or her own psychological world and how particular meanings are imputed to it. To an illiterate a well-stocked library means nothing; for someone else it could provide an inexhaustible source of diversion and instruction. Again, for a primitive aborigine a bicycle has no use. For someone else it might offer a useful means of transportation. Each individual perceives and responds to environmental stimuli differently, depending on previous learning or experience, present interests and needs, and the life situation in which the person finds himself or herself. "All behavior, without exception, is completely determined by, and pertinent to, the perceptual field of the behaving [human] organism . . ." observed Arthur W. Combs and Donald Snygg, speaking to the same point.[94]

The most basic reason why people respond differently to environmental forces is, simply, that persons themselves differ. The most salient characteristic of a human being is his or her own uniqueness and individuality, Gordon Allport noted.[95] Each strives "to become characteristically human at all stages of development," but always in a fashion specific to that particular individual.[96] Consequently, any account of human activity that leaves out internal dispositions or, as in the case of behaviorism, excludes questions of purpose and intentionality from consideration, must be not only dehumanizing but fundamentally incomplete.

In a similar connection, sociologist Edgar Friedenberg offered a relevant observation:

> It makes a profound difference to the total personality and to the meaning one finds in life itself whether the subjective or the objective approach to the world predominates; or whether, to speak in more fundamental terms, one's sense of who one is in relation to the rest of the universe is felt to depend ultimately on one's dexterity and precision in responding to observable features of the environment.[97]

For Allport, as for Maslow, a conception of personhood based only upon responsiveness to external forces would be hopelessly inadequate because it omits the most important feature of all—the internal human drive for self-actualization.

Present in everyone, Maslow held, is a hierarchy of drives, ranging from the most basic and potent survival needs, such as satisfying thirst and hunger, up a scale encompassing progressively higher needs such as personal safety, love and belongingness, esteem, cognitive growth (the quest for knowledge and understanding), and, ultimately, esthetic fulfillment (the desire for beauty). A normal, healthy person strives to satisfy all of his or her needs at the highest level possible. To the extent that drives are actualized and the person's fullest potentiality unfolds, the result is a balanced, integrated personality. Maslow found that self-actualized persons, as he described them, tended to be realistic, self-accepting and accepting of others, problem-centered rather than self-centered, autonomous and independent, creative, loving, altruistic, and often quite nonconformist in their approach to life.[98] Spontaneous and natural in all things, the self-actualizing individual, he claimed, is purposive, goal-directed, and "fully functioning" in every dimension of personality.[99]

A mature, psychologically developed person is one who is free from neurosis, has a positive self-image, exhibits a healthy outlook on life, shows tolerance, and has a capacity for accepting others. She or he feels competent to deal effectively with the exigencies of life, both now and in the future.[100] As Carl Rogers described the self-actualized human being, he or she "is a person functioning freely in all the fullness of his [or her] organismic potentialities; a person who is dependable in being realistic, self-enhancing, socialized, and . . . creative . . . ever changing, ever developing . . . in each succeeding moment of time."[101] Such a person always lives life to the very fullest, with joy, confidence, and intensity.[102]

Not surprisingly, humanistic psychological theorists were agreed that individual growth or self-actualization represents the ultimate goal of education. It can only occur, as Carl Rogers was to argue, in an atmosphere free of coercion and pain. Young children thrive in an environment where there is no harsh discipline or intense competition. Only in a situation that is nonpunitive and nonthreatening can each child grow to understand his or her own needs and values. Only where the environment offers encouragement and acceptance can a learner begin to take charge of his or her own experiences.

The best hope for children, Rogers emphasized, was classrooms where learners could experiment, manipulate objects, ask questions, compare the results of their exploration, and discover their own answers. Social interaction among peers was likewise essential, he felt. More important still, as Harold C. Lyon and others pointed out, was a type of learning that unites intellect and feeling, that integrates cognition and affect. The child is a holistic entity. Learning, therefore should also be holistic in the sense that rationality and emotionality are brought together.[103] Unless learning is to remain purely formal and hence meaningless, the child must come to *care* about whatever he or she is learning. The student must *feel* as well as "know" that his or her own learning has personal relevance and importance.

Teaching, in the conventional sense of that term, Rogers declared in *Freedom To Learn,* is "a relatively unimportant and vastly over-rated activity."[104] The assumption that what is taught is what is learned, that what is presented by a teacher is what the student assimilates, he stressed on numerous occasions, is "obviously untrue."[105] No one can "teach" anything to anyone. One can only attempt to facilitate learning on the student's part. It is necessarily a "do-it-yourself" project. Education therefore should not be looked upon as a process of imparting ready-made knowledge to others through talking and lecturing. Rather, it should be seen as an effort to create the circumstances for encouraging "self-initiated, significant, experiential, 'gut-level' learning by the whole person."[106]

We know, Rogers claimed, that the initiation of such learning does not depend upon teaching skills, or curriculum planning, or the use made of books, or the scholarly expertise of an instructor. The facilitation of significant learning, in his words, "rests upon certain attitudinal qualities which exist in the personal *relationship* between the facilitator and the learner." The attitudes or qualities required include "realness" or "genuineness," a kind of "non-possessive caring" or "prizing" of the learners' feelings and opinions, trust and acceptance by the facilitator, and "empathic understanding" of students' needs.[107] Basically, the relationship between teacher and learner should very much resemble that between a client and a therapist; and the best kind of education, according to Rogers, should produce a person quite similar to one produced by good psychotherapy.[108]

Combs and Snygg similarly felt that "real" or "meaningful" learning of the sort encouraging self-actualization was most likely to occur where the right to a free exercise of choice was respected. Once again, the teacher should not try to purvey information as such. The true pedagogical task is to foster conditions in which students learn on their own, by and for themselves. In experiencing themselves and their own phenomenological worlds, the latent potential within each human person comes to fruition.[109]

Where some humanistic writers disagreed was on the kind and amount of freedom needed for self-discovered learning. John Holt, for example, argued that because all children are naturally curious and will explore on their own if given the chance, undue structuring of learning activities is unnecessary. The danger is that in trying to protect children from their own mistakes, adults can actually increase their dependence and fear of failure. Virtually complete freedom from adult interference or guidance is essential if children are to become creative and effective learners.[110] Maslow, on the other hand, foresaw hazards in permitting a total lack of restrictions. Unless or until the learner acquires self-control, an immature child might fail to realize that the pursuit of certain goals can be harmful or destructive. In order to become a self-actualizing person, the learner must accept certain limits or conditions upon need gratification.

Generally speaking, Rogers adopted a similar position, except that for him freedom was an internal subjective phenomenon largely unrelated to issues of external restraint. "Freedom is essentially an inner thing," he noted, "something which exists in the living person quite aside from any of the outward choices of alternatives which we so often think of as constituting freedom...." It is "the discovery of meaning from within oneself," coupled with "the burden of being responsible for the self one chooses to be."[111] To be truly free is to come to the realization that "I can live myself, here and now, by my own choice." The correlative experience of "freedom" for a teacher inheres in the experience of sharing it with others. "To free curiosity; to permit individuals to go charging off in new directions dictated by their own interests; to unleash curiosity; to open everything to questioning and exploration; to recognize that everything is in process of change—here is an experience I can never forget," Rogers exclaimed.[112]

Taken as a whole, contemporary humanistic psychology applied to education bore more than a superficial resemblance to earlier forms of humanistic pedagogical theory. It shared with romanticism a faith in the innate goodness of human nature and a belief in the spontaneous curiosity of the child. Rogers and Holt, for example, sounded very Rousseau-like in their enthusiasm for total freedom and undirected learning. Maslow's concept of growth, all things considered, was not unlike that of Dewey's; and most modern humanist theorists endorsed the same themes of informality, learning by discovery and problem-solving methods, self-directed exploration, and stress upon affective development expressed earlier. Whether the writings of Allport, Maslow, Rogers, and others prompted a popular reawakening of interest in humanistic education, however, or whether they simply reflected that concern *ex post facto* is relatively unimportant. What does matter is that when humanism in education once again found acceptance in the late sixties, a body of theory was at hand to give it legitimacy and definition.

## THE AQUARIAN AGE

When interest in humanistic education reappeared, it very much bore the impress of events of the day. As the decade of the sixties opened, the nation's mood seemed almost euphoric. A new President had just been elected—young, bright, and charismatic. A feeling of heady idealism prevailed, a sense of commitment very different in spirit from the apathy and conformism typical of the fifties. With a "New Frontier" at hand, Americans looked to the future with renewed hope and confidence.

The staccato report of gunfire in Dallas a scant three years later, however, abruptly brought the dream to an end. Energetic optimism began to turn into doubt. It would end up as deep disenchantment before the decade was over. Few could have foreseen the series of traumas into which the country would be plunged over the next few years, shaking it to its very foundations.

The first seismic tremor came when the nation's 19 million blacks served notice that they would endure no longer the humiliation they had suffered since the days of Emancipation. Deprived of the right to vote by poll taxes and trumped-up literacy tests, consigned to segregated housing, and isolated by schools that prepared only for menial employment, blacks were now resolved to gain for themselves the basic civil rights to which they were entitled under the Constitution and which had been so long denied them. The crusade for social justice and equality of opportunity had many beginnings. It originated with lunch-counter sit-ins in Greensboro, North Carolina, and elsewhere throughout the South. The movement drew strength from a successful economic boycott staged in Montgomery, Alabama. More protest followed. At first scores, then hundreds, then thousands, and eventually hundreds of thousands joined in the marches and demonstrations that were spreading across the country.

Meanwhile, the United States found itself embroiled in a bitter civil war half a world away. What had begun years before as a small-scale effort to "contain" Communist aggression in southeast Asia now threatened to become a major debacle. Americans grew disheartened and increasingly confused as the nation's commitment escalated, each step inexorably drawing the country in deeper. Costs and casualties rose steadily. Scattered antiwar demonstrations broke out in various parts of the country. Still the conflict dragged on, seemingly without purpose or resolution. The prospect of defeat was unthinkable. Yet military victory remained as elusive as ever. Time and time again officialdom offered bland assurances that the end was in sight. Skeptics believed otherwise, however, and their misgivings were to prove contagious. By the late 1960s, with peace still not achieved, antiwar sentiment grew stronger. Pacifist sit-ins, open resistance to the draft, and expanding youth dissent threatened to tear the nation apart.

One social cause interacted with another in synergistic fashion, building momentum; and in the process many American youths were radicalized. College campuses became scenes of feverish activity as students marched and staged protest rallies. At Berkeley in 1966 the issue was "free speech." Elsewhere the conflict was over the right of students to have a meaningful voice in academic governance. A frequent target of protest was higher education's involvement in lucrative war-related research. Above all, students opposed the Viet Nam War itself.

Events culminated finally in a massive, bloody confrontation at the Chicago National Democratic Convention in 1968, where youthful, long-haired demonstrators fought pitched battle in the streets. Shouting antiwar slogans and hurling invectives at the police, self-styled revolutionaries of the New Left assaulted the barricades, hoping desperately to score a victory against the hated Establishment. To some observers, it seemed the world had gone mad.

Especially bewildering to many was the emergence of a youth counter-culture utterly contemptuous of traditional middle-class values.[113] Most of the renegades, it was pointed out, were themselves products of the "Middle America" they so despised, a world of economic security and social respectability. Yet for the first time in memory, high-school adolescents and college students alike (a vocal segment of them, at any rate) were in open rebellion against the Protestant ethic of hard work, social status, and competition for material success. They rejected with derision and scorn all the established verities of the past, opting instead for an ill-defined ethic of radical individualism and self-absorption. They were, some feared, anarchists on the loose in the midst of an otherwise well-ordered technocratic society.

The contagion spread even into the suburbs. Parents barely recognized their offspring. The young men wore their hair indecently long. Garbed in tattered fatigues, baggy pants, and ankle-length skirts, these youth adorned themselves with beads and luminous body paint. They were everywhere, not just in New York's East Village or the Haight-Ashbury section of San Francisco, long-time meccas for hippies and assorted "flower children." What was incomprehensible to many was how young radicals deliberately turned their backs on most of the creature comforts of modern civilization, living by choice amidst the squalor of the inner city or venturing off into the wilderness to form primitive rural communes. Equally troubling were the preachments of the gurus of the movement, with their strange credo of universal love, peace, and harmony.

They were, many hippies proclaimed, the vanguard of a dawning new era—an Aquarian age of human liberation and fulfillment for all. Celebrating the advent of the millennium, many American youths turned increasingly to the hallucinatory pleasures of drugs, to astrology, to meditation and other forms of Eastern mysticism. Their music was hard acid rock; their art was psychedelic; and their religion was conformity to nonconformity. They were an enigma, and a direct frontal challenge to almost everything traditionalists held dear.

Not surprisingly, with the efflorescence of an anti-establishment counter-culture came resurgent agitation for school reform. Part of the protest was a reaction against the manic obsession in the early sixties with packaged learning, automated instruction, accountability, and behaviorism. On a deeper level, calls for more humane education reflected a profound and abiding antipathy toward technocracy and all its underlying cultural assumptions. Before the furor had subsided, educational theory and practice would be subjected to the most radical reexamination they had received in over half a century.

## A LITERATURE OF PROTEST

The attack upon mainstream educational thought was already underway in the mid-sixties, and it would reach epidemic proportions in the early years of the decade following. Even the major titles of what grew to become a massive body of literature defy complete enumeration. John Holt's *How Children Fail* (1964) was a typical early statement in its criticism of the more subtle forms of psychological oppression in schools. Holt's first book was followed three years later by *How Children Learn* (1967) and elaborated in *The Underachieving School* (1969) and *What Do I Do Monday?* (1970). Outrage at the alleged "destruction" of the hearts and minds of children in inner-city ghetto schools found expression in Nat Hentoff's best-selling *Our Children Are Dying* (1966), Herbert Kohl's *36 Children* (1967), in James Herndon's *The Way It Spozed To Be* (1968), Sunny Decker's *An Empty Spoon* (1969), and in *Diary Of A Harlem Schoolteacher* (1969), by Jim Haskins. Best known among the many books of the genre was an award-winning exposé by Jonathan Kozol, entitled, *Death at an Early Age* (1967). Each in its own way bore eloquent testimony to the rigid authoritarianism and systematic suppression of genuine learning said to characterize most of the nation's classrooms.

In much the same vein were numerous collections of shorter writings, including Diane Divoky's anthology of high-school underground newspaper articles, *How Old Will You Be In 1984?* and a similar collection by Libarle and Seligson called, *The High School Revolutionaries* (1969). Student alienation was analyzed at length by Edgar Friedenberg in *Society's Children: A Study of Ressentiment in the Secondary School* (1967). A memorable assortment of beginning teachers' reminiscences edited by Kevin Ryan and entitled, *Don't Smile Until Christmas* (1970) illustrated from another point of view the trauma of life working in an inhumane and insensitive system. *Radical Ideas and the Schools* (1972), by Nelson, Carlson, and Linton, offered a useful compendium of typical writings in the literature of dissent, as did a volume assembled by Ronald and Beatrice Gross entitled, *Radical School Reform* (1969).

In higher education, criticism from Paul Goodman in *Compulsory Miseducation/The Community of Scholars* (1962) enjoyed renewed popularity. Also much discussed was a book by John Keats, *The Sheepskin Psychosis* (1965). An anthology by John and Susan Erlich, *Student Power, Participation and Revolution* (1970) testified to the extent and vigor of collegiate activism; so too did Harold Taylor's *Students Without Teachers: The Crisis in the University* (1970). One of the most widely discussed books of the period, a work supplying the student protest movement with something akin to an "underground classic," was a slim volume authored by Jerry Farber, a former English teacher at Los Angeles State College. Published in 1969, it was called *The Student as Nigger.*

Angry and vitriolic in tone, the essay's central metaphor of the student as a subservient oppressed black aroused a storm of protest. Two Los Angeles high-school teachers were summarily dismissed for sharing it with their classes. A prominent California state senator attacked the book in a newspaper editorial as an "almost incredible abuse." Dozens of campus newspaper editors foolhardy enough to reprint it promptly found themselves in trouble with administrative officials. Farber's work was denounced before the Canadian parliament as a "suppurating sore on the body politic." In Montana, it figured as an issue in a statewide campaign to defeat a higher-education tax levy referendum. "A dirty, filthy source of moral poison," "degenerate writing," and "obscene pornographic smut" were some of the kinder epithets applied.[114]

"Students are niggers," Farber began. "When you get that straight our schools begin to make sense." The question is why they are so treated, he argued. If an answer could be found, one could begin considering seriously whether it might be possible for students ever to come up from "slavery."[115] So far as he was concerned, the most salient fact of college life was student disenfranchisement. Old enough to vote in national elections, to marry and raise families, students still lacked any voice in decisions affecting their own academic lives. "The students are, it is true," he observed, "allowed to have a toy government run for the most part by Uncle Toms and concerned principally with trivia.'' But most student governments lacked real political power. ''The faculty and administrators decide what courses will be offered; the students get to choose their own Homecoming Queen.'' If students get uppity and rebellious, ''they're either ignored, put off with trivial concessions, or maneuvered expertly out of place.''

Students, he alleged, are expected to know their place. They call members of the faculty ''Dr.'' or ''Professor'' and they smile and shuffle as they await permission to enter an advisor's office. The faculty tells the student what courses to take, which electives are permitted; they tell him or her what to read, what to write, and what format to use in writing term papers. ''They tell him what's true and what isn't. Some teachers insist that they encourage dissent but they're almost always jiving and every student knows it. Tell the man what he wants to hear or he'll fail your ass out of the course.''[116] When a teacher says, ''jump,'' students jump. The only question is, ''How high?''

For Farber, the most discouraging aspect of the master-slave approach to education was that students accepted it. ''They haven't gone through twelve years of public schooling for nothing,'' he noted sarcastically.

> They've learned one thing and perhaps only one thing during those twelve years. They've forgotten their algebra. They've grown to fear and resent literature. They write like they've been lobotomized. But, Jesus, can they follow orders! Freshmen come up to me with an essay and ask if I want it folded, and whether their name should be in the upper right hand corner. And I want to cry and kiss them and caress their poor tortured heads.[117]

Students do not ask that orders make sense, Farber claimed. Generally, they have given up expecting things to make sense long before they leave elementary school. They have learned to accept as true—or at least of giving the appearance of believing as true—whatever the teacher as unquestioned authority declares is true. From kindergarten on, students learn that the name of the game is survival. The important thing is to please the teacher. ''You found out,'' he wrote, ''that teachers only love children who stand in nice straight lines. And that's where it's been at ever since. Nothing changes except to get worse. School becomes more and more obviously a prison.'' Schools are run as penal institutions. Twelve or more years' of formal education amounts to a course ''in how to be slaves.'' For Farber, the evidence was overwhelming. Entering college freshmen, he alleged, had ''that slave mentality: obliging and ingratiating on the surface, but hostile and resistant underneath.''[118]

Students varied in their awareness of servitude. A few were rebellious. Most simply played the game. As many others had been more deeply brainwashed, Farber believed. ''They swallow the bullshit with greedy mouths. They honest-to-God believe in grades, in busy work, in General Education requirements. They're pathetically eager to be pushed around.'' But however they reacted, by turning their anger inward against themselves or by trying to work the system to their own best advantage, he asserted, all were slaves. And the problem, as Farber saw it, was that "damn little education takes place in the schools. How could it? You can't educate slaves; you can only train them. Or," he added, "to use an even uglier and more timely word, you can only program them."[119]

Worse yet, Farber argued, emancipation was not achieved when students graduated. "As a matter of fact," he noted,

> we don't let them graduate until they've demonstrated their willingness—over 16 years—to remain slaves. And for important jobs, like teaching, we make them go through more years just to make sure. What I'm getting at is that we're all more or less niggers and slaves, teachers and students alike. This is a fact you might want to start with in trying to understand wider social phenomena, say, politics, in our country and in other countries.[120]

How to fight educational oppression? Farber offered no concrete answers. Schools tend to get rid of troublemakers. "Rebel students and renegade faculty members got smothered or shot down with devastating accuracy," he observed. "Others get tired of fighting and voluntarily leave the system." But dropping out was a mistake, he thought. "You can't really get away from it so you might as well stay and raise hell." Writing at the height of the civil rights crusade of the late 1960s, Farber drew an analogy between dissident students and protesting minorities. He asked, "What have black people done? They have, first of all, faced the fact of their slavery. They've stopped kidding themselves about an eventual reward in the Great Watermelon Patch in the sky. They've organized; they've decided to get freedom now, and they've started taking it." Students oppressed by an overbearing school system, he felt, could draw their own inferences.[121]

Elsewhere, Farber argued that "it's not *what* you're taught that does the harm but *how* you're taught." The real lesson is the method; and the medium is, ultimately, coercive. Students are "bullied into docility and submissiveness," he alleged. The form of instruction offers a structure of rules, punishments, and rewards whose influence far transcends any particular subject matter conveyed.[122]

Schools are exploitive, Farber argued, because they encourage—indeed, insist upon—unquestioning adjustment to the System. A great show is made over teaching "critical thought," but only within the narrow limits prescribed by authorities. By molding the young and rewarding "good" behavior, he alleged, schools reinforce existing norms and thus perpetuate the social order. The rebel who refused to conform or who drops out is punished. He or she forever after is excluded from power, denied access to a good job, and relegated to an inferior position in society. The successful graduate of the system, on the other hand, is anxious to please and infinitely accepting of whatever rules and regulations are imposed. He or she is so used to following orders, deferring to others and "playing the game" that the person eventually cannot do otherwise. He or she is positively *addicted* to authority.

Schooling does not have to be so destructive of personal autonomy, he concluded. If it were not compulsory, and if schools were controlled by the people in them, students might be able to learn "without being subdued and stupefied in the process." Finally, if students en masse would learn to say "no," change would become possible, he believed. "Students can have the kind of school they want," Farber insisted, "—or even something else entirely if they want—because there isn't going to be any school at all without them." [123]

Dissent, or saying "no," appeared as a common theme in the literature of school reform. Like Farber, Postman and Weingartner, in their celebrated *Teaching as a Subversive Activity* (1969), went so far as to say that rebellion could be a positive and constructive response to social "entropy"—the inevitable tendency of a system to decline and degenerate. A strategy essential for survival in the modern world, they wrote, was to challenge tradition. Always the conventional wisdom should be questioned and brought to account. The "necessary business" of the schools should be to subvert attitudes, beliefs, and assumptions that are obsolete and outworn. [124]

"Our intellectual history," they observed, "is a chronicle of the anguish and suffering of men who tried to help their contemporaries see that some part of their fondest beliefs were misconceptions, faulty assumptions, superstitions, and even outright lies." Milestones along the road of intellectual development, however, were marked at those points "at which some person developed a new perspective, a new meaning, or a new metaphor." Borrowing a phrase from Ernest Hemingway, Postman and Weingartner stated: "We have in mind a new education that would set out to cultivate just such people—experts at 'crap detecting.' " [125]

The most important intellectual ability humankind has yet developed, they argued at length, is the art and science of asking questions. Yet the school environment is arranged and managed in such a way that significant question-asking is not valued. Agreeing with Farber that "the critical content of any learning experience is the method or process through which the learning occurs" (that is, the medium of instruction *is* the message conveyed), they noted that schools typically require students to take in information passively. They sit and listen to teachers. Or they read books. Mostly, they are required to *remember.* "They are almost never required to make observations, formulate definitions, or perform any intellectual operations that go beyond repeating what someone else says is true. They are rarely encouraged to ask substantive questions, although they are permitted to ask about administrative and technical details." [126] But rarely are they allowed at any age to play a role in determining what problems are worth studying or what procedures of inquiry ought to be used. Mainly, what students learn is how to please the teacher, how to conform to someone else's expectations, and how to locate the "right answer" as predefined for the learner.

Postman and Weingartner warned that the new kind of education they advocated was not unopposed. "In our society," they observed, "as in others, we find that there are influential men at the head of important institutions who cannot afford to be found wrong, who find change inconvenient, perhaps intolerable, and who have financial or political interests they must conserve at any cost." Such persons, they further claimed, would much prefer that the schools do little or nothing to encourage youth to question, doubt, or challenge any aspect of society, especially its most vulnerable parts.

"We believe," they wrote, "that the schools must serve as the principal medium for developing in youth the attitudes and skills of social, political, and cultural criticism." But powerful vested influences had a stake in preserving the status quo at all costs. Determined effort, including withdrawal of support from existing institutions, would be needed before a new kind of education would be possible, one having as its purpose "the development of a new kind of person . . . who . . . is an actively inquiring, flexible, creative, innovative, tolerant, liberal personality who can face uncertainty and ambiguity without disorientation, who can formulate viable new meanings to meet changes in the environment which threaten individual and mutual survival." [127]

Helen K. Billings, founder of the Montessori Institute of America, in a 1975 volume, *Are Schools Destroying Our Children?* marveled over the apparent lack of common sense in conventional school usage. "Does it make sense," she asked rhetorically, "that a young, eager child of four teaching himself to read via TV, supermarkets, and billboards must be forced to delay his 'education' until six years, by which time his peak of interest and motivation may have passed . . . ?" Again,

> Does it make sense that we say each child is unique and individual, and then we put them into an assembly-line situation where they are all treated like machines that need bolts tightened and paint applied, so that all should look and act alike? . . . Does it make sense that during the most important years of a child's development—the first five—it is left to chance whether he develops the habits, skills, attitudes, and values that will largely determine the degree to which he will "succeed" in life? . . . Does it make sense that at age six we put children into a highly competitive situation where a child soon learns what his chances of success are? . . . Does it make sense that the child who has learned to hate school at age ten is forced to stay there until he is sixteen, a full-fledged rebel whose ambition is to break every window in the school? [128]

Children do not "fail" in schools, she charged; rather, schools "fail" children. We profess to believe that every child is unique and individual and has a right to be himself or herself. Yet immediately "we lump all children together, trying to make them all as much alike as possible." We claim to value "self-realization" as an educational goal. But the conditions of school life are so ordered as to make the aim unattainable. We laud "good interpersonal relations" as an objective but then pit one child against another in a scramble for good grades. Formal schools, Billings insisted, "are *not* geared to produce healthy-minded, productive, happy individuals." [129] A decent, humane education, she asserted, would be based on respect for individual differences; it would be continuous year-round; it would start in the child's early formative years; and it would be based on appreciation for how meaningful learning actually takes place. Moreover, in its effects it would ultimately transform society itself:

If we had children who loved learning, who found joy in experimenting, who had in the very earliest years developed habit patterns to instill in them a sense of order, of sequence, of a scientific approach to learning itself, then we would no doubt have happier citizens. . . . We propose that the chaotic and illogical conditions in the world today are largely due to the faulty, haphazard, and negative manner in which we "educate" our children! [130]

Radical school critics set themselves against practically all the assumptions upon which prevailing pedagogical wisdom depended. Schools do not enlighten, they charged; they indoctrinate. Passivity is dressed up as social adjustment, and conformity as respect for authority. Teachers give more attention to rules and regulations than to learning. Schools miseducate—they provide children with practically no freedom to practice the very behaviors expected of them as reasonable, mature adults. Thus, for example, educators preach democracy and practice despotism. They laud creativity but reward pedantry. They endorse divergent thinking but penalize students whose work betrays creativity. In their obsession with order and routine, schools make real education impossible.

Ronald Gross, attempting to sum up the propositions most frequently embodied in the recommendations of radical reformers, cited ten basic recommendations:

1. Students, not teachers, must be at the center of education;
2. Teaching and learning ought to emphasize students' real concerns, not artificial disciplines, bureaucratic requirements, or adults' preconceived notions about what children need to learn;
3. The paraphernalia of standard classroom practice should be abolished: mechanical order, silence, tests, grades, lesson plans, hierarchical supervision and administration, homework, and compulsory attendance;
4. Most existing textbooks should be thrown out;
5. Schools should be much smaller and much more responsive to the diverse educational needs of children and their parents' preferences;
6. Teacher certification requirements should be abolished;
7. All compulsory testing and grading, including intelligence testing and entrance examinations, should be eliminated;
8. All tax-exempt or public educational institutions should be prohibited from imposing entrance examinations;
9. Legal barriers to the formation of independent schools by parents should be removed;
10. The schools' monopoly on education should be broken, such that parents are enabled to exercise a free choice in how best to secure an education for their children. [131]

Among the more thoughtful critics of the period was Charles E. Silberman, author of a Carnegie Corporation-sponsored study entitled, *Crisis In The Classroom, The Remaking Of American Education* (1970). "It is not possible," he observed, "to spend any prolonged period visiting public school classrooms without being appalled by the mutilation visible everywhere—mutilation of spontaneity, of joy in learning, of pleasure in creating, of sense of self.'' Public schools, he avowed, are the kind of institutions ''one cannot really dislike until one gets to know them well.'' They are, as a rule, he alleged, ''grim, joyless places,'' governed by petty rules, ''intellectually sterile'' and ''esthetically barren'' in their atmosphere.

Yet it need not be so, Silberman insisted: ''Public schools *can* be organized to facilitate joy in learning and esthetic expression and to develop character—in the rural and urban slums no less than in the prosperous suburbs.'' It was not a utopian hope; as he argued, what makes change possible is that what is mostly wrong with public schools is due not to venality or stupidity, or to indifference, but to ''mindlessness''—the failure or refusal to think seriously about educational purpose and a reluctance to question established practice.[132] The real challenge as he saw it in 1970 was not how to devise alternatives to public schools but how to infuse those same public educating institutions with a greater sense of purpose. If American education had a model offering a clear-cut vision of what schooling *should* be like, he felt confident, the common tendency to confuse day-to-day routine with goals or aims could be overcome and the system could be made truly functional once again.

## THE BRITISH EXAMPLE

By the early 1970s attempts to build a ''new pedagogy'' were well advanced. On a descriptive level, efforts to show how learning in schools could be made more exuberant and relevant were forthcoming from Herbert Greenberg's *Teaching With Feeling* (1969), from Terry Borton's *Reach, Touch and Teach* (1970), Herbert Kohl's *The Open Classroom* (1969), Barbara Blitz's *The Open Classroom, Making It Work* (1973), Postman and Weingartner's *The Soft Revolution* (1971), Sylvia Ashton-Warner's *Teacher* (1971), and a host of other works too numerous to mention.[133] The single greatest source of inspiration, however, came from British experiments with ''open education.''[134]

Between 1963 and 1967 a ''Central Advisory Council for Education,'' consisting of twenty-five members, had undertaken to complete the first major reassessment of Britain's elementary schools since 1931. The 1967 report of the Council, popularly known as the Plowden Report, endorsed sweeping changes throughout the country's elementary-school system.[135] It was unequivocal, for example, in its support for reforms aimed at fostering ''the whole personality'' of the child, a ''full and satisfying life,'' the ''full development of powers,'' and the promotion of such qualities as curiosity, confidence, perseverance, and alertness in children.

The educational environment, the Council affirmed, should provide always ''a happy atmosphere'' for learning. The school, it said, ''is not merely a teaching shop, it must transmit values and attitudes. It is a community in which children learn to live first and foremost as children and not as future adults. . . . The school sets out deliberately to devise the right environment for children, to allow them to be themselves and to develop in the way and at the pace appropriate to them.'' It lays stress on ''individual discovery, on first hand experience and on opportunities for creative work.'' Furthermore, ''it insists that knowledge does not fall into neatly separate compartments and that work and play are not opposite but complementary.''[136]

Vincent Rogers, an observer of Britain's informal schools, who returned to the United States to urge the adoption of their features in American education, summed up a central theme: the British primary school, he wrote, ''is committed to the notion that children should live more fully and more richly *now*, rather than at some ill-defined time in the distant future. Education, then, is not preparation for life; rather, education *is* life with all of its excitement, challenge, and possibilities.''[137] Beatrice and Ronald Gross, writing for *Saturday Review* in 1970, noted how the ''new approach'' taken in many British schools discarded ''the familiar . . . classroom setup and the traditional, stylized roles of teacher and pupil for a far freer, highly individualized, child-centered learning experience. . . .'' Open education in the British mode, they suggested, might hold the key to a ''radical reformation'' of elementary education in the United States as well.[138]

American educators and journalists descended in droves upon British schools to observe the new pedagogy at firsthand. What they found were decentralized classrooms with open, flexible spaces divided into functional learning areas rather than rows of desks and chairs fixed to the floor. They saw children free to move about as individuals or in groups, choosing their own activities. They found learning spaces filled with resources, including books, concrete materials, and other media. Teachers and aides worked most of the time with individual students or with small groups of three or four; rarely did teachers present the same material to the entire class at one time.

Unlike Neill's Summerhill, which was based on the premise that children would learn automatically if left alone, most open-space schools offered considerable structure and direction. Yet there was far greater freedom than commonly found in their American counterparts. The evident concern was for learning, as opposed to teaching. Curricula emerged through the mutual interests and explorations of children and teachers working together; very little content was predefined as ''basic'' or ''essential'' and required for all. Many American observers were impressed by the general atmosphere of excitement. At the same time they found that individual freedom or flexibility in learning was not incompatible with the development of responsibility and self-control among students.

Some commentators, however, voiced skepticism over whether open education could work in the United States. Joseph Featherstone, for example, an early proponent of the concept whose articles in the *New Republic* did much to popularize the British movement, warned against uncritical adulation or slavish imitation of practices borrowed from a somewhat different cultural milieu.[139] Another writer noted how ''fundamental differences'' in bureaucratic structures governing the two educational systems worked against the wholesale adoption of open education. Without the autonomy accorded principals and teachers in Great Britain, he claimed, building an informal, open system of education in an American setting might prove impossible.[140] A typical caveat was issued by Beatrice and Ronald Gross:

> In the present climate of American education, the open classroom approach sometimes seems like a flower too fragile to survive. The demands on the schools today are harsh and often narrow. . . . In such a climate, the open classroom seems precariously based on a kind of trust little evident in education today. Teachers must trust children's imagination, feelings, curiosity, and natural desire to explore and understand their world. They also must learn to trust themselves—to be willing to gamble that they can retain the children's interest and respect once they relinquish the external means of control: testing, threats, demerits, petty rules and rituals. School administrators, in turn, must trust teachers enough to permit them to run a classroom that is not rigidly organized and controlled but, rather, is bustling, messy, flexible, and impulsive. Parents must trust school people to do well by their children, without the assurance provided by a classroom atmosphere recognizable from their own childhoods and validated, however emptily, by standardized tests.[141]

## OPEN EDUCATION

Cautionary warnings notwithstanding, the vogue for open education spread rapidly. Professional education journals were soon filled with articles on humanistic learning and open-space classrooms. At national conventions, a major topic of conversation among educators was humanizing education. The outpouring of books continued.[142] Besides reports of what was going on in English schools or pleas for the American adoption of similar reforms, there appeared numerous analyses of the burgeoning open-education movement in the context of its historical precedents and philosophical or psychological underpinnings. For those with a more practical orientation, "how-to-do-it" manuals offering specific advice on implementing open education in American schools were produced in abundance.

As interest in open education grew, so too did confusion over its meaning or import. Sometimes changes were purely cosmetic, involving little more than the installation of carpeting and the tearing down of walls and acoustical barriers between classrooms. Otherwise curricula and instruction of a traditional variety remained intact. Some enthusiasts, for example, seemed more concerned with physical space than with attitudes or values. To them, the term "open" had only an "architectural" meaning; what went on *pedagogically* in those open spaces remained much the same.[143] Elsewhere, more substantive changes were attempted as innovative school districts (in varying degree) tried to establish open environments.[144] In the more successful experiments, participants heeded Silberman's point that "openness" should be understood as "less an approach or method than a set of shared attitudes and convictions about the nature of childhood, learning, and schooling."[145]

Definitions and characterizations of open education abounded.[146] Summarizing an emergent consensus among many educators, Robert A. Horwitz, of

Yale University, claimed that the term referred primarily to "a style of teaching involving flexibility of space, student choice of activity, richness of learning materials, integration of curriculum areas, and more individual or small-group than large-group instruction."[147] As Vito Perrone, of the University of North Dakota, explained it, advocates of open education favored practices consistent with the belief that "learning is a personal matter that varies for different children, proceeds at many different rates, develops best when children are actively engaged in their own learning, takes place in a variety of settings in and out of school, and gains intensity in an environment where children—and childhood—are taken seriously."[148]

Roland S. Barth, principal of the Angier School, Newton (Massachusetts) Public Schools, in an often-quoted piece in the October 1971 issue of *Phi Delta Kappan*, attempted to get behind the superficial rhetoric of "integrated day," "Leicestershire Plan," "informal classroom," "open education," and so on, and to identify the most basic assumptions about learning and knowledge reflected in a true open-classroom situation.[149] Altogether, he was able to assemble over two dozen statements to which proponents invariably gave their assent. Among them were certain fundamental convictions about children's learning: that children are innately curious and will explore their environment without adult intervention; that natural exploratory behavior is self-perpetuating if it is not threatened; that such active exploration facilitates learning; that self-confidence is highly related to one's capacity for learning and for making choices; and that children have both the competence and the moral right to make significant decisions concerning their own learning.

As to children's intellectual development, Barth suggested that open-education advocates held many beliefs and convictions in common. Most accepted the fact that young children learn and develop intellectually and emotionally not only at varying rates but according to different styles, each in his or her own way. Verbal abstractions should follow direct experience with objects and ideas, not precede or substitute for them. Growth is best facilitated through a sequence of concrete experiences followed by abstractions.

In terms of evaluation, Barth found proponents of open education were agreed that "objective" measures of performance could have a negative effect upon learning, that learning is best assessed intuitively, by direct experience, and that "those qualities of a person's learning which can be carefully measured are not necessarily the most important." Concerning knowledge itself, Barth's study suggested once again that open-classroom supporters generally accepted certain basic postulates: that the structure of knowledge is "personal and idiosyncratic" and is a function of the synthesis of each individual's experience with the world; and that "little or no knowledge exists which it is essential for everyone to acquire."[150]

Other attempts to formulate the controlling precepts of humanistic or open education differed only in minor details. Herbert Walberg and Susan Thomas, for example, listed eight major themes: individualized instruction; continuous diagnosis, provisioning for a wide range of materials and equipment; subjective evaluation; "humanness"—respect for and trust in individuals; emphasis upon personal growth; faith in the natural curiosity of children and their capacity for independent exploration; and a warm affective relationship between teacher and students.[151]

Charles Rathbone in, *Open Education,* similarly cited six major articles of faith: the importance of active learning and direct experience; "personalized" knowledge as the only meaningful product of instruction; teaching children how to learn and emphasis upon their individual needs in developing independence, self-reliance, trust, and responsibility; the teacher as diagnostician, facilitator, and resource person; openness and trust in the classroom; and respect for the right of children to be treated with kindness and respect.[152]

Yet another summary of humanistic goals and practices offered the following statements:

1. Learning takes place under facilitative conditions indicative of warmth, genuineness, acceptance, and lack of judgment and threat on the part of the teacher. Effective interpersonal relationships are necessary for learning. There is a relationship of mutual respect and confidence between the teacher and the learner.
2. The learning situation is structured mutually by the teacher and the learner. The objectives of education are mutually agreed upon by the teacher and the learner.
3. The teacher does not control or dominate the learning situation. He or she is the facilitator of learning and in this role acts as a resource person who is available for personal consultation.
4. There are multiple learning alternatives for the student. Each individual learner pursues educational activities of his or her own choice. The teacher does not specify lesson tasks. Children are encouraged to express themselves in various ways depending on their own developmental level.
5. The educational program is judged on the basis of its ability to develop the maximum potential of the individual and to release his or her creative talent. The essence of learning is the cumulative subjective experience that pervades human life, augmenting the richness of each new experience and broadening the horizon of meaning.
6. The teacher does not evaluate and criticize unless requested by the student, and he or she does not assume total responsibility for grades. The nature of curricular experiences, the quality of pupil performance, and the modes of evaluation are jointly worked out by the teacher and the learner. Self-evaluation on the part of the learner is maximally emphasized.
7. The school program is characterized by facilitative experience-centered and problem-oriented learning environments, interpersonal relationships, cooperative planning and evaluation, self-initiated learning, freedom with responsibility, interdisciplinary approaches related to the satisfaction of human needs, and self-regulated modes of discipline.[153]

At a relatively early point in the movement, Perrone offered a prophetic comment about its future. There was a danger, he warned, that open education would become another fad, "a new gimmick to sweep over the American landscape, only to end up a few years from now on the educational junk heap of once-promising reforms.''[154] Attempting to forestall just such an eventuality, supporters in the early 1970s launched an effort to document the efficacy of open-space classrooms. A considerable body of research on the effects of individualized instruction and learning followed. Unfortunately, results were mixed or inconclusive.

---

ON HUMANISM IN EDUCATION

Humanistic education seeks to foster values like interdependence, collaboration, equality, and intimacy, rather than technocratic values like dependence, competition, hierarchy, and control over others. From a humanistic perspective, these technocratic values now bear a dangerously high price tag in terms of their long-term human consequences. . . .

Humanistic educators attempt to be skillful practitioners of genuine dialogue and to foster it among others. They have learned that the atmosphere that best motivates people to think and act creatively is one in which there is real listening, openness, trust, constructive feedback, and free speculation; in which people feel free to think metaphorically, analogically, and absurdly; in which there is tolerance of fantasy, ambiguity, and novelty. . . .

The humanistic perspective arises from a particular view of the nature of humankind. A basic humanistic assumption is that humans are free creatures. This does not imply that human behavior is uncaused, random, or uncontrollable, nor does it mean that people are uninfluenced by their environments, personal histories, or experiences. Rather, it means that they are able to make significant personal choices, to frame purposes, to initiate actions, and to exercise a degree of management over their own lifes.

—Paul Nash, "A Humanistic Perspective,"
*Theory Into Practice* 18 (December
1979): 325–326.

---

Of all the variables investigated, greatest attention was given to academic achievement. The overall pattern of findings failed to suggest a clear superiority of open or informal methods in the teaching of basic skills, but neither did studies reveal any substantial inferiority either. Some evidence in other areas suggested few differences between open and traditional schools in how favorably students regarded themselves or the extent to which respondents had a "positive" self-concept. Some research indicated that open classrooms seemed to be more enjoyable for children, that more creative activity occurred in open classrooms than in conventional ones, and that children in open classrooms exhibited increased independence, greater curiosity, less anxiety, and more cooperation.

Overall, as one writer summarized the findings, "evidence from evaluation studies of the open classroom's effects on children is not sufficiently consistent to warrant an unqualified endorsement of that approach . . . as decidedly superior to more traditional methods." However, he felt there was sufficient evidence to defend the idea that "the open classroom should be supported as a viable alternative when teachers and parents are interested in such a program." He added, perceptively, that further research was unlikely to resolve growing debates between proponents of more open teaching styles and advocates of the so-called back-to-basics approach. Opponents of open education, he believed, would be unlikely to be swayed in their opinions by additional research.[155]

## CRITICISM

Even those supportive of humanistic educational reforms entertained doubts about the open-education movement as it developed. Joseph Featherstone felt that in the clamor for open schools, the need to address recurring, fundamental problems in society at large might be overlooked. "The most pressing American educational dilemma is not the lack of informality in classrooms," he observed. "It is whether we can build a more equal, multiracial society." Open education, in his opinion, would become a sham unless those favoring it also remained sensitive to the societal context in which it was sustained.[156]

James W. Bell, of Arizona State University, noted that the open-education movement had been confined mainly to elementary schools. Its impact on secondary education was limited at best, centering primarily on facilities, organization, and course offerings. "Very little has been changed," he commented, "in other key concepts . . . such as individualized instruction, integration of content, vertical grouping, creativity, and self-direction."[157] In higher education, more than a few well-intentioned but disillusioned professors reported it was easier to criticize traditional education than to make humanistic reforms actually work in a college classroom.[158]

Many were angered by what one New Jersey social-studies coordinator termed the "relentless and patently uncritical attack on all public education" that had been waged since publication of Silberman's *Crisis in the Classroom*.[159] The vehemence and unreasonableness of the criticism, and the absence of an effective counterattack, prompted William Goetz to offer a rebuttal. Most critics, he alleged, had succumbed to a romantic sentimentality about children, painting a picture of eager young learners tyrannized by classroom despots that was altogether untrue. He further claimed open-education advocates were oblivious to the egregious failure of many experiments with informal education. Above all, school critics appeared to be astonishingly naive about the need for rules in schools. The problem, Goetz said, was not order itself that bothered students; most wanted and needed structured stability of some sort. The real issue was the inconsistent or arbitrary exercise of authority in enforcing rules and regulations.

Especially irksome to Goetz was the "aristocratic insouciance" of those who issued sweeping indictments and unreservedly proclaimed all schools as failures. It depends, he noted, on what prior values or assumptions control the analysis, and by what criteria American education is judged. He conceded, however, that in trying to be all things to all people, schools had left themselves open to abusive attacks. "In this the silly season of educational criticism," as he put it, it is well to recall that there have been many silly seasons of educational bombast about what the schools should and could do—a process which . . . has snared the schools in their own rhetoric and made them vulnerable to attack. . . . The lesson should be clear: Institutions that claim they can do almost everything should not be surprised if they are accused of "failing" to do anything.[160]

Purdue University's S. Samuel Shermis, in contrast, thought the schools were all too effective in carrying out their tasks. He appeared to accept at face value critics' claims that schools were impersonal factories: large, cold, and inhumane. Yes, he agreed, students' rights are often callously disregarded. The typical curriculum *is* irrelevant and boring. Teachers *are* dull. But practices labeled irrelevant, dull, indoctrinative, unjust, mechanical, and depressing, he claimed, are actually quite *useful:* "they serve to prepare students for life in a realistic and accurate manner."[161] The schools' internal conditions are most like what students will find in the world without. Hence schools do provide functional preparation for life in society as presently constituted.

Ritualism in school is important because it conditions children to endure the boring work they will engage in later on. Schools do not teach "critical thinking" because society is organized in such a way that the *last* thing it wants or needs are intelligent, discriminating citizens. The school's emphasis on procedure and administrative detail is likewise adaptive because it teaches students to cope with a thoroughly bureaucratized social order. In these and countless other ways, schools accurately reflect the cultural values and patterns found in the larger society. What goes on in education, Shermis emphasized, is neither accidental nor forced upon the schools by a willful minority of reactionaries. "Those who have focused on joy, spontaneity, inquiry, meaning, and relevance," he argued, "have simply not perceived the point that if schools are to prepare children realistically for life, then life in school should be consonant with what exists in the culture."[162]

Criticism leveled against schools therefore was misdirected, he felt. What libertarians perceived as repression was simply an expression of important patterns which the larger community in fact seeks to maintain. Public-opinion polls, for example, regularly show that most people feel their schools are functional and that in some valid sense they prepare young people appropriately for their future social roles. Critics, then, should look not to the schools but to the dominant culture in attempting to understand the character of American education as it exists today, he concluded.

Jonathan Kozol, unimpressed by all the rhetoric of "individualized instruction," "self-paced learning," and "classroom freedom," was scathing in his denunciation of "open-structured" education. It was, he admitted, less repressive, less directly manipulative, and certainly more enjoyable than anything offered by traditional pedagogy. But he denied it was truly "open" in any meaningful sense. Left intact was the overriding purpose of the schools; namely, socialization to the existing social order. Open education, in his judgment, should be seen for what it was: a clever ploy on the part of the dominant interlocking power structures of society, designed to co-opt students and "buy out" dissent.

The amiable myth behind the notion of the open classroom, he claimed, has to do with the imagined "authenticity," the "spontaneity," and the "autonomy" of the child's initiative in a supposedly "open" learning situation. A child, after all, does not "ask" to learn about anything to which he or she has not been previously exposed. The learner will not "explore" what he or she has already been trained subtly to avoid as "inappropriate or awkward or unpopular or dangerous, or morally contaminated." The child can "discover" only what the teacher supplies. The child is not really "free" to inquire except within whatever limits authority is willing to tolerate. What open education offers, then, said Kozol, is merely the illusion of free choice. In a "closed kingdom of confined and narrow options, guided stimuli, and calculated access to alternative ideas," the concept of learner freedom becomes meaningless.

Nor is open education ideologically and ethically "neutral." It purports to offer unlimited choices, and to honor equally all value claims so that children can make decisions for themselves. In reality its neutrality is spurious. It is sustained only within the context of the "managed framework of controlled ideas and preference-manufacture" upon which the nation's economic system depends. If and when schools succeed in their work, one can be assured they will graduate good capitalists, loyal citizens, and avid consumers. The end result is always the same—compliant, accepting conformists.

In an unjust society, Kozol argued, schools inevitably find use as tools "to quiet controversy, to contain rebellion, and to channel inquiry into accepted avenues of discreet moderation." Their task is not to provoke controversy, to further dissent, or to encourage honest scrutiny of society. Rather, they serve as agents of indoctrination. Their task is to inculcate allegiance to the system and to perpetuate the status quo. In the final analysis, as Kozol saw it, there was nothing "revolutionary" about open education at all. In his judgment it failed to challenge "the basic anesthetic character of public school, its anti-ethical function . . . its inculcation of the sense of vested interest in credentialized reward, its clever perpetration of a sense of heightened options in a closed and tightly circumscribed arena." In this sense, at least, Kozol concluded, open classrooms were reactionary. They represented at best a new way of doing an old job—protecting the established social order.[163]

## ALTERNATIVE SCHOOLS

Allen Graubard, author of *Free the Children: Radical Reform and the Free School Movement* (1972), agreed with the position enunciated by Samuel Shermis. It is probably true, he observed, that radical critics represented only a small dissenting minority. A substantial majority of Americans in all times *approve* of the schools' conservatism, including an authoritarian structure, heavy stress on discipline and punishment, motivation by testing and grading, required curricula, and emphasis on skill training for employment. Most people basically endorse the methods, values, and stated purposes of the public-school system.

In the main, he continued, most parents *want* schools to shape their children into loyal, patriotic, obedient, literate, and employable citizens. Far from opposing the imposition of attitudes and forms of behavior so much decried by humanistic radicals, the public generally approves of the values transmitted by educational institutions. As he phrased it, mothers and fathers

> want their children to be good Americans—and this means being able to get a job; not being a troublemaker; not criticizing or seriously questioning the dominant values of American life; accepting the so-called free enterprise system; and that the U.S. only fights wars for good, moral reasons; that the distribution of property and wealth is reasonably just; that people who succeed earn their positions and that those who don't succeed had their fair chance but just didn't have the stuff or were too lazy.[164]

Essentially, most Americans like the school system and the way it operates. They are satisfied with the job being done. The only reforms they want or approve of are those that would increase the schools' effectiveness in doing what they are now supposed to do. They want changes not so much in form or content, but in improved results. They want schools to foster discipline in children, to keep them out of trouble, to teach them whatever it is they need to know, and to help them to become potentially good candidates for employment and college. If more concentration on skills or more stringent discipline is required to accomplish these ends, so be it.

Assuming this to be the case, Graubard traced the origins of the so-called "free school" movement of the late sixties to the desire on the part of a minority of teachers, parents, and students for a much freer learning environment than that provided in almost all public schools. Private alternatives, as he saw it, were founded on a belief that public institutions, by their very nature, could never be truly "free." Given the circumstances of political control under which they operated, anything more than cosmetic alterations would be impossible. Staffed by officially credentialed teachers, obliged under law to insist upon compulsory attendance, and charged with a mandate to indoctrinate, public institutions at best would be allowed little leeway. They might assume the more superficial trappings of "openness," but otherwise everything else would remain unchanged. Basic goals and processes would stay the same.

Unwilling to settle for mere surface changes, many parents therefore elected to open their own alternative schools. Beginning with a handful of "free" or "community" schools around 1965 or 1966, private institutions grew, until they numbered in the hundreds by the early seventies.[165] Most were quite small, with enrollments ranging from half a dozen or more upwards to perhaps a hundred students. All were supported exclusively or primarily by tuition monies and by the fund-raising efforts of dedicated staff and parents. Varying in style and spirit, they shared mainly a critique of the methods, forms, content, and results of their public-school counterparts.[166]

On a continuum of permissiveness, "free" private education tended toward much greater freedom than even "open" public education. Whereas in public schools teachers typically retained significant control over what students were to learn, in free schools students often were allowed to decide when, how, what, and if they would learn.[167] What some permissive middle-class parents wanted, basically, was a Summerhillian experience for their children—a place where learners would be allowed to be spontaneous, uninhibited, creative, happy. They would be released to do "their own thing." Extreme informality was the rule, with very little direction or guidance offered. The environment was left as unstructured as possible.

Other free schools were much more directive in character and more oriented to political change. In style and tone they took on the character of the counterculture that had inspired their founding in the first place. The values they promoted were self-consciously and deliberately at odds with dominant mainstream values. Essentially they existed to nurture revolutionary consciousness and to pave the way for societal reconstruction.

In between the two extremes fell the majority of private free schools. Some were closely patterned after the British open-education model. Others harkened back to Montessori or experiments of the progressive era. Most featured an enriched learning environment, active parent-teacher collaboration in program planning and supervision of learning activities, and individualized instruction and assessment.

Unfortunately, perhaps, most private experimental free schools proved short-lived. Begun on a shoestring, most succumbed to financial problems after only a few years of operation. More viable and enduring by far were efforts to create alternatives *within* public-school systems, supported by local, state, and federal aid.[168] Philadelphia's Parkway, which opened in 1969 after two years of intensive planning, for example, was among the first public alternative schools, as was the Wilson Open Campus School, in Mankato, Minnesota, and the Murray Road School, in Newton, Massachusetts. In a very real sense these and others that followed were intended to serve as laboratories where open education, experiential education, "individualized-continuous-progress education," and other reforms urged by humanistic critics could be tried out. Alternative schools, in other words, would provide sites for the field-testing and validation of new innovations. To the extent that they were successful, it was expected, they would point the way toward the reform of all American education.

If anything, alternative schools continued to grow in substance and number throughout the seventies. As the movement spread, national and state associations sprang up by the dozens. New research projects were launched in an effort to compare and evaluate the results of differing learning environments. Under the leadership of such groups as the National Consortium on Options in Public

Education, more experimentation, development, and documentation took place in public education than had occurred in decades.[169]

But with the growth in number of public alternative schools came a shift in focus. Gradually the idea arose that no one single model was adequate to provide public schooling with the diversity it needed. Increasingly, experimental schools came to be looked upon less as pilot projects for the ultimate transformation of all schools along the lines of open education and more as permanent *options* within the public-school system. Experimentation with a broader range of concerns followed. Schools were used as places for the development of curricula for gifted and talented students, for developing special programs geared to the diverse needs of children from different ethnic backgrounds, and for organizing career-related training programs. In response to the flight of whites from the inner city to the suburbs, many so-called alternative schools were organized as "magnets" to help retain middle-class children in urban school districts. Alternative schools were pressed into service to assist with desegregation; to help reduce school violence, vandalism, and disruption; and to increase parent and community involvement in public schools.

---

### HUMANISM OR THE BASICS?

Sometimes educators throw around terms that leave parents confused. We don't have their training; yet our children are involved; so we give the words meanings of our own, and often communication problems arise.

Take the matter of the humanistic curriculum and basic education. I'm not sure I know what either one is. We see the words but we don't know what they mean.

While visiting my mother, her neighbor invited me to attend a home and school meeting at which 80 mothers and fathers, two teachers, and the principal were present. When the president called for discussion, one father complained that humanism has replaced the basics. He said that basic education has been put in second place to a humanistic curriculum.

After he sat down, a mother said that she didn't understand what is meant by a humanistic curriculum. Could someone explain it? Another mother said it sounded as if it were a study of humans and, if so it seemed important.

The father then grabbed the microphone and said that both mothers had it all wrong. He said humanistic education is nothing but "progressive life-adjustment studies." He insisted teachers had to get back to the basics. At no time, however, did he explain what "progressive life-adjustment studies" are.

Another parent said her son had had a six-week minicourse in the humanities. He had studied art, music, and literature; so maybe that was what the humanistic curriculum meant—more of those subjects. Immediately the "basics" man was on his feet again, shouting that that was what he was saying—no spelling, no writing, no mathematics; just socialization and frills.

The president of the association felt totally inadequate to handle the discussion for he had thought the purpose of the Home and School Association was to give parents a chance to ask teachers about their children's work. All this discussion was too involved for him and the meeting was getting out of hand.

One of the older, respected parents tried to restore order. She said she wasn't sure what humanistic education means but whatever it is, she didn't see any signs that their school was turning to social or psychological growth, or to just art, music, and literature. She had been reading about the need for a humanistic curriculum and thought that the principal and teachers could advise parents of what was involved so parents knew the balance between the skill areas and the humanistic areas. (Loud applause as she sat down.)

The principal agreed that children need both humanistic experiences and basic skills but did not pursue the matter further. He commended the parents for their interest and the meeting concluded. Temporarily, a Band-Aid covered the parents' bewilderment.

I don't have any children in that school, but I feel empathy for those parents. I don't know what the humanistic curriculum is myself and I'm not sure many parents do. Just what is it? Is it the opposite of basic education, as the man said?

If you know, let the parents in your school in on the secret. Maybe the answer will gradually reach the town where I live.

—Dorothy Thompson, "Humanism or the Basics?" *Instructor* 87 (January 1978): 36. Reprinted from *Instructor,* January 1978. Copyright © 1978 by The Instructor Publications, Inc. Used by permission.

Along with the idea of broadening objectives came another idea: the notion that the concept of an "alternative" school cut both ways. That is, if an "open" school was an "alternative" to a conventional school, a "traditional" school could as easily serve as an "alternative" to overly permissive education. Thus, what began as an effort to infuse schooling with the spirit of humanistic reform gradually changed from a radical initiative into a conservative reaction. More and more the idea of the alternative school was adopted by back-to-basics advocates. By the mid-seventies, for example, there were as many "traditional" schools offering themselves as alternatives within public education as there were "open" schools. A decade later the number of "schools without walls" had dropped dramatically. For every school offering individualized instruction and free learning, there were twice the number emphasizing formality, deference to authority, and traditional curricula. Greatly outnumbering open-space schools were institutions dedicated to drill, recitation, and rote learning.

By the mid-eighties it was clear that the idea of institutional pluralism had achieved widespread acceptance. Equally clear was the fact that the entire character of the alternative-school movement had changed. The same interest in experimentation and exploration of alternatives was evident. But the nature of the alternatives sought was now different. Consistent with the nation's growing political and educational conservatism, humanistic reform—once the motivating force for the development of alternative schools—clearly no longer enjoyed the popular support it had once received. For all practical purposes, the humanistic education movement was moribund. In the aftermath, all that remained was the need to account for its apparent demise.

## IN RETROSPECT

Writing toward the end of the decade of the seventies, Carl Rogers voiced optimism over the future of humanistic education. "I firmly believe," he wrote, "that innovative, humanistic, experiential learning, whether taking place in or out of the classroom, is here to stay and has a future." American education, he claimed, had passed a watershed. He spoke confidently about "an increasing flow of movement into an education more fit for humans. Every city has its alternative schools, free schools, and open classrooms." [170] Arthur W. Combs, a professor at the University of Northern Colorado, felt the same. "The humanist movement is no fad," he insisted, "destined to come into being for a short time and quickly fade away." [171]

Quite the contrary, Combs asserted, humanistic education was only one expression of a much larger worldwide movement in human thinking, paralleled by humanistic movements in psychology, sociology, anthropology, political science, theology, philosophy, and medicine. To skeptics who believed that humanistic education was a nice idea but much too "soft" to prepare youth for the tough world of reality, Combs's response was that there were at least three major reasons why the humanistic trend would endure and achieve still greater prominence.

First, he claimed, the interdependence of people in a complex, technological civilization has made *human* problems more pressing than ever. To live successfully in an increasingly interdependent world requires, at the very least, intelligent citizens who understand themselves and the dynamics of interaction with others, and who can behave as responsible, problem-solving human beings. The gravest problems in contemporary society—problems of population, pollution, energy, starvation, health, terrorism, the threat of nuclear destruction—are all "essentially human" problems. They can be solved, but only if people are educated with a clear understanding of the personal skills necessary for living with one another.

Secondly, according to Combs, the future demands educational processes that deal not only with student behavior but also with their "inner life," especially with self-concepts, values, and feelings. To suppose that one must choose between education for intellectual development or affective growth, for example, he insisted, is a serious error. It is as though one must choose between "smart psychotics or well-adjusted dumbbells." Such either-or thinking is "not only inappropriate, it can be destructive." [172] An educational system that ignores or rejects affect—attitudes, feelings, and emotions—as an important facet of the learning process consigns itself to impotence. [173]

The only kind of education, therefore, that can hope to meet such objectives as instilling civic responsibility, good mental health, moral conduct, and a desire to learn is one that recognizes and takes into account the central importance of subjectivity in learning—"the characteristics that make us human." An education system that treats students as objects or strives for total objectivity, on the other hand, Combs claimed, cannot meaningfully address the most important goals for which education exists. [174]

Not only is it true that modern life demands citizens capable of coping with the human problems they will inevitably face, and that the causes of behavior lie in the qualities that define us as human beings—our feelings, attitudes, beliefs, values, hopes, understandings, and aspirations—but, thirdly, humanistic education is essential because learning itself is, as Combs put it, "a deeply human, personal, affective process." He emphasized his point as follows:

> Humanistic education is no fad, no flash in the pan. It is firmly rooted in new conceptions of the nature of the human organism, the causation of behavior, and the processes of learning. These are facts of life. They will not go away, and they cannot be ignored because they are inconvenient. To do so is as silly as saying, "I know my car needs a carburetor, but I'm going to run mine without one!"

Humanism in education, he emphasized once again, is no "fragile flower, too tender for a tough world." Quite the contrary, it is, Combs insisted, "a systematic, conscious attempt to put into practice the best we know about the nature of human beings and how they learn."[175]

Others were not so sure, at least insofar as "open" education or "open-space" classrooms were to be taken as examples of education humanism applied in actual practice. Many questioned whether all children could benefit from open education, in either a cognitive or an affective sense; and the paucity of hard research to support the more extravagant claims of humanistic educators troubled many observers.[176] In particular, the apparent failure of research to document the relative advantages of open-space schools over more conventional or traditional schools led to rising skepticism.[177]

Roland Barth, for example, alleged that experience had shown "quite contrary to open educators' assumptions about children that trust in children's capacity to make choices is unwarranted and will be abused."[178]

One writer expressed a common sentiment in observing,

> The concerns of those who want to "look before they leap" will not be eliminated by arguments that the open classroom is like poetry or religion and must be accepted by faith and intuition alone. Neither poetry nor religion is supported by tax dollars. . . . The lack of consensus and the limitations characteristic of the present research call for teachers to proceed cautiously, not moving "too far, too fast" in their experimentation.[179]

Indicative of the increasing mood of caution in the seventies was the advice offered by Fred M. Hechinger: "Common sense suggests that there are grave psychological disadvantages in the polar extremes of drill-master traditionalism and super-permissive progressivism."[180]

By the mid-seventies, early glowing reports implying humanistic education was a panacea for a host of ills had given way to a more sober reassessment of recent school ferment. In the wake of a taxpayers' revolt and declining financial support for public schools, the fact that the direct costs of open education were higher than in regular schools proved disquieting. Open space classrooms required a lowering of the student-teacher ratio, a move many school districts were unwilling or unable to contemplate. The need for more and better teacher preparation also became apparent. Open-structured schooling, as one observer noted, required "so much of the teacher that one wonders how many individuals [are] capable . . . of meeting its awesome challenge, no matter how good-willed and energetic the person."[181] Managing individualized instruction, as others pointed out, "was an exhausting endeavor and a major physical and psychological drain."[182] In order to succeed, an open-education format needed a special kind of highly dedicated teacher, one possessing prior, highly specialized training. Such exceptional personnel, however, were always in short supply.

Assessments differed as to why open education seemed to be faltering. Some blamed administrators for simply grafting a new innovation onto a traditional system, with all of the inevitable compromises entailed. Others felt that overcrowding and poor facilities were responsible for a lack of success. Others felt the problem lay with educators who failed to grasp the vast differences in the philosophical underpinning of the open classroom as opposed to that of traditional schools. Still other critics placed blame on teacher-educators for their failure to provide adequate preservice and in-service training.

Again, some analysts saw the erosion of support for open education as a special instance of a much larger trend: a loss of public confidence generally in the institution of schooling. Hofstra University's Mary Anne Raywid went so far as to claim that school criticism had grown so pervasive and pronounced as to assume the dimensions of a "legitimacy crisis" in American education. Evidence of failure abounded: reports of declining achievement and falling test scores, school violence, vandalism—the list of problems, as she noted, "is now long and all too familiar."[183]

What struck some commentators were the eerie parallels between the fate of progressivism in the 1930s and 1940s and open education in the 1970s and 1980s. "Open education is well on its way down the same path the progressive education movement followed to its demise," two writers concluded.[184] In 1930 John Dewey had issued both a warning and a challenge to progressive educators. "If," he argued, "progressive schools become complacent with existing accomplishments, unaware of the slight foundation of knowledge upon which they rest, and careless regarding the amount of study of the laws of growth that remains to be done, a reaction against them is sure to take place."[185] So far as Robert P. Mai, executive director of the Educational Confederation of St. Louis, Missouri, was concerned, the same need and the same reaction now confronted advocates of humanistic open education.[186]

The problem, as Mai saw it, was that like progressivism, open education had already degenerated into an orthodoxy offering its own rigid formula for school reform. It too was inadequately based on an understanding of human development and how to provide for it in the schools. Open education originated in much the same way as did progressivism, with "simplistic, sentimental, and unrealistic self-image making.'' It began with a polemical approach to the analysis of educational problems, which, although perhaps necessary to overcome inertia and apathy, proved insufficient for the hardheaded and dispassionate analysis that should have followed. The strength of humanistic reformers, according to Mai, was their effectiveness in drawing attention to the tedium, the mechanical rigidity, and the senseless authoritarianism characteristic of American schooling. But what critics failed to provide was a solid body of knowledge upon which to draw in formulating strategies for change. Righteous indignation, a sense of moral urgency, and a rhetorical desire for freedom were never enough for organizing more defensible educational programs, any more than the same qualities were for the early progressivist. What was needed was reliable information about how children develop, how they learn, and how learning can best be challenged.

"Open education must be humanistic, but not foolish and sentimental," Mai avowed. "Nor can it afford to be psychologically naive or socially irresponsible."[187] In particular, terms such as "need," "interest," and "freedom (all too often used with no more exactitude than necessary to convey essentially libertarian sentiments)," he argued, should be defined more rigorously. Thus, for example, is a learner's "need" the same as an "interest"? Is there a difference between "interest" and "impulse"? *What kind* of freedom is needed in education: freedom *from* some set of inhibiting circumstances or freedom *for* achieving certain goals? Are constraints uniformly oppressive? Is teacher-directed instruction always meaningless or ineffective? Does freedom inevitably lead to learning?

The typical humanistic position declares itself for the rightness of discovery learning, freedom of choice, children's rights, and individual needs. Unhappily, the rhetoric all too often remains at the level of appealing clichés—for instance, "child-centered" and "experienced-based" curriculum—that among progressivists initially expressed the promise of important change but ended up as little more than slogans. "I find it . . . difficult to hold . . . that children can learn only that which seems to them relevant, or learn best when given their heads," Mai objected, "for this simply ignores our own varied experience as a learner, and all that we know and have found interesting only because circumstances pressed us to examine and explore." He continued, "Indeed, it often seems that the role of the school-as-social-institution to cultivate traditions and provide training in practical skills like counting is entirely overlooked by humanistic apologists for open, informal classrooms."[188]

Richard Hoftstadter, writing about the early progressive educators, commented on their tendency "to set up an invidious contrast between self-determining, self-directed growth from within, which was good, and molding from without, which was bad." His conclusion was:

> The notion that the authoritative classroom would of necessity produce the conformist mind and that sociable learning would produce the ideally socialized personality is at first appealing, but there is about it a kind of rigid rationality of the sort that life constantly eludes. . . . To expect that education would so simply produce a hoped-for personal type was to expect more than past experience warranted.[189]

Mai quoted Hoftstadter approvingly, arguing that the latter's judgment applied with equal force to contemporary open-classroom advocates. We are, said Mai, still guilty of feeding on a rhetoric generating the same sort of unrealistic expectations, a rhetoric of assumptions and explanations that, in its efforts to persuade, obscures realities serious educators must confront.[190]

Neil Postman, a professor of media ecology at New York University, put forth a quite different analysis. In his account, the alleged lack of hard research data supporting open-education reforms had little or nothing at all to do with the decline of the humanistic-education movement.

It had all begun, he noted, when dozens of articulate young critics entered schools, were repelled by the situation they uncovered, and set out writing angry tracts demanding a halt to the "intellectual and emotional carnage." Initially, they were tough, reality-oriented analysts who recognized a pedagogical horror show when they saw it. John Holt, for example, wrote eloquently of the boredom, confusion, and fear experienced by schoolchildren—"fear of not having the right answer, of not understanding things the way everyone else does, of being singled out, of not being singled out, of reproach, of ridicule, of failure." For many children then and now, Postman declared, the school is a "House of Fear, no matter how charming its architecture, or open its halls, or contemporary its materials."[191]

Some critics proposed concrete, specific changes, as exemplified by the more successful adaptations of the British open-space classroom. Others offered alternatives. But the free-school movement was never widespread enough to offer relief to millions of children attending regular public schools, and the scores of alternative schools that grew up did not always prove helpful in showing how public education itself could be reformed. "And then suddenly it was over," Postman mused. "The situation has not been much improved or even very much clarified. Everything, as of today, looks quite the same as before."[192] What happened? Where did all the critics go? And what happened to all the angry, spirited defenses of the oppressed so common in the sixties? How did an educational reform movement that had begun so promisingly, he wondered, end up becoming so ineffectual?

Postman offered several intriguing explanations. First, he claimed, the end of the war in Viet Nam had a great deal to do with declining interest in school reform. More than anyone suspected, the two were connected. In a sense, the movement to humanize education was a spillover from the antiwar movement. Once the war was over, critics lost interest in trying to change the nation's school system.

Next, many critics who were genuinely interested in educational reform underestimated the difficulty of their task. They failed to appreciate the complexity of the school as a social institution, the multiplicity of forces shaping or otherwise impacting upon it, and the complications involved in attempting to introduce major structural alterations. The fact that many reformers were utopians unwilling to settle for anything less than radical transformation compounded the problem.

Oftentimes, they exaggerated the degree of public support behind them. When schools proved resistant to change, they were overwhelmed by the magnitude of the problem and soon turned their attention elsewhere.

In addition, some critics, according to Postman, had a well-developed contempt for administrators and teachers, the very people who would have to bear responsibility for carrying through proposed reforms. Burdened by a crippling self-righteousness and contemptuous of those who they considered beyond redemption, they cut themselves off from their most influential constituency, the adults who run the schools.[193] Besides, the more militant critics contented themselves with diatribes against formal education—they made no effort to provide the instructional materials and methods needed to make reforms work.

Next, Postman suggested, too few critics had sufficient in-depth experience with the daily workings of schools. Most were outsiders, lacking any official connection with state departments of education, teacher-training institutions, or other agencies that could provide them with a "power base." "This meant that they could not *make a living* as educational critics. This, in turn, meant that many of the best critics had to repair fairly quickly to their natural sources of income and interest."[194] The result was twofold: external criticism could not be sustained long enough to make a difference; and within the system, official routes of influence remained relatively uncontaminated by the new proposals.

Postman also felt that many school critics were naive. Their view of children was Rousseau-like and, ultimately, woefully unrealistic. "Typically, a school was imagined to be a place of obtuse, malignant adults, dedicated to oppressing purehearted, liberty-seeking, instinctively humane children." With such "cartoon imagery" as this, he judged, it was no wonder so little was accomplished and that it all ended so soon.[195]

Concomitant with the emergence of the school-reform movement, Postman continued, there arose a spirit of psychic self-absorption, a kind of narcissistic turning-inward—"getting in touch with your feelings, shedding layers of inhibition, exorcising guilt, never saying yes when you mean no, doing your own thing and no one else's, and in general minimizing such demands as may intrude on your heightened consciousness."[196] In the Age of Self-Improvement, prevailing throughout the seventies and the first half of the eighties, school criticism lost its focus and high energy. Without cadres of disciplined, committed young people to carry forward the critical tradition, radical reform was bound to falter.

Finally, Postman pointed to the nation's worsening economic condition as a major factor responsible for the expiration of a school-reform movement. Coupled with the demographic reality of a diminishing school-age population, education (like the railroads, as one wit had it) became a declining industry. School closings, cutbacks in staffing, reduced expenditures for educational institutions, and lack of employment opportunities for prospective teachers all made a difference. "It is a principle universally to be observed," Postman declared, "that when people are worried about getting or holding jobs, they do not make first-rate social critics."[197]

## SUMMARY

"Humanism" in the Western cultural tradition originated in Graeco-Roman antiquity as an outlook affirming the inviolability or sanctity of the individual, the inherent dignity of personhood, and the importance of self-directed human development within the frame of civilized culture. As revived among leading thinkers of the Renaissance, humanism reaffirmed the worth of human interests and concerns and the near-infinite possibilities of personal self-fulfillment. Western humanism found various expressions in subsequent eras, most notably in the eighteenth-century Enlightenment, and again in the modern period.

As a basic philosophic perspective or outlook on life, humanism is claimed as the unique possession of a broad range of contemporary movements and ideologies. Likewise, as applied to education, humanism has been subject to variant interpretations, though typically associated with certain recurrent themes having to do with human freedom, dignity, personal autonomy, and individualism. Humanism in education emphasizes teaching and learning to promote self-actualization, humane methods of instruction, individualization, and maximal freedom for self-initiated, self-directed learning. Contemporary educational humanism is descended from, or shares features with, both "romanticism" in educational thought and the reform movement known as progressivism.

The "romantic" tradition in education arose in response to a centuries-old pattern of cruelty and insensitivity toward children. Originating primarily in the writings of Jean-Jacques Rousseau, romanticism came to be defined as a doctrine stressing the goodness of human nature, the spontaneous curiosity or will to learn of young children, and the desirability of child-centered instruction. As extended and elaborated upon by Pestalozzi, Froebel, Tolstoy, and in the contemporary period by Homer Lane, A. S. Neill and John Holt, the romantic impulse urged unfettered child growth, freedom in learning, the importance of intuition and feelings, and trust in the child's natural unfolding or development. Less sentimental in its conception of childhood and more directive in its recommendations for practice was the educational theory of Maria Montessori, who also emphasized spontaneity and discovery learning in a "prepared" environment. Especially important in her view was adapting the learning situation to developmental stages of growth of each child.

Progressivism in the American experience expressed a long-standing article of faith that education was a powerful instrumentality for social progress. Progressivist educational reform, as part of a much broader program for societal renewal, was aimed at providing opportunities for the children of immigrants and the urban disadvantaged. What early proponents termed the "new education" combined vocational training, daily-living skills, and a child-centered pedagogy, in its efforts to improve upon the traditional educational usages of the past. In the writings of such reformers as Joseph R. Buchanan and Francis W. Parker, the burgeoning progressive-education movement found clear expressions of a humanistic approach to the instruction of the young.

The special targets of progressivist reform were the authoritarianism and rigidity of prevailing pedagogy. John Dewey, for example, who more than any other single figure was identified in the popular consciousness as spokesman for the new educational humanism, spoke out strongly against passive learning, curricular uniformity, and the mechanistic character of most conventional instruction. Reacting to all forms of traditionalism in education, his plea was for learning by doing, discovery through experience, and active learner participation in the work of schools. It was Dewey also who did the most to popularize the concepts of a child-centered curriculum, the teacher as a facilitator and resource guide, and education for human growth and development.

Later progressivists, including Harold Rugg, John Childs, George Counts, William Heard Kilpatrick, and Boyd Bode became increasingly divided over questions having to do with the larger social ends of formal education. Whereas some theorists tended to confine their attention to the conditions affecting humane classroom learning, others grew more concerned over the potential role of the school in facilitating social reform. Dewey, who profoundly opposed all dualisms and dichotomies, rejected the supposed need to choose between the two positions.

By the late 1930s, progressivism as an organized reform movement in education had lost much of its earlier force. In the postwar period of the 1940s and early 1950s, political reaction placed progressivists on the defensive. Thanks in part to internecine struggles among adherents of the movement over goals, and partly because of an apparent failure to develop a defensible pedagogy capable of widespread application, progressivism fell into disrepute. It was succeeded by a resurgence of traditionalist feeling and renewed popular support for educational conservatism.

Toward the end of the 1950s the nation's political mood turned still more conservative. In education the shift was mirrored by a near-hysterical concern to exploit schools in the pursuit of national and international policy aims. In the aftermath of the furor over the Soviet launching of *Sputnik,* the focus of attention was upon greater educational accountability. The so-called "structure-of-the-disciplines" movement led by Jerome Bruner, for example was one indication of the shift in emphasis. With the opening of the decade of the sixties, conventional wisdom had it that public schooling should become more rigorous, more cost-effective, and, above all, more efficient. In calls for the application of "systems analysis" and efficiency criteria, an earlier concern for humanistic teaching and learning was seemingly lost sight of altogether.

Around the same time that technocratic values were coming to the fore, behavioristic approaches to instruction and evaluation enjoyed a new vogue. B. F. Skinner, for example, proved to be an articulate and persuasive defender of the notion that education could be managed as an exercise in behavioral engineering. Professional interest in so-called "teaching machines" and programmed instruction reached fever pitch, prompting expectations that a technological revolution in schooling was at hand. Hence, the reaction against technocracy, born of the social turmoil of the late 1960s, when it took place, was as unexpected as it was pronounced.

Coalescing out of the several diverse social currents and reform movements of the sixties was a youth counter-culture whose members set themselves at odds with practically all mainstream values and mores. Interacting with the phenomena of sociopolitical activism was a chorus of protest directed at American education. So-called radical critics assailed the schools for a host of ills; and most of the grievances recapitulated complaints levied much earlier by progressivist reformers against traditional education. Although differing in style or tone from their predecessors, what humanistic critics of the sixties and seventies wanted was not altogether different: more "relevant" curricula, greater individualization of instruction, and more humane classroom treatment of children.

In the example of the British infant and primary schools, many humanistic reformers found an ideal model for what came to be known as open education. Unfortunately, American attempts to adapt that model in a dissimilar social setting all too frequently proved inconsistent or superficial. Nonetheless, under the banner of educational humanism, much valuable experimentation was begun. Although its impact was felt primarily on elementary-school classrooms, neither high schools nor colleges and universities remained unaffected. Altogether, efforts to "humanize" or "individualize" or "personalize" education assumed many different forms, constituting the main agenda for reform in school systems throughout the country for a least a decade and more.

Definitions of humanistic education varied. One important formulation was offered by the Working Group on Humanistic Education, sponsored by the Association for Supervision and Curriculum Development (ASCD). The ASCD group defined it as follows: humanistic education is a commitment to educational practice in which all facets of the teaching/learning process give major emphasis to the freedom, value, worth, dignity, and integrity of persons. More specifically, humanistic education

1. accepts the learner's needs and purposes and develops experiences and programs around the unique potential of the learner;

2. facilitates self-actualization and strives to develop in all persons a sense of personal adequacy;

3. fosters acquisition of basic skills necessary for living in a multicultural society, including academic, personal, interpersonal, communicative, and economic proficiency;

4. personalized educational decisions and practices (to this end it includes students in the processes of their own education via democratic involvement at all levels of implementation);

5. recognizes the primacy of human feelings and uses personal values and perceptions as integral factors in education processes;

6. develops a learning climate that nurtures learning environments perceived by involved individuals as challenging, understanding, supportive, exciting, and free from threat; and

7. develops in learners genuine concern and respect for the worth of others and skill in conflict resolution.[198]

From its inception, the drive to "humanize" the schools never lacked for critics. Some alleged American schooling had never been as oppressive and stultifying as its radical critics had claimed. Some questioned the efficacy of open classrooms as compared with their more traditional counterparts. Others questioned the seeming social irrelevance of much that passed for humanistic reform; the issue, it was argued, was not simply classroom informality but the ties between schools and the larger social order. Still other critics reversed the argument, asserting that society gets the schools it wants and deserves. In an inhumane society, one can predict the kind of schooling that will prevail. Finally, certain critics such as Jonathan Kozol denied that "free" learning was possible in a society that was not itself "free" in any meaningful sense of the term.

Among the more radical educational experiments of the late 1960s were efforts to create alternatives to public schools. So-called "free" schools were begun by private groups in order to provide children with a less-rigidly structured form of education than public schools were able to offer. Some were apolitical, Summerhill-like institutions, where learners enjoyed virtually total freedom. Others were more directive, incorporating some of the best features of British open schools. Still other free schools were highly politicized places of learning, dedicated to political activism and the values of the counter-culture. With the exception of those supported by upper-middle-class parents, most free schools floundered after only a few years of operation. Financial exigency was chiefly responsible for their closings.

More durable by far were public "alternative" schools, founded originally as laboratories for designing and field-testing educational innovations. A great many attempted to pioneer open-education reforms; as many more became involved in other kinds of social-engineering experiments. By the 1980s, the concept of an educational "alternative" had shifted in the direction of traditionalist or "fundamental" schools, where back-to-basics and rigid discipline were the order of the day.

If "relevance" was the rallying cry for educational reform between the mid-sixties and mid-seventies, in the late 1970s and early 1980s the call was for basic learning and essential skills. Like the progressivist movement in the forties, the impulse to humanize education born of earlier social turmoil began to weaken. By the mid-eighties, concern over declining academic achievement, failing test scores, and school violence greatly overshadowed interest in open education and other humanistic initiatives. The rhetoric of "meeting learners' needs" and "individualizing instruction" remained as strong as ever, but the substance had disappeared. Certain minor changes had taken place in public education—especially in the organization of elementary-school classrooms—but otherwise everything remained much the same.

Explanations for the apparent failure of the school-reform movement were varied. Open education, some claimed, had been overpromised and underdelivered. Reformers allegedly had failed to develop a coherent body of practices upon which a new pedagogy could be developed. Other writers accounted for the demise of humanistic education in terms of broader social currents and trends, including the rise of privatism in the 1970s, deteriorating economic circumstances, the eclipse of radical leftist political activism and several other factors. Such proponents of humanism in education as Arthur Combs and Carl Rogers, however, continued to believe that the conditions of modern life, now more than ever, warranted a thoroughgoing resuscitation of humanistic educational endeavor.

## REVIEW QUESTIONS

1. How was the spirit of "humanism" expressed in Graeco-Roman antiquity? What was "classical humanism"? What were the *most* important themes in the development of the humanistic tradition in Western culture?

2. How are modern religious and secular humanism similar? How do they differ? Upon what ground respectively does each base a belief in the importance of humanity and of individual persons?

3. What are the main themes or emphases associated with modern humanism in education?

4. What is the "romantic" tradition in education? Who have been its foremost exemplars? What specific features distinguish romanticism in education?

5. Summarize briefly Rousseau's view of the child and of learning. In what sense did his views allegedly represent a kind of watershed or "Copernican Revolution" in the history of educational thought?

6. What did A. S. Neill accept as the ultimate goal of life, and how was his concept of freedom related to the achievement of that goal?

7. Why did Maria Montessori believe that conventional schooling failed to develop the child's full human potential? What specific experiences led her to develop her own theories of child development? How did she view the activity of teaching? In what sense was her methodology "child-centered"? What did she mean by a "prepared environment," and how was this related to her concept of the child as an "absorbent being"? How did she understand the concept of "liberty" or "freedom" in learning?

8. How did progressivism as a social-reform movement begin? Under what circumstances did it arise? What were the specific stimuli for educational reform? What were the major elements of the so-called "new education"? To what groups or constituencies were early progressivist efforts directed?

9. What common themes appeared in the educational writings of Joseph Buchanan, Franklin Parker, William James, and John Dewey? What were the main outlines of progressivist pedagogy as it was developed?

10. What were John Dewey's basic objections to traditional schooling? How did he define such terms as "curriculum," "pedagogy," and "education" itself? What did he view as the primary aim or goal of education? How did he conceive the teacher's task? Why did he claim that educational processes must be understood simultaneously from both a psychological and a social perspective? How did Dewey define the relationship between the school as an institution and society?

11. Identify or define the major issues dividing "child-centered" progressivists from those interested in societal reform. What position did Harold Rugg and George S. Counts promote, and why? How did Dewey attempt to reconcile the two positions?

12. Boyd Bode repeatedly voiced criticisms of the progressive-education movement in the 1920s and 1930s. What were they? In what ways did Dewey share Bode's concerns?

13. What were the most important factors responsible for the gradual decline and eventual eclipse of progressivism? How did the reaction against progressivism in education find expression? What forms did it assume?

14. What was the so-called "cult of efficiency" in American education in the 1960s? Upon what assumptions about schooling did it depend? How did technocratic reformers view people, the process of education, and the nature of knowledge? To what ends did they wish to direct schools? What is "systems analysis" as applied to education? What appeared to be the dominant values of educational reform in the early sixties?

15. Why did behaviorists attempt to redefine psychology as a "behavioral science"? How did John Watson or B. F. Skinner view internal mental states or consciousness? what did Skinner stipulate as the proper concern of psychology as a discipline? How was "behavioral engineering" applied to problems of teaching and learning? How did Skinner define "freedom" in education? What specific forms did behaviorism assume as applied to educational theory and practice?

16. Why did such humanistic psychologists as Carl Rogers and Abraham Maslow object to behaviorism? How did they explain or account for human development and action? What is meant by "needs hierarchy" and "self-actualization"? What allegedly are the distinguishing characteristics of the self-actualizing person?

17. In what ways were the educational ideas of Carl Rogers similar to those of the progressivists or the romantics? Why did Rogers claim "no one can teach anything to anyone"? In what ways, according to Rogers, are psychotherapy and education alike?

18. How was the emergence of a so-called youth "counter-culture" in the sixties related to a resurgence of interest in humanistic education and school reform?

19. Summarize the main allegations or criticisms of schooling levied by radical school critics of the late 1960s and early 1970s. Why, for example, did Farber believe students were oppressed? Why did Postman and Weingartner believe that teaching should be a "subversive" activity? Why did critics claim that schools were "failing" children?

20. What was the Plowden Report? Why was it important in the context of American educational reform? What were the basic underlying assumptions of "open" education? What specific practices characterize "open-space" or "open-structured" classrooms?

21. What were the major objections raised against open education? What was the main point of the argument offered by S. Samuel Shermis? Why did Jonathan Kozol so bitterly attack open education? What was the nature of the "deception" it allegedly represented?

22. What is a "free" school? How and why did the free-school movement begin? How did free schools differ, typically, from "alternative" public

schools? What happened to the free-school movement? How did the character and aims of alternative schools change in the seventies and eighties?

23. What explanations were offered regarding the causes of the apparent decline of popular interest in, and support for, humanistic education? What parallels were drawn between the fate of progressivism and that of the open-education movement?

## SOME QUESTIONS FOR DISCUSSION

1. Throughout most of recorded history, formal education typically has been, in the words of an old-time rhyme, "'readin' and writin' and 'rithmetic, taught to the tune of a hickory stick." Why? What accounts for the fact that in every age, schooling has been a relatively unpleasant affair, marked by regimentation, endless drill, and harsh punishments? Was it the low socioeconomic status of the traditional schoolmaster? Ignorance about human growth and development? A lack of psychological knowledge about how to facilitate learning? Cultural attitudes and expectations? All of these? What other factors may have been involved?

2. A person claims to be a "humanist." As opposed to what—a nonhumanist? What attributes, characteristics, values, or beliefs define a humanist? What might be *excluded* from a definition of humanism in education?

3. The English word "educate" derives from the Latin *educare,* "to bring up," while "education" is cognate with *educere,* "to lead, to draw forth, to bring out," as in "educe," to elicit something latent. On etymological grounds, then, is it plausible or convincing to argue, as some writers have done, that "education" should be viewed as a process of "drawing out" from within, rather than as an external imposition of something upon a learner? Phrased differently, do the origins of the word "to educate" or "education" suggest any particular way of managing instruction?

4. Child psychologists, counselors, and psychiatrists often allege that the institution of schooling is the most anxiety-producing influence in the life of a child, outweighing even the impact of the home environment. Is this true? If so, why?

5. Some writers view the difference between "open" and "traditional" schooling as one of *structure*; that is, "low-structure" teaching (education through experience and discovery) versus "high-structure" instruction (stress on drill in the basics). Is this an adequate way of conceptualizing the difference between the two formats? Is an "open-space" classroom *less* structured than a more traditional one, or is it simply structured *differently*?

6. A cardinal tenet of educational humanism is that learning must be adapted to the individual child. Does this mean the *pace* or *rate* of learning is the major relevant variable? Or are there other equally important variables that should be taken into account (for instance, learning "style," learning modality, and so on)? What does it mean to individualize instruction or learning? What are the realistic limits of individualization in a classroom with one teacher and upwards of twenty or thirty children?

7. Can or should all school learning be pleasant, enjoyable, and free of tedium or drudgery? When—under what specific conditions—might drill or rote memorization be defensible? Must a young child always fully understand why he or she is expected to learn something? What makes learning meaningful? What make learning relevant or irrelevant?

8. Is corporal punishment in school ever justified? If so, when, or under what circumstances? If not, why not? Review the arguments, pro and con, concerning physical punishment. Can punishment find use as an acceptable means of enforcing discipline? What might be the alternatives? Which are most effective as determinants of behavior—rewards or punishments? What about "psychological" punishment? What forms does it assume?

9. Assume for the sake of argument (all things being equal) that children tend to want to learn what interests them most. Therefore, or so it is said, they should be allowed to pursue their own interests. They are self-motivated. They will engage in the sorts of activities that most fully satisfy their own curiosity. What happens then if children fail to learn what teachers and adults consider to be most important? What is the difference between "interest" and "need"? Do children *need* to learn some things which happen not to interest them? Who defines an educational need? On what basis? Does the concept of "need" justify compulsion or coercion in learning? Why or why not?

10. Can people be *forced* or compelled to learn something? What is the difference between "compulsion" and "exposure" in learning? Are there circumstances when it is appropriate to attempt to force a person to learn something?

11. Does it really matter what specific information is acquired in school? After all, with sufficient need and motivation on a learner's part, anything can be learned if and when it is needed—even basic skills such as reading and writing. If this is true, why impose learning in school?

12. Some enthusiasts for humanistic education have argued that liberalizing the allegedly "repressive" atmosphere of schools will automatically lead to greater human liberation and more meaningful learning. At the opposite extreme are critics who argue that classroom informality is incompatible with academic achievement and intellectual excellence. What are the real issues involved in this perennial debate?

13. A venerable cliché in education insists on teaching "the whole child." What does this mean? One can "teach" in the sense of conveying information. One can also help foster certain skills. What about feelings and emotions? Can these be taught? How are values acquired? What is "affective education"? What specific teaching practices might be expected to *reinforce* the age-old dichotomy drawn between reason and emotion, intellect and feeling (illustrated perhaps in the comment, "I learned algebra but I also learned to hate algebra").

14. React to, and comment upon, the following: "There are matters beyond the intellectual which are in desperate need of attention. To focus entirely upon objectivity and the development of the outer person fulfills but half the responsibility. It becomes equally essential to attend to the subjective aspects of the inner person which include: interest, attitudes, values, appreciation, and adjustment. Objectives which represent the cognitive domain, through the development of intellectual abilities and skills, re-

main important, but they must be set in proper balance and perspective with those affective or subjective aspects of the person which are of profound significance if a complete educational experience is to be provided" (cited in *ASCD News Exchange* 19 (January 1977): 6). What implications follow for the management and assessment of school instruction?

15. Robert Rosenthal and his associates have argued for the existence of a so-called "Pygmalion effect" in schools, such that students tend to conform to their teachers' expectations of them. Thus, for example, allegedly students do better with teachers who create a warm social-emotional classroom environment, who provide extensive "feedback" to student performance, who vary instructional materials, and who offer ample opportunities for students to respond to questions. Assuming these findings are accurate, are they more consistent with one type of classroom management system than another? Does the Pygmalion effect provide any special warrant for an "open" format over a more traditional one? Or could a teacher exploit the phenomenon in *any* type of teaching-learning situation?

16. Is classroom competition necessarily undesirable? Or can it be a healthy way to stimulate student motivation? Under what circumstances can it prove psychologically damaging or injurious to learning? When might it be helpful?

17. How important is the "interpersonal relationship" between teacher and learner? Does its importance differ, depending on the age of the learners involved? Is it always necessary for teachers to be warm, accepting, and supportive in order for learning to take place?

18. Legal considerations aside, what inalienable moral rights should children of all ages enjoy in school? What student rights or prerogatives must a teacher respect and never infringe upon? Correlatively, what responsibilities are all schoolchildren morally bound to observe? Do teachers also have moral rights, and if so, what are they?

19. Does the concept of "learning readiness" have any validity or special meaning for the organization and sequencing of school curricula? For example, it is often claimed that learning to read or acquiring a foreign language should begin well before the age of six. If so, why is so little support and concern given to early-childhood education? Why are certain learning activities delayed past the point of maximum readiness?

20. In what sense may be said that the distinction between "curriculum" and "instruction" is fundamentally mistaken or artificial? Is it true, as some have claimed, that *how* you are taught is *what* you learn? Is the "medium" of instruction really the educational "message" as well? Does a method of instruction predefine the content of a curriculum? Can the two concepts be treated separately or are they indistinguishable from each other?

21. Some critics claim that the issue of "freedom" in education is usually misconstrued. The removal of adult authority from a given group of children does not necessarily free them—they are simply sentenced to the tyranny of their peers or their own impulses. Likewise, education as something developed from within, as opposed to something formed from without, is said to be a "phony" distinction—*active* teaching, building upon a child's experience, but *directing* its subsequent development, it is claimed, is essential for socially relevant learning. Others claim adult in-

tervention constitutes an invasion of a learner's freedom. Discuss and evaluate these arguments.

22. Upon what does the "authority" of a teacher in a classroom depend? Is there a difference between being "authoritarian" and being "authoritative"? If so, what is the significance of the distinction? What is the difference between legitimate authority and its illegitimate exercise in education?

23. Is "behaviorism" in education inherently antihumanistic? Why or why not? Might one not argue, for example, that programmed instruction, mastery learning, behavioral contracts, criterion-referenced assessment and evaluation, classroom token economies and so forth, all represent valuable ways of individualizing and promoting success in learning and hence are supportive of humanistic values in education?

24. From an anthropological or sociological point of view, one of the major roles of the school is to pass on the culture. To each new generation a cultural inheritance or set of traditions is imparted. Civilization depends upon some measure of intergenerational continuity in terms of a shared culture. Is open or informal or humanistic education sufficiently responsive to this age-old imperative?

25. Can open or free or informal education in the humanistic tradition have any aim or goal beyond that of individual personal development and self-actualization? Why or why not? For example, could humanistic learning have larger social import, affecting society at large?

26. The idea of open education at the elementary-school level is reasonably well defined, both in theory and practice. Less well developed, perhaps, is the idea of an "open" high school. How might educational humanism as an outlook or perspective on schooling find concrete, tangible expression in a college or university? How might one recognize or define "humanistic" education at the collegiate level? What institutional characteristics best exemplify "humane" postsecondary education?

27. Many humanistic reformers have attempted to experiment with open, individualized education, only to end up thoroughly disillusioned, arguing that "kids can't be trusted." Many students thrive on responsibility but find it difficult to accept. What are the necessary conditions for "trust" in formal schooling—as exemplified by an "honor" system to safeguard against cheating, an "open shelf" system for the school library or media center, student mobility in hall corridors, and so on? When does trusting students work and when does it fail? Under what circumstances—or within what limits—can or should teachers trust their students?

28. Radical school critics argue that truly "free" learning is possible only in schools independent of the social, economic, and political controls exercised over education by a basically conservative establishment. Assess this claim.

29. Who runs public education in this country? Who are the people in federal, state, and local agencies that help shape public policy affecting schools? What kinds of people hold administrative positions of responsibility in colleges, universities, and public elementary and secondary schools? Who make up the membership of boards of trustees or orators, or boards of education? Are any generalizations about their members possible? Are "leaders" in education likely to be representative of the nation's population as a whole in terms of sex, age, race, ethnic orgin, socioeconomic

class, occupation, religious affiliation, or political persuasion? Do schools generally reflect the interests and values of those who govern or manage them?

30. Some writers on education argue that the school as a social institution is simply a microcosm of the larger society that sustains it. The values, beliefs, assumptions, procedures, and behaviors reinforced in schools more or less "correspond" with those found to prevail within the surrounding social order. Hence, it is claimed, it is futile to attempt to change schools without accompanying changes occurring in society. Schooling, in other words, affords no leverage for social change. And since inducing large-scale societal change is extraordinarily difficult, if not impossible, reforms aimed at effecting internal changes within schools are likewise impossible, futile, or self-defeating. Critique this argument.

31. Students from a very early age onward are under pressure to perform well and to get good grades. They learn the importance of "psyching out" the teacher, of getting the "right answer," of giving back whatever he or she wants. They study less to learn than to pass the test. When they are successful, they become extraordinarily adept at strategies for survival. They come to appreciate the value of credentials. Under such a system, one emphasizing competition, grades, and credentials, is it possible for learning to be "free" or "open"? If schools—and society at large—penalize certain behaviors and reward others, and if the desired behaviors are antithetical to real or meaningful learning, how can education be "humanized"? Is reform possible? Are humanistic changes in schools that run counter to the technocratic or materialistic values that dominate the undergirding culture possible or even desirable?

32. Several years ago a *New York Times* editorial cited the comment of a student who, reacting to pressures to decide upon a career, remarked sadly, "Adolescence has been an American luxury, but we can't afford it anymore." The editorialist's point was that today's adolescents have fewer opportunities for leisure, for social life, and for self-exploration than a generation ago. Does your own personal experience bear out this contention? How "serious" a student were you in elementary school or in high school? What about in college? To the extent that it is possible to generalize, how have pressures to prepare for adulthood affected your own schooling and your responses to school experiences?

33. If you were the parent of a school-age child, what kind of school would you prefer for that child? Assuming a choice were available between a permissive open school and a more traditional school, which would you select and why? What factors would weigh most heavily in your decision? What kind of school would you personally most like to have attended as a child?

## FURTHER READING

ARCHAMBAULT, REGINALD D., ed. *Dewey on Education, Appraisals.* New York: Random House, 1966.
———. *Dewey on Education, Selected Writings.* New York: Modern Library, 1964.
ASHTON-WARNER, SYLVIA. *Teacher.* New York: Bantam, 1971.

BARTH, ROLAND S. *Open Education and the American School.* New York: Agathon Press, 1972.
BENDINER, ROBERT. *The Politics of Schools, A Crisis in Self-Government.* New York: Mentor, 1969.
BILLINGS, HELEN K. *Are Schools Destroying Our Children?* Columbia, S.C.: Southeastern University Press, 1975.
BIRMINGHAM, JOHN. *Our Time Is Now: Notes from the High School Underground.* New York: Praeger, 1970.
BLACKIE, JOHN. *Inside the Primary School.* New York: Schocken, 1971.
BLITZ, BARBARA. *The Open Classroom, Making It Work.* Boston: Allyn & Bacon, 1973.
BODE, BOYD H. *Fundamentals of Education.* New York: Macmillan, 1921.
———. *How We Learn.* Boston: Heath, 1940.
———. *Modern Educational Theories.* New York: Macmillan, 1927.
———. *Progressive Education at the Crossroads.* New York: Newsome and Company, 1938.
BORTON, TERRY. *Reach, Touch and Teach.* New York: McGraw-Hill, 1970.
BOYD, WILLIAM. *The Educational Theory of Jean-Jacques Rousseau.* New York: Longmans, Green, 1964.
———, ed. *The Emile of Jean-Jacques Rousseau.* New York: Teachers College Press, Columbia University, 1960.
BROWN, GEORGE ISAAC. *Human Teaching for Human Learning, An Introduction To Confluent Education.* New York: Viking, 1971.
BULL, RICHARD E. *Summerhill U.S.A.* New York: Penguin, 1970.
CASS, JOAN, and D.E.M. GARDNER. *The Role of the Teacher in the Infant and Nursery School.* London: Pergasson Press, 1965.
CHILDS, JOHN L. *American Pragmatism and Education.* New York: Holt, Rinehart & Winston, 1956.
———. *Education and the Philosophy of Experimentalism.* New York: Century, 1931.
COMBS, ARTHUR, ed. *Humanistic Education: Objectives and Assessment.* Alexandria, Va.: Association for Supervision and Curriculum Development, 1979.
CRARY, RYLAND W. *Humanizing the School.* New York: Knopf, 1969.
CREMIN, LAWRENCE A. *The Transformation of the School.* New York: Knopf, 1962.
DAVIS, DAVID C. L. *A Model for Humanistic Education.* Columbus, Oh.: Chas. E. Merrill, 1971.
DECKER, SUNNY. *An Empty Spoon.* New York: Harper & Row, 1969.
DEGUIMPS, ROGER. *Pestalozzi: His Life and Work,* trans. J. Russell. New York: Appleton-Century-Crofts, 1895.
DENNISON, GEORGE. *The Lives of Children.* New York: Vintage, 1969.
DEWEY, JOHN. *Democracy and Education.* New York: Macmillan, 1916.
———, and EVELYN DEWEY. *Experience and Education.* New York: Macmillan, 1938.
———. *Schools of To-Morrow.* New York: Dutton, 1915.
DIVOKY, DIANE, ed. *How Old Will You Be in 1984?* New York: Avon, 1969.
DOOB, HEATHER SIDOR. *Evaluations of Alternative Schools.* Arlington, Va.: Educational Research Service, 1977.
DWORKIN, MARTIN S., ed. *Dewey on Education, Selections.* New York: Bureau of Publications, Teachers College, Columbia University, 1964.
ERLICH, JOHN, and SUSAN ERLICH, eds. *Student Power, Participation and Revolution.* New York: Association Press, 1970.
FANTINI, MARIO. *Public Schools of Choice.* New York: Simon & Schuster, 1973.
FARBER, JERRY. *The Student As Nigger.* New York: Pocket Books, 1970.
FEATHERSTONE, JOSEPH. *Schools Where Children Learn.* New York: Avon, 1971.
FISHER, ROBERT J. *Learning How to Learn.* New York: Harcourt, Brace, Jovanovich, 1973.
FRIEDENBERG, EDGAR Z. *Coming of Age in America.* New York: Vintage, 1967.
———. *The Dignity of Youth and Other Atavisms.* Boston: Beacon Press, 1966.
GLASSER, WILLIAM. *Schools Without Failure.* New York: Harper & Row, 1969.
GONZALEZ, GILBERT G. *Progressive Education: A Marxist Interpretation.* Minneapolis: MEP Publications, 1982.
GOODMAN, PAUL. *Compulsory Mis-education/The Community of Scholars.* New York: Vintage, 1962.
———. *Growing Up Absurd.* New York: Random House, 1960.
———. *New Reformation: Notes of a Neolithic Conservative.* New York: Random House, 1970.
GRAUBARD, ALLEN. *Free the Children: Radical Reform and the Free School Movement.* New York: Pantheon, 1972.

GREENBERG, HERBERT M. *Teaching with Feeling.* Indianapolis: Pegasus, 1969.
GREENE, MAXINE. *Teacher as Stranger.* Belmont, Cal.: Wadsworth, 1973.
GROSS, RONALD, and BEATRICE GROSS, eds. *Radical School Reform.* New York: Simon & Schuster, 1969.
HART, HAROLD H., ed. *Summerhill: For and Against.* New York: Hart, 1970.
HASKINS, JIM. *Diary of a Harlem Schoolteacher.* New York: Hart, 1970.
HEARN, D. D., J. BURDIN, and L. KATZ, eds. *Current Research and Perspectives in Open Education.* Washington: American Association of Elementary-Kindergarten-Nursery Educators, 1972.
HENTOFF, NAT. *Our Children Are Dying.* New York: Grove Press, 1969.
HERDON, JAMES. *The Way It Spozed to Be.* New York: Simon & Schuster, 1968.
HERTZBERG, ALVIN, and EDWARD STONE. *Schools Are For Children: An American Approach to the Open Classroom.* New York: Schocken, 1971.
HILL, BRIAN V. *Education and the Endangered Individual.* New York: Dell, 1975.
HOLT, JOHN. *How Children Fail.* New York: Dell, 1965.
———. *How Children Learn.* New York: Pitman, 1969.
———. *The Underachieving School.* New York: Pitman, 1969.
———. *What Do I Do Monday?* New York: Dutton, 1970.
KEATS, JOHN. *The Sheepskin Psychosis.* New York: Dell, 1965.
KELLY, EARL. *In Defense of Youth.* Englewood Cliffs, N.J.: Prentice-Hall, 1962.
KOHL, HERBERT. *The Open Classroom.* New York: New York Review Books, 1969.
———. *36 Children.* New York: New American Library, 1967.
KOZOL, JONATHAN. *Free Schools.* Boston: Houghton Mifflin, 1972.
———. *The Night Is Dark and I Am Far from Home.* Boston: Houghton Mifflin, 1975.
LEEPER, ROBERT R., ed. *Humanizing Education: The Person in the Process.* Washington, D.C.: Association for Supervision and Curriculum Development, 1967.
LEMBO, JOHN M., ed. *Learning and Teaching in Today's Schools.* Columbus, Oh.: Chas. E. Merrill, 1972.
LEONARD, GEORGE. *Education and Ecstasy.* New York: Delacorte, 1970.
LERNER, MAX. *Education and a Radical Humanism.* Columbus, Oh.: Ohio State University Press, 1962.
LYON, HAROLD C. *Learning to Feel—Feeling to Learn.* Columbus, Oh.: Chas. E. Merrill, 1971.
MACRORIE, KENNETH. *Up Taught.* New York: Hayden, 1970.
MARSHALL, SYBIL. *An Experiment in Education.* Cambridge, England: Cambridge University Press, 1966.
MAYHEW, KATHERN C., and ANNA CAMP EDWARDS. *The Dewey School.* New York: Appleton-Century-Crofts, 1936.
MCCALLISTER, WILLIAM J. *The Growth of Freedom in Education.* London: Constable and Company, 1931.
MONTESSORI, MARIA. *The Absorbent Mind.* Wheaton, Ill.: Theosophical Press, 1964.
———. *The Montessori Method.* New York: Schocken, 1964.
———. *The Secret of Childhood.* Calcutta: Orient Longmans, 1963.
———. *Spontaneous Activity in Education.* New York: Schocken, 1965.
———. *What You Should Know About Your Child.* Wheaton, Ill.: Theosophical Press, 1963.
MURROW, CASEY, and LIZA MURROW. *Children Come First: The Inspired Work of English Primary Schools.* New York: American Heritage Press, 1971.
NEIL, A. S. *Summerhill, A Radical Approach to Child-Rearing.* New York: Hart, 1960.
NORDSTROM, CARL, *Society's Children: A Study of Ressentiment in the Secondary School.* New York: Random House, 1967.
NYQUIST, EWALD B., and GENE R. HAWES, eds. *Open Education, A Sourcebook For Parents and Teachers.* New York: Bantam, 1972.
O'GORMAN, N., ed. *The Storefront.* New York: Harper Colophon, 1970.
PEPENOE, J., ed. *Inside Summerhill.* New York: Hart, 1969.
PERRONE, VITO. *Open Education: Promise and Problems.* Bloomington, Ind.: Phi Delta Kappa Educational Foundation, 1972.
POSTMAN, NEIL, and CHARLES WEINGARTNER. *Teaching As A Subversive Activity.* New York: Delta, 1969.
———. *The School Book.* New York: Delacorte Press, 1973.
———. *The Soft Revolution.* New York: Delta, 1971.

PRATT, CAROLINE. *I Learn From Children.* New York: Cornerstone Library, 1970.
RATHBONE, CHARLES, ed. *Open Education: The Informal Classroom.* New York: Citation Press, 1971.
REICH, CHARLES A. *The Greening of America.* New York: Random House, 1970.
REVEL, JEAN-FRANCOIS. *Without Marx or Jesus.* New York: Doubleday, 1970.
ROGERS, CARL R. *Freedom to Learn.* Columbus, Oh.: Chas. E. Merrill, 1969.
———. *On Becoming a Person.* Boston: Houghton Mifflin, 1961.
ROGERS, VINCENT R., ed. *Teaching in the British Primary School.* New York: Macmillan, 1970.
ROSZAK, THEODORE. *The Making of a Counter Culture.* New York: Anchor Books, 1969.
RYAN, KEVIN, ed. *Don't Smile Until Christmas.* Chicago: University of Chicago Press, 1970.
SCHRAG, PETER. *Village School Downtown.* Boston: Beacon Press, 1967.
SILBERMAN, CHARLES E. *Crisis in the Classroom, The Remaking of American Education.* New York: Random House, 1970.
———. *The Open Classroom Reader.* New York: Vintage, 1973.
SILBERMAN, MELVIN L. *The Experience of Schooling.* New York: Holt, Rinehart & Winston, 1971.
SODERQUIST, HAROLD O. *The Person and Education.* Columbus, Oh.: Chas. E. Merrill, 1964.
TAYLOR, HAROLD. *Students Without Teachers: The Crisis in the University.* New York: Avon, 1970.
TROOST, CORNELIUS J., ed. *Radical School Reform.* Boston: Little, Brown, 1973.
WALBERG, HERBERT J., and SUSAN C. THOMAS. *Characteristics of Open Education—A Look at the Literature for Teachers.* Newton, Mass.: Education Development Center, 1971.
WALMSLEY, JOHN. *Neill and Summerhill, A Man and His Work.* New York: Penguin, 1970.
WEBER, LILLIAN. *The English Infant School and Informal Education.* Englewood Cliffs, N.J.: Prentice-Hall, 1971.
WEES, W. R. *Nobody Can Teach Anyone Anything.* New York: Doubleday, 1971.
WIRTH, ARTHUR. *John Dewey as Educator.* New York: John Wiley, 1966.

## NOTES

1. Jacques Maritain, "A New Approach to God," in Ruth Nanda Anshen, ed., *Our Emergent Civilization* (New York: Harper & Row, 1947), pp. 286, 287.

2. Gordon Childe, *Man Makes Himself* (New York: Mentor, 1951).

3. In Julian Huxley, ed., *The Humanist Frame* (London: Allen and Unwin, 1961), p. 44.

4. Julian Huxley, *Religion Without Revelation* (New York: Mentor, 1957), p. 195.

5. See Eugene Kevane, *Augustine the Educator* (Westiminster, Md.: Newman Press, 1964), p. 33.

6. C. C. Swinton, *The Autobiography of Guibert, Abbot of Nogent-sous-Couey* (New York: E. P. Dutton, 1926), p. 24.

7. Cited in William J. McCallister, *The Growth of Freedom in Education* (London: Constable, 1931), p. 67.

8. Cited in ibid., pp. 11–112.

9. Quoted in Pierre Villey, *Montaigne devant la posterite* (Paris: Boivin, 1935), p. 147. See also the commentary in Michel Joubert, "Montaigne the Educator," *Contemporary Review* 146 (December, 1934): 722–729.

10. Cited in McCallister, *Growth of Freedom,* p. 84.

11. Quoted in ibid., p. 163.

12. M. W. Keatinge, trans., *The Great Didactic of John Amos Comenius* (New York: Russell and Russell, 1907), p. 250.

13. See McCallister, *Growth of Freedom,* p. 231.

14. William Boyd, ed., *The Emile of Jean-Jacques Rousseau* (New York: Teachers College Press, Columbia University, 1960), p. 180.

15. Ibid., p. 178.

16. See Jack H. Broome, *Rousseau: A Study of His Thought* (New York: Barnes and Noble, 1963); Thomas Davidson, *Rousseau and Education According to Nature* (New York: Scribner's, 1898); William Boyd, *Emile for Today* (London: Heinemann, 1964); William Boyd, *The Educational Theory of Jean Jacques Rousseau* (New York: Longmans, Green, 1964).

17. Roger DeGuimps, *Pestalozzi: His Life and Work,* trans., J. Russell (New York: Appleton-Century-Crofts, 1895), pp. 47, 48.

18. Cited in Christopher J. Lucas, *Challenge and Choice in Contemporary Education* (New York: Macmillan, 1976), pp. 178, 179; and Christopher J. Lucas, *Our Western Educational Heritage* (New York: Macmillan, 1972), pp. 445, 446.

19. Quoted in Herold H. Hart, *Summerhill: For and Against* (New York: Hart, 1970), pp. 49, 50.

20. A. S. Neill, *Summerhill: A Radical Approach to Child-Rearing* (New York: Hart, 1960), p. 12.

21. Ibid., p. 293.

22. Ibid.

23. Hart, *For and Against*, p. 8.

24. Maria Montessori, *The Secret of Childhood* (Calcutta: Orient Longmans, 1963), p. 114.

25. Ibid., p. 129.

26. E. M. Standing, ed., *The Child in the Church* (St. Paul, Minn.: Catechetical Guild, 1965), p. 7.

27. Maria Montessori, *The Montessori Method* (New York: Schocken, 1964), p. 15.

28. Ibid., pp. 95-98.

29. Maria Montessori, *The Absorbent Mind* (Wheaton, Ill.: Theosophical Press, 1964), p. 205.

30. Maria Montessori, *Spontaneous Activity in Education* (New York: Schocken, 1965), p. 43.

31. Ibid., p. 70.

32. Montessori, *Montessori Method*, p. 87.

33. Maria Montessori, *What You Should Know About Your Child* (Wheaton, Ill.: Theosophical Press, 1963), p. 131.

34. Timothy L. Smith, "Progressivism in American Education, 1880-1900," *Harvard Educational Review* 31 (Spring 1961): 169.

35. See Paul Douglas, *American Apprenticeship and Industrial Education* (New York: Columbia University Press, 1921), pp. 53-85; and Oscar Handlin, *The Uprooted: The Epic Story of the Great Migrations that Made the American People* (Boston: Little, Brown, 1951), pp. 63-116.

36. Smith, "Progressivism," p. 171. See also Gilbert G. Gonzalez, *Progressive Education: A Marxist Interpretation* (Minneapolis: MEP Publications, 1982).

37. Smith, "Progressivism," p. 171.

38. See Joseph Buchanan, *The New Education* (New York: Outlook, 1903), pp. 104ff.

39. Quoted in Smith, "Progressivism," pp. 186-187.

40. William James, "Talks to Teachers," in R. B. Perry, ed., *The Thought and Character of William James* (Boston: Little, Brown, 1935), pp. 23-24.

41. Ibid., pp. 36, 87, 96, 125.

42. G. Max Wingo, *Philosophies of Education: An Introduction* (Lexington, Mass.: Heath, 1974), p. 148. See also Lawrence A. Cremin, *The Transformation of the School* (New York: Knopf, 1962), chapter 1.

43. John Dewey and Evelyn Dewey, *Schools of To-Morrow* (New York: Dutton, 1915), p. 294.

44. See Lawrence A. Cremin, "John Dewey and the Progressive Education Movement, 1915-1952," in Reginald D. Archambault, ed., *Dewey on Education, Appraisals* (New York: Random House, 1966), pp. 10-25.

45. Ibid., p. 13.

46. John Dewey, "The School and Society," in Martin S. Dworkin, ed., *Dewey on Education, Selections* (New York: Bureau of Publications; Teachers College, Columbia University, 1964), pp. 50-51.

47. See John Dewey, *Democracy and Education* (New York: Macmillan, 1916), p. 138; and Dewey, *The School and Society* (Chicago: University of Chicago Press, 1899), pp. 124-125.

48. Dewey, "The Child and the Curriculum," in Dworkin, *Dewey, Selections,* p. 95.

49. For an account of the Chicago Laboratory School, see Kathern C. Mayhew and Anna Camp Edwards, *The Dewey School* (New York: Appleton-Century-Crofts, 1936).

50. See Reginald D. Archambault, ed., *Dewey on Education, Selected Writings* (New York: Modern Library, 1964), pp. xxiii–xxiv.

51. Dewey, "The Child and the Curriculum," in Dworkin, *Dewey, Selections,* p. 96.

52. Ibid., p. 96.

53. Dewey, *Democracy and Education,* p. 231.

54. Dewey, "My Pedagogic Creed," in Dworkin, *Dewey, Selections,* p. 21.

55. Ibid., pp. 21–22.

56. Dewey, *Democracy and Education,* p. 126.

57. Ibid., p. 62.

58. Dewey, "My Pedogogic Creed," in Dworkin, *Dewey, Selections,* pp. 22–24.

59. E. C. Moore, "John Dewey's Contributions to Educational Theory," in *John Dewey, the Man and His Philosophy* (Cambridge, Mass.: Harvard University Press, 1930), p. 23.

60. See William Heard Kilpatrick, *Foundations of Method* (New York: Macmillan, 1925).

61. George S. Counts, *Dare the School Build a New Social Order?* New York: Harper and Row, 1932.

62. Cited in James Bowen, *A History of Western Education,* vol. 3 (London: Methuen and Company, 1981), p. 434.

63. John Dewey, "Education and Social Change," *The Social Frontier 3* (May 1937): 237.

64. Ibid., p. 238.

65. Ibid.

66. Boyd H. Bode, *Fundamentals of Education* (New York: Macmillan, 1921), pp. 241–242.

67. Boyd H. Bode, *Modern Educational Theories* (New York: Macmillan, 1972), p. 163.

68. Boyd H. Bode, *Progressive Education at the Crossroads* (New York: Newsome and Company, 1938), pp. 43–44.

69. Dewey, *Experience and Education* (New York: Macmillan, 1938).

70. Quoted in Bowen, *Western Education,* p. 439.

71. Jerome Bruner, "After John Dewey, What?" in Archambault, *Dewey, Appraisals,* p. 213.

72. Ibid., pp. 214–215.

73. Note the commentary in Edward J. Power, *The Transit of Learning* (Sherman Oaks, Cal.: Alfred Publishing Company, 1979), pp. 366–367.

74. Neil Postman and Charles Weingartner. *The School Book* (New York: Delacorte Press, 1973), p. 5.

75. See Julius Menacker and Erwin Pollack, "The Challenge of Accountability," in Julius Menacker and Erwin Pollack, eds., *Emerging Educational Issues, Conflicts and Contrasts* (Boston: Little, Brown, 1974), pp. 357–398; and Leon M. Lessinger and Ralph W. Tyler, eds., *Accountability in Education* (Worthington, Oh.: Chas. A. Jones Publishing Company, 1971), pp. 1–6.

76. John L. Hayman, Jr. "The Systems Approach and Education," *Education Forum* 38 (May 1974): 493–501.

77. See Ludwig von Bertalanffy, *General System Theory: Foundations, Development, Applications* (New York: George Braziller, 1968), p. 4; and Mohammed A. A. Shami, Martin Hershkowitz, and Khalida K. Shami, "Dimensions of Accountability," *NASSP Bulletin* 58 (September 1974): 1–12.

78. Belatti Banathy, *Instructional Systems* (Palo Alto, Cal.: Fearon Publisher, 1968), *passim.*

79. See H. Thomas James, *The New Cult of Efficiency and Education* (Pittsburgh: University of Pittsburgh Press, 1969).

80. W. Robert Houston and Robert B. Howsam, eds., *Competency-Based Teacher Education* (Chicago: Science Research Associates, 1972); and W. David Maxwell, "PBTE: A Case of the Emperor's New Clothes," *Phi Delta Kappan* 55 (January 1974): 306–311.

81. Consult B. F. Skinner, *Science and Human Behavior* (New York: Macmillan, 1953).

82. John B. Watson, *Behavior, An Introduction to Comparative Psychology* (New York: Holt, 1914).

83. B. F. Skinner, "Behaviorism at Fifty," in T. W. Wann, ed., *Behaviorism and Phenomenology* (Chicago: University of Chicago Press, 1964), p. 79.

84. B. F. Skinner, *Science and Human Behavior*, p. 33.

85. Ibid., p. 402.

86. See B. F. Skinner, *The Technology of Teaching* (New York: Appleton-Century-Crofts, 1968); and Skinner, "Are Theories of Learning Necessary?" *Psychological Review* 57 (July 1950): 192–193ff.

87. Quoted in Lucas, *Contemporary Education*, p. 79. See B. F. Skinner, "The Science of Learning and the Art of Teaching," *Harvard* Educational Review 24 (Spring 1954): 86–97.

88. See, for example, Michael Scriven, "A Study of Radical Behaviorism," in Herbert Feigland and Michael Scriven, eds., *The Foundations of Science and the Concepts of Psychology and Psychoanalysis* (Minneapolis: University of Minnesota Press, 1963), p. 121ff.; Harvey Wheeler, "Social and Philosophical Implications of Behavior Modification," *Center Report* 5 (1972): 3–5; Michael B. McMahon, "Positivism and the Public Schools," *Phi Delta Kappan* 51 (June 1970): 515ff.; L. B. Resnick, "Programmed Instruction and the Teaching of Complex Intellectual Skills," *Harvard Educational Review* 33 (Fall 1963): 467–468; Fred Guggeheim, "Curriculum Implications and Applications of Programmed Instruction," *School Review* 73 (Spring 1965): 60–64; the discussion on Skinner in James McClellan, *Toward an Effective Critique of American Education* (Philadelphia: Lippincott, 1968); and the critique in Van Cleve Morris and Young Pai, *Philosophy and the American School* (Boston: Houghton Mifflin, 1976), pp. 330–349.

89. James F. Day, "Behavioral Technology: A Negative Stand," *Intellect* 102 (February 1974): 304–305.

90. B. F. Skinner, "The Free and Happy Student," *New York University Education Quarterly* 4 (Winter 1973): 2–6. See also B. F. Skinner, *Beyond Freedom and Dignity* (New York: Knopf, 1971) p. 42.

91. Skinner, *Beyond Freedom*, pp. 102–104.

92. Abraham H. Maslow, *The Psychology of Science* (Chicago: Henry Regnery, 1966), pp. 9–10.

93. Maslow, *Toward a Psychology of Being* (New York: D. Van Nostrand, 1962): pp. 170–200.

94. Arthur W. Combs and Donald Snygg, *Individual Behavior* (New York: Harper & Row, 1959), p. 20.

95. Gordon W. Allport, *Personality: A Psychological Interpretation* (New York: Holt, Rinehart & Winston, 1937), p. 3.

96. Gordon W. Allport, *Becoming* (New Haven: Yale University Press, 1955); p. 28; and Gordon W. Allport, *The Nature of Personality: Selected Papers* (Cambridge, Mass.: Addison-Wesley, 1950), pp. 128–129.

97. Edgar Z. Friedenberg, *The Dignity of Youth and Other Atavisms* (Boston: Beacon Press, 1966), p. 23.

98. Abraham H. Maslow, *Motivation and Personality* (New York: Harper & Row, 1954), chapters 5 and 12. Maslow, *Psychology of Being*, p. 129.

99. Maslow, *Motivation*, chapter 12. p. 197.

100. Combs and Snygg, *Behavior*, p. 45.

101. Carl R. Rogers, *Freedom to Learn* (Columbus, Oh.: Chas. E. Merrill, 1969), p. 295.

102. Abraham H. Maslow, *The Farther Reaches of Human Nature* (New York: Viking, 1971), p. 189–190.

103. See Harold C. Lyon, *Learning to Feel—Feeling to Learn* (Columbus, Oh.: Chas. E. Merrill, 1971). Note also the relevant discussions in Herbert Greenberg, *Teaching With Feeling* (Indianapolis: Pegasus, 1969); Terry Borton, *Reach, Touch and Teach* (New York: McGraw-Hill, 1970); and in George Isaac Brown, *Human Teaching For Human Learning, An Introduction to Confluent Education* (New York: Viking, 1971).

104. Rogers, *Freedom to Learn*, p. 153.

105. Carl R. Rogers, "The Interpersonal Relationship in the Facilitation of Learning," in Rogert R. Leeper, ed., *Humanizing Education: The Person in the Process* (Washington, D.C.: Association for Supervision and Curriculum Development, 1967), p. 1.

106. Ibid., pp. 2–3.

107. Ibid., pp. 7–12. For a critique of Rogers's views, consult R. S. Peters, "On Freedom to Learn," *Interchange* 1 (1970): 111–114.

108. Rogers, *Freedom to Learn,* p. 279.

109. Combs and Snygg, *Behavior,* p. 412.

110. John Holt, *How Children Fail* (New York: Bell, 1965), pp. 207–210; and John Holt, *How Children Learn* (New York: Pitman, 1969), p. vii.

111. Rogers, *Freedom to Learn,* p. 269.

112. Rogers, "Facilitation of Learning," p. 3.

113. Theodore Roszak, *The Making of a Counter-Culture* (New York: Anchor Books, 1969).

114. Jerry Farber, *The Student As Nigger* (New York: Pocket Books, 1970), pp. 13–15.

115. Ibid., p. 90.

116. Ibid., p. 91.

117. Ibid., p. 92.

118. Ibid., pp. 92–93.

119. Ibid., pp. 95, 98.

120. Ibid., p. 99.

121. Ibid.

122. Ibid.

123. Ibid., p. 17.

124. Neil Postman and Charles Weingartner, *Teaching As A Subversive Activity* (New York: Delta, 1969), pp. 14–15.

125. Ibid., p. 3.

126. Ibid., p. 19.

127. Ibid., pp. 2, 218.

128. Helen K. Billings, *Are Schools Destroying Our Children?* (Columbia, S.C.: Southeastern University Press, 1975), pp. ix–x.

129. Ibid., p. 72.

130. Ibid., pp. vii, 42.

131. Ronald Gross, "From Innovations To Alternatives: A Decade of Change in Education," *Phi Delta Kappan* 53 (September 1971): 23.

132. Charles E. Silberman, *Crisis In the Classroom, The Remaking of American Education* (New York: Vintage, 1971), pp. 10, 11.

133. See also William Glasser, *Schools Without Failure* (New York: Harper & Row, 1969); George Dennison, *The Lives of Children* (New York: Vintage, 1969); George Leonard, *Education and Ecstasy* (New York: Delacorte, 1970); Sybil Marshall, *An Experiment in Education* (Cambridge, England: Cambridge University Press, 1966); and W. R. Wees, *Nobody Can Teach Anyone Anything* (New York: Doubleday, 1971).

134. The Plowden Committee, *Children and Their Primary Schools* (London: Her Majesty's Stationery Office, 1967). See also Joseph Featherstone, *Schools Where Children Learn* (New York: Avon, 1971); and Vincent R. Rogers, ed., *Teaching in the British Primary School* (New York: Macmillan, 1970); and Lillian Weber, *The English Infant School and Informal Education* (Englewood Cliffs, N.J.: Prentice-Hall, 1971).

135. Plowden Committee, *Children,* cited in Ewald B. Nyquist and Gene R. Hawes, eds., *Open Education, A Sourcebook For Parents and Teachers* (New York: Bantam, 1972), p. 25.

136. Ibid., p. 28.

137. Cited in ibid., pp. 46–47.

138. Ibid., p. 9.

139. Featherstone, *Schools,* p. 111ff.

140. Robert J. Taggart, "Open Education Without Professional Autonomy? The English Head Versus The American Principal," *Elementary School Journal* 74 (March 1974): 336–343. See also Robert J. Fisher, *Learning How to Learn* (New York: Harcourt, Brace, Jovanovich, 1972), p. 7.

141. Cited in Nyquist and Hawes, *Open Education,* p. 18.

142. See John Blackie, *Inside the Primary School* (New York: Schocken, 1971); Alvin Hertzberg and Edmund Stone, *Schools Are For Children: An American Approach to the Open Classroom* (New York: Schocken, 1971); Casey Murrow and Liza Murrow, *Children Come First* (New York: American Heritage Press, 1971); Charles Rathbone, ed., *Open Education: The Informal Classroom* (New York: Citation Press, 1971); Charles E. Silberman, *The Open Classroom Reader* (New York: Vintage, 1973); and Roland S. Barth, *Open Education and the American School* (New York: Agathon Press, 1972).

143. See L. G. Katz, "Research On Open Education: Problems and Issues," in D. D. Hearn, J. Burdim and L. Katz, eds., *Current Research And Perspectives In Open Education* (Washington, D.C.: American Association of Elementary-Kindergarten-Nursery Educators, 1972).

144. See Ronald Linder and Daniel Purdom, "Four Dimensions of Openness in Classroom Activities," *Elementary School Journal* 75 (December 1975): 146–151.

145. Silberman, *Crisis In the Classroom,* p. 208.

146. See, for example, Herbert J. Walberg and Susan C. Thomas, "Defining Open Education," *Journal of Research and Development in Education* 8 (1974): 4–13.

147. Robert A. Horwitz, "Psychological Effects of the 'Open Classroom,'" *Review of Educational Research* 49 (Winter 1979): 72–73.

148. Vito Perrone, *Open Education: Promise And Problems* (Bloomington, Ind.: Phi Delta Kappa Educational Foundation, 1972), p. 8.

149. Roland S. Barth, "So You Want To Change To An Open Classroom," *Phi Delta Kappan* 53 (October 1971): 97–99.

150. Ibid., p. 99.

151. Walberg and Thomas, *Characteristics of Open Education—A Look at the Literature for Teachers* (Newton, Mass.: Education Development Center, 1971).

152. Rathbone, *Informal Classroom.*

153. M. Hanif, M. Nawaz, and S. A. Tanveer, "Open Education Versus Back to Basics: An Analysis of the Issues," *Contemporary Education* 50 (Winter 1979): 106–107.

154. Perrone, *Promise and Problems,* p. 7.

155. Horwitz, "Psychological Effects," p. 83.

156. Joseph Featherstone, "Tempering A Fad," cited in Lucas, *Contemporary Education,* p. 204.

157. James W. Bell, "Open Education, Are High Schools Buying It? *Clearing House* 48 (February 1974): 337–338.

158. Alton Harrison, Jr., "Humanism and Educational Reform—The Need for a Balanced Perspective, *Educational Forum* 38 (March 1974): 331–336.

159. William W. Goetz, "The Schools And Their Critics: An Angry Comment From Within The System" *Phi Delta Kappan* 56 (December 1974): 268.

160. Ibid., p. 270.

161. S. Samuel Shermis, "Educational Critics Have Been Wrong All Along: Long Live Tradition!" *Phi Delta Kappan* 55 (February 1974): 403–404.

162. Ibid., p. 406.

163. Jonathan Kozol, "The Open Schoolroom: New Words for Old Deceptions," *Ramparts* 2 (July 1972): 38–41. See also the expanded version of this article as chapter 10 in Jonathan Kozol, *The Night Is Dark and I Am Far from Home* (Boston: Houghton Mifflin, 1975), pp. 95–105.

164. Allen Graubard, "Radical School Reform: Some Ambiguities," in John Martin Rich, ed., *Innovations in Education: Reformers And Their Critics,* 3rd ed. (Boston: Allyn and Bacon, 1981), pp. 286–287.

165. See Allen Graubard, "The Free School Movement," *Harvard Educational Review* 42 (August 1972): 352–355.

166. For a history of the movement, consult Allen Graubard, *Free the Children: Radical Reform and the Free School Movement* (New York: Pantheon, 1972); and for a critique, Jonathan Kozol, *Free Schools* (Boston: Houghton Mifflin, 1972).

167. Richard L. Hopkins, "Open Schools, Free Schools," *School and Community* 50 (March 1974): 28.

168. See Mary Anne Raywid, "The First Decade of Public School Alternatives," *Phi Delta Kappan* 62 (April 1981): 551–554; Barbara J. Case, "Lasting Alternatives: A Lesson in Survival," *Phi Delta Kappan* 62 (April 1981): 554–555; and Robert D. Barr, "Alternatives for the Eighties: A Second Decade of Development," *Phi Delta Kappan* 62 (April 1981): 570–573.

169. See Mario Fantini, *Public Schools of Choice* (New York: Simon & Schuster, 1973); National School Boards Association, *Research Report: Alternative Schools* (Washington: NSBA, 1976); Ford Foundation, *Matters of Choice: A Ford Foundation Report on Alternative Schools* (New York: Ford Foundation, 1974); and Heather Sidor Doob, *Evaluations of Alternative Schools* (Arlington, Va.: Educational Research Service, 1977).

170. Carl R. Rogers, "Beyond the Watershed: And Where Now?" *Educational Leadership* 34 (May 1977): 623.

171. Arthur W. Combs, "Humanistic Education: Too Tender for a Tough World?" *Phi Delta Kappan* 62 (February 1981): 446.

172. Arthur W. Combs, "Affective Education or None at All," *Educational Leadership* 39 (April 1982): 495.

173. Arthur W. Combs, "A Humanist's View," *Educational Leadership* 55 (October 1977): 55.

174. Combs, "Humanistic Education," p. 448.

175. Ibid., p. 449.

176. See Donald L. Halsted, Anne Marie Bober, and Fred Streit, "Open Classroom: A Panacea?" *Educational Forum* 41 (May 1977): 487–491.

177. Ronald L. Williams, "What Happened to the Schools of the Future?" *NASSP Bulletin* 61 (October 1977): 42–46.

178. Roland S. Barth "Open With Care: A Case Study," in Vincent R. Rogers and Bud Church, eds., *Open Education, Critique and Assessment* (Washington, D.C.: Association for Curriculum Development and Research, 1975), p. 55.

179. Thomas E. Gatewood, "How Effective Are Open Classrooms? A Review of the Research," *Childhood Education* 51 (January 1976): 176.

180. Fred M. Hechinger, "Reappraising the Open Classroom," *Saturday Review* 3 (March 1977): 6.

181. Thomas C. Hunt, "Open Education: A Comparison, An Assessment, and a Prediction," *Peabody Journal of Education* 53 (January 1976): 111.

182. Leonard Sealey, "Open Education: Fact or Fiction?" *Teachers College Record* 77 (May 1976): 617–623.

183. Mary Anne Raywid, "The Novel Character of Today's School Criticism," *Educational Leadership* 31 (December 1979): 200.

184. Thomas C. Hunt and Lowell C. Yarusso, "Open Education: Can It Survive Its Critics?" *Peabody Journal of Education* 56–57 (July 1979): 294.

185. John Dewey, "How Much Freedom in New Schools?" in Joseph Ratner, ed., *Education Today* (New York: Greenwood, 1969), p. 222.

186. Robert P. Mai, "Open Education: From Ideology to Orthodoxy," *Peabody Journal of Education* 55 (April 1978): 231–238.

187. Ibid., p. 234.

188. Ibid., p. 233.

189. Richard Hofstadter, *Anti-Intellectualism in American Life* (New York: Vintage, 1966), pp. 373, 385.

190. Mai, "Ideology to Orthodoxy," pp. 234, 236.

191. Neil Postman, "Where Have All The Critics Gone?" *New York Education Quarterly* 9 (Fall 1977): 28–31.

192. Ibid., p. 20.

193. Ibid., p. 21.

194. Ibid.

195. Ibid.

196. Ibid., p. 22.

197. Ibid., p. 23.

198. See Arthur W. Combs, ed., *Humanistic Education: Objectives and Assessment* (Alexandria, Va.: Association for Supervision and Curriculum Development, 1979).

# CHAPTER SEVEN
# SOCIAL RECONSTRUCTION AND FUTURISM
## Education for Human Survival

## INTRODUCTION

Oftentimes it is said that formal education should be "above politics." Schools—especially public institutions—must avoid divisive issues and partisan entanglements. In fact, however, at no time are educational agencies isolated from larger currents, trends, and reform movements in society. Often they figure at the very center of a major social controversy, as when courts must pass on questions having to do with students' rights, admissions policies, tax exemptions, liability, or race relations. The historic 1954 Supreme Court decision in *Brown* v. *Topeka Board of Education* affords a case in point. Repudiating the "separate but equal" doctrine as unconstitutional, the Court held that a dual system of racially segregated schools was illegal. Schools ever since have been embroiled in turmoil surrounding the struggle for racial integration and equality. Scores of other legal decisions on as many different issues might be cited to illustrate how politics and education constantly interact in American society.

Inevitably, political considerations enter into the formulation of local, state, and federal policy affecting education. The same holds true for state and federal legislation influencing everything from program funding and personnel development to school construction and student financial aid. Questions of power, access, and control invariably shape both what schools teach and how they are managed as institutions.

Schools perform numerous social services. Some, such as requiring school-children to be inoculated against disease, are hardly ever challenged. Other measures aimed at furthering some larger external objective are more controversial: mainstreaming, busing, affirmative action, and so on. Nevertheless, pupil assignments to achieve racial "balance" in schools, the placement of handicapped children in regular classrooms, admissions quotas, and so forth mostly concern how schooling is organized or administered. More problematic by far are explicit efforts to gear teaching and curricula to a social need or issue.

On the face of it, trying to solve a social problem directly through formal education seems preposterous. The idea that a teacher in a classroom can say or do anything that might contribute to the resolution of some monumental issue in society appears so farfetched as not to be worth considering at all. But the truth of the matter is that schools are commonly looked to for addressing societal needs extending well beyond the classroom. Some initiatives (such as services rendered in the interest of public health and safety) are relatively innocuous. Others become subjects of lively debate.

Insurance-industry statistics indicate those who successfully complete a driver-education program are less likely to be involved in a fatal accident than those who have not received training. Pressure is applied to include driver education in the school curriculum. Alcohol and drug abuse are common among teenagers. Preventive programs are urged upon schools. Unwanted pregnancies and venereal disease run rampant in the adolescent population. Sex education is offered as a response. Heightened racial tensions suggest a need for human-relations training. The struggle of ethnic minorities for cultural legitimacy and identity prompt calls for multi-cultural education or for programs in, say, Hispanic or Black Studies. Alarmed over an apparent decline in standards of public and private morality, the public appeals for greater emphasis in schools on moral training or "values clarification." Secularism leads to demands in some quarters for "nonsectarian" religious instruction. When surveys reveal widespread ignorance among youth about the workings of the nation's economic system, appropriate education is touted as a possible remedy. Lack of patriotism implies a need for better citizenship instruction.

Environmentalists want more teaching about ecology. Peace activists view the school as the logical place to house peace-and-world-order studies. Feminists push women's studies and the elimination of sexist bias in curricula. Gay-rights defenders make comparable demands. Consumer-protection organizations lobby vigorously for programs of consumer-oriented education, and so on. Sooner or later every group with a social agenda turns to education as a way of furthering its cause.

Business and industry invest considerable sums to produce "free" instructional materials for use in schools. Most subtly endorse the sponsor's products as they promote business values. Unions do the same to advance the views of organized labor, as does the military in its efforts to bolster enlistments. Commercial interests commonly direct public-relations campaigns to children in schools.

Any number of reasons account for efforts to use formal education to promote particular causes. First, schools *are* the places where young people are assembled en masse. Secondly, it is where they are exposed to information. Students may not always assimilate the official curriculum intended, but learning of one sort or another *does* take place. It is unreasonable, for instance, to suppose the average youngster has not acquired *some* knowledge over the course of twelve or more years of instruction. Thirdly, education has public "resonance." Learning is, after all, *for* something—it has consequences that impact upon society. And while an individual teacher with twenty or thirty children in one classroom may not make much of a social difference, hundreds of thousands instructing millions of youngsters might. Hence, the school's potential for helping to bring about social change is rarely overlooked. Out of this appreciation arises the impetus to enlist the aid of education to effect change.

Attempts to use schools to advance specific interests have a long (if not always honorable) history. The inclination to exploit educational institutions for leverage on some larger social problem—prejudice, discrimination, socioeconomic inequality, and so on—is well established in American society. The early colonists, for example, looked to education to foster morality and allegiance to denominational creeds. The nation's founding fathers were sensitive to the need for popular instruction to buttress the fledgling republic. Jacksonian democrats hoped the spread of learning would eradicate lingering vestiges of aristocratic prejudice. Horace Mann, founder of the common-school movement, proclaimed public education was "a great equalizer of the conditions of men, the balance wheel of the social machinery. . . ." Post–Civil War progressivists worked hard to involve the schools in a crusade for social reform.

Besides fostering literacy and maintaining social control, schools have been expected to acculturate immigrants, to promote public morality, to buttress a work ethic, to inculcate patriotic sentiment, to strengthen allegiance to democratic principles, to solve unemployment problems and train the work force, to defuse social conflict, to facilitate interpersonal relations, to encourage protection of the environment, and otherwise further a multitude of social objectives. Sometimes pressure comes from politically conservative forces struggling to preserve the status quo or to return to an antecedent state of affairs. Just as often political liberals and those of a socialist orientation have tried to link educational efforts with major social change. In the latter instance, the elements of something approximating a "tradition" can be discerned. Its major component elements, recast as a formal argument about educational aims and the school's role in society, suggest a series of syllogistic-like propositions, as follows:

1. The province of education is knowledge;
2. Knowledge (as Bacon once observed) is "power";

3. Schools exist to impart knowledge;
4. Therefore, schools should "empower" people.
5. What is most worth knowing is whatever promotes social justice and human survival;
6. The existing social order is unjust and endangers human survival;
7. Radical societal change is required to achieve justice and to secure conditions that make decent human survival possible;
8. Therefore, formal education should be geared to social change.
9. Education as a catalyst for change requires:
    a. supportive attitudes and values; that is, receptivity to change;
    b. relevant information aimed at promoting popular awareness and "consciousness raising" about social issues;
    c. psychological skills needed to anticipate, to adjust to, and to effect needed change;
10. Therefore, schools should emphasize futuristic, change-oriented, "survival" knowledge.

No single rubric or label serves to identify the outlook or perspective implied by the argument. The term "reformism" is perhaps too general and all-encompassing, though it serves to denote a characteristic interest in utilizing education (in conjunction with other forces) to bring about social improvement. Much the same objective applies to a graceless term like "activism." The term "radicalism" offers itself as a convenient possibility: "of, pertinent to, or proceeding from the root; original, fundamental, reaching to the ultimate source" of something. Its virtue is that it suggests a magnitude of reform transcending amelioration or minor adjustments to "business as usual" in society. So does the term "utopianism." Least satisfactory in certain respects but at one time most commonly employed by educational philosophers has been the term "social reconstructionism," designating a point of view stressing the role of education in a "reconstruction" of the social order. Another candidate is "futurism," with its emphasis upon the forward-looking character of the education proponents support. For present purposes, any of these labels will suffice, depending on context and intended emphasis, with the idea of "reconstruction" in the social order as the implicit unifying theme.

## "SOCIAL FRONTIER" THEORY IN EDUCATION

The rise to prominence of a "radical" strain in pedagogical theory was a gradual phenomenon. By the late 1920s, however, tensions within the prevailing progressivist camp were beginning to surface. On the one side was a "child-centered" wing, which retained its long-standing interest in individualized instruction and the psychological growth of children. On the other was a small but distinguished coterie of progressive educational theorists who had begun to move away from preoccupation with questions of freedom for children in schools and to take up issues associated with the *social* conditions upon which such freedom was thought to depend. By 1927 an informal discussion group had been formed around William Heard Kilpatrick at Teachers College, Columbia University. Members included George S. Counts, John L. Childs, R. Bruce Raupp, Harold Rugg, Goodwin Watson, and other notable luminaries of the day. This small group met regularly over the next seven years and intermittently thereafter up until about 1939, when it disbanded. Public expressions of the self-styled ''frontier'' association were to appear in the pages of a journal called *The Social Frontier* (1934–1943), the 1933 yearbook of the National Society of College Teachers of Education entitled *The Education Frontier,* publications of the Educational Policies Commission of the National Education Association, and the American Youth Commission of the American Council on Education. Individual members also drafted numerous articles and books on their own.

The basic thesis shared by all members of the group was that experience-based, pupil-planned activity in the Deweyan mold had proved inadequate in the Depression era. The central task of education, it was explained in *The Educational Frontier,* should be ''to prepare individuals to take part intelligently in the management of conditions under which they will live, to bring them to an understanding of the forces which are moving, [and] to equip them with the intellectual and practical tools by which they can enter, into a direction of these forces.''[1] The key to meeting society's changing requirements was to provide teachers and students with a more profound understanding of pressing issues of the day.

Whereas earlier it had seemed enough to give students opportunities for creative self-expression and growth through a curriculum based upon their own felt needs and interests, the present imperative was to inform students about the larger political, social, and economic forces working in society, about the dislocations brought about by uncontrolled laissez-faire capitalism, and the apparent failure of the nation's economic system to guarantee a stable social order. School programs, as John Dewey and John L. Childs argued, ''should have definite reference to the needs and issues which mark and divide our domestic, economic, and political life in the generation of which we are part.''[2]

The plea they issued was for a new, more directive kind of education, which would send into society persons better able to understand the social order, to live intelligently as effective citizens within it, and upon an intelligent appraisal of its future needs, to change it to suit the vision of a better life for all. Educational change could only be ''correlative and interactive'' with political change, but without the help of education no social innovations would be likely to succeed or endure. The public school, in essence, should serve as an instrument of social reconstruction, bringing about a new form of social organization grounded in intelligent foresight, rational planning, and respect for the moral equality of all persons.

No one was a more forceful and eloquent defender of the new radicalism in educational thought than George S. Counts. In 1922 he published a study of high-school dropouts, *The Selective Character of American Secondary Education,* in which he indicted schools for perpetuating gross inequalities based on racial, ethnic, and class origins.[3] A similar study five years later documented class bias in the composition of school boards, showing domination by attorneys, physicians, bankers, and merchants. A 1929 volume entitled *Secondary Education and Industrialism* advanced the argument that while schools could never be direct agents of change in society, they still had a crucial role to play in making change possible. All of these themes were brought together in a remarkable manifesto-like work published in 1932, *Dare the School Build a New Social Order?* Written over half a century ago, much of it sounds as fresh and pertinent today as when first written. Here Counts supplied a sort of credo for the radical strain in American educational thought. Subsequent proponents, it might be said, have only elaborated upon or refined the basic thesis he first enunciated.[4]

Counts opened his argument with the claim that American education was in the grip of the ''forces of social conservation and reaction'' and served the cause of perpetuating ideas and institutions suited to a bygone age.[5] He conceded the strengths of the more progressive schools of the day, noting how they focused attention on individual student needs, activity learning, and personal freedom. Yet he felt they too reflected a narrow conception of the meaning of education, one no longer adequate to society's changing needs. In its preoccupation with ''motion'' or activity, progressivism lacked a sense of direction, a coherent orientation, or clearly defined purposes. ''Like a baby shaking a rattler,'' he observed sarcastically, ''we seem to be utterly content with action, providing it is sufficiently vigorous and noisy.''

Liberal, experimental schools of the 1930s, as he saw them, mirrored

the viewpoint of the members of the liberal-minded upper middle class . . . persons who are fairly well-off . . . who pride themselves on their open-mindedness and tolerance, who favor in a mild sort of way fairly liberal programs of social reconstruction, who are full of good will and humane sentiment, who have vague aspirations for world peace and human brotherhood, who can be counted upon to respond moderately to any appeal made in the name of charity, who are genuinely distressed at the sight of *unwonted* forms of cruelty, misery, and suffering . . . but who, in spite of all their good qualities, have no deep and abiding loyalties, possess no convictions for which they would sacrifice over-much, would find it hard to live without their customary material comforts, are rather insensitive to the accepted forms of social injustice . . . rarely move outside the pleasant circle of the class to which they belong, and . . . will follow the lead of the most powerful and respectable forces in society and at the same time find good reasons for so doing.[6]

Education, Counts avowed, needed to emancipate itself from the dominance of this upper middle class. It should ''face squarely and courageously every social issue, come to grips with life in all of its stark reality, and establish an organized relation with the community, develop a realistic and comprehensive theory of welfare, fashion a compelling and challenging vision of human destiny, and become less frightened . . . at the bogies of imposition and indoctrination.''[7]

Counts felt the specter of indoctrination was easily banished. ''My thesis,'' he wrote, "is that complete impartiality is utterly impossible, that the school must shape attitudes, develop tastes, and even impose ideas." Some form of imposition is inescapable. Public education inevitably inculcates dominant values, norms, and ideals in society; and bias in instruction cannot be avoided. Choices always must be made. "The real question," he argued, "is not whether imposition will take place, but rather from what source it will come."[8]

His answer, basically, was that on all genuinely crucial matters, "the school follows the wishes of the groups or classes that actually rule society; on minor matters the school is sometimes allowed a certain measure of freedom." But this might change in future, Counts hoped, if teachers "could increase sufficiently their stock of courage, intelligence, and vision. . . ."[9] Educators might become "a social force of some magnitude" if they but aroused themselves to their moral obligation to work collectively for the realization of a true democratic vision of society. The root of the problem as he saw it was apathy:

> Nothing really stirs us. . . . We are moved by no great faiths; we are touched by no great passions. We can view a world order rushing rapidly towards collapse with no more concern than the outcome of a horse race; we can see injustice, crime and misery in their most terrible forms all about us and, if we are not directly affected, register the emotions of a scientist studying white rats in a laboratory. And in the name of freedom, objectivity and the open mind, we would transmit this general attitude of futility to our children. In my opinion this is a confession of complete moral and spiritual bankruptcy.[10]

Counts was under no illusion that "teacher power" or professional control over education would come easily. "To expect ruling groups and classes to give precedence to teachers on important matters . . . is to refuse to face realities." Just as a spring never rises higher than its source, "so the power that teachers exercise in the schools can be no greater than the power they wield in society." Yet in a time of crisis, he felt confident, if educators would assume a leadership role in making the schools places "for the building, and not merely for the contemplation, of our civilization," organized professionalism in education might find popular acceptance.[11]

More than once Counts stressed the point that educational values and goals are socially derived. "There can be no good individual apart from some conception of the character of the *good* society; and the good society is not something that is given by nature: it must be fashioned. . . . This process of building a good society is to a very large degree an educational process."[12] He hastened to add that this did not mean that the educational system should attempt to promote particular reforms directly. Instead, educators should strive, as he put it, to give to children "a vision of the possibilities which lie ahead and endeavor to enlist their loyalties and enthusiasms in the realization of the vision."[13] In the process, all social institutions and practices would have to be critically examined.

Counts did not hesitate to spell out in broad terms the vision of a reconstructed social order he had in mind. Educators, he commented, would have to help create an ideal "that has its roots in American soil, is in harmony with the spirit of the age, recognizes the facts of industrialism, appeals to the most profound impulses of our people, and takes into account the emergence of a world society."[14] A good society would be one "in which the lot of the common man will be made easier and his life enriched and ennobled." Traditional ideals of unrestricted free enterprise, extreme competition, and rugged individualism, he stressed, had serviced, not the democracy of the original American dream, but a system founded on feudal economic arrangements. It was time to revive the concept of genuine social, economic, and political democracy.

As in the case of most leftist critics of Depression America, Counts was haunted by its injustice and gross inequality: "Here is a society that manifests the most extraordinary contradictions: a mastery over the forces of nature, surpassing the wildest dreams of antiquity, is accompanied by extreme material insecurity; dire poverty walks hand in hand with the most extravagant living the world has ever known; an abundance of goods of all kinds is coupled with privation, misery, and even starvation...." The human race has within its grasp the power to usher in an age of plenty, to "make secure the lives of all, and to banish poverty forever." Future possibilities are limited only by "our ideals, by our power of self-discipline" and by the political will to devise social arrangements in which the common welfare of the people takes precedence over the interests of the privileged few.[15]

Harold Rugg, an equally vocal critic of conventional progressivism, denounced prevailing school theory for being "obsessed with the halo of the past, blind to the insistent problems of the present, and impotent to project alternative solutions" to society's pressing needs for the future. What was needed, he asserted, was a new curriculum arising "directly out of the problems, issues, and characteristics of our changing society." With astonishing prescience, Rugg identified as major concerns of the years ahead such issues as global overpopulation, unplanned urbanization, uncontrolled technological growth, nationalism, the ecological hazards of acquisitive materialism, and the increasing interdependence of world trade and culture. Schools, he held, should have a part in helping people to address these concerns. When critics complained that radical social reconstructionists were really trying to use the schools to promote extra-educational objectives, Rugg responded acidly that an educational system that did not attempt to shape learners toward specified ideological and social ends was a contradiction in terms.[16]

John L. Childs, another member of the "social frontier" group at Teachers College, took much the same position. Schooling is a social phenomenon, he argued, whose vitality depends on its dealing "with the specific affairs of modern technological, scientific, economic, political, family, and religious life." It must be oriented "primarily to that which lies ahead, rather than to a culture which is in process of disintegration and disappearance." In the nature of things, the curriculum cannot be wholly impartial. The school functions as "an agency of cultural selection" in picking out which elements will be emphasized and which neglected. Although it is "highly important," said Childs, for an educational program to respect the uniqueness of each individual student and his or her interests, it cannot stop there. Societal values, ultimately, determine what interests, dispositions, and allegiances will be nurtured. Some conception of the social welfare therefore sets the standards served by education.[17]

The fact that the school is an agent of society is *not* equivalent to its being an agent of the state, and still less to its being the servant of whatever particular groups dominate in the social order. Neutrality amounts to support for the most reactionary and predatory interests to be found in society, Childs argued. Nor is criticism enough; that is, education cannot be reduced to a bare process of criticizing existing social arrangements. In order to be significant, any critique must invoke standards, ethical judgments, and social values. "Ultimately, criticism must rest on something other than criticism." Hence, the school cannot stop short at teaching "process"—*how* to think. It must to some extent suggest *what* learners are to think. No school leaves the young neutral respecting various social alternatives. Consequently, a decision must be made as to what constructive interpretations of events and issues will be offered in school:

> In spite of all that is said about social neutrality, the school controlled by this conception of its social function is not actually socially neutral. As long as the school is content merely to make an exposition of various social alternatives and to commit itself to the advocacy of no positive social policies, it tends to throw its support on the side of the arrangements and groups which are now entrenched in power.[18]

The alternative is not for schools to impose upon the young some blueprint for a new society. But the implication that follows from the impossibility of neutrality is that educators must become more fully aware of the "social presuppositions" upon which education rests. Teachers should come to share in a "new social orientation," Childs maintained, so that the school "may do its share in helping the young to adjust to that which lies ahead."[19]

Early social reconstructionists seemed vague about precisely what new vision of society, based on "the democratic ideals and aspirations of the American people," could be promoted in schools; and they were even more imprecise in specifying exactly *how* education might contribute to the building of a new social order. Apart from arguing that the school could not be a neutral forum where all views were presented impartially, and that radical social transformation was required, they offered practicing teachers little detailed guidance or direction. John Dewey, for one, supported many of the ideals of the social-reconstructionist perspective, though he felt Counts, Rugg, Childs, and others exaggerated the potential for social change in public education. His considered judgment seems to have been that the school's role was to form the understanding and dispositions needed for facilitating change. But education could never be a direct agent of change or the *primary* determinant of societal reform.

On one point, at least, however, he agreed wholeheartedly. "Perhaps the most effective way of reinforcing reaction under the name of neutrality," he observed, "consists in keeping the oncoming generation ignorant of the conditions in which they live and the issues they will have to face. This effect is the more pronounced because it is subtle and indirect; because neither teachers nor those taught are aware of what they are doing and what is being done to them." The basic issue, Dewey affirmed, could be expressed as a question: "Where shall the social emphasis of school life and work fall, and what are the educational policies which correspond to this emphasis?"[20]

## EDUCATION AND THE CULTURE-CRISIS THESIS

Reconstructionism as the expression of a radical-reformist strain in educational thought enjoyed little influence over the next two decades; and those such as Rugg, Childs, B. O. Smith, William Stanley, and others who continued to promote the theme of education for social renewal were viewed more as eccentrics than proponents of a viable position. In the forties and fifties, there was little popular interest in, and even less support for, a point of view emphasizing sweeping alterations in the social structure. After all, critics noted, the Depression was safely in the past and a postwar boom was on. Society had survived, and there appeared to be little warrant for any drastic change in the course of American education. Almost alone in the 1950s was a handful of activist critics who persisted in claiming a need for radical societal and educational transformation.

Perhaps the most insistent and eloquent defender of the reconstructionist perspective was Theodore Brameld, one-time vice-president of the Progressive Education Association (1941–42) and a nationally prominent professor of educational philosophy at Boston University. His writings, spanning more than three decades, consistently advanced the thesis that formal education could be a major engine for social reform. Echoing complaints against progressivism levied by Rugg, Childs, and Count a decade or more earlier, Brameld criticized child-centered pedagogy for being "dilatory" and "inefficient." The greatest weakness of progressive education, he declared, was that it had not clearly or unequivocally focused upon either the content or meaning of educational goals. Like the American culture with which it was ideologically allied, progressivist thought had been much more concerned with delineating an effective pedagogical method than with formulating appropriate educational goals.[21]

"The fear that any kind of substantive commitment to ends will lead to dogmatism and then to immoral means for achieving them has haunted progressivists," Brameld observed. "My opinion is that progressivists sometimes avoid and evade the responsibility [for affirming definite objectives] . . . because they are conditioned perhaps often quite unconsciously by the milieu of a culture which has actually discouraged even defensible commitments in favor of the more comfortable and safer stance of methodology and process."[22]

The adequacy of any theory about education, Brameld argued, must be judged by how well it meets the needs of its own time. "It was earlier thought, for example, that education should aim primarily to instill in the minds of the young a reverent acceptance of traditional patterns of culture."[23] Today, he declared, any such view was clearly outmoded. In an era of cataclysmic upheaval, the only adequate philosophic orientation for education is one that is responsive to the cultural situation as it now exists, that can gear learning to human betterment, and is amenable to translation into concrete programs of action. Especially at the present juncture, the queries that ought to shape schooling at all levels are: what kind of world do we want and what kind of world is achievable? Toward what goals must human civilization move in order to meet the challenges of the future?

Brameld's thesis was breathtaking in its scope and ambition. The entire purpose and process of education should be reconstructed, he announced in *Education As Power* (1965). Humanity lives in a period fraught with the greatest peril it has ever encountered. The human species faces a crisis in its age-old struggle to satisfy basic physical, social, emotional, and spiritual needs. The problem is that technology has developed to the point where a truly utopian order of existence is a live possibility, yet that same technological capacity may also be misused to reduce human civilization to a slag heap of radioactive ruins. As yet it is not at all clear which course will be pursued: the road to destruction or to utopia. But, given its current drift, human culture, left unreconstructed, he warned, "will almost certainly collapse of its own frustrations and conflicts."[24]

Time is short, and humankind is caught unprepared in a trap of its own making. "The central critique of modern culture contends that . . . the major institutions and corresponding social, economic, and other practices that developed during preceding centuries of the modern era are now incapable of confronting the terrifying, bewildering crisis of our age," Brameld argued. Because the world's major political, social, and economic institutions are based upon destructive, exploitative uses of technological power, they are tending to lead mankind closer and closer to the brink of final disaster. They must be radically reconstituted if the inertial drift toward chaos is to be reversed.

Education, he continued, can do no less than to help people participate fully and actively in the dynamics of cultural reconstruction. It must assist in the transformation of the existing social order, and thereby prevent its eventual annihilation. Society must be reconstructed, not simply through political action, but more fundamentally through the education of its members to the grave dangers of the present situation. Education must lay claim to a vision of a new and more viable social order. It must "attempt to build the widest possible consensus about the supreme aims that should govern mankind in the reconstruction of world culture."

Ultimately, the need is for "a world in which the dream of both ancient Christianity and modern democracy are fused with modern technology and art into a society under the control of the great majority of the people who are rightly the sovereign determiners of their own destiny."[25] The fundamental goal is "a world civilization and an educational system which in all ways supports human dignity for all races, castes, and classes; self-realization; and the fullest vocational, civic, and social cooperation and service.''[26] The full significance of this paramount aim, Brameld said, should be stated both in the negative terms of the alternative—probable death to the human race—and in positive terms of the technological revolution that, for the first time in history, makes a world civilization both imperative and workable.[27]

Specifically, Brameld hoped that in years to come ''a vast range of now largely neglected or incompetently treated areas of study'' would receive greater attention. Centering in the crisis of the age, they would need a ''realistic appraisal'' so that people everywhere would become more fully aroused to the dangers confronting humanity and more fully aware of the prospects for averting catastrophe. We must, he stressed, ''tear away the curtains that conceal from so many learners the most vexing questions of our time—political, social, economic, moral, scientific, religious, cultural.''[28]

Brameld asserted over and over again that solutions to humanity's most urgent problems could not be imposed. Nor could the new civilization he envisioned be realized or brought into being except through democratic processes of decision making. ''The majority of peoples should, through their freely chosen representatives, control all fundamental economic, political, and social policies, and they should do so on a planetary scale,'' he proclaimed. ''This is the supreme goal of education for the current decades.''[29] All members of the human race, without regard for present national boundaries, would have to share without hindrance in the projection of utopian goals for all humanity. They would have to be free to test those goals in the light of the best available evidence, and, ultimately, to engage in concerted action to achieve the goals to which a convergent humankind becomes committed. Far from being ''utopian'' in the pejorative sense of unattainable or impractical, Brameld claimed, nothing less would be adequate to halt the world's headlong rush toward planetary extinction.

To critics who objected that Brameld was simply calling for another form of indoctrination, he posed the principle of ''defensible partiality.'' Educators, he said, need not maintain a sterile neutrality with respect to the issues around which the present world culture crisis revolves. Instead, in the process of freely examining divergent ideas, they should examine the evidence, identify alternative solutions, and help define the basic thrust of proposed reforms. Ultimately, he believed, decisions could be reached by democratic consensus, an agreement based not on dogma or arbitrary authority but upon the relevant findings of scientific investigation. Developments in the social sciences particularly would supply the ''facts'' upon which collective action would be taken.[30] He was confident that people could arrive at ''defensible'' conclusions and commitments if these were validated by evidence and tested through exhaustive consideration of the alternatives. They would be ''partial'' insofar as they would lead to one course of action rather than another.

Brameld anticipated his critics' objections that it was unrealistic to expect educators to initiate or lead the wholesale ideological and social revolution required for cultural reconstruction. In defense, his claim was that education was not a "sufficient" solution to world problems, only that its influence was "a necessary condition of prime importance." As he phrased it, "Actually, education becomes a constructive force only when it fuses with the economic, political, socially creative forces of the culture. . . ."[31] In the final analysis, Brameld pointed out, education as a social institution can only function in one of two ways. Either it will be used to thwart change and obscure the urgent necessity for far-reaching societal transformation or it will be enlisted in the cause of effecting society's positive and orderly transition into the future. No other choices exist.

Brameld's summation of the argument, appearing in many different places, is worth quoting in his own words. In a 1973 essay he phrased it as follows:

> In spite of reactions of ridicule and cynicism . . . that one immediately anticipates from many citizens, increasing minorities of other citizens are already shifting toward affirmative and transformative commitments. For them, only a world community that aspires no longer to war but rather to global peace, no longer to national and class arrogance but rather to transnational democratic authority, no longer to the deprivation and exploitation of multitudes but rather to full sharing of the earth's prolificity—only such a world community . . . can still justify man's ultimate choice of alternative features.

Education, "viewed in the only perspective any longer tenable—a global perspective—confronts the . . . choice of reconfirming our human limitations," or serving as a way "to build *for* something"—a decent, humane world in which human survival is both possible and worthwhile.[32]

## CRITICISM

Brameld's revolutionary thesis, first expounded in his *Ends and Means in Education* (1950); extended in *The Use of Explosive Ideas in Education* (1965), *Education as Power* (1965), and *Education for the Emerging Age* (1965); and reiterated in *Patterns of Educational Philosophy in Culturological Perspective* (1971), came in for much criticism. Hobert W. Burns, dean of the School of Education at Hofstra University, summarized Brameld's position as follows:

> The *raison d'être* of his concern and anxiety lies implicit in the basic premise that we are facing the very end of civilization as we know it (the crisis-culture thesis), upon the analysis that salvation can come only through a reconstructed world order (the end), which would be the consequence of a dramatic, radical alteration in the structure, function, and purpose of education throughout the world (the means).[33]

The "gut issue," as Burns saw it, was twofold. First, what is the warrant for the assertion of a culture crisis? Is there any such social consensus that contemporary human culture is in a state of crisis and that it is of planetary proportions? Secondly, what are the grounds for claiming that the most desirable end to be sought is a worldwide democratic social order? As a matter of fact, he objected, "there is no impelling social consensus that things are all that bad, so bad as to compel a further social consensus on the need to abolish war and establish universal democracy." Indeed, Burns observed, "the operative social consensus seems to be that war is evil-in-the-abstract but necessary-in-the-particular—witness every nation's opposition to war but the willingness to engage in it when it is means to certain ends. The social consensus seems to be *for* war." [34]

James McClellan, of Temple University, on the other hand, accepted Brameld's argument that human culture *is* in a state of crisis. "Western civilization," he agreed, "still suffers from war and the hangover of wars, depression, and an established precedent for genocide. Over-hanging every effort to secure peace and justice on this planet is the Damocles' Sword of nuclear holocaust. And each time we seem to have made a little progress in escaping the threat of the Big Bang, our attention is caught by the ominous whimper of too many newborn babies." He further endorsed the reconstructionist's point that what passes for public schooling is positively *mis*-educative, as systematically and devastatingly as if it were deliberate. It offers the appearance of democratic control, but the substance of control lies "with a minority class and with a bureaucratic structure which is quite unresponsive to the real needs of the people." The dominant minority has deeply vested interests in the existing economic and political system, and, most importantly, "in a system of education which projects the *status quo* onto the next generation." [35]

In other words, McClellan agreed with two fundamental precepts: that civilization is in trouble, and that education isolates or insulates the young from an understanding of why culture confronts a crisis. Yet he remained highly critical of Brameld, calling him an "architect of confusion."

Brameld's proposals, McClellan alleged, were "historical oddities" or "curiosities," not worth taking seriously. Brameld was neither effective nor influential as a critic, he claimed, for several reasons, most of them having to do with a lack of reasons and argument for his specific policy recommendations. "Even though he is treating, literally, the great issues of human life or death," McClellan complained, "his imagination does not open any genuinely new perspective on the human condition nor on the nurture of human values through education. On the other hand, his sense of prophetic mission prevents him from participating directly and effectively in helping school teachers and administrators do their jobs just a little better." [36]

In essence, McClellan, like many others, appeared to feel that Brameld had paid insufficient attention to the realities of power and the structure of control in education, the relative powerlessness of classroom teachers, and the ubiquity of the political forces in society that shape school curricula. On one side, Brameld had added little if anything original to the common-sense observation that the world has become a dangerous place in which to live. On the other side, he had—or so it was claimed—failed to show how, given present conditions, education could help change matters. "The Reconstructionist," McClellan asserted, "refuses to be bound either by the present administrative structure or the legal and financial disabilities under which present schools operate."[37] It might be thought-provoking to project an imaginative vision of what education could do to create better human beings and a better world for them to live in. But without an argument to show *how* a utopian vision might be translated into practice, the exercise was likely to be futile. Faith and good intentions alone, McClellan implied, were insufficient.

## THE PLANETARY CRISIS RECONSIDERED

For whatever reasons—its seeming naiveté about the realities of social change, confusions in theory, conceptual ambiguities, or lack of practical policy recommendations—reconstructionism as a formal viewpoint about education attracted little attention and even fewer adherents in the fifties and early sixties. It was and remained a minor thread among the strands of mainstream educational theory. Brameld himself professed disappointment on many occasions that his proposals had attracted so little comment and discussion. But if his faith in the transformative power of education to create a better world order was not widely shared, his analysis of the planetary crisis was increasingly echoed in the writings of social commentators. Among those who attempted to assess the conditions of the planet and humanity's prospects in it, pundits tended to divide themselves into cornucopians or Malthusian Cassandras. The former foresaw years of abundance for everyone; the latter envisioned a plundered planet running out of time and resources. By the late 1960s, however, pessimists appeared to outnumber the more hopeful.

"Confident articles on the future," historian Kenneth Clark observed, "seem to me, intellectually, the most disreputable of all forms of public utterance."[38] Norman O. Brown likewise admitted, "Today even the survival of humanity is a utopian hope."[39] To the question as to whether humankind even has a future, Desmond King-Hele, in *The End of the Twentieth Century?* (1970), answered in the negative. "Probably not," he conceded, or, to be more specific, "Man has many possible futures but the most likely ones are disastrous."[40] Biophysicist John Rader Platt was equally insistent with his reminder that "the world has now become too dangerous for anything less than Utopia."[41] Novelist Arthur Koestler spoke for many in the closing words of *The Ghost in the Machine* (1967): "Nature has let us down, God seems to have left the receiver off the hook, and time is running out."[42] Commenting on the phenomenon of worldwide student protest in the 1960s, Harvard biologist George Wald remarked, "What we are up against is a generation that is by no means sure it has a future."[43] For the first time in history, a generation had come into its own facing the stark realization that it might be the last.

Philosopher Kai Nielson felt the modern predicament was one of spiritual saturation or "psychic overload," brought on by a succession of crises that left people feeling powerless and overwhelmed. The crux of the problem was not apathy per se (a form of predigested pessimism; that is, "Nobody can do anything anyway—why try?") so much as it was simple confusion:

> The fear is very deep, and a cynical, often bitter, conviction is pervasive, that in our society we have lost the capacity to shape our collective destinies, to control our lives together as social beings, or even, in any proper sense, to understand them so that we can see where we are going and try to forge a rational and human society where human beings can flourish. We have a sense that our collective lives are out of control, propelled by deep and complex forces whose workings we only very dimly understand. The fear of, or at least the apprehension about, the future is very considerable. There is the nagging anxiety—an anxiety that a conversation with an informed futurist will only reinforce—that we may have passed the point of no return and that from now on it may be all downhill. . . . Many have come to believe that . . . nothing that human beings can collectively do can save us. There is, many think, no rational hope for changing society and, indeed, we would not even know how to change it if we could.[44]

Meanwhile, dire predictions for the future continued. Speaking of future possibilities for war, a 1955 manifesto jointly authored by Bertrand Russell and Albert Einstein warned bluntly, "We have found that the men who know the most are the most gloomy."[45] After weighing the possibilities latent in a situation in which unlimited power to destroy is available and yet the world is still divided into over one hundred feuding nations, Desmond King-Hele concluded that large-scale war was not only possible but even probable. Discussing the chances of an error of judgment, he predicted, "The logical conclusion is that the weapons are likely to be let loose, probably before the end of the twentieth century."[46]

The prestigious Stockholm International Peace Research Institute in 1977 felt driven to the same conclusion: all-out nuclear war remains a likely possibility in this generation. There is little time left, warned George Wald, a 1968 Nobel Prize winner in physiology and medicine:

> We live in a highly lethal society. No society in human history has cultivated the technology of killing and destruction as has Western society. . . . We now have it in our hands to wipe out all humanity and much of the rest of life on earth. The stockpiles of nuclear weapons in the United States and the Soviet Union several years ago reached the explosive equivalent of ten to fifteen tons of TNT for every man, woman, and child on the planet. You might think that enough; but we are now—both superpowers—in the middle of a huge escalation, replacing all the single warheads by multiple warheads, and devising new and more accurate guidance systems.[47]

Countless warnings were sounded. Jonathan Schell, writing in *The Fate of the Earth* (1982), saw nuclear weapons as the ultimate threat capable of ending human history itself. "They are a pit into which the whole world can fall—a nemesis of all human intentions, actions, and hopes," he declared. And yet, as he saw it, "at present, most of us do nothing. We look away. We remain calm. We are silent.

We take refuge in the hope that the holocaust won't happen, and turn back to our individual concerns. We deny the truth that is all around us.''[48] Sidney Lens made much the same point:

> Because of its catastrophic scope, the nuclear menace is neither believable nor believed by the general public. It has been absorbed, grain by grain, over a period of thirty years, so that its impact has been lost. Americans have been immunized to the permanent emergency. . . . Yet, we are confronted by a lunatic process, in which every participant is sane but all collectively are trapped in psychosis. The process propels itself, like a machine gone mad.[49]

As if nuclear war were not a sufficiently fearsome prospect, prognosticators could point to other dilemmas of almost equal urgency confronting humankind in the waning years of the twentieth century. A particular discomfiting picture was painted by Donella H. Meadows and others in the Club of Rome's 1972 report, *The Limits of Growth*. Utilizing a computer model of the ecosystem based on the major variables of the world's environment—population, resources, pollution, per capital industrial output, and food per capita—a research team at MIT ran projections of how these variables would interact and the probable consequences, decade by decade, extending into the twenty-first century. In each case the results were bleak. Only by assuming zero population growth, zero industrial growth, and the *immediate* implementation of rigorous environmental policies (''resource recycling, pollution control devices, increased lifetime of all forms of capital, and methods to restore eroded and infertile soil'') was it possible to create a scenario in which systemic collapse on a global scale was averted.[50] The last computer run supplied a chilling indication that preventive action would have to begin *well before* the year 2000 if catastrophe were to be avoided in the next century. Only slightly more ''hopeful'' was another writer's direful prediction: ''The human race has, maybe, thirty-five years left.''[51]

The Club of Rome's analysis was only one of many predicting probable disaster. A 1976 doomsday report from the Central Intelligence Agency, for example, cautioned that if present trends continued, prospects were for widespread hunger, political disarray, and general calamity within a matter of decades. Summing up the bleak profile of the future, CIA soothsayers solemnly anticipated planetary upheavals ''beyond comprehension.'' Years before, C. P. Snow had posed the peril, in a 1959 Rede Lecture. ''Isn't it time we began?'' he asked. ''The danger is, we have been brought up to think as though we had all the time in the world. We have very little time. So little that I dare not guess at it.''[52]

Much the same sort of declarations of gloom were forthcoming in a 1980 document prepared by the U.S. State Department and the Council on Environmental Quality entitled, *The Global 2000 Report to the President: Entering the Twenty-First Century.*[53] Its focus was on population, material resources, food, and environmental contamination. Once again came the claim that, should current patterns prevail, the world a few short years hence will be more crowded, more poisoned, less stable ecologically, and more vulnerable to political chaos than it already is now. Population continues to soar. The gap between "have" and "have-not" nations is fast becoming a yawning chasm. Developed nations will consume a grossly disproportionate share of energy and irreplaceable resources, further aggravating Third World poverty. A predatory international economic order will exacerbate global tensions. Famine will increase. Mass starvation will intensify. Forests and arable land will diminish or become polluted. Potable water will become scarce. Much animal and plant life will face extinction as civilization invades wild habitats. Pollutants raining down on the land coupled with particular degradation of the atmosphere from the burning of fossil fuels promise to wreak permanent damage. And always, of course, looms the grim specter of a nuclear Armageddon.

In 1979, in observance of the International Year of the Child, Estefania Aldaba-Lim, Assistant U.N. Secretary General, commented on the kind of world the present generation was leaving to the next. "It is," she observed sadly, "a world of predominantly military priorities, where nuclear bomb inventories of the two superpowers, already sufficient to destroy every city in the world seven times over, are still growing at the rate of three bombs a day." She noted the world had become a place "where human survival and health appear to be increasingly endangered by environmental pollution on a scale which makes control ever more complex and difficult." She spoke of "a shrinking privileged minority of these living in the highly industrialized areas of the world" which continues to consume the greatest share of the earth's material goods and to reap the benefits of industrial production, world trade, and technology. She wondered what human values would survive when children are daily confronted with gross social and economic inequities and priorities favor more effort and ingenuity expended on destruction than human survival.[54]

Author Isaac Asimov, responding to the same question, offered a pessimistic assessment. "The kind of world we are leaving to our children is one in which all the leaders are concerned with short-range goals—the next election—the next diplomatic coup—the next step in outreaching the neighboring power economically, militarily, or both," he commented. "In such a world of short-range goals only, it may be that the long-range goal of survival will be lost and our children with it—and it is that sad possibility our children are inheriting."[55]

H. G. Vonk, of Florida Atlantic University, summed it up:

> Man has been too clever by half: He has devised a magnificent engine of technology—and lost control of it. Its exhausts and by-products threaten to choke and poison him; but man seems no more able to seize control of his engine than a lowly moth is able to seize control of his urge to visit the flame. Ironically, man possesses much of the engineering know-how needed to escape his destiny, but very little of the social know-how. In the end, this may result in the final triumph of means over ends.[56]

## ANESTHETIC EDUCATION AND ITS CRITICS

Meanwhile, Vonk alleged, back in schools pupils were "being readied for the crucial challenge via guided tours through the historical dustbin. The dead issues of the distant, cold past are marched in and out of the classroom like so many obedient tin soldiers." In large part, he felt, dead issues are tractable because "nobody gives a damn." He wrote, "Nobody gets worked up over whether some war ended in 1864 or 1865, because they weren't there and none of their friends were there. Even when someone does get excited, it only turns his head from the present (where his problems are) to the past (where his problems are not)." Vonk compared the typical school curriculum to the kiki bird: "The kiki bird, you will recall, used to fly backwards so he could find out where he had been. This habit had the decided advantage of keeping his mind off where he was going." He added, "But the kiki is now extinct."[57]

School critic Jonathan Kozol, in a 1975 diatribe entitled *The Night Is Dark and I Am Far from Home,* damned American schooling as a consumer fraud. It purports to offer education, he wrote, but actually seeks to indoctrinate.[58] Its function is not to educate humane and decent people, but "manageable voters, manipulable consumers and, if need be, in the case of war or crisis, willing killers."

Public education as a whole, he believed, is by no means an inept, disordered construction, as is sometimes alleged. On the contrary, it is an extremely efficacious mechanism for cooption and domestication wielded by a "rich, benevolent, sophisticated, murderous, well-mannered and exquisite social order." Its primary objective and most consistent consequence is the perpetuation of a value system founded on hypocrisy and deceit.[59] Schools control student inquiry, narrowly circumscribe discussion, preordain answers, and, overall, serve to suppress or divert children's ethical impulses. Public education sustains the pretense of free options with consummate skill and nurtures the illusion that schooling is conducted against the backdrop of a decent nation, of a democratic culture, and a well-intentioned corporate structure.

The best measure of the system's effectiveness, Kozol claimed, was the palpable fact that in this country "we live with evil, and do so moreover with a fair amount of ease and skill and even with a certain amount of self-congratulation on the reasonable nature of our own response."[60] The pious lies purveyed in schools are manifold: there are no social ills that will not admit of eventual technological correction. Injustice comes, never from "doing wrong," but only of not "doing good" fast enough. There are no oppressors, only oppressed people. There are two sides to every question. Conflict must be "resolved." Values should be "clarified"—but only rarely acted upon, and then without "excessive" moral fervor. Never criticize anything without being prepared to supply a better alternative. Reasonability is better than intemperate passion. Social progress is possible without danger, sacrifice, or pain. An individual can never do anything to combat injustice. Things are getting better. Heroic figures should be admired, never emulated. Political leaders always have the best interests of the people at heart.

A class is "studying about" racism, poverty, social injustice, or economic oppression. The teacher says, "The least we can do, children, is care." The term "least," of course, means "most," Kozol asserted; and "care" is a code word for not taking action. Ultimately, the purpose of the ritual of examining social ills in schools is to *display* feelings and analyze them so they can be placed safely at arm's length.

Likewise with "research," whether it is the contrived recapitulation of what is already known, as engaged in by schoolchildren doing their preplanned lessons, or the more elaborate inquiry conducted by university scholars. The point always, according to Kozol, is not to advance effective action, but to postpone it. "The more powerful and more persuasive the existent body of raw data and hard evidence," as he put it, "the more inexorable our obligation to go back and start again at Intellectual Zero."[61] As the myth has it, we can never know enough to decide upon a concrete course of action.

In its practical effects, Kozol avowed, the objective of schooling in the present-day corporate order is spiritual and ethical lobotomy. Although the realities of the world persist, children allegedly must not be allowed to grow up feeling enraged over sickness, poverty, or war machines. They must be made to feel powerless in the face of systematic economic exploitation and needless human misery. They must be *taught* to believe in the simulation of democratic options by a ritual of meaningless election choices between candidates of virtually identical position. It is essential that no identifiable connection ever be discerned between personal privilege or affluence and the cost to the less privileged. Hunger or starvation in the world need to be perceived as uncaused ordeals, products of benign misfortune or honest human errors.

Kozol concluded his indictment with a word to practicing educators. Teachers, he wrote,

> should not delude themselves about the task ahead. The walls that stand around the unjust world in which the U.S. schools now toil, exist and thrive will not be leveled by the sound of trumpets or by another research project. . . . Ethical struggle, in an unjust nation, cannot fail to take on the dimensions of a revolutionary labor. No matter how we long to see it in less formidable lines, there is no way to get around the high stakes that are now before us.

True revolutionaries might elect to remain in the system, attempting to undermine it from within, all the while posing as quiet, passive, and subservient acolytes of nation, state and social order. Nonetheless, he warned:

> To the degree that he [the teacher] elects to stay *within* the public education apparatus, to this degree . . . his function, from this moment on, is to assign connections, to demonstrate the fraudulence of empty options, to undermine the walls of

anaesthetic self-protection, to take out low-watt issues and replace them by high-voltage questions, to generate the confidence for insurrectionary actions, to instigate the capability to build up lines of strong and lasting loyalties among like-minded souls—then, too, and at the proper time, to build the readiness for stark and vigorous acts of intervention in the face of pain.[62]

For Kozol, the alternatives were inescapable. "Power knows where its own interest lies; so too do those machineries that serve and strengthen power," he emphasized. "School indoctrination is the keystone of a mighty archway in this land. It will not be removed without grave consequences for the struggle it supports. Nor will it be taken out without the kind of struggle and the kind of sacrifice that great events and serious human transformations always call for." Either one must accede to the system and to "anesthetic" education or one must seek to destroy it. His book, he wrote, was a call for "tactics, plans, scenarios of clear and conscious and intentional subversion of the public schools." The object was not "amelioration but sophisticated and prepared rebellion."[63] Not until schools were utterly transformed, he stated, could there be any hope for a form of education competent to engage the challenge of human survival and justice.

Kozol's unrelieved pessimism, his angry moralism, and his uncompromising condemnation of American society as lacking any redeeming features whatsoever won him few followers—significantly, his book was out of print a few short years after its publication. But the allegation that schooling was an "anesthetic" influence in the lives of children could not be easily dismissed. Nor could the claim that conventional schooling was out of touch with social reality, that it failed to address life-and-death questions of war, peace, injustice, environmental deterioration, the energy crisis, and so on. Little or anything was being done, critics complained, to counter the tendency of people to turn inward, to avoid recognition of social problems, and to disavow responsibility for action in the public arena.

Formal education has failed to challenge learners with a vision of what a new world could be like, argued New York University's Frederick L. Redefer. Higher education especially, he claimed, had neglected to "make students aware of the dangers of the present drift; the crucial shortages the world will face in energy, resources, foods; the effects of overpopulation. . . ." College and university faculties, he charged, "are participants in a built-in system protecting the time-encrusted administrative arrangements and practices of higher education that inhibit change." Was it not time, Redefer asked, "to develop purposes for education and to create a new education for some students in some schools and colleges by some of the faculty? Is it not a time when a social purpose for education can be found and a commitment to an improved world accepted? Must we wait for society to change before colleges do?"[64]

Responding affirmatively, Leon Hymovitz, a Philadelphia school principal, acknowledged the message to schools was "loud and unmistakable." The need, he claimed, was to reform all institutions of instruction at all levels, making "survival education" and "catastrophe management" the primary focus of schooling.

Children, he wrote, "need a vision and a version of the future, ways of thinking about the future, problem-solving, and decision-making." Youth should be offered global perspectives, news of politics, economics, war and peace, science and technology."[65] If humanity is not to blow itself up "in a crapshoot at the turn of this century . . . it is the infant in the crib who must be readied to reason, discover, and decide how to save and preserve us from the best and the worst that is in us." To do otherwise, Hymovitz warned, "is to continue to drift, to tempt the fates, to court disaster, and to condemn us to a future not worthy of our precious past."[66]

# EDUCATIONAL REFORM AND SOCIAL CHANGE

Analyses of how schools should respond to crisis in the social order differed. Some, like John P. DeCecco, of San Francisco State College, believed reform would have to begin on a piecemeal basis, involving attempts to stimulate students to do "real" things—to think and write and act upon personal and social dilemmas—and with the development of curricula promoting "searching for complex and sophisticated qualitative improvement in human life and aspiration." A social studies curriculum, for example, he argued, "need not simulate or simply verbalize conflict, debate, mediation, negotiation, and so on, but should practice it in the reality of genuine school and community conflict."[67] The forms and processes of schooling would need to be restructured drastically. Some, like Jean Anyon, of Rutgers University, felt an "honest pedagogy" would aim at the development in students of informed opinions and critical social thought based on exposure to a multiplicity of views on society, history, and social thought. Heretofore, she observed, school book reports of social development, political reform, economics, and labor had not been "neutral" in any meaningful sense, but had expressed the interests of the wealthy and powerful.[68]

Fannie R. Shaftel, on the other hand, felt the great lack was not lack of information or even misinformation, but misplaced priorities and the absence of guiding values. "Our problem of how to survive and grow into a humane community," she observed, "is not so much the result of lack of available knowledge as it is first of all a *crisis in values.* The priorities essential to survival demand a new ordering, based upon *the valuing of human progress rather than material progress.*"[69]

Author Herbert Kohl, in a 1980 article, offered a provocative interpretation of the problem as he saw it. The problems present-day educators face in the eighties, he was convinced, were no different than those the schools have faced since the first attempt to provide free education for all children. Then, as now, the basic question has been, What can the schools contribute to the creation of a social and economic democracy? Harkening back to George Counts's 1932 appeal for schools to build a new social order, Kohl reviewed five major assumptions in the argument:

1. social and economic democracy is good;
2. the schools potentially have the power to change society;
3. teachers are capable of being major agents of social change;
4. the school should not be a neutral place, but one advocating a socially and economically democratic view of society
5. propaganda on the good side is part of good educational practice; and this implies changing the curriculum and the social role of the teacher.[70]

Kohl professed support for economic democracy, which he construed as "humane, community-oriented socialism," but he conceded that "socialism" is a dirty word in contemporary American society, and "using socialism in a positive context is likely to get you fired." From his perspective, it was far better than capitalism, with its elevation of selfishness to the level of a universal moral value. Yet he felt opportunities for like-minded teachers to express their personal political convictions in classrooms were limited, and perhaps properly so. He felt it was possible to educate people to believe in socialist values, but by force of example rather than by direct instruction, and not necessarily in schools.

As for whether schools can change society, Kohl's answer was negative. "From my current perspective," he observed, "the view that the schools can build a new society is akin to the idea that the world will be redeemed by children or that the children will somehow save us adults. I believe that both those ideas are incorrect. We cannot give our children the responsibility for redeeming the world we either messed up or at least witnessed being destroyed."[71]

Kohl's argument ran as follows: teachers who attempt to lead social movements through their work at school simply will not survive. The system cannot tolerate it. Secondly, individuals working for change need a support system. But teachers' organizations are dominated by educationally conservative people, and are not easily turned around. Thirdly, while teachers do influence students, that influence is limited and sometimes unpredictable. One cannot predict what students will take from school or how they will translate learning into action years hence. As he commented, "Many of the most progressive schools have produced more corporate lawyers than social activities."[72]

Could the school forswear neutrality and advocate a social-economic democratic view of society? Here Kohl offered two reactions. In the first place, the school is not and cannot be a neutral place, he judged. "The system itself," he noted, "all the way from the textbook manufacturers, to the companies that supply the buses, to the people who serve on the school boards and the screening committees that hire teachers and administrators, is not neutral." Given its bias, schooling "embodies training for the acceptance of capitalism in most of its public manifestations." The likelihood of its changing is small.

Yet, secondly, there *is* something teachers could do, he suggested. "Perhaps the most important thing we can do *at present* is point out [bias in the system] and expose our students to the biases of texts in all subjects as well as in the structure, management, and financing of schools. . . . The system itself is an object worth studying with our pupils.'' He advised,

> Let them find out what it is, how it works, who serves it, and whom it serves. Let them research and find out for themselves, and let us as teachers and educators find out for ourselves, since often we are as ignorant as our students. And then we will draw conclusions about what the schools we work in do, how they relate to the rest of the political and economic system, and how there might be other ways to do things.[73]

On the issue of propagandizing, Kohl said he was not convinced that it was good educational practice, no matter what side of an issue one advocates. The aim of education is to help people to think through a problem, to weigh factual and moral considerations, and to come to their own informed conclusions. Propaganda, however, uses techniques to persuade, convince, and induce compliance with a particular viewpoint. Not that propaganda is now absent from schools— but, said Kohl, no defensible purpose is served by adding to it. A teacher may reveal his or her own beliefs after students have studied a subject, but only when alternative views have been fairly presented and learners have begun to form their own judgments. At the same time, Kohl stressed, students must be brought to understand that the issues are real, not merely academic abstractions, and that the logical fruition of coming to a conclusion is to act upon it.

## THE MEANING OF CITIZENSHIP IN AN AGE OF ANONYMITY AND GLOBAL INTERDEPENDENCE

One prominent issue in explorations of the theme of education for social reconstruction pursued in the seventies and eighties had to do with the meaning of public ''citizenship.'' William Ophuls, of Northwestern University, observed, ''To state the point baldly, there is no longer any such thing as citizenship in the modern industrial world.'' Few people, he claimed, truly enjoy the status of citizenship, along with all its attendant rights, duties, and privileges. ''The vast majority simply go along for the ride.'' The idea that a group of self-reliant individuals having a common set of elevated political ideals would be actively involved in governing themselves—the original American ideal of citizenship— Ophuls felt had disappeared or been lost sight of.[74] David Mathews, one-time Secretary of the Department of Health, Education, and Welfare, made much the same point with his comment, ''Being a citizen today is essentially a spectator sport. Citizenship education is little more than learning what others do to make and execute the policies of government.''[75]

Mathews attributed public apathy to popular disillusionment with the nation's major political institutions, as shown by sinking voter registrations and public-opinion polls that reflected a failing confidence in government. ''We may well be witnessing," he noted, "the kind of citizenship dropout that Thomas Jefferson imagined when he asked, in his First Inaugural Address, if the American experiment in self-government might be withering for lack of energy to sustain it."[76] Ophuls, in contrast, felt that ambiguity surrounding the meaning of citizenship stemmed from confusion over values, and that "citizen dropout" was the product of very basic cultural factors.

Nineteenth-century political liberalism (today's conservatism), as Ophuls analyzed it, rested on the notions of atomistic individualism, innate selfishness, and government as a mere referee in the political struggle over private ends. "Privatism is a corollary of liberalism," he argued. "According to liberal principles, the ends of man are *private* ends—that is, ends that are privately determined, privately attained, and privately enjoyed. The community is seen as little more than a necessary evil, nothing but an arena for ego's quest." Thus, when people *do* participate in public life, there is a strong tendency for them to turn their participation into a vehicle for the pursuit of private ends.[77] But as the public arena comes to be dominated by the politics of organized selfishness, the scope and meaning of citizenship are thereby reduced.

Genuine participation in the policy and the performance of public duty are rendered difficult, if not impossible, given the scale and complexity of contemporary social institutions, he alleged. First, anomie and anonymity are rife in the gigantic impersonal world of the megalopolis or the suburb. It is almost impossible in such a setting to preserve any sense of "community." Secondly, important political action occurs at such a remote psychological "distance" from the potential participant that it is difficult to comprehend, much less deal with effectively. Thirdly, the major issues with which citizens are supposed to be involved are so esoteric and awesomely complex—economic policy, nuclear energy, international relations—that only specialists can hope to understand them. The basis for real comprehension as an essential prerequisite for exercising responsible citizenship is thereby eroded. The net result, as Ophuls phrased it, is that "individuals have been demoted to hapless consumers in the political as well as in the economic market place."[78]

Considering the cost in time and energy demanded for political participation, harried individuals understandably settle for passivity. Already overburdened by private concerns, the political consumer runs up against Robert Dahl's "criterion of economy," which operates more and more strongly as social pace, scale, and complexity increase.[79] "Simply put," Ophuls wrote, "the difficulty is that genuine participation takes time, with the time required increasing disproportionately with the difficulty and complexity of the problems; today, this is more time than all but a few professionals can spare, so that there is inevitably little exercise of informed citizenship by the individual."[80]

Passivity aside, another result that follows is illustrated by the so-called "tragedy of the commons." The phrase describes the plight of all who use common property resources, such as the environment. The "tragedy" arises because, as Ophuls explained:

It is always rational for individuals to abuse the commons even when they are fully aware (and they rarely are) that this will cause long-term ruin. The reason is simple: If an individual exploits, he stands to receive all the gain, but others absorb most of the resulting environmental damage; on the other hand, if he abstains, he exposes himself to the risk that others will exploit the commons for their own gain and thereby force him to suffer environmental damage without any corresponding benefit. Being damned if he doesn't, the individual typically decides to do, even if this involves eventual damnation, because he gets at least some benefits along the path to perdition.[81]

So long as resources were inexhaustible, land was readily available, and there were no adverse effects from increasing technological productivity, the unrestrained exploitation of the "commons" seemed harmless. The problem, however, is that continuing exploitation has run up against the limits posed by declining resources, diminishing technological returns, and ecological degradation. "In sum," Ophuls noted, "after a brief hiatus of several centuries during which it was possible to have our cake and eat it too, we are about to re-encounter a situation of scarcity that calls into question every premise of a political system predicated on the assumption of perpetual abundance. . . ."[82]

The paramount need today, he argued, is for "ecological citizenship." The problem is that it is difficult to imagine an educational system and a culture less well adapted to promoting a new ethic responsive to ecological scarcity. In the first place, "the industrial system needs technocrats and bureaucrats the way armies need cannon fodder, and our educational factories are by and large engaged in training and certifying students for positions in the industrial army." A good organizational soldier is neither capable nor willing to entertain questions that might be fundamentally subversive of the system. It follows, then, that current education must be "narrowly economic and technical in its content and methodology."[83]

The typical curriculum, Ophuls alleged, encourages students to take a materialistic approach to knowledge and life. Even the structure of the system reinforces the curriculum, leaving little opportunity for creating "the common basis for social and political discourse that is necessary if citizens are to talk intelligently to each other about the issues facing them." Formal education tends to be value-free (or, more precisely, it emphasizes economic rationality and technical efficiency); it promotes passivity; it is overly theoretical and academic in the worst sense of those terms; and, finally, it is dominated by those whose vested interests are utterly inimical to ecological responsibility.[84] Meanwhile, however, he judged, the coming generation would need an altogether different set of values and beliefs for "citizenship" in a world where, as a book by E. F. Schumacher put it, "small is beautiful."[85]

For some writers, "ecological consciousness" defined the major element of any viable conception of contemporary citizenship. Others, in growing numbers, stressed "internationalism" as an equally important ingredient. "All civic education at this juncture in human history should be set in a global perspective; and this global perspective must be informed by just world order values," declared the authors of a section of the 1977 Report of the National Task Force on Citizenship Education, cosponsored by the Danforth Foundation and the Charles F. Kettering Foundation.[86] Henceforth, it was said, the school as an institution must devote itself "to the creation of a climate favorable to drastic change in the international system," to teaching about global "interdependence," and possibilities for the eventual creation of "a humanitarian world order."

Specifically, the report announced, in devoting themselves more vigorously to the study of international relations and world affairs, educational institutions should involve students with such questions as (1) How can the likelihood of international violence be reduced significantly? (2) How can tolerable conditions of worldwide economic welfare, social justice, and ecological stability be created? (3) How can a warless and more just world be achieved and maintained? and (4) How can the quality of human life be improved on a planetary scale?[87]

Ranking among the most trenchant critiques of American education from an internationalist perspective was a work by Edwin O. Reischauer, former U.S. ambassador to Japan, entitled, *Toward The 21st Century: Education For A Changing World.* The most pressing problems of the next century, he argued, will be universal and planetary in scope—environmental pollution, the exhaustion of natural resources, overpopulation. They will be solved (if at all) only through international cooperation, supported by informed citizens who have been educated in a new and radically different way. Moreover, considering the inevitable time lag in effecting change through education, reforms must begin immediately. "We need a profound reshaping of education if mankind is to survive in the sort of world that is fast evolving," Reischauer asserted; and he proceeded to lay out in detail the concrete changes he felt would be needed. The burden of his argument was that education faces "some stupendous tasks" in fostering a "generalized understanding of world problems and a sense of world citizenship."[88]

Today, he claimed, American schoolchildren "absorb little real knowledge of peoples and nations with different cultural backgrounds and gain little perception of the growing interdependence of mankind and the necessity of developing a sense of world community." The implicit frame of reference for most social education is the sovereign nation-state, a political unit that is fast losing its relevance in the emergent global economic order. Above and beyond the specialized technical skills needed by the few in tomorrow's world, educational institutions must diffuse more widely among all students "skills in communication and knowledge about other countries and cultures." Summing up, Reischauer concluded, "A reorientation of education so as to give young people everywhere a sense of the shared interests and basic oneness of mankind and to prepare them for effective participation as members of a world community is, I believe, a clear necessity for human survival in the twenty-first century."[89]

That Americans have shown little enthusiasm as a people for learning about other cultures or learning foreign languages is well known. Moreover, given the ability of pollsters and opinion analysts to demonstrate that the public is "appallingly" ignorant about almost any foreign people or international problem, commissions concerned with international understanding have little trouble discovering many causes for alarm. This was certainly the case in the early 1980s, when several "blue ribbon" groups charged with assessing American's knowledge of and capacity to understand and communicate with peoples from other nations and cultures issued reports. Among them was a 1979 report of the President's Commission on Foreign Language and International Studies, entitled, *Strength Through Wisdom;* the report of the National Assembly on Foreign Language and International Studies, *Toward Education with a Global Perspective;* the Council on Learning's Task Force on Education and World View report, *Statement on Education and World View;* and the Atlantic Council's policy entitled, *The Successor Generation: Its Challenges and Responsibilities.* [90]

Noting the widening gap between needs associated with global interdependence and the competence to meet them, the President's Commission urged strengthening foreign-language and international-studies instruction at all levels of formal education, from kindergarten through graduate school, and programs to enhance the international awareness and participation of U.S. business and organized labor. Also recommended was the creation of regional research-demonstration centers for pedagogical and curriculum development in international-studies areas. The Commission further called for the reinstatement of foreign-language requirements in higher education, a required international-education component in teacher certification, and the inclusion of at least two or three international-studies courses in all undergraduate-degree programs.

Both the Task Force report and that of the National Assembly dealt with reforming education in order to increase American capabilities for competing with interdependence. The Assembly's document, for example, defined "global perspective" as "the ability to conceptualize and understand the complexities of the international system; a knowledge of world cultures and international events; and an understanding of the diversity and commonalities of human values and interests." As a major focus of educational effort, such a perspective was to include "the competence to live and work with other peoples, cultures, and issues, not just to understand them." [91] Similarly, the Council on Learning's Task Force felt "global understanding" was of paramount importance, and ought to include "a fundamental understanding of the key elements of global and national interdependence; a deeper knowledge and understanding of another culture; and general competency in a second language." [92]

The Atlantic Council's *The Successor Generation* spoke of the "frightening degree of ignorance" and apathy among American youth revealed in recent polls regarding democratic principles and "the need to strengthen and defend them in an interdependent and turbulent world." [93] It also called upon the nation's educational system to develop an ethical base, or "set of beliefs and principles that can serve as bulwarks against which the claims of conflicting value systems can be assessed.''[94] Only through an affirmation and reaffirmation of shared values, the Council stated, could young people be guided toward a better understanding of global interdependence and its impact on human society everywhere.

At the same time that high-level commissions were beginning to urge more attention to international education, professional educators' associations were issuing similar appeals. The American Association of School Administrators, for example, in February of 1980 adapted an official resolution urging the establishment of educational programs that would ''reflect an international point of view and engender respect for and appreciation of the diversity of the world's cultures and its people.'' In addition to providing more opportunities for students to acquire competence in foreign languages, schools were called up to ''promote knowledge concerning various peoples and problems that relate to the world community.''[95]

A similar policy resolution on educator preparation issued by the Association for Supervision and Curriculum Development (ASCD) held that ''teacher education should help teachers acquire deeper understanding of other cultures and peoples, greater insight into world affairs and world problems, and broader understanding of the need for support of democratic ideals.'' The ASCD document also lamented the decline in enrollments in foreign-language classes. ''This trend should be reversed,'' it was said, ''as it is imperative that today's students develop understanding of and sensitivity to other cultures and gain the ability to communicate with the diverse peoples of . . . the world.''[96]

A 1980 policy statement from the Council of Chief State School Officers likewise voiced strong support for ''education for global interdependence.'' Two years earlier, the National Association of Elementary School Principals (NAESP) had acknowledged ''the need for understanding of peoples at home and abroad and for intelligent leadership in global matters.'' Schools, the NAESP acknowledged, must establish programs designed to promote ''increased global awareness'' and that ''engender respect and appreciation for the diversity of the world's cultures and promote knowledge concerning various peoples and problems that relate to the world community.''[97] Over a four-year period extending into the eighties, the National Association of Secondary School Principals issued a series of resolutions affirming its commitment to educational programs that ''lead to a greater understanding of other peoples and other cultures throughout the world and to a fuller appreciation of the increasing realities of global interdependence.''[98]

The most detailed statement was forthcoming in April of 1981, from the National Council for the Social Studies (NCSS). ''Growing interrelatedness of life on our planet has increased the need for citizens to possess the knowledge and sensitivity required to comprehend the global dimensions of political, economic, and cultural phenomena,'' the NCSS declared. ''The purpose of global education is to develop in youth the knowledge, skills, and attitudes needed to live effectively in a world possessing limited natural resources and characterized by ethnic diversity, cultural pluralism, and increasing interdependence.'' The foundation of popular understanding, the Council's document emphasized, would have to be built at the elementary and secondary levels; and programs of "citizen education in a global age" were held to be of sufficient importance as to warrant being considered more than a mere addition to the curriculum.[99]

Overall, by the early eighties, attempts to redefine the meaning of citizenship in a dawning era of global interdependence and to give the concept a more internationalist cast were well advanced. Implicit throughout was the assumption that global "cooperation" would follow from "awareness" and "understanding." Special conferences on global education convened regularly. Reports, curriculum guides, instructional materials, and bibliographies of topical literature were produced in abundance, both by professional education associations and by politically active special-interest groups. Conspicuous by its absence, however, was any emergent consensus on what place international problems or concerns

---

### THE HUMAN MANIFESTO

Human life on our planet is in jeopardy. It is in jeopardy from war that could pulverize the human habitat. It is in jeopardy from preparations for war that destroy or diminish the prospects of decent existence. It is in jeopardy because of the denial of human rights. It is in jeopardy because the air is being fouled and the waters and soil are being poisoned. It is in jeopardy because of the uncontrolled increase in population. If these dangers are to be removed and if human development is to be assured, we the people of this planet must accept obligations to each other and to the generations of human beings to come.

We have the obligation to free our world of war by creating an enduring basis for world wide peace. We have the obligation to safeguard the delicate balances of the natural environment and to develop the world's resources for the human good. We have the obligation to place the human interest above the national interest, and human sovereignty above national sovereignty. We have the obligation to make human rights the primary concern of society. We have the obligation to create a world order in which people neither have to kill nor be killed.

In order to carry out these obligations, we the people of this world assert our primary allegiance to each other in the family of humankind. We declare our individual citizenship in the world community and our support for a United Nations capable of governing our planet in the common human interest.

The world belongs to the people who inhabit it. We have the right to change it, shape it, nurture it. Life in the universe is unimaginably rare. It must be protected, respected and cherished.

We pledge our energies and resources of spirit to the preservation of the human habitat and to the infinite possibilities of human betterment in our time.

—Norman Cousins, with Don Keys, *Credo of Planetary Citizens,* as cited in *The Caravan for Human Survival* (Arlington, Va.: World Federalists Association, 1981), p. 1. Reprinted with permission of Planetary Citizens.

should occupy in school programs. Rarely were efforts made to assign priorities or to assign responsibilities within school systems for internationally oriented education. Ironically, as more official attention was paid to foreign-language instruction and global-education curricula, however, federal support for research, curriculum development, and programs in these areas was diminishing steadily.

Meanwhile, however, burgeoning interest in "futuristics" or "futurism" was coming to define a new phase in the reconstructionist tradition launched by Counts, Rugg, Childs, and Brameld. Depending on how it was conceived, in its educational bearings, futurism promised a far more detailed agenda for how formal schools could be harnessed to the task of enhancing prospects for human survival in the years ahead. Although no less apocalyptic in how it contemplated the thrust of current trends, futurist thought tended to be more hopeful in tone, more optimistic, more positive in its assessment of reform possibilities. Nowhere was this more true than in the writings of best-selling author Alvin Toffler, whose books *Future Shock, Learning For Tomorrow,* and *The Third Wave,* more than anything else, were responsible for popular ferment over futurism.

## FUTURISM

"Future shock," as Toffler defined it, refers to "the shattering stress and disorientation" individuals experience when they are subjected to too much change in too short a time. It is, he claimed, "the disease of change," and as a socio-pathology it is no longer a distantly potential danger, but a "real sickness from which increasingly large numbers already suffer." The roaring currents of change, he alleged, are already upon us, overturning institutions, assaulting time-honored values, and shriveling our psychological roots. Change is "the process by which the future invades our lives." [100] Yet for all the rhetoric about the need to help people survive the buffeting of rapid and continuous change, Toffler declared, what passes for education today is a hopeless anachronism, facing "backward toward a dying system, rather than forward to the emerging new society." Schools devote their energies to cranking out people "tooled for survival in a system that will be dead before they are." [101]

"All agree," he claimed, "that our educational system is rocketing toward disaster and that we cannot redirect it, no matter what innovations we introduce, unless we take a fresh look at the role of the future in education." [102] Looking back over the past hundred years or more, as Toffler saw it, in preindustrial society the past crept forward into the present and repeated itself in the future. It was sufficient to school the young in the skills, knowledge, and values of the past, because those were what they would need to know in the future. Social change was virtually nonexistent or advanced at an extremely slow pace. It was safe to assume that as the present resembled the past, the future would substantially conform to the present.

Everything changed with the advent of the Industrial Revolution. Mass education was the product of industrialism; and it was designed to adapt people for "a new world of repetitive indoor toil, smoke, noise, machines, crowded living conditions, and collective discipline." [103] The emergent educational system simulated this industrial world: it assembled masses of students (raw material) for processing by teachers (workers) in a central school (the factory) run by an administrative bureaucracy modeled after the structure of industrial hierarchies (management). Even the organization of knowledge into fixed disciplines was grounded on the assumptions of industrialism.

"The inner life of the school," Toffler explained, "thus became an anticipatory mirror, a perfect introduction to industrial society. The most criticized features of education . . . the regimentation, lack of individualization, the rigid systems of seating, grouping, grading and marking, the authoritarian role of the teacher . . ." were precisely what made mass public education adapted to its place and time. Those who were processed through the educational machine entered an adult society whose structure of jobs, roles, and institutions was not dissimilar to that of the school itself. Children did not simply learn material for subsequent use; they *lived* as well as learned a life resembling the one they would lead in the future. [104] The "covert" curriculum taught three courses: punctuality, obedience, and rote work. "In this sense, the schools of the industrial age were a highly efficient anticipation of what life would hold later on. They offered an advanced simulation of adult life. And that was, perhaps, a sensible thing for schools to do." [105]

The problem, Toffler argued, is that the system still teaches the same covert curriculum, even though the world the child will enter no longer requires the same virtues. Today's schools, in other words, simulate the past, not the future. As he phrased it,

> All of us in the high-technology nations are caught up in one of the great revolutions in human history. We are in the process of creating a new civilization which will demand new ways of life, attitudes, values, and institutions. The young people in our schools today are going to live in a world radically different from the one we know—and a world that will be undergoing continual and in all likelihood, accelerating change. [106]

The pace of life in the contemporary postindustrial era is quickening at an ever-increasing rate; the scope and magnitude of changes are growing larger; and the accelerative thrust of society is toward still greater change.

For Toffler, the lesson was plain: education must have as its prime objective increasing people's ability to cope with continuous change. The more change, Toffler wrote, the greater the need to extend one's attempt to cope with the environment into the future:

> It is no longer sufficient for Johnny to understand the past. It is not even enough for him to understand the present, for the here-and-now environment will soon vanish. Johnny must learn to anticipate the directions and rate of change. He must . . . learn to make repeated, probabilistic, increasingly long-range assumptions about the future. And so must Johnny's teachers. [107]

Serving much the same point was a comment offered by Warren Ziegler:

> The children of this decade will be inhabitants of the 21st century—our future, but *their* present. If, like past generations through the recorded history of mankind, we could still safely assume that the future will be like the present, we could rest easy with the application of past verities to the existential present. But there is a growing suspicion . . . that the future is going to be sufficiently unlike the past to raise a portentous question about the present aims, contents and structures of education.[108]

"I can think of no more important role for education," Toffler asserted, "than to serve as one of the great adaptive mechanisms both for the social system as a whole and for the individual within it."[109] Assailing the present-day curriculum as "a mindless holdover from the past," he argued that nothing should ever be included in a required curriculum unless it could be justified incontrovertibly in terms of the future. A "super-industrial education," he held, would be devoted to helping young people generate successive, alternative images of the future: assumptions about new types of jobs and professional vocations, changing human relationships, shifting ethical norms, sociological and technological innovations, and novel life-styles. "It is only by generating such assumptions," he remarked, "defining, debating, systematizing and continually updating them, that we can deduce the nature of the cognitive and effective skills" needed to survive the onslaught of tomorrow.[110]

Both the content and process or structure of instruction would need to change, he predicted. Besides revamping curricula, he urged a move to "ad-hocratic" forms of educational organization, management, and administration stressing dispersal, decentralization, mobility, and flexibility. New contingency programs, the teaching of new skills under the most imaginative circumstances possible, the fostering of new values better adapted to a fast-changing world, a comprehensive reorientation of the schools from their past-oriented focus to concentration on the future—these he cited as major imperatives confronting educators in the modern world.

As evidence of the need for education to counter "the dizzying disorientation brought on by the premature arrival of the future," as he put it, Toffler cited numerous instances of situations in which young schoolchildren were asked to imagine what the future might be like, and the roles people would play in the world of tomorrow. In almost all cases, students left *themselves* out of their forecasts. For the most part the kinds of futures they saw themselves moving into were simply extensions of the type of lives their parents were living at present. "They did not foresee," he commented, "that the rather shattering or monumental world events they themselves forecast—including revolutions, technological upheavals, and ecological catastrophes—would have any impact on their own lives. In short, they seemed to make a sharp distinction between a swiftly changing future 'out there' and a more or less unchanged personal future."

This suggested for him a need to refocus the temporal horizon in education. "If our young people are not encouraged to think of the future as something likely to require change in *their own* lives,'' he warned, ''then we are producing millions of candidates for future shock.'' Today's society, Toffler emphasized, is undergoing a process of radical fragmentation. It is beginning to require not merely many thousands of new occupations that never existed in the past, but new personality types, new roles, and new skills. Schools would need therefore to find new ways to transmit those skills from old to young—''and in the opposite direction as well.''[111]

Futurists repeatedly stressed the point that today's world is historically unique. ''A favorite cliche of historians,'' observed University of Maryland sociologist Jean Dresden Grambs,

> is that those who do not remember the past are condemned to repeat it, but I believe there are conditions today that have no precedent in the past. . . . The reality of nuclear armaments is that human beings now have the potential for destroying most of the civilizations on this planet or poisoning the whole earth so that viable life is impossible. Nothing in the annals of diplomacy or state craft, nothing in the rulebooks on protocol tells how to negotiate with total annihilation.[112]

Toffler, however, saw room for optimism. ''Life will be what we make it,'' he insisted. ''The decisions we make today will determine what our life will be like.''[113]

The argument he presented in *The Third Wave* was that there was no need to succumb to despair or to become paralyzed by pessimism. Constructive personal and social options are still available. Linear thinking, he argued, can lead people into a dangerous cul-de-sac in which they reject any possibility of a hopeful future, not to mention the will to work for a decent tomorrow for humankind. At least some modicum of optimism is needed, Toffler declared, some image of a possible, plausible, and hopeful future for the new generation. ''Today,'' he noted, ''we either send children through the schooling process and they come out ignorant—without a thought in their heads about the complex problems that we all face, from crises in food supply and energy to international relations, and so on—or else they are given so extremely pessimistic an image of our present dilemmas that they are paralyzed.'' Both of those approaches produce people who are inadequate and incapable of coping. Both undermine society's capacity to face up to its challenges and to deal with them. ''Schools that fail to give kids a vision of a workable future are crippling those kids,'' he claimed, ''and are doing something extremely dangerous to democracy.''[114]

Howard F. Didsbury, Jr., executive director of Kean College's futuristics program, agreed. ''There are two perilous attitudes toward the future,'' he remarked,

> one is belief in a ''technological fix''—the notion that science and technology will snatch us back from the abyss just in time; this attitude tends to encourage complacency. At the other extreme—and equally dangerous—is the great temptation to exaggerate or overemphasize the complexities and difficulties that lie before us. Such an overemphasis tends to make the problems seem so great that students grow apathetic or feel completely ineffectual.[115]

## FUTURIST IMPERATIVES FOR EDUCATION

Either way, observed Ervin Laszlo, the most crucial problem of contemporary education is that while society is changing and in a generation will be very different from the present, "education in matters of social concern is hardly changing and seems to be bent on remaining what it has been for the last generation or two." This, he predicted, "will create an increasing gap between society and the educational establishment, making the latter irrelevant and the former dangerously adrift in the absence of widespread and reliable knowledge." [116]

Most futurist writers acknowledged the difficulty of "shifting education into the future tense," as Toffler put it, but they were agreed that failure to make the attempt could prove disastrous. "I'm deeply convinced," wrote R. Buckminster Fuller, "that the subject of Learning Tomorrows contains within it the answer as to whether humanity is going to be able to continue much longer on our planet—for we are going to have to acquire an almost entirely new educational system and do so almost 'overnight.' " [117]

Solon T. Kimball weighed in with an identical opinion: "We can no longer assume that the knowledge or the practices that served us adequately in the past are sufficient for either the present or the future. . . . We must continually construct an educational system to serve a society that is in a continuous state of emergence." [118] Offered Edgar Dale: "A mature society is one that plans ahead for at least one generation. . . . It uses its best brains to forecast the long-range effect of its daily decisions. Such a society is constantly saying, 'If we do this today, then *that* will happen ten, twenty, or thirty years from now.' And it sets up the self-correcting feedback system which enables us to change plans as unexpected conditions arise." [119]

Specific prescriptions varied on how to bring school and society closer together. Almost all analysts were agreed that traditional curricula and methodologies offered little help in creating future-focused education, though they differed on what replacements were required. "We should recognize," one writer observed, "that today's curriculum is the residue of traditions dating back thousands of years, and generally reflects what teachers want to teach more than what young people need to learn. Teachers have invented many ingenious arguments for their subjects, because they want to protect their livelihoods, but we should not let ourselves be deceived." Edward Cornish, of the World Future Society, accordingly foresaw grave difficulties in bringing about educational reform; and he counted obstructionism on the part of teachers and academic scholars as the chief worry. [120]

Robert Theobald felt that students should be taught survival skills to cope with risk, uncertainty, and stress. He also urged the inculcation of values implied by a finite universe. [121] As characterized by E. Paul Torrance, the new value orientations to be stressed included a shift from homogeneity to heterogeneity; from standardization to destandardization; from competition to interaction; from conquering nature to living in harmony with nature; from material satisfaction to cultural satisfaction; from efficiency to esthetics and ethics; and from thinking in categories to "thinking in social context."[122] Dennis Van Avery, Director of the Graduate Program in Education at Utah's Westminster College, thought the abilities students would need would include "a tolerance for multiple interpretations and the ability to explore and create alternatives." They would need a tolerance for ambiguity, and adaptability to change.[123]

Glen Heathers, of Philadelphia's Research for Better Schools, outlined what he considered the psychological requirements for living in the future. In the economic realm, he argued, the increasing proportion of jobs in service occupations portend a need for greater skills in human relations. In the political sphere, the need is for social awareness and a sense of responsibility for active participation in dealing with acute societal problems. Socially, the increasing need, Heathers claimed, is for individuals to acquire the attitudes, values, and skills required for effective interpersonal and intergroup relations. In the personal sphere, each person will need to develop qualities of individuality that can withstand societal pressures toward conformity and anonymity. Building a rich inner life is an important purpose at any time, he observed. It becomes all the more important in a mass society whose social life tends to become more impersonal, homogeneous, and in some sense dehumanizing. Paradoxically, perhaps, the uniformity of contemporary culture gives rise to the need for greater diversity in life-styles, closer identification with some personal reference group (cultural, ethnic, racial, religious, and so on), and tolerance for interpersonal or intergroup differences.[124]

Louis J. Rusin, of the University of Illinois, was unwilling to try to spell out the substance of future curricula, but he believed that "in the period ahead we will need a curriculum based more upon active and less upon inert knowledge." Whatever its content, subject matter that was "purely decorative or steeped in tradition" would have to be abandoned in favor of knowledge "that helps the young to better understand their world." Schools of the future, he wrote, must emphasize decision-making skills: "It is precisely because the citizenry of the future will be called upon to make agonizingly difficult choices in priorities, lifestyles, and social aspirations that the instructional program of the schools must treat, in varying contexts, the processes through which people examine problems, gather evidence, project probable consequences, and reach decisions."[125]

Humanist educator Arthur Combs took much the same approach. Preparation for the future has *always* been a primary function of education, he argued. But until recently the future to be prepared for was generally stable and predictable. Consequently the curriculum could be based on precisely defined skills and subject matter. But with accelerated social change, it is no longer possible to predict with exactitude what knowledge and skills will be needed in the future. The only "certainties" ahead, Combs believed, have to do with the information explosion, the increasing pace of change, the primacy of social problems, and the increasingly important need people will feel for personal satisfaction and fulfillment in their own lives. The implications that follow for education, as he viewed them, were that it would never again be possible to design a curriculum to be required of everyone, that tomorrow's educational system would have to concentrate on producing effective problem-solvers, that questions of value would become paramount, and that social change would require education as a lifelong process.[126]

"We now have the knowledge and the technology to feed, clothe, and house the entire world," Combs asserted, "only to find ourselves faced with a new problem: how to use this knowledge and technology for the general (i.e., worldwide) welfare." The crux of the issue as he defined it was that "the major problems we face today and the primary problems we shall face in the future *have to do with learning to live effectively with ourselves and other people.*" [127] Problems of overpopulation, environmental pollution, poverty, food distribution, energy, health, crime and violence, terrorism, aging, socioeconomic inequality, and basic human rights are all essentially *social* problems, he emphasized. Even the nuclear bomb is no problem in itself; "it is the people who might use it with whom we must be concerned." [128]

In an increasingly interdependent era, societal stability becomes ever more precarious. Even a single individual armed with modern technology can wreak unimaginable havoc through an act of terrorism or sabotage. The power of people for good or evil is being magnified. Those who feel frustrated or alienated can pose hazards for everyone. Hence, personal fulfillment is a necessary ingredient for society's continuing welfare and safety: "More than ever, societies of the future will be dependent upon caring, responsible citizens. . . ." Combs summarized the educational imperative as follows: "The future demands effective problem-solvers and citizens willing and able to deal effectively with themselves and each other in the solution of human problems. It requires open-system thinking and an emphasis on values, processes, human problems, and the human condition." An adequate system of schooling, he concluded, "must be concerned with student feelings, attitudes, beliefs, understandings, values—the things that make us human. . . ." [129]

Futurists continued to wrestle with the question of what substantive content and skills offered the longest-range survival value. "Cognitive skills" required for living in a world of resource shortages, obsolescent social systems, uncontrolled technological innovation, and increasing global interdependence, according to Christopher Dede and Dwight Allen, would likely include: (1) reading/writing/editing; (2) listening/seeing/computer usage; (3) speaking/logic; (4) mathematics/analytical problem-solving; (5) proficiency in scientific method; (6) pattern recognition/managing information overload; (7) forecasting and prediction; (8) media usage; and (9) decision making.[130] Another pair of writers denied that basic skills, understandings, and attitudes that have the greatest survival potential could be identified with any great precision. They acknowledged, for example, the likelihood that the traditional three R's would remain essential, but, as they pointed out, "even now their position is being challenged by the growing importance of becoming fluent in the various computer languages." Computers, television, and other electronic innovations, they predicted, would soon diminish the importance of conventional word-based literacy.[131]

For Robert Fitch and Cordell Svengalis, writing in *Futures Unlimited: Teaching About Worlds To Come* (1979), a publication of the National Council For The Social Studies, school curricula in future would need to emphasize to a much greater degree analysis of major social issues and the development of skills through which students deal with issues, manage the exponential growth of information, and sort out social priorities and moral questions. Finally, however, they alleged, the need was to "emphasize learning strategies which develop creative and imaginative thought processes, rather than methods which emphasize little more than the acquisition of facts." The discrete study of possible futures—building scenarios—would likewise "provide additional strength to the implementation of inquiry strategies."[132]

Many writers detected great promise in the study of the future as a subject *in its own right,* analogous to studies of the past or present. "I am convinced," one curriculum specialist observed, "that children are naturally interested in studying the future and have a variety of apparently natural, spontaneous ways of investigating the future. These include: imagining, fantasying, asking questions, guessing, experimenting, and experiencing. To teach children to study the future we must understand these natural tendencies, build upon them, and make them more powerful tools."[133]

The point, of course, as futurists saw it, was not to think of the future as fixed and unalterable, but as an array of possibilities dependent upon, and as outgrowths of, present-day choices. "Orienting a course toward what might happen in the future turns students from antiquarians into planners, that is, from passive research into the past to active participation in shaping the future," wrote Edward Cornish.[134]

Many advocates of courses in futuristics made the point that the future in a very real sense already affects the present as much as does the past, because current beliefs about what is in store profoundly influence the attitudes and hence the behavior of people in the here and now. And what people believe and do *at present* inevitably helps shape what is to come. The future is not predetermined; it depends upon how it is anticipated and decided upon in advance. If for no other reason, then, study *into* the future is as important as study *of* the present or *about* the past.

Courses in futuristics or "futurology," as proponents envisioned them, could assume many different forms. Studies in such diverse fields as anthropology, economics, political science, psychology, sociology, and philosophy at the collegiate level might incorporate consideration of likely trends and developments, with particular attention paid to the ways in which new discoveries are likely to impinge upon existing disciplines and organized bodies of subject matter. Whole courses might be devoted to imaginative projections of the future. Alternatively, an important focus might be on the complex relations between human values and technological change, as in "bio-ethics," which deals with the moral implications of burgeoning medical technology—genetic engineering, cloning, artificial insemination and "test-tube" babies, cybernetics, *ad infinitum.*

Futurists called for new courses devoted to war and peace, leisure, population control and eugenics, ecology, social planning, forecasting, utopianism, and other topics. Their need, as Irving Buchen insisted, would only increase with time; and he was confident that a future-orientation in education would eventually be recognized as something more than a passing fad that could be easily dismissed. "Futurism," he argued, "is neither super-gadgetry nor salvationist ideology. It does not traffic in hysterics or lullabies. It does not seek to change human nature in manipulative fashion, but rather to encourage awareness of the rich changes inherent in its own multiplicity. Above all, futurism does not now, and never will, possess an assured or fixed body of content that exists apart from what it seeks to comprehend."[135] The crucial factor, he and others implied, was not the specific content of educational programs, but how well they helped young people prepare themselves for an uncertain and problematic succession of tomorrows.

Among the most important attempts to identify "what young learners need to understand, not merely to survive in the years ahead but to live humanely as well" was undertaken in conjunction with a 1980–81 Phi Delta Kappa Diamond Jubilee curriculum project funded by the Lilly Endowment. Opinions were solicited from an international panel of 135 scholars on what young learners would need to know growing up in the waning years of the twentieth century. Reporting on the results was Harold G. Shane, of Indiana University, a long-time proponent of future-focused curricula in education.[136] Nearly all the scholars who were interviewed agreed on the existence and nature of such global problems as environmental pollution, the growing energy deficit, and the widening gap between industrialized and nonindustrialized nations. But they differed widely on how such problems could be addressed or resolved. Major consensus came only on the point that the next quarter-century would bring continued turbulence or unrest. Major factors responsible cited by panelists included population growth, poverty and hunger, political instability, the nuclear-arms race, and the electronic assault on people's lives and sensibilities.

"Competing values and ideologies proved to be the epicenter of ominous problems of the next several decades," Shane recounted. Value conflicts took various forms, but all reflected a major split between those who believe "the biosphere must be exploited to satisfy basic human needs and those who see the earth as a closed ecosystem that requires a better balance between humans and nature."[137]

Panelists predicted mounting pressures from developing nations for a new global economic order favoring a more equitable distribution of resources. Worldwide inflation, increasing public and private debt, and unemployment were repeatedly identified as phenomena that threaten to lower the world standard of living. Political fragmentation on a planetary scale was also mentioned as an obstacle to peace, as was proliferation of nuclear-weapons technology. The social irresponsibility of multinational conglomerates, the world's underinvestment in research for alternative energy sources, the likelihood that a global revolution of rising aspirations would flounder in frustration and disappointment, and a dozen or so other trends were cited as formative influences upon the near future.

Against this background, panelists tried to pick out the elements of a viable curriculum for the dangerous years ahead. As Shane summarized their views, interviewees identified certain basic "survival concepts" from the natural sciences worth emphasizing. These included the concept of limits to future growth, the importance of conservation, the reality of growing interdependence, and the idea of "entropy" as applied to resource utilization (for example, when fossil fuels are consumed to produce energy, the process is irreversible—resources are "degraded from useful to useless forms" and irretrievably lost).

---

In an age when men have invested machines to melt cities, an age in which war has become the norm and in which the only question is how hot or cold it is to be, it should hardly be necessary to speak of the seriousness of the future. . . . Yet I do not believe that most of us take the future very seriously.

> —Robert L. Heilbroner, quoted in
> Gordon Feller, Sherle R. Schwenninger, and
> Diane Singerman, eds., *Peace And World
> Order Studies, A Curriculum Guide* (New
> York: Transnational Academic Program,
> Institute for World Order, 1980), p. 131.

Insights about nuclear weapons are of the utmost importance to the younger generation—for preventing nuclear war, and for creating social forms which take into account man's radically changed relationship to his world because of the potentially terminal revolution associated with these weapons.

> —Robert Jay Lifton, *History And Human
> Survival* (New York: Random House, 1970),
> p. 371.

We are set, irrevocably, I believe, on a path that will take us to the stars—unless in some monstrous capitulation to stupidity and greed, we destroy ourselves first. And out there in the depths of space, it seems very likely that, sooner or later, we will find other intelligent beings. Some of them will be less advanced than we; some, probably most, will be more. . . . There will be a great deal of growing up required of the infant human species.

> —Carl Sagan, *Broca's Brain* (New York:
> Random House, 1979), p. 314.

---

From the life sciences, scholars recommended attention to the "holistic" quality of basic natural laws, the phenomenon of synergistic combination, and the complexity of interrelationships among biological life systems. In the social sciences, a number of those interviewed felt that global or world history should be taught, as well as comparative politics. In economics, the issue of growth versus "small is beautiful" should be stressed, and the idea of "trade-offs" in making decisions. Sociologists on the panel spoke of the need for "new forms of mutual comprehension and solidarity" in global society. Anthropologists agreed, citing the urgent need to foster greater awareness of cultural diversity, pluralism, and relativism. The importance of knowing at least one language other than one's mother tongue for cross-cultural communication and understanding was also underscored.[138]

Archictectonic values "to counter the raw self-interest and savagery that lurk beneath the thin veneer of 20th-century civilization in much of the world," as Shane phrased it, included social responsibility, altruism and public service, ethical interpersonal relationships, equality, and egalitarianism. He concluded his report with two points: "First, to help our youth to survive and to live humanely, we must recognize that the most important social decisions in human history must be made soon—within the next 20 or 25 years—and they can only be made wisely by *educated* persons."

Secondly,

> we can no longer ask why don't *they* do something to improve our schools, rather, we must say, what are the ways that *we* can shape a humane and decent future by the way *we* reorder the attitudes, values, and behaviors that are prerequisite both to better ecological relationships with our physical world and to better human environments in the home, the school, and the community.[139]

## CONTRA FUTURISM

When it was not simply ignored, futurism in education attracted more than a few sympathetic critics. Historian Herbert J. Muller, of Indiana University, agreed that much of what has come down from the past in the universities is of questionable value for contemporary needs, and has been unquestioned simply because it has long been customary, "as comfortable to academics as old habits, and as mindless as the ivy on the college walls."[140] He conceded too that much of what passes for scholarship is pedantry: "I have myself dwelt wearily on the too many thousands of Ph.D. dissertations and learned articles in the professional journals, the great bulk of them written by specialists only for other specialists, with little relevance to basic issues of value judgments, still less to education for the future."[141]

Muller also endorsed the futurist contention that young people have more need for flexibility, adaptability, and resourcefulness than any generation before them. Echoing sentiments expressed many times before, he declared that education should promote such characteristics through a fuller awareness of present-day social change and the probable future consequences of current trends. Students need to know what they are up against, the very real dangers, the good reasons for alarm that exist. They also need to retain a spirit of guarded optimism and to become aware of the more hopeful possibilities ahead. The trouble with traditional curricula, he felt, was that they had not focused enough on the most *relevant* uses of the past, on understanding the present, or anticipating the future.

Muller further endorsed the idea of whole courses devoted to the study of possible futures. Besides classes in ecology, war and peace, futurist sociology, economics, and psychology, he cited the obvious possibility of a study of utopias, ranging from Thomas More or Francis Bacon, through Edward Bellamy, Paul Goodman, Lewis Mumford, Karl Marx, and B. F. Skinner (*Walden II*). Such study might likewise illustrate the revulsion against the utopian tradition, as in *Brave New World, The Tomorrow File, 1984,* and much science fiction. In view of humanity's growing technological capabilities, visions of ideal or nightmarish possibilities become especially pertinent, he alleged.

His support for futurism notwithstanding, however, Muller was troubled by the apparent tendency of writers such as Toffler to assume that education should mold people who are well adjusted to the increasingly rapid pace of life, to instant obsolescence, to constant transience and novelty. Not only did he find their faith in technology naive and their embrace of change dangerous; he felt that the futurist thesis was too ready to dismiss the past as irrelevant. If indeed the past is "dead," as many have alleged, he wrote, "I should still say so much the worse for the future." Orienting education toward the future need not entail a neglect of history; in fact, a future focus not grounded in appreciation for the past, he implied, was both shortsighted and ultimately self-defeating.

"I would concentrate instead," he remarked, "on efforts to give the young a better idea of what civilized life has meant and can mean at its best, so that they might help to shape a [decent] future. . . ."[142] While accepting the inevitability of much change, it is still important to ask how much is *necessary* or *desirable,* and as judged by *what* standards. Unwilling to allow technicians to make all the decisions and to strive for the sort of utopian superindustrial future forecast by Toffler, Muller insisted it was worthwhile studying basic human values and judgments inherited from the past. The need, he claimed, is to widen the range of choices in possible futures by introducing students to the wealth of possible answers about how to live and what to live for suggested by the diverse cultures of the past, in both East and West, as embodied in the great works of art and thought the human race has inherited.[143]

In the search for significance, for ways of ordering life and giving it meaning, Muller argued, there may be better alternatives illustrated in history than a culture characterized only by transience, impermanency, and manufactured experiences. Unthinking acceptance of a future world dominated by technique and technology would be shallow and superficial. A major human failure, he observed, is the inveterate, unreasoned tendency to resist change. But an equally undesirable alternative—sometimes encouraged by futurists—is the inclination to accept change uncritically. In the final analysis, he judged, the danger latent in much futurist thought, bereft of historical perspective, was that it might actually hasten the advent of a civilization resembling the frightening horrors conjured up by such dystopian novelists as Orwell and Huxley.

A somewhat different tack was taken by Lloyd P. Williams, of the University of Oklahoma. Like Muller, he assented to the proposition that planning for the future is important. People *should* try to anticipate pending developments. Alternative possibilities in human affairs *do* need to be formulated and held in mind. All this is common sense explicitly in the forefront of the educated mind; it is by no means the exclusive insight of futurists, he observed. Only a fool, for example, is oblivious to the fact that if current trends continue, the world is headed for ecological disaster and may eventually become uninhabitable. Together with the possibility of a thermonuclear war, these trends make human survival a problem for the first time in history. "Will the world dissolve into atomic dust," he asked, "or simply wither from petro-chemical induced stagnation, or perhaps just soften into a morass of insensitive, wallowing aimless human amoebas?"[144]

Yet even if we need to be concerned with the tendencies and consequences of our present-day actions, can the future be predicted with any certainty? Williams professed skepticism. The future, he avowed, "is less amenable to comprehension and even less subject to control than is generally recognized by the reformer. In a very real sense the future is absolutely unknown and our endless projections, extrapolations, and guesses are just as often wrong as not."[145] The notion that the future can be controlled, he alleged, "while understandable, is a charming, self-deceptive presumption." The future is almost "totally vagrant." Planning often goes astray, and efforts to control events typically end up in failure or produce totally unforeseen consequences. This is especially the case the longer the range of planning efforts: "The validity of an idea varies inversely with its projected distance into the future, so the more deeply we seek to penetrate the future the less precise our image. This . . . should keep us vividly aware of the need for restraint and caution, as predictions are notoriously subject to error."[146]

Williams found the "aura of assurance" surrounding futurists' predictions unpersuasive. More importantly, he felt it betrayed insensitivity or indifference to the persistent imperatives of human existence. Not all change represents progress; and it is easy to overestimate our ability to control social events in the same way or to the same degree that we manipulate physical phenomena. As he put it, "Several centuries of dramatic success in the natural sciences have made us believers in progress. That belief in turn has produced a dangerous strain of ingenuousness in modern people, innocently and gratuitously translating scientific success into social, scientific certainties."[147] The trap into which futurists fall, many of them, is to assume that scientific efforts to deal with people or society will prove as effective as have achievements in the natural and physical sciences.

For example, Williams hypothesized, the future may demonstrate something of the immutability or resistance to change of human nature, just as does the past:

> With history the long story of endless bloody war and exploitation, with politics a narrative of endless political oppression, with economics the tale of mad pursuit of wealth at any price, with social disorganization rife throughout the world, with the bomb

builders at work around the clock, with the family steadily disintegrating, with crime and terrorism widespread in the world, is it so unreasonable a conclusion to say that humans are selfish, predatory, savage creatures and only the accidental development of technology has alleviated our lot and thus, by diminishing suffering, permitted intermittent periods of civilized, restrained behavior? The four horsemen of the apocalypse have their steeds saddled and appear relatively typical men ready to ride again.[148]

In other words, perhaps human nature is a "given." If so, and if savagery and selfishness are intrinsic to it, then the nature of human beings sets limits upon future possibilities, limits that some futurists are unwilling to face up to and confront honestly.

Williams's most fundamental disagreement with futurists, however, was over the role of the school in social change. He dismissed as "idealistic fancy" the rational-democratic idea that education can be an instrument of social reform. Schools, Williams stated emphatically, do not reform society. They transmit dominant cultural patterns and values to the young; they cannot be sufficiently directive to reorder society. Furthermore, Williams felt, the hard truth of the matter is that strong governmental or military authority is needed to implement reforms on the scale demanded in today's disordered world. "One problem futurists need to face," he declared, ". . . is deliberately to decide whether they merely want to discuss social change, or democratically to play at social change, or rigorously to support that hard and concentrated authority necessary to avoid impending tragedy by forcing social change."[149] Naked power is required. Only in an authoritarian society can schools be used to reshape the social order; otherwise the effort is random, piecemeal, incidental, and relatively ineffective.

Thus, Williams believed, in order to maintain their credibility, futurists would either have to demonstrate that tough, realistic democratic change is possible to resolve the world's thorny problems or they would have to accept authoritarian solutions. "The alternative," he alleged, "is for futurism to become just one more historical curiosity buried in the massive graveyard of educational theory."[150]

In the meantime, his recommendation for education was to concentrate upon "the humanization of the young" and the "cultivation of sound character." We should, he said, approach the future with explicit recognition of the conjectural nature of our predictions and a sense of the highly improbable fulfillment of our loftier aspirations. Anything else would be self-deceptive or presumptuous. "Judicious people flow with the currents of history, living with quiet resignation. They use their influence constructively whenever possible, but they do so with a clear sense of the modest consequences likely to result." A "charitable providence" blinds us to the future and we should be grateful; otherwise we might all suffer mental derangement in our frenetic efforts to keep the globe habitable. Only one thing is certain, Williams wrote, and that is "the future is unfathomable and the wise person lives serenely in the present."[151]

## IN RETROSPECT AND PROSPECT

A half century or more of radical reformism in educational thought suggests a definable "tradition" of sufficient continuity to allow its restatement as a position or argument. In basic outline, the social-reconstructionist–futurist perspective may be said to incorporate the following tenets:

1. *Education is a social, political, and moral phenomenon.* The process of education is neither autonomous nor self-sufficient. That is, education takes its significance and direction from the social order and from the ways of living for which learners are prepared. Learning is inescapably social. Both the process and the content of instruction arise out of, and are products of, societal ideals, values, and purposes.

2. *Heretofore schooling has served as a mechanism of social reproduction and cultural transmission.* In its formal institutionalized expression, education is a refractory phenomenon, more or less mirroring the sociocultural milieu of which it is an integral part. Traditionally, schools have been employed as agencies for passing on a cultural inheritance and thereby sustaining intergenerational continuity. A related task has been to define, organize, and impart the knowledge, skills, and values necessary for effective participation in a social community. Consequently, insofar as educational endeavor is necessarily a long-term undertaking, schools have always tended to "lag behind" the forces of social change.

3. *Schooling tends to be a conservative and conserving influence in the maintenance of the social order.* Historically, schools have been—and continue to be—conservative institutions, in the dual sense of "conserving" and transmitting received knowledge, and in the political sense of being dominated or controlled by, and hence serving the needs of, dominant groups whose interest is the preservation and perpetuation of the existing order. Continuance of this domination is tantamount to a prescription for disaster.

4. *Education is never socially neutral.* Schools are instruments of cultural selection and discrimination. They reflect value choices in myriad ways: by how they are organized and administered, by the structure and content of curricula, and by the methods of instruction employed in formal classroom settings. Neither the structure nor the process of schooling is wholly impartial or objective. Bias is inevitable. It is revealed in what is selected to be taught, how it is taught, and what learning is most heavily emphasized. Typically, both the content and management of instruction buttress or reinforce the dominant assumptions, values, and belief systems of those who exercise power in society.

5. *The present world situation is historically unique.* War, injustice, poverty, inequality, despoilation of the environment, and overpopulation have dogged humankind throughout history. These are by no means new problems. But what is *absolutely* unique about the current world situation is the crisis brought on by the rapid acceleration of the pace of social change, on an unprecedented scale, and the uncontrolled development of technology. For the first time ever, humanity has at its disposal the technical capability for self-extinction and the virtual destruction of the bio-sphere. Whether by accident, miscalculation, or deliberate design, the unleashing of a nuclear holocaust could obliterate the human species and render the planet uninhabitable for most other higher life forms as well. The fact that Armaggedon has been avoided for the past four decades or so—the blink of an eye in the span of history—affords no guarantee whatsoever that a final cataclysm can be avoided indefinitely without drastic preventive measures.

  Hazards of nuclear war aside, the sheer growth in numbers of the planet's total human population appears to be straining the world's ecological carrying capacity. Technological growth has made possible an ever-increasing material standard of living for a sizable proportion of the global population. However, the benefits of technological innovation have been differential, further widening the gap between haves and have-nots, in the process generating incredible social stress. Moreover, the price of affluence has been the depletion of irreplaceable finite natural resources and ecological devastation. Conceivably, technology can continue to expand the limits of growth, and postpone a time when growth must cease (for example, through extraterrestrial importation of natural resources). But the margin for error is getting slimmer; and the social edifice erected upon a technological foundation is a precarious one, increasingly susceptible to disruption.

6. *Human survival demands social reconstruction.* In an era of worldwide crisis, there exists as never before an imperative to create a new social order, probably on a planetary scale. Global interdependence necessitates a broader frame of reference than that supplied within the context of sovereign, autonomous nation-states. If the world's problems are to be alleviated to any significant degree, collaborative and cooperative efforts will have to be undertaken on an international basis. They can be resolved only within such a framework. It is no longer possible, for example, for any country to solve its problems or to meet its own domestic needs without impacting upon the interests of other countries. Although it may not be possible to determine the precise shape and character of a reconstructed social order, it is likely that far-reaching systemic change must happen soon, within the span of the next generation or so.

   Whether societal reform can be achieved, through democratic or authoritarian means, is equally uncertain. What remains clear, nevertheless, is that societal reconstruction, if it occurs, will be accompanied by wrenching, even convulsive, political, economic, and cultural change. The new social order to come will demand a fundamental shift or reorientation in human values: from predatory competition to cooperative communalism, from elitism to egalitarianism, from exploitation to conservation, from inequality to equality. The only alternative is probable extinction of the human species or the rise of a totalitarian police state on a global scale.

7. *Education is related to social change.* The role of education in society must expand from one of cultural conservation to social adaptation. Schooling must become more socially relevant, more engaged with societal issues, more directly involved in effecting long-range change. As measured by these standards, conventional education today is woefully inadequate. It amounts in many cases to a desensitization process that inures the young to human suffering and injustice. To the extent that schools insulate learners from social reality, such institutions are morally irresponsible. To the extent that they misrepresent reality, they are positively obstructive. To the degree that they fail to engage students' energies in addressing that reality, they are soporific.

8. *Schools can and should help facilitate desirable social change:*
   a. Politically conscious educators should organize themselves to achieve power. In their collective awareness they should strive to achieve a shared vision of a reconstructed social order. Professional responsibility demands that such a vision be "imposed" upon schoolchildren and that learners' loyalties and enthusiasm be enlisted by teachers in working toward the realization of that vision (Counts); and/or
   b. Educators should become more fully aware of the "social presuppositions" upon which present-day schooling rests and labor to make them explicit in the consciousness of the young. Children should be offered a "new social orientation," so that they can arrive at their own reasoned conclusions and plans for action in addressing societal issues (Childs, Kohl); and/or
   c. Social-science research (most notably findings from social psychology and

cultural anthropology) is capable of providing the relevant empirical basis for decisions about social change. Schools are the logical forum for building an empirically grounded democratic consensus as to the desirability and necessity of a reconstructed planetary civilization. The method of "defensible partiality" implies that teachers should actively seek to promote the formation of such a consensus (Brameld); and/or

d. Educators should forswear the conservative bias that poses as ideological neutrality. They should acknowledge frankly the need to help a new generation comprehend, anticipate, adjust to, and ultimately control social change. The survival of humanity itself may well depend upon the success with which this task is carried forward. Although the school cannot *lead* social change, it need not follow it blindly either. While the school cannot (or should not) indoctrinate to any specific point of view, it still has a critical change-oriented role to perform. It must present relevant information around which informed opinion can coalesce. It must teach the skills and values needed for coping with social transformation. And above all, it must help facilitate societal renewal by assisting the young to make imaginative projections into alternative possible futures, so that they can select from among them and commit themselves to a livable tomorrow (Toffler).

9. *The future is open.* Past, present, and future are all interrelated. Contemporary culture is a product of what has been. But the present decreasingly resembles the past. The discontinuity between the present and the future is likely to be even greater. The future is built out of the present as the product of tendencies, trends, movements, and decisions taking place in the here and now. Yet, reflexively, the future also affects the present insofar as expectations about what lies ahead help shape what happens (or fails to happen) in the present moment. Neither fatalism nor despair constitutes an appropriate response to social change. The future remains to be decided upon. Education must become involved simultaneously in combating the pessimism that leads to paralysis and generating the concerned awareness that preserves hope.

10. *Change is inevitable.* The only knowable certainty is the prospect of greater and more rapid social change. The structure, process, and content of education will change accordingly. Whether it will change rapidly enough and in an appropriate direction may very well help determine what kind of future humanity has in store or, indeed, whether it has any future whatsoever.

## SUMMARY

The impulse to use schools for solving social ills—racial or ethnic discrimination, prejudice, sexism, socioeconomic inequality, and so forth—is deeply rooted in the American tradition. Throughout the nation's history, formal education has been enlisted to advance larger social ends or to address issues ranging from unemployment and juvenile delinquency to cultural assimilation and the preservation of religious or political ideals. As a social institution the school has never been insulated from societal turmoil. It invariably has been shaped by larger trends, currents, and reform movements in the undergirding social order. Oftentimes, schools are affected in terms of how they are supported, administered, or controlled, or through demands for ancillary services they render outside formal curricula. Almost as frequently, schools are called upon to offer explicit instruction directed toward some external interest or cause.

The first major attempt to recruit schools as direct agents of large-scale social change came in the 1930s, when such radical progressives as George S. Counts, Harold Rugg, and John L. Childs issued appeals for a new and more politically engaged type of education. These social reconstructionists, as they were later termed, denied the possibility of social or ideological neutrality in schooling. Either educational institutions would continue as they had since time immemorial, reflecting the interests of conservative, politically dominant interests in society, it was argued, or they would become engines of societal renewal. In the Depression era, when the American capitalist-corporate order seemed on the verge of collapse, proponents of "social frontier" education urged educators to help build a new socialist order.

Counts, Rugg, and others appeared to stop short of claiming that schools should or could promote specific social reforms directly. But they did say that institutionalized instruction should go well beyond simple "exposure" to competing values and beliefs. Educators, they affirmed, had a professional and moral responsibility to assume a more directive role in promoting the desirability of social change and outlining the type of societal transformation demanded by the times. On the whole, radical reformers had in mind a vision of an ideal social order founded on economic democracy or socialism and a communitarian system of values.

A direct spiritual descendent of the early reconstructionists was Theodore Brameld, who, throughout the 1950s and 1960s, offered a restatement of the position first enunciated twenty and thirty years before. Human culture today, he argued, confronts a crisis of planetary proportions. The risk of nuclear war is increasing. Growing world interdependence requires movement toward a new planetary civilization whose institutions and values are freely decided upon through democratic means, based upon relevant empirical considerations supplied through social-science research. If education were to prove itself adaptive to modern world conditions, Brameld insisted, it would be used systematically, in a conscious and deliberate way, to build the necessary consensus of opinion required in paving the way for a reconstructed global order.

Critics attacked the reconstructionist thesis on several grounds. Some denied the existence of a world culture crisis or rejected Brameld's analysis of the nature of that crisis. Others admitted that the crisis was real but were unpersuaded that educational endeavor could make any effective contribution in alleviating or resolving the crisis. Some critics faulted Brameld and his followers for their alleged failure to spell out in explicit detail how schools could be harnessed to the task. Still others argued that the policy recommendations offered by reconstructionists were either unsubstantiated, naive, or oblivious to the complex realities of effecting social change.

Meanwhile, predictions of impending doom were becoming more frequent. Some declarations of concern were forthcoming from intellectual leaders whose stature made dismissal increasingly difficult. The threats of nuclear devastation, global environmental pollution, depletion of resources, overpopulation, and international political anarchy were impossible to deny. Unfortunately, even the so-called experts disagreed among themselves as to what steps would be needed to avert catastrophe. There was even less agreement on how such gargantuan social problems as world hunger, poverty, human-rights violations, war, and ecological devastation were related to education. Many critics assailed traditional schooling for its seeming irrelevance. Yet there was little in theory or past experience to indicate how formal education could be brought to bear on complex social issues.

School reformers throughout the sixties and seventies repeatedly attacked conventional schooling as a form of indoctrination subservient to politically reactionary norms. It served, they charged, as an intellectual, moral, and spiritual ''anesthetic,'' numbing learners to the hard realities of oppression and social injustice. Through the illusion of freedom and choice, it purveyed ''lies'' calculated to serve corporate-industrial and military interests; in no meaningful sense could the learning offered through schools facilitate human liberation. While few analysts offered prescriptions for managing wholesale change—indeed, many radicals despaired of school reform short of total societal revolution—in their condemnation of American public education for its lack of social conscience and political conservatism, they stood squarely in the same reformist tradition as Counts, Rugg, Stanley, Childs, Brameld, and many others.

The recurrent refrain from critics was that schooling needed to be infused with a renewed sense of social purpose. Given the magnitude of the problems to be faced and the demands imposed on the next generation, it was said, formal education should play a more directive role in society's transformation. Few believed schools themselves could change the social order in any direct or immediate fashion on their own accord. The plea most often made, rather, was for an end to the pious fiction of neutrality and greater social awareness on the part of educators everywhere.

Some commentators drew attention to the need for more and better citizenship education. Despite the very formidable obstacles to meaningful political participation in contemporary mass society, there was general agreement that the meaning of ''citizenship'' itself was overdue for drastic revision. Some analysts urged greater emphasis upon environmental issues and ''ecological'' responsibility. Others argued for a more global, international perspective. More than a few professional educational organizations lent official support for foreign-language instruction, courses in foreign affairs and current events, and programs of international education.

If the potential of education lies with ''consciousness-raising'' and promoting ''awareness'' rather than with narrow partisan advocacy of a position on divisive issues, the futurist movement of the seventies and eighties could be construed as an outgrowth or logical extension of the social reconstructionist tradition. Beginning with Toffler's *Future Shock,* the term ''futurism'' entered into public consciousness. With it arose burgeoning interest in its applications to educational theory and practice. Once again, the same interest in social change was evident, this time framed in a somewhat broader context than ever before.

The task of schools, proponents of futurism claimed, is less a matter of exercising control over current trends in society and more a matter of extending the temporal horizon of classroom instruction by educating learners about the probable future consequences of present-day trends and events. Whereas previously the role of schooling was to pass on a culture more or less intact, and subsequently to service the needs of industrial society, henceforth, as Toffler put it, education would need to shift into the future tense.

Precisely how education was to discharge so awesome a responsibility became a matter of dispute. Many writers spoke of the need to overhaul traditional curricula, to scrutinize their content with a view toward probable future utility, and to refocus students' attention, toward the study of alternative futures. A typical argument was that all education springs from some image of the future. If that image turns out to be grossly inaccurate, children have been ill-served by their instruction and are rendered still more susceptible to the socio-pathology of future shock. If schools fail to grapple with the issues at all, the consequences can be equally disastrous.

One suggestion advanced was that teaching should concentrate on coping, or "survival skills" required in an era of unprecedented social change—skills for dealing with stress, uncertainty, and risk. Another was that schools should help students identify and give allegiance to new values, most particularly those having to do with communication and effective interpersonal relations, tolerance for diversity, empathetic understanding, cooperation, ecological responsibility, and global interdependence. In a few instances, however, writers were willing to attempt a delineation of the substance of a curriculum they felt could prepare learners for life in the twenty-first century.

Futurism never lacked for critics. Some detractors dismissed it as a passing fad. A number of skeptics felt it was an exercise in futility, either because the future is wholly unpredictable or because schools can do little if anything to deflect the course of social events. Some were troubled by the implicit assumption of certain futurists that the study of the past—as a guide to any desirable future—has become irrelevant. For whatever reasons, at least a few observers concluded that worrying about an uncertain tomorrow divested the present of its own special significance. Their best advice was to leave the future to unfold by itself.

## REVIEW QUESTIONS

1. In what specific ways do schools become involved in partisan political issues? How do larger societal currents, trends, and reform movements affect the process, organization, and content of schooling?

2. Why do special-interest groups tend to look to schools for ways of advancing their respective social causes?

3. Explain or characterize the difference in outlook between educational progressivists in the 1930s and social reconstructionists. What was the

"social frontier" group centered at Teachers College, Columbia University (circa 1927–49)?

4. Why did George S. Counts criticize the experimental progressive schools of the 1930s? In what ways did he find them deficient? How did he propose to reform them?

5. Why did Counts discount the hazards of "imposition" or indoctrination in schools? Why did he feel the school as a social institution could not maintain a posture of complete ideological neutrality? What did he propose as an alternative, and why?

6. Review briefly Counts's view of professionalism in education and "teacher power." How did he assume teachers could exercise political leadership in schools?

7. What were the defining characteristics of an ideal reconstructed social order as envisioned by Counts?

8. Why did John L. Childs agree with George Counts that neutrality or impartiality in school curricula and instruction is an impossibility?

9. How did John Dewey view the role of the school vis-à-vis social change and reform?

10. Why did Theodore Brameld criticize progressive education? To what social factors did he ascribe its alleged weaknesses or shortcomings? What did he claim should be the basic goal of contemporary education? How did he believe formal schools could contribute to cultural reconstruction? How did he define and justify the idea of "defensible partiality" in teaching? How did this concept differ from the notion of "imposition" cited by George S. Counts?

11. What were the chief criticisms to which Brameld's culture-crisis thesis was subjected? Why did some critics allege Brameld's brand of reconstructionism was naive or unrealistic?

12. Why did Jonathan Kozol assail American education as a "consumer fraud"? Outline the basis for his specific charges against schooling, with reference to his allegation that it purveys "pious lies." What did he mean when he charged that the aim of education is "spiritual and ethical lobotomy"? What is meant by the term "anesthetic" education?

13. How did Herbert Kohl assess the power of schools to change society and of teachers to serve as agents of social change? How did his views differ from those of Counts or Brameld?

14. Did Herbert Kohl believe social neutrality in schools was possible? Why or why not? How did he feel teachers should respond to bias in the educational system?

15. What is meant by the term "global interdependence"? Upon what basis have some writers called for an internationalist redefinition of citizenship and citizenship education?

16. Why did William Ophuls believe effective citizenship is difficult, if not impossible, in contemporary society? What is the so-called tragedy of the commons? What did Robert Dahl imply by his "criterion of economy" in terms of individuals' efforts to involve themselves in social issues and reform movements? What is "ecological citizenship" as mentioned by Ophuls and other writers?

17. What does Alvin Toffler mean by the term "future shock," and how can it allegedly be avoided or minimized? According to his analysis, how did the

function of schooling change with the transition from a preindustrial social order to an industrial society? In what specific ways do today's schools mirror industrial life and values?

18. Why did Toffler believe today's "covert" or latent curriculum in schools has become obsolete? What criterion would he employ for deciding upon curricular content? Why, specifically, has he argued for a greater future focus in education?

19. Why do futurists argue that contemporary world problems are historically unique in character? In other words, what is allegedly different about today's global crisis?

20. What values and skills are most frequently cited by futurists as having the greatest utility or survival potential for the future? Why are these particular values or skills emphasized so frequently?

21. Explain why Arthur Combs believes "humanistic" education offers the most adequate agenda for the future. Why does he appear to believe effective interpersonal communication and cooperation offer the keys to addressing tomorrow's critical issues?

22. In what sense is it possible to argue that the future affects the present?

23. Summarize the main objections raised by such critics of futurism as Herbert J. Muller and Lloyd P. Williams. For example, how did Muller justify the role of history in futurist education? What implications did Williams draw from his allegation that the future is essentially unknowable?

## SOME QUESTIONS FOR DISCUSSION

1. Review Counts's characterization of the upper middle class. Is his description applicable today? Is it a fair assessment? Why or why not? Does it describe adequately the people you know in your own socioeconomic class and that of your parents?

2. Counts once alleged that people "are moved by no great faith" and "touched by no great passions." As a generalization, does this reflect your own personal experience? Do you feel the public generally is indifferent to, ignorant of, and apathetic about pressing social issues? If so, why? From what sources do most people gain their information about current events?

3. Social critics often claim that the values of rugged individualism, competition, and free enterprise have outlived their usefulness and should be replaced by values of cooperation and communalism. Further, many futurists argue that schools should be involved in promoting this shift in values among youth. Do you agree or not? Evaluate the issues involved. For example, as presently organized and administered, how likely is it that public schools would be effective in teaching communitarian values and ideals?

4. It is sometimes said that the school is an agency of society and should serve the public interest. But *which* public interest? As defined by whom?

5. Brameld and other social reconstructionists have argued, basically, that the treatment accorded social issues in school instruction should be

based on "relevant" scientific evidence. Consider, then, the phenomenon of global population growth. How should teachers handle this issue? The "facts" suggest rapid, almost exponential growth in the world's number of people. The *meaning* or *significance* of the so-called population bomb, however, is in dispute. Questions of interpretation and values deeply divide opinion. What is an appropriate educational response?

6.  Reserve Officer Training Corps (ROTC) programs are a fixed feature on many college and university campuses. Are institutions of higher learning morally obligated to give equal support and attention to Peace Studies as well? After all, if a college grants academic credit for the study of warfare, why not give equal emphasis to the study of peace?

7.  What is the meaning of the term "democracy"? What is a democratic political system? Given the influence of well-funded political action committees and lobby groups on the formation of public policy, is it possible to claim we live in a democracy? Why or why not? What is meant specifically by democratic ideals in education?

8.  Construct examples to illustrate the alleged "tragedy of the commons" as cited by William Ophuls. On a local, national, or international basis, what specific trends dramatize the uncontrolled exploitation of the environment for purely private ends? What are the consequences? How might teachers explain this phenomenon to young children?

9.  Is teaching about social issues and problems the unique or exclusive responsibility of the social-studies teacher? How might instruction in science, mathematics, art, music, or physical education become more socially and politically relevant?

10.  Many critics believe schoolchildren should be obliged to attain fluency in a foreign language. Insofar as English is fast becoming an international language, is it necessary or desirable to expend the time and energy needed to acquire fluency in some other language? Few people are likely to live or travel abroad extensively (except perhaps as tourists) or to be engaged directly in international trade or diplomacy. Most of the contacts North Americans have with people from other countries are limited. Therefore, are there adequate grounds for insisting that students study other languages and cultures? Why or why not?

11.  How plausible or convincing is the futurist's contention that in light of the accelerated rate of social change, education must acquire a future orientation and emphasize the study of possible alternative futures?

12.  Young schoolchildren from a very early age are socialized to identify themselves with the interests of a sovereign nation-state and to define themselves as citizens of a particular country. Is it true, as some internationalists allege, that the concept of an independent sovereign state has become anachronistic, and that in an era of increasing global interdependence, a new international socioeconomic and political order is needed? If, as some critics claim, we have today a system of global "feudalism," what might be the alternatives? How can the human race move toward the creation of a more unitary planetary order?

13.  Some people view the environment as a domain to be exploited and subjugated to human interests. With appropriate technological intervention, it is held, there are virtually no limits to growth. Others tend to see the ecosystem as closed, finite, and limited. Most public debate over ecological issues nowadays reflects this fundamental divergence of perspective.

How might students in elementary and secondary education best be introduced to the problems, issues, and questions thereby generated?

14. When pollsters periodically circulate a copy of the American Bill of Rights, most people reportedly do not recognize the document. Often respondents are asked if they support its provisions. A *majority,* if asked to vote on the Bill of Rights today in a referendum, indicate they would reject one or more of the amendments. If so, what does this suggest about the political attitudes and values of many American citizens and about present-day citizenship education?

15. The highest national expenditure in most countries is for armaments. Currently some $400 billion is spent annually by national leaders for military purposes. Each year, the amount escalates. Funds are expended, on the average, at the rate of $30 million to $50 million *per hour* on "defense." By the mid-eighties the total annual outlay—in constant-value dollars—represented a 3,500 percent increase over spending levels in 1900. Less than 1 percent of world military costs are allocated to international peace-keeping; and total world economic aid is less than 6 percent of military expenditures. Should this information be taught to students in schools? If so, how and why?

16. In a recent national survey, half of all twelfth-graders polled could not identify an Arab country, given four choices. One in every four seventeen-year-olds could not identify Congress as a part of the *legislative* branch of government. About 15 percent of those interviewed thought the term "Cold War" referred to Hitler's invasion of Russia in the winter of 1941. In another government-sponsored national study, it was concluded that 85 percent of all schools lack appropriate educational programs in international affairs. Less than 10 percent of all collegians tested had ever completed a course in international affairs. More than one-third professed total indifference to international matters. The lowest scorers on a test designed to measure awareness of foreign affairs and events were education majors—the nation's future teachers. Discuss the possible implications of these findings.

17. Research studies conducted since 1959 consistently suggest that prospective and experienced teachers harbor antidemocratic values, attitudes, or beliefs, and to a greater degree than the general population. Many (upwards of 25 percent) endorse government censorship of speech and press. Almost one-fifth in a 1966 study supported suspension of the right of habeus corpus. (Another fifth failed to recognize the term.) In another poll, one-third of all experienced teachers felt educators should be required to sign loyalty oaths. There was widespread agreement that "a large mass of the people" are incapable of determining what is and is not good for them. Many supported involuntary sterilization of "criminal and moral misfits." Teachers, it has been found, consistently score higher than nonteachers on scales purporting to measure authoritarianism. Assuming the pattern of findings holds true today, what implications follow for assessing prospects for school reform and social change?

18. Is it necessary or even desirable for schools to help generate greater public awareness of current U.N. statistics suggesting the following?
    a. If present trends continue, almost half of the world's children will never live to reach the age of sixty;
    b. An estimated 42 percent of the world's children lack minimally adequate medical care;

  c. Approximately 16 percent of all children throughout the world suffer from undernourishment and malnutrition;

  d. An estimated 35 percent of all those aged five to fourteen are denied access to formal schooling;

  e. World illiteracy, in both relative and absolute terms, is on the increase.

19. Analyze or assess each of the following quotations:

  a. "I know how to change the world—one person at a time."
(seventeen-year-old community service volunteer)

  b. "My wife and I tried to raise our kids with decent values. Now it's up to them. Sure, I care about what's going on in the world. I read the newspaper, watch the news on TV. But you know what? I can't do a damn thing about it—wars, pollution, poor people, rip-offs—that stuff. I'm just one person and I'm powerless."
(forty-eight-year-old retail store manager)

  c. "The political dinosaurs in this town are trying to ban *Fire On Ice* and *Catcher In The Rye,* for cryin' out loud. The school board's running scared and our local superintendent is 'king' of the local reactionaries. We teachers do what we're told—we need the jobs. No way am I going to rock the boat. I shun controversy like the plague. I follow the curriculum guide and don't make waves. Controversial issues? Hell, liquor by the bottle is a hot issue in *this* county!"
(twenty-eight-year-old high-school social-studies teacher)

  d. "These futurists say we should be talking about big social problems. Okay, but they don't tell us *how.* I mean . . . they're not specific enough. Have these so-called experts been in a real-life classroom lately? My kids are into video games. They don't care about ecology or conditions in Third World countries. They can't relate to anything beyond themselves and their own private lives. What am I supposed to do as a teacher—work miracles?"
(twenty-three-year-old elementary-school teacher)

  e. "I'll probably go to college when I graduate. My father wants me to go into engineering like he did. . . . I haven't decided yet. But I can't afford to worry about ten or twenty years from now. What I want to know is, will there be a good job out there waiting for me when I finish college? That's the future I'm worried about—my own!"
(eighteen-year-old high-school senior)

  f. "There's one main reason why the world hasn't blown up yet or fallen apart. That's because everybody's too scared to think about it. Or they're apathetic. I believe thoughts have power. Thought creates reality. If everybody began thinking nuclear war was inevitable—it would be. Thinking about it would *make* it happen. I'm *glad* the public is ignorant or uninvolved, myself included!"
(twenty-year-old college student)

  g. "I think our teachers should tell us more about the world. Sometimes we talk about things. Mostly we do our workbooks so we can have recess."
(nine-year-old elementary-school child)

20. Discuss and evaluate each of the following propositions:

  a. The future is not fixed, but consists of a variety of alternatives, among which people can choose those they want to realize.

  b. Choice is necessary. Refusing to choose is itself a choice.

   c.   Small changes through time can become major changes.

   d.   The future world will probably be drastically different in many respects from the present world.

   e.   People are responsible for their future; it does not just happen to them.

   f.   Methods successful in the past may not work in the future, owing to changed circumstances.

## FURTHER READING

BJORK, ROBERT M., and STEWART E. FRASER. *Population, Education, and Children's Futures.* Bloomington, Ind.: Phi Delta Kappa Educational Foundation, 1980.

BRAMELD, THEODORE. *Education As Power.* New York: Holt, Rinehart & Winston, 1965.

———. *Education for the Emerging Age.* New York: Harper and Row, 1965.

———. *Patterns of Educational Philosophy.* New York: World Book Company, 1950.

———. *Patterns of Educational Philosophy in Culturological Perspective.* New York: Holt, Rinehart & Winston, 1971.

———. *Philosophies of Education in Cultural Perspective.* Chicago: Holt, Rinehart & Winston, 1955.

———. *The Use of Explosive Ideas in Education.* Pittsburgh: University of Pittsburgh Press, 1965.

BROWN, B. FRANK, ed. *Education for Responsible Citizenship, The Report of the National Task Force on Citizenship Education.* New York: McGraw-Hill, 1977.

CORNISH, EDWARD. *The Study of the Future.* Washington, D.C.: World Future Society, 1977.

COUNTS, GEORGE S. *Dare the School Build a New Social Order?* New York: Harper and Row, 1932.

———. *The Selective Character of American Secondary Education.* Chicago: University of Chicago Press, 1922.

FELLER, GORDON, SHERLE R. SCHWENNINGER, and DIANE SINGERMAN, eds. *Peace and World Order Studies, A Curriculum Guide,* 3rd ed. New York: Transnational Academic Program, Institute for World Order, 1981.

FITCH, ROBERT M., and CORDELL M. SVENGALIS. *Futures Unlimited: Teaching About Worlds to Come.* Washington, D.C.: National Council For The Social Studies, 1979.

KAUFFMAN, DRAPER. *Futurism and Future Studies.* Washington, D.C.: National Educational Association, 1976.

———. *Teaching the Future.* Palm Springs, Cal.: ETC Publications, 1976.

KIERSTEAD, FRED, JIM BOWNAN, and CHRISTOPHER DEDE, eds. *Educational Futures: Sourcebook I.* Washington, D.C.: World Future Society, 1979.

KING, DAVID C., JAMES M. BECKER, and LARRY E. CONDON. *Education for a World in Change: A Report.* New York: Intercom #96, Global Perspectives in Education, n.d.

KOZOL, JONATHAN. *The Night Is Dark and I Am Far from Home.* Boston: Houghton Mifflin, 1975.

MEAD, MARGARET. *Culture and Commitment.* New York: Doubleday, 1970.

MULLER, HERBERT. *The Uses of the Future.* Bloomington, Ind.: Indiana University Press, 1974.

NATIONAL ASSEMBLY ON FOREIGN LANGUAGE AND INTERNATIONAL STUDIES. *Toward Education with a Global Perspective.* Washington, D.C.: Association of American Colleges, 1981.

REISCHAUER, EDWIN O. *Toward the 21st Century: Education for a Changing World.* New York: Vintage, 1973.

ROSSMAN, MICHAEL. *On Learning and Social Change.* New York: Random House, 1972.

RUBIN, LOUIS, ed. *The Future of Education.* Boston: Allyn and Bacon, 1975.

RUGG, HAROLD. *American Life and the School Curriculum.* Lexington, Mass.: Ginn, 1931.

———. *Culture and Education in America.* New York: Harcourt Brace Jovanovich, 1931.

———. *That Men May Understand.* New York: Doubleday, 1941.

SHANE, HAROLD. *Curriculum Change toward the 21st Century.* Washington, D.C.: National Educational Association, 1977.

————, M. BERNADINE TABLER, and ANNE INGRAM MERKEL, eds. *Educating for a New Millennium*. Bloomington, Ind.: Phi Delta Kappa Educational Foundation, 1981.

————. *The Educational Significance of the Future*. Bloomington, Ind.: Phi Delta Kappa Educational Foundation, 1973.

SHIMAHARA, NOBUO, ed. *Educational Reconstruction, Promise and Challenge*. Columbus, Oh.: Chas. E. Merrill, 1973.

TOFFLER, ALVIN. *Future Shock*. New York: Random House, 1970.

————. *Learning for Tomorrow, The Role of the Future in Education*. New York: Vintage, 1974.

————. *The Third Wave*. New York: William Morrow, 1980.

WAGSHAL, PETER H., and ROBERT D. KAHN, eds. *R. Buckminster Fuller on Education*. Amherst, Mass.: University of Massachusetts Press, 1979.

————. *Learning Tomorrows: Commentaries on the Future of Education*. New York: Frederick A. Praeger, 1980.

WORKING GROUP ON THE SUCCESSOR GENERATION. *The Successor Generation: Its Challenges and Responsibilities*. Washington, D.C.: Atlantic Council of the United States, 1981.

## NOTES

1. Cited in Lawrence Cremin, *The Transformation of the School* (New York: Knopf, 1961), pp. 229–230.

2. Ibid., p. 230.

3. George S. Counts, *The Selective Character of American Secondary Education* (Chicago: University of Chicago Press, 1922).

4. For commentary, see Sidney Hook, *Education for Modern Man: A New Perspective* (New York: Knopf, 1963) p. 105ff.

5. George S. Counts, *Dare the School Build a New Social Order?* (New York: Harper and Row, 1932), pp. 5, 24.

6. Ibid., pp. 7–8.

7. Ibid., pp. 9–10.

8. Ibid., pp. 19, 27.

9. Ibid., p. 17.

10. Ibid., pp. 22–23.

11. Ibid., pp. 30, 37.

12. Ibid., p. 15.

13. Ibid., p. 37.

14. Ibid., p. 39.

15. Ibid., pp. 33–36, 45.

16. See Harold Rugg, *Culture and Education in America* (New York: Harcourt Brace Jovanovich, 1931); Harold Rugg, *American Life and the School Curriculum* (Lexington, Mass.: Ginn, 1931); and Harold Rugg, *That Men May Understand* (New York: Doubleday, 1941). See also Sandford W. Reitmann, "The Reconstructionism of Harold Rugg," *Educational Theory* 22 (Winter 1972): 488ff.

17. John L. Childs, "Should the School Seek Actively to Reconstruct Society?" *Annals of the American Academy of Political and Social Science* 182 (November 1935): 1–6.

18. Ibid., p. 9.

19. Ibid.

20. John Dewey, "Education and Social Change," *The Social Frontier* 3 (May 1937): 238.

21. Theodore Brameld, *Philosophies of Education in Cultural Perspective* (New York: Holt, Rinehart & Winston, 1955), pp. 183–184.

22. Unpublished correspondence between Theodore Brameld and Richard J. Anderson (November 30, 1965).

23. Theodore Brameld, *Education for the Emerging Age* (New York: Harper and Row, 1965), p. 72.

24. Ibid., p. 1.

25. Ibid., p. 25.

26. Theodore Brameld, *Education As Power* (New York: Holt, Rinehart & Winston, 1965), p. 103.

27. Theodore Brameld, *Patterns of Educational Philosophy in Culturological Perspective* (New York: Holt, Rinehart & Winston, 1971), p. 356.

28. Brameld, *Education for the Emerging Age,* pp. 12–13.

29. Brameld, *Education As Power,* p. 6.

30. Brameld, *Education for the Emerging Age,* p. 83.

31. Ibid., p. 157.

32. Theodore Brameld, "Self-Fulfilling Prophecy as an Educational Perspective," in Nobuo Shimahara, ed., *Educational Reconstruction, Promise and Challenge* (Columbus, Oh.: Chas. E. Merrill, 1973), pp. 28, 34.

33. Hobert W. Burns, "Brameld's Reconstructionism Reviewed," *Phi Delta Kappan* 47 (November 1965): 147. See also Takeo Taura, Kazuhisa Hiramitsu, and Yutaka Hibi, "Recent Developments in Reconstructionist Theory," *Phi Delta Kappan* 47 (November 1965): 150–152.

34. Burns, "Reconstructionism," p. 149.

35. James E. McClellan, *Toward an Effective Critique of American Education* (Philadelphia: Lippincott, 1968), pp. 179–180.

36. Ibid., p. 152.

37. Ibid., p. 133.

38. Kenneth Clark, *Civilization* (New York: Harper and Row, 1969), p. 345.

39. Norman O. Brown, *Life Against Death* (London: Sphere Books, 1968), p. 267.

40. Desmond King-Hele, *The End of the Twentieth Century?* (New York: Macmillan, 1970), p. 1.

41. J. R. Platt, *The Steps to Man* (New York: John Wiley, 1966), p. 196.

42. Arthur Koestler, *The Ghost in the Machine* (London: Hutchinson and Company, 1967), p. 339.

43. George Wald, "A Generation in Search of a Future," *The New Yorker* (March 22, 1969): 29–31.

44. Kai Nielsen, "Religiosity and Powerlessness," *The Humanist* 37 (May-June 1977): 46–47.

45. Quoted in Nigel Calder, *Technopolis* (London: MacGibbon and Kee, 1969), p. 60.

46. King-Hele, *End of Twentieth Century?* p. 24. See also Gerald Mische and Patricia Mische, *Toward a Human World Order: Beyond the National Security Straitjacket* (New York: Paulist Press, 1977), pp. 14–18.

47. George Wald, "There Isn't Much Time," *The Progressive* 39 (December 1975): 22.

48. Jonathan Schell, *The Fate of the Earth* (New York: Borzoi Books, Knopf, 1982), pp. 3, 230.

49. Sidney Lens, "The Doomsday Strategy," *The Progressive* 40 (February 1976): 34.

50. Donella H. Meadows, D. L. Meadows, J. Randers, and W. W. Behrens, *The Limits of Growth* (New York: Universe Books, 1972).

51. David Lyle, "The Human Race Has, Maybe, Thirty-Five Years Left," *Esquire* 68 (1967): 116–118.

52. C. P. Snow, *The Two Cultures and the Scientific Revolution* (New York: Cambridge University Press, 1959), p. 54.

53. *The Global 2000 Report to the President, Entering the Twenty-First Century* (Washington, D.C.: U.S. Government Printing Office, 1980).

54. "What Kind of World Are We Leaving to Our Children?" *Social Education* 43 (October 1979): 470.

55. Ibid., p. 471.

56. H. G. Vonk, "Education and the 27-Year Countdown," *Phi Delta Kappan* 54 (April 1973): 514.

57. Ibid.

58. Jonathan Kozol, *The Night Is Dark and I am Far from Home* (Boston: Houghton Mifflin, 1975), pp. 9–11.

59. Ibid., pp. 1, 9, 181.

60. Ibid., p. 45.

61. Ibid., p. 140.

62. Ibid., pp. 184, 186.

63. Ibid., pp. 188–189.

64. Frederick L. Redefer, "A Call to the Educators of America?" *Saturday Review/World* (July 27, 1974): 49–50.

65. Leon Hymovitz, "Schools for Survival in the Twenty-First Century," *Clearing House* 55 (September 1981): 33.

66. Ibid., p. 34.

67. John P. DeCecco, "Tired Feelings, New Life-Styles, and the Daily Liberation of the Schools," *Phi Delta Kappan* 53 (November 1971): 171.

68. See Jean Anyon, "Issues and Voices From the Past: Whose History in American Classrooms?" *Journal of Education* 162 (Summer 1980): 67.

69. Fannie R. Shaftel, "The Elementary School Social Studies We Need," *The Social Studies Professional* (January 1972): 3.

70. Herbert Kohl, "Can The Schools Build A New Social Order?" *Journal of Education* 162 (Summer 1980): 58.

71. Ibid., p. 60.

72. Ibid., p. 61.

73. Ibid., p. 62.

74. William Ophuls, "Citizenship and Ecological Education," *Teachers College Record* 82 (Winter 1980): 217.

75. Quoted in B. Frank Brown, "Introduction, The Case for Citizenship Education," in B. Frank Brown, ed., *Education for Responsible Citizenship, The Report of the National Task Force on Citizenship Education* (New York: McGraw-Hill, 1977), p. 3.

76. Ibid.

77. Ophuls, "Citizenship," p. 223.

78. Ibid., p. 225.

79. See Robert A. Dahl, *After the Revolution? Authority in a Good Society* (New Haven: Yale University Press, 1970).

80. Ophuls, "Citizenship," p. 225.

81. Ibid., pp. 228–229.

82. Ibid., p. 230.

83. Ibid., p. 237.

84. Ibid., pp. 237–239.

85. E. F. Schumacher, *Small is Beautiful: Economics as if People Mattered* (New York: Harper and Row, 1973).

86. Saul H. Mendlovitz, Lawrence Metcalf, and Michael Washburn, "The Crisis of Global Transformation, Interdependence, and the Schools," in Brown, *Education*, p. 139.

87. Ibid., pp. 198–205. See also Gordon Feller, Sherle R. Schwenninger, and Diane Singerman, *Peace And World Order Studies, A Curriculum Guide,* 3rd ed. (New York: Transnational Academic Program, Institute for World Order, 1981).

88. Edwin O. Reischauer, *Toward The 21st Century: Education for a Changing World* (New York: Vintage, 1973), pp. 3, 135, 139.

89. Ibid., pp. 12, 137, 195.

90. President's Commission on Foreign Language and International Studies, *Strength Through Wisdom: A Critique of U.S. Capability* (Washington, D.C.: U.S. Government Printing Office, 1979); The National Assembly on Foreign Language and International Studies, *Toward Education with a Global Perspective* (Washington, D.C.: Association of American Colleges, 1981); The Council on Learning, *Task Force Statement on Education and World View* (New York: Council on Learning, 1981); Working Group on the Successor Generation, *The Successor Generation: Its Challenges and Responsibilities* (Washington, D.C.: Atlantic Council of the United States, 1981).

91. National Assembly, *Global Perspective,* p. 2.

92. *Task Force Statement on Education and The World View,* p. 6. See also Paul Simon, *The Tongue-Tied American: Confronting the Foreign Language Crisis* (New York: Continuum, 1980).

93. Working Group, *The Successor Generation,* p. 13. See also *Issues and Options: The Work Program of the Atlantic Council* (Washington, D.C.: The Atlantic Council, 1981), p. 4.

94. Working Group, *The Successor Generation,* p. 21.

95. Cited in H. Thomas Collins, *Working Draft, A Preliminary Compilation of Selected National Membership Organizations and K-12 Global/International Education* (New York: Global Perspectives in Education, n.d.), p. 2.

96. Ibid., p. 3.

97. Ibid., pp. 5–7.

98. Ibid., p. 8.

99. Ibid., p. 9.

100. Alvin Toffler, *Future Shock* (New York: Bantam, 1971), pp. 1–2.

101. Ibid., p. 399.

102. Toffler, in an interview reproduced in June Grant Shane and Harold G. Shane, "The Role of the Future in Education," *Today's Education* 63 (January-February, 1974): 72.

103. Toffler, *Future Shock,* pp. 399–400.

104. Ibid., p. 400.

105. Toffler, in an interview reproduced in Andrew Smith, "Education and The Future: An Interview with Alvin Toffler," *Social Education* 45 (October 1981): 424.

106. Quoted in Shane and Shane, "Role of the Future," pp. 73–74.

107. Toffler, *Future Shock,* p. 403.

108. Warren L. Ziegler, "The Potential of Educational Future," in Michael Marien and Warren L. Ziegler, eds., *The Potential of Educational Futures* (Worthington, Oh.: Chas. A. Jones, 1972), p. 3.

109. Shane and Shane, "Role of the Future," p. 75.

110. Toffler, *Future Shock,* p. 403. See also Alvin Toffler, ed., *Learning for Tomorrow, The Role of the Future in Education* (New York: Vintage, 1974).

111. Shane and Shane, "Role of the Future," p. 76.

112. Jean Dresden Grambs, "Forty Years of Education: Will the Next Forty Be Any Better?" *Educational Leadership* 38 (May 1981): 651.

113. Quoted in Smith, "Education and the Future," p. 424.

114. Ibid., p. 426.

115. Quoted in Edward Cornish, *The Study of the Future* (Washington, D.C.: World Future Society, 1977), pp. 213–214.

116. Ervin Laszlo, "The Education of Educators," in Fred Kierstead, Jim Bowman, and Christopher Dede, eds., *Educational Futures: Sourcebook I* (Washington, D.C.: World Future Society, 1979), p. 49.

117. Peter H. Wagshal and Robert D. Kahn, eds., *R. Buckminster Fuller on Education* (Amherst, Mass.: University of Massachusetts Press, 1979), p. 161.

118. Solon T. Kimball, "Culture, Class, and Educational Congruency," in Stanley Elam and William P. McLure, eds., *Educational Requirements for the 1970's* (New York: Frederick A. Praeger, 1967), p. 8.

119. Edgar Dale, *The News Letter* 36 (May 1971): 3. See also Don M. Beach, "Futurism and Implications for Education," *Contemporary Education* 52 (Summer 1981): 228–231.

120. Cornish, *Study of the Future*, p. 209.

121. Robert Theobald, "The Nature of Education: A Fundamental Reconsideration," in Kierstead et al., *Educational Futures*, pp. 29–35.

122. E. Paul Torrance, "Creativity and Futurism in Education Retooling," *Education* 100 (Summer 1980): 299.

123. Dennis Van Avery, "Futuristics and Education," *Educational Leadership* 37 (February 1980): 441–442.

124. Glen Heathers, "Education to Meet the Psychological Requirements for Living in the Future," *Journal of Teacher Education* 25 (Summer 1974): 108–112.

125. Louis J. Rusin, "Whither Goest the Curriculum?" *Journal of Teacher Education* 25 (Summer 1974): 117.

126. Arthur W. Combs, "What the Future Demands of Education," *Phi Delta Kappan* 26 (January 1981): 369–371.

127. Ibid., pp. 371–372. Italics added.

128. Ibid., p. 372.

129. Ibid.

130. Christopher Dede and Dwight Allen, "Education in the 21st Century: Scenarios as a Tool for Strategic Planning," *Phi Delta Kappan* 62 (January 1981): 366.

131. Robert M. Fitch and Cordell M. Svengalis, *Futures Unlimited: Teaching About Worlds To Come* (Washington, D.C.: National Council for the Social Studies, 1979), p. 22.

132. Ibid., p. 22.

133. Torrance, "Creativity and Futurism," p. 305.

134. Cornish, *Study of the Future*, p. 211.

135. Irving H. Buchen, "Humanism and Futurism: Enemies or Allies?" in Toffler, *Learning for Tomorrow*, p. 140.

136. Harold G. Shane, M. Bernadine Tabler, and Anne Ingram Merkel, *Educating for a New Millennium* (Bloomington, Ind.: Phi Delta Kappa Educational Foundation, 1981). See also Harold G. Shane, "A Curriculum for the New Century," *Phi Delta Kappan* 62 (January 1981): 351–356.

137. Ibid., p. 352.

138. Ibid., pp. 353–354.

139. Ibid., p. 356.

140. Herbert J. Muller, "Education for the Future," *The American Scholar* (Summer 1972): 377–378.

141. Ibid., p. 380.

142. Ibid., p. 378.

143. Ibid., pp. 381–386.

144. Lloyd P. Williams, "Some Friendly Criticisms of Futurism," *Educational Studies* 12 (Spring 1981): vi.

145. Ibid., p. v.

146. Ibid., pp. vi, vii.

147. Ibid., p. x.

148. Ibid.

149. Ibid., p. xiii.

150. Ibid., p. xiv.

151. Ibid., pp. vi, vii, xv.

# INDEX